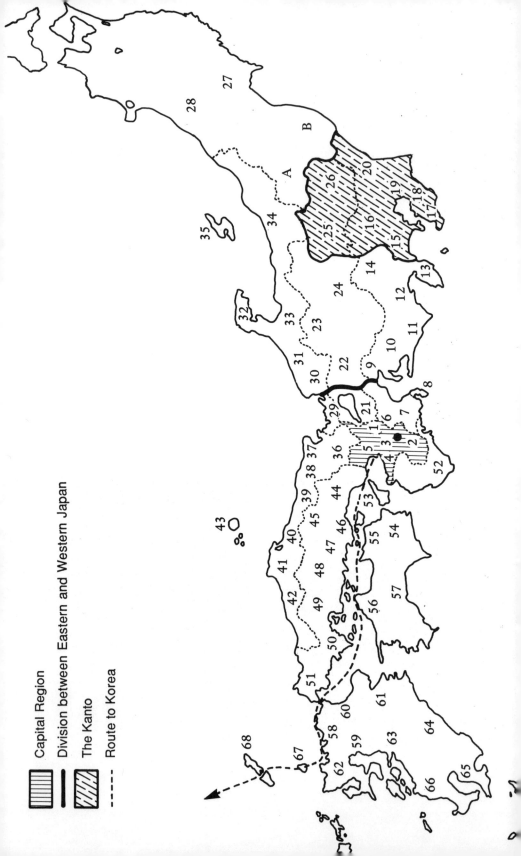

Capital Region

Division between Eastern and Western Japan

The Kanto

Route to Korea

Map 1. THE PROVINCES AND CIRCUITS OF EIGHTH-CENTURY JAPAN

Kinai	*Tōsandō*	*San'indō*	*Nankaidō*	*Islands*
1. Yamashira	21. Ōmi	36. Tamba	52. Kii	67. Iki
2. Yamato	22. Mino	37. Tango	53. Awaji	68. Tsushima
3. Kawachi	23. Hida	38. Tajima	54. Awa	
4. Izumi	24. Shinano	39. Inaba	55. Sanuki	
5. Settsu	25. Kōzuke	40. Hōki	56. Iyo	
	26. Shimotsuke	41. Izumo	57. Tosa	
Tōkaidō	27. Mutsu	42. Iwami		
6. Iga	28. Dewa	43. Oki	*Saikaidō*	
7. Ise			58. Chikuzen	
8. Shima	*Hokurikudō*	*San'yōdō*	59. Chikugo	
9. Owari	29. Wakasa	44. Harima	60. Buzen	
10. Mikawa	30. Echizen	45. Mimasaka	61. Bungo	
11. Tōtōmi	31. Kaga	46. Bizen	62. Hizen	
12. Suruga	32. Noto	47. Bitchū	63. Higo	
13. Izu	33. Etchū	48. Bingo	64. Hyūga	
14. Kai	34. Echigo	49. Aki	65. Ōsumi	
15. Sagami	35. Sado	50. Suō	66. Satsuma	
16. Musashi		51. Nagato		
17. Awa				
18. Kazusa				
19. Shimōsa				
20. Hitachi				

Source: Aoki Kazuo, *Nihon no rekishi 3 Nara no miyako* appended map.

Heavenly Warriors

William Wayne Farris

Distributed by the HARVARD UNIVERSITY PRESS, Cambridge (Massachusetts) and
London   1995

Heavenly Warriors

The Evolution of Japan's Military, 500–1300

Published by the COUNCIL ON EAST ASIAN STUDIES, HARVARD UNIVERSITY

The Council on East Asian Studies at Harvard University pub-
lishes a monograph series and, through the Fairbank Center for
East Asian Research and the Reischauer Institute of Japanese
Studies, administers research projects designed to further scholarly understanding of China, Japan, Korea, Vietnam, Inner Asia,
and adjacent areas.

The Library of Congress has catalogued the hardcover edition as
follows:

Library of Congress Cataloging-in-Publication Data

Farris, William Wayne.
    Heavenly warriors : the evolution of Japan's military,
500–1300 / William Wayne Farris.
        p. cm. – (Harvard East Asian monographs ; 157)
    Includes bibliographical references and index.
    ISBN 0-674-38703-1
    1. Japan–History, Military–To 1868.   2. Japan–
History–To 1333.   I. Title.   II. Series.
DS838.5.F37   1992
952–dc20   92-11200
                                                          CIP

Paperback ISBN 0-674-38704-X

To Jane and Nat

Contents

Contents

Figures

Maps

Acknowledgments

I am grateful to many persons for their help with this book. Professor Albert Craig encouraged my research and asked important questions early on. The late Professor Kishi Toshio supported my research in Kyoto while I was on a Fulbright Faculty Research Abroad Grant for 1983–1984. Professor Uwayokote Masataka of Kyoto University provided encouragement and a tutor for Heian sources, Motoki Yasuo. When I returned to Japan in the summer of 1986 to study at Tokyo University, I was expertly guided by Professor Ishii Susumu. Hongō Kazuto of the Historiographical Institute helped to introduce me to Kamakura records while I was at Tokyo University. My research in 1986 was funded by the American Philosophical Society and the University of Tennessee. A Summer Stipend from the National Endowment for the Humanities supported the final stages of writing. I should also like to thank Professors Sasayama Haruo, Nagahara Keiji, Gomi Fumihiko, Toda Yoshimi, Amino Yoshihiko, Yasuda Motohisa, and Fukuda Toyohiko for conversing with me for hours on the origins of the warrior. Professors David Herlihy and Carol Lansing helped me in making comparisons with the medieval European military. I should also like to thank Professor Harold Bolitho of Harvard University and Doris Gove of the University of Tennessee for numerous suggestions about style and presentation. Of course, any mistakes are the responsibility of the author.

Finally, I wish to thank my wife, Jane Park Farris, for reading and commenting on the entire manuscript. Jane and my son, Nat, sustained me through some difficult times with their inspiration and merriment.

Preface to the Paperback Edition

Books are often likened to children because both entail sustained work and continue the line of the author. Yet there is an essential difference between the offspring of these two creative activities. Children change and mature from the day they are born. When a writer composes a monograph, the book remains forever the same while the author is usually the one who undergoes a gradual transformation.

I constructed the argument of *Heavenly Warriors* in reaction to what I termed "the Western analogue theory," which had a long history and was almost universally popular among scholars of Japan and the United States until the 1950s and early 1960s.[1] The Western analogue theory held that European historical development was paradigmatic and that although Japan had started out under the influence of China, continental institutions had quickly failed. Japan entered an era of anarchy by 900, which resulted in the formation of powerful new engines of economic growth (private estates) and a nascent class (the samurai) to protect them. In 1185, the inevitable occurred when Yoritomo overthrew the effete Kyoto aristocracy and founded his shogunate. Feudalism was born in Japan.

Two major revisions of "the Western analogue theory" form the backbone of "the evolutionary thesis" presented in *Heavenly Warriors,* and remain fundamental to my thinking today. First, the defining characteristics of the late-Heian samurai—basic fighting technology, social organization, economic standing, and political function—combined long before the year 900 to create a class of regional strongmen playing a significant role in local society. Mounted archers from designated lineages formed a critical element in the ancient Japanese military by the time that horse-riding technology spread across the archipelago in the sixth century. The court's fear of invasion from the continent in the late 600s and a forty-year war against the people of northeastern Japan toward the end of the 700s encouraged further development, especially in the Kanto.

The district magistrate of the late seventh and eighth centuries constitutes the prototype of the late-Heian samurai. These officials of the Chinese-style state were local strongmen who fought on horseback with bow and arrow, held a sizable parcel of land, and passed their office, status, skills, and land on to their offspring. The contention that the samurai had ancient forerunners, including the district magistrate, is not new to the world of Japanese scholarship, and Amino Yoshihiko has recently reiterated it.[2]

Second, the evolution of the warrior class after 850 took place in conditions of economic hardship, not growing prosperity. Previous interpretations emphasized population pressure on the land, but *Heavenly Warriors* argues that pestilence and primitive agricultural technology were critical. Repeated epidemics and occasional famines depopulated villages, provinces, and—in extreme cases—the entire archipelago. Taxes went unpaid. Because the court had become accustomed to a certain level of revenue, it became more aggressive about collecting its share of the declining yield. The result was violence caused by both tax evaders and collectors.

The growth of this type of violence put the warrior in an advantageous position because his skills were necessary to ensure the court its share of revenues and, conversely, to protect the evader. Military men were performing this service even before 800. For example, one record suggests that the court used the Ōmi militia to collect revenues which were past due to the temple Tōdaiji in 763.[3] During the tenth and eleventh centuries, warriors served as provincial governors and tax-farmers; after a harsh cycle of epidemics and bad harvests ending in the mid-eleventh century, more fighters assumed positions as managers of estates (big farms; *shōen*) paying rent to members of court.

While garnering revenues for the court, individual warriors accumulated valuable political experience and some wealth. They also continued the age-old tradition of forming patron-client relationships with civil aristocrats and clerics at court. By the twelfth century, two magnificent military leaders emerged: Taira no Kiyomori, who dominated the civil aristocracy, and Minamoto no Yoritomo, who manipulated it. As a result of the Great Civil War of 1180–1185, which pitted the Taira against the Minamoto, warrior-tax collectors stipulated that if they filled the coffers for the elite in Kyoto, they would like more secure tenure of their offices and a greater percentage of the harvest.

The civil aristocracy and religious institutions represented in Kyoto did not allow these prerogatives to go unchallenged. From its inception, the government in Kamakura was fragile and the incomes samurai derived from their positions were minimal outside the Kanto. The warrior class was small. In 1221, the imperial house questioned the right of the shogunate to exist. The supremacy of the samurai became assured only in the late thirteenth century when the Mongols assaulted Japan and forced the court, along with the rest of western Japan, to become almost completely dependent on the political and military power of Kamakura.

When I undertook the *Heavenly Warriors* project, I sought to immerse myself in the primary sources and the numerous debates contained in Japanese secondary works, hoping thereby to give the reader a glimpse of the sophisticated world of Japanese historiography. In the process, unfortunately, I overlooked several valuable works in English. Since publication, I have attempted to redress that oversight, and the experience has caused me to modify my thinking.

The most fundamental modification has been to recast the English-language debate over the rise of the samurai. Further reading has indicated that as early as the late 1960s Cornelius Kiley, John Hall, Hori Kyotsu, and other historians were beginning to question the Western analogue theory in important ways. By the time *Heavenly Warriors* appeared in 1992, the number of historians employing other perspectives had grown considerably. In particular, many scholars—Jeffrey Mass, Karl Steenstrup, Bruce Batten, Martin Collcutt, Cameron Hurst, and others—were questioning whether the twelfth-century founding of the Kamakura shogunate was really the turning point that previous authors had described. And in terms of "the rise of the samurai," Karl Friday recently published *Hired Swords: The Rise of Private Warrior Power in Early Japan,* which made fine use of research by Japanese historians.

In this English-language material, one can see a spectrum of views on the formation of the warrior class and its ascent to political prominence. The venerable Western analogue theory is still alive among a few senior historians in Japan (Yasuda Motohisa is an example), although it has declined greatly in influence; it persists in many English-language world- and Japanese-history textbooks that refer to the founding of "feudal Japan" in 1185. Several scholars, such as Mass, Friday, Hurst, Varley, and Hall, occupy an intermediate position, rejecting parts of the Western analogue theory but still embracing other aspects. *Heavenly Warriors* attempts to provide a fundamental alternative to that theory.

Three further modifications in my analysis pertain to specific historical matters. In an article that deserves a wide readership, Peter Arnesen has significantly undermined the documentary evidence for the lone case of a Taira land steward (*jitō*), a samurai manager and tax collector assigned to elite estates.[4] Upon further reflection, I agree with Arnesen—and with Mass—that the land steward was most likely an institution invented by the Minamoto, and not one previously used by the Taira, a possibility that I raised on pp. 285–286. There still seems, however, ample reason for a high assessment of the Taira and their contributions to Japan's early military development.

Second, an article by Kenneth Butler examines samurai war tales in detail and makes a point relevant to my argument on late-Heian and Kamakura battle tactics.[5] Butler has shown that most of the stories of heroic individual combat preserved in *The Tale of the Heike* and other samurai literature are probably later accretions. Because the stories date from several decades after the battles took place, they cannot be used, as I did on pp. 270 and 272, to support the idea that late-Heian fighting involved one-to-one combat. It still seems reasonable to argue, however, that there was little mass combat among the samurai in the twelfth and thirteenth centuries.

Finally, *Heavenly Warriors* follows the Japanese consensus that the aristocratic elite adopted the Chinese-style military system of the late seventh and early eighth centuries out of fear of invasion (see Chapter 2). Was that the real reason? Could the supposed danger have been an excuse used by the court to create a military system capable of bringing recalcitrant local strongmen under its sway? John Hall has implied as much in his writing on Bizen province, and it seems a point worthy of more emphasis than I gave it in *Heavenly Warriors.*[6]

I would like to take this opportunity to thank the Council on East Asian Studies at Harvard University for suggesting a paperback version of this book. My thanks also go to Executive Editor Katherine Keenum for seeing to the task. I am particularly grateful to Al Craig, Hal Bolitho, and Conrad Totman for their encouragement and for the useful criticisms and suggestions that they have provided throughout this project.

NOTES TO THE PREFACE

1. *Heavenly Warriors,* pp. 2–3 and note 2, pp. 399–400.

2. Amino Yoshihiko, *Higashi to nishi no kataru Nihon no rekishi,* pp. 71–76.

3. *Dai Nihon komonjo,* XVI, pp. 390–399. On this point, note Yoshida Takashi, *Ritsuryō kokka to kodai no shakai* (Iwanami shoten, 1983), p. 306.

4. Peter Arnesen, "The Struggle for Lordship in Late Heian Japan: The Case of Aki," *The Journal of Japanese Studies* 10:101–141 (Winter 1984).

5. Kenneth Butler, "The *Heike Monogatari* and the Japanese Warrior Ethic," *Harvard Journal of Asiatic Studies* 29:93–108 (1969).

6. John Hall, *Government and Local Power in Japan, 500 to 1700,* pp. 45–98.

Figure 1. A CHRONOLOGY OF JAPANESE MILITARY
HISTORY, 500–1300

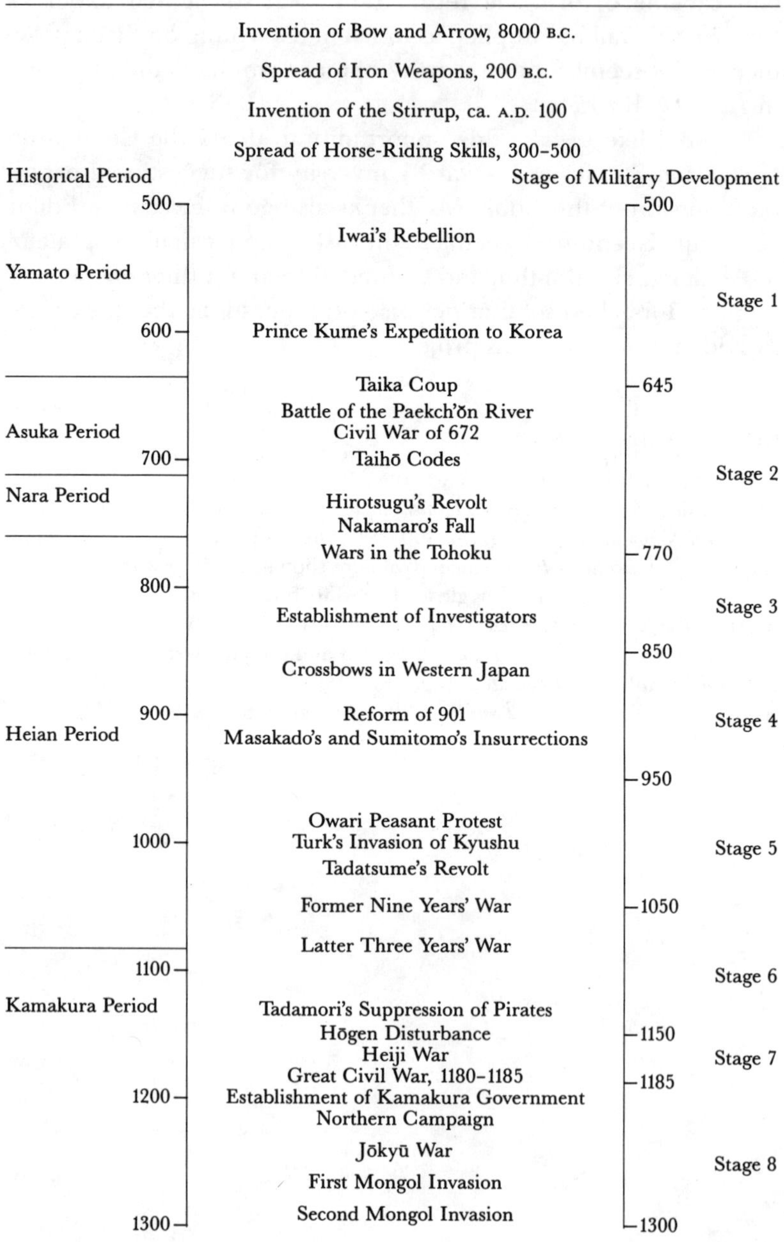

Invention of Bow and Arrow, 8000 B.C.

Spread of Iron Weapons, 200 B.C.

Invention of the Stirrup, ca. A.D. 100

Spread of Horse-Riding Skills, 300–500

Historical Period		Stage of Military Development
500		500
	Iwai's Rebellion	
Yamato Period		
		Stage 1
600	Prince Kume's Expedition to Korea	
	Taika Coup	645
	Battle of the Paekch'ŏn River	
Asuka Period	Civil War of 672	
700	Taihō Codes	
		Stage 2
Nara Period	Hirotsugu's Revolt	
	Nakamaro's Fall	
	Wars in the Tōhoku	770
800		
		Stage 3
	Establishment of Investigators	
		850
	Crossbows in Western Japan	
900	Reform of 901	Stage 4
Heian Period	Masakado's and Sumitomo's Insurrections	
		950
	Owari Peasant Protest	
1000	Turk's Invasion of Kyushu	Stage 5
	Tadatsume's Revolt	
	Former Nine Years' War	1050
	Latter Three Years' War	
1100		Stage 6
Kamakura Period	Tadamori's Suppression of Pirates	
	Hōgen Disturbance	1150
	Heiji War	Stage 7
	Great Civil War, 1180–1185	1185
1200	Establishment of Kamakura Government	
	Northern Campaign	
	Jōkyū War	
		Stage 8
	First Mongol Invasion	
1300	Second Mongol Invasion	1300

Introduction

In a government, military matters are the essential thing.
—The Emperor Temmu, 684

Temmu needed a strong army. Victor in a civil war in which he had forced his own nephew and rival to commit suicide, he had learned that arms and men were necessary to his survival. But this Japanese Emperor, posthumously hailed as "the Heavenly Warrior," also meant his dictum to have a national application. Temmu had been alive when a combined Chinese and Korean host had annihilated a Japanese army in Korea, opening the door to an invasion of his homeland.

Five hundred years passed before another fighting man, Minamoto no Yoritomo, interpreted Temmu's aphorism in his own way by founding a new martial government in Kamakura (near modern Tokyo). It is unlikely that Yoritomo had Temmu's principle in mind when he launched his rebellion in 1180, but he, too, had learned its truth through personal ordeal. Placed under house arrest as a child, Yoritomo had grown to rally ⸱⸱is father's allies to his cause and secured his military administration ⸱n 1185 only after a bitter civil war that lasted 5 years.

The careers of these two martial leaders from disparate eras, regions, and classes indicate the crucial importance of soldiery throughout Japan's early history. Despite this, the study of Japan's premodern military — its weapons and organization, and its place in society, politics, and the economy — is surprisingly underdeveloped, especially in English. The samurai (a lightly armored mounted archer characteristic of Japan after 1100) may have been a critical figure in Japanese history, but the story of his origins and development is still largely untold.[1]

One reason for the neglect of military matters is the way schol-

1

ars have conventionally viewed Japan's past. Since Japan rapidly assimilated Western political and economic forms in the nineteenth century, many scholars began to think that Japan and Western Europe must have experienced parallel historical developments. Because the mounted fighters who founded the martial government in Japan in the late twelfth century reminded many Japanese and Western historians of European knights, it was assumed that Japan, too, must have had a feudal past.

By the turn of the twentieth century, many leading Japanese scholars had "discovered medieval Europe in Japan," explaining their own early history according to a "Western-analogue theory."[2] This interpretation stated that, although both Japan and Western Europe possessed tribal fighting specialists in the sixth century and before, those early sprouts of Japanese feudalism were all but wiped out by the adoption of Chinese-style institutions beginning in the mid-seventh century. The Taihō Codes of 702, a set of statutes written in Chinese and inspired by Chinese models, mandated a stable, centralized state in control of a reformed military system emphasizing peasant infantry. The eighth-century Japanese government took on the public and civilian character of Chinese law, which seemed, according to the theory, analogous to Roman institutions. At the apogee of the Chinese-style state in 750, the army was so docile and impotent that no one could have guessed that Japan would eventually come under martial rule.

But conditions began to change. In less than a century, the entire Chinese-style system started to decline; the result was a situation in the countryside similar to the political vacuum created in the West by the fall of the Roman Empire after the barbarian invasions. In the absence of an effective Japanese central government between 900 and 1100, local strongmen were forced to arm themselves in order to survive. Rebellions became commonplace. The new military men of the countryside soon formed bands, linked together by ties of dependence and based in private estates on land they had cleared themselves. Eventually the effete Court aristocracy came to rely upon these fighting men for control of rural Japan. Finally, in 1185, Yoritomo seized the leadership of the new class of fighters, successfully usurped political power from the Court, and established a feudal government which allotted land to samurai in exchange for their martial services. The Western-analogue theorists thus hold that within about 500 years, Japan had moved from the public, civilian system of the Chinese-style law codes to private, feudal rule, just as the West had gone from the Roman Empire to Charlemagne.

Although Japanese historians have dramatically rewritten their own early history since the beginning of the twentieth century, aspects of the Western-analogue theory have lingered there; authors in Western languages have remained almost totally under its sway. The result has been that the role of the military in early Japanese history has been distorted in two important ways. First, students have neglected soldiery before the year 1050. This criticism is much less true of Japanese scholars than their Western counterparts; yet one leading Japanese historian has recently argued that the gap separating fighters of 900 from the samurai of 1200 was so wide that the former could be safely ignored.[3] His opinion is common among many Japanese, who stress that the twelfth-century samurai (*bushi*) was a new elite of country landholders, rather than a direct descendant of the mounted archers of yore.

Second, scholars on both sides of the Pacific have groped for the economic and social underpinnings of Yoritomo's regime. If the Kamakura Shogunate represented Japan's conversion to a new way of life (feudalism), then the new ruling class (the samurai) must have had their own economic base (land). This reasoning has been carried to the ultimate by many postwar Japanese historians, who portray the samurai of 1200 as a newly ascendant class which led Japan's "age of widespread land clearance."[4]

In contrast to the Western-analogue theory, this book will offer an evolutionary model to explain the origins and development of martial power in early Japan. The evolutionary model emphasizes the underlying continuities in the early Japanese military by maintaining that an equestrian martial elite was a critical factor in society, economy, and politics as early as about A.D. 500. Such an interpretation differs in 3 fundamental respects from the Western-analogue theory. (1) Rather than assuming that the adoption of Chinese-style institutions undercut military development, the evolutionary model asserts that the new government of the late seventh and early eighth centuries was an administration driven by martial purposes, and actively encouraged military affairs, relying upon mounted combat led by local strongmen in addition to conscript peasant footsoldiers. (2) Fighting men of the late ninth, tenth, and eleventh centuries were not a product of a political vacuum, but continued to work within a modified government and military framework, refining the technology of war, honing political skills, and carving out economic bases. (3) The founding of Yoritomo's Shogunate in Kamakura in the late twelfth century did not mean a sea change for soldiers, or for Japanese society as a whole, but represented underlying continuities in the war-making techniques, social organization, economic base, and political status of fighting men.

This book will focus on almost a millennium of Japanese history, from 500 to 1300. Its 8 chapters divide that stretch of time into definable periods in the evolution of the early Japanese military. The starting point is the era from 500 to 645, before the advent of Chinese-style institutions in Japan. A limited number of artifacts, uncovered from archeological sites, dated both before and after A.D. 500, and a few extant written sources help scholars pinpoint and describe the origins of weapons, war, and Japan's early military during this time. What kinds of weapons did Japanese fighters employ? How did the Japanese come by their technology? What was the relative importance of local leaders as compared with the Japanese king in raising and leading troops? Were there regional variations in war-making techniques?

The period from 645 to 770 was the apogee of Chinese-style institutions and culture in Japan and is the second stage of martial history, when political leaders promoted martial affairs to defend the archipelago. Why did a strong army and navy become an overriding goal for Japanese leaders? How was the military armed, raised, organized, and led, according to Japan's first comprehensive set of laws, the Taihō Codes of 702? What do actual battles reveal about issues such as the relative importance of mounted and other forms of combat, or the role of the local elite? How were fighters employed in capital politics?

From 770 to 900, the political and military system established by the Emperor Temmu and others slowly decayed. The Court turned to two technological wonders, the mounted archer and the crossbow, to serve its needs in an era of population decline. What was the role of the 40-year war in northeastern Japan in this transformation? How did technology, conscription, and leadership change? What new solutions were offered to the problem of defending Japan in the ninth century?

A fourth step in the evolution of the samurai covers the century from 850 to 950, which saw a shift from defense against foreigners to domestic peacekeeping. The level of internal violence increased, and subjects took aim at their government. What were the causes of this new violence? How did the Court respond? How were armies and navies armed, raised, and organized during the revolts of Taira no Masakado and Fujiwara Sumitomo? What was the character of the soldier's economic base and political ties?

In the fifth period, from 950 to 1050, a modified military establishment emerged from the rubble of rebellion, providing the "missing link" between the fighters of Temmu's day and those of the late twelfth century. How were troops organized and led in the capital and provinces? How did the revolt inspired by Taira no Tadatsune in the Kanto region (the area around modern Tokyo) between 1028 and 1031 sow the seeds for a further shift in the system of the middle Heian era?

A sixth phase in the evolution of Japan's military power spanned the years 1050 to 1150. The major question of this era for students of martial affairs revolves around the tie between fighting men and land, specifically the new systems of land tenure, village administration, and taxation established after 1050. How did these new institutions affect the economic base of the samurai? Was there an "age of widespread land clearance" and what was the samurai's part in it? How did these new systems influence warfare and the raising of troops?

The years from 1150 to 1185 form a seventh phase when samurai became prominent leaders of the capital elite, first in Kyoto, then in Kamakura. The quest for an independent military government was finally realized in 1185 when samurai developed the political skills to contend with the civil aristocracy. How did the

Taira family of martial aristocrats come to power? What was the basis of their strength and what innovations did they make in the military? How were troops organized and armed during the monumental Civil War of 1180–1185? Why did Yoritomo win and the Taira lose?

A conventional study of the ascent of the fighting man to the center stage of Japanese history would end at 1185. But stopping the story with Yoritomo's victory assumes that the samurai reached the pinnacle of power with the establishment of a separate government. As is always so in history, an assessment of one's assumptions is in order. How did the military of the 1200s fight? How was it organized and commanded? How strong was the martial government in Kamakura? How many samurai were there and how did their incomes compare with other members of the ruling class? Is *feudalism* an appropriate term to describe the Kamakura regime?

Before these issues can be examined, some attention should be paid to terminology and theories of weaponry, war, and soldiering. The term *warrior* is deceptively simple, usually referring to a specialist in the techniques of war. There are several terms in Japanese that may be translated as *warrior,* and some conjure up a more specific meaning than *warrior* can convey. Among these are *mononofu* (a soldier of the 500–800 era), *tsuwamono* (a fighter from 900–1300), and *bushi* (a military man, usually a mounted archer, as early as 750, used mostly after 900).[5] In addition, the primary sources of the 500–1300 era mix in almost at random other words with similar connotations, like *mosa* (lit. "fierce one"), *musha* (warrior), *heishi* (soldier), and *kyūba no shi* (mounted archer).

The question is how do these various terms for an expert in warfare relate to one another? This problem has surfaced in Japanese academic circles as a debate over the definition of *bushi,* the military specialist who helped lead Japanese society for about 700 years. One camp, located mostly in western Japan, views *bushi* as a technical expert in war, especially mounted combat.[6] If one accepts this definition, then the *bushi* has a long string of progenitors dating back several centuries. Another group, however, centered in the Tokyo area, follows Marxist models and construes *bushi* to have been a class of rural landholders that came into existence only in the late eleventh century.[7] Recently, one authority has attempted to resolve the debate by suggesting that a *bushi* was both a mounted archer and a country lord possessing land.[8] There is no end in sight to this controversy.

It is the central contention of this book that the twelfth-century warrior (*bushi*) was not a new figure but had roots that dated back to A.D. 500 or thereabouts. The *bushi*, like many of the *manonofu* and *tsuwamono* before him, was merely one variant of the Asian-style mounted archer predominant in the Middle East and the steppe; similarities among all the fighting men of these early centuries of Japanese history far outweigh the differences. In order to prove this contention, this study will examine (1) the skills and weapons by which fighters made their reputations; (2) the social organizations they formed; (3) their economic basis, especially ties to the land; and (4) martial men in the political structure.

I shall use the word *warrior* as a general term to denote a specialist in the technology of warfare, applicable to any epoch. When I need a more specific meaning, I shall refer to a time interval, or use Japanese terms such as *bushi* or *mononofu*, either alone or in parentheses after an English equivalent. Since the most prominent military experts after 1100 were the lightly armored, mounted archers known as *bushi*, my usage of the term *warrior* will inevitably have considerable overlap with *bushi* in the last three chapters. The term *samurai* will mean "the lightly armored, mounted archer of the twelfth century and after," or as an appropriate equivalent of *bushi*.

Another thorny problem is feudalism. Despite voluminous research, the concept has not been satisfactorily defined by historians of Western Europe, much less scholars of Japan.[9] Though I do not find the controversy over feudalism very interesting or enlightening, it is relevant because the construct is invoked in the Western-analogue theory. This work will hold that a traditional society was feudal when three conditions obtained: stable agrarian economy, a martial ruling class, and the predominance of ties of loyalty binding fighting men together.[10]

The debate over feudalism has usually been more confusing than helpful; social scientists have therefore embraced anthropological theories of weapons and war as a more productive method of studying the military in history. Many scholars currently believe that human beings may have a genetic predisposition for making weapons, which are defined as "instruments or devices used primarily in attack or defense in combat, fighting, or war."[11] The creation of weapons about 2 million years ago was a great breakthrough for humanity, as it put us on an equal, and in some cases superior, footing with wild animals naturally "armed" with sharp teeth and claws.

Organized human aggression is probably as old as weapons themselves, as when a group of Paleolithic men surrounded a woolly mammoth and beat it to death. But war, by which I mean organized aggression between or within communities of human beings, is a more recent invention. It is not natural to humans, but the product of settled, agricultural civilization which first sprang up in the Middle East about 10 thousand years ago.[12] Disparities arising from the fluctuations of traditional farming economies, such as famines or epidemics, led to a desire for a neighbor's wealth, land, or laborers. William McNeill actually views war as a type of parasitism, analogous to a plague raging out of control.[13]

Anthropologists have identified two types of warfare between groups of human beings, based on observations of the animal kingdom.[14] These should be viewed as opposite ends of a continuum; any conflict may contain elements of both. One is predatory, the human equivalent to a pride of lions attacking and killing an antelope. The killer, either male or female, acts coldly and ruthlessly to secure food with prosaic weapons. An example of a predatory war might be Hitler's partial conquest of France in World War II or the Roman victory over Carthage in the Punic Wars: Strong centralized states directed well-organized and efficient militaries to seize territory or people. In most cases, predatory conflict among human beings takes place between distinct groups, such as two kingdoms or modern nation-states.

The other form of warfare is called intraspecific, because it is modeled on behavior frequently taking place between two animals of the same species, as when two deer lock horns in combat over a female. Intraspecific war differs from the predatory type in both its means and purpose. In intraspecific combat, ritual, individual battle among males involves elaborate weapons, and aims to secure dominance or the continuation of the males' contribution to the gene pool, usually *within* a group such as a family, region, or class. The best examples of intraspecific warfare come from times when the state was weak and combat deteriorated into individual tests of strength and bravery, such as the jousts of medieval European knights to win the admiration of a lady or the battles of Homeric heroes to secure the fair Helen. In both these cases, the style of combat — individualized and highly ritualized — are sure signs that the wars were intraspecific. Usually social scientists base the distinction between predatory and intraspecific conflicts as much on the means of combat as on the goals of either side. Aspects of traditional weaponry and war that appear irrational to the modern eye may have originated as parts of intraspecific conflict.

Historians of war and the military have also focused their attention on technology and tactics, primarily in the West.[15] Although the pace of technological change was slow in early times, weaponry tended to vary more than other factors, such as organization. The principles of counter-response and symmetry — the tendency of one antagonist to reproduce the same kind of weapon as the enemy — dominated much of martial thinking in the premodern era as it does today.[16] This law of development applied to both field warfare, offensive in nature, and defensive siege combat.

Tactics and battle formations counted for almost as much as weapons to traditional armies and navies. For this reason it is important to distinguish between men who made war as individuals, and those who moved and fought as a single unit, employing tactics that made the whole greater than the sum of its parts. When individual foot soldiers engage in combat as a disciplined, organized entity, they are called infantry; when single-mounted fighters enter combat as a group, they are acting as cavalry.

Of course, technology and tactics amounted to only part, albeit the most visible part, in the success of an army or navy. It is also important to comprehend the entire military system, by which is meant the way men and women were called to duty, equipped, organized, deployed, and rewarded. Politics, the economy, social structure, and culture were interlocking and mutually reinforcing factors.

The era between 500 and 1300 in Japan has a technological unity. It coincides with the era of the horse, when mounted warfare was the preferred mode of combat. Light, mobile equestrian warfare as practiced by Japanese soldiers throughout these years was probably the most deadly form of battle known to humanity before the advent of gunpowder.[17]

chapter one

The Origins of Weapons, War, and Japan's Early Military, 500–645

*Let us, I pray you, go over to the royal domain of Fukakusa, and thence on
horseback towards the Eastern Provinces. Let us make Mibu our headquarters
and having raised troops come back and fight. Our success is not in doubt.*
— Miwa no Fumiya no Kimi, a military advisor
plotting rebellion in 643

Miwa and his lord, Prince Yamashiro of the Imperial House,
never reached the Eastern Provinces, and their revolt was
doomed. But they had the right idea. To secure the loyal military
following, which buttressed political power even before the
advent of Chinese institutions, contenders for the throne were
increasingly obliged to seize the Eastern Provinces for the area's
two most famous products, horses and skilled fighters. A large
concentration of talented mounted warriors made the Eastern
Provinces, an area corresponding to the Kanto plain plus the old
province of Mutsu, an important martial center from the mid-
sixth century on and the last refuge for rebels, scoundrels, and
dissidents of every description.

Evidence for the era before 645 is scarce, but historians have
been able to piece together fragments that supplement this picture of Japan's earliest military. Archeologists have found spears,
shields, and heavy armor in excavations, suggesting the existence
of foot soldiers in addition to mounted combatants. Both types of
fighters used arrows launched from sophisticated bows, the most
popular and deadly weapon devised by the Japanese. Evidence of
naval warfare also survives, centering on the area near the Inland

Sea and northern Kyushu. Royal bureaucrats, military aristocrats, and court-appointed local strongmen commanded forces
that ranged from 10,000 to 25,000 soldiers. Patterns that would
last for centuries were already emerging.

JAPAN'S EARLIEST MILITARY TECHNOLOGY

PREHISTORIC ARMS, ORIGINS TO A.D. 300. The bow and arrow may
not have been the first weapon made by a Japanese, but it soon
became the most popular.[1] The earliest hunters hurled stone-
tipped spears or axes at pigs and wooly mammoths during the
Old Stone Age (150,000–200,000 years ago), but, as the Neolithic
period dawned about 10,000 B.C., the Japanese quickly learned
the advantages of archery. Archeologists have discovered chipped
arrowheads in profusion all over Japan, from Hokkaido to Kyushu, which testifies to the leading role of the bow and arrow in the
Neolithic hunt.

The first archers in Japan used simple, small bows, averaging
about a meter in length.[2] These bowmen rarely polished their
stone arrowheads, and they made their bows from a single piece
of wood, often cut from a tree trunk.[3] But the bow and arrow
were so crucial for survival that soon the drive was on to build a
better bow. Archers added lacquer and bark to improve flexibility
and preserve their weapons, and, by the end of the Neolithic era,
the compound bow, made of several pieces of wood glued
together, was already in use in northern Honshu.[4] Japan's Neolithic hunters were so adept at bow making and archery that their
arrows could pierce a pig's pelvis bone or a human ulna.[5]

Some historians have asserted that the compound bow did not
evolve in Japan until the eleventh and twelfth centuries.[6] They
point to compound bows made of wood, bamboo, and mica portrayed in works of art and literature from that period. They also
argue that, prior to A.D. 1000, all bows were made of one piece of
wood, such as those preserved in the Shōsōin Treasure House in
Nara dating from the mid-eighth century. But archeologists who
study the Neolithic period have shown that Japan's first archers
were in fact quite sophisticated; bow making in Japan had nearly
reached its zenith by the end of the Neolithic era, about 300 B.C.[7]

Later marksmen could manage only minor modifications as the technique of compound bow making spread throughout the archipelago.

Why the late Japanese hunter preferred the compound bow and arrow over other weapons is something of a mystery. Certainly Japan's environment played a role: Trees and stones were plentiful and iron almost non-existent. Neolithic Japanese hunters tracked relatively small game, such as pigs and deer, which could be killed by a single bowman. Anthropologists believe that the early Japanese preferred to hunt alone or in units of no more than 10 men, and that archery served the needs of the lone huntsman better than a spear or other weapon.[8]

Even after the Bronze and Iron Ages began simultaneously about 300 B.C., bringing with them the ability to make new kinds of armaments, the bow and arrow remained the weapon of choice.[9] Bows became larger and arrowheads heavier, so that archers could launch their missiles with greater power. But most arrowheads were still made of stone, even after the Japanese smelted their first iron-tipped arrows in northern Kyushu at the beginning of the Christian era.[10] The Japanese preference for the bow and arrow stands in strong contrast to the Homeric custom, which favored swordplay and deemed archery unmanly.[11]

During the early Bronze and Iron Ages, immigrants and traders supplied metal arms from China and Korea to the archipelago. Soon residents of the island learned to forge their own bronze weapons for the first time, providing the first example of counter-response and symmetry in arms technology in Japanese history. Bronze armaments, which strongly resembled continental prototypes, included spears, pikes, and double-edged swords; the most functional bronze weapons were actually imported from Korea.[12] Archeologists have uncovered bronze arms chiefly in northern Kyushu. Their owners prized the new metal weapons for ceremonial purposes, such as burial with a village chief.[13] By A.D. 100, blacksmiths in Japan were producing pikes, spears, and double-edged swords of iron, armaments that soon supplanted production in bronze.[14]

The Bronze and Iron Ages also brought a revolution in livelihoods, at least in the western half of the archipelago. New farming techniques entered Japan from the continent, and the first evidence of war dates from about A.D. 100. At Doigahama, an archeological site on the western tip of Honshu, scholars have discovered the skeletons of war victims, one pierced by 15 arrows.[15] Most Japanese archeologists and historians agree that the introduction of farming resulted in a class system of haves and have-nots, and that poorer residents organized campaigns to steal their neighbors' surplus grain.[16] War became widespread, as evidenced in the charred remains of late-Iron-Age villages and in references to war in Japan in Chinese sources of the mid-third century A.D.[17]

The Japanese armies that marched in A.D. 300 seem to have been composed of a few foot soldiers wielding bows, swords, and spears. A recent discovery of a wooden shield riddled with holes from arrowheads suggests that these fighters must also have had bodily protection.[18] Naval technology consisted of simple boats constructed from dug-out tree trunks.[19]

WEAPONRY FROM A.D. 300 TO 500. All late-Iron-Age Japanese soldiers had a common problem: Their country was iron-poor. The shortage of iron probably enticed the Japanese to become involved in politics on the Korean peninsula in the fourth century.[20] Unfortunately, the historical record for the period between A.D. 300 and 500 is so murky, and the subject of Japanese-Korean relations so sensitive, that scholars may never satisfactorily illuminate the date, extent, and reasons for Japanese entanglement on the continent.[21]

The wars on the Korean peninsula between Japan (called Wa or Yamato), and the Korean kingdoms of Silla, Paekche, and Koguryŏ provided the Japanese with valuable lessons about fighting and the military (see Map 2, p. 24). Japanese arms makers quickly learned to make the armaments wielded by continental soldiers, demonstrating the principles of counter-response and symmetry.

One weapon found among the Koreans was so new and terrifying that it eventually caused a revolution in warfare in Japan: the horse. Japanese scholars are unanimous in the opinion that Yamato footsoldiers fled headlong from Korean mounted troops about A.D. 400, when the Japanese engaged the northern kingdom of Kogŭryŏ in southern Korea.[22] Equestrian skills, the birthright of every samurai, originated with the hated and feared Koreans.

The horse added a horrifying new dimension to war because soldiers on horseback were much more mobile than foot soldiers. If they fired arrows and had an avenue of escape, they could annihilate well-organized and disciplined infantry while sustaining few casualties. Even heavily armored Roman legions were no match for the mounted archers of Persia.[23] It is little wonder that, once Japanese fighters learned equestrian skills, the horse was used almost exclusively for war, and gradually came to dominate war strategy, until the fourteenth century and the appearance of a pike-bearing (yari) peasant infantry.[24]

The cavalry revolution originated in the Middle East about 900 B.C. and had several implications. First, making war from a galloping horse was a dangerous occupation. In order to be effective, the warrior on horseback needed both hands free to wield a weapon; yet letting go of the reins seemed to guarantee that the fighter would end upon the ground, bruised and helpless.[25] The only alternative was to guide the horse with one's feet and legs, perhaps using the voice to direct a trained horse. Training both horse and rider took time and practice.

Moreover, a horse was expensive, and not everyone had the leisure time to practice. A horse could consume as much grain as 6 to 8 persons, and the owner was responsible for mating and training the animal.[26] Furthermore, the horse was not very useful aside from its war-making capacities: Its meat and milk could not compare to the cow's, and it could not pull a plow until the Europeans invented the horse collar about A.D. 1000.[27] Therefore, civilized societies that utilized the horse extensively tended to have specialized fighters. In some cases, the warriors might be aristocrats, in others, slaves; but always the big question was how to pay for such an expensive military system.

Although horse-riding was new to the Japanese in A.D. 400, the horse had more ancient origins.[28] Neolithic Japanese knew of the horse, which they ate and used in religious rituals. Archeologists have established that the horse was introduced to Japan via two routes, from southern China into Kyushu, and from northeastern

Asia through Korea. During the Bronze and Iron Ages, the Japanese did not ride horses, but used them as beasts of burden.

Early Japanese horses were small by Western standards. Bones excavated from tombs of the late fifth century suggest that the Japanese horse averaged about 130 cm. at the shoulder (about 4.25 feet), whereas European thoroughbreds stand about 160 cm.[29] Recently discovered horse bones from the Kamakura period (1185–1333) indicate that war horses could have been as short as 100 cm. at the shoulder; the Japanese horse remained small even into the twentieth century. The small build of the Japanese horse may derive from genetic factors, or could mean that owners did not feed their steeds with hay or alfalfa in the winter when natural forage was scarce. The size of the Japanese horse mitigated against a fighter's putting the weight of armor on his mount, as the Parthians (Persians) did in the first centuries after the birth of Christ.[30] The use of vulnerable, unarmored horses in battle necessitated an emphasis on speed and mobility in fighting tactics.

The process by which Japanese foot soldiers learned to ride horses is not clear; written records are scarce and unreliable. *The Chronicles of Japan,* the country's first Court history, compiled in 720, says that Korean kings donated horses and horse gear to the Japanese, but the source is not reliable for that era.[31] Some entries from the late 400s speak of the establishment of state-supported horse keepers in Japan, here again a question of credibility.[32]

Archeology provides valuable evidence in tracing the development of equestrian skills. While a few horse trappings may be found in large tombs dating from the 400s, most gear dates from around A.D. 500, when the practice of horse riding seems to have become widespread.[33] Typically, bridles are found, often with the horse's tooth marks in the metal. In addition, the tombs contain wooden saddles decorated with precious metals.

Because the foot-stirrup was invented in China sometime soon after the birth of Christ, Japanese soldiers were familiar with the device from the time they first began to ride, unlike Europeans who did not learn of it until the eighth century.[34] The first Japanese stirrups were wooden, or made of metal hammered into a circle and attached to a leather strap; despite their simplicity, these ensured a rider's stability on the mount. By the seventh century,

Japanese artisans had developed pouch-shaped stirrups, a form so successful at keeping the rider in his saddle that they were popular until 1853.

YAMATO MILITARY TECHNOLOGY, A.D. 500 TO 645. Finds of horse trappings show how equestrian skills spread through Japan after A.D. 500. The earliest artifacts of mounted warfare come from the Kinai (Kyoto-Osaka) region and northern Kyushu, and may be dated at the second half of the fifth century. The location of this evidence along the route from Korea to the Yamato Court supports the theory that the Japanese learned to ride from continentals. By 500, however, horse gear became less common in Kyushu and western Honshu and appeared in greater and greater quantity in eastern Honshu, especially in the Kanto. Many superb examples of workmanship, such as the golden bit uncovered from a tomb in Miyazaki city, Gumma prefecture, or the gold and silver saddle excavated from a mound in Ashikaga city, Ibaraki prefecture, originated from the sixth-century Kanto.[35] Craftsmen of this area even sculpted clay figurines of horses complete with riding equipment. Japan's leading expert on tombs believes that, by the 500s, mounted warfare was probably most popular in eastern and northern Honshu.[36]

Eastern Honshu, especially the Kanto region, was ideally suited for the development of mounted archery. The Kanto Plain is the largest flat area in Japan, perfect for grazing horses; and, even in mountainous regions, valleys might be used to pasture horses, with the ridges serving as natural fences. It is little wonder that most horse pastures were situated in central and eastern Honshu in later historical times. Furthermore, horse manure could be employed in dry farming, a common activity in eastern Honshu. Hunting had been a popular livelihood in eastern Honshu ever since Neolithic times; archery skills were as sophisticated in eastern Honshu as anywhere in the world.[37]

As Japanese soldiers learned to ride horses, they improved their skills and weapons for mounted combat. It is probably true that Korean fighters swung swords from their mounts as they swooped in on their prey, and the Japanese undoubtedly copied this tactic.[38] But even in the sixth century, Japanese mounted warriors probably preferred the bow and arrow. Archery had always been the most popular and most advanced form of combat, and, while sixth-century bows had grown to almost two meters in length, earlier bows had been just the right size for mounted archery.[39] By 500 or so, bamboo arrows were 80–85 cm. long, with iron tips weighing 25 gm.[40] One Japanese authority has argued that an archer could knock a rider off his mount at 100 meters.[41]

Historical sources disclose that sixth-century Japanese horse riders quickly realized the potential of mounted archery. A story of the Emperor Yūryaku, thought to have reigned about A.D. 500, portrays the monarch as an avid hunter shooting at pigs and deer from horseback with a bow and arrow.[42] By far the most convincing evidence comes from *The Chronicles of Japan* for the year 553. Emissaries of Paekche, the kingdom located in southwest Korea and allied with the Japanese, requested aid from the Emperor Kimmei:

> . . . the lands beyond the sea [Korea] are very scarce of bows and horses. From old times until now, they [Paekche] have received them from the [Japanese] Emperor, and have therewith defended themselves against their powerful enemies. I humbly pray the Celestial Bounty to bestow on us a large supply of bows and horses.[43]

The Chronicles of Japan is an unreliable source, especially where Koreans are concerned. Yet there can be little doubt that the Japanese Court bestowed military aid upon the King of Paekche, or that the Japanese actually dispatched troops to Korea.[44] Furthermore, Paekche was an isolated state in southern Korea where horses may not have been as plentiful as in the north. The Paekche request for horses and bows from Japan indicates that mounted archery, the fighting style later to become emblematic of the samurai, had already evolved by the sixth century.

In addition to mounted archery, Japanese soldiers of the sixth and seventh centuries also employed other weapons, mostly of continental design.[45] Fighters wielded offensive weapons, such as the sword and spear, while armor and shields were the major protective armaments. Iron was essential to the manufacture of all these arms, but who manufactured the weapons, and how, remains unclear.[46] Korean immigrants probably furnished much of the expertise, and, after Japan's ally the Kaya States were destroyed in 562, immigrant artisans then residing in the archipelago learned to manufacture armaments with increased efficiency and simplicity.

The spear (*hoko*) was the long weapon employed by foot soldiers, as it had been since the Bronze and Iron Ages. The tip was of iron, often with a tongue for attaching it to a wooden or bamboo pole. Spears measured about 4 meters, and were used to stab or to be hurled at fighters, either mounted or on foot. Yamato spears derived their basic shape from Korean prototypes.

The standard sword (*tachi*) for Yamato fighters was a straight piece of tempered iron sharpened on one side. Blacksmiths also forged double-edged swords (*tsurugi*), but their use was largely ceremonial. Artisans formed sheaths of leather or even hemp cloth, sometimes with bone or horn added. Archeologists distinguish between two types of swords: the ring-pommeled sword imported from China via Korea (*kantō tachi*) and a straight sword (*kubu tsuchi tachi*) found mainly in the Kanto (see Figure 2). Mounted and foot soldiers alike employed swords as stabbing weapons.

The major defensive arms were the shield (*tate*) and armor (*katchū*). Shields were built of wood and leather, sometimes coated with lacquer, and carried by foot soldiers. Clay figurines of warriors molded in the 500s often hold shields. A Japanese historian has estimated that a shield of the sixth or seventh century was larger than the horses of that time, measuring 150 cm. high and 60 cm. wide.[47]

There were two types of armor: the solid iron cuirass (*tankō*) and lamellar armor (*keikō*). The former may have been introduced from Southeast Asia and is seen on many clay figurines of sixth-century fighters. Although it was composed of separate pieces of metal fastened together by leather or bolts, the cuirass permitted little freedom of movement, and lost its popularity after the year 400 (see Figure 3).

Lamellar armor was of Northeast Asian origin and was the accepted battle wear after 500 because it was lighter than the cuirass and allowed greater mobility. It was especially well-suited for mounted warfare. About 800 pieces of iron went into each suit. Fighters wore helmets with metal visors with both types

Figure 2. SWORDS OF EARLY JAPAN

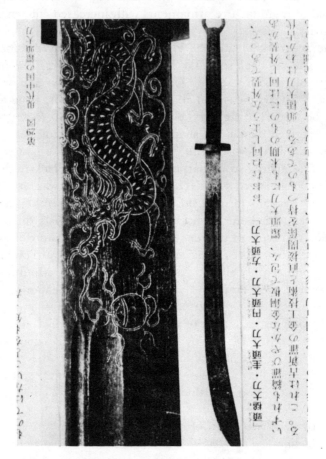

Ring-Pommeled Sword (*kantō tachi*)

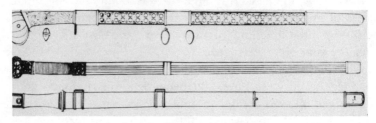

Straight Sword (*kubu tsuchi tachi*)

Figure 3. ARMOR OF EARLY JAPAN

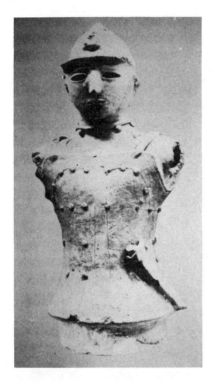

Iron Cuirass

Lamellar Armor (Tibetan Example)

of armor. Decoration of armor with colored thread, leather, and cloth was common.

Although scholars are certain about the weapons used by early Japanese soldiers, little evidence survives to reveal tactics and battle formations before 645. *The Chronicles of Japan* sometimes describes Korean armies as using drums, bells, and gongs to indicate movements, implying that foot soldiers and horsemen moved and fought not as individuals but as units of infantry and cavalry.[48] Yet there are cases of individual combat among the Koreans as well.[49] One Japanese historian has suggested that a typical Korean battle might consist of two armies drawing up infantrymen behind planted shields, who would rain arrows on their enemies. Then cavalrymen would ride out from an opening in the line, and attack the other camp with swords.[50]

If the laws of symmetry and counter-response were at work, then the Japanese might well have fought in a similar manner, but the rare descriptions of battles in which Japanese took part are so sketchy that no one can be sure of tactics. Indeed, the emphasis is often on individual skills and heroism, as in the story of a famous archer who challenged an entire government army.[51] Japanese topography, mostly sharp peaks and swift-flowing streams, also undoubtedly limited the usefulness of large formations of numerous warriors. Thus it is doubtful that, even by 645, the Japanese had developed disciplined field tactics to a high degree.

While in Korea, the Japanese had a chance to learn about siege as well as field warfare.[52] The typical Korean fortress used the mountainous terrain of the peninsula to the advantage of the defenders. A dirt wall 1 to 1.5 meters in height surrounded the summit, which was relatively flat, while, at the bottom, stone walls blocked the easiest routes to the top. Gates made of timbers sunk in the ground permitted entrance to friendly troops. These fortresses were simple to build and often covered several square km. in area.

The palaces of Yamato kings were located in the Kinai on the Inland Sea, across the Tsushima Straits from Korea, and therefore a navy was vital to kingly interests in Asia. But construction of the boats that were supposed to have carried expeditions to Korea is a subject of controversy. Some scholars believe that Japanese boats were nothing more than scooped-out logs spliced together to make rafts (in some cases nails may have been used).[53] Others point to clay models of boats and argue that these vessels were built entirely of planks by the year 600.[54] The most widely accepted view, however, is that boats were made of several hollow logs tied together, with planks attached to the sides and top of the logs to enhance seaworthiness.[55]

A typical vessel measured 10 to 20 meters long, 1 to 2 meters wide, and 0.5 to 1 meter deep. Builders favored cedar and camphor. Japanese boats usually contained a compartment for the crew and helmsman, and were driven by both oars and sails, but they were not safe for a voyage to the continent and rarely plied the ocean at night. The unseaworthy and inefficient construction was a result of the Japanese environment: Trees were plentiful, and the Inland Sea between Honshu, Shikoku, and Kyushu was calm.

Artisans constructed most vessels of the Yamato navy in what is modern Wakayama prefecture, then known as Ki (lit., "tree"). The Court enlisted navigators of Yamato expeditions to the continent from the families of local strongmen also named Ki, who claimed relatives all along the Inland Sea and in northern Kyushu. When these families went to war in their boats, they loaded their horses in with the rest of their weapons. A picture from a tomb in southern Kyushu shows a red horse riding in a boat.[56] An entry in *The Chronicles of Japan* lists one boat as carrying on average 25 men and 2 horses.[57]

JAPAN'S EARLIEST MILITARY ORGANIZATION

The most important martial undertakings of the sixth and early seventh centuries were predatory campaigns to seize territory, usually in Korea (see Map 2). While evidence for most expeditions is scarce, a late crusade against Yamato's rival, Silla, provides a catalogue of early Japanese military organization. *The Chronicles of Japan* describes the 602 expedition of Prince Kume to Korea:

> Prince Kume was appointed General for the Invasion of Silla, and was allotted Shinto priests, local strongmen [*kuni no miyatsuko*], and bureaucratic servants [*tomo no miyatsuko*], and 25,000 troops.[58]

23

Map 2. KOREA, C. A.D. 500

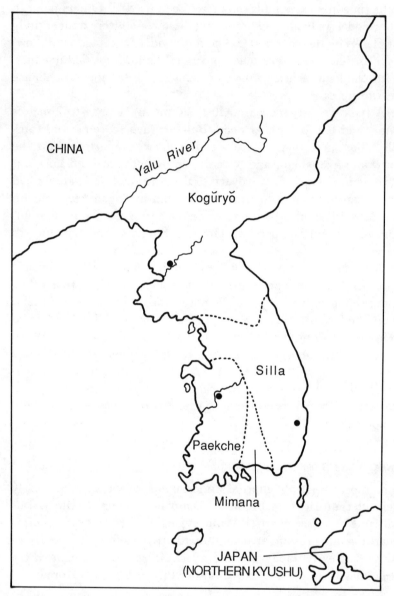

Even though they did not fight, the Shinto priesthood was an essential element in any campaign. These men and women offered prayers for victory and blessed weapons before battle, ceremonies in which the commanding general often participated. Numerous myths and genealogies bear out the close relationship between Japan's first religion and the military, a tie that implies the antiquity of martial occupations in Japan.

The first and most important contingent of Prince Kume's fighting forces was led by regional strongmen with special royal titles of authority (*kuni no miyatsuko*, lit., "local servants of the Court"). These men were essentially kings of their bailiwicks. By the early 600s, the Yamato Court had selected between 120 and 150 of these leaders throughout Japan, each wielding varying degrees of political, military, economic, and religious power over territories of different sizes. These specially designated chieftains shared 3 common characteristics. (1) Their powers were derived from and limited to their local bases. (2) Their status was considerably lower than that of either the Yamato King or other nobles at his Court. (3) They were not major players in Court politics, despite personal ties to some courtly aristocrats or the monarch.[59]

Although each Court-recognized strongman was without peer in his area, increasingly in the sixth and seventh centuries they were being drawn into a loose federation linked to the Court and the King who was based near the modern city of Nara. The Yamato Court demanded tribute from its strongmen in the form of grain, cloth, local products such as fish or iron, and personal servants. In return, the Yamato King recognized and supported his local chieftains' right to rule.

Little is known of how the Yamato regional leaders raised, equipped, fed, or organized their forces. One specialist has argued that a strongman's troops comprised two groups: a peasant majority serving as foot soldiers, and elite mounted warriors belonging to the strongman's family.[60] It is reasonable to believe, as most Japanese scholars do, that royally designated regional strongmen fought as horsemen and commanded units of peasant foot soldiers, since these local chieftains had the wealth to buy and raise horses, and had the time to practice equestrian skills. Furthermore, evidence from the eighth and ninth centuries shows that the descendants of regional strongmen who held royal titles were mounted fighters, usually skilled in archery.[61]

The number of soldiers raised by local servants of the Court is hard to estimate, but *The Chronicles of Japan* lists 10,000 to 25,000 for expeditions to Korea. If one assumes that the Court historians who compiled *The Chronicles of Japan* meant that the Court itself and its appointed local strongmen each provided half the force, and that every strongman provided troops for an expedition, then each regional leader would have been responsible for fewer than 100 soldiers. Most local strongmen associated with Court expeditions came from western Honshu, especially Kyushu, because they were nearest the continent and the Court, and were experienced in naval warfare.

The revolt of Tsukushi no Kimi Iwai, a local strongman once recognized by the Yamato King as the leader of northern Kyushu, furnishes one of the few examples of military forces commanded by the regional chieftain. Iwai plotted rebellion after taking a bribe from the Koreans in 527, blocking the way for a Japanese expedition to Korea, refusing to pay taxes, and intercepting shipments of goods from Korea to the Yamato King. Iwai's forces were probably both naval and land-based.[62]

Modern scholars think Iwai took bribes from a Korean kingdom (Silla) to stop the Japanese expedition. Court historians writing in the early eighth century emphasized Iwai's jealousy of the commander of the expedition, another local chieftain who had once been his friend and equal:

> Iwai lifted up his voice in abusive language, saying: "You [the strongman selected to lead the campaign] who have now become an envoy were formerly my companion. We rubbed shoulders and touched elbows; we ate the same food from the same vessels. How can you lightly be made an envoy and make me come freely and prostrate myself before you!"[63]

This conversation implies that competition among royal strongmen to lead campaigns for the King was fierce; it is difficult to tell whether such was indeed the case, or whether Court historians of the early eighth century were rewriting the record to enhance the prestige of the Imperial Family. The power of the Yamato monarch

over his local leaders was certainly not so great as to prevent strongmen from refusing duty and rebelling against him. Eventually
Iwai's resistance was crushed by another expedition:

> The flags and drums approached close to each other, the dust [from
> both armies] became mingled. The critical moment for the two armies
> arrived, and the position was such that 10,000 deaths seemed unavoid-
> able. At length Iwai was killed.[64]

The description of the conflict in which Iwai perished is reminiscent of earlier Chinese sources, and therefore may not accurately
portray Japanese battle tactics. But insofar as this source has
instructional value, the battle appears to have taken place between
foot soldiers. The reference to flags and drums could indicate the
existence of true infantry, moving and fighting as a unit.

Japan's first history, which reveals precious little about the
armies under the command of regional strongmen, depicts the military roles and armies of Court artistocrat-bureaucrats (*tomo no miyatsuko*) in greater detail. By the time of the 602 expedition to
Korea, the Court bureaucracy that served the Yamato monarch
had become elaborate enough for certain noble familes to specialize in the martial arts. These military aristocrats (*gunji shizoku*)
included the Mononobe no Muraji, who began as Shinto priests
leading prayers before battle and then assumed military duties;
the Ōtomo no Muraji, who oversaw archers guarding the Yamato
palace; and the Saeki no Muraji. The appearance of noble families who monopolized military commands at Court was an important development in Japanese martial organization, a fundamental
pattern that would recur in early Japanese history.

Two units of troops which served the Yamato King and members of the royal family are especially well documented.[65] The
quiver-bearers (*yugei*) and royal retainers (*toneri*) had some features
in common: Both were relatives of local strongmen sent as tribute
to the Yamato King and both served under military aristocrats like
the Ōtomo no Muraji and the Saeki no Muraji.

But the differences between the two units were also significant.
The quiver-bearers came into being in the late fifth century.[66] The
Ōtomo no Muraji supervised these units of bowmen through per-
sonal ties, as *The Chronicles of Japan* suggests in its description of the

mythical origin of these guards.[67] The *yugei* hailed from western Honshu and protected the palace of the Yamato King.

The band of retainers fighting for the house of Yamato, the *toneri*, were nominally under the administration of the Ōtomo no Muraji, but were really personal attendants attached to various members of the king's family. The following excerpt describes the fighting prowess of one such guard in the employ of Prince Yamashiro:

> Hereupon the slave Minari and several tens of royal retainers (*toneri*) came forth and fought in their [Prince Yamashiro's] defense. Hashi no Saba no Muraji was hit by an arrow and died, and the troops were afraid, and retreated. They said to one another: "The saying 'One man as good as a thousand' is applicable to Minari."[68]

Referring to Minari as a "slave" indicates the close personal tie of loyalty between each royal retainer and his master.

The tale of Prince Yamashiro and his rebellion against the Japanese Court continues:

> Therewith Prince Yamashiro and his companions tarried on the mountain for 4 or 5 days. They had nothing to eat or drink. Miwa no Fumiya no Kimi advanced and advised him, saying: "Let us, I pray you, go over to the royal domain of Fukakusa, and thence on horseback towards the Eastern Provinces [Tōgoku]. Let us make Mibu our headquarters and having raised troops come back and fight. Our success is not in doubt."[69]

Two points about this story are significant. First, the royal retainers with ties to Prince Yamashiro all rode horses. The chroniclers do not mention weapons, but it seems likely that Miwa and his fellow warriors used the bow and arrow, as suggested by the archery battle joined by Minari earlier. Since Miwa, Minari, and the other retainers serving Prince Yamashiro were members of the families of local strongmen before they came to Court, their use of mounted archery implies the practice was widespread among regional chieftains.

Second, Prince Yamashiro sought refuge in and reinforcements from the "Eastern Provinces," a term that then meant the Kanto and northeastern Honshu. Japanese historians have traced the origins of individual royal retainers (*toneri*) and found that the overwhelming majority hailed from that area.[70] Although this source does not say as much, Prince Yamashiro and his band probably wanted to escape to these hinterlands because the region offered a plentiful supply of horses, weapons (especially bows and arrows), and fighters. The same "Eastern Provinces" soon gained a reputation as a refuge for rebels in search of an army.

Japanese historians differ on the political status of eastern Honshu, one source of the Yamato Court's men and arms. Inoue Mitsusada believed the Kanto was a backward military and economic base subjugated by the first Yamato kings.[71] He thought the Yamato dynasty had concentrated on making the Kanto in particular into its main martial base after the fall of Japan's ally in Korea (the Kaya States) in 562. The discovery of a sword excavated from a Kanto tomb and inscribed with the name of a late-fifth-century monarch ruling in the Kinai has strengthened this position.[72] But other scholars have noted a myth in *The Chronicles of Japan* that gives a prominent Kanto family status equal to the Yamato rulers and have argued that the Eastern Provinces from earliest times formed an independent kingdom that may have had many weapons and fighters but could not possibly have served as the Yamato military base.[73] Although the standing of this region in the early Japanese political hierarchy is controversial, most agree that eastern Honshu already had its own identity, as suggested by the use of unique geographical terms like the "Eastern Provinces" or "the East" (*azuma*). The scholarly consensus in Japan is that archeological and historical evidence makes it clear that eastern Honshu already had a special military significance by 600.

In addition to the forces under the control of royally designated local strongmen and the Yamato King, most aristocrats possessed considerable personal military might as well. The following incident, which occurred in the late fifth or early sixth century, arose from competition between two brothers for the hand of an aristocratic woman:

> [One suitor] blazed out into a great rage, and forthwith, on that same night, proceeded to the house of Ōtomo no Kanamura no Muraji, where he levied troops and concerted his plans. Ōtomo no Muraji waylaid Shibi no Ōmi [the other suitor] with a force of several thousand men, and slew him at Mount Nara.[74]

Since Ōtomo no Muraji also served as a military official for the Yamato King, he may have been leading government forces, and not his own personal soldiers.

By the early seventh century, a new aristocratic family, the Soga, were masters of the Court. Avid supporters of the new religion of Buddhism, they had won out over the Mononobe no Muraji and other devotees of Shinto in a war in 587. According to *The Chronicles of Japan,* the Soga had prayed to the four Heavenly Kings of Buddhism before battle, and the gods had favored their side with victory. And so a new faith gained the patronage of the Court through its efficacy on the battlefield.

The obituary of the first Soga leader describes him as having "a talent for military tactics," and his progeny inherited their father's concern for armed power:[75]

> He [Soga no Ōomi Emishi] built a house on the east side of Mount Unebi and dug a pond, so as to make of it a castle. He erected an armory, and provided a store of arrows. In his goings and comings he was always surrounded by an attendant company of 50 soldiers. These sturdy fellows were called the Eastern Company.[76]

The name given to Emishi's guards, the Eastern Company, implies that they came from the Eastern Provinces, further evidence of the military character of early eastern Honshu. It is likely that the Soga family achieved dominance of the Court in the early 600s because of their armed might.

CONCLUSION

As the first phase in the development of the Japanese military came to a close in 645, some basic patterns had begun to emerge. Much of the technology used by the samurai of later times had already come into existence, and mounted archery was widely practiced, especially in the Kanto and adjacent areas. At Court a few aristocratic families had specialized in the martial arts, and, although it is difficult to prove that these military noblemen were horse-riding bowmen, they undoubtedly commanded fighters who were. Even in the countryside, mounted combat had become the privilege of a few well-to-do strongmen.

Military men had also assumed an important role in the political structure. Martial experts reported to the Court to serve the Yamato King, either as royal retainers, or through their political status as Court-recognized regional strongmen. Many of the King's attendants were mounted archers, and came from rough-and-tumble country in the Kanto and northeastern Honshu. The same region was fast becoming famous as a land of rebels and outlaws.

When scholars ask how the Japanese paid for their earliest military ventures, however, answers are more difficult to find. Some specialists believe that the Court provided the King's attendants like the *toneri* with cooks, supplies, food, and even a salary, but the evidence is thin.[77]

The dearth of knowledge about the economic base of Japan's first fighters has shaped the debate over the origins of the Japanese warrior (*bushi*) and feudalism. Historians who see the samurai as military experts have no trouble in viewing horse-riders of the sixth- and early-seventh-century as their ancestors. But those who define the *bushi* as a feudal landlord overseeing peasant cultivators disagree. Without land, there could be no warriors (*bushi*), they would argue. While it is too early in this study to draw unshakable conclusions, it seems fair to say that the evolution of basic technological, social, and political structures in the Japanese military before 645 raises doubts about the wisdom of defining the samurai simply as a class of rural landlords. Equating the *bushi* with certain patterns of landholding may have its advantages when looking into samurai-peasant relations, but, when it comes to uncovering the lineages of Japan's fighting men, it will not do.

Problems also await those Western-analogue theorists who hold that Japan appeared to be on the road to feudalism before 645. In the Introduction, I described feudalism as obtaining when a military ruling class bound together predominantly by ties of loyalty ruled over an agrarian economy. In characterizing pre-645 society, Western-analogue theorists would probably stress the importance of the mounted warrior relying on personal ties of loyalty; but without knowledge of the rural economy, use of the term *feudalism* seems premature. The number and power of military specialists in the ruling class is similarly difficult to discern, and raises another objection to the use of *feudalism* to describe this era. The widespread deployment of peasant foot soldiers (not just mounted knights) and the importance of royal bureaucrats rather than feudal lords as military commanders are further arguments against calling this epoch feudal. All these facts suggest that supporters of the Western-analogue theory are reading the data in a selective way. Basic patterns may have already begun to take shape in the Japanese military, but they were pointing in a different direction.

chapter two

Obeying the Imperial Command: The Military from 645 to 770

The dread imperial command
I have received: from tomorrow
I will sleep with the grass,
No wife being with me.
— Mononobe Akimochi, a Border Guard in 755

Soldiering has always been a lonely duty. When Mononobe composed this poem in 755, however, his desolation must have been particularly intense. He was leaving his home in eastern Honshu, possibly forever, for the windswept beaches of northern Kyushu, forfeiting his position as a local strongman (*kuni no miyatsuko*) with an ancient pedigree, to obey the "dread imperial command." Mononobe was just one of many men who in the eighth century dared the mountainous terrain of central Honshu and the tranquil waters of the Inland Sea in a long and perilous journey to defend the Imperial Court against an attack from China or Korea.

In a span of less than 30 years in the mid-seventh century, Japan was beset by a bloody and successful coup d'état, a disastrous foreign campaign in Korea, and a civil war. Defeat abroad and rebellion at home drove the former Yamato kings, now elevated to the rank of emperor, to build a powerful army and navy. The model for the new military, spelled out in law codes compiled in 702, was based largely on Chinese prototypes: The Japanese Court authorized itself to draft and train peasants to form a disciplined army composed mainly of infantry. The government intended to arm its soldiers with the latest continental weapons, such as the crossbow, and dispatch them to guard northern Kyushu or the new imperial palaces in the Kinai region.

Yet neither Court lawgivers nor local officials charged with carrying out the new statutes could alter the social and economic realities of eighth-century Japan. By 702, when the first set of comprehensive Chinese-style laws came into force, the Japanese had already had long experience with weaponry, war, and military organization; in actual battles, the "new" military fought much like its predecessor. Local strongmen, many of them descendants of Court-appointed chieftains (*kuni no miyatsuko*) from before 645, continued the tradition of mounted combat, commanding peasant foot soldiers who were often undisciplined and unreliable. These mounted warriors, who swung swords and fired arrows, constituted the backbone of both the provincial militia in the countryside and aristocratic forces in the capital. In their drive to strengthen the Japanese military against outside threats, Court officials did not alter the previous patterns so much as legitimize them and allow them to become entrenched.

FORGING THE NEW CHINESE-STYLE SYSTEM

INITIAL ATTEMPTS AT REFORM, 645–660. In 645, Prince Naka, his fellow-assassin Nakatomi (later Fujiwara) no Kamatari, and the soon-to-be Emperor Kōtoku murdered the leader of the Soga family during a palace ceremony before the eyes of a startled Empress. Most historians once believed that the assassination occurred simply because of Japan's domestic political squabbles. In this view, the conspirators carried out their coup d'état to punish the Soga, who had dominated the Court for over a half century, and to reestablish the power of Japan's rightful rulers, the imperial line. The palace revolution of 645 became a symbol of a rejuvenated imperial institution, which would now lead Japan on the path to civilization and enlightenment.

In the last 15 years, however, Japanese scholars have criticized such a view for overemphasizing the benevolence of the imperial line and failing to consider the coup d'état in the context of international politics in East Asia. For most of their rule, Yamato leaders had benefited from disunity in China and Korea. During the late sixth and early seventh centuries, however, the political and military balance of power on the Asian continent shifted dramatically. The great Sui (589–617) and Tang dynasties (618–907) unified China; both were aggressive and expansionist in their foreign policy and began to extend military power towards the border lands, especially Korea. As Chinese peasant armies invaded the Korean peninsula in the 630s, rebellions threw the small Korean kingdoms of Koguryŏ, Paekche, and Silla into upheaval. Eventually new rulers instituted native military dictatorships to defend their kingdoms against the Chinese.[1]

Although there were over 100 miles of ocean between Japanese shores and Korea, the Court had once possessed territory on the mainland, and still had interests and allies there. Students and official emissaries to the continent reported the advance of Tang armies and the battles in Korea to the Japanese Court, and many Japanese courtiers began to wonder whether the mighty Chinese armies would stop at the Straits of Tsushima. Every government decision took place with one eye on the upheavals in Korea.

By the early 640s, Japan was particularly vulnerable because the Court could not agree upon who was best suited to lead in formulating a response to the military action on the continent. The throne was occupied by the Empress Kōgyoku, a woman whose chief virtue lay in her ties to the Soga family, the most powerful aristocrats at Court. It was hoped that the Empress could hold the throne until the Court could make a final decision on which man would make the best ruler.

Soga no Iruka, the iron-fisted leader of his family, supported a close relative to be the next monarch, but most of the Court (including some members of the Soga) sided with the cause of Prince Yamashiro, who had been passed over for the throne once before. Iruka, however, determined that Yamashiro lacked a talent for foreign affairs, so crucial to Court deliberations in the 640s. And so, in 643, Iruka pressured Prince Yamashiro into an abortive coup, described in Chapter 1. Prince Yamashiro was forced to commit suicide.

Opposition to Iruka's high-handed methods grew at Court. By 645, Nakatomi no Kamatari and Prince Naka, both of whom knew of the increasingly dangerous military situation in Korea and concluded that the Court could not unite behind the fractious Iruka, had become the focus of an anti-Soga conspiracy. In the 6th month of 645, the conspirators assassinated Iruka and executed most of the rest of the Soga family. Japan's own militaristic and centralizing cabal had thus taken power, determined to respond to the growing Chinese menace and the Korean coups. The Imperial Family may have benefited from the murder of the Soga, but Japan's increasing vulnerability to invasion supplied the real motivation for the conspirators.

Like their counterparts in Korea, Japan's new rulers immediately focused on military affairs. Before the blood had dried on their hands, the new ruling clique, headed by Prince Naka, turned its attention to weapons and security. Immediately after the coup in 645, the new Emperor appointed 8 governors (*kuni no mikotomochi*) for Japan's military base, the Eastern Provinces (the Kanto and Mutsu). He directed them to erect arsenals where all swords, armor, and bows and arrows in the Kanto and northeastern Japan could be collected and put under state supervision. The only persons permitted to keep arms were those who might face raids from the "barbarians" (*emishi*) of northeastern Honshu.[2] Less than a month later the Emperor issued a similar command "to collect weapons of all kinds" throughout the rest of Japan.[3] The edict to dispatch governors to the Eastern Provinces and collect the weapons there reflected both the military importance of the region and official fears about rebellion.

In 646, the Emperor recalled the governors to reprimand two of them for abuse of authority, but soon made new appointments to all 8 posts. According to *The Hitachi Gazetteer,* a source compiled in the early eighth century, lawgivers recognized the Kanto portion of the Eastern Provinces as a distinct entity, defining it as the area east of the Ashigara Pass (on the border of the eighth-century provinces of Sagami and Suruga).[4] To control this vital region, the rulers of Japan divided the Kanto into 8 parts and named a governor general (*sōryō*) to oversee each.[5] Two Japanese historians have argued that the appointment of governors general was meant to bring the independent kingdom of the Kanto more firmly under the control of the new faction at Court.[6]

While the new rulers concentrated on the Eastern Provinces

because of their historical military importance, Prince Naka and company also attempted to seize control of other regions. In the aftermath of the coup, they began establishing new units of local government called *kohori* (also *hyō*, lit., "military district").[7] Japanese historians are unanimous in the view that the Court borrowed this term from the Koreans, and that the new office was military.[8] Later records indicate that the establishment of these new units was a Court attempt to reduce the power of pre-645 local strongmen (*kuni no miyatsuko*) by carving up their jurisdictions (*kuni*) and dividing their authority into military, administrative, and religious components. Little is known of the appointees to the new military districts; many seem to have been relatives of the local strongmen from the Yamato era, while some may have been newcomers. In 645, however, the new leaders at Court were still too weak to push their divide-and-rule strategy too far.

In early 646, the recently anointed Emperor Kōtoku and his loyal clique promulgated the Taika Reform Edict, according to *The Chronicles of Japan.*[9] Though there is considerable controversy about the authenticity of the 646 Edict, which mandated a wholesale transformation of Japan on Chinese legal models, two provisions of Articles 1 and 4 were probably part of the original decree:

(Article 1) . . . Let . . . Border Guards (*sakimori*) . . . be provided . . . (Article 4) As to weapons, each person shall contribute a sword, armor, bow and arrows, a flag, and a drum. . . .[10]

Border Guards, such as Mononobe Akimochi, the poet-soldier mentioned earlier, traveled from eastern Honshu to protect northern Kyushu from invaders later in the eighth century. Historians are uncertain how well Court officials could have implemented this system so soon after the coup in 645, but the reference to Border Guards is a reflection of Japanese anxieties about foreign attack.[11]

Article 4 is the first evidence of state desires to control all weapons, a policy greatly elaborated in the 680s and included in the Chinese-style law codes adopted in 702. It is notable that flags and drums, which could have been used to signal coordinated movements, are mentioned. In 646, the new ruling clique issued another command to repair arsenals throughout Japan, a policy undoubtedly related to the previous order demanding the collection of private weapons in the Eastern Provinces in 645.[12] Military matters were clearly on the minds of the members of the new ruling faction.

DISASTER ABROAD AND MORE REFORMS, 660-672. Meanwhile events on the continent were moving rapidly against the Japanese Court. The powerful Tang empire began invading the northern Korean kingdom of Koguryŏ, but it soon became clear that to defeat Koguryŏ the Tang also had to destroy Koguryŏ's ally, the southwest Korean kingdom of Paekche. In the 3rd month of 660, the Tang mounted a massive offensive against Paekche, sending 100,000 troops by land and sea. In the 7th month, Silla, the third Korean kingdom, added its forces as a staunch ally of Tang. Paekche fell shortly thereafter, and the Tang took more than 700 prisoners, including most of the Paekche ruling class.[13]

Even after the King of Paekche had surrendered to Tang and Silla, his partisans continued to fight in the field. One of the leaders of the resistance movement sent 100 Tang prisoners to the Japanese Court and begged for aid. Aristocratic leaders like Prince Naka and the Empress Saimei (r. 655–661, formerly the Empress Kōgyoku) could not bear to see their friend and military ally destroyed; the next year both moved to a temporary palace in northern Kyushu to organize preparations for a fleet.

The Court sent 3 expeditions to the mainland: a special army of 5,000 men in the late summer of 661, a fleet of 170 ships in the spring of 662, and an army of 27,000 under the famed general Abe no Hirafu in 663. Later historical records suggest that the Japanese expeditions to aid the Paekche partisans were similar in fighting technology and organization to many late Yamato excursions to Korea, such as Prince Kume's ill-starred attempt to cross the ocean.[14] Japanese court histories show that a majority of the troops hailed from western Honshu, Shikoku, and especially from Kyushu, though some soldiers marched and rode to battle from the Kanto and northeastern Japan.[15] Records also suggest that most of the leaders of the campaign held titles normally reserved for the local strongmen (*kuni no miyatsuko*) of Yamato times. Almost two decades after the coup of 645 and the commitment to Chinese-style institutions, the means of raising, equipping, and organizing a Japanese army showed little change.

For a time the foreign war went well; during the latter half of 662, the Japanese army and Paekche partisans even engaged Silla and Tang forces near the former Paekche capital. However, when the third Japanese contingent arrived in Korea, both Tang and Silla sent reinforcements. Dissension broke out in the Japanese-Paekche ranks. As the tide of battle turned in favor of Silla and Tang, the Korean and Chinese allies planned a knock-out punch. In the 8th month of 663, a pitched battle was fought just outside the main Japanese-Paekche fortress on the Paekch'ŏn River:

> The hostile generals arrived before Chuyu [the former Paekche capital] and surrounded the royal city. The Tang generals, in command of 170 fighting ships, drew up in line of battle in the Paekch'ŏn River. The Japanese warships that first arrived engaged the Tang fleet, but had not the advantage, and therefore retired. Great Tang stood on its guard in strict order of battle.
>
> . . . The Japanese generals and the Paekche King, regardless of the aspect of affairs, said to one another: "If we struggle which shall be first [to kill the enemy], they [the Tang and Silla forces] will naturally retire of themselves." So they again led forward the routed Japanese ranks, and troops of the Middle Division of their force, to attack the Great Tang fleet. But Tang closed upon them [the Japanese] from right and left, and engaged them from all sides. In a short space of time, the imperial [Japanese] force was defeated, and many fell into the water and drowned. The ships were unable to maneuver either astern or ahead. Echi no Takutsu [a Japanese general] looked up to heaven and made oaths; he gnashed his teeth, and in his rage slew several tens of men. He then fell fighting.[16]

The Battle of the Paekch'ŏn River was the worst defeat for the Japanese in their premodern history. Chinese and Korean sources both stress the heavy losses on the Japanese side, perhaps as many as 400 ships, 10,000 men, and 1,000 horses.[17]

There were many reasons for the debacle in Korea. The Chinese forces were more numerous and better armed, and employed mass tactics in a way Japanese generals had never witnessed. Although the account of the battle in *The Chronicles of Japan* is brief, it suggests that the Japanese relied more on individual skill and bravery, as implied in the phrase "struggling to be first," a term later used to describe samurai man-to-man combat.[18] In addition, the Japanese generals quarreled amongst themselves, a sign that they lacked unified command.[19]

The loss at the Paekch'ŏn River was a bitter blow to the Japanese Court. For over a century, Japan's foreign policy had depended on support of Paekche over Silla on the Korean peninsula; now it seemed likely that the whole peninsula would fall under the domination of Tang and Silla. The worst Japanese fears were substantiated in 668 when the Tang used Kogŭryŏ disunity to destroy the northern Korean kingdom. Korea had fallen into the hands of powers hostile to Japan.

The scope of the military emergency that gripped Japan in the wake of the disaster at the Paekch'ŏn River is best portrayed by an incident of 671. The Tang dispatched a mission to Japan to release a high-ranking Paekche official held captive in China during the war, but, before the embassy sailed from Tsushima, the island way-station between Japan and Korea, the mission sent some Japanese prisoners-of-war ahead to Kyushu. The Tang ambassador's reasoning was:

> The ships of our people [the Tang party] are numerous, and if they suddenly arrived [in Japan], it is to be feared that . . . [the Japanese] guards would be alarmed, and engage us in a battle of archery. So . . . [we] sent on [the Japanese prisoners] to give . . . some notice in advance of . . . [our] intention of proceeding to the Court.[20]

The new Emperor Tenji managed to smooth out relations with the Tang during his tenure on the throne, but tension still underlay the expressions of friendship.

In the aftermath of defeat, Tenji's government hastened to prepare Japan for a Korean or Chinese assault. Courtiers of all degrees took to wearing long swords and daggers or carrying shields and bows and arrows.[21] Tenji moved his Court and capital further inland to Ōmi on Lake Biwa, a safe distance from any possible invasion route, and conducted military exercises there. In 670, Tenji ordered the first nationwide census as an initial step towards conscription of the populace.

Ably assisted by refugees from Korea, Tenji's government hurriedly fortified northern Kyushu, the Japanese island where an invasion force would land first. In 664, the Court specified that beacon fires and Border Guards be placed on the islands of Tsushima and Iki between Korea and Kyushu. Tenji then planned a complex of Korean-style fortresses to defend northern Kyushu. He had a great embankment (*mizuki*) 40 meters wide and 15 meters high built across the small plain facing Hakata Bay; Court strategy probably included constructing a moat on the seaward side of the wall to forestall an advance by enemy troops.[22] A few months later, Korean engineers oversaw the raising of stone and dirt fortifications (Forts Ōno and Ki) in the mountains behind the dirt embankment. The Court then appointed a military governor of Kyushu to command the complex. Korean-style siege works soon appeared in Nagato, Takayasu (near Nara), and Yashima, strategic mountains along the route from Kyushu to Tenji's capital at Ōmi.

FORGING THE CHINESE-STYLE SYSTEM, 672–702. The defeat in Korea had drained the Emperor Tenji of his popularity among local strongmen (*kuni no miyatsuko*) formerly appointed by the Yamato Court. These men were still so vital to the Emperor's control of the country that no thorough overhaul of the military system could be undertaken without their support. Tenji's son, Prince Ōtomo, was the choice to assume the imperial dignity upon his father's death in 671, but Tenji's younger brother, Prince Ōama (later the Emperor Temmu, r. 672–686), had other ideas.[23] In 672, civil war broke out.

Japan's first well-documented conflict over the throne lasted about one month and unfolded in three stages.[24] In the first and crucial phase, which lasted from the 22nd through the 27th day of the 6th month, Prince Ōama escaped from self-imposed exile at Yoshino, enlisting the aid of his personal retainers (*toneri*) and military men from Yamato province. Traveling on horseback with little food, Ōama and his band secured the cooperation of a few strategically situated local strongmen and seized the two important passes of Suzuka in Ise and Fuwa in Mino (see Map 3). Ōama thus had access to the men and weapons of the Eastern Provinces

Map 3. THE CIVIL WAR OF 672

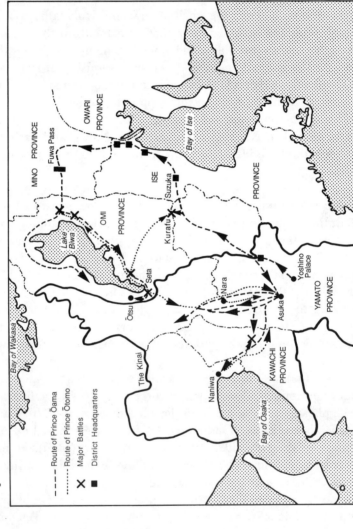

Source: Ienaga Saburo et al., eds., *Zusetsu Nihon bunka shi taikei 2 Asuka jidai,* p. 124.

while sealing the region off from Prince Ōtomo and the Court. Prince Ōama soon assembled a large army commanded by several military aristocrats.

The Ōmi Court under Prince Ōtomo panicked. Ōtomo attempted to raise troops in the Eastern Provinces, Yamato, Kyushu, and western Honshu, but his efforts came to naught. Meanwhile Ōama tightened his control of central and eastern Honshu. On the 4th day of the 7th month, a small army under an Ōmi general managed to win a victory near the palace in Yamato.

In the final stage, Prince Ōama divided his forces into 3 armies. The first retraced the route of Ōama's escape through Mino and Ise and reinforced his flagging troops in Yamato, where they eventually prevailed. The second and main army proceeded from Fuwa Pass southwest along the southern shore of Lake Biwa, while the third corps went northwest over the top of Lake Biwa to cut off Ōtomo's retreat. Although one of Prince Ōtomo's most innovative generals surprised Ōama's force at Kurafu with a night attack comprising exclusively horse-riders, Ōtomo was soon faced with a last stand at Seta. When Ōama's second army smashed through Ōtomo's lines at Seta, Ōtomo's force fled headlong in retreat. Ōama's generals presented Ōtomo's head to their leader at Fuwa on the 26th day of the 7th month. Prince Ōama completed mop-up operations in the Kinai region by the end of the month.

The Civil War of 672 reflects patterns of the old military technology and organization more than the new. First, it shows the importance of eastern Honshu in military strategy. Prince Ōama's initial thrust was directed at the Fuwa and Suzuka Passes to block his enemy's access to the Eastern Provinces. Once these passes were secure, only Prince Ōama was able to raise troops in that region. While the evidence on the geographic origins of Ōama's soldiers is slim, historians have been able to determine (1) that two of Ōama's main generals commanded armies hailing from the Eastern Provinces, and (2) that these fighters came from as far away as Shinano and Kai.[25] The army that turned the tide for Ōama in Yamato was composed of mounted troops from the Eastern Provinces.[26] When one considers other indications of the military importance of the Eastern Provinces mentioned throughout Chapters 1 and 2, these facts show that Prince Ōama's initial trek

from Yoshino did not stop in Mino and Ise, but was aimed at recruiting an army of warriors from the Eastern Provinces. Ōama's
ability to attract these men to his cause proved decisive in the final
campaign.

Second, weapons and tactics appear to have begun to change in
the wake of the defeat in Korea. *The Chronicles of Japan* describes
Prince Ōtomo's forces as banging drums and gongs and firing
crossbows during a decisive battle near the end of the war, suggesting that his army had begun to copy Chinese ideas of mass infantry attacks. He may have tried to discipline his foot soldiers into
units that launched "arrows that fell like rain."[27] A Korean expert
in the ways of group warfare led Ōtomo's troops at Seta, while a
Tang prisoner-of-war advised Ōama and his men.[28] References to
shields and fortifications are also common in the account of the
Civil War.[29]

But there can be no doubt that the decisive edge in battle went
to the side with the best mounted fighters.[30] Prince Ōama's plot to
seize the passes would never have been possible without horsemen,
who speedily escorted him from exile at Yoshino and rallied the
troops around him. The counterblows of the Ōmi court began
when Prince Ōtomo commenced to "assemble . . . [his] choice
horsemen and pursue in . . . [Ōama's] track."[31] Ōtomo's last victory at Kurafu was the product of a special division of immigrant
mounted troops.[32] Horse-riding fighters, commanded by generals
from the Eastern Provinces, won several battles for Ōama.[33]

The command structure also shows relatively few changes from
the early sixth century. At Prince Ōama's camp, royal retainers (*toneri*) such as Murakuni no Muraji Oyori, who was sent to Mino to
rally local strongmen to Ōama's cause, planned and executed campaigns. The same aristocratic military families (for example, the
Ōtomo family, not related to Prince Ōtomo) who commanded
forces in the sixth and seventh centuries assembled and supervised
Ōama's armies in 672. In the field, local chieftains (*kuni no miyatsuko*) recognized and supported by the Yamato monarch a century
earlier gave Prince Ōama the edge at major battlegrounds like
Mino and Owari.[34] In contrast, Prince Ōtomo's cause suffered
from a lack of support from local strongmen in his base in western
Honshu, presumably because these same regional leaders had

been cajoled into sending troops to Korea to fight in the disastrous Battle of the Paekch'ŏn River and felt they had been overtaxed.

The one new element evident in military organization during the Civil War of 672 was the role of the provincial governors (*koku-sai*) who had been appointed by the Emperor Tenji from the ranks of Court aristocrats. These officials had arrived in the countryside during and after the defeat in Korea, and held considerable military power. They gave Ōama's cause its first boost in critical regions like Ise and Mino.[35]

In the 2nd month of 673, Prince Ōama ascended the throne to become the Emperor Temmu. His victory had eliminated many Court aristocrats and pre-645 local strongmen who opposed strengthening imperial power, while at the same time the new Emperor was regarded with the awe normally reserved for a successful military commander. Temmu wasted no time in using his unprecedented power to make sweeping changes in the political order.

His concerns naturally included reform of the fighting establishment, along three lines. First, he saw to it that government officials were well armed and able to defend themselves. Temmus' reign is filled with references to archery tournaments and laws demanding the provision or inspection of weapons and horses for courtiers as well as lower-ranking officials. His military emphasis is apparent in a 684 edict directed to officials at Court:

> In a government, military matters are the essential thing. All civil and military officials should therefore diligently practice the use of arms and riding on horseback. Be careful to provide an adequate supply of horses, weapons, and articles of personal costume. Those who have horses shall be made mounted soldiers; those who have none shall be foot soldiers. Both shall receive training. Let no obstacle be thrown in the way of their assembling for this purpose.[36]

The decree expressed Temmu's goal of military preparedness against both foreign and domestic enemies. The Emperor assembled and trained officials in the hopes of creating an expert and disciplined fighting force that would wage war as units of infantry and cavalry.

Second, Temmu confiscated weapons from persons not employed in his government. He gave orders to the provinces that all such things as great and small horns, drums, fifes, flags, crossbows, and stone-throwing engines should not be kept in private houses but stored in local district offices.[37] As a man who had betrayed his nephew and stolen off secretly to the Eastern Provinces to raise his own army, Temmu knew the danger inherent in independent military force. In the district offices, local men of influence friendly to Temmu held power and controlled men and arms. The weapons cited in the order, such as flags, crossbows, catapults, and noisemakers, were central to an army that utilized mass tactics, like Chinese peasant armies the Japanese had faced in Korea.

Third, Temmu continued Tenji's policy of defense against a continental invasion. It was the "Heavenly Warrior Emperor," as he was posthumously known, who initiated the practice of ferrying Border Guards who came from eastern Honshu to northern Kyushu.[38] In addition, Temmu maintained the fortifications built in northern Kyushu during previous reigns.

The victor in the Civil War of 672 was always careful to maintain close ties with the region that had catapulted him to power. A large portion of Temmu's revenues originated from the Eastern Provinces, and many of his closest advisors were from the same region. At one point Temmu may even have considered the radical proposal of relocating the capital to Shinano, deep in the mountains of central Honshu. Temmu had won victory in 672 through the control of the Eastern Provinces, an important military center for the Yamato kings of the late sixth century, and he was not about to allow his heirs to lose the throne by ignoring its importance.[39]

Efforts at reform continued under Temmu's successors, his consort, the Empress Jitō (r. 686–697), and her grandson, the Emperor Mommu (r. 697–707). In 693, the Court sent "professors of the art of war . . . to give instruction and training in the various provinces."[40] These men had studied Chinese-style battle tactics as elaborated in Sun-tzu's *The Art of War* and other classics. Later the government established the first state pastures to supply horses to the military.[41]

Jitō and Mommu also completed the divide-and-rule reform of local government initiated soon after 645. By 690, the Court had established two layers of administration over the peasantry: the province (*kuni*, not to be confused with the earlier unit), and the district (*kohori*, *hyō*). The Emperor appointed aristocrats from the Court to be governors of the 60-odd provinces, while magistrates, named from among the heads of locally prominent families, oversaw about 400–500 districts. In practice, the Office of Ceremony (Shikibu shō) and the provincial governor worked in tandem to select the magistrates, who were often descendants of pre-645 local strongmen (*kuni no miyatsuko*). The district post was most unusual, even "un-Chinese," since magistrates held their office for life, received a large allotment of land, and could usually assume that their office would devolve upon an heir.[42] In 702, the Emperor Mommu changed the Chinese character used for the district from *hyō* to *gun*, thus matching current Chinese usage.

In 689, the Court required local officials to compile registers of the population, a crucial prerequisite for drafting commoners to fight. Functionaries divided the populace into four groups and had them "trained in warlike exercises."[43] Most authorities agree that the implementation of a comprehensive census was the most important prerequisite for the formation of a Chinese-style conscript army.[44]

THE CHINESE-STYLE SYSTEM OF 702

THE CHINESE MODEL. In 702, a committee of Court aristocrats compiled the Taihō Codes, Japan's first set of comprehensive, Chinese-style laws. Although only fragments of the 702 compendium now exist, legal commentators of the ninth century preserved almost every article in a nearly identical set of statutes, the Yōrō Codes of 718. Lawgivers wrote both Codes in Chinese, and many statutes repeat verbatim articles found in Chinese compendia. Thus it is possible to view Japanese legal development over time and to compare Japan's laws to China's.

All Codes, both Chinese and Japanese, laid out the framework for political, social, and economic institutions. According to the statutes, every person was required to register in a periodic census, thereby receiving a parcel of land to farm and becoming liable for head taxes in kind and labor, including military service. Taxes supported the refined lifestyle of the aristocracy in the capital and a bureaucracy scattered throughout the country.

In both Japanese and Chinese Codes, legal minds outlined their ideas for the military in the Chapter on the Army and Defense (in Japanese, *Gumbō-ryō*). This contained the most advanced and up-to-date Chinese thinking in the early eighth century on how to operate a successful army and navy.[45] Chinese views on the military were a direct result of their recent historical experience. For about 400 years after the fall of the Han Dynasty in A.D. 220, the Chinese suffered barbarian invasions and political disunity. Violence was endemic, and the barbarians, who lived in hereditary military households, commanded the armies of China's cultural heartland, the north. Because most Chinese avoided service, and the government had to reward these hereditary fighters, the system was expensive and armies relatively small and unreliable.

A reformed military system helped reunify China by the end of the sixth century. The essence of the revised Chinese model was to conscript commoners (mostly peasants), place them under strong centralized control, and mold them into a highly disciplined force of infantry and cavalry using coordinated tactics. Officers trained the peasant-soldiers relentlessly after the fall harvest was over.

Such a military design had 4 advantages. (1) It was cheap. The soldiers were supposed to be commoners, who received tax exemptions in lieu of payments, and, because peasants provided many of their own weapons, the government also saved on arms outlays. (2) Although the Emperor could raise huge forces (over a million men in the early 600s), fighters could stay on campaign only for a short time, since they were also farmers. Brief campaigns suited commoners and civilian leaders alike. (3) The Chinese military was primarily defensive in nature. Chinese officials arranged their commoner guard units around the capital to keep uncivilized tribesmen away. (4) Perhaps most important, the Chinese system severely restricted the role of locally powerful, hereditary military families. These households, many of them barbarian, had evolved during the age of disunity which began in A.D. 200, and, since they relied upon personal loyalties, they could be difficult for the state to control. In 590, the Chinese Emperor tried to eliminate the distinctions between military and commoner families by making everyone liable to the census and martial service.[46] This practice continued in the seventh and eighth centuries: Laws barred locally powerful men from command of the regional militia, although some rural aristocrats may have served as officers anyway.[47] The Chinese government even refused to allow a soldier to use his own horse; the state raised and allocated the animals.[48]

These highly trained Chinese peasant-soldiers proved to be a formidable force in the field, conquering new territories from Korea to central Asia. The large majority of Chinese troops in the 500–800 era fought on foot, using crossbows and wearing heavy iron armor. But cavalrymen, firing a crossbow that could shoot 200 paces, were also an essential element of Chinese mass tactics. In one battle, Chinese cavalry scattered enemy mounted forces of up to 10 times their own number.[49] Like the infantry, horsemen became conditioned to respond precisely to horn, drum, and flag signals; they could advance and retire from battle under perfect control.[50] It is little wonder that the Japanese, who already had a long tradition of mounted archery themselves, would copy this successful model.

CONSCRIPTION AND ORGANIZATION IN JAPAN. The Japanese laws on the military system which were implemented in 702 are a classic example of the principles of counter-response and symmetry, the tendency of one antagonist to duplicate the enemy's weapons and organization. Like their Chinese rivals, the Japanese dictated that commoners belonging to a household listed in the census should form the backbone of the army. The authors of the Taihō Codes sought to draft 1 soldier for every 3 adult males 21 to 60 years old in a household, rather than 4, as specified in the 689 Law Codes.[51] In actual practice, the proportion came closer to one quarter, which usually meant that 1 adult male per household went into the military. Most Japanese historians now believe that the households noted in the population registers were artificial units created expressly to provide the Court with troops.[52] Because an administrative village (ri or sato, also an artificial unit) contained 50 households, 20 such villages could produce 1 unit of provincial militia (gundan), about 1,000 men.[53]

Every soldier was expected to furnish most of his own equipment:

> Each person shall provide one bow, one bag for bowstrings, two additional bowstrings, 50 campaign arrows, one quiver, one great sword, one knife, one whetstone, one straw helmet, one pouch for rice, one water cup, one salt container, one set of leggings, and one pair of straw sandals.[54]

Supplying one's own arms must have been burdensome, but in return the Court exempted soldiers from other labor duties.[55] In comparison with the Chinese, Japanese soldiers lacked many sophisticated weapons: They used little iron and possessed only 2 crossbows for every 50 men.[56]

The basic unit within the provincial militia was the squad (*ka*) of 10 men. (A 10-man band was also the smallest building block for the Assyrian army, the Mongol Horde, and the Chinese.)[57] Five Japanese squads formed a platoon (*tai*) of 50 men, which might be composed of foot soldiers or horsemen, "those good at mounted archery" in the words of both Chinese and Japanese laws.[58] Two platoons comprised a company (*ryo*) of 100 men, and 5 to 10 companies made up 1 unit of provincial militia. Ideally, every province was supposed to have its own militia.

Japanese historians have uncovered evidence of 25 militia outposts scattered throughout 13 provinces ranging from Kyushu to northeastern Honshu.[59] Seven militia protected the province of Mutsu, a part of the Eastern Provinces and home to rebellious barbarians (*emishi*). Some scholars have estimated that the Court could conscript about 100,000 to 120,000 troops in an emergency under this system, but these figures would surely have strained the limits of the Japanese peasantry.[60]

LEADERSHIP. The Taihō lawmakers' intention as to how centralized command of the provincial militia should be is a crucial point hotly debated by Japanese historians. Some argue that the Law Codes gave responsibility for the unit to the provincial governor, a Court aristocrat and civilian sent from the capital to the countryside for a set term.[61] The provincial government was expected to "examine and test weapons" every year, submit documents detailing where soldiers had campaigned or traveled, and even escort them to their destinations.[62] Each governor also supervised the drums and noisemakers, beacons, fortifications, pastures, and horses and cattle within his jurisdiction.[63] Governors also had a hand in selecting and promoting the officers (*gunki*) in charge of the provincial militia, subject to ratification by the Court.[64] In addition to the day-to-day administration of the local military, the governor was duty-bound to call up troops both for major engineering projects and for apprehending criminals.

The governor's office (hereafter called the provincial headquarters) was also a major strategic center. Besides maintaining records on the military and other political matters, the provincial headquarters operated granaries, collected taxes, oversaw the government transportation system, and encouraged agriculture. State-supported artisans at the provincial capital also manufactured weapons, such as straight swords, bows and arrows, breastplates, chain mail, and quivers, according to government specifications.[65] If one agrees with those Japanese scholars who argue that aristocratic governors and their provincial administrations had charge over the militia, then the Taihō system would have been centralized and duplicated the Chinese injunction against local strongmen leading the military.[66]

The governor was not, however, the only official charged with military duties in the countryside. Each unit of provincial militia had its own leadership beginning with captain (*taishō*) and rising to colonel (*gunki*), and most scholars believe that lawgivers had no choice but to allow these officers, who were of local origins, to be the real commanders of the militia.[67] Proponents of this view point out that these officers held their ranks for life and usually passed the office on to their heirs, while governors served only a 4- or 6-year term. Moreover, the Codes say that the colonels' duties included "inspecting soldiers (*heishi*), preparing weapons, practicing mounted archery, and inspecting ranks and lines."[68] Finally, according to the Codes, the governor and the Court jointly selected officers such as the captain or colonel from "jobless holders of Court rank, military rank recipients, and commoners who are said to excel at the military arts," men far more qualified to lead an army than an aristocratic governor or his underlings.[69]

Two points suggest that the local officers and the provincial governor probably shared the legal privilege of militia command. First, the provincial headquarters was a new office in 702, only a decade old; it seems unlikely that courtiers would have expected the governor to penetrate and control the countryside so quickly without the assistance of the local elite. Second, it is improbable that lawmakers intended local men of influence to have the sole right of command, because the Codes gave local officers low official status.[70] These men did not receive salary or land, and most spent their time bowing and scraping before the governor, who held limited powers of appointment and promotion. Lawgivers probably intended to use local expertise and gain community support, while allowing the provincial government a general supervisory power.

Yet it is significant that local officers received the right of day-to-day command from the Court. For, even though the officers themselves may not have received impressive perquisites, such as land, salary, or high status, their social standing in the community more than made up for these disadvantages. Historical documents have shown that most officers were members of the same local families who had produced the pre-645 strongmen (*kuni no miyatsuko*).[71] Because the government had appointed most prominent men from the same families to the powerful lifetime post of district magistrate (*gunji*), officers in the militia were likely to have a close relative who controlled the area politically as well. Thus, although it appeared as if the pre-645 local strongmen had lost much of their power because of the divide-and-conquer strategy of Temmu and the Court in the late seventh century, in fact control of the populace stayed "all in the family." Hiring a district magistrate's relative to command the militia would have aided in enlisting his support for the Court in the district. By authorizing these local officers to command the troops of the militia, the Court was both making a concession to pre-645 Japanese military organization and also violating an important Chinese principle against control of the military by local leaders.

OBLIGATIONS OF THE RANK-AND-FILE. The duties of soldiers in the provincial militia included the apprehension of outlaws, the protection of barrier posts and fords, and the occasional extraordinary expedition. If the Court had followed the Chinese model to the letter, a soldier would have spent most of his time standing guard or in training. However, the Japanese Codes lack a rule mandating or describing regular training procedures, and, although the Chinese Codes do not contain such an article either, other sources indicate that Chinese officers forced their troops to practice group tactics every winter.[72]

Japanese historians are divided on the issue of regular winter training for peasant recruits. One historian has noted that household and tax registers occasionally describe the weapons and duties of soldiers as well as battle wounds that may have resulted from mock combat, while another scholar has argued that the provincial headquarters manufactured and stored weapons to guarantee that soldiers could train.[73] In addition, there are 13 examples of the Court's stipulating that peasant-soldiers should train.[74] In 5 cases, the authors state that the training would be in Chinese-style mass tactics, mentioning "rules of line formation," or in one instance stating that soldiers should "swing swords, stab with spears, fire crossbows, and catapult stones."[75]

But another scholar has raised strong doubts about each of these cases.[76] Two orders to drill soldiers appeared in the late seventh century during the height of fears about invasion and before the compilation of the Taihō Codes. The Court issued two other edicts during Fujiwara no Nakamaro's abortive campaign against Korea; these decrees could also have been temporary measures. The law that describes swords, spears, crossbows, and catapults did not come into effect until 753, again during a crisis with Korea, and does not specifically require regular winter drilling sessions.

Most of the laws that discuss training soldiers for the new military contain the vague phrase that recruits should practice "the martial arts" (*bugei*). For example, not long after the implementation of the Taihō Codes in 702, the Court mandated that soldiers should go on rotation, serving at militia or provincial headquarters 10 days out of every 100 and "learn the martial arts."[77] One young Japanese scholar studying the Chinese-style military has suggested that "learning the martial arts" really meant individual training in how to use weapons.[78] He has further pointed out that orders that mention learning the martial arts usually specify drilling in mounted archery.[79]

On this issue, like many in early Japanese history, there is no evidence to support a sure judgment. But two points seem clear: First, that Japanese commoner foot soldiers probably received some training in group fighting tactics; and, second, that mounted fighters practiced their trade relentlessly, even under a system that supposedly favored infantry. The former point is obvious from the size of armies raised under the Taihō system, while the latter can be inferred from descriptions of combat.

Soldiers in the provincial militia drilled so that they would be ready when called upon to serve at the installations in northern Kyushu or in the capital. Border Guards (*sakimori*) were liable for 3 years' duty in northern Kyushu.[80] The Taihō Codes specified how to provision the troops on the road and rotate them while on duty; described the procedure should a Guard fall ill on the road or at his post, or commit a crime; discussed how Guards received lands to farm while stationed away from home; and allowed private slaves to men on guard duty.

The most interesting statute on the Border Guards stipulated that provincial governors escort these troops as far as Naniwa (present-day Osaka) in their journey to Kyushu. The Codes are silent on the origins of the Border Guards. The question then arises: Where did they come from? The consensus of Japanese scholars is that they hailed from the Eastern Provinces, especially the Kanto, although some writers believe that other provinces provided some support.[81] The primacy of the Kanto as the homeland of the Border Guards was probably true from the beginning of the system in the days of the Emperor Temmu.

Three considerations argue strongly for eastern Honshu as the nearly exclusive source of men serving in the Border Guards. (1) It would have made no geographical sense to send men from western Honshu and Kyushu eastward through Naniwa and then dispatch them westward along the same route to Kyushu; Naniwa made a logical transshipment point only if the Border Guards came from eastern Honshu. (2) Ninety poems in *The Man'yōshū* written by Border Guards give 10 eastern Honshu provinces as the homes of the poets. Seven of 8 provinces in the Kanto are represented. (3) Financial records from the Shōsōin in Nara list both the total number (2,300) of Border Guards for 737 and their final destinations on their return home. Two documents were written in western Japan (Chikugo and Suō), but they merely show that the Guards were escorted eastward out of the province and had not yet arrived home. The only record that contains the destinations of the homeward-bound Guards comes from Suruga, in eastern Honshu itself. Nearly half the Guards (1,082) mentioned in the Suruga document hailed from the eastern Honshu provinces of Izu, Kai, Sagami, Awa, Kazusa, Shimōsa, and Hitachi. The same Japanese historian who analyzed the financial records argues that the remaining 1,218 Border Guards of 737 probably came from other known Border Guard homes in eastern Honshu such as Shinano, Kōzuke, Shimotsuke, and Musashi.[82] All these arguments suggest that the consensus among Japanese scholars that most Border Guards originated from eastern Honshu, as well as the emphasis in this book upon the Eastern Provinces as an important military base from the late sixth century, is correct.

The Codes were silent on the matter of how the Border Guards fought, but 3 points suggest that most were archers, some mounted. (1) They hailed from the Eastern Provinces, an area historically associated with this type of combat; later in the eighth century, when the Court abolished the system of Border Guards, the same men waged battles as mounted archers in northeastern Honshu (Tōhoku). (2) Poems composed by Border Guards in the mid-eighth century mention horses and archery. (3) Archeologists recently have uncovered numerous arrowheads from an excavation on a small island off the western tip of Honshu, possibly a station for Border Guards.[83] The arrowheads probably belonged to bowmen rather than crossbow specialists.

Provincial militiamen could also become Capital Guards, liable for 1 year of service.[84] While at the capital they comprised the 800-man Right and Left Capital Guard (Sa eji fu, u eji fu), and defended the imperial residence and office buildings in the capital. Documents indicate that the government supplied these men with provisions such as rice, salt, and hemp cloth, charged them with duties such as catching criminals.[85] The Codes also detailed off-duty activities and provisioning, restricted comings and goings, banned simultaneous conscription of father and son, and required regular weapon inspections. An article in the Codes specified that Capital Guards should practice mounted archery, sword-play, spear-fighting, and firing crossbows and catapults.[86] The Court later set aside the produce from certain lands specifically to reward Capital Guards who excelled at mounted archery.[87]

Working along with the peasant conscripts at the capital were Palace Guards called Hyōe, a native Japanese institution. Law-givers wrote a detailed provision describing how these soldiers were to be chosen:

> Provincial governors shall select Palace Guards (Hyōe) from among those sons and relatives of the district magistrates who are strong and skilled in archery and horsemanship.[88]

Palace Guards served the same function and belonged to the same class as the early-sixth-century royal retainers known as *toneri*. In addition to those chosen from the families of district magistrates, the Codes also designated that male heirs of capital aristocrats might serve, provided that they were "strong and good at archery and horsemanship."[89] Altogether there were 800 Palace Guards in 2 divisions (Sa hyōe fu and U hyōe fu). Because they were officials, and not mere commoners like the Capital Guards, the Codes ordered that the government evaluate the Palace Guards regularly and that they be permitted satisfactory rest. The 200 Gate Guards (E mon fu) were a similar institution which also drew its men from among those families with pre-645 military credentials (*yugei*).[90]

OTHER ASPECTS. The Chinese-style military system of the Codes was meant to defend Japan from foreign menaces.[91] Thus a section of the chapter on the military described in general terms siege warfare, the maintenance and protection of fortresses and bar-riers. Authors also discussed the location and organization of a complicated system of beacons (*tobuhi*).[92] The laws on beacons derive not from the Chinese Codes but from lesser legal works, and are so difficult to understand that it is doubtful that such a sys-tem of communication could have worked. Gazetteers and other sources indicate, however, that the Japanese did use signal fires to link northern Kyushu with posts along the Inland Sea all the way to the capital.[93]

As Chinese expeditions against the Koreans had proven, peasant-soldiers could wage short-term predatory wars to seize territory, as well as defend their homeland. Thus legislators established the procedures for campaigning, including the unified, bureaucratic command which had been sorely missing at the Battle of the Paekch'ŏn River. Lawgivers also compiled rules for encampment, the granting of a ceremonial sword (*settō*) to the commander, the appointment of a great general (*dai shōgun*), punishment for disobeying orders, care for the wounded and sick, a ban on women accompanying the troops on campaign, and the bestowal of merit ranks (*kun'i*) upon worthy fighters.[94] Many articles repeat the wording of Chinese laws almost exactly.

The Codes also outlined other facets of the Chinese-style military. Statutes specified the proper way to distribute, store, and replace weapons, and continued the Emperor Temmu's ban on private ownership of such goods. Laws elaborated methods for the selection and evaluation of the quasi-military royal (*chōdai*) and aristocratic (*shijin*) attendants, and imperial retainers (*toneri*). The Codes distinguished between civilian and military officials, in theory giving military men separate and lower ranks and status. In practice, however, the Japanese government regularly conferred civilian ranks and offices on military men and appointed civilian officials to command campaigns.

HORSE-RAISING IN THE EIGHTH CENTURY

> Horses and cattle are resources of the provincial militia and should not be wanting for even a short while.[95]

> Horses are utilized in the provincial militia and are a preparation against an emergency.[96]

> Nothing is superior to the horse for use in the provincial militia.[97]

> In case of an emergency, the horse has the most immediate use.[98]

Horses were necessary to carry warriors and military supplies. After the Battle of the Paekch'ŏn River and the Civil War of 672, Court officials knew that they had to encourage horse raising.

PASTURES IN THE CODES. To ensure a sufficient supply of horses, Taihō legislators required that governors establish and administer pastures where cattle and horses could be bred. According to law, a head (*bokuchō*) and at least 3 other officials were responsible for each pasture. These functionaries received rewards for increasing the fold, and were personally liable for making up any losses. Each pasture had a horse stable (*umaya*) and corral where trainers could break horses for riding. Grooms tended to the animals at the officially sanctioned rate of one person for each high-grade horse.

The governor visited the provincial pastures annually, inspected the animals, and branded foals with the word *government*. The provincial headquarters then submitted a record listing state and private animals in their jurisdiction to the Council of State, the supreme advisory board of aristocrats in the capital. In his report, the governor described the color and health of each horse, even down to the number of teeth for each animal.

The Codes gave specific instructions on the care of horses. Caretakers provided fodder for every animal according to its grade: One statute states that good horses ate beans, rice, barley, dried grasses, and leaves, although a commentator known for his realism indicates that few horses were fortunate enough to feed on grain in the eighth century.[99] Regulations also spelled out procedures for the care of sick and dead animals, with a permissible attrition rate of 10 percent per year. Officials burned the pasture every spring to produce the best growth for the summer.

MATING. Breeding numerous horses as quickly as possible was a major concern for a government determined to build a strong military, and both institutional and cultural factors tended to encourage frequent foaling. Laws specified that officials could expect a promotion if mares bore foals at a rate of 60 or more per 100 females. Anxious for quick rewards, the pasture head and his assistants did very little to limit reproduction.

Furthermore, castration and spaying, two means of restricting foaling, have never been popular among the Japanese, probably because the act of cutting flesh was seen as unclean, resulting in the spiritual pollution of the cutter. Therefore, instead of neutering their livestock, officials merely kept mares and stallions separate when foals were not wanted.[100] Usually, caretakers released males and females into the pasture and nature took its course. According to a Japanese scholar, horses can sustain a high reproductive rate in the wild; he believes that between 70 and 80 percent of the mares would bear foals in a year.[101] Because pasture officials were required to breed mares from ages 3 to 19, the Court may soon have had a population problem of a unique kind.[102]

LOCATION. Historical records indicate that pastures were situated far away from civilization, on islands or in mountainous regions.[103] A report from 754 describes one pasture as a wide open space, bounded on one side by a river, and containing perhaps 300 animals.[104] One historian has investigated an area thought to have been a pasture in Ibaraki prefecture in the Kanto; herdsmen divided the land into two parts, each partially marked off by walls and ditches.[105] One division measures about 50 hectares (125 acres) and another at 300 hectares (750 acres) of mountains and valleys.

Another region well suited to pasture was Shinano province, where geographers and archeologists have discovered a site believed to have been Haibara Pasture.[106] There were 16 pastures in Shinano by the 800s, and approximately twice that number by the thirteenth century. The province is estimated to have produced 1,000 horses a year in the ninth century. At Haibara, the pasture was over 200 hectares (500 acres) and supported over 100 horses. It contained three types of land: pasture; dwellings and rice paddies for the maintenance of officials; and horse stables for wintering and breeding the animals. Moats and dirt walls surrounded pastures and stables. The area used for stables is apparent even today; each corral and stable resemble steps on a staircase as they rise up a low incline. Archeologists have excavated the area believed to have been the site of the chief official's residence, and have concluded that the giant foundation stones could belong only to a government building.

Historians believe that the Codes originally required that every province have a state-run pasture, but have found evidence for only 44 grazing lands in about a third of the provinces, mostly in western Honshu and Kyushu.[107] However, as the system developed in the eighth century, the location of pastures naturally shifted to less populated regions. Both Kyushu and the Eastern Provinces became the focus for state efforts at horse raising, while cattle were bred in the region west of the capital.[108] By the ninth century, pastures sent about 500 stallions a year to the Court.

HORSE-RAISING AND THE LOCAL ELITE. A legal source from the early ninth century states that a good horse could cost 500–600 sheaves of rice.[109] This price was prohibitive for most Japanese: It was 5 times greater than the yield from the parcel allocated to the average adult male by the government. Because horses were so expensive, and care of the animals was time-consuming, the Court once again ignored Chinese restrictions on local men of influence and turned to them to take the lead in horse raising. Pasture heads in Japan were normally from the households of the district magistrates or other locally powerful persons; the Codes suggest that pasture heads held military rank (*kun'i*) or the Outer 6th Court Rank (Court aristocracy began at the Inner 5th Court Rank).[110] In addition, when the pasture head shipped a horse to the provincial militia, officials selected a wealthy local family to care for the animal.[111] These powerful families also must have raised their own herds of horses that could be ridden in battle, a practice that would not have been tolerated in China.[112]

Most historians stress agricultural land when they write of the origins of the samurai, probably because many twelfth-century fighters took their surnames from the fields they farmed. But one should not exaggerate the tie between warriors and cultivated land, especially in the eighth century. Rather than pursuing agricultural activities, many of Japan's early warriors chose to breed horses and to hunt. It was no accident that twelfth-century warriors (*bushi*), such as the Shida, Chichibu, Mochizuki, Sara, and Kodama, had their origins in pastures established under the Taihō system.

THE REVOLT OF FUJIWARA NO HIROTSUGU
AND THE PROVINCIAL MILITARY

There can be no greater test of a military system than action on the battlefield, and the revolt of Fujiwara no Ason Hirotsugu in northern Kyushu in 740 provided just such a trial for the Chinese-style army of the Taihō Codes. The middle years of the reign of the

Emperor Shōmu (r. 724–749) were a time of unparalleled hardship in Japan. In 735 a great smallpox epidemic struck the islands, killing as many as 40 percent of the population. The epidemic coincided with a period of bad harvests and affected peasants and nobles alike. The pestilence was disastrous for the aristocratic Fujiwara family, which lost all 4 of its sons — Umakai, Maro, Muchimaro, and Fusasaki. The loss was especially tragic because the Fujiwara brothers had rotated the most powerful positions at Court amongst themselves; not long after the death of the Fujiwara, their bitter rival Tachibana no Moroe stepped into the political vacuum and assumed control at Court.

Umakai's son, Fujiwara no Ason Hirotsugu, was most harshly affected by Fujiwara misfortunes.[113] In 738, Hirotsugu had assumed the coveted governorship of Yamato province, the cradle of Japanese civilization. But only one year later the new leadership banished him to the lonely port of Dazaifu in northern Kyushu.

In 740 Hirotsugu vented his frustration in a remonstrance to Court, in which he pointed out "the failures of recent policy, described catastrophes of heaven and earth," and demanded the ouster of his enemies.[114] Four days after the Court received his views, on the 3rd day of the 9th month, Hirotsugu raised the flag of rebellion. The Court responded by appointing the civilian aristocrat Ōno no Ason Azumabito to be the Great General in a unified command structure over an army of 17,000 soldiers, drawn from both eastern and western Japan, except Kyushu. On the 4th day of the 9th month, the government dispatched 24 natives of southern Kyushu (the Hayato) to serve as a reconnaissance team.

Court histories confirm that Hirotsugu divided his army of 12,000 to 15,000 men into 3 units, two under his subordinates Tsunade and Komaro and one directly under Hirotsugu's command. The rebel Hirotsugu then ordered each to advance along separate routes to northeastern Kyushu, where he hoped to push the government force back into the sea[115] (see Map 4). Along the way, Hirotsugu stopped at Oka district headquarters "to make camp, set up his crossbows, raise beacon signals, and conscript soldiers from the province [of Chikuzen]."[116] At last Hirotsugu arrived at fortifications (*chinsho*) in the Miyako district of Buzen province, just across a narrow channel from the likely invasion route.

Map 4. THE REVOLT OF FUJIWARA NO HIROTSUGU

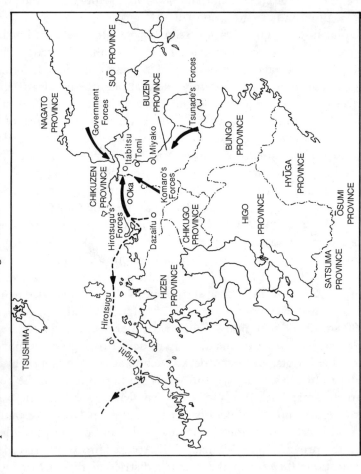

Source: Aoki Kazuo, *Nihon on rekishi* 3, *Nara no miyako*, p. 324.

But Hirotsugu's plan for a coordinated attack soon began to unravel. One army of several thousand men failed to appear, and the other was late. The leader of the government army reported a successful landing to relieved Court officials:

> We have killed and captured [one] bandit . . . of the Junior 8th Court Rank, Senior Grade, Secretary (*shishō*) at Dazaifu, Chief of Fortifications in Miyako district, Buzen province, and [another] . . . , his Second-in-Command at the Itabitsu Fort in Kiku district. But the First-in-Command . . . was struck by two arrows and fled into the wilds. We took alive 1,767 men from 3 camps located at Tomi, Itabitsu, and Miyako and captured 17 weapons.[117]

On the 21st and 22nd of the 9th month the court reinforced its army with over 4,000 troops, including 40 fine soldiers (*jōhei*) led by the magistrate of Toyoura district in Nagato province. The army of Hirotsugu was in full retreat.

Hirotsugu's allies surrendered one after another to Azumabito's forces. On the 25th, 4 district officials betrayed the rebellion and led 500 mounted warriors into battle on the government's side. On the same day, a citizen of Buzen province killed another of Hirotsugu's confederates. Later the magistrate of another district in Buzen brought his trophies from battle — several "bandits"' (rebels') heads. Hirotsugu tried to make a last stand at the Itabitsu River with a reported 10,000 horse riders, but, when his army was unable to make a crossing, Hirotsugu fled and his army disintegrated. On the 23rd of the 10th month, the government captured Hirotsugu; a week later he was beheaded.

Despite sparse documentation, Japanese historians have drawn important conclusions about early Japanese military technology and organization from accounts of Hirotsugu's revolt. First, it is clear that armies on both sides consisted of foot and mounted soldiers. Commanders must have used foot soldiers, as indicated by the size of the forces and some references to crossbows and battle lines. Thus it appears that the reforms of the Japanese military according to the Chinese model had had some effect on technology and tactics by 740, almost a century after the decision to adopt Chinese-style tactics.

But the changes were not so far-reaching as a superficial reading of the sources might lead one to believe: Major battles still turned on the strength of each army's mounted troops.[118] Even before the first arrow had been fired, Azumabito and the Court probably had a great advantage in horsemen, because they drew a sizable portion of their army from eastern Honshu, where many good mounted archers could be found, whereas Hirotsugu was limited in his recruiting to Kyushu. Moreover, Hirotsugu lost many horse riders to betrayal, as when his erstwhile allies, the 4 district magistrates of northern Kyushu, joined the Court's army and brought 500 mounted soldiers with them. Court annals also note the movement of small bodies of elite troops, such as the 40 fine soldiers who joined the government from Nagato province; these fighters could well have been mounted archers, too. Forces for both Hirotsugu and the Court may have been listed in the thousands, but battles were won or lost by a small number of mounted fighters.

Second, Japanese historians also agree that the organization of the armies on both sides had changed little since the early seventh century. To be sure, Hirotsugu used his official position and the provincial-level military facilities in Kyushu to raise troops. As the second-in-command at Dazaifu, Hirotsugu held considerable personal power; he also commandeered fortifications (*chinsho*) in the Miyako area where provincial militias were probably located.[119] A court chronicle further suggests that Hirotsugu availed himself of the military resources of the provincial headquarters of Ōsumi, Satsuma, Chikuzen, Bungo, Hizen, and Chikugo, the most powerful military centers according to the Codes.[120]

In spite of these references to more recently established offices like the provincial headquarters, it seems likely that the district office, staffed by families of local strongmen accustomed to mounted combat and military leadership from before 645, played a much more important role in martial conscription and organization.[121] According to John Hall, "The adoption of a centralized conscription system had technically disarmed the provincial aristocracy," but the evidence from Hirotsugu's rebellion raises strong doubts that local strongmen ever parted with their weapons.[122] For example, Hirotsugu stopped to raise troops at Oka district headquarters as he made his way to the first battlefield; later, another district magistrate, leading 40 fine soldiers, reinforced government troops. Hirotsugu's army also surrendered in district units to Azumabito's forces. Although the Taihō Codes had given a prominent role to provincial governors in military organization and leadership, district magistrates and their relatives were the true commanders during combat. Many of these men belonged to the same families who had supervised regional forces before the decision to copy the Chinese model in the late seventh century. Some historians argue that a law abolishing the provincial militia in 739 was responsible for the low profile of the governors, but it is unlikely that the 739 order applied to strategically located Kyushu. [123]

The preeminence of the district magistrate in Hirotsugu's rebellion also raises an important question about the command structure employed by both sides. Official chronicles of the war make it clear that the district, not the provincial militia, was the standard unit of combat. Magistrates led their men into battle and surrendered in district units. If one assumes that the magistrates were horse riders — an assumption supported by most data of the eighth century — then the pre-645 command structure in which local strongmen rode into battle as horsemen overseeing units of foot soldiers would have remained unaltered almost a century after the first attempt to adopt Chinese mass warfare.

Therefore, the battles that occurred during Hirotsugu's rebellion imply relatively little change had taken place with the adoption of the Chinese-style military. Armies used some continental weapons and tactics, but the mounted fighter still played a critical role. And the leaders of these forces were district magistrates, many descended from local strongmen (*kuni no miyatsuko*) from the sixth and seventh centuries. Even after the crushing defeat at the Paekch'ŏn River in Korea, old patterns were difficult to change.

Other evidence strongly supports similar conclusions about military organization and leadership in the eighth century. One scholar has analyzed three government expeditions against the Hayato people of southern Kyushu in the early eighth century and found that there is almost no evidence for the existence of a provincial militia as mandated in the Taihō Codes. But documentation does indicate the considerable power of local strongmen (district magistrates) in the conscription and organization of troops. [124]

The most cogent evidence of the district magistrate's military power comes not from Kyushu but from the Eastern Provinces. *The Man'yōshū*, a poetry collection from the eighth century, contains 90 verses written by Border Guards (Sakimori) on their way to duty in northern Kyushu. These men hailed from 10 provinces in eastern Honshu, and were traveling under official escort to the port of Naniwa in the year 755:

> The dread imperial command
> I have received; from tomorrow
> I will sleep with the grass,
> No wife being by me.
>   — By Mononobe Akimochi, Lower Naga District;
>   a guard from a *kuni no miyatsuko* family.[125]

> The steep mountain-road of Ashigara
> I will travel, the good god granting,
> And never will turn back homewards;
> The Pass of Fuwa I will cross,
> Where well a reckless man might fear to stand;
> I will go as far as my horse can take me,
> Even to the uttermost point of Tsukushi—
> There I will stop and thus will pray:
> "May those I love be well till I return!"
>   — By Shidoribe Karamaro[126]

> Praying to the gods of heaven and earth,
> And thrusting hunting arrows in my quiver,
> For the far isle of Tsukushi
> Now I depart—yes I!
>   — By Ōtabe Aramimi, a noncommissioned
>   officer (*kachō*)[127]

A Japanese specialist on the early military has examined the poems in detail and pointed out that each poet signed his verse according to his rank. The signatures rank soldiers in the following order from the top down: local strongman (*kuni no miyatsuko*); assistant (*jotei*); secretary (*shuchō*); squad leader (*kachō*); and, finally, draftee (*jōtei*). This investigator believes the use of terms is no accident; he asserts that the descendants of Yamato-era local strongmen conscripted and organized their subordinates into groups, just as they had done in the early seventh century and before.[128]

The historical record does not include a detailed example of a district magistrate's conscripting or organizing an army within his jurisdiction, but it is possible to envision how the "new" Chinese-style military must have worked. The heart of an eighth-century army would have been the extended family of the district magistrate, most of whom were the descendants of the pre-645 local nobility and passed their lifetime appointments on to their heirs. The magistrate's wealth and political power in his bailiwick would have required the provincial governor to cultivate good relations with him. The district magistrate would have maintained horses and weapons both officially and personally; his mounted forces, staffed primarily by his relatives and close friends, would have been the elite of his troops. In addition, his economic and political powers would have allowed him to draw upon the peasantry for foot soldiers.

The power the district magistrate of the eighth century exerted over the residents in his region was social, economic, and political. [129] One might represent the regional strongman's sphere of influence as 3 concentric circles, after a model developed by a Japanese historian to describe warrior power in the tenth century and later [130] (see Figure 4). The innermost circle consisted of the magistrate's household, which would include several residential buildings, storehouses, and land. A fence with a gate surrounded the whole complex. There may have been as many as 100 residents, including the magistrate's immediate family, slaves, and dependent families and individuals.

The next circle contained the land directly farmed by his household. As district magistrates, most local leaders automatically received 6 *chō* of land (about 18 acres), over twice as much as held by the aristocratic provincial governor. The magistrate also controlled parcels of 3 to 6 acres set aside to promote and reward superior bowmen, both on foot and horse. [131] Allotments to other household members and newly cleared land increased the magistrate's holdings many times. Moreover, his wealth comprised such things as cattle, horses, cash, facilities to manufacture salt, cloth, or iron, and thousands of sheaves of rice. Any magistrate with such combined resources could easily have raised a small army.

The third circle consisted of the magistrate's jurisdiction, the district. The center of activity was the district office itself, again

Figure 4. A REGIONAL STRONGMAN'S SPHERE OF
INFLUENCE

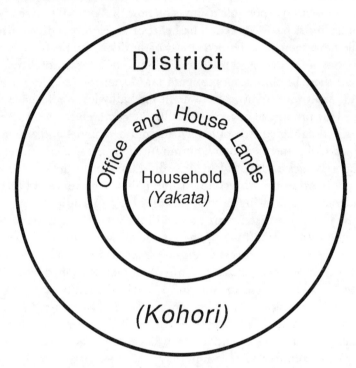

Source: Adapted from Ishii Susumu, *Nihon on rekishi* 12, *Chūsei bushi dan,* p. 111.

containing several residential and storage buildings; the district
office even served as the magistrate's permanent lodging in some
cases. More than 100 functionaries such as secretaries (*shoshō*),
cooks, papermakers, horse tenders, and as many as 50 laborers
served him. As tax collector, the district magistrate had an iron
grip on his subjects, particularly through a system of annual seed
loans that cultivators were obliged to repay. From this circle the
magistrate would raise the bulk of his forces, especially foot soldiers. The magistrate's relatives, many of whom would have been
leaders of the provincial militia, helped enforce his rule.[132]

The schema is admittedly hypothetical, since there are few
records to describe how the district magistrate used his personal
and familial economic power, some of which lay in land, to raise

and possibly even reward horsemen and foot soldiers to fight for a distant central government. To be sure, the Court sanctioned the magistrate's authority publicly, and rewards were more likely to come from the Court and to be in the form of commodities rather than land, but these two points do not undermine the fact that the basic model is similar to one seen in the tenth or twelfth century.

The foregoing analysis of the district magistrate is also germane to longstanding controversies over how one defines a warrior (*bushi*) and when this figure first appeared in Japanese history. Historians in Japan belong to one of two schools, some preferring a functional definition based on fighting technology, while others see the samurai as a rural landlord. The group using the functional definition has no trouble seeing eighth-century magistrates as a close relative of the twelfth-century warrior, but scholars who incline towards the landlord view conventionally reject any close affinity between the two. Yet the district magistrate, who usually fought as a horseman and served as a local official in charge of land, would seem to satisfy the requirements of the landlord camp as well. There were, of course, still some differences between the eighth-century warrior and his twelfth-century counterpart.

There can be no question that, during the 700s, local command lay with the district magistrate, and that, far from being a centralized, despotic state, the Chinese-style imperial government was highly dependent upon the cooperation of all 550 local strongmen. A magistrate's power displayed an overlap of personal and official authority, and personal ties reinforced his authority even at the outer extent (district) of control.

FUJIWARA NO NAKAMARO AND MILITARY POWER IN THE CAPITAL

While the provinces were the chief source of military manpower in the eighth century, the greatest demand for martial expertise arose at the capital. Nara was home to 10,000 bureaucrats, the most influential of whom commanded small personal armies and indulged in countless political intrigues. Every shift of political fortunes brought a new array of military power to support the ascendant aristocrat. The very number of soldiers in the capital constituted a war waiting to happen.

Of all eighth-century courtiers, no man knew the value of force better than Fujiwara no Ason Nakamaro (706–764), cousin of the rebel Hirotsugu. A famed scholar of the Chinese classics and mathematics, Nakamaro showed little aptitude for politics in his early years. As the son of a high official (Muchimaro), Nakamaro made his debut as a royal retainer (*udoneri*), and then proceeded to the University in Nara, where would-be officials studied writing, mathematics, and Chinese classics. At the rather advanced age of 29, he progressed into the circle of true aristocracy with the rank of Junior 5th Rank, Lower Grade.

Nakamaro first tasted military action with the outbreak of Hirotsugu's revolt in 740. Fearing the ill effects of the rebellion, the Emperor Shōmu made a pilgrimage to the sacred Imperial Shrine at Ise to pray for the welfare of the realm. Shōmu feared for his life, and traveled to Ise with an escort of 400 soldiers. Even though he was not of military lineage, Nakamaro was appointed the Great General of the Forward Cavalry to lead this escort.[133] Nakamaro may have seen for the first time that military power buttressed political authority.

For the next several years Nakamaro patiently waited. Between 740 and 746 his career as a Court bureaucrat took wing; he moved from the 5th to the 3rd Court Rank and assumed the exalted post of Advisor (*sangi*) within the highest advisory body, the aristocratic Council of State. Nakamaro also carefully cultivated his aunt Kōmyō, consort of Emperor Shōmu. In 749, Kōmyō established a special office (*shibi chūdai*) to oversee her affairs and appointed Nakamaro as head. Because laws issued from the new office carried the same weight as imperial edicts, Nakamaro's ascendancy at Court was assured.

The year 749 saw other changes at the capital. The Great Buddha, a statue constructed for the new state temple at Tōdaiji, was at last nearing completion, and the Emperor Shōmu used the occasion to retire. He placed his daughter by the Consort Kōmyō, the Empress Kōken (r. 749–758) on the throne. As was the custom in such successions, Shōmu reinforced her political authority by creating a special unit of mounted soldiers (*tachiwaki no toneri*) to serve and protect her; according to this edict, they were men from the Eastern Provinces:

The men from the East always say: "Even though an arrow may strike us in the forehead, it will never pierce our backsides. With single-minded devotion we will serve our ruler."[134]

While there is no corroborating documentary evidence to link these fighters with the Eastern Provinces, Japanese historians who have studied the *tachiwaki no toneri* find no reason to doubt Shōmu's words.[135]

In 756 the Emperor Shōmu died, but not before trying to raise one of the Emperor Temmu's grandsons to the rank of Heir Apparent. Shōmu's nomination had little support, however, and the Court soon split into rival factions, each backing a different candidate for Emperor.

Nakamaro immediately organized the military to protect the person he favored for the imperial dignity. First, Nakamaro had himself made the General of the Middle Guards (Chū efu), a unit that had previously housed personal retainers for the Fujiwara family.[136] Next he took over a position (*shibi naishō*) that oversaw military affairs throughout the country. Finally, he issued a 5-point edict which limited the martial power of his aristocratic rivals:

(1) Heads of aristocratic families (*uji*), though not entrusted with state affairs, assemble their relatives as they please. Hereafter let this not be so.

(2) The number of horses for aristocrats has already been restricted by regulation. Let them not keep horses above the limit.

(3) According to the Codes, there is a legal limit on the number of attendant soldiers for each rank. Again let them not exceed the limit.

(4) Previously We Ourselves have issued a ban which prohibits the carrying of weapons in the capital by any but military officers. But still the practice does not stop. We Ourselves ought to announce to the concerned officials to issue another strict ban.

(5) Groups larger than 20 horsemen should not gather in the capital.[137]

The decree not only implies that the capital was an armed camp but also underlines the importance of mounted warfare in aristocratic military planning. Four hundred years before samurai such as the Taira and Minamoto battled in the streets of Kyoto, control of mounted fighters was already the key to political power.

Presented with Nakamaro's new powers, and confronted with limits on their own ability to gather troops, Nakamaro's enemies made a feeble attempt to enlist military aristocrats like the Ōtomo and Saeki in their cause, hoping to assassinate the Fujiwara leader in his home and capture the routes to the Eastern Provinces to prevent Nakamaro from enrolling soldiers there.[138] But Nakamaro's control of the military had given him the edge; his enemies fled or committed suicide.

Nakamaro placed his candidate on the throne as the Emperor Junnin and ruled the Court as he wished for the next 4 years. But, in 760, his supporter, the Consort Kōmyō, died, and things began to go wrong. Famines and epidemics plagued the land. A planned invasion of Silla and the construction of a new palace at Hora in Ōmi province added mightily to Court expenses and the burdens of the peasantry.

In 762, Nakamaro's sister, the Former Empress Kōken, fell in love with the Buddhist monk Dōkyō. Relations between the Retired Empress and Nakamaro's favorite, the Emperor Junnin, deteriorated rapidly as Dōkyō and Kōken tried to dominate the Court. Once again the capital would be the scene of conflict.

Nakamaro hurriedly began military preparations. He filled the ranks of the Middle Guards, which he controlled, with supporters. He had his son named to a key position in the Palace Guards and placed another partisan at the head of the Swordbearers (*tachiwaki no toneri*), which oversaw the Former Empress's military base at the capital. Other sons assumed the governorships of the strategic provinces of Echizen and Mino on the route to eastern Honshu. Finally, on the 2nd day of the 9th month of 764, Nakamaro asked the Former Empress to name him Supervisor of Military Messengers from the Four Provinces of the Kinai, the Three Provinces of the Passes (Ise, Mino, and Echizen), and Ōmi, Tamba, and Harima. In this capacity, Nakamaro reviewed the skills of 20 soldiers from each province, who rotated to the capital every 5 days.[139] Nakamaro hoped that his new supervisory position would give him control of the capital region and the three major routes to the military bases in eastern Honshu.

Kōken's faction was not to be outdone. She called the aged Kibi no Makibi, a well-known expert in Chinese strategy, out of retirement to prepare forces, and sent construction gangs to the Seta River in Ōmi province to raise embankments and defensive works, a move that would conveniently cut Nakamaro off from the Eastern Provinces. Then, when Nakamaro's hand-picked leader of the Sword-bearers died suddenly, Kōken replaced him with her own man.

War began when the Retired Empress attempted to remove the imperial seal and travel passes from the possession of Nakamaro's confederate, the reigning Emperor Junnin.[140] Nakamaro had a son hurry to protect the symbols of imperial power, while the Retired Empress replied by sending two crack soldiers in her Sword-bearers unit to intercept and kill Nakamaro's son. Nakamaro responded and further escalated the violence by ordering the Captain of the Middle Guard to recapture the seals and passes. Finally, with the symbols of imperial majesty as well as a pretender to the throne in his caravan, Nakamaro escaped eastward towards the provincial headquarters of Ōmi (see Map 5).

As Nakamaro fled, the Former Empress stripped him of rank, position, and surname; she ordered the passes of Fuwa, Arachi, and Suzuka closed to keep Nakamaro from reaching the all-important Eastern Provinces. She raised an army and offered rewards to those who would follow. The Retired Empress also countermanded false orders which Nakamaro had issued with the stolen seals.

Nakamaro first tried to conscript troops in Ōmi province, but Kōken maintained control of the province by constructing defensive works and stationing men there. Her soldiers captured a rebel messenger, and, when Nakamaro arrived in Ōmi, his "face lost its color" upon finding the bridge at Seta burnt and the provincial headquarters in the enemy's hands.[141] He then turned to Echizen province, where he expected his son the governor would welcome him with open arms. Once again Kōken's generals (especially Makibi) struck first, organizing the local elite there against the revolt. They killed Nakamaro's son and blocked Arachi Pass which led to eastern Honshu. Trapped between two pincers north and south, Nakamaro and company tried to cross Lake Biwa, but the winds blew in the wrong direction, and the boat nearly sank.

Map 5. THE REBELLION OF FUJIWARA NO NAKAMARO

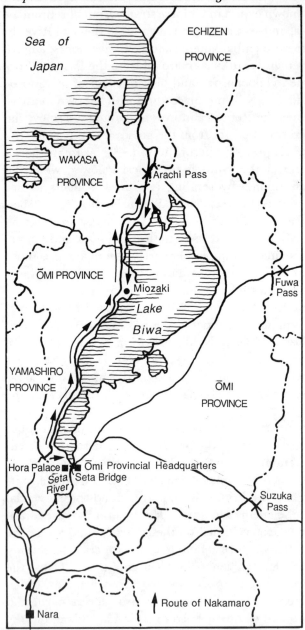

Source: Kishi Toshio, *Fujiwara no Nakamaro,* p. 398.

At last the two armies engaged in an archery battle at Miozaki in Ōmi province. From 1 a.m. until 3 p.m. on the 18th, soldiers of each side vied for the advantage amidst torches and the banging of drums. As Nakamaro appeared to gain the upper hand, reinforcements from the capital arrived and the rebel army retreated. Nakamaro and his family were captured as they attempted to flee by boat to eastern Honshu. Jubilant troops transported Nakamaro's head to the capital, and Kōken reassumed the throne as the Emperor Shōtoku (r. 764–770; she purposely used the male title to emphasize her power). The greatest revolt in almost a century had ended in failure.

The way in which each side attempted to raise an army was critical to the outcome of Nakamaro's rebellion. Despite his position as Supervisor of Military Messengers, the appointment of his son as provincial governor, and even the forging of documents to call out the provincial militia, Nakamaro's ties to the local elite were weak, especially in the strategic provinces of Ōmi and Echizen. He failed to create a viable alternative to assembling an army through the personal loyalty of district magistrates.

On the other hand, the Retired Empress secured support from local strongmen (district magistrates) in Ōmi and Echizen, where mounted warriors made the difference in combat.[142] Then she was able to block the passes to the Eastern Provinces and prevent Nakamaro from doing what the Emperor Temmu had done successfully in 672. Once again, the Codes may have made the provincial headquarters the main military center in the countryside, but reality was different. Evidence from Nakamaro's revolt reinforces the view of the local military gained from analysis of Hirotsugu's insurrection.

But the most interesting aspect of Nakamaro's rise and fall is the picture it presents of the military in the capital. Historians are accustomed to thinking of the Chinese-style institutions of the eighth century as public, bureaucratic, and civilian; they look at officials as individuals, rather than as operating in cliques. But Nakamaro's career shows that there was a private and military facet to the Chinese-style system as well. Indeed, the numerous personal ties of loyalty between Nakamaro and his fighters suggest those established in feudal societies.

Throughout his life, Nakamaro organized units of loyal retainers and gave them legitimacy as state institutions like the Middle Guards or the Sword-bearers. These aristocratic armies of professional warriors were half-public and half-private in character, and personal ties of loyalty were crucial to their formation and operation. Such bonds were formed not between aristocrats and peasant foot soldiers, but between high-ranking courtiers and military specialists, especially mounted warriors from the families of district magistrates. Such military specialists saw the bearing of arms as a privilege and an art (*bugei*); in *The Man'yōshū*, these men were called warriors (*mononofu*), written with the same characters as the medieval term for warrior (*bushi*).[143] The practice of bringing local martial specialists to the capital to serve the aristocracy, originating long before the era of heavy Chinese influence, continued almost unaltered.

One Japanese scholar has cited 4 occasions when these horsemen from prominent local families played an essential role in Court ceremony: the greeting of a foreign dignitary, an imperial procession, the New Year's Day military formation, and mounted archery rites conducted on the 5th day of the 5th month.[144] Sources show how personal ties were formed between aristocrats and military specialists:

> The Emperor [Shōmu] observed the hunt. Those wealthy houses from the 1st rank of imperial princes to those with no rank at all, as well as district magistrates and their offspring, soldiers, and those brave and colorfully dressed commoners who hail from the . . . Capital, the Five Provinces of the Kinai, and Ōmi, have them all carry out the hunt.[145]

> An order was issued to the . . . Capital to assemble 800 persons from the offspring of those holding the 6th Rank and below who could act as horsemen for the arrival of the Tang guests.[146]

During Court ceremonies, aristocrats of the 5th Court Rank and higher mingled with lower-ranking locals, the courtiers providing equipment, horses, and costumes, while regional military specialists displayed their skills.[147] The chances for ties of loyalty to form must have been legion. Aristocrats created their armies of bodyguards, and the relatives of district officials received a chance to breathe the cosmopolitan air of the capital. If one considers personal ties of loyalty to be a major feature of feudal society, then these military cliques of the supposedly public eighth century were as feudal as anything created later in Japanese history. Even the rank of the local specialists, the 6th Court Rank and below, was the same status preferred by warriors of the twelfth century, when they became known as "samurai," or "those who serve."

In fact, eighth-century aristocrats enjoyed creating their own armies of military specialists so much that the government was forced to set limits early on. In 721, the Court restricted the number of horses (and by implication mounted fighters) that each aristocrat might possess:

> Princes, aristocrats, and rich people provide for many strong horses. Competition for the animals is without limit. This competition does not just reduce family wealth, but in the end makes for rivalry and fighting.[148]

The Court's reasoning was correct, but it then set limits too high — as many as 20 mounts for a powerful official. High-ranking aristocrats with 20 horsemen could have overwhelmed a provincial headquarters. Competition among aristocrats for horses and skilled fighting specialists resulted in a military presence in the capital that made life in Nara exciting and dangerous.

CONCLUSION

Momentum for reform of the Japanese military developed during the second half of the seventh century. Threatened first by the Tang campaigns in Korea in the 630s and 640s, and then by the destruction of its own expedition against the Tang in Korea in 663, the Japanese Court placed high priority on the development of a strong military establishment. The government hurriedly tried to bring the Eastern Provinces under its sway in 645; after 663, the Court had defensive works constructed and manned in northern Kyushu to secure the country from invasion by Korean or Chinese armies.

All efforts to strengthen the military, however, amounted to little until the accession of the Emperor Temmu. The "Heavenly

Warrior Emperor" won the throne with a smashing victory in the Civil War of 672, when he seized the Eastern Provinces and used the mounted fighters there to overwhelm his rival. He indicated the military nature of his rule when he said that "in a government, military matters are the essential thing"; he ordered the militarization of the capital aristocracy while bringing recalcitrant local strongmen (*kuni no miyatsuko*) under his thumb by confiscating their weapons.

Those who followed Temmu to the throne also focused on military matters. The Court culminated a half-century of reform in 689 when it implemented a nationwide census whose main purpose was the raising of troops. The government organized households and local government on the basis of their ability to produce soldiers, thus creating Japan's first martial government.[149]

The Chinese army served as the model for political reformers in a Japan anxious to strengthen the military. A Chinese-style military had several advantages: It was inexpensive and defensive in character, and it restricted the power of local strongmen. Since commoners provided the manpower, armies could be huge and yet easily demobilized. Most important, Chinese armies were successful and aggressive, especially in the tactics of mounted warfare.

Yet the Taihō system set up in 702 was a compromise between Chinese models and Japanese social reality. To be sure, the Court conscripted commoners into the provincial militia, and these recruits were supposed to bring their own weapons. Aware of the advantages of group tactics and a unified command after the loss to the Chinese and Koreans in 663, lawgivers made efforts to adopt both practices. They also established a system of state pastures to increase the horse population.

But Japanese social norms dictated that the Chinese-style system would have a distinctly Japanese cast. Rather than restrict the role of the pre-645 hereditary military elite in the countryside, courtiers gave the local strongman a crucial place in leading the provincial militia. The provincial headquarters, housing the offices of aristocratic governors, oversaw the operation of the local military, but day-to-day decisions remained in the hands of the same families who commanded armies prior to the Chinese model. Moreover, relatives of local strongmen also ran the state pastures, contributed their own horses and weapons for practice, and ran the district office. The important function devoted to locally powerful families may be considered a flaw in the system, but it is hard to imagine how the Japanese Court could have acted differently.

Taihō legislators departed from the Chinese ideal in other ways as well. They allowed members of district magistrates' families to come to the capital to serve as Palace and Gate Guards, an old practice in Japan which would never have been permitted in China. Border Guards were often elite mounted fighters drawn from the traditional military base in the Eastern Provinces. Although it is not clear how frequently Japanese commanders drilled their soldiers in group tactics to make them into real infantry and cavalry units, officers were not bashful about training their men on an individual basis in horse riding, archery, swordplay, and other aspects of the martial arts.

The Taihō system in action shows even greater departure from the Chinese ideal. In the revolt of Fujiwara no Hirotsugu in 740 and again in the organization of Border Guards from the Eastern Provinces, local strongmen raised and organized armies through their position as district magistrates. Most magistrates and their relatives fought from horseback, and they, not the peasant foot soldiers, provided the backbone of the eighth-century military. District magistrates acted as commanders in actual battle because they had the economic base, primarily through their offices and lands, to maintain horses and drill in mounted tactics. One is tempted to argue that little had changed in the provinces in the century since the Court adopted the Chinese model as a goal.

In the capital, military power was essential to political authority, as seen in the case of Fujiwara no Nakamaro. High-ranking aristocrats formed private military forces made up of provincial specialists by using personal ties of loyalty, and legitimized their bands of assassins through the use of office. The eighth-century Court had a strong martial, feudal, and private aspect.

Western-analogue theorists have characterized the Chinese-style institutions of the late seventh and eighth centuries as a public and civilian system which undercut Japan's military development and the rise of feudalism. But the motivation for such reforms derived from Japan's military failures, and the first focus of lawgivers was on military affairs. By giving a major role to local strongmen and other specialists in the martial arts, and emphasizing horse raising and practice in mounted warfare, the Court inadvertently paved the way for the rise of the twelfth-century samurai.

chapter three

War in the Northeast and Technological Remedies, 770–900

> *. . . the barbarians' custom is battle as mounted archers; ten of our commoners*
> *can not rival one of the enemy.*
> — a Court historian, 837

The lesson of the Battle of the Paekch'on River in 663 had been that organization and numbers won battles. The Chinese had long practiced coordinated tactics using well-drilled units of infantry and cavalry; indeed it was the celebrated strategist Sun-tzu who had warned that a disciplined and capably led body of troops would always prevail over individual warriors, no matter how skilled or brave.[1] The lawgivers of the Taihō Codes had hoped to transplant just such a military establishment to their native land in 702.

By the late eighth and ninth centuries, Japanese experience led to a different outcome. Between 774 and 812, the Court engaged in a series of predatory expeditions to subjugate the people of northeastern Honshu (the Tohoku). True to the Codes, the refined aristocrats of the Kinai dispatched huge armies of horsemen and peasant foot soldiers to bully the "barbarians" (as the people of the Tohoku were rudely called) into submission. But the barbarians, employing the hit-and-run tactics of mounted warfare against a government host, proved to be a obstinate opponent who yielded only after exhausting the Court's treasury. The 40-year war in northeastern Honshu placed an even greater emphasis on warriors specializing in mounted tactics, both on the local level and at the capital. The Court raised many horsemen from the Kanto, thus militarizing the long-time martial center even more thoroughly, and the technology of combat was subtly altered to favor the rise of mobile, horse-riding troops.

Lacking the financial base and manpower to raise conscript armies in the ninth century, the central government stopped drafting commoners to serve in the provincial militia, the Capital Guards, or the Border Guards, institutions adopted only a century earlier, thus starting a trend of giving up tight control over the military in favor of a system that worked better and was less costly, but had even more risks than the Taihō Codes. To replace conscription, the Court turned to the elite of the Taihō army, mounted soldiers from the families of district magistrates, to serve in the countryside. When these forces proved inadequate, lawgivers at the capital reached for a technological remedy, the crossbow, to defend their homeland.

By the end of the northeastern wars and the ninth century, Japan's military looked different. The government had curtailed conscription of unskilled, cumbersome armies, while local martial specialists had become even more firmly established. Combat against the barbarians had improved horsemanship, armor, bows, and swords to allow rapid movement in battle. These technological and cultural innovations were now available to military specialists out of whose number would eventually spring the samurai.

PRELUDE TO THE WARS IN NORTHEASTERN JAPAN, ORIGINS TO 774

THE PEOPLE. The earliest contact between the Court and the natives of northeastern Honshu reached far back into mythological times. For example, in the reign of the legendary Emperor Keikō (estimated at the fourth century A.D.), an account of the exploits of the warrior-hero Takechi no Sukune implies the extent of the northeasterners' barbarism and what should be done about it:

> Takechi no Sukune returned from the East Country and informed the Emperor, saying: "In the Eastern wilds there is a country called Hidakami [the basin of the Kitakami River]. The people of this country, both men and women, tie up their hair in the form of a mallet, and tattoo their bodies. They are of fierce temper, and their general name is

the "toad barbarians of the East" (*emishi*). Moreover, their land is wide and fertile. We should attack them and take it."[2]

The identity of the people whom Takechi no Sukune called "Eastern barbarians" is the subject of a heated debate among Japanese scholars.[3] Some historians and ethnologists cite two reasons for believing that these people were really Ainu, a group of indeterminate race who dwell in Hokkaido today. First, many place-names in northeastern Honshu are of Ainu origin. Second, an alternative interpretation for the Chinese characters for Eastern barbarians (*emishi*) is *ezo*, a term used to refer to the Ainu after the year 1200.

A second opinion argues that the natives of northeastern Honshu were not Ainu but were identical to the Mongol-like people in the rest of Japan. Supporters of this view discount the alternative interpretation for the term *emishi* as testimony that appeared much later. In addition, autopsies performed on the mummified remains of persons from the twelfth century who were supposedly descended from the Tohoku "barbarians" revealed no trace of Ainu characteristics.[4]

The controversy over the identity of the early natives of northeastern Honshu raises a broader question: How developed was Tohoku society in the eighth century? Court records suggest that the residents of northeastern Honshu were culturally different from the people of western Japan, that they lived primarily by hunting and fishing, enjoyed horse riding, spoke a language unfamiliar at Court, and possessed strange and wondrous customs.[5] But many recent scholars emphasize archeological evidence that metalworking, rice agriculture, and the practice of burying the dead in large earthen tombs had already reached northeastern Honshu by the eighth century, thus making the Tohoku resemble western Honshu in the sixth century.[6] These scholars claim that official historians undoubtedly wrote biased accounts meant to exaggerate the crudeness of those outside the cultivated sphere of the Court.

Three points about early Tohoku society seem clear. (1) The residents of northeastern Honshu lived in a less-developed region of Japan, even though agriculture and metalworking may have been known there by 700. Hunting and fishing were popular livelihoods throughout Japan in the early era, but especially so in the Tohoku.[7] These lifestyles would affect the battle tactics of the "barbarians" in the wars to come. (2) The natives of northeastern Honshu were comparatively uncivilized, even more mobile and less agrarian than their neighbors to the southwest. Division of labor had taken place to a much smaller extent, and writing seems to have been unknown. (3) The Tohoku natives considered themselves politically independent of the Court.[8]

The refined aristocrats residing in the capital considered the populace of the distant northeastern Tohoku to be brutish barbarians. The term *emishi* soon became synonymous with untrustworthy, immoral, and violent behavior, as in this account (also probably from the fourth century A.D.):

> So the Emperor [Keikō] took a battle-axe and, giving it to Yamato Takeru no Mikoto, said: "We hear that the eastern savages are of a violent disposition, and are much given to oppression; their hamlets have no chiefs, their villages no leaders; each is greedy for territory, and they plunder one another. . . . Amongst these eastern savages the *emishi* are the most powerful; their men and women live together promiscuously; there is no hierarchy of father and child. In winter they dwell in holes, in summer they live in nests. Their clothing consists of furs, and they drink blood. Brothers are suspicious of one another. In ascending mountains they are like flying birds; in going through the grass they are like fleet quadrupeds. When they receive a favor, they forget it, but, if an injury is done them, they never fail to revenge it. Therefore they keep arrows in their topknots and carry swords within their clothing. . . . If attacked, they conceal themselves in the foliage; if pursued, they flee into the mountains.[9]

The Court believed its duty was to bring the civilizing influences of the imperial state to these misguided people, and from time to time took its duty seriously. The fertile lands and wealth of the region also played a large part in inspiring civilizing efforts by the Court.

EARLY ATTEMPTS TO ESTABLISH GOVERNMENT CONTROL. The leading Japanese expert on the early history of northeastern Honshu and the "barbarians" believes that there were cultural contacts between the Yamato Court located in the Kinai and the people of the Tohoku in the period before the introduction of Chinese civilization began in 645.[10] These contacts were not necessarily warlike, as suggested by myths in *The Chronicles of Japan* and *The Record of Ancient Matters* (which often stop with the surrender of the "barbarians" just short of battle, after they recognize the cultural superiority of western Honshu). Local strongmen (*kuni no miyatsuko*) from the Eastern Provinces, such as the Kenu and Abe families, claimed loose control over the Tohoku, and the Court held them responsible for law and order in the region.[11]

The first verifiable documentation of fighting between the Court and residents of the Tohoku occurs in the reign of the Empress Saimei (r. 655–661). Abe no Ōmi Hirafu led several expeditions to the Tohoku, into the modern-day prefectures of Akita and Niigata.[12] In 658, Abe commanded 180 ships against the "barbarians," who surrendered without battle; the defeated natives of northeastern Honshu asserted that they carried bows and arrows everywhere to hunt, not to threaten the Court.[13] Later, when 200 docile "barbarians" paid court to the western Japanese, the differences in culture were apparent in the government's gifts of heavy armor, flags, and drums to their visitors.[14] Such weapons belonged to units that fought in the large Chinese-style armies organized by the Court; the "barbarians" must have accepted the items as a gesture of friendship without knowing how to use them.

Not all early contacts were so friendly. In one encounter, when Abe refused to accept the surrender of the "barbarians," they put their own wives and children to death.[15] Abe's expeditions in the 650s showed that the new clique headed by Prince Naka, who had helped assassinate the previously ruling family, the Soga, was serious about controlling and civilizing all of Honshu. The campaigns served as a symbol for the Court's assertion of its authority and may have secured the Eastern Provinces from attack, although it is doubtful that all resistance was crushed.

Court histories report that, after Abe's victories, the government vigorously began to establish administrative centers throughout northeastern Japan in the late seventh and early eighth centuries. During his expedition, Abe had founded several district headquarters and set up palisades at Nutari and Iwafune along the

Japan Sea (see Map 6). In 708, the government set up Dewa district to the north of Iwafune, and shipped weapons to that region the following year. Less than two weeks later the Court renamed the district with the hopeful title the Dewa Office for the Conquest of the Northern Barbarians. In 712, the government reorganized Dewa as a province, transferring two districts from the province of Mutsu to Dewa's jurisdiction. The rapid creation of palisades, districts, and provinces in the Tohoku along the Japan Sea shows that the region had reached a new level of strategic importance in the Court's eyes.[16]

But such administrative outposts should not be equated with firm imperial control; they needed support to be useful, leading to the creation of colonies in the early and middle eighth century. Three rebellions spurred this trend. In 709, the "barbarians" revolted, requiring the dispatch of an expedition complete with special military law and a ceremonial sword. In 720, the assassination of a government official provoked the Court to similar action.[17] Little else is known about these campaigns, except that they aimed at restoring control over terrorized areas. In 724, a more serious rebellion took place in what is now northeastern Miyagi prefecture. The revolt required 8 months to put down and resulted in the capture of over 600 prisoners.[18]

Finally, in 737, Ōno no Azumabito, soon to be the hero of Hirotsugu's insurrection, set out on an ambitious campaign with 1,000 mounted soldiers from 6 Kanto provinces.[19] First, Azumabito subdued the area north of the recently erected Fort Taga (modern Sendai). He then raised 6,000 more soldiers and marched from Shikama Palisade in Mutsu to Tamano in Dewa, thus joining the two provinces for the first time. At Tamano, Azumabito joined the Governor of Dewa with about 700 soldiers, and together they opened a road to Mt. Hirahoko, 50 km. due north. The two leaders then overwhelmed isolated Okachi village in the far north without a fight and returned to their respective posts. Azumabito's expedition undoubtedly provided new information about an area that courtiers from western Honshu had never before seen.

For the next 37 years, until the beginning of the wars in northeastern Honshu in 774, relative peace prevailed in the region. But the Court was busy settling and fortifying the region in an attempt

Map 6. NORTHERN JAPAN IN THE EIGHTH AND NINTH
CENTURIES

Source: Takahashi Tomio, *Emishi,* p. 207; Ienaga Saburō et al., eds., *Zusetsu Nihon
bunka shi taikei* 4, *Heian jidai (jo).*

to strengthen its weak control. Colonization had been a policy even in the early eighth century: "[The Court] had 1,000 wealthy households from 6 [Eastern] provinces . . . move and distributed them throughout Mutsu province."[20] It was assumed that wealthy families would use their personal ties to the Court to extend government control into the hinterlands. Court-sponsored migration continued throughout the middle of the eighth century, although the colonists usually were poor individuals rather than wealthy families: "[The Court] allotted 233 confiscated male slaves and 277 females to Okachi Palisade."[21]

The court also constructed many fortifications. By the time of Azumabito's expedition in 737, laborers had already built strongholds at Fort Taga and Fort Akita, as well as points such as Ojika, Niita, Shikama, and Tamatsukuri. Fort Taga, also the provincial headquarters for Mutsu, was particularly important, since it served as the military headquarters for the entire Tohoku region. In the second half of the eighth century, the government completed new bastions at Monofu in Mutsu and Okachi in Dewa with a total labor force of over 8,000 persons.[22] Both horsemen and foot soldiers manned the new fortifications. In 767, the Court finished Fort Iji, almost due north of Taga, an action that soon provoked the "barbarians" to violence.[23]

Archeologists have excavated several fortifications, revealing something of what life was like at the strongholds. Northeastern bastions consisted of inner and outer rectangular dirt walls supported by wooden posts and surrounded by moats; at Fort Monofu, for example, the outer wall encircled an area of 2.8 square km., while the inner wall measured 72 meters north to south and 116 meters east to west.[24] Fortifications generally commanded plains, although some, like Fort Taga and Hotta Palisade, rested on hills. At Fort Taga, engineers arranged structures such as temples, office buildings, and storehouses within the second wall, like a provincial headquarters. Archeologists have discovered many artifacts buried in small dwellings located both inside and outside the outer walls of forts. At Fort Akita, many pit dwellings contained iron knives, arrowheads, axes, and reapers, which suggests that the colonists (*sakko*) may have served as both farmers and soldiers.[25]

The forts of northeastern Honshu were much simpler and more primitive structures than the Korean-style bastions of northern Kyushu. Builders in the Tohoku never used stone for walls or foundations; the roof was thatched rather than tiled. Northeastern strongholds probably had fewer residents, even though they were normally laid out on plains, not on mountains like Korean-style forts. The primitive construction of Tohoku fortifications may indicate that the "enemy" (the *emishi*) tended not to lay siege as continental fighters did so that Korean-style strongholds would not have been necessary.

One archeologist has argued that the structures in northeastern Honshu were not really fortifications at all.[26] Despite the use of terms like *fort* and *palisade* by Court officials, the archeological remains of the buildings look more like provincial headquarters than military strongholds.[27] The resemblance between Tohoku bastions and provincial headquarters may mean that the primary function of the forts was political, not military, or could hint at the strong military character of provincial offices in other parts of the country. Or, the initial purpose of the forts may have been military, but the administrative role followed closely, to consolidate the Court's authority. Building separate forts and provincial headquarters would have been a waste of resources in a distant area only weakly controlled by the Court.

By the last quarter of the eighth century, the Court could claim that it had influence in most of northeastern Japan, except for the regions north of Akita in the west and north of Fort Iji in the east. Forts, palisades, districts, and provinces symbolize both the determination of the Court to control the Tohoku and the potential threat of native resistance. Consider Fort Okachi in Dewa province as an example of Court plans to administer the region.[28] In 737, during Azumabito's expedition, Okachi was a hamlet for the "barbarians," who submitted of their own accord to the Court. In 759, the government at Nara ordered the construction of Fort Okachi, and soon thereafter divided the area around the stronghold into Okachi and Hiraga districts. Later Yamamoto district was added; Fort Okachi served as the local administrative and military center for all three districts and came under the supervision of the governor at Fort Akita further north.

THE WARS IN NORTHEASTERN JAPAN, 774-812

The Court conducted 5 expeditions in Mutsu and Dewa during 38 years of warfare, in 776, 788, 794, 801, and 811. Historians have found causes for the conflict between the Tohoku and western Honshu on both sides. One cause was certainly the desire of Court leaders to display their power by bringing the "barbarians" to heel; the same urge also led the government to build new capitals at Nagaoka and Heian in the Kinai. The Court may also have been attempting to direct attention away from the unwise fiscal policies of the last decade: The Emperor Shōtoku and Dōkyō in particular had pursued spendthrift ways while revenues from western and central Japan decreased. As the Court built new bastions in northeastern Honshu, local residents could hardly have been enthusiastic about new taxes instituted with the arrival of government control; some resistance probably stemmed from this.[29] Tohoku society had matured since the early eighth century, and the wars were also a struggle for control between Court officials and native chieftains.[30]

The 40 years of warfare began when the residents near Fort Monofu in Mutsu province revolted in 774.[31] The Court immediately turned to the 8 provinces of the Kanto (called the Bandō after 750, to distinguish the region from the Tohoku) to furnish between 500 and 2,000 troops apiece. (The term *Bandō* literally means the area east of Ashigara Pass on the border between Sagami and Suruga and includes the 8 provinces of Sagami, Musashi, Kōzuke, Shimotsuke, Hitachi, Shimōsa, Kazusa, and Awa [see Map 1].) Fighting was so fierce the next year that land went uncultivated in Mutsu, and the rebellion spread to Dewa. Ōtomo no Sukune Surugamaro, a military aristocrat who was serving as the General of the Military Government in Fort Taga (*chinju fu shōgun*), led the counterattack by striking against the *emishi* base at Toyama hamlet. In 776, Ōtomo led an expedition allegedly on the scale of 20,000 soldiers against rebels in Mutsu. Meanwhile, Dewa could produce only 4,000 troops to quell an uprising at Shiriwa hamlet; the Kanto again came to the rescue by providing mounted fighters. The campaign was prolonged into 777, and, while the situation in Mutsu quieted, the province was so exhausted that the government granted tax relief. The fighting in Dewa continued, with heavy losses to the Court. Over 2,220 men received military promotions for the capture of about 750 "barbarians." A new leader with military forebears, Saeki no Sukune Kuramaro, assumed a generalship for the fight in Dewa, but the situation remained volatile.

In 780, the Court ordered the erection of Fort Kakubetsu just north of Fort Iji; it appeared as though pacification of the Mutsu frontier was a reality. But, in the 3rd month, as a new Court-appointed general proceeded to the construction site at the head of supposedly friendly native (*emishi*) troops, a trusted lieutenant, Iji no Kimi Azamaro, magistrate of Jōji district, ambushed the state army. Azamaro, who was of *emishi* stock, was reputedly resentful of aspersions cast on his ancestry; after killing the leader of the army, he turned the rebellious troops south and pillaged and burned Fort Taga, frightening off the defenders.

The Court immediately appointed another expedition headed by three aristocrats, among them a military man, Ōtomo no Masutachi. The government made elaborate preparations, shipping helmets and grain to the empty shell of Fort Taga, but the commanders dallied. What is more, the leaders failed to answer Court requests for progress reports. Then they demanded more grain and clothing and set the date of the 5th day of the 9th month for Bandō fighters to assemble at Taga. In the meantime, Dewa officials discussed the possible abandonment of Fort Akita, made untenable by local rebellions. Still the expedition delayed at Fort Taga until, by the end of the 10th month, a request to postpone the campaign arrived at Court.

Despite presumably commanding tens of thousands of troops, the leaders cried that "in the summer the grass was too thick and in the winter uniforms were too few."[32] As more supplies poured into Fort Taga, the generals asked for permission to march victoriously through the streets of Nara. This request ignited the wrath of the Emperor, who claimed that the expedition had killed only 70 of more than 4,000 rebels. Yet the leaders returned to the capital and even received prizes.[33]

There was little fighting while first one commander and then another stalled at Fort Taga, and the battle was always on the rebels' terms:

> . . . the barbarians' custom is battle as mounted archers; 10 of our commoners can not rival one of the enemy.[34]

> They swarm like bees and gather like ants . . . But when we attack, they flee into the mountains and forests. When we let them go, they assault our fortifications. . . . Each of their leaders is as good as 1,000 men.[35]

Lightning swift and familiar with the terrain, the rebels used guerrilla tactics to their clear advantage.

For the next few years, the new Emperor Kammu (r. 781–806) had other concerns and devoted limited attention to the northeastern campaigns. In 784, he appointed the famous poet Ōtomo no Yakamochi to lead another expedition. Kammu also decreed that the provinces of the Kanto should establish forces composed of military specialists (including relatives of district magistrates, unemployed officials, and vagrants good at mounted archery), ranging from 500 to 1,000 per province. This edict, coming at perhaps the lowest point of Japan's military preparedness against the barbarians, indicated a growing reliance on the expertise of military families from the Kanto area. The frontier was quiet for another three to four years, while the Court strengthened its military resources.

Ōtomo no Yakamochi, the designated commander of the next campaign against the barbarians, died late in 785, and so preparation for the next battle began in earnest in 786. In that year, Saeki no Katsuragi, another man from a family of martial aristocrats, inspected weapons of the provinces along the Eastern Sea Route (Tōkaidō). In 788, the Court sent 35,000 bushels of provisions to Fort Taga. On the 3rd day of the 3rd month, Kammu issued orders to assemble a force of 52,800 foot soldiers, horsemen, and porters at Fort Taga.[36] The troops were specialists: Most had experience in fighting in the Tohoku or were particularly skilled at mounted archery. Late in 788, the Court appointed a Great General to Campaign in the East; he set out from the capital with a warning from the Emperor Kammu that "the safety of the Bandō resides in this one expedition."[37]

The army gathered at Fort Taga in the spring of 789 and invaded hostile territory. But once again the expedition stalled, this time along the banks of the Koromo River. After an angry message from the Emperor, the force began to advance farther into barbarian country:

> The three armies adopted the same battle plan and pooled their strength. We set a time to cross the river and strike the bandits. According to the plan, we chose 2,000 men from the middle and rear armies and together they crossed the river at the same time. When they reached the dwelling of the bandit chief Aterui, about 300 brigands came out to meet us and we engaged each other. The government troops were strong, and the bandits withdrew. The government soldiers fought and burned all the way to Sufushi hamlet, and were about to join forces with the forward army. But the forward army was held up by the bandits and could not cross the river. At this point about 800 more bandits came forth and joined the fight. Their strength was quite great, and the government troops gave way somewhat. The brigands struck straightway, and about 400 more bandits appeared who came out of the eastern mountains and cut off the rear of the government army. We faced the enemy on the front and rear; the brigands attacked furiously. The government was forced into full retreat. General . . . Hasetsukabe Yoshigoto, seasoned fighters Takada Michinari, Ezu Somaro, Asukabe Yoshitari, and Ōtomo Monotsugu died in battle. Altogether we burned 14 bandit hamlets of about 800 houses. . . . Those who died in battle for the state were 25. While 245 were struck by arrows, those who drowned in the river were 1,036. Those who returned without belongings were 1,257.[38]

Japanese generals had violated at least 3 cardinal rules of military strategy. (1) Even after the experience of the Korean debacle, they had divided what should have been a unified command and failed to organize their movements tightly. As a result, when the enemy attacked, panic ensued and most soldiers drowned. (2) They had advanced into unknown enemy territory, a move the master strategist Sun-tzu would never have approved. (3) They had believed that the spectacle of a Chinese-style army, moving according to banners and drums, would frighten the *emishi* into submission. The same commanders had badly underestimated the strength and mobility of barbarian troops. The Battle of the Koromo River would take its place among Japan's military disasters, seared into the memory by the pain of defeat at the hands of a barbarian people.

After the disaster at the Koromo River, the generals sent another report to the Court complaining of the difficulty of supplying such a great force, and then dissolved the expedition. The Emperor Kammu condemned his generals for their inability to kill even 100 brigands while losing several thousand of their own. An inquiry fixed the blame for the defeat on subordinates and rewarded those who fought with valor.

The Court immediately began to outfit another expedition. Kammu authorized the construction of armor and the portage of grain, although complaints arose that the burden fell inequitably upon the poor and those residing in the Kanto. Kammu then asked people throughout Japan to aid in the preparations, including the wealthy, vagabonds, and estate officials.[39] He even requested that courtiers have armor manufactured.

In 791, the Court appointed officers to inspect the soldiers of the Kanto provinces once again. The Emperor Kammu named another scion of the military aristocracy to be the head of the expedition, but among the assistants was one Sakanoue no Tamuramaro. He also belonged to a family of military aristocrats (*gunji shizoku*), but with Korean origins. Tamuramaro's ancestors had served the Emperor Temmu in the Civil War of 672; his father had assisted the Former Empress Kōken in the suppression of the revolt of Fujiwara no Nakamaro.[40] Later records describe Tamuramaro as having a "red face and yellow hair" and "retainers beyond number."[41]

Through 792 and 793, chronicles note the surrender of various hamlets in the Tohoku to Court representatives. Then in 794, the same year that construction of the new capital at Heian began, the expedition was under way. Because the Court annals for these years are lost, however, it is impossible to describe the campaign in detail. The army, which is supposed to have numbered 100,000, was probably designed to frighten the enemy to death; the casualties it inflicted—"beheaded 467, captured 150, collected 85 horses, and burned 75 villages"—seem minor compared to the giant attacking force.[42] What is more, in 792 the Court had ended the draft; the difficulties Tamuramaro would have encountered in assembling 100,000 men in an age of recurrent epidemics without state conscription seem insurmountable. There can be little doubt that the figure is an exaggeration, probably by several thousand. In any case, Kammu at long last had a victory of sorts over the fighters of the frontier, and resistance seemed to be quelled.

There were 3 results of the military success in Mutsu. (1) The Court was able to reinitiate colonization, as noted in a 796 order which shifted 9,000 residents of the Kanto, Echigo, and Dewa to Fort Iji in Mutsu.[43] (2) The government resettled many residents of northeastern Japan in western Honshu and used them as guards. This policy caused some problems, because the outsiders enjoyed "stealing horses and cattle and riding them as they pleased."[44] The Court also granted special stipends and surnames to residents of the Tohoku who submitted. (3) The victory brought fame and power to Tamuramaro, who became the Governor of Mutsu, Inspector (*azechi*), and General of the Military Government (*chinju fu shōgun*). His total control contrasted with the division of authority which had occurred in 789 during the Battle of the Koromo River.[45] In 797, the Emperor picked Tamuramaro to be Great General Who Quells the Barbarians (*sei i taishōgun*).

Yet the conquest of northeastern Japan was still incomplete. While the region around Fort Iji had been pacified, the area known as Izawa was still a center of rebellion.[46] As long as this stronghold remained unconquered, neither Fort Taga nor Fort Akita was safe. And so, in 801, Tamuramaro reportedly led an expedition on the order of 40,000 men to wrench this territory from the barbarians. Little is known of the encounter, except that the Court was again victorious, even marching as far north as Hei (northern Iwate prefecture). Tamuramaro oversaw the construction of Fort Izawa, and also captured Taibo no Kimi Aterui, who had plotted the strategy for the Court's defeat at the Koromo River. Tamuramaro advanced to Senior 3rd Court Rank in a ceremony that also featured Aterui's execution. Later, in 803, Tamuramaro oversaw the construction and provisioning of Fort Shiwa north of Izawa, and the headquarters of the military government (*chinju fu*) moved to Izawa.

The Emperor Kammu was not finished yet. In 804 Tamuramaro was reappointed Great General Who Quells the Barbarians, and Mutsu province received more military provisions. The government also built a post station between Shiwa and Izawa. But then, in 805, because in the words of Advisor (*sangi*) Fujiwara no Ason Otsugu, "At present all under heaven suffer from military expeditions and construction," Kammu gave up his plans of conquest.[47] The state's coffers were empty, and the Court postponed the Tohoku campaign.

The Mutsu-Dewa frontier was quiet for some time after Tamuramaro's victories. The Court concentrated its efforts on strengthening Fort Izawa and provisioning northeastern Japan from Kanto stores, revising the tax system, rewarding military officials and protecting civil ones, and securing land rights for the native populace. In 810, Fumiya no Watamaro, a friend and protégé of Tamuramaro, became head of the political machinery in the north. Watamaro applied early in 811 to launch an expedition against the inhabitants of Hei and Nisate in what is today northern Iwate prefecture. He originally requested 26,000 troops, but soon accepted a reduction of almost 10,000 men. Unlike previous campaigns, however, the troops did not come from the Kanto, but originated from Mutsu and Dewa.

In the 4th month, Watamaro succeeded Tamuramaro to the title Great General Who Quells the Barbarians. Tamuramaro's son obtained an appointment as a general during this campaign, thus assuring the Sakanoue family's status as a military house. By the 5th month, the expedition had gathered food, weapons, and uniforms. After warning Watamaro not to arouse those natives who had already submitted, the Court cautioned that "the safety of the province lies in this expedition."[48] On the 14th day of the 7th month, the main contingent of government soldiers, 1,000 local barbarians who had previously submitted (*ifu, fushū*), engaged the residents of the rebel Hei hamlet and won a victory for which historical sources provide few details. On the 13th day of the 10th month, the Emperor praised Watamaro as worthy of the mantle of Tamuramaro and rewarded him with advancement into the rank of the high aristocracy. The number of permanent troops (*chimpei*) in northeastern Honshu fell to just a few thousand as 38 years of warfare came to an end.[49]

CHARACTER AND EFFECTS OF THE NORTHEASTERN WARS

Historians have long suspected that the wars in Mutsu and Dewa were an important watershed in the development of Japan's early military.[50] But examination of the evidence suggests that these conflicts really served as a subtle deviation rather than a major break from the past.

CONSCRIPTION AND FIGHTING STYLE. According to John Hall, "The Nara experiments with a conscript army were probably the least successful aspect of the Taika reforms."[51] However, draft and combat during the wars in the Tōhoku, over a century after Taika, took place entirely within the framework of the Chinese-style system mandated in the Taihō Codes. A recently discovered wooden tablet from an excavation at Fort Taga shows that the government conscripted troops through the provincial militia as specified in the Taihō Codes:

Shirakawa Provincial Militia presents:
A list of archers.
Total: 44 men. . . .[52]

Another document preserved in a lacquer bucket at Fort Taga and dated 780 also mentions an officer with the Namekata Provincial Militia in Mutsu, while similar records from a site in old Hitachi province list the weapons carried by each soldier, just as the Taihō Codes required.[53] Even after the abolition of the universal draft in 792, the prescriptions of the Taihō Codes remained in effect in frontier areas such as Mutsu and Dewa. The wars of the late eighth and early ninth centuries were a turning point, but not because Court leaders had suddenly abandoned the Chinese-style system.

The size of the Court armies dispatched to the Tōhoku also confirms the government's commitment to the Chinese-style model: The 5 armies reportedly averaged 46,560 people. Of course, objections may be raised to the credibility of sources that mention huge expeditions; when one considers the difficulties of moving and provisioning such large armies, it is easy to share these objections, especially about the third campaign which allegedly involved 100,000 troops in 794.

Yet there are 3 good reasons for accepting the figures in the official histories as a general indication of the size of Court forces, even if the sources overestimate the dimensions of state armies to enhance the prestige of a government at war. (1) All the tabulations on army size appear in official Court histories, sources compiled according to the high standards of Chinese-style historiography, usually much more reliable when it comes to numbers of men in combat than later medieval war romances such as *The Tale of the Heike* or *Mirror of the East (Azuma kagami)*. (2) In the case of the second expedition of 788, which totaled 52,800, not only is the count a precise number, but one source indicates the makeup of the army, 27,470 soldiers and 12,400 porters. (3) Even for the two campaigns of Tamuramaro, when the totals were suspiciously round numbers like 100,000 or 40,000 men, another measure is available to support the general credibility of military head-counters. The usually reliable Court history, *The Latter Chronicles of Japan,* lists exact numbers for officials charged with commanding divisions within these large hosts. For the 100,000-man campaign, the number of supervisors (*gunken*) was 16 and secretaries general (*gunsō*) 58, while, for the 40,000-man army, the totals of *gunken* and *gunsō* were 5 and 32, respectively. In the army of 100,000, every lieutenant general would have overseen 1,725 men while the ratio would have been one *gunsō* for every 1,250 men in the 40,000-man army. These numbers mean that the Court was providing more administrators per combatant for these two expeditions than required by the Codes.[54] Surely the use of such precise figures for the command structure of these giant hosts reinforces a general aura of reliability for the official figures for the whole army.

The degree to which the Court was able to conscript peasants for duty in the northeastern wars is impressive, and it is important to note that many of the draftees were not fighters. If the second expedition can be taken as an example, only about half (27,470) of an army of 52,800 actually participated in battle; there were 12,440 porters. Given this ratio of laborers to fighters, the largest number of combatants raised for the Tohoku wars would have been about 50,000, if one accepts the figure 100,00 for the third expedition. The conscription of even half this number of persons would have been an impressive achievement, strong evidence that the Taihō system was not defunct.

The fighting style of the Tōhoku expeditions also points to the continued use of the Chinese-style model as laid out in the Taihō Codes. Conscription orders indicate that both foot soldiers and horsemen participated in combat.[55] Although there are no references to drums, banners, or other accoutrements of continental warfare, armies totaling in the tens of thousands must have fought according to Chinese-style coordinated mass tactics. The Battle of the Koromo River shows that commanders from western Honshu sometimes applied the precepts of Chinese strategy poorly; the giant, noisy, colorful armies undoubtedly hoped their mere presence would frighten the enemy into surrender.

Another example of the operation of the Codes during the wars is the role of the provincial headquarters. At the opening of hostilities in 774, the provincial headquarters in the Kanto served as staging areas for the Court army. In 784, as the poet Yakamochi prepared a campaign, the provincial headquarters in the Kanto once again funneled soldiers to the front. Two years later, in 786, inspectors traveled to each provincial headquarters in the Kanto to oversee the manufacture of weapons. In 791, during Sakanoue no Tamuramaro's first expedition, the provincial headquarters acted as draft centers for a third time. The provincial office had begun to play the crucial military role envisioned by the authors of the Taihō Codes, and it is no accident that the provincial headquarters was the preeminent military center in the Kanto from this period on.

At the same time, the growing importance of the provincial headquarters was a subtle shift away from the way the Chinese-style army had functioned earlier in the eighth century. When Hirotsugu revolted or when the Border Guards went to northern Kyushu from their homes in eastern Honshu, the district magistrate, and not the provincial officials, had played the crucial role in conscription. The leadership of the former local strongman (*kuni no miyatsuko*) was a pattern left over from the pre-645 era. The all-out effort to crush the barbarians placed a new emphasis on the provincial headquarters, and a slow transformation in the Taihō system began to take place.

SOCIAL ORIGINS OF THE COMBATANTS. The battles in northeastern Japan also resulted in other seemingly minor but significant changes in the operation of the Chinese-style system. The wars placed an even heavier reliance on those social groups that led the armies of the Taihō system. In 783, the Court issued orders to the 8 provinces of the Kanto to "select children of jobless bureaucrats, the relatives of district magistrates, and vagabonds, as well as those who are able to be soldiers"; in 788, the army included "those who could practice mounted warfare."[56] Many, if not most, of these soldiers belonged to the same class of district officials who fought in the rebellion of Fujiwara no Hirotsugu in 740.

But the fighting in the Tohoku began to open the way for other military specialists in addition to the district magistrates. A decree of 788 states that preference was given to "those who had entered the army, experienced the war, and received military rank."[57] Unemployed officials and even vagabonds may have achieved fame and status by joining the army. In using such persons, the Court ensured that skilled fighters would come to the fore, even if they were not from the families of district magistrates. The Court regularly handed out ranks and rewards to those who performed well in the northeastern wars, and a correlation between excellence in battle and political and economic rewards became established. This pattern was even more pronounced after 900.

Yet another Taihō pattern that gained renewed emphasis was the use of military aristocrats to fill leadership positions. At first the Court turned to inexperienced civilian aristocrats, along with martial families from the sixth century like the Ōtomo and Saeki, to command the expeditions against the barbarians; the result was delay and failure. Success resulted only when the government appointed Sakanoue no Tamuramaro, a man of seventh-century military lineage, to lead the troops.[58] Some recent Japanese historians have begun to doubt the legend that has grown up around Tamuramaro and have emphasized instead the economic reasons for the barbarians' collapse, but most scholars admit that victory would have come much more slowly without Tamuramaro's leadership.[59] Fumiya no Watamaro was another able general leading an expedition in the wars, and he used his experience to initiate his own martial house. Both Tamuramaro and Watamaro received high civilian rank and office, once again proving that in Japan there were no limits to what a talented military officer could achieve.

TECHNOLOGY. There were also modifications in fighting technology. According to documents of the eighth century, the provincial headquarters manufactured swords, bows, arrows, and armor based on designs established at Court.[60] In 781, in the midst of the wars against the *emishi*, the government decided to alter the material for armor to a significant degree:

> The Council of State Orders:
> That we should put an end to iron armor and make leather armor.
> Concerning the above, we have received an order from the Inner Councillor (*nai daijin*): "I have received an imperial edict: 'It has been heard: The armor of the provinces has all rusted through after some years. Most can not be used. Once in three years we establish a precedent and repair them. As we repair them they are damaged; this is an extreme waste of labor. Now leather is tough and lasts for as long a time as armor. When put on the body it is light and convenient; when struck by an arrow, it is difficult to penetrate. When the amount of labor is measured, it is especially easy to make. Henceforth the armor made annually by the provinces should all be leather. As in previous precedents, submit designs. But the previously made iron armor should not be simply destroyed. Every three years have them repaired, as in the past.'"
>
> —Ten'ō 1/4/10 (781)[61]

Officials reasoned that leather armor was preferable because it was tough, long-lasting, and easy to make, whereas iron lamellar armor or cuirasses rusted quickly and were difficult to make and maintain. But it is important to note that the government handed down this order just after the revolt of Iji no Azamaro in 780; fighting the *emishi*, who "took hunting and fishing as their living" and "roamed about just like the clouds," had provided the stimulus for change in military technology.[62] The relative lightness of leather armor made the Court's horsemen more mobile, a necessity when fighting the quick, mounted archers of the Tōhoku. Once again a change in Japanese fighting technology followed the principles of counter-response and symmetry.

Swords also underwent subtle modification as a result of the

Figure 5. THE *WARABITE TŌ*

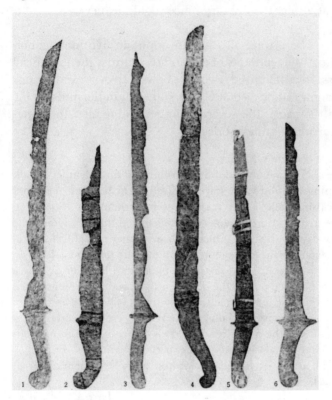

Source: Ishii Masakuni, *Warabite tō,* frontispiece.

wars.[63] The sword carried by the Chinese-style armies was straight, sometimes with both edges sharpened. The Court had imported it from the continent, yet another example of the principle of counter-response and symmetry in military technology. Soldiers used straight swords to stab an opponent, either in the saddle or on the ground.

Archeologists have uncovered, however, a different type of sword in the tombs and dwellings of northeastern Japan. Named the *warabite tō,* this sword is curved and has been dated as no older than the eighth century (see Figure 5). Fighters must have used the curved sword of the Tōhoku to slash their enemies, similar to the samurai swordplay of later eras. Experts on weapons have surmised that the *warabite tō* was the direct ancestor of the samurai sword; *emishi* guards spread its use to the rest of Japan by the ninth century. Thus the curved sword, known as "the soul of the samurai" in later ages, was a gift of the northeastern barbarians.

Lynn White has argued that there are certain technological preconditions for warrior rule in premodern societies.[64] In Western Europe, the basis for feudalism was the stirrup. In Japan, the technological preconditions for the victories of the warrior over the civil aristocracy after the twelfth century were in place by the late eighth century with the end of the wars in northeastern Honshu. By the early ninth century, Japanese mounted military specialists used the bow and arrow, swung curved swords, and wore light armor. Technologically, the development of the samurai was complete.

THE WARS AND ECONOMIC TROUBLES. In addition to these subtle shifts in certain aspects of the Chinese-style system, the wars in northeastern Honshu also contributed towards one major change: national exhaustion of manpower and resources[65] (see Appendix Tables 1 and 2). The wars required provisions of rice and other foods, as well as uniforms, arrows, and armor, most of which came from outside Mutsu and Dewa. The government constantly drafted men: "People from the provinces who enter the army and go to Mutsu and Dewa have been exhausted by their soldierly duties and many have suffered the destruction of their family enterprise."[66] Along with massive expenditures for construction and deteriorating economic conditions, the wars were responsible for the bankruptcy of the Chinese-style state and the abandonment of the Taihō system of commoner conscription in 792.[67]

The burden fell especially heavily on the provinces of the Kanto plain. In the middle of the eighth century, the Court had recognized this region as being a separate geographical entity; a new unified system of transportation, developed in the late seventh and eighth centuries, also helped promote the unique identity of the region.[68] As a traditional military center, the Kanto bore the brunt of provisioning and draft orders. "The provinces of the Bandō have frequently adhered to military duty; because of this they are afflicted with epidemic and drought."[69] The wars contributed to a rising tide of violence in the Kanto, an area which already had a reputation as a land of rebels.

PRUNING THE TAIHŌ SYSTEM

The mighty Emperor Kammu (r. 782–805) was devoted to strengthening imperial power and prestige. He built two great new Chinese-style capitals at Nagaoka and Heian (Kyoto) and crushed the barbarians of the Tohoku. Both projects cost vast amounts of money and manpower, but Temmu and the emperors of the eighth century would have approved of Kammu's grand imperial designs.

But, by the year 800, the Court faced serious political and economic problems. Because of expenditures for the construction of the new capitals and the wars against the barbarians, the government was near bankruptcy. In addition, repeated outbreaks of epidemics from abroad and poor farming conditions made for a declining tax and manpower base. Kammu and the rest of the Court knew that radical retrenchment was in order, and that, with foreign enemies in abeyance, external defense was a logical target for budget cutters.

ENDING THE UNIVERSAL DRAFT. In 792, on the eve of the third and largest expedition to the Tohoku, the Court abolished the heart of the Chinese-style system, conscription of commoners for the provincial militia (except for areas of current or potential military activity like northeastern Honshu and northern Kyushu). Government officials complained in the edict that "provincial governors and colonels (*gunki*) of the militia . . . use soldiers as forced laborers, . . . and wastefully cause the Court expenses."[70] Therefore, "in order to reduce the . . . [burden] . . . of corvée labor" on commoners, the state would do away with the draft. Already suffering from depopulation due to repeated epidemics, Japan could no longer afford to conscript people for huge expeditions and the construction of new capitals.

Although official venality and the scarcity of labor were immediate causes for the demise of the provincial militia, the conscription of peasant soldiers, in contrast to the drafting of military specialists, had always been difficult. Military service required peasants to spend a long time away from home and to provide most of their own weapons and provisions. The prologue to one law of the early ninth century stated that, "if one man is drafted, the whole household will consequently be destroyed."[71]

By the late eighth century, those peasants who were drafted did not meet official specifications:

> Their [the recruits'] bodies are naked and their heads are bald. They know how to use only sickles and hatchets; how can their weak backs and tired shoulders bear to pull a bowstring? They come without provisions and, when we ask about this, they flee. If we feed these hungry recruits, then they vie in becoming habitual offenders. If we charge them according to law and make arrests, our jails are full. They seek food by performing forced labor and then quickly run off to the mountains and wilds.[72]

Poor commoners came to the army looking for a way out of poverty.

The Court also charged that provincial officials abused their power over peasant recruits. A 753 report said that "provincial functionaries work soldiers on private projects in violation of law; the conscripts all throw away their bows and arrows and instead take up spades and hoes."[73] In 813, the Court decried "provincial officials" who were "not of good character" and "employed soldiers as they please[d] at their private houses."[74] It was no wonder that men's "physical powers became exhausted and they could not stand up to being a soldier." A later lawmaker wrote that "the servile nature of the conscript makes him no different from a slave."[75]

The end to the peasant draft came at the culmination of a century of reforms. In 719, only 17 years after the establishment of the Taihō system, the Court had seen fit to reduce the number of provincial militia, officers, and soldiers.[76] While bad relations with Silla induced lawmakers to increase the military establishment in 732, only 7 years later the Court stopped the draft (except in Kyushu and the Tōhoku) in the wake of the Great Smallpox Epidemic of 735–737.[77] In 746, the government once again reestablished conscription for the provincial militia, but in 780 the Court announced a reduction in the size of forces in accordance with a general policy of financial retrenchment.[78] The construction of capitals and the wars in northeastern Honshu dealt the final blow to the draft of commoners.

To be effective, a Chinese-style army had to drill regularly every year, a difficult task when recruits fell victim to so many problems. For this reason, the Taihō system had relied on the political and economic clout of district magistrates to convince commoners to come out and fight in the army. Although it would be incorrect to say that the drafting of commoners to fight as units of infantry was a total failure in Japan, it was clearly the weakest link in the system.

The abolition of the draft in 792 also meant an end to related institutions, such as the Border and Capital Guards. In 795, the Council of State declared it was doing away with the transportation of Border Guards from eastern Honshu to northern Kyushu, except for the two tiny islands of Iki and Tsushima in the strait between Korea and Japan. Lawgivers left each province to decide on its own how best to defend itself. The Court abandoned the system of Border Guards because the defenders "tired of their defensive positions after a long time" (that is, deserted). Desertion may have been a problem because the absence of the man of the house meant economic hardship for his family. In addition, Border Guards were expensive, and bureaucratic entanglements were very numerous.[79]

Initiated in the years after the disaster at the Paekch'ŏn River in 663, the practice of sending soldiers from eastern Honshu to guard the shores of northern Kyushu seems to have functioned fairly well for half a century, as long as the threat from China and Korea seemed real. But, beginning in 730, the Court gradually withdrew its defensive support from Kyushu. In 730 and again in 737, officials handed down orders ending the transfer of Kanto warriors to northern Kyushu.[80] Despite several requests from Dazaifu, a military headquarters located in northern Kyushu, Kanto warriors returned to Kyushu soil only for the years 755–757. The government terminated Border Guards for Iki and Tsushima in 835, and Kyushu relied on its own populace for defense for the remainder of the ninth century.

Historians cite 3 reasons for the end of the Border Guards system. (1) After 750, China fell prey to internal rebellions and decline and no longer posed a major military threat; Korea also grew weaker in the eighth century. (2) The wars against the barbarians of the Tohoku so drained the manpower and resources of the Kanto that the region could not provide soldiers to defend northern Kyushu. (3) Domestic economic and demographic problems weakened the resolve of the government to sustain a defense for the entire archipelago.

As early as 723, the Court acknowledged that the idea of raising Capital Guards (Eji) from the ranks of the peasantry was unworkable. Capital Guards "came to work in their best years and returned home as white-haired old men; they were separated from their parents forever and in the end fell into wrongdoing."[81] Peasants made better laborers than they did Capital Guards, and the actual soldiers were taken from among low-ranking officials and relatives of district magistrates who had always served as attendants and retainers (*toneri*).[82] By the ninth century, most "Capital Guards" were working as porters, messengers, gardeners, and diggers.

The other offices for the defense of the capital, the Palace Guards (Hyōe fu) and Gate Guards (Emon fu), also lost their standing as military units during the early and middle ninth century.[83] In 811, the Court reorganized protection of the capital to consist of the Left and Right Offices of the Palace Guards, the Left and Right Offices of the Gate Guards, and the Left and Right Offices of Imperial Attendants (Sa u konoe fu). Coordination among these offices was poor, and, as the status of district magistrates deteriorated in the ninth century, the Palace Guards weakened greatly. The Gate Guards supplied some police, but a new Office of Investigators (Kebiishi chō) soon absorbed the Gate Guards' function (see Chapter 5). The Office of Imperial Attendants became the bailiwick of mighty civil aristocrats, the northern house of the Fujiwara, who engaged in poetry contests and ignored their military duties. By the mid-ninth century, the duties of the Imperial Attendants became non-military and the number of lower officers shrank. Peasants began to claim positions just to avoid paying taxes.

THE MOVE TOWARDS MILITARY SPECIALISTS. With the draft, Border Guards, and Capital Guards abolished, Japanese rulers were once again vulnerable to foreign and domestic enemies, and the Court realized that it could not leave the government undefended. One week after the abolition of the provincial militia in 792, political leaders authorized a new military system:

> The Council of State Orders:
> That "Strong Fellows" (*kondei*) ought to be conscripted.
> . . . Concerning the above, . . . "Strong Fellows ought to be conscripted and allotted to protect weapons storehouses, bell repositories [passes to use the official system of transportation], and provincial headquarters. Sons and brothers of the district magistrates ought to be chosen. Rotations should be formed."[84]

The government planned to replace a military composed primarily of commoners with martial specialists called Strong Fellows, who would be drawn from the same class that had provided leadership for the Taihō armies, the local strongmen ("sons and brothers of district magistrates").

The 792 decree was not the first occasion on which the Strong Fellows had appeared in East Asian history. The term had originated in China, and the Japanese Court used the phrase at least three times in the seventh century to describe military specialists.[85] In 733, the Court had authorized the creation of provincial Strong Fellows, only to rescind the order for most of Japan in 738 in the wake of the Great Smallpox Epidemic.[86] In 762, Nakamaro had established a similar system for the strategically located provinces of Ise, Ōmi, Mino, and Echizen, raising his troops from among district magistrates; his company was also short-lived.[87] A 780 edict required the Court to select "wealthy persons with talent for mounted archery," a possible reference to the families of district magistrates.[88]

Because the decree establishing the Strong Fellows specified the class from which they were to be drawn, the 792 order provides a crucial clue for understanding the social origins, organization, and fighting style of Japan's early military. The Court enjoined the relatives of district magistrates, the same group that had crushed the rebellion of Fujiwara no Hirotsugu and had supplied countless fighters for capital aristocrats, the Border Guards, and the Tōhoku armies, to form the new military of the late eighth and ninth centuries. The government may have decided to do away with the systematic conscription of commoners, but it would retain the backbone of the early Japanese military—local fighting specialists.

There can be little doubt that the Strong Fellows were mounted soldiers, because the 733 edict which first established the guards specified that each Strong Fellow be granted two grooms.[89] When battle lines were drawn, these grooms probably acted as foot soldiers. Since there are no examples of the Strong Fellows in combat, it is difficult to determine whether they used mass or individual tactics, but the command structure in which each equestrian trooper led 2 foot soldiers into war is identical to that used by the twelfth-century samurai.

Thus, the 792 edict establishing the Strong Fellows allows historians to infer several points about the early Japanese military. First, because the Strong Fellows were mounted troops and most of the fighters were from the families of district magistrates, it seems fair to assume, then, that many district magistrates must have also fought as horsemen. Furthermore, since most district magistrates belonged to families that had been local strongmen (*kuni no miyatsuko*) in the period before the heavy influx of Chinese-style institutions in 645, and since mounted combat was important before 645, the 792 decree lends further credence to the argument made in Chapter 1 that many pre-645 local chieftains were also mounted fighters.

The 792 order reinforces the interpretation made throughout this book: that pre-645 local strongmen (*kuni no miyatsuko*) gave rise to the later district magistrates, both of whom traditionally fought from horseback. The establishment of bands of Strong Fellows merely recognized what had always been a given under the Taihō system—the importance of local powerholders and their horses in warfare. This basic structure, in which local men of influence led the army as horse-riding military specialists, was an old pattern based on political and family relationships. The pattern would retain its importance for at least four more centuries, until after the founding of Japan's first samurai government in Kamakura in 1185.

The 792 edict also provides another clue to understanding the rise of the samurai: It lists the number of Strong Fellows stationed in each province (see Appendix Table 3). The distribution of troops clearly favors the Kanto. Seven of 8 Kanto provinces are represented in the 13 provinces with 100 or more mounted fighters, while only 2 western Honshu provinces contain that many. Three of 4 provinces with more than 100 Strong Fellows were in the Kanto. The weight given the Kanto reflects the large number of horse pastures in eastern Honshu and the Kanto's role as a military base from Yamato times.[90]

But the official figure for Strong Fellows demonstrates more than the relative importance of the Kanto. The total number of mounted soldiers listed in the 792 order is about 3,200 men. This figure is at least as large as (if not larger than) estimates for the total number of housemen (*goke'nin*) who bolstered Yoritomo's shogunate in Kamakura in the late twelfth century (see Chapter 8).

To be sure, there are those who will rightly suggest that comparing Strong Fellows to Yoritomo's housemen and drawing conclusions about relative military strengths in 792 and 1185 is a hazardous business. First, the number 3,200 most likely does not represent all the mounted fighters in Japan in 792; nor does any similar count for Yoritomo's housemen in 1185. Second, the figure of 3,900 Strong Fellows for 905 found in *The Ordinances of Engi* shows a 22-percent increase in the number of Strong Fellows over the 792 count and could be used to argue for a large growth in Japan's strength in mounted fighters just over the course of the 800s. On the other hand, *The Ordinances of Engi* is also known to be a source compiled long after the heyday of the Taihō system and may not accurately reflect reality.

If one keeps these objections in mind but still credits the figures for Strong Fellows of 792 and housemen of 1185 as being generally instructive, then it seems apparent that the rise of the samurai to a position of political power did not take place because of a dramatic overall increase in mounted fighters. Yoritomo's victory in 1185 was no revolution of numbers. Until 1300, it seems unlikely that the Japanese economy ever supported more equestrian fighters than it did in 792. These points underline the evolutionary character of the changes which led to the assertion of samurai power with the founding of the Kamakura government.

The 792 system has often been portrayed as weak and ineffective, partly because there were relatively few Strong Fellows. In addition, there are other signs that the new institution did not function well. Not long after the 792 edict, Nagato and Yamashiro provinces returned to the conscription of peasants, because Nagato was next to northern Kyushu and Yamashiro contained the imperial capital.[91] An 866 order of the Council of State said that "the Strong Fellows raised by the provinces have lacked ability; they are emptily called the 'defense of teeth and claws' but are no different from a guard of grasshoppers."[92]

Four points indicate that the Strong Fellows were not so impotent as some historians have believed. (1) Although 3,200 men may seem like a small number, they were mounted fighters, who were especially effective because of their combat style.

(2) The Court did not intend the Strong Fellows as a defense against foreign invasion. These men protected provincial headquarters, transportation centers, and weapons repositories. They guarded strategically located centers which might have been the target of thieves and brigands. (It is interesting to note that the Court singled out provincial headquarters for protection, a sure sign of that local office's growing importance.)

(3) The 866 order, which condemns the Strong Fellows as a defense of "grasshoppers," must be viewed in the context of its times. The 860s saw renewed threats of invasion from the Korean kingdom of Silla, and the Court believed that it should attend to external defense as well as internal rebellions. In 863, the Japanese government deported 60 Silla merchants who had sailed to Hakata Bay. By 870, Silla pirates were stealing tax shipments bound for the capital, and the Court responded by dispatching weapons and troops to Kyushu. The Strong Fellows who guarded provincial headquarters against troublemakers were naturally seen as inadequate for foreign defense, and the 866 order merely states this fact.

(4) Japanese scholars have produced evidence of the longevity of the 792 system of Strong Fellows. One historian has uncovered a record of a special office for the Strong Fellows in Hitachi province as late as the 1300s.[93] Aristocratic diaries and other administrative documents also mention the Strong Fellows department in various provinces in the tenth and eleventh centuries.[94] Thus, the men who made up the Strong Fellows system of 792 should be seen for what they were — the backbone of the Taihō army and a missing link be-

tween early mounted fighters and the samurai of the twelfth century.

The Court at first limited the Strong Fellows to the more settled areas of Japan, but later the Tohoku and Kyushu added their own versions of the 792 system. In Kyushu there were 1,740 troops:

> When your servants consider it, we should dismiss peasant conscripts and abolish the post of colonel (*gunki*); we will newly choose wealthy, mobile fellows. Their names shall be called "Select Warriors" (*senshi*) . . .
>
> Recently, the people's customs are greatly distant from the skills of mounted archery. But the districts of Ōno and Nahori in Bungo province produce mounted hunters. They are useful as soldiers.[95]

The occupation and social origins of the Select Warriors are important. In Kyushu as in northeastern Honshu, the government drew its horsemen from among mounted hunters, who skinned and dressed game for a living (*tokai no tagui*) in opposition to Buddhist teachings. Moreover, it is interesting to note that the districts of Ōno and Nahori are regions suitable mostly for horse raising, hunting, and forestry.[96] One is again reminded that many military men practiced professions other than farming.

Kyushu's Select Warriors came from a different class from the Strong Fellows of central Japan. They were "wealthy, mobile" people, not from families with long pedigrees like the district magistrates who joined the Strong Fellows. Select Warriors also received provisions, grooms, and exemptions from taxes to entice them into service. Some historians have seen this system as the start of the institution of paid military volunteers.[97]

Northeastern Japan followed the trend towards mounted specialists. Before the wars of the late eighth and early ninth centuries, a combination of peasant-soldiers and "fortress soldiers" (*chimpei*) imported from the Kanto had guarded the Tohoku. In 769, there were about 3,000 fortress soldiers, who received provisions from the government. With the outbreak of war in the area, the Court shipped more soldiers north, mostly from the Kanto. In 815, the government sent the fortress soldiers home and recruited veterans of the wars in the Tohoku.[98] Called "Strong Warriors" (*kenshi*), these soldiers numbered 2,000 and guarded Fort Izawa and the Tamazukuri Palisade. By the early tenth century, northeastern Japan possessed its own military specialists who had volunteered because of their martial skills and experience (see Appendix Table 3).

The Court also drafted barbarian (*emishi*) prisoners-of-war to serve as special mounted units.[99] The state had resettled these captives in 35 provinces in central Japan after the Tohoku wars; they may have numbered as many as 10,000 in the Kanto alone. Their skill at archery and their mobility made them valuable recruits, and enlistment excused them from taxes. They also acted as guards at provincial headquarters in exchange for provisions.[100] In 869 and again in 895, the Court sent some barbarian guards to Kyushu to practice archery and await a possible invasion from Silla.

THE CROSSBOW AND JAPAN'S DEFENSE IN THE NINTH CENTURY

In 837, Mutsu officials reported to the Court on the value of the crossbow:

> Mounted archery is the custom of the barbarians. Ten commoners can not stand up against one of them. But when it comes to crossbow warfare, even though there are bandits coming from 10,000 directions, they can not resist the flying arrows of even one crossbow. This weapon is the best for overwhelming the barbarians.[101]

The weapon which merited such high praise has a long history, invented in China, where infantrymen used the crossbow as early as the Warring States period (403–221 B.C.). The northern Korean kingdom of Koguryŏ introduced the weapon to Japan in 618 when it delivered two Chinese prisoners-of-war and several military accoutrements.[102] Japanese soldiers must have recognized the value of the crossbow; by the Civil War of 672, there is a report of crossbows shooting arrows "just like rain."[103]

The authors of the Taihō Codes attached a special significance to the crossbow. Lawgivers required that both the provincial militia and capital have experts familiar with its manufacture and use. The Codes specified that each militia was to have crossbow experts at the rate of 2 "strong men" for every unit of 50.[104] Both sides employed the weapon in the revolt of Fujiwara no Hirotsugu in 740.

Despite the prominence of the crossbow in pre-800 sources,

scholars know little about the mechanics of the weapon. The general shape of the crossbow of the ninth century is well-known, but it is difficult to be precise about its structure.[105] Archeologists have yet to discover a crossbow in excavations in Japan.[106] The absence of artifacts may imply that the weapon was not as widely used in Japan as in China.

Early Japanese artisans made both stationary and hand-held weapons primarily of wood, with metal triggers. *The Ordinances of Engi* from the early tenth century stated that 633 units of labor were necessary to manufacture the relatively sophisticated machine.[107] The trigger mechanism was especially complex; the 837 Mutsu report noted that the crossbows in government storehouses were "either out of kilter, or the trigger was not aligned properly."[108]

Yet the crossbow was an effective weapon. William McNeill has noted that a Chinese crossbow could unseat a mounted fighter at 400 meters.[109] Thus it might be thought of as an ancient version of the handgun: a weapon easy to use but complicated to manufacture and maintain. In this regard, the crossbow provides a contrast with the long bow employed by horse-riding archers, which was relatively easy to manufacture but much more difficult to master.

In 835, a Court-sponsored artisan improved upon Chinese prototypes by inventing a new stationary crossbow:

> Shimaki no Fubito Makoto of the Outer Senior 5th Rank, Lower Grade, greatly surpassed the crowd of artisans in his thinking on machine design. He wanted to prepare a frontier weapon and by himself developed a new design for the crossbow. It even can be shot from four directions; it rotates and is easy to set off.
>
> On this day, from the Great Minister (*daijin*) on down, powerholders summoned the Capital Guards to Suzaku Gate and they gave a trial shooting using the new crossbow. It faced to the south and was fired. We could only hear the sound of the weapon firing and did not see the shadow of the arrow flying. We did not even know where the arrow stopped.[110]

Three years later, in 838, Mino province ordered 4 of the new machines to replace 20 of the old issue.[111]

As noted previously in this chapter, the Japanese government became alarmed about a possible invasion from Silla beginning in the 860s. To defend against foreign encroachment the Court adopted a policy of locating crossbows and crossbow experts (*doshi*) throughout the endangered areas on the Sea of Japan. For example, one order from 871 did away with a provincial clerkship (*shishō*) and established in its stead a crossbow expert in Hōki province, western Honshu.[112] During the latter half of the ninth century, the Court appointed crossbow experts to 18 provinces in Kyushu, western Japan, and northeastern Honshu.[113] In Tsushima, geographers have uncovered an archaic placename called Crossbow at the entrance to a Korean-style fortification which may date from this era.

Crossbow experts saw action several times in the late ninth century. In 866, the magistrate of Kii district in Hizen province conspired with some Koreans to teach "the skills of the crossbow" to Silla fighters and attack Tsushima, but the plot failed.[114] In 894, Japan actually joined battle with 100 Silla ships holding 2,500 soldiers; the turning point in the battle came when the Governor of Tsushima "raised shields and arranged crossbows."[115]

The crossbow also made its mark in the Tōhoku. In 880, a revolt of barbarians took place; the rebels seized and burned Fort Akita. Among the weapons they destroyed were 29 stationary crossbows and 100 of the hand-held variety.[116]

Three points are especially important when considering the role of the crossbow in the early Japanese military. (1) The high technological requirements for its manufacture meant that the state played a significant part in its development and deployment. Few private individuals could afford to build one; therefore the crossbow helped to focus military power in the hands of the central and (especially) provincial governments. As the state weakened after 900 and could no longer hire artisans to make crossbows, however, defenders gravitated towards other, less complicated weapons.

(2) This technological remedy reinforced the trend towards the use of military specialists already seen in the adoption of special mounted units in the 792 system. It is noteworthy that the surnames of military aristocrats such as Fumiya and Sakanoue appear among those using the crossbow in Kyushu and the Tōhoku, respectively. Crossbow experts were probably of different social origins from horse-riding archers; those skilled at the crossbow were low-ranking officials who received a salary for practicing their trade.

(3) The crossbow gave foot soldiers a weapon to use on the battlefield and helped keep alive the Taihō tradition of commoners' marching off to war. Several Japanese scholars now believe that local officials were still able to draft small numbers of commoners into the army as foot soldiers even after the abolition of universal conscription in 792.[117] These historians read the scarce evidence (about a half dozen government orders) in different ways: Some argue that the district magistrate led these troops beginning around the year 800; others assert that provincial officials commanded foot soldiers after 850. The slim documentation, encompassing only Mutsu, Kyushu, and Kazusa, suggests that the ability of local officials to raise peasant foot soldiers in this period must have varied widely according to province. It seems most likely that the foot-soldier tradition forged during the eighth century under the Taihō Codes continued in some areas, but certainly not as a systematic, nationwide draft.

Although armies had shrunk in the face of the dwindling pool of manpower, the ninth-century military still probably fought much like its predecessors. Horse-riding bowmen, crossbow experts, and common foot soldiers all went to battle, occasionally even employing mass tactics. Yet the emphasis was swinging towards mounted specialists. This can be seen in the rapid decline in crossbow use by the early tenth century. A famous Court aristocrat wrote in 914 that "[crossbow] experts simply debated the amount of their salary, and no one asked about the quality of their skills."[118] Difficulty of manufacture probably also played a role in the eventual decline of the crossbow on Japanese soil. An interesting historical question is what would have happened if the Japanese had possessed the technological expertise, personnel, and official will to continue the deployment of the crossbow after 900. Would the crossbow have wiped out the mounted archer in Japan as it did in China?

CONCLUSION

The late eighth and ninth centuries were a critical stage in the development of military power in premodern Japan. In the late eighth century, the scene focused on northeastern Japan. The Court had colonized the Tohoku since the early seventh century, seeking to capture the wealth and people of the region. During the era from 774 to 812, the government conducted 5 major expeditions against the residents of northeastern Japan, thought to be brutish barbarians. For 20 years after the Court made its determination to "civilize" the area, the barbarians resisted so successfully that huge Chinese-style armies made no progress. As many as 100,000 men reportedly set out at one time to conquer the region, but small guerilla forces of mounted archers defeated the Court's host, as in the Battle of the Koromo River. At last in 794, the Court achieved victory after naming the military aristocrat Sakanoue no Tamuramaro to command; for nearly 20 years thereafter pacification continued.

The government fought the wars in northeastern Honshu within the framework of the Taihō system. The Court drafted peasants to supply labor and fight as foot soldiers and the same military aristocrats who had been active earlier in the eighth century commanded expeditions. Yet the war also caused the Court to place a heavier reliance upon military specialists, especially those raised by the provincial headquarters of the Kanto region. Many military experts were mounted fighters, since this was the favorite combat style of northeastern Japanese residents. By and large, specialists came from the same families that produced district magistrates. Battlefield experience honed their fighting skills and the Court rewarded veterans with prizes.

The wars brought about subtle but important changes in soldiery. The natives of the Tōhoku were superb mounted archers, and warriors for the Court gained in horse-riding skills by their experience on the battlefield. In particular, the wars effected a move from heavy iron armor to light leather protective gear. The sword, adopted from the continent as a straight weapon, probably received its curve from the barbarian fighters. Thus the wars in northeastern Japan led to the adoption of the technology associated with the samurai of the twelfth century.

The major effect of 40 years of hostilities was to exhaust the Court's reserves of men and matériel. Officials felt the burden even more keenly, since the government was also in the midst of building new capitals at Nagaoka and Heian. The region of eastern Japan known as the Bandō (the Kanto), which supplied warriors and other resources, was hardest hit.

Partially as a result of 40 years of campaigns, the government abandoned the nationwide conscription of peasants. The corruption of militia and provincial officials, the shortage of manpower, and the decline in the quality of recruits were all cited as reasons for the end to the universal draft of commoners. Most of these abuses were not sudden occurrences, but had afflicted the Chinese-style system of the Taihō Codes almost from the beginning. Of course, the abolition of peasant conscription also meant the end of the Capital and Border Guards.

The system the Court used to replace the Taihō conscription arrangements was two-pronged. On the one hand, the Court spelled out its increasing reliance on the use of the bow and horse by creating a class of provincial horsemen known as the Strong Fellows. These forces came from the same group that had comprised the backbone of the Chinese-style system, the local strongmen (district magistrates). The numbers of Strong Fellows listed per province show the importance of the Kanto as a military base even in the ninth century, while the total of 3,200 horsemen for 792 may well have been higher than the number of samurai who fought to establish Yoritomo's government in 1185. The Strong Fellows were thus also a link to the samurai of later times.

The duty of the Strong Fellows was to guard provincial storehouses, which suggests the growing importance of the provincial governor in local military affairs. Although some historians have portrayed the Strong Fellows as a failure, evidence shows that remnants of the 792 system were apparent in some areas well into the 1300s. The 792 system suited the Court so well that it created similar institutions in Kyushu and northeastern Japan in the ninth century. Taken together, these systems suggest that the rise of military men occurred within, not outside, the purview of the government.

Crossbow-bearing foot soldiers composed the second prong of the ninth-century army. Despite its sophisticated technology and consequent difficulty of manufacture, the crossbow was easy to use. An artisan devised an advanced version of the machine, and it was deployed throughout the latter half of the ninth century to defend Japan against the threat of invasion. Even with an end to the universal draft of commoners in 792, officials conscripted some peasants to serve as foot soldiers and laborers in the ninth century, continuing the Taihō tradition on a much smaller scale.

By the year 900, several essential features of samurai life were already in place. The weaponry of the twelfth-century warrior had basically completed its evolution thanks to the barbarians, who added light armor and the curved sword to the repertoire of the horse-riding archer. The early evolution of this fighting technology put the Japanese mounted archer on a par with or even ahead of the heavily armored Western European knight, with whom the samurai is so often compared.

In addition, military houses, the basic unit of samurai social organization, existed in Japan in 900. The mounted warriors of the ninth century handed their fighting style down to their children, just as the samurai would three centuries later. At the local level, the families of district magistrates made use of the technology of the horse and bow; famous ninth-century military aristocrats included the Fumiya and the Sakanoue. But the more renowned military houses who would contend for power in the 1100s, such as the Taira and Minamoto, ascended into the aristocracy after the rebellions of Masakado and Sumitomo in the late 930s.

It is harder to be certain about another aspect of samurai life — the economic base. Although land seems to have been a component in ninth-century-warrior economic holdings, the Court usually paid for its military establishment with appointment to office or even salary. Surely these rewards included access to the products of the land, as when the district magistrate received a hereditary parcel with his position; but it is unclear whether he then divided his parcel among his retainers as a guarantee of their loyalty.

In the realm of politics, fighting specialists were just as far away from power as they had ever been. While the military aristocracy was evolving, a civilian nobility also came into existence, and the latter estate monopolized political power for three centuries. One hallmark of the samurai's rise to political dominance was that, even though the weapons, social organization, and numbers of fighters necessary to form a separate military government existed from early on, it would take four more centuries for the warrior to gain the political acumen necessary to assert autonomy.

chapter four

From External Defense to Internal Peacekeeping, 850–950

"My destiny lies in the martial arts. Come to think of it, who among my comrades can rival Masakado!"
—Taira no Masakado, warrior-rebel of the tenth century

The original Emperor [Suzaku] descended from his throne and raised his palms to his forehead in supplication. All officialdom performed ablutions and offered a thousand prayers . . . Priests attached images of the bandit [Taira no Masakado] beneath thorny trees to bring him bad luck. . . .
— Description of Court reaction to the revolt in 939

Masakado's rebellion of 935–940 was the longest, most serious insurrection Japan had ever endured, and it came at a time when slow changes of economic decline, hardship, and discontent— trends that had been growing for two centuries—weakened the Court and increased the impetus towards rebellion. Repeated epidemics and famines in the eighth and ninth centuries had resulted in short-term instabilities in and long-term stagnation of the economy and population, and, by 900, resources were so scarce that improvement in (or even maintenance of) an individual's standard of living was accomplished only at another's expense. In the new zero-sum game, there were winners (some high-ranking aristocrats and clerics and most upper-level provincial officials) and losers (most district magistrates and many peasants); both sides turned to violence to survive.

Framers of the Taihō Codes had mandated an elaborate military system to defend the Court from foreign invaders, not to deter domestic violence. To cope with new attacks from within against provincial officials, in 901 the Court relaxed its tight control of conscription and troop organization and granted new martial powers to provincial governors, strengthening the role of the provincial headquarters as a military center. With this reform, peace reigned for a few decades in the violence-plagued Kanto and Tohoku.

In 935, however, war erupted in the Kanto, and soon residents of northeastern Japan and pirates in the Inland Sea turned against the government as well. These conflicts challenged Japan's imperial control and forced the Court to focus on internal strife. At the head of forces, which varied only slightly in composition and technology from Taihō armies, the eastern rebel Taira no Masakado fought a war to resolve a family dispute, trying to ensure his own survival and that of his family. At the same time, the pirate leader Sumitomo led a tax revolt in western Japan. The Court rallied its forces by 940, but won out more through political cunning than by military might. The nationwide revolts caused unprecedented destruction and gave birth to the Kanto Independence Movement, many new houses of military aristocrats, and a reformed rural military system aimed at keeping peace through the provincial headquarters.

GROWING DOMESTIC VIOLENCE AND REFORMS IN THE MILITARY SYSTEM

In 866, people of the two adjoining provinces of Mino and Owari went to war over a ditch. The relocation of a water course apparently would have favored one province over another, and, rather than negotiate a settlement, residents of the two areas sought a solution in violence. A Court historian described the conflict at the mouth of the Hirono River:

> Earlier Owari provincial officials reported: "We received an authorization from the Council of State and were digging open the mouth of the Hirono River to have it run in its former riverbed. But Kagami Yoshio, the Magistrate (*tairyō*) of Kagami district in Mino province and Kagami Yoshimune, the Magistrate of Atsumi district [also in Mino], led a military force of over 700 foot soldiers and horsemen and attacked at the mouth of the river. They killed and wounded [our]

district officers and shot and killed [our] forced laborers. The river flowed red with blood and the grasslands were littered with gore."[1]

The incident at the Hirono River was just one example of the increasing strife that afflicted many areas and groups in Japan by the end of the ninth century. The 866 conflict on the border between Mino and Owari was representative in that it involved district and provincial officials using their military powers, not against external enemies or political rebels, but in a domestic setting to correct an economic situation they felt was unfair. The internal violence was intimately bound up with deteriorating social and economic conditions in the countryside, and the troops that fought on both sides were raised by local officials acting within the framework of Taihō institutions.

ECONOMIC DECLINE AND LOCAL POLITICS. The Chinese-style system of the late seventh and eighth centuries is often characterized as a centralized, despotic state. But the power of the Court was based on the consent and cooperation of local strongmen who served as district magistrates in the countryside. Court aristocrats provided official recognition for the local lord's economic and social position in his home region, as well as training at the capital for his relatives. In return, the magistrate collaborated in administering the census, land allocation, and revenue collection. This arrangement functioned well for about three decades after the promulgation of the Taihō Codes in 702, but, by the 730s, problems arose that eventually led the interests of the two groups to diverge.

From the local strongman's point of view, the problem was how to obtain an appointment to a district post, which was essentially hereditary and included great administrative and military powers. Local men of influence were numerous even in the 600s: how was the Court to choose? The Codes had dictated that the two qualifications for district appointment were to be talent and a lineage derived from the first local officials who had served under the Emperor Kōtoku after the coup d'état of 645.[2]

Despite stiff competition within designated families, the selection of district magistrates ran rather smoothly until the outbreak of the Great Smallpox Epidemic of 735–737. Many candidates for office from families of former district magistrates perished in the plague, and the Court broadened the pool for official appointments to include families who had never before filled the office.[3] The new law suddenly thrust into consideration many who previously had no hope for district office or political advancement. In 749, the government attempted to bring to the fore the descendants of pre-epidemic officeholders, but the damage was already done.[4] Now there were several candidates for each office, and fierce competition ensued.

These local rivalries occurred in the context of stagnant, or even worsening, economic conditions in the countryside. The underlying cause of the prolonged economic slump was the repeated outbreak of epidemics throughout the late seventh, eighth, and ninth centuries.[5] Plagues slowed population growth, which in turn meant a shortage of labor for farming. Pestilence also fostered population mobility which was not conducive to the settled rice agriculture preferred by Court aristocrats. The Court had trouble governing shifting and dispersed settlements, and the continuing epidemics and famines made the peasantry even harder to control, count, and tax. Repeated disease outbreaks also seem to have hindered the conversion of wastelands into productive fields and the development of agricultural technology.

By 763, deteriorating economic conditions and local rivalries over official appointment to district posts exploded into violence. Faced with dwindling stores of grain, local strongmen began to rob and burn government grain storehouses. The first Court law on the subject shows the connection between disease, worsening farming conditions, and arson:

> Those who have died in epidemics are many in number; rain and dryness are out of rhythm. "Divine fires" (*jinka*) occur frequently and result in wasteful damage to state revenues.[6]

At first, district magistrates blamed the incineration of storehouses on the gods, calling them "divine fires." Amazingly, the Court initially accepted this explanation, but eventually learned the truth: Its appointed officials in the countryside were taking the grain, then destroying the evidence. Arson of district and provincial storehouses remained a serious problem from the second half of the eighth into the early ninth century.[7]

Local men of influence not named to office also found a way to take advantage of the widespread arson. Families who had been overlooked in the appointment process set storehouses ablaze; the Court punished the incumbent, and the arsonist received his cherished nomination to the magistrate's position.[8] "Divine fires" sparked by official rivalry occurred most frequently in the Kanto, where violence was becoming a way of life.

Worsening economic conditions resulted in a growing maldistribution of rural wealth, which led to increased competition for district posts. From the late eighth through the ninth centuries, sources speak of "the rich" (*fugō no tomogara*), a shadowy term referring to local strongmen and wealthy peasants.[9] Many of the rich were also district magistrates.[10] The litany of Court complaints against the rich included the hiring of laborers away from poor peasants during planting and harvest, and paying for exemption from forced labor, and the hoarding of cash.[11] In addition, the rich cheated starving peasants of their official grain dole during famines; they monopolized fertile lands; they bribed provincial officials to evade taxation.[12] In 822 and again in 830, the country suffered from a severe epidemic, and the Court berated the rich for accumulating large caches of grain while poor victims starved.[13] Local strongmen further profited from famine by making rice loans at high interest to needy farmers.[14]

The wealthy class created by the exploitation of the economic crisis increased the field of candidates for district positions. The Court tried desperately in 798–799 to bring magistrates back under its direct supervision by requiring that all nominees obtain training in the capital, but the attempt failed because local strongmen would not risk leaving their districts and interests long enough for the experience.[15] During the ninth century, the Court surrendered power over the district to the provincial headquarters, which solved the problem of appointments by creating new offices and naming all candidates to posts. As the number of district positions increased, their power decreased and fragmented, and the provincial office became more powerful. The stage was set for violent confrontation between local men of influence, many of them district magistrates, and newly appointed provincial officers.

As the power and goodwill of the district appointees declined, other important changes occurred. Without the cooperation of district magistrates, the census system quickly broke down; runaways and vagrants fled to the protection of temples, aristocrats, and the rich. The institution of state land allocation became unworkable. District and provincial officials began to hold back for themselves a greater portion of the revenues they collected for the Court, lining their own pockets with a healthy cut of tax items like hemp cloth, iron, and sea products. The quantity and quality of revenues entering the capital declined dramatically over the period 750–900.

Aristocrats at the capital reacted to the fiscal crisis in 5 ways. (1) The Court adopted retrenchment policies. The government eliminated offices and limited the number of aristocrats and imperial relatives who could draw salaries. (2) The Court scolded and punished provincial and district officers who failed to send sufficient revenues to the capital. A representative policy was the establishment of Investigators of Provincial Dismissal Notices (*kageyu shi*), who checked provincial tax documents to guarantee governors' honesty. If his records were not in order, the aristocratic governor would not receive the proper papers to return to the capital.

(3) Individual capital aristocrats cultivated personal political and economic ties with local strongmen and others to ensure a source of revenue independent of the government. In return for a share of the harvest, capital aristocrats invested in local agriculture and supported the strongmen politically. These ties overlapped with eighth-century institutionalized links between the capital and the district magistrate. One cause of violence in the countryside was attempts by aristocratic messengers or household officials to collect taxes unlawfully or resist the demands of provincial officials.[16] The creation of early estates (*shōen*) is an example of aristocrat-strongman cooperation.[17] (4) The Court conducted raids on provincial storehouses and other assets to keep the central government in operation. By the late ninth century, the government adopted new financial measures, such as the assignment of special lands to individual offices, to ensure continuing revenues.

(5) Aristocrat-bureaucrats at the capital increased the powers of the provincial office and turned its staff into tax-farmers. These officials became tax collectors who accumulated as much revenue as possible, turned over a set percentage to the government, and kept the rest. This practice was already well under way by the mid-eighth century, when officials built tax-farming into the system of provincial rice loans.[18] In the ninth century, the Court required provincial headquarters to pass on only 70 percent of the 3-percent rice tax, permitting the staff to keep the rest as an incentive to collection.

The new emphasis on the provincial administration as the only base of imperial power in the countryside necessarily affected the office itself.[19] The highest-ranking officers, the governors (*kami*), took up residence in the capital and visited their provincial headquarters only occasionally. The size of the staff increased and, despite repeated prohibitions, many lower-ranking officials stayed on past their appointments to build bases in the provinces. These ex-officials were listed as "rich vagrants" by the government and often formed bands to resist taxation.[20] In many cases they joined forces with district magistrates and other strongmen through intermarriage. Lower Court aristocrats and imperial relatives also ignored the ban on taking up residence in the provinces, since the government could no longer provide them with an income in the capital.[21] The increased size, power, and economic role of the provincial government required protection; the establishment of the Strong Fellows (*kondei*) to guard the provincial office in 792 undoubtedly reflected this need.

Thus, from the mid-eighth through the ninth century, Japanese society was caught up in a zero-sum game. The winners were the rich, a few Court aristocrats and powerful temples, and high-level provincial officials. The biggest losers were traditional local strongmen who had held the magistrate's position, lower-ranking Court aristocrats, and average peasants, the vast majority of the population, who were often victimized by the rich. Competition for scarce agricultural and labor resources and the growing maldistribution of wealth were essential elements in the increasing domestic violence in Japan in the late ninth and early tenth centuries.

THE RISING TIDE OF INTERNAL CONFLICT. The Battle at the Hirono River in 866 is one of the earliest examples of anti-government disorder, but usually violence focused on the provincial headquarters. In 884, another district magistrate, Ihogibe no Atai Yasumichi, attacked the Governor of Iwami province with a force of 217 men, surrounding the provincial headquarters and stealing official seals and storehouse keys.[22]

It should come as no surprise that most of the violence of the late ninth century occurred in the Kanto. The area was separated from the Court and its neighbors by high mountains, lending a sense of geographic insulation. From the late sixth century, the Kanto region had been one of the Court's military bases, which meant that weapons were easy to obtain; during the eighth century, a system of roads unified the Kanto and made it possible for criminals to move around freely. The wars in northeastern Japan had further militarized the region, and caused social upheaval. The Kanto also had a reputation as the last refuge of criminals and rebels. In 889, the revolt of Mononobe Ujinaga ushered in a quarter-century of rebellion in the Kanto.[23]

One of the most intriguing examples of lawlessness in the Kanto comes from an order dated 899.[24] After noting that robberies were especially prevalent in the Kanto province of Kōzuke, provincial officials complained about a "band of horse employers" (*shūba no tō*), people who used packhorses to move others' possessions. These moving specialists were really mobile thieves; they stole people's horses in one area and then used them as packhorses in another. Such conduct "harmed the livelihood of those people with just one broken-down nag," as well as violated state laws on transportation.[25]

Three points about "the band of horse employers" are especially noteworthy. (1) According to one Japanese scholar, the activities of these bands coincided with a spate of epidemics and famines.[26] Once again it seems that deteriorating economic circumstances gave rise to violence and lawlessness. (2) The 899 order emphasizes the Kanto as a region with many horses. One archeologist has linked bands of movers to pastures in the mountains of Shinano, just outside the Kanto.[27] (3) The order states that the horse thieves came from among the ranks of the rich, and were difficult to catch since they formed bands strong enough to threaten an entire province but able to disperse at a moment's notice. One Japanese historian has argued that such bands included different classes of people from vagrants to aristocrats, and that these organizations both resisted the government and oppressed residents, just like warrior bands (*bushi dan*) of later times.[28]

Historians know much less about violent crime occurring in other areas of the Kanto and eastern and central Honshu. Robberies occurred in Musashi province in the same year as the horse bandits bedeviled Kōzuke province. Disorder prevailed in Shinano, Kai, Musashi, and Kōzuke from 895 to 900. In 901, brigands attacked the Governor of Echizen; in the same month, a criminal robbed and burned a district storehouse in Suruga. "Evil bands" murdered the Governor of Hida and his wife in 905. Ten years later, in 915, a lesser provincial official conspired to murder his superior in Kōzuke. In 916, the government made a feeble attempt to stop the crime wave by banishing Fujiwara no Hidesato and his band for unnamed transgressions against the state. In 919, a former minor provincial official stole tax items, burned official warehouses, and attacked the headquarters of Musashi.[29]

The late ninth century also saw a special type of disorder: revolts of former residents of the Tohoku (*emishi*) now dispersed throughout the country. After the final expedition against these people in 811, the Court had enacted a policy of moving them to provinces in the south and west, partly to break up their resistance in Mutsu and Dewa and partly to employ them as police. According to *The Ordinances of Engi,* thought to reflect conditions of the ninth century, as many as 10,000 of the erstwhile natives of northeastern Honshu may have been located in the Kanto alone.[30]

The defeated barbarians openly resisted the Court's relocation policy. The earliest revolt took place in Izumo province, where the rebels eventually surrendered to Court-appointed peacemakers of their own kind.[31] Uprisings also occurred in Kazusa in 848, 875, and 883; an order from the Council of State directed especially to Kazusa states that the barbarians still had "untamed hearts." The order goes on to stress that the former residents of the Tohoku committed arson and robbery, thus enhancing the formation of bands of thieves.[32]

The barbarians still living in northeastern Honshu also opposed the government; by far the worst revolt occurred in 878 in Dewa province. During the wars of the late eighth and early ninth centuries, most of the fighting had taken place in Mutsu, but, in the third month of 878, a revolt broke out in Dewa which lasted more than 6 months. It is notable that the rebellion followed a bad harvest and famine, confirming the link between poor economic conditions and violence.[33] The incident began with the storming of Fort Akita and the burning of storehouses, homes, and the fortress itself. The Court advocated a peaceful settlement to the hostilities and dispatched reinforcements from Mutsu and the Kanto. In the 4th month, official troops engaged the rebels near the Akita River but suffered a humiliating defeat in a deep fog, even though the insurgents were outnumbered 2 to 1. The defeat of the imperial forces temporarily turned the northern half of Dewa into an independent country.[34]

The Court responded by naming Fujiwara no Yasunori as the new Governor and appointing Ono no Harukaze, a martial aristocrat with experience in Tohoku affairs, to be General of the Military Government at Fort Taga. Sakanoue no Yoshikage, a descendant of Tamuramaro, assisted Ono. Eventually Yasunori directed Ono and Sakanoue to make a show of force (their army included some friendly *emishi* troops) and then to convince the rebels to surrender by pointing out that the Court had appointed a new, more understanding Governor who doled out grain to famine victims. The two leaders accomplished their tasks, and peace returned to Dewa late in 878. A show of force and diplomacy had proved less costly and more effective in dealing with the people of the Tohoku than had the huge armies of the eighth century.

GOVERNMENT RESPONSE TO LAWLESSNESS. The mounting domestic violence of the late ninth and early tenth centuries prodded the Court to enact countermeasures. First, it reinforced the police power of the provincial office. The government carried out this policy primarily during the mid-ninth century by establishing Investigators (*kebii shi*) in central and eastern Japan.[35] Second, sometime between 889 and 898, lawmakers responded by dispatching a military aristocrat, Prince Takamochi, to the most rebellious area, the

Kanto. The Court granted Prince Takamochi the surname Taira (written with the character "to pacify") and named him Vice-Governor of Kazusa. He took up residence in the provinces; the Court granted this unusual privilege to Takamochi even though other aristocrats were denied the same right. According to one Japanese scholar, this indicates both Takamochi's military ability and the seriousness of disorders in the Kanto.[36]

Despite these actions, upheavals continued unabated. When in 901 serious but unspecified violence once again engulfed the Kanto, the Court decided to enact a third reform, an overhaul of the way provincial governments handled crime and rebellion.[37] The Taihō Codes had spelled out in detail the circumstances under which officials were to raise troops to police their jurisdiction. The laws in force before 901 included a provision for the arrest (*tsuibu*) of prisoners, A.W.O.L. soldiers, laborers and, most important, traitors, by the nearest government agency. Law required the provincial office making arrests under this statute to issue a report to the Council of State in the capital.[38] Another regulation provided a complicated bureaucratic procedure for raising troops and tracking down killers and robbers as they crossed into different jurisdictions.[39]

Two provisions in the Codes dealt with the conscription of soldiers in case of a rebellion or crime wave. One appeared to grant great latitude to the provincial office organizing a force to suppress bandits or killers, but in fact restricted local officials by requiring them to file a request to draft soldiers with the Council of State via emergency post.[40] Another law stated that the governor could raise no more than 20 troops on his own; if he needed more, he was forced to apply to the central government and obtain an imperial edict.[41]

In other words, the Taihō Codes made provincial officials responsible for law and order in their jurisdictions, but intervened at various stages in provincial administration to keep the governors from conscripting troops too freely. To make sure that the provincial government did not overstep its bounds, the Codes required the governor to report his every move to the Council of State and await an imperial edict if he contemplated using more than 20 soldiers to quell an uprising. The Court forced provincial officials to comply with these rigorous standards during an outbreak of piracy in 862 and again during a revolt of the residents of northeastern Honshu in 883.

The new 901 system significantly increased the power of provincial governors to deal with domestic troublemakers. Instead of requiring a dispatch by the emergency post and the receipt of an imperial edict for raising troops, the Court now asked for a normal report and request of an arrest order (*tsuibu kampu*) from the Council. The government lifted all restrictions on the number of troops a governor might conscript. Under the Taihō Codes the provincial governor had had the right of command over the provincial militia, but had rarely exercised it because of the power of the district magistrate. With the decline of the magistrates, the end to limitations on the governor gave rise to a modified military system focused on the province. The concentration of tax and land powers already in the governors' hands reinforced the trend. The opportunity soon would arise for members of the provincial staff to specialize in military and police affairs. The provincial headquarters were becoming the Court's islands of fiscal and military safety in a sea of violence.

How well did the new local system work? Rather well, if we can judge by its longevity. For nearly 35 years after the implementation of the 901 institutions loosening restrictions on the provincial headquarters, relative peace reigned over the Kanto, a real accomplishment in light of the region's martial traditions and continuing economic hardships. Then two new figures came onto the scene and changed Japanese history forever.

THE REVOLT OF TAIRA NO MASAKADO

The major reference for the rebellion of Taira no Masakado, which lasted from 935 to 940 and ultimately shook the Japanese Court to its foundations, is *The Tale of Masakado (Shōmon ki).*[42] As the ancestor of later Japanese war romances, *The Tale of Masakado* includes imaginative reconstructions of battles and idealizations of characters, and, while it was once thought that the author wrote this piece of literature only a few years after the end of the revolt in 940, it is now widely suspected that in fact *The Tale of Masakado* was not composed until sometime after the beginning of the eleventh century.[43]

There are, however, several good reasons to make critical use of this source for analyzing the insurrection and Masakado's military organization. First, there can be little doubt that the author worked from many historical materials of excellent quality, including a letter sent from Masakado to the Court in 939. Second, according to one Japanese specialist in Masakado and his era, even though *The Tale of Masakado* may have been written around 1000, the social and economic conditions it describes probably come close to those of the Masakado's era.[44] In my analysis of the revolt, I have followed the work of Fukuda Toyohiko, a leading historian, who bases his account of the rebellion on *The Tale of Masakado* but distinguishes between sections supported by reliable records and those that are plainly later accretions.

Masakado's revolt began as a family squabble.[45] According to *The Tale of Masakado*, the soon-to-be rebel was first incited to violence because of his Uncle Yoshikane's opposition to the marriage of his daughter to Masakado. In tenth-century Japan, convention often dictated that a husband go to live with his wife's family; such a practice was especially prevalent among erstwhile aristocrats like the Taira family. But a later passage in *The Tale of Masakado* indicates that Masakado refused to go to Yoshikane's residence; instead, Yoshikane's daughter went to live with Masakado against her father's wishes. As the conflict wore on, other issues divided Masakado from his enemies, but the original reason for both sides' taking up arms seems to have been Yoshikane's daughter.

Two men fighting over a woman is hardly new in history, but in this case the *casus belli* is particularly noteworthy because it denotes a subtle shift in the nature of conflict in Japanese history. Until Masakado's insurrection, Japan's wars had seen a relatively strong central government direct large numbers of troops that tried to seize territory or people from an enemy which was frequently an out-group, as in Japan's earlier expeditions to Korea or the wars in the Tōhoku. In the Introduction, I noted that anthropologists call this type of violence "predatory," because of its similarity to a pack of predators coldly killing their prey.

But social scientists recognize a second kind of warfare termed "intraspecific," because it resembles fighting between two males of the same species. In these conflicts, combat is ritualized and individualized and often carried out with elaborate weapons. The goal of such fighting is as important as the method: Males attempt to assert dominance or achieve the survival and continuation of their line by securing females, usually within an in-group.

Masakado's rebellion of 935–940 marks the beginning of a transition in Japanese history from "predatory" to "intraspecific" warfare. Rather than seeking territorial aggrandizement, Masakado was fighting for a woman, his own survival, and the continuation of his line, while his uncle, Yoshikane, was battling to avenge an insult, thus showing his dominant position over Masakado and the rest of his family. The war between Masakado and Yoshikane was fought to determine hierarchy and dominance among males within an in-group, the Taira family, much as a duel between two bucks decides the leadership of a herd.

To be sure, Masakado's rebellion still contains elements of "predatory" violence: Combat does not seem to have yet become individualized or stylized, especially when compared to warfare in the twelfth and thirteenth centuries. But the original cause of the fighting, a woman, and the ultimate goal of the anti-Masakado forces, to kill Masakado, both suggest that the real issue for the combatants was dominance within an in-group. From the early tenth century on, such "intraspecific" violence became more frequent in Japan, and combat tended to become increasingly ritualized and individualized, until one reaches the elaborate one-on-one battles of the samurai age. Because of its intraspecific causes and goals, Masakado's rebellion deserves consideration as Japan's first samurai conflict.

Combat in the revolt began in the 2nd month of 935, when Masakado marched from his base in Shimōsa to Hitachi province against an array of forces led by Minamoto Mamoru (a former provincial official and Yoshikane's father-in-law) and Yoshikane's brother, Kunika (another ally of Mamoru) (see Map 7). Masakado may have borne ill will towards Mamoru because of his relationship to Yoshikane, but it is also likely that Masakado joined these hostilities at the behest of Taira Masaki, a local strongman who was quarreling with Mamoru.[46] *The Tale* states that Masakado

Map 7A. MASAKADO'S REVOLT, 935–940

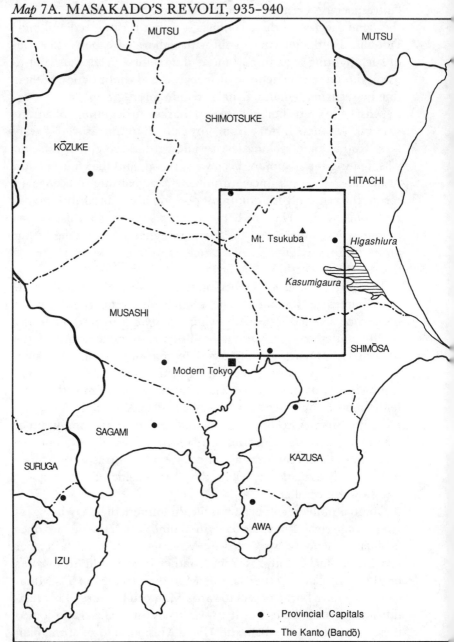

MUTSU

MUTSU

SHIMOTSUKE

KŌZUKE

HITACHI

Mt. Tsukuba

Higashiura

Kasumigaura

MUSASHI

SHIMŌSA

Modern Tokyo

SAGAMI

KAZUSA

SURUGA

AWA

IZU

● Provincial Capitals

—— The Kanto (Bandō)

Source: Fukuda Toyohiko, *Taira no Masakado no ran,* p. vi.

Map 7B. MASAKADO'S REVOLT, 935–940 (blow up)

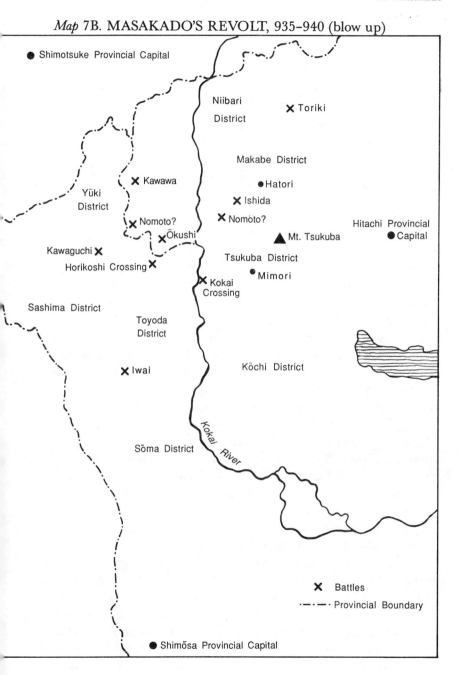

● Shimotsuke Provincial Capital

Niibari District

✕ Toriki

Makabe District

✕ Kawawa

Yūki District

● Hatori

✕ Ishida

✕ Nomoto?

✕ Nomòto?

Hitachi Provincial
● Capital

✕ Okushi

Kawaguchi ✕

Horikoshi Crossing ✕

▲ Mt. Tsukuba

Tsukuba District

● Mimori

✕ Kokai
Crossing

Sashima District

Toyoda District

✕ Iwai

Kōchi District

Kokai River

Sōma District

✕ Battles

·—·—· Provincial Boundary

● Shimōsa Provincial Capital

135

engaged in battle with flags fluttering and bells ringing, a sure sign that he intended to use foot soldiers in coordinated tactics as envisioned by the authors of the Taihō Codes. He won an archery contest at Nomoto, killing his uncle, Kunika, and Mamoru's children. As the victor, Masakado

> set fire to everything, beginning with the residences at Nomoto, Ishida, Ōkushi, and Tōriki, down to the small houses of dependents (*yoriki*). . . . Five hundred residences of allies (*banrui*) in the three districts of Tsukuba, Makabe, and Niibari were burned down to the last one.[47]

Mamoru was so angry after his defeat at Nomoto that he called upon his son-in-law, another of Masakado's uncles named Yoshimasa, to engage Masakado. Masakado won again, in a battle in which most of Yoshimasa's forces fled. After his defeat, Yoshimasa requested aid from his elder brother, the Vice-Governor of Shimōsa, Yoshikane. Yoshikane was not just the man who had opposed Masakado's marriage; he was the eldest living son of Prince Takamochi, the Taira progenitor and head of the family. As such, he had many military resources at his disposal. He raised forces from Shimōsa and Kazusa provinces in such numbers that officials at the two provincial headquarters attempted to prevent their dispatch, but later withdrew official protests because "the incident was a family matter" beyond the sphere of state affairs. At his camp at Mimori in Hitachi, Yoshikane met with Taira no Sadamori, one of the sons of the murdered Kunika. Yoshikane argued that "a soldier (*tsuwamono*) considers his reputation foremost" and convinced Taira no Sadamori to join his forces.[48] Masakado was infuriated because Sadamori had earlier promised from his military post in the capital that he would not take up arms.

Masakado assembled about 100 mounted warriors and met Yoshikane's forces near the Hitachi-Shimotsuke border. Despite being exhausted and outnumbered, he mustered his foot soldiers against Yoshikane's line of implanted shields and captured 80 men. Yoshikane fled to the Shimotsuke provincial headquarters with Masakado in pursuit, and Masakado surrounded his uncle and his army. Although he could have killed Yoshikane, Masakado reasoned that to do so would bring censure from his family and the

Court; he released Yoshikane through a gap in his western line. According to *The Tale of Masakado,* many soldiers fled with their leader.

Not long after his victory in the 10th month of 936, the Court called Masakado to the capital to give testimony about a complaint lodged by Minamoto Mamoru over the battle at Nomoto in 935. According to a letter later written by Masakado, Regent (*kampaku*) Fujiwara no Ason Tadahira, Masakado's lord and the highest aristocrat in Japan, intervened in the case and lightened Masakado's punishment. Early in 937, the government granted Masakado a full pardon when a nationwide amnesty was declared.

Back in the Kanto, Masakado quickly discovered that the pardon had little effect. Still smarting from his defeat, Yoshikane once again raised troops and engaged Masakado at Kokai Crossing. Yoshikane placed a statue of Prince Takamochi, the progenitor of the Taira line, in front of his troops. Perhaps because of this psychological ploy, Masakado and his forces "withdrew, carrying their shields."[49] To weaken Masakado's ability to make war, Yoshikane burned a critical stable and houses at Masakado's base in the nearby Toyoda district of Shimōsa province.

Following his defeat at Kokai Crossing, Masakado doubled his troop strength and equipped them with 370 spears and shields, again indicating the presence of foot soldiers. As he prepared to attack Yoshikane at the Horikoshi Crossing in Toyoda district, Masakado fell ill with beriberi:

> Just before the battle, his allies (*banrui*) scattered like divining sticks. The enemy burned all the remaining homes. Both people and horses used for planting were damaged.[50]

While Masakado hid in the mountains, for safety's sake he put his wife (Yoshikane's daughter) on a boat, which Yoshikane captured on his way back to Shimōsa. In the 9th month of 937, her younger brothers allowed her to escape back to Masakado to live with him against her father's wishes.

When Masakado's beriberi relented, he came out of the mountains and took aim at Yoshikane again. He raised 1,800 troops and proceeded to burn "the houses of (Yoshikane's) allies (*banrui*) and dependents (*yoriki*) down to the last one."[51] Yoshikane fled to the mountains; Masakado pursued and set up his shields to do battle. Despite Masakado's efforts, the contest quickly settled down into a war of attrition during the winter. The marauding troops destroyed that season's harvest, and both sides finally broke off the engagement. In the 11th month of 937, Masakado applied to the Court for orders to arrest Yoshikane, Mamoru, Sadamori, and their allies, but the governors of the Kanto paid no attention.

Late in 937, Yoshikane hit upon a plan to destroy Masakado. He lured one of Masakado's messengers, a man named Hasetsukabe Koharumaru, to his camp. Yoshikane argued that

> if you [Koharumaru] really plot against Masakado and injure him, you will be relieved of the harsh duties of a packman and will be made a horse-riding vassal. Even more, I will pile up grain to increase your bravery and divide up clothes for a prize.[52]

Koharumaru agreed and led one of Yoshikane's field hands to Masakado's camp at Iwai; Koharumaru showed him where Masakado kept his weapons, where he slept, where he tethered his horses, and where the entrances to the camp were. Before Yoshikane could execute his stratagem, however, Masakado discovered the trick, rallied his forces, and defeated Yoshikane. Once again, Yoshikane's troops "threw away their shields and fled like clouds."[53]

Meanwhile, Taira no Sadamori decided to return to the capital (Heian) to plead his case against Masakado early in 938. Masakado attempted to prevent this by sending about 100 horsemen more than 200 km. to intercept his enemy, but Masakado failed to win a decisive victory and Sadamori escaped to Heian. In the meantime, the Court sent a messenger to summon Masakado to the capital, also probably in the spring of 938. Masakado felt uneasy: How had he offended the Court? Masakado sent a message justifying his behavior in the conflict with Yoshikane, Sadamori, and his other relatives, but did not travel to the capital.

Meanwhile, Sadamori arrived at Heian in the summer of 938 and complained about Masakado's depredations to the Council of State. In the summer of 939, Sadamori returned to the Kanto with a summons for Masakado to appear in the capital.[54] Masakado became outraged because the Court chose to investigate him on the word of Sadamori, who was himself the object of a government arrest order. While Sadamori was still en route to the Kanto, however, Yoshikane died. Sadamori attempted to hide in the Tohoku with the aid of the Governor of Mutsu, who was probably dispatched to put down a revolt of Dewa natives, but Masakado blocked Sadamori's path. Sadamori lived a day-to-day existence in the mountains, fleeing from Masakado until the end of 939.

While Masakado and Sadamori were doing battle in early 938, an affair was taking place in Musashi province that would eventually be important to all. The temporary Governor and Vice-Governor of the province, Prince Okiyo and Minamoto no Tsunemoto, respectively, were involved in a dispute with Adachi District Magistrate Musashi Takeshiba. According to *The Tale of Masakado,* the Governors were trying to collect taxes to which Takeshiba said they had no right. When Takeshiba refused their request, "the Governors said in a biased fashion that the Magistrate was without scruple, raised soldiers as they pleased, and forced their way into his jurisdiction."[55] Takeshiba fled; the citizens of his district were attacked and their homes sacked. The conflict between District Magistrate Takeshiba and the Provincial Governors was a repetition of a scene that had played throughout most of Japan for a century.

Early in 939, Masakado heard about the dispute and decided to arbitrate, perhaps to curry favor with the Court. Takeshiba and Prince Okiyo freely entered into negotiations with Masakado, and they seemed to resolve the problem. But Takeshiba, who commanded some troops, had his line surround Tsunemoto's camp without provocation, and the shocked Tsunemoto fled. While Masakado returned to Shimōsa thinking he had provided valuable services in the dispute, Tsunemoto went to the capital and reported that Masakado, Prince Okiyo, and Takeshiba had plotted against him. He further claimed to the Council of State that Masakado was intent upon state treason.

The Court responded to the allegations with a mixture of prayers and policies. As in all natural and man-made disasters, it initiated prayers at shrines and temples. The government also began to take pragmatic measures against Masakado and the increasing violence in the Kanto. First, it appointed as new governor for Musashi a man who had previously held other posts in the Kanto.

In addition, the Court ordered three other officials with military resources and reputations — the Vice-Governor and Overseer (ōryō shi) of Sagami, the temporary Vice-Governor of Musashi and head of an official horse pasture at Ono, and the temporary Vice-Governor of Kōzuke and the head of Chichibu pasture — to arrest robbers in their respective jurisdictions. The Court was closing in on Masakado.

In the 3rd month of 939, Regent Fujiwara no Ason Tadahira, Masakado's lord, sent a personal letter to Masakado asking him about the charges. Masakado sent replies through the 5 provincial headquarters of Hitachi, Shimōsa, Shimotsuke, Musashi, and Kōzuke to persuade Tadahira that the talk of treason was unfounded. The Court threw Tsunemoto in jail, but was now even more on its guard against Masakado. [56] To add to Masakado's troubles, the government also dispatched inquisitors (suimon shi) in the 6th month of 939 to investigate his reported treasonous behavior. The Court gave the inquisitors the power to raise troops, which indicated the gravity of the situation.

As Masakado waited for the arrival of the inquisitors from the Court, an incident broke out that would ultimately spell his doom. In Hitachi province there lived one Fujiwara no Haruaki, who fit the description of "the rich" to a tee. He never granted famine relief to his cultivators, even under the direst circumstances. He robbed the poor and disdained provincial messengers seeking taxes. The Governor of Hitachi, Fujiwara no Ason Korechika, several times sent requests (ichō) to Haruaki, but he resisted; eventually the central government issued an arrest order for him, but he fled with his wife and a few followers to Toyoda district in Shimōsa, near Masakado's base. Along the way to Shimōsa, Haruaki burned several district storehouses. The Hitachi Governor asked Masakado to capture Haruaki and hand him over, but Masakado refused, partly because he always preferred the underdog. Eventually, in the 11th month of 939, Masakado compounded his refusal by raising 1,000 troops to help Haruaki defend himself in Hitachi. Masakado asked the province to drop its arrest order and allow Haruaki to live in Hitachi, but Korechika refused. Masakado defeated a force three times greater than his own and surrounded the provincial headquarters. According to a letter included in *The*

Tale of Masakado, the leader of the provincial forces was the Governor's son, Tamenori, who had allied himself with Masakado's old enemy, Sadamori. It seems likely that Masakado's real reason for going to Hitachi was not to aid Haruaki, but to prevent Sadamori from linking up with Tamenori.

Once Masakado had taken over the Hitachi headquarters, he proceeded to rob, pillage, and rape. He stole the official provincial seals and keys to the warehouses and took the defeated Provincial Governor Korechika back to his (Masakado's) headquarters in Shimōsa province. But Sadamori and Tamenori, the Governor's son, escaped. As Masakado's army headed back for Shimōsa, Prince Okiyo, who had been partly to blame for Masakado's involvement in the incident between District Magistrate Takeshiba and Provincial Official Tsunemoto in Musashi province in 938, suggested that,

> even though we have struck down only one province, censure from the state will not be light. Let us take over the Bandō in the same fashion and watch the situation for awhile.[57]

Apparently, Prince Okiyo felt that the rebels had a better chance of winning a full-scale revolt that encompassed the entire Kanto region, now that they had already committed a serious offense against the Court in Hitachi. Masakado agreed, citing his own imperial bloodline as reason enough for his thirst for power. In the 12th month of 939, he attacked Shimotsuke, took the seals and keys, and chased the Governors back to Heian. Four days after he took the Shimotsuke headquarters, on the 15th of the 12th month, Masakado captured the capital of Kōzuke and dealt with the Governors in the same way.

According to *The Tale of Masakado,* three important events occurred while Masakado encamped at Kōzuke. First, he met a shaman who declared Masakado the "new emperor" (*shinnō*). Despite the criticism of his brother and an "imperial" servant, Masakado argued that he had "made a soldier's name for himself" in the Kanto and should be emperor.[58] He furthermore said that, "if all the troops of the Court attack, then we can close off Ashigara and Usuhi Passes" and defend the Kanto.[59] Then, as befit a new emperor, Masakado established an imperial capital in Shimōsa and a port in Sagami. He also named his own Council of State and set patterns for official seals and records. Masakado made a tour of Sagami and Musashi provinces, and confiscated the provincial keys and seals. By controlling all the provincial headquarters of the Kanto, Masakado had become the first head of the Kanto Independence Movement; Yoritomo would bring the movement to fruition by hijacking the same military centers (the provincial headquarters) in the late twelfth century.

Second, Masakado appointed new officials for the provinces of the Kanto. Of interest among the new appointees are Prince Okiyo as the Vice-Governor of Kazusa, and Masakado's brother, the rebel Masatake, as the Governor of Izu. Third, Masakado wrote a letter to his lord at Heian, Fujiwara no Tadahira, justifying his position. In the note, which drips with bravado, Masakado blamed Sadamori and Tamenori for his transgressions and pointed out that "my destiny lies in the martial arts (*bugei*). Come to think of it, who among my comrades can rival Masakado!"[60]

Early in 940, Masakado journeyed once again to Hitachi to wipe out his remaining enemies. Although he failed to find Sadamori or Tamenori, he did capture Sadamori's wife. In an exchange of poems with the woman, Masakado attempted to learn Sadamori's whereabouts, but was elegantly rebuffed. The troops of the "new emperor" soon dispersed for spring planting.

REBELLIONS EAST AND WEST

The news of Masakado's attacks on first Hitachi and then Shimotsuke and Kōzuke reached the court in the 12th month of 939. As officials prepared to hear the case against Masakado from the provincial governors who had fled the Kanto, more disturbing news entered the capital from the provinces on the Inland Sea. Fujiwara Sumitomo, the administrator (*jō*) of Iyo province on the island of Shikoku and leader of his own pirate band, had "heard rumors of Masakado's treason from afar" and plotted his own rebellion.[61] Sumitomo established a communications network that included the capital, where men "set fires for consecutive nights" and "spent evenings on roofs."[62] Just as Sumitomo was about to attack, the Vice-Governor of Bizen province, Fujiwara no Kodaka, caught wind of this [Sumitomo's plans] and, in the last 10 days of the 12th month of Tengyō 2 (939), made an overland trip with his wife and family to warn [the Court] of these facts. Sumitomo heard of this [action] and wanted to do harm to Kodaka. Using his vassals Fumimoto and others, he caught up with them [Kodaka's party] at Suki post station in Uhara district in Settsu province; on the 26th of the 12th month between 3 and 5 A.M., Sumitomo and his retainers unleashed arrows like rain. In the end they captured Kodaka and cut off his ears and sliced his nose. They stole his wife and carried her off; the children were killed by the pirates.[63]

Sumitomo and his pirates also took the Vice-Governor of Harima prisoner. Thus, before knowledge of Masakado's actions could fully sink in, the Heian Court faced another rebellion that could not be ignored or settled with diplomacy. Sumitomo's revolt also followed hard on the heels of a disturbance in northeastern Honshu which had lasted from the late spring to the fall of 939.[64]

The year 939 was not the first time the Court had encountered trouble from pirates. The Inland Sea formed the center of a trade network that stretched from Lake Biwa to Dazaifu in northern Kyushu, and pirates had plagued the region since at least the middle of the ninth century.[65] Until 900, pirates had often allied themselves with traders and officials of Silla. Unlike the bandits of the Kanto, pirates tended to operate on a small scale as fishermen or traders, often in league with aristocratic retainers, estate officials, or "rich vagrants." They covered great distances quickly in boats (which often also served as their homes) and could hide easily for long periods of time.

Beginning in the 930s, pirate activity increased. In 931, the Court issued orders to guard the roads and rivers of Yamashiro; in 932, it published an arrest order, but did not enforce it even at the end of 933.[66] In 934, the Court raised troops from among aristocratic retainers and Musashi provincials, but apparently to no avail, for late in the year pirates robbed and burned an official granary at Iyo.[67] In 936, Sumitomo, "chief of the pirates," formed a band in his home province of Iyo.[68] Reports stated that he commanded as many as 1,000 ships to rob and pillage, until the Court appointed a Governor of Iyo who rewarded the pirates for turning themselves in:

> The bandits heard of his [the Governor's] magnanimous behavior, and over 2,500 admitted their sins and submitted to punishment. Pirate chiefs . . . altogether 30 in number, folded their arms, offered lists of names, and submitted. So we allotted them land, clothes, and food, granted seeds, and urged them to [take up] agriculture.[69]

It is interesting to note that the year 936 was a bad year for disease and famine, and that pirate activities seem to correlate with these misfortunes. According to a later record, the government actually put Sumitomo, probably the son of a local strongman with ties to the Fujiwara, in charge of arresting pirates in 936.[70]

A year of drought and disease followed in 938, and pirates began to infest the waters of the Inland Sea once again in 939. Sumitomo and his men were also on the prowl, and on the 17th of the 12th month of 939, the Regent Fujiwara no Tadahira received word that Sumitomo was preparing to head for the high seas.[71] On the 21st, the Court officially called Sumitomo to the capital, but his response was the attack on the Settsu official Kodaka and his family just outside modern Osaka.

Faced with revolts both to the east and west, the capital was thrown into an uproar:

> The original Emperor [Suzaku] descended from his throne and raised his palms to his forehead in supplication. All officialdom performed ablutions and offered a thousand prayers. . . . Priests tied figures of the bandit [Masakado] beneath thorny trees to bring him bad luck.[72]

The Court also took the practical measures of closing the Three Passes that lay between the Kanto and the capital at Heian and securing other strategic positions in the provinces. The government placed the capital on military alert, conducting New Year's Day ceremonies under guard and constructing watch towers in the city. The situation was so serious that the Regent Tadahira himself named the soldiers who policed the capital.[73] Finally, Court aristocrats appointed two search-and-destroy missions (*tsuitō shi*) for eastern Honshu, led by Fujiwara no Tadanobu and Ono no Koremoto, and one for the Inland Sea, led by Ono no Yoshifuru. The new policies had a sense of urgency about them, especially when compared to the actions taken after the reports of Masakado's initial transgressions.

In addition to general steps, the Court also initiated specific countermeasures against each rebel. On the 9th day of the 1st month, it released Minamoto no Tsunemoto from jail and rewarded him with the Junior 5th Court Rank, Lower Grade. The Court also fired the inquisitors whose job it had been to question Masakado. On the 11th, officials issued an order to the provincial offices of eastern Honshu to destroy Masakado. The command sought to gather the best soldiers of the land by specifying that provincial governors offer aristocratic rank and land to the brave warrior who could cut Masakado's throat. Undoubtedly the Court had in mind the rich and local men of influence who had until now spent their time resisting taxation and causing civil strife. The state established a policy of setting a thief to catch a thief, just as it had used barbarians to pacify barbarians in the eighth century.

In the 1st month, the Court named new governors for the 8 provinces of the Kanto. The appointments exemplify the principle of using bandits to catch Masakado. Among them were Taira no Kimimasa and his brother Kimitsura, sons of Masakado's longtime enemy Yoshikane and themselves objects of arrest orders. Sadamori also received a governor's post. The state made Fujiwara no Hidesato an overseer (*ōryō shi*) in Shimotsuke, even though he had been banished for fighting with a provincial governor. Other officials appointed to Kanto gubernatorial posts had similar credentials.

On the 19th of the 1st month, Fujiwara no Tadafumi assumed his title as the Great General to Campaign in the East, just as the Codes mandated. On the 8th day of the 2nd month, the expedition left the capital, with Minamoto no Tsunemoto among Tadafumi's adjutants. The size of Tadafumi's force is unknown, but the government gathered soldiers from the capital and the provinces.

Meanwhile, the situation in the Inland Sea became critical. On the 16th of the 1st month, Ono no Yoshifuru, commander of the search-and-destroy mission sent to western Honshu, left the capital, but only 4 days later pirates made a successful attack on Bitchū.[74] At this point, the Court made an important decision.

Rather than face two enemies at once, Heian lawgivers concluded that they would try to buy off Sumitomo by offering him the 5th Court Rank, a sign of entrance into the nobility. The messenger carrying the certificate of Court rank left the capital on the 3rd day of the 2nd month. Pirate raids continued for some time after that: On the 5th day of the 2nd month, Sumitomo attacked Awaji near present-day Osaka, and on the 22nd there was a report that Sumitomo intended to sail to the capital. The next day the Court established watchguards (*keigo shi*) for Yamazaki and Kawajiri, two ports near the capital. The Court dispatched troops for Yamazaki on the 25th, but, on the following day, Yamazaki burned, a deed probably performed by arsonists friendly to Sumitomo.[75] Fires consumed sections of the capital late in the month, and officials posted guards throughout the capital to prevent more arson. On the 2nd day of the 3rd month, Sumitomo notified the Court of his pleasure at being promoted to the 5th Rank, and from this point on the direct threat to Heian subsided. The Court was now free to deal with Masakado militarily.

Masakado had spent most of the 1st month in Hitachi province with 5,000 soldiers, searching for his enemies Sadamori and Tamenori. As the 2nd month approached, however, his forces dwindled to 1,000; on the 1st he marched to Shimotsuke, where he heard that both Sadamori and the new official, Fujiwara no Hidesato, were lying in wait for him. Before Masakado and the forward lines detected the enemy, the rear guard led by an overly enthusiastic leader engaged Hidesato's numerically superior forces. Using this "old stratagem" to divide and conquer, Hidesato defeated the rear guard; he split his forces into three units and cut down his enemy in great numbers.[76]

Sadamori and Hidesato pursued Masakado ever closer to his base, near a small settlement named Kawaguchi. Despite brave fighting by Masakado and his forces, he lost once again and retreated further into his own bailiwick. Hidesato and Sadamori burned Kawaguchi and the other villages they conquered to cut Masakado off from his base. Fearing that Masakado would regroup and recruit more soldiers before they could finish him off, Sadamori drove his troops forward with promises of great rewards.

On the 13th of the 2nd month, Sadamori and his troops arrived in Shimōsa. Masakado took to hiding, and Sadamori countered by burning everything in sight, including Masakado's camp at Iwai. According to *The Tale of Masakado*, Masakado began to lose the support of his allies, who "simply cried out at Masakado's maladministration."[77]

On the morning of the 14th, Masakado donned his armor for the last time, to make a stand at a northern mountain at about 3 in the afternoon. He had only 400 men with him. At first he was fortunate to have the wind at his back, an aid in archery warfare. The wind was so fierce that "the new emperor's southern shields fell over forwards; Sadamori's northern shields collapsed on the faces of his troops."[78] The two sides abandoned fixed positions, taking to individual combat, and Masakado's horsemen ripped into Sadamori's central line. Masakado pursued and forced nearly 3,000 of his enemies' troops to flee; Sadamori had only 300 men left, most of them milling around in confusion.

But then the wind changed, and Hidesato and Sadamori took the advantage. According to *The Tale of Masakado*, a divine arrow killed Masakado; it is more likely that an arrow from Sadamori's quiver destroyed him. Hidesato quickly beheaded the rebel as proof of their victory.[79] Sadamori and company killed almost 200 of Masakado's allies and collected an assortment of swords, shields, quivers, and bows. Unlike earlier commanders, Masakado did not try to hide, flee, or commit suicide; never before had a Japanese general gone down fighting in his last battle.

The expedition that had left Heian under Fujiwara no Tadafumi arrived too late to deal with Masakado but finished off the remnants of his forces. When Tadafumi entered Sagami province, he dispatched Masakado's brother and other rebels; on the 8th day of the 4th month, the expedition entered Shimōsa, and Fujiwara no Tadanobu and Taira no Kimitsura cleaned up there. Kimitsura, whose positions included that of overseer (*ōryō shi*) in Shimōsa, is given credit for capturing Prince Okiyo, Masakado's confederate, who first suggested embroiling the entire Kanto in rebellion. The expedition executed Fujiwara Haruaki and others in Hitachi.

On the 25th of the 2nd month, the first report of Masakado's defeat reached the Court. As promised in the arrest order, the government granted the victors rewards. Sadamori received the

Junior 5th Court Rank, Upper Grade, and a post in the capital. Hidesato accepted an even higher rank, Junior 4th, Lower Grade, and later the governorship of Shimotsuke. Minamoto no Tsunemoto became an official at Dazaifu with the Junior 5th Rank, Lower Grade. The Court appointed Taira no Kimimasa to be the new Governor of Musashi at Junior 5th, Upper Grade. Japan's leaders proudly displayed Masakado's head in the capital on the 25th of the 4th month; on the 15th of the 5th month, Tadafumi arrived home and the Court expedition concluded.

Fortunately for the Court, Sumitomo and his henchmen had remained quiet from the 3rd through the 5th months of 940 when the expedition was subduing rebels in the Kanto. As soon as the threat from Masakado subsided, however, Heian aristocrats turned their full energies to suppressing Sumitomo's band. On the 18th of the 6th month, the Regent Tadahira authorized an arrest order for Sumitomo's followers. The Court omitted Sumitomo from the order because he was a member of the aristocracy at the 5th Court Rank. Before the government could act, Sumitomo struck against the provincial troops of Sanuki with 400 ships on the 20th of the 8th month. Vice-Governor Fujiwara no Kunikaze suffered defeat and fled with a watchguard (*keigo shi*) to a secret hiding place in Awa province in western Honshu. Government troops lost several hundred men to Sumitomo's archers. Sumitomo burned the provincial headquarters and private houses and stole government items.

The Court reacted to the most recent defeat two days later on the 22nd of the 8th month when Ōmi provincial soldiers marched to Awa. The state also named Ono no Yoshifuru chief officer and Minamoto no Tsunemoto an assistant for a new search-and-destroy mission dispatched to the Inland Sea. On the 2nd of the 9th month, a report stated that one pirate chief had been captured in Sanuki.

But these actions did not stop Sumitomo, especially since the harvest in 940 had once again been poor. On the 22nd of the 10th month, he won a victory at Dazaifu; the next month, pirates burned the government mint in Suō. In the 12th month, an engagement took place in Tosa.

Even as Sumitomo won these victories, however, the Court

counterattacked. In the first month of 941, Iyo provincial officials presented the head of one pirate leader who was also a former official of Yamashiro. Fujiwara no Kunikaze, who had fled Sanuki in an earlier pirate attack, rallied 200 ships around him and joined battle with the pirates at their base in Iyo province. Although Sumitomo's forces outnumbered Kunikaze's almost 8 to 1, one of Sumitomo's chiefs went over to Kunikaze and betrayed all of Sumitomo's secret hiding places and waterways. Kunikaze won a smashing victory. Although he was able to cut off most escape routes, Kunikaze eventually hit rough seas, and some of his quarry evaded him.

For 3 months, until the 5th month of 941, pirate activity abated. In the 5th month, Sumitomo made his greatest gamble by again attacking Dazaifu. He succeeded in capturing the official headquarters, burning it, and pillaging the area. The defeat caused the Court to establish another expedition to campaign in western Honshu, once again headed by Fujiwara no Tadafumi and composed of forces from Ōmi, Mino, and Ise and the personal retainers of Taira no Sadamori. On the 20th of the 5th month, Yoshifuru gathered his bravest troops and assaulted Sumitomo on land while his adjutants oversaw sea forces. In Hakata Bay, state forces engaged Sumitomo and fought the decisive battle. The Court army and navy defeated the pirates under Sumitomo, who lost 800 ships and several hundred soldiers. An uncounted number of Sumitomo's family and friends threw themselves overboard as the defeat became inevitable.

In the 6th month, the government captured Sumitomo in his native province of Iyo, and a watchguard and veteran of the revolt in the Kanto put the pirate leader to the sword. The victors proudly showed off Sumitomo's head in the capital three weeks later, and Ono no Yoshifuru, leader of the government forces, returned to Heian early in the 8th month. Because of the wide area over which the pirate activity ranged, and because Sumitomo's organization from the beginning had been an alliance of local strongmen and wealthy migrants, mop-up operations took over 4 months, until the last outlaw fell to a traitor's knife late in the 10th month of 941. The state amply rewarded each of the government fighters for putting an end to Sumitomo and his band. At long last the revolts of Masakado and Sumitomo had ended.

MASAKADO, SUMITOMO, AND THE EVOLUTION OF
THE MIDDLE HEIAN MILITARY SYSTEM

The insurrections of the 930s and 940s reveal much about Japanese society and the military. In particular, 5 areas are worthy of note: the social origins of soldiers, military technology and organization, the fighters' economic base, regional social and political differences, and military institutions.

SOCIAL ORIGINS OF WARRIORS. Detailed accounts of battle disclose much about tenth-century military men, especially in the Kanto. The most widely accepted view among Japanese scholars is that the armies of Masakado and his rivals were composed of 3 parts: relatives (*innen*) and rich migrants, dependents (*jūrui*), and allies (*banrui*).[80] Relatives tended to band together into units composed of economic and social equals, as when Yoshikane, Sadamori, Yoshimasa, and Minamoto no Mamoru joined to fight Masakado in the early battles. In this case, the leaders were related through marriage, which tended to be a strong link, whereas blood ties, especially distant ones amongst large families like the Taira or Minamoto, were weaker. An exception to this rule was apparent when Yoshikane placed a statue of Prince Takamochi, erstwhile chief of all the Kanto Taira, in the front of his lines in order to dissuade Masakado from attacking.[81] Included in the same category as relatives were rich migrants such as the troublemaker Fujiwara no Haruaki. These soldiers may have farmed a bit of land, but basically relied on robbing and pillaging to keep themselves supplied. It is probably safe to assume that relatives and rich migrants were mounted fighters, as indicated by Masakado's leading mounted assaults on his enemies' lines, and donning armor and riding a horse in his last battle.

The great leaders, such as Masakado and Sadamori, supplied and directly commanded the second category of fighters, the dependents. As noted in the description of Masakado's camp, the residences of soldiers (*tsuwamono*) like Yoshikane and Masakado were complex, with numerous homes, storage bins, corrals, sentry posts, weapons containers, forges, looms, and other functional areas. A wall surrounded the entire complex; entry or search was illegal. Such residences were so large that they were on a par with a provincial headquarters, and they carried out both private and state functions.[82]

Within the residence the dependents had a variety of servile duties, one of which was to fight for their lord. Japanese historians have generally argued that dependents served as highly skilled horsemen, few in number, who often turned the tide in battle.[83] When Yoshikane attacked Masakado's camp at Iwai, he commanded only 80 horsemen, described by the author as being so skilled that "one is as good as a thousand."[84] A Japanese scholar has asserted that those 80 mounted fighters must have been dependents.[85] Since nearly every battle recorded in *The Tale of Masakado* included archery, it seems logical to conclude that many dependents were mounted archers.

The story of Hasetsukabe no Koharumaru, traitor to Masakado on Yoshikane's behalf, also supports the view that most great Kanto lords had a coterie of dependents who fought as mounted archers. Hasetsukabe was originally a peasant who desired to improve his lot in life. Yoshikane offered him material rewards and a position as a horseman for his act of betrayal, suggesting that elite fighters were mounted soldiers who depended on their lords for economic support.

The third component of Kanto fighting forces was the allies.[86] Unlike dependents, an ally was relatively free and only partially reliant on the leaders' economic and social functions. Before he accepted Yoshikane's bribe and became a dependent, Koharumaru was probably one of Masakado's allies. In addition to performing guard duty for Masakado, he farmed and sold charcoal before his act of betrayal. Minor local strongmen from the families of district magistrates were undoubtedly also included among the allies.

Allies provided the bulk of all Kanto fighting forces; they were foot soldiers who carried spears, shields, and other weapons into battle. As soon as the tide of battle began to turn against them, the allies were quick to disperse. Generals such as Masakado and Sadamori adopted a scorched-earth policy to destroy their enemies' power to raise allied foot soldiers.

Some Japanese scholars have been eager to draw comparisons between the dependents (*jūrui*) and allies (*banrui*) and Western models. For one, the dependents were serfs and mercenaries relying on their lords for sustenance and returning absolute loyalty, while the allies were mostly powerful serfs (*nōdo shu*), who hauled their reluctant underlings out to fight for a distant lord.[87] Another has likened the dependent to the Roman *colonus*, a cultivator tied to the land.[88] While such comparisons may be intriguing, including the widely held views on the distinctions between dependents and allies, such a comparative exercise assumes parallel historical development in Japan and Western Europe towards the same end (feudalism); Japanese history is thus forced to correspond to Western standards. Actually, Japanese peasants of the tenth century moved too freely to have been called serfs.

ORGANIZATION AND TECHNOLOGY. A more fruitful and interesting debate concerns the fighting style of Masakado and his rivals. The opening battle of *The Tale of Masakado* mentions bells and banners, and combat usually involved lines of shields and foot soldiers.[89] According to one Japanese specialist on Masakado and the tenth-century military, it is apparent that the Taihō tradition of mass tactics using units of commoners as foot soldiers was still very much alive at this time, despite the critical role in battle of mounted archers.[90]

To be sure, tenth-century foot soldiers could not have been too disciplined, because they fled as soon as the tide of battle turned against them; it is doubtful that they ever drilled as units. In Masakado's last battle, coordinated attacks quickly disintegrated, and fighters took to individual dueling. Yet it is important to note that the battles fought by Masakado and other Kanto lords are reminiscent of eighth-century wars using the fighting technology, style, and organization of the Taihō system.

An important question then arises: How could Masakado have been the ancestor of the samurai, who fought from horseback in single combat, if he attempted to employ Chinese-style mass tactics? A senior twelfth-century scholar and advocate of the Western-analogue theory argues that Masakado's military organization and technology, which included soldiers moving according to signals like a Chinese army, disqualifies him as a warrior (*bushi*) because this fighting style bore little resemblance to the individual battles of samurai of later times.[91] The same historian bolsters his

conclusion by noting that the forces of both Masakado and his enemies were largely made up of peasants, and that tenth-century
armies did not perform on the basis of feudal ties of dependence.
Warriors of the twelfth and thirteenth centuries had developed feudal ties in which land was exchanged for military service, and no
longer used commoners in Chinese-style tactics, so the argument
goes.

But there is second, preferable way to fit Masakado's military
organization into the evolution of the samurai. Rather than setting up Western feudalism and Chinese-style warfare as polar
opposites and describing Masakado as not feudal enough (as advocates of the Western-analogue theory inevitably do), it makes
more sense to see the Taihō system as giving birth to the fighting
technology, style, and organization of the twelfth-century warrior.

Japanese soldiers probably learned of Chinese-style mass tactics
for the first time in the sixth and seventh centuries, and, even during the Sinophilic eighth century, may not have practiced such
combat very seriously. Masakado was heir to the Taihō ideal of
mass warfare using peasant foot soldiers, but he was also a direct
descendant of the mounted fighters who guarded the Kyushu coast-
line against foreign invaders, or battled the barbarians of the
Tohoku. The Taihō system had the potential to evolve into either
mass armies of commoners, as in China, or into elite units of specialized mounted fighters; while Japan eventually took the latter
alternative, in the mid-900s both elements were still present.

Thus, one should not dismiss the armies of the tenth-century
Kanto as being completely unrelated to warrior forces of the
twelfth and thirteenth centuries just because Masakado used peasant foot soldiers and elite mounted forces in mass tactics. As
another historian has pointed out, the distinctions between Masakado's forces and samurai armies of the twelfth century are slight;
peasants served as foot soldiers in late Heian armies, and Masakado also utilized ties of dependence among his elite fighters (especially the dependents), often in exchange for commodities rather
than land.[92] The difference between Masakado and a samurai of
the twelfth century was a matter of small degree, not kind. Therefore it is best to view Masakado as having had characteristics that
resembled both fighters in the Taihō armies and the medieval

samurai. This view of his fighting organization implies that the difference between forces of the eighth and thirteenth centuries was much less than might be expected.

The type of warfare in which Masakado was engaged also points to his status as a transitional figure. His motive for battling his primary adversary, his uncle Yoshikane, was a desire to bring Yoshikane's daughter to live with him, against her father's wishes. Thus Masakado was fighting for his own survival and the continuation of his line; he was attempting to prove his own dominance in the Taira family, and among Kanto warriors. Such intraspecific conflicts were standard in the age of the samurai in the twelfth and thirteenth centuries, and helped produce the highly ritualized, individualized combat for which the samurai is so well known.

Masakado's family origins also show him to have been a transitional figure. He was a member of the Taira, and his paternal forebear Prince Takamochi was a military aristocrat. The Taira became one of Japan's most famous warrior lines, and eventually dominated the Court in the late twelfth century. According to one Japanese historian, Masakado's mother also had martial ancestors. She may have been Agata Inukai Harueme, descended from Agata Inukai no Sukune Kiyondo, a local strongman of the Kanto who served as a soldier in the Kyushu defense forces in the mid-eighth century.[93] If this is so, then Masakado derived his military talents from both sides of his family. Many medieval warrior lines also sprang from ancient roots.[94]

ECONOMIC BASE. Historians generally agree that there was little real difference between the military forces of Masakado and his enemies. The same is not true of the economic base which supported their armies. One scholar has pointed out that Masakado's base was in low-lying, swampy lands, presumably prime rice fields, while Sadamori's economic foundations lay in a more mountainous area.[95] These different bases helped account for the seasonal cycle evident in Masakado's campaigns and also for Sadamori's ability to hide out after his defeats.

Japanese historians, many of whom adhere to the Western-analogue theory, have worked out a taxonomy wherein both Masakado and Sadamori have been grouped together as soldiers (*tsu-*

wamono) who were also great private landlords (*shieiden ryōshu*).[96] In this view, Masakado, Sadamori, and the other chiefs of the tenth and early eleventh centuries can not qualify as warriors (*bushi*) because their hold on their widespread domains was too weak, their cultivators too independent, and because the lords were directly involved in farming themselves. These economic factors dictated that the great private landlords' military organization would be simple, that their peasant fighters would readily flee battle, and that campaigns had to be short.

It is too early in this study to compare the warrior landlords of the tenth century with their counterparts of the twelfth century, who are known as "country lords" (*zaichi ryōshu*, see Chapter 6). But the distinctions between these two categories are small and arbitrary. In both cases, warrior landlords exercised personal control over men who farmed as well as fought; they also could command peasants outside their domains to go to battle for them. Moreover, it is doubtful that either landlord engaged in cultivation himself or held secure tenure over his lands, and, even in the twelfth century, a cultivator had the legal right to leave his lord's lands. Campaigns were brief and fighters disloyal in the thirteenth century as well as in the tenth. There is a direct line that runs from the district magistrate, the military lord of the eighth century, through Masakado and the other "great private proprietors" of the tenth century, to the "country lords" of the twelfth and thirteenth centuries. Differences among all three categories are minimal in economic and military matters.

In addition, focusing so exclusively on agriculture accepts a basic premise of the Western-analogue theory, that land is the only form of wealth that counts. Recent Japanese scholars have been increasingly critical of the emphasis on Masakado and his enemies as landholders. One has noted that Masakado's lands did not become productive rice fields until the seventeenth century. Masakado's base most likely consisted of pastures for horses.[97]

Iron production was also crucial for Masakado and his fighters.[98] Prior to 800, the primary centers for iron smelting were in western Honshu, but a technique for producing iron out of iron sand spread to the Kanto in the ninth century. At a site near Masakado's base, archeologists have uncovered the remains of 3

155

furnaces, 4 smelters' homes, charcoal repositories, and iron residue, all dating from the ninth century. The technique for smelting was primitive, because it used no bellows, and as much as 60 percent of production was so low in quality that it had to be rejected. Yet this technology helped close the gap between the Kanto and western Honshu; prices listed in *The Ordinances of Engi* indicate that, by the tenth century, iron was about the same price in the eastern Honshu as in traditional western centers of smelting.[99] Masakado and his fellow warriors lived at least as much by iron and horses as they did by rice farming.[100]

REGIONALISM. A fourth major question raised by the rebellions of Masakado and Sumitomo concerns regional social and political differences. Scholars have often looked upon the revolt of Masakado as an attempt to form an independent state in the Kanto.[101] This area had indeed been distinctive ever since the late sixth century when it had served as a military base for the Yamato kings. Unified by its transportation system and relatively cut off from the capital by mountains, the Kanto had achieved a separate identity by the tenth century. The role the Kanto played as a staging area for the wars against the barbarians of the Tohoku undoubtedly assisted this process.

Despite Masakado's zeal, however, the Independence Movement for the Kanto failed for 2 reasons.[102] (1) Masakado did not establish a political administration with its own identity separate from the Heian Court. After Masakado conquered the Kanto, he created offices for his fellow rebels, but they were all copies of ministries already functioning in Heian. Moreover, even though he named himself the "new emperor," Masakado neglected the first chore of all sovereigns—the appointment of a calendar-maker. These cosmological experts divined the name of the emperor's reign period, blessing a virtuous leader with peace and abundant crops by the name that they chose. Without the calendar-maker and a proper title for the period of his rule, Masakado lacked legitimacy, and his kingdom had no separate identity.[103]

(2) Masakado failed to achieve unified support, even though he faced a formidable enemy. His declaring himself the new emperor

challenged and antagonized the Heian Court; unity was imperative if he was to win against the more economically and culturally advanced areas of western Honshu, Shikoku, and Kyushu. But the rebel-warrior gave no tax reductions and simply appointed an alternate set of rapacious aristocrats to be provincial governors. It was no accident that Masakado was finally laid low by fighters from the Kanto such as Hidesato and Sadamori, who felt they could not support the new administration.

In contrast, the insurrection of Sumitomo lacked even revolutionary potential. In western Japan, military units were small, vertical ties between local strongmen and Court aristocrats were common, and people were highly mobile. Because the Court had many estates in western Honshu, however, the rebellion of Sumitomo represented a clear threat to the aristocracy, and the central government in Heian acted much more quickly to put down Sumitomo than it did Masakado.[104] Like the periodic epidemics and famines that broke out in western Japan, Sumitomo's revolt meant a reduction of the economic surplus; but the Court could do something about Sumitomo and his pirates. Perhaps Masakado's being distantly related to the imperial line inhibited the Court's determination to waylay him.

THE MILITARY SYSTEM OF THE 900S. The upheavals of the tenth century, as disastrous as they were, helped solidify the military system drawn up in outline in 901. Utilizing reports from the provincial governors, the Council of State handed down arrest orders (*tsuibu kampu*) enabling the governor to raise troops. The Council twice issued arrest orders appointing overseers (*ōryō shi*) to deal with the rebel Masakado, once in the 6th month of 939, and again in the 1st month of 940, when the Court selected Hidesato, Sadamori, and others among Masakado's enemies to fill official positions. It is notable that the government gave all the overseers posts in the provincial government as temporary vice-governors (*gon no suke*) or administrators (*jō*). Eventually, the state chose overseers for many provinces in eastern Japan and Kyushu; the revolt of Masakado marked the concrete realization of the system based on the provincial headquarters and ordained by the provisions of the 901 Reform.

The revolt of Masakado also changed the way overseers performed their jobs. According to one historian, overseers were orig inally escorts for troops such as the Border Guards of northern Kyushu.[105] Overseers had sedulously avoided combat both when fighting erupted in Dewa in 878 and in 894 when Silla attempted an invasion of Tsushima. Now a new type of overseer was evident, one who had provincial ties and specialized in combat, like Taira no Kimitsura.[106]

The renewed emphasis on the provincial headquarters as the heart of the military system of the tenth century is also apparent in the rebellion of Sumitomo. Sources repeatedly mention troops raised through the provincial headquarters (*shokoku no heishi*) in the suppression of his insurrection, including those from Bitchū, Sanuki, Bizen, Bingo, Tosa, and Iyo.[107] The Court also raised troops from Ōmi, Musashi, Mino, and Ise. It did not give the military leaders of these soldiers the title of overseers, but called them watchguards (*keigo shi*). The two offices differed in little except name; in both cases persons with local influence filled military posts to keep the peace.[108] According to one Japanese specialist, the watchguards originated in the mid-eighth century, more evidence of the early origins of the tenth-century military system.[109] With the defeat of Sumitomo, the system of watchguards ended, and the state established arrest officers (*tsuibu shi*) in many provinces in western Japan, paralleling the overseers of the eastern Honshu.

Exactly how provincial officials raised soldiers is unclear, but it is apparent that the Court relied on the offer of rewards to gather troops. The dependence upon reward honed the mercenary instincts of the tenth-century warrior, although the rewards were usually in the form of appointments to office or Court rank, not gifts of land. Political appointments meant revenues, since most local officials were really tax-farmers. Hidesato, Sadamori, Minamoto no Tsunemoto, and Ono no Yoshifuru are the best-known beneficiaries of the reward system. Like Hidesato, many obtained appointment to a provincial governorship, whence they built military bases and gained valuable political experience. A military system that emphasized mounted archery was expensive, but, rather than pay for it with land, the Court used appointment to office and revenue sharing.

The revolts of the 930s and 940s helped secure select status for at least three families. The Seiwa Genji (Minamoto), the Kammu

Heishi (Taira), and Hidesato's line of the Fujiwara all became warrior houses (*tsuwamono no ie*), after the model of the military families (*gunji shizoku*) of the pre-645 and later eras. The government expected these martial families to provide military service when the situation warranted and secured their loyalty with political favors. Their most famous members maintained the status of military aristocrats with followers. As in the case of Masakado, many of the tenth-century military aristocrats married into local families with martial credentials going back to the eighth century and earlier.

Officials termed the followers of the new military aristocrats, along with the troops tied to the civil aristocracy, "the soldiers of noble houses" (*shoka no heishi*); they formed the second pillar of the tenth-century military system, the first being the troops of the provincial office. The Court called upon Sadamori's soldiers in the course of Sumitomo's revolt, and aristocratic followers also helped to guard the Court when Sumitomo was thought to be nearby. Masakado himself pledged loyalty to an aristocratic lord, Fujiwara no Tadahira. The state's recognition of aristocratic troops as part of the military was one of the legacies of Masakado's and Sumitomo's rebellions and is reminiscent of the public guise used for private aristocratic armies during the eighth century.

CONCLUSION

The military system of the mid-Heian period evolved during a period of protracted internal violence in the second half of the ninth and first half of the tenth century. A stagnant economy racked by repeated epidemics and famines set aristocrat against local strongman and local strongman against peasant in efforts to maintain their standards of living. The winners of the zero-sum game were some high-ranking aristocrats and temples, a group called "the rich," and upper-level provincial officials; the losers were many peasants and traditional local men of influence (district magistrates) whose powers eroded against the growing influence of the provincial office. From about 870 until 920 the provincial headquarters was the target of violence, as it was the central office responsible for the collection of taxes.

The Court first relied upon increased police forces to counter growing violence. When this proved inadequate, aristocrats in the capital at Heian sent Prince Takamochi, a new military aristocrat, to the violence-plagued Kanto to effect peace. His appointment late in the ninth century to a position in provincial government initially met with success. The Court also enacted a far-reaching reform of the military system in 901 when it simplified the procedure for reporting violence at the provincial level to the central government and removed the limitations on provincial governors trying to raise troops. Just as provincial tax-farmers became the chief revenue officials, so provincial military powers expanded to make the provincial headquarters an island of Court law and order in a sea of violence.

In 935, the Kanto once again became the center of violence as Taira no Masakado, a descendant of Prince Takamochi, fought against his relatives in a marriage dispute. This conflict was intraspecific in character, the issue being Masakado's own survival and the continuation of his line. Masakado skirmished with his kin for 4 years, causing widespread destruction, while the Court in Heian took little notice. But in 939, when he intervened first in Musashi and then in Hitachi in quarrels over taxation, the Court was shocked into action. Eventually Masakado conquered the entire Kanto and made himself the "new emperor."

A pirate of the Inland Sea, Fujiwara Sumitomo, was also in rebellion in 939. Sumitomo's forces were composed of an alliance of several pirates throughout western Japan, and had troubled the Court since at least 932. In 939 and 940, the violence focused on the provincial headquarters and intensified as famine and epidemics encouraged farmers to turn to piracy.

The Court responded to the twin rebellions by appointing military officials at the provincial level to take on the rebels and issuing a request for fighters which promised rewards. Court countermeasures bore fruit; Masakado was beheaded in the 2nd month of 940 and Sumitomo in the 5th month of 941.

The rebellions of Masakado and Sumitomo reveal much about tenth-century Japan. Masakado's military organization comprised (1) relatives and rich migrants, (2) dependents, and (3) allies. Dependents were loyal mounted fighters, while allies were foot soldiers who fled battle when the tide turned against them. Masakado employed foot soldiers in Chinese-style mass tactics as well as elite mounted fighting specialists, like commanders in the eighth century. Masakado's fighting style suggests that the samurai evolved out of the Taihō system, and that there is relatively little difference between armies of eighth-century and twelfth-century Japan.

Many Japanese scholars describe Masakado and his rivals as "great private landlords" who cultivated their own lands and had loose control over the peasants on their domains. As a result of their weak economic position, the lords of the tenth century could manage to fight only brief campaigns with simple organizations that disintegrated quickly. Yet the distinctions between Masakado and the samurai of the twelfth and thirteenth centuries are fine and somewhat arbitrary. Office, pastures, ironworks, and other economic enterprises were at least as important as land to warriors of the mid-900s.

The twin revolts of Masakado and Sumitomo suggest that Japan in the tenth century comprised distinct regions, some, like the Kanto, possessing an identity of their own. Yet Masakado was too naive politically to use his military prowess to establish an enduring separate kingdom. He had no program like that of the later Yoritomo to tie local men of influence to him by their purse strings.

Finally, the revolts of Masakado and Sumitomo elaborated and consolidated the military system established in 901. The two pillars of the new system were the aristocratic warriors of the capital and fighters based in the provinces. In the capital, the state recognition of private aristocratic forces was reminiscent of the policies of the eighth century. In the provincial headquarters, the revolts produced military specialists who went by titles derived from the Taihō Codes. Military skills continued to be the prerogative of an hereditary elite headed by aristocratic warriors who held high office, a pattern reminiscent of the eighth century and before.

The central government in Japan in the late ninth and early tenth centuries was declining. Economic conditions were worsening, and the population had stagnated, perhaps even shrunk. State revenues were decreasing, and the power of the central government to enforce law and maintain order had weakened somewhat. Domestic violence and rebellions were becoming increasingly common.

Yet it is not correct to suppose that Japan lacked all vestiges of an effective central administration, as advocates of the Western-analogue theory maintain. The Court in Heian was still vigorous enough to establish new systems of taxation and military organization based indirectly on laws contained in the Taihō Codes. The reformed military system of 901 was the result, and it helped lay the groundwork for the rise of the samurai in the twelfth century. Warriors were free to build their economic bases and hone their political skills within the system, and most of them did that. The existence of such a military system for the 900s, even as flexible as it was, raises doubts about following the Western-analogue theory to describe Japan at this time.

Another important link between early Japanese fighters and the twelfth-century warrior was forged at this time. As a result of the twin rebellions of Masakado and Sumitomo, two new military houses ascended into the ranks of the aristocracy. The descendants of Tsunemoto (Minamoto) and Sadamori (Taira) were new to the nobility, but, during the next two centuries, they would acquire the wealth and political experience to contend for leadership over all Japan's warriors.

chapter five

The "Missing Link": The Military of the Middle Heian Era, 950–1050

> *The expanse of bows could be seen glittering in the morning sun for about a mile and a half along the broad white beach. The Provincial Governor was accompanied by the men of his residence and the warriors of the province, and he commanded a force of about 2,000 men.*
>
> —from *Tales of Times Now Past*, about 1016

One of the major tenets of the Western-analogue theory is that, with the decline of the Taihō system after 900, Japan lacked an effective central government. As the fall of the Western Roman Empire created a political vacuum in Europe, Japan of the tenth and early eleventh centuries was also assumed to be "without law and order just as if there was no state control at all."[1] Under these conditions, heretofore law-abiding local men of influence began to arm themselves for self-defense; they soon formed bands of mounted warriors linked by ties of loyalty, and paid for their armies with land.[2] As in Western Europe, the absence of a strong polity gave birth to a new class of fighting men, and their system of rule was thought to be feudalism.

Reference to scattered documents, legal sources, and literary works has shown that Japan of the middle Heian era was much more like the Eastern Roman Empire, where a capable administration continued despite invasions and rebellions. Japanese historians have been able to sketch the martial system of the era 942–1050, the "missing link" between the institutions of the Taihō Codes and the twelfth-century warrior. The new military had two pillars: forces of the aristocrats in the capital; and warriors of the provincial headquarters in the countryside.

The military of the capital was composed of a small coterie of capital police, including the Imperial Guards and Investigators, and stronger and better-organized units of aristocratic troops. Martial aristocrats were a special category of noble retainers; they belonged to houses that had the privilege of practicing the martial arts, pledged loyalty to several high civil aristocrats at the same time, and maintained economic bases outside the capital city of Heian.

In the countryside, the governor commanded personal retainers, provincial officials, and "soldiers of the provinces." Personal retainers were mercenaries who bullied the populace for revenue, while lesser officials operated out of the provincial headquarters as the Strong Fellows had done in the ninth century. Every province kept lists of its ablest fighters; a man might become a "soldier of the province" by serving guard duty, riding in the provincial hunt, acting in a local religious ceremony, or obtaining appointment as an overseer or arrest officer. Most governors also relied upon assistance from wealthy local strongmen who had often married into older military houses from the eighth century, and who owed loyalty to a mighty civil aristocrat.

The dual system of the capital and the provinces that lasted from 900 to 1050 came to an end during a severe crisis in the mid-eleventh century, when epidemics, drought, and the 3-year revolt of Taira no Tadatsune, a tax rebel, disrupted Japanese farming for decades. Yet out of the rubble would come reforms in land tenure, taxation, and village administration that led to further modifications in the military of the twelfth century.

THE MILITARY SYSTEM OF THE CAPITAL, 942–1050

Japanese capitals have always been exciting and dangerous centers of military intrigue, even in the eighth century, when aristocrats like Fujiwara no Nakamaro bolstered political power with personal armies. Fujiwara no Sanesuke, a leading Court aristocrat and descendant of Nakamaro, described one violent act in Heian in his diary in 1023:

At some time between 10 P.M. and 2 A.M., the Nakamikado home of the Governor of Tamba . . . burned. Over 10 mounted soldiers came and set fire to it. The people in the house challenged them, but the power of the gang of robbers was great and so they did it, people say. The Governor was in the province, it is said. . . . Well, the capital is no different from the Bandō (the Kanto)![3]

This example of brute force used against an official resident of the capital is only one of many such incidents occurring during the century after the defeat of Masakado and Sumitomo. As Sanesuke bewails, by the early eleventh century, the capital seemed to be as much the scene of daily violence as was the home of warriors in the Kanto. The constant conflict in Heian was a by-product of a military system that concentrated many troops there.

Fighting men of the capital between 942 and 1050 came from two organizations: the capital police, which included the Imperial Guards (Efu) and Investigators (Kebii shi), and aristocratic soldiers (*shoka no heishi*). On the surface, it appears as through this division distinguishes public from private troops, but the public-private dichotomy is really inadequate to describe the system.

IMPERIAL GUARDS. According to the Taihō Codes of 702, protection for the capital was in the hands of Imperial Guards, who could have been commoner-soldiers sent to the capital from the provincial militia (Capital Guards), or the relatives of capital aristocrats and district magistrates (Palace and Gate Guards). The conscription of commoners from the countryside to serve as Capital Guards did not function well even in the early eighth century, since these peasants had no tradition of military training and usually made better porters or diggers than soldiers. The Court abolished the Capital Guards in 792 when it did away with nationwide conscription. By the early to mid-ninth century, the status of the district magistrate had deteriorated, and the Palace and Gate Guards had also declined.

In 811, the Court reorganized the Imperial Guards into the Left and Right Offices of the Palace Guards (Sa, U hyōe fu), the Left and Right Offices of the Gate Guards (Sa, U emon fu), and the Left and Right Offices of Imperial Attendants (Sa, U konoe fu). Yet, during the 800s, these offices continued to lose power and, according to one Japanese historian, by 900 the Palace Guards and Imperial Attendants no longer served a primarily military function.[4] This was also true of another small force (*tachiwaki no toneri*) established in 776 to guard the Heir Apparent.[5]

It is still possible, however, to catch glimpses of the Imperial Guards protecting the capital during this period, mostly in diaries and chronicles. For example, in 948 the Court requested that the Guards take up their bows and search out criminals throughout the capital.[6] Later in the same year, when robbers plagued the capital, these units made special rounds at night.[7] In 976, the government commanded Guards from the office of assistant (*suke*) to attendant (*toneri*) to take part in a great search (*ōasari*) in the capital.[8] In this activity the Imperial Guards assisted "those of the 5th Rank and below who had martial courage," that is, warriors of hereditary lineage. It is fair to say that the various units of the Imperial Guards were not a major source of protection for the capital by the 900s.

INVESTIGATORS. In the early ninth century, the Court recognized the need for a better defense of the capital against crime and upheaval. Lawgivers first conceived the Office of Investigators (Kebii shi chō) somewhere between 815 and 834 to provide the necessary services.[9] Throughout its existence the Office of Investigators had a close relationship with the Office of Gate Guards, and officials often served concurrently in both.[10] In the ninth century, legislators restricted the duties of the Office of Investigators; the Office only really became active on a day-to-day basis in 895. By the early tenth century, the Court had organized the Office of Investigators in 4 tiers, like other Chinese-style ministries and bureaus. In addition, the Investigators employed secretaries, policemen, legal experts, even released prisoners.

The duties of the Office of Investigators varied considerably. They arbitrated conflicts between opposing sides, such as individuals or temples. They collected late taxes, or they might survey land, go on guard duty, or seize a citizen's property that was for some reason forfeit. Many times tax-collection or land-survey duties required 20 or so Investigators to leave the capital for a nearby province.[11] They regulated and oversaw the customs of the capital, as when they challenged a person for wearing clothing or using a cart improper to his or her status. Investigators possessed many judicial duties. Most important, the Office of Investigators arrested persons, and for this purpose maintained a police force.

Historical records preserve many instances of the Investigators in action, but none is more colorful than the following excerpt from 1056:

> Today between 7 and 9 A.M., all of a sudden from the northern hill within the temple precincts 70 or 80 mounted and foot soldiers came out, wearing armor and sedge hats and carrying bows and arrows and swords and spears. They surrounded the Eastern Second Building from the horse trail of the Northern Quarters. In some cases they rode horses, in some cases they ran on foot; using loud voices they cried out. Those in a nearby building heard this and were afraid. . . .
>
> People throughout the temple ought not to have thought this strange. This incident was . . . a case of arresting a criminal according to the Office Order (*chōsen*) of the Investigators.[12]

The reason for the arrest by the Investigators and the eventual outcome of the case are unknown, but this description shows that investigators could number as many as 70 or 80 men, and used both mounted and foot soldiers.

The strength and social composition of the police in the Office of Investigators is a matter of some controversy among Japanese scholars. According to one, the Investigators' Office had a fairly powerful police force which employed men of military talent on its lower levels.[13] Another has argued that the Investigators were actually not strong at all, and what police force they possessed was made up of commoners.[14] The controversy is important: A weak Investigators' Office would raise doubts about the strength of the Court in the tenth and early eleventh centuries.

Historians will probably debate these points for some time in the future, but recent research suggests that the Investigators had a small police force that contained relatively few warriors in the tenth and eleventh centuries. The task of estimating the size of the police force is difficult because officials often took personal followers with them on their missions; these assistants may or may not have been policemen. A careful reading of the historical record indicates that the police force of the Investigators numbered perhaps a few hundred at most.[15] Normally the Office made only one excursion outside the capital at a time, and the Investigators took only about 20 or 30 people. The largest force mentioned in the years 900 to 1050 is about 70 or 80 (see above). If this number went on a trip to the countryside just outside the capital, then some must have stayed behind in the city, perhaps as many as 200 police to oversee Heian, a city of approximately 100,000 people, and deal with other disturbances. In addition to policemen, the Investigators also included higher-ranking functionaries, and in the 940s there were about 30 of these upper-level officials. Thus the Investigators must have been a small organization, certainly fewer than 500.[16]

Analysis of the social origins of the Investigators also raises doubts about the role of trained military specialists in the organization. One historian has counted all the persons who appear in the records as Gate Guards, a position normally held concurrently with posts in the Investigators' Office. He finds that at the level of administrator (*jō*), a position most believe was usually held by those of warrior lineage, practically none of the persons had such a background.[17] Another tenth-century specialist supported this research by tracing all the arrests made by the Investigators and finding that the responsible administrators were not of martial lineage.[18]

But it would be a mistake to dismiss the Investigators as entirely unrelated to the warrior of this time (*tsuwamono*). Two scholars have agreed that, while the administrator was not of military background, the next lowest levels, the secretary (*sakan*) and clerks (*fushō*), could in some cases be military men.[19] In addition, one of the first advocates of the Investigators as a source of fighters has found that, in many cases when the Investigators went on a mission to arrest a criminal, the officials took personal followers with them. For example, at some time between 1023 and 1028 when Investigators went to Yamato province, 4 officials took along 9 followers (*jū*) and 7 lower-level police.[20] The followers were not official members of the Investigators; the scholar who discovered this case has argued that the followers were private retainers with military backgrounds. The presence of followers not only suggests that warriors may have played some role in the Investigators, but also demonstrates how tenth-century Japanese offices mixed public and private functions.

A document from 997 may reveal much about the behavior and military power of the men employed as Investigators.[21] In this account, Minu Kimitada, a resident of Kawachi province, formed a league with other hereditary warriors named Sakanoue, Tami, Mamuta, Ochi, and Yuge. On orders from an official of the Imperial Consort, whose motives were unknown, the league attacked the home of Minu Kanetomo with "15 or 16 mounted soldiers and over 20 foot soldiers."[22] The record further states that Kimitada himself was fleeing an arrest order, had gathered about him various unsavory henchmen (*dōrui*) who prevented Kanetomo from cultivating his fields, and had built towers for archers on his residence.

Surnames like Minu and Tami were common among employees of the Investigators' Office; the historian who analyzed this record believes that these warriors were representative of the type of men who joined the Investigators. They were mainly small landholders based in the capital region and migratory members of the class called "the rich." The document indicates not just the small size of their forces (15 or 16 horsemen and about 20 foot soldiers), but also the fluid way in which such forces could gather and then melt away.

WARRIORS OF THE ARISTOCRACY. The second and more powerful part of the capital military consisted of soldiers owing loyalty to a civil aristocrat. Because every aristocrat worthy of the name had numerous attendants and followers, including many with military skills, the capital was almost always the scene of conflicts between different nobles. The following 6 accounts from various aristocratic diaries describe a variety of conflicts:

1. A quarrel led to the demolition of an aristocrat's house.

969 — 7th day, 2nd month: On this day, a houseman (*kenin*) of the Minister of the Right Morotada fought with a houseman of the Middle Councillor (*chūnagon*) Kaneie. An attendant (*toneri*) of the

Minister was killed. Several hundred housemen of the Minister came out and wrecked the house of the Middle Councillor.[23]

2. Warriors kidnapped an aristocrat.

988 — 4th day, 12th month: The new Middle Councillor (Fujiwara no Michinaga) dispatched some followers who could be brave [i.e., warriors] and captured Lesser Vice-Minister of Rites [Tachibana no] Yoshinobu.[24]

3. An aristocratic dispute led to a pitched archery battle in the streets of the capital.

995 — 24th day, 7th month: The Minister of the Right (Michinaga) and the Inner Minister (Fujiwara no Korechika) had an argument . . . It was almost as if they came to blows. . . .

— 27th day: People are saying that there was a battle on the 7th Avenue. This was the action of the follower (*bokujū*) of the Middle Councillor Takaie (a friend of Korechika). . . . In this incident a follower of the Middle Councillor led forth many archers, and, while they were summoning and catching them, [Taira no] Noritake . . . released his arrows and shot 2 men. The officials of the Investigators' Office went to the spot where the incident had occurred, but the various people had scattered. . . . They captured Noritake. . . .

— 2nd day, 8th month: Some say: Because of yesterday's tumult (an attendant [*zuishin*] of the Minister of the Right Michinaga was killed), Takaie will not be coming to Court. . . . The Minister of the Right [Michinaga] says that if Lord Takaie does not hand over a suspect, then he ought not come to Court.[25]

4. A policeman was murdered.	1005 — 16th day, 2nd month: Last night an attendant of the Minister of the Left, a Rotation Head (*banchō*) of the Right Imperial Attendants, Mitobe Yasutomo, was shot and killed.[26]
5. An archery tournament was scheduled.	1005 — 13th day, 5th month: . . . Yesterday it was discussed at the residence of the Minister of the Left [Michinaga]: On the 13th each aristocrat should meet at his residence, bringing a follower. On the next day there will be an exhibition of mounted archery.[27]
6. An Investigator and a member of an aristocratic household quarreled.	1013 — 27th day, 1st month: . . . A follower of low rank in the Investigators' Office (*kachō*) was struck by a lower-class person of the house [of Michinaga]. . . . The Minister of the Left (Michinaga) had a member of the Investigators' Office, [Minamoto] Yorikuni no Ason, capture and send a suspect [to the Investigators]. . . . [But] Yorikuni locked the suspect in jail, it is said.[28]

The Court issued bans on the private possession of weapons from time to time to prevent outbreaks of violence, but the prohibitions proved ineffective.[29]

These 6 incidents give some insight into the size, technology, organization, and social composition of aristocratic armies. They show that aristocratic soldiers must have abounded in the capital. The first incident mentions "several hundred"; it would not be surprising if the warriors for a high-ranking aristocrat were more numerous and effective than the police force of the Office of Investigators.

Second, many fighters were mounted archers. The third and fourth incidents state that battles between aristocratic soldiers were archery contests, while in the 5th excerpt, high-ranking nobles had warriors perform in mounted tournaments. Just as in the eighth century, aristocrats may have provided the horses and weapons for their talented minions. The aristocratic preference for mounted archers must have convinced many a fighter to take up the "horse and bow," because the skills of a foot soldier were just not impressive enough for Court displays.

Third, what little is known of the organization of aristocratic military forces suggests that Taihō models served as a precedent. According to one scholar, "private" aristocratic soldiers fought in units of 10 men (*ka*), just like the eighth-century provincial military.[30] Many aristocratic fighters wore clothing of the same color as the Imperial Guards, again suggesting the borrowing of state models for weaponry and organization.

Fourth, these conflicts reveal much about the social composition of aristocratic forces. Although it is difficult to know how the aristocracy raised their armies, many must have also served as low-ranking officials in the Imperial Guard or Investigators. In fact, ties between aristocrats and "official" soldiers in the Investigators or Imperial Guards were probably more common between 900 and 1050 than they had been in the 700s, because, by the tenth and eleventh centuries, government posts did not provide a good living, as indicated by demands of Imperial Guards for back wages.[31] The temptation for these trained soldiers to become attendants for a wealthy aristocrat must have been great. In the 4th and 6th incidents, state offices provided some of the manpower for aristocratic armies, again showing the mixture of public and private operations. Many aristocratic troops probably belonged to the same class economically as the lower-ranking police of the Investigators' Office, such as the Minu discussed earlier. Some may have been low-ranking estate officers, although the evidence for this is slim.[32]

MILITARY ARISTOCRATS. One type of aristocratic warrior deserves separate attention: the hereditary military aristocrat. While many of the military aristocrats who resided in and guarded the capital in the tenth and eleventh centuries were relatively new to their jobs, such as the Seiwa Genji (Minamoto) or Kammu Heishi (Taira), some were not, and the idea of a hereditary military elite living in the capital was old. In the eighth century, if not earlier, there were hereditary houses which specialized in the military arts (*bugei*), such as the Ōtomo, Saeki or Sakanoue; in the ninth century, one might classify the Ono and Ōkura as such military experts.

By the tenth and eleventh centuries, however, newer hereditary lines of martial specialists had become firmly fixed, and anyone who wielded a bow or sword without being from a military house was widely scorned. For instance, in 1028, a member of the Left Gate Guards named Fujiwara Norimoto, a man not from a warrior family, killed one of his followers. A leading civil aristocrat stated his disapproval in his diary: "Norimoto enjoys the martial arts (*bugei*), but people do not approve. . . . He is not of warrior (*musha*) blood."[33]

By the early eleventh century, there were those who practiced military skills who did not belong to hereditary houses, but they did so without social approval. Amateurs like Norimoto may have known how to use weapons, but they could not comprehend a warrior's honor and customs. Many of the stories contained in the early twelfth-century collection *Tales of Times Now Past* begin with the statement that the main character of the tale belonged to an hereditary warrior house (*tsuwamono no ie*).[34] Such lineages normally specialized in the art of mounted archery.

By the tenth century at the latest, the Heian Court froze official society into hereditary houses, with those achieving the 6th, 5th, or sometimes 4th Court Rank and specializing in mounted archery being known as military aristocrats. A proclamation from 1046, submitted by the warrior Minamoto no Yorinobu to a shrine of Hachiman, the Shinto God of War, shows how one military house conceived of its duties and lineage.[35] As the head of the Minamoto from Kawachi province near the capital, Yorinobu began by describing Japan's mythological military heroes, such as the Emperor Ōjin (period of rule estimated at the end of the fourth century A.D.) who had subjugated Korea, or his mother, the Empress Jingū, who also supposedly invaded that same country. He then explained his own lineage, and listed the 21 generations that reached back through several emperors to the God of War Hachiman. Finally, he boasted of his own military feats and argued that the Court must rely upon both the literary and martial arts (which Yorinobu and his progeny would master) in order to rule effectively. The proclamation of Yorinobu may not be accurate history, but it is good evidence of the way in which military aristocrats of the tenth and eleventh centuries legitimized their status by claiming a long line of prominent ancestors (much as the imperial line had done in the sixth century) while seeking their own unique identity as martial specialists.

Military aristocrats led the most important and most effective of the forces in the capital. For example, in 960, when a rumor arose that Masakado's offspring were about to enter the capital, the Court enjoined the Office of Investigators to carry out a search, but also wisely appointed the greatest warriors of the hereditary houses to help: Minamoto no Mitsunaka, son of Tsunemoto, who gained fame in the Masakado rebellion; and Ōkura Harunori, a veteran of Sumitomo's revolt. Later, in 973, when bandits broke into Mitsunaka's house in the capital, the order was not for the Investigators but for "those who were able in the martial arts."[36] In the eleventh century and after, when the monks of the great temples like Enryakuji and Kōfukuji made it their regular practice to raid the capital, it was the leaders of the most skilled military houses, not the Investigators or the Imperial Guards, who formed the main force against the monks' advance.

Occasionally, a source will provide a close look at the military aristocrat and his activities. This example of an assassination may be found in the diary of the great Fujiwara no Michinaga:

1017 — 11th day, 3rd month:
The captain (*kami*) of the Right Gate Guards came and said: "At somewhere between 3 and 5 P.M., when the imperial procession was underway, there was a person named Kiyowara no Munenobu staying at a small residence near the intersection of Rokkaku and Tomi avenues. . . . But then 7 or 8 horsemen and more than 10 foot soldiers surrounded and killed him. I sent the Investigators and had them make a record of the incident as you see here. . . ."

Thus after inquiring about the particulars, I [Michinaga] found it was [Minamoto no] Yorichika's deed. People widely say: This Yorichika is good at killing people. This kind of act happens frequently.[37]

It is unclear whether Yorichika himself killed Munenobu, or simply ordered his henchmen to commit the crime, but a final comment indicates that Yorichika wanted to assassinate Munenobu because the victim was a member of the band that had murdered one of Yorichika's men at his base in Yamato province. Yorichika was a good example of a military aristocrat who had his economic base in the provinces, but kept contacts in the capital.

For his murder of Munenobu, the Court stripped Yorichika of the governorship of Awaji and the captaincy of the Right Horse Office (Meryō). But one can almost see Michinaga make a mental note to himself when he wrote that Yorichika was "good at killing people." In fact, Yorichika was probably a follower of Michinaga's when Munenobu's murder took place. At the same time, Yorichika also worked for Fujiwara no Sanesuke, another leading civil aristocrat, again showing that it was possible for a Japanese warrior to serve two masters at once.[38] Yorichika's brand of soldier must have been in great demand among the aristocrats of the capital; many military aristocrats were nothing more than hired assassins.

An attachment to a great civil aristocrat such as Michinaga, ranked at the 3rd Court Rank or higher, must have been essential for maintaining status as a military aristocrat. Those military men who did not acquire such ties could not obtain high office and all the perquisites that attended it. One could always develop a base in the provinces, but there was a large difference between a military aristocrat who was active in capital politics and one who was not.

It would be a mistake to presume that the Minamoto and Taira, who gained great fame in the twelfth century, were the only houses of military aristocrats. One historian has listed some lesser military nobles, including the house of Fujiwara Motokata, originally of Kazusa in the Kanto, which produced such warriors as Yasusuke and Yasumasa (a follower of Michinaga). Other military aristocrats included the Montoku Genji, the Nagara Fujiwara, the Ōkura, the Tachibana, and the Hidesato Fujiwara. All these warrior houses originated before Masakado's rebellion.[39]

Yet the Minamoto and the Taira were the most well-known military aristocrats, even in the tenth century. According to a contemporary record, "among warriors (*bushi*), [Minamoto no] Mitsunaka,

[Minamoto no] Mitsumasa, [Taira no] Korehira, [Taira no] Muneyori, and [Minamoto no] Yorimitsu, all of these are the best under heaven."[40] Perhaps the most renowned was Minamoto no Mitsunaka, who reached the coveted 4th Court Rank and held 8 governorships and numerous military offices in the capital. Mitsunaka used high rank and offices (notably the governorship of Settsu) to establish a provincial base and martial following for himself.[41] He gained favor in 969, when he helped the Fujiwara banish their rivals from the capital and reserve the highest offices in the land to themselves. Mitsunaka showed a keen sense of Court politics, since, by cooperating with the Fujiwara, he not only gained for himself and his offspring the privilege of serving the most powerful Fujiwara leaders for more than 100 years, but he also eliminated a competing warrior family from capital politics.

Another capital military aristocrat is Taira no Korehira, founder of the Ise Taira.[42] The first mention of him is in 998, when he fought with his relative Muneyori in Ise. The Court punished both warriors for fighting, but meted out the more severe penalty to Muneyori. One reason for the difference was that Korehira contributed to the construction of a residence for the daughter of the Minister of the Right, who probably interceded on Korehira's behalf.

In 1006, Korehira was on the verge of taking office as the Governor of Ise, once again owing to the good offices of his patron, the Minister of the Right. However, Michinaga, the chief aristocrat at Court, objected because of Korehira's violent activity in the province; instead of the governorship of Ise, Korehira became the Vice-Governor of Kōzuke in the Kanto. In 1010, the year after Korehira ended his stay in Kōzuke, he presented Michinaga with a gift of 10 horses, an act that symbolized Korehira's becoming a follower of Michinaga. In return for his submission, Michinaga had Korehira named to a position in Kyushu. Not long after his appointment, Korehira also went to work for Fujiwara no Sanesuke, thereby serving more than one lord, as Yorichika had done earlier.

As reward for his service to the most powerful civil aristocrats, the Court had Korehira appointed to several governorships. According to his genealogy, Korehira assumed governorships in Kōzuke, Hitachi, Ise, Mutsu, Dewa, Izu, Shimotsuke, and Sado.

As he moved from post to post, he accumulated valuable political experience that almost put him on a par with Mitsunaka. Korehira also gained great wealth, and sources allude to a greed so consuming that whole provinces suffered. Korehira's store of political experience strongly contrasts with Masakado, the warrior who rebelled and naively declared himself the "new emperor." Korehira acquired great wealth and office by working through the system, rather than against it.

Something is known of Korehira's fighting organization and economic base. According to one scholar, many of his followers were members of the Imperial Guard or the Investigators' Office, again demonstrating the mixture of public and private roles.[43] Most ties between Korehira and his followers were loose, contractual arrangements like the connections he had forged with his aristocratic mentors, and they worked fairly well as long as the patron could provide rewards to the warrior. Korehira accumulated most of his wealth through the offices he held. He undoubtedly had a residence in Ise that was as large as an eighth-century district office, complete with storehouses, offices, and other buildings.

Relatively little is known of the Taira after Korehira disappeared from the records in 1038. During the early eleventh century, the Taira in Ise continued to fight among themselves; the conflict that originated between Korehira and Muneyori lasted for at least two generations.[44] Like other military aristocrats of the tenth and eleventh centuries, the Taira of Ise must have been busy accumulating wealth, enrolling followers, and increasing their political influence in the provinces.

THE MILITARY SYSTEM OF THE PROVINCES, 942–1050

Ever since the implementation of the Chinese-style system of the Taihō Codes in 702, the Court had appointed provincial governors from among the lower ranks of the aristocracy to oversee the countryside. Since they came in from the outside and collected taxes, the governors faced a potential conflict with the residents of the province, especially with local strongmen. Disputes between district magistrates and governors were common in the eighth century, and, by the ninth and tenth centuries, as anti-government violence led by tax rebels and the rich focused on the provincial headquarters, governors of necessity became the leaders of sizable military forces. In some provinces, conflicts were so common that the Court took to naming prominent military aristocrats to the governorships to deal with local warriors.

Tales of Times Now Past contains a description of how the warrior-governor Minamoto no Yorinobu punished the bandit Taira no Tadatsune. The incident probably occurred sometime before 1016, and opens as follows:

> So Yorinobu became the Governor of Hitachi and went down to that province. While he was there, there was a warrior (*tsuwamono*) called Taira no Tadatsune in the province of Shimōsa. As this warrior's military force was extremely great, he did as he pleased throughout Kazusa and Shimōsa, and he even took no heed of taxes (*kuji*). Again, he was also negligent even about the things that the Governor of Hitachi ordered. The Governor greatly censured this and was impatient to cross over into Shimōsa and correct him.
>
> Now there was in the province a man called Saemon no Taifu Taira no Koremoto. When he heard about this matter, he advised the Governor: "Tadatsune is a powerful man. Moreover, his lair is not a place that people can approach easily. Thus he cannot be set upon with a small force. So prepare an army in great numbers and cross over."
>
> The Governor listened to this advice and then observed: "That may well be so, but I cannot leave matters like this."
>
> And so he set out in a hurry and crossed over into Shimōsa. At this Koremoto assembled an army of 3,000 horsemen, and came up and met him in front of Kashima Shrine.
>
> The expanse of bows could be seen glittering in the morning sun for about 20 *chō* [2.5 kilometers] along the broad white beach. The Governor was accompanied by the men of his residence (*tachi no monodomo*) and the warriors of the province (*kuni no tsuwamonodomo*), and he commanded a force of about 2,000 men. . . .[45]

According to a specialist at Tokyo University, the final paragraph of this description contains a catalogue of the military forces most provincial governors had at their disposal: (I-A) those associated with the governor's official residence in the provinces (*tachi no monodomo*), and (I-B) the warriors known only as fighters of the province (*kuni no tsuwamonodomo*).[46] One may further subdivide the soldiers associated with the governor's official residence in the provinces into: (I-A-1) the governor's personal retainers; and (I-A-2) those fighters who held posts in the provincial headquarters. In addition to their own military forces (I), every governor also forged uneasy alliances with local strongmen who lived in his jurisdiction but remained beyond his official control. In Yorinobu's case, this was Taira no Koremoto (II). (Figure 6 provides a graphic representation of the provincial military.)

(I-A-1). PERSONAL RETAINERS. By 900, the governors (*zuryō*) of the provinces were tax-farmers who saw their appointments as ways to get rich.[47] They built lavish homes in the capital and spent most of their time enjoying life in the city. Every governor maintained a coterie of followers and dependents who would accompany him on journeys to the provincial capital to rake in his wealth. The followers included not just fighting men, but also secretaries, accountants, and relatives.

The greed of governors of the tenth and eleventh centuries was legendary, but none was more notorious than Fujiwara no Motonaga of Owari. His behavior was so rapacious that the district magistrates and people of his province gathered in 988 and wrote a 31-article grievance to the Court to protest his conduct. Their complaint stated that, "when Governor Motonaga came down from the capital, he led employed and unemployed officials, dependents, and similar unsavory characters," including "two previously employed Palace Guards (*takiguchi*)." These troublemakers "scattered and filled the jurisdiction like clouds," and most "lived in the neighborhood of the provincial headquarters like swarming bees." The poor people of Owari protested that, "while mounted on horses," these men "had their followers and dependents wreck doorways and throw open shutters to look for and take various items." The residents of the province further asserted that Motonaga's henchmen falsified land records to claim taxes for unproductive (or non-existent) fields; "they robbed people of their possessions and moved them to [Motonaga's] capital residence." According to one passage in the grievance, the relatives and retainers of Governor Motonaga were "essentially no different from barbarians."[48]

Figure 6. PROVINCIAL MILITARY FORCES

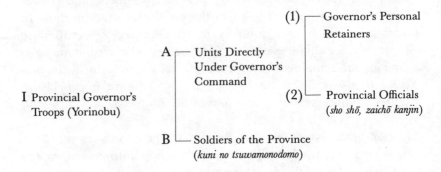

II Local Strongman's Troops
(Koremoto)

Source: Ishii Susumu, "Chūsei seiritsu ki gunsei kenkyū no ichi shiten," *Shigaku zasshi* 78:1–21 (December 1969).

The Court dismissed Motonaga, although one source says that he continued to play a prominent role in capital life thereafter.[49] It is interesting to note that his personal retainers included two former members of the Palace Guards, persons of military background. They must have been particularly helpful to Motonaga as he exploited the peasants of Owari and kept the provincial officials under his thumb. These members of the Governor's following were similar to the retainers of capital aristocrats, as both groups held minor government posts in addition to their work for their lords.

The number of retainers commanded by a governor must have varied considerably with the wealth and personality of the office-holder. Because Yorinobu was a warrior himself, it is likely that his retainers in Hitachi were relatively numerous as he set out to chastise Tadatsune. Governors from non-military backgrounds must have commanded fewer, and less reliable, personal troops. If he was lucky, a new governor might gather around him as many as 5 men with prior military backgrounds, some perhaps with rank and job experience. Otherwise, he might simply hire raw recruits, many of them former migrants living by their wits.[50] A twelfth-century compilation suggests the ephemeral nature of the governor's personal military coterie when it states that "the term of office ended emptily and each person went his own direction with no one to serve morning and night."[51] Loyalty was temporary when the lord could not provide employment and a source of income to his mercenaries. The same record shows that the success of a governor's term, defined by the amount of revenue he was able to collect, rested largely on his obtaining as few as 1 or 2 personal retainers to enforce his rule.

(I-A-2) PROVINCIAL OFFICIALS. The Taihō Codes of 702 did not spell out how many or what kind of bureaucrats were to work at the provincial headquarters; they merely listed the high-ranking office-holders such as the governor, vice-governor, administrator, and secretary. Because day-to-day command of the provincial militia in the eighth century was in the hands of the district magistrate and his family, it seems likely that the provincial government did not have many administrators specializing in military affairs when law-givers compiled the Codes in the early eighth century.

As noted in Chapters 1 and 2, however, the provincial governor was responsible for the annual inspection of the provincial militia (*gundan*) and the manufacture of weapons. Abundant evidence indicates that, based upon this legal authority, some governors began to expand the military role of the provincial headquarters as early as the late eighth century. The provincial headquarters of the Kanto were the primary staging ground for the wars in northeastern Honshu between 774 and 812. One archeological site dated at the late eighth and early ninth century has yielded the foundations of office buildings and residences, pottery, and lacquer-covered documents. These records list many military activities, such as the conscription of troops and the manufacture of weapons. This excavation is located not far from the area long associated with the Hitachi provincial headquarters in the Kanto.[52] An early-ninth-century regulation that lists workers employed at the provincial headquarters states that for the construction of weapons provinces used between 30 and 120 persons of a total staff of about 600.[53] A record from 997 details the contents of the provincial headquarters of Kōzuke and tallies almost 23,000 arrows, 2,400 bows, and 200 swords.[54] The provincial headquarters in Musashi and Hitachi were of crucial importance for Masakado in his rebellion between 935 and 940.

As economic conditions deteriorated and internal violence became more prevalent in the late ninth and tenth centuries, provincial officials, once limited to non-military duties, began to arm themselves and gather retinues. In the eighth and early ninth centuries, the government did not permit provincial officials outside of the frontier in Kyushu or officials of the three provinces with passes that led from the capital to eastern Honshu (Mino, Ise, and Echizen) to carry weapons. In the late ninth century, the Court allowed the provinces of Izumo and Hōki, just across the ocean from Korea, to arm their officials; by the early tenth century *The Ordinances of Engi* added Musashi, Awa, Kazusa, Shimōsa, Hitachi, Kōzuke, Shimotsuke, Mutsu, Dewa, Echigo, Sado, Inaba, Iwami, Oki, and Nagato provinces to the list.[55] When officials of Kai, Shinano, and Suruga provinces also received permission to arm themselves in the mid-tenth century, most of eastern Honshu, as well as the strategic provinces on the Japan Sea, had officials in minor and major positions carrying weapons.[56]

The twelfth-century compilation *Tales of Times Now Past* portrays the life of these minor provincial officials:

> Now a long time ago there was a lone secretary (*shoshō*) from Higo province (northern Kyushu). Day and night he went to the provincial headquarters (*tachi*), and he passed some years working at state affairs. While he was working, there was an urgent matter; he left the house early one morning and made his way to the province office. He went without followers, and simply rode along on his horse alone. The distance from the secretary's home to the office was over 10 *chō* [about 1.3 km.].[57]

The provincial secretary of this story did not employ a retinue, but another tale describes a secretary as commanding 4 or 5 powerful fellows who "guarded him day and night."[58]

One historian has analyzed the changing composition of provincial staffs over the era 700 to 1200.[59] He first depicts the metamorphosis in provincial government which has been outlined in this book: the increase in staff, the absence of the governor from day-to-day administration, the transformation of the province into a financial resource, and the growth of hereditary positions for lower-level staff (*zaichō kanjin*). In particular, he has noted 2 significant trends. (1) Many of the lower-ranking staff who obtained hereditary posts in the provincial headquarters were concurrently district magistrates whose status had declined and whose independent powers had weakened. These hereditary local strongmen of the seventh and eighth centuries were the main military commanders of the Taihō system and must have contributed to the militarization of the provincial office in the tenth and eleventh centuries. In other words, one source for the warrior of 1185 was the district magistrate of 750. (2) Many of these lower-ranking officials had access to land controlled by the province (*kokuga ryō*). Permission for all land clearance had to proceed from the provincial headquarters, and low-ranking staffers were often in a position of power, bargaining over land rights, capital, and control over the local peasantry for labor.

Historians know little about the internal workings of the provincial headquarters in the era 942–1050, but they can make inferences based upon documents from later eras. A record from the fourteenth century shows the composition of the Hitachi provincial office, which contained many bureaus that dealt with land, taxation, records, religion, and other matters.[60] Two bureaus related to military affairs were the Investigators' Department (Kebii sho) and the Department of Strong Fellows (Kondei sho). The Court established the former office between the latter half of the ninth century and first half of the tenth century in various provinces. One scholar argues that its function was more judicial than military, while another emphasizes the Investigators' martial character by pointing to two references to provincial Investigators' leading troops in the late ninth and early eleventh centuries.[61] Unfortunately, so little is known of this position until the twelfth century that no conclusion is possible.

The appearance of a Strong Fellows Department in a fourteenth-century document is most surprising. This finding contradicts the conventional view that the system of Strong Fellows was inoperative almost from the time it began in 792. In provincial

183

records, capital handbooks, and diaries, the system of the Strong Fellows first discussed in Chapter 2 comes across as a long-lived institution.[62]

Governor Yorinobu could not have defeated Tadatsune with just the officials of the provincial headquarters, because their forces were undoubtedly meager. Yet their signficance can not be measured by numbers alone. Taken together with the evidence on the militarization of the provincial headquarters, the existence of military officials in the regular provincial staff proves that a major point of origin for the samurai of medieval Japan was the eighth-century Chinese-style system itself.

(I-B) SOLDIERS OF THE PROVINCE. It is doubtful that Minamoto no Yorinobu could have matched the strength of Taira no Tadatsune with his personal retainers and minor provincial officials alone. He also needed the support of the soldiers of the province, described in this excerpt from *Tales of Times Now Past:*

> Now a long time ago, a person called Middle General Sanekata became the Governor of Mutsu. Because he was of exalted noble house, when he went down to that province, the important soldiers of the province (*kuni no uchi no shikaru beki tsuwamonodomo*) provided enter-tainment for this Governor unlike any for his predecessors. Day and night they did not fail in their service at his official residence.[63]

Unlike the fighters discussed so far, these soldiers of the province were not directly under the Governor's command. Yorinobu needed some extraordinary means to enroll these men in his service.

There were 4 ways the governor convinced soldiers of the province to join his army: enlist them in the provincial watch, send them on an official hunt, have them perform in a religious cere-mony, or appoint them to office.[64] Guard duty took place at the governor's official residence, and was a privilege that allowed local warriors a chance to curry favor with the leaders of the provincial headquarters. For example, in the 10th month of 1039, the Gov-ernor of Mikawa province died in the capital. According to the diary of Councillor (*sangi*) Fujiwara no Sukefusa, "boarders from that province as well as attendants (*samurai*) of the province" were to wait for the burial ceremonies and go back to Mikawa, on orders of the Regent (*kampaku*).[65] Most scholars believe that the boarders and attendants were in the capital to serve as guards for the deceased Governor's family.

Once again, most documentation on this practice comes from later periods, and historians make inferences about the tenth and eleventh centuries. There are several examples from the thirteenth century of soldiers of the province providing guard duty for governors in Heian and for the provincial headquarters, and one historian has argued that the origins of such service lay in the tenth or eleventh century.[66] Presumably the constable (*shugo*), the chief warrior in each province during the Kamakura era (1185-1333), merely took over the practice of the provincial governors when he granted the soldiers of the province the privilege of guard duty at the provincial capital.

An eleventh-century governor wishing to bring the military power of soldiers of the province under his control could also invite them to go on a provincially sanctioned hunt. A document from around the year 1000 tells the story of one Kanooka who acquired "a name for being handy at archery" and served "generations of governors" when they commanded that "for three days all the persons of the province should go on a hunt."[67] Like guard duty, participation in the provincial hunt was a practice still popular in the thirteenth century, when the constable organized provincial warriors for hunts. It is interesting to speculate, as one scholar has, that killing game was the original occupation for many warriors, a specialization which only later drew the condemnation of peasants and Buddhist prelates.[68]

A third means available to Governor Yorinobu for enlisting soldiers of the province was to have them perform in provincial religious rites. Warrior participation in Shinto rites originated in the tenth century or thereabouts; the duties of fighters might include wrestling (sumo), dancing, or mounted archery contests (*yabusame*). In the same period, governors began to designate one Shinto preserve as the leading shrine (*ichi no miya*) in the province, and Shinto officials often became members of the provincial staff, actions aimed at consolidating religious and military power under the governor.[69] By the thirteenth century, service in Shinto rites at such famous shrines as Izumo or Suwa in Shinano was a privilege that helped distinguish a person as being of martial lineage. The strong association of military skills and families with Shinto confirms that the ties between warriors and rulers go way back; one is reminded of the pre-645 local strongman (*kuni no miyatsuko*) who combined military with Shinto duties. Such a combination suggests the militaristic nature of Japan's earliest faith and the integral role played by the military in premodern Japanese culture.

A fourth method for bringing soldiers of the province into the governor's ranks was to appoint them to office, especially to military posts such as overseers (*ōryō shi*) and arrest officers (*tsuibu shi*). The appointment to a provincial office carried with it prestige, and warriors were hungry for recognition of their hereditary military prowess. As noted in Chapter 3, the Court named overseers, arresting officers, and search-and-destroy missions during the revolts of Taira no Masakado and Fujiwara Sumitomo, and, even though the state terminated some of those specific appointments after the revolts, the practice of naming soldiers of the province permanently to these posts expanded after 942.

Examination of the historical record shows that there were nearly 100 warriors named to military posts within the provincial headquarters, with slightly over half the appointments between 900 and 1050. These positions fell into four categories: (1) provincial overseers and arrest officers; (2) search-and-destroy missions; (3) camp overseers; or (4) overseers of transport.[70] The provincial overseer (*shokoku ōryō shi*) and provincial arrest officer (*shokoku tsuibu shi*) were the most common and important, and differed only in the area of appointment, the arrest officers taking posts in the Kinai and the Inland Sea area, the overseers on the frontier in eastern Honshu or Kyushu.[71]

A good example of the appointment of an overseer comes from Izumo province in the year 952. According to the provincial request, "violent persons are going where they please" and "tax-paying people form bands" and "rob people's possessions." But Kiyotaki "Shizuhira is equipped with both ability and drive and also is able at martial skills; he is of an upright character and laboring for the state is in his heart." If the Court would name Kiyotaki to be an overseer, "he not only would put an end to the evil fellows but also see that there were good and peaceful customs" in Izumo.[72]

It is noteworthy that to become a provincial overseer or arrest officer, one had to be "able at martial skills," as Shizuhira was. Provincial offices possessed "lineage charts" (*fudai zu*) which told them who the best soldiers of the province were.[73] One historian examined several individuals named as provincial arrest officers and overseers and noted that many of them came from the families of former district magistrates.[74] Once the Court made the appointment, it often became hereditary; the twelfth-century history *Mirror of the East* (*Azuma kagami*) states that members of the family of Fujiwara Hidesato, the warrior primarily responsible for killing Masakado, handed down his overseer position for 13 generations.[75]

The general way in which provincial overseers and arrest officers went about their jobs is clear, but few details are available.[76] After the commission of a serious crime, such as murder or theft of government property, district and provincial officials investigated and made a report to the Court. In turn, the Court issued an arrest order (*tsuibu kampu*), which gave the provincial headquarters (and through the headquarters the provincial overseer or arrest officer) the power to arrest and punish bandits, raise troops, and reward soldiers. It is difficult to say exactly how the officer raised troops, but one expert has argued that the district magistrate submitted a list of names to the provincial office; the provincial headquarters in turn solicited the warriors in their jurisdiction through a circular (*megurashibumi*). When the governor concurrently held the position of overseer or arrest officer, he could employ between 20 and 30 fighting men, and most reported directly to him. The provincial headquarters could hold men of the province who did not participate in the battle to apprehend the criminal to be legally responsible. Once the transgressor was caught or killed, the provincial arrest officer or overseer recommended worthy warriors for awards of Court rank or office.

The Court named soldiers of the province to be a second type of martial officer and sent them out from the capital. Organized into 4 tiers like all Chinese-style offices, the search-and-destroy mission (*tsuitō shi*) was composed mainly of Imperial Guards until after the revolt of Taira no Tadatsune in 1028. Most missions were small and not of much interest to the student of military affairs.

A third military appointment was the camp overseer (*shojin ōryō shi*). His duty was to lead during battle, and the small body of evidence that exists shows that they operated only during the revolt of Masakado, the Former Nine Years' War from 1051 to 1062, the Hōgen Disturbance of 1156, and the Great Civil War of 1180–1185.

The fourth martial office was the overseer of transport (*unjō butsu ōryō shi*). One record from around the year 1000 speaks of a certain Matsukage, Overseer of Moving Official Rice to the Capital, who was "the offspring of a warrior." In another case, a soldier who was called general (*shōgun*) in his province was also the Overseer of Moving Rice, an hereditary post that enabled the holder to commandeer men and boats during wartime. The connection between the militarization of the transportation system and the development of warrior strength is again apparent.[77]

(II) LOCAL STRONGMAN'S TROOPS. The final group from which Yorinobu obtained his forces was the local strongmen, the same class that led the pre-645 and the Taihō military. In this case, the influential local was Taira no Koremoto, and, according to *Tales of Times Now Past*, the 3,000 men he supplied were more than Governor Yorinobu could manage.

Koremoto had personal reasons for joining forces with the Governor. Evidence suggests that he and Tadatsune belonged to warring factions of the Taira family, and that the bad blood between them went back at least to their fathers' generation — perhaps once again an example of a conflict to achieve dominance within a family of warriors. One is reminded of Masakado's revolt and the role played by personal and family enmity among local warriors in the 930s.

Little is known of Koremoto's family background, but it is likely that he and his relatives intermarried with local families, such as those appointed to be district magistrates. Unfortunately, most genealogies do not show the intermarriage because of the changing nature of kinship over the premodern era (500–1850). In the Heian era (784–1185), governors and other warrior-nobles like Prince Takamochi brought the marital customs of Heian aristocratic families to the Kanto; these customs included nightly visits by the man to his mate's family and the eventual adoption of the husband into the bride's family in cases where the bride's family held higher status than the prospective husband's.[78]

Most genealogies, however, date from the fourteenth century when the old customs had died out and the ideal Japanese family had become patrilineal. If an aristocratic Taira man married a woman from a magistrate's family, then the authors of fourteenth-century genealogies followed patrilineal practice and omitted the bride's (magistrate's) side of the family from the charts. When a man from a magistrate's family married a Taira woman, then he changed his surname to Taira as a result of adoption, and genealogy experts did not usually note his family origins in their documents. Thus the role of older district magistrates' families as the source of spouses for the families of local strongmen like Koremoto has gone largely unnoticed.

Another point about Koremoto is of interest. Scholars know that he actively sought liaisons with Heian aristocrats; in fact, he made presents to Fujiwara no Sanesuke and became one of his followers. Later, Sanesuke protected one of Koremoto's sons from the charge of raping a governor's wife. There was little practical difference between Koremoto, a provincial strongman, and his relatives like Korehira who were capital aristocrats, held more official posts and higher rank, and resided mostly in the capital in Heian. Each possessed considerable wealth and political influence with important civil aristocrats. However, Koremoto probably had closer ties to leading Court officials than did the local strongmen (district magistrates) of the eighth century.

Koremoto was an especially wealthy local warrior, who is said to have made one Governor of Hitachi envious with the lavish gifts he gave. He inherited the property once held by Sadamori, not far from Mt. Tsukuba and the scene of Masakado's insurrection. According to one historian, Koremoto's living quarters looked much like Masakado's: a fortified residence on high ground surrounded by the fields of his followers and peasants.[79] There is no way to know the composition and organization of Koremoto's forces, but they were probably similar to Masakado's and also to those raised by the district magistrates in the eighth century. Kore-

Figure 7. ECONOMIC AND MILITARY BASE OF
KOREMOTO

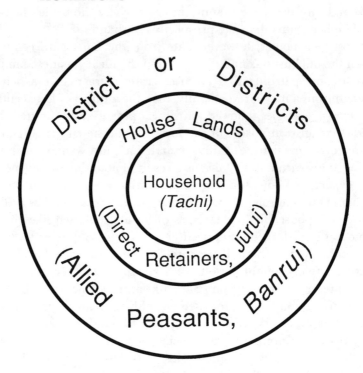

Source: Ishii Susumu, *Nihon no rekishi* 12, *Chūsei bushi dan,* p. 111.

moto's army undoubtedly included both personal dependents, who
lived with their lord in his residence and were strongly loyal, and
peasant allies, who dwelled in the surrounding region and dropped
their weapons at the first sign of adversity in battle. A basic pattern
from the eighth century remained intact (see Figure 7).

Figure 6 displays the military forces the Governor of Hitachi,
Minamoto no Yorinobu, had at his disposal to punish Taira no Tadatsune. The troop strength of Yorinobu was so great that Tadatsune submitted to the Governor without a fight, and the prowess of
Yorinobu so impressed Tadatsune that the bandit offered a signed
pledge of loyalty (*myōbu*) to Yorinobu and became his follower.

Although it is difficult to be certain, it is likely that fighting units in other provinces comprised the same elements. An incident from the 4th month of 1019 provides an opportunity to analyze military forces in the countryside. At this time foreign invaders known as the Toi people (really the Jurchens, a tribe from Manchuria) raided northern Kyushu. The incursion lasted for about one week, and the military forces used by the Japanese originated entirely in northern Kyushu. According to a record submitted by the main government outpost at Dazaifu, on the 7th of the 4th month, about 3,000 foreign invaders pillaged Iki and killed the Governor.[80] On the 8th, the invaders landed on Noko Island in Hakata Bay, and were engaged in fierce fighting by troops led by former officials and soldiers (*kenjō*) of Dazaifu. On the 9th, the foreigners tried to burn the Japanese defense post near Dazaifu, but shield-bearing Japanese foot soldiers forced them to retreat after a brief landing. On the 10th and 11th, a storm halted battle. On the 12th, a sea battle took place; records show that the Vice-Governor of Dazaifu provided 10 boats, while ex-officials and wealthy residents of the area launched nearly 30. On the 13th, the Jurchens moved on to Hizen, where the previous Vice-Governor led troops of the district (not the province) and forced the aggressors to retreat to the continent. An epidemic broke out as the battles ended, and the Court received word of considerable agricultural disruption.

One historian has analyzed the local units which engaged the foreign invaders and found a pattern similar to the one outlined in Figure 6.[81] The forces of Dazaifu consisted of (1) those directly under the command of the Vice-Governor, such as the "weapons-bearers" (*kenjō*) mandated in the Taihō Codes, and (2) ex-officials and residents of northern Kyushu who were called "generals" (*shō-gun*) and belonged to military houses.

Notable among the ex-officials and local strongmen of northern Kyushu was Ōkura Tanemochi, grandson of Haruzane who had fought against Fujiwara Sumitomo. Tanemochi was in his seventies when he engaged in battle with the Jurchens, but the Court rewarded him with an appointment to the governorship of Iki for his efforts. The soldiers provided by Tanemochi and other ex-officials and strongmen were the main body of troops used to repel the invaders. It is interesting to note that Tanemochi was a follower of Fujiwara no Sanesuke; the opportunity for rewards and liaisons with Heian aristocrats must have been the driving motive for men like Tanemochi. As Fujiwara no Sanesuke wrote in his diary: "If there are no prizes, in future incidents there will be no way to promote fighting men (*shi*)."[82]

THE REBELLION OF TAIRA NO TADATSUNE AND REFORM OF THE SYSTEM OF 900–1050

Despite his chastisement in the early eleventh century by Governor Minamoto no Yorinobu, Taira no Tadatsune continued to be a troublemaker. A record of 1046 describes Tadatsune's behavior in 1027:

> . . . the lawless rat bespread himself over the Eastern capital, looked down upon the governors of the Bandō, and displayed his power. He treated the tax-paying forced laborers cruelly and possesseda barbaric heart of evil intentions. He overturned Court strictures and caused taxes to suffer; he . . . neglected state orders, and resisted messengers carrying imperial edicts. . . .[83]

Late in 1027, the leading aristocrat at Court, Fujiwara no Michinaga, died; Tadatsune used the opportunity created by the transition in leadership in the capital to rebel in his home base in Kazusa and Shimōsa provinces.[84] Sometime in the first half of 1028, Tadatsune attacked the provincial headquarters of nearby Awa, burning the Governor to death. Tadatsune had managed to get by with his earlier tax evasion and abuse of laborers, but the Court could not ignore an open attack on a provincial headquarters. Such actions demanded a response and also provided a good opportunity for warriors to advance their careers. Competition for leading roles was keen.

Aristocrats in Heian first discussed the punishment of Tadatsune on the 5th day of the 6th month of 1028.[85] On the 21st of the same month, courtiers suggested 4 candidates to head the expedition against Tadatsune: Minamoto no Yorinobu, Taira no Masasuke, Taira no Naokata, and Nakahara Narimichi (a legal expert in the Investigators' Office). Finally the government decided to make Naokata the leader with Narimichi second-in-command. According to recent research, Yorinobu, who had already dealt with Tadatsune on the provincial level, had originally been the top candidate. However, Naokata and his father Koretoki used their standing as vassals of Michinaga and Naokata's position as a follower of the new leader at Court (Fujiwara no Yorimichi) to obtain the appointment.

Naokata and Koretoki had two reasons for pressuring the Court on Naokata's appointment, one based on a political career and the other on a family feud. First, Naokata had a base in the Kanto provinces of Sagami and Izu, and a victory over Tadatsune could only increase Naokata's power in the region. Second, Naokata and Tadatsune belonged to warring factions of the Taira family.[86] The revolt of Taira no Tadatsune takes on a different shade: It is no longer just a question of Tadatsune's rebellion against the state, but really a personal, intraspecific battle between Naokata and Tadatsune for dominance within the Taira family. Tadatsune would have to fight for his life.

Early in the 7th month of 1028, Naokata and Narimichi made preparations for the expedition. Narimichi, a legal expert and not a military man, resisted going on the expedition by making outrageous requests of the Court. On the 10th of the 7th month, the Minister of the Right and influential aristocrat, Fujiwara no Sanesuke, bargained him down from 9 to 3 conditions and began the process of having Court diviners forecast a propitious day for the expedition. After much debate, the Court decided that the army would depart on the 5th day of the 8th month in 1028; during the 2-week debate, Sanesuke worried that "weeks and months would pass by" and "the bandits would come up with a plot."[87]

As the expedition delayed, Tadatsune's fury against the provincial government grew worse. A messenger from Kazusa reported on conditions in the Kanto:

> The people of the province more and more refuse to listen to the provincial office. The office is under Tadatsune's control, and the Governor's life or death rests with his [Tadatsune's] heart. Disorder does not stop day after day. Tadatsune's followers have poured into the offices and have tied up the Governor's followers.[88]

Tadatsune directed his ire against the Kazusa provincial headquarters, and specifically against the Governor. He may well have been leading local resistance to provincial tax-farmers, as Masakado had done 80 years earlier. It is interesting to note that, on the 23rd, Sanesuke ordered Naokata to give the Governor's family an escort in their trek back to the capital because the people of Kazusa would not.[89]

At the same time, Tadatsune was careful not to antagonize directly the Court and leading policymakers like Sanesuke. Thus Tadatsune allowed the Vice-Governor's horse groom free passage back to the capital to deliver a present of two horses to Sanesuke. Tadatsune hoped the government would see that his "insurrection" was in fact a protest against excess taxation and not a full-scale revolt against the Court.

Incidents immediately preceding the departure of the expedition emphasize Tadatsune's desire to escape the punishment of the Court. Early in the 8th month of 1028, rumors flew around the capital that followers of Tadatsune were transmitting messages from their chief to the Investigators, to the all-powerful Regent (Fujiwara no Yorimichi), and to Tadatsune's patron in the capital, the Inner Minister Fujiwara no Norimichi, to halt the expedition. It is clear that, like Masakado, Tadatsune was trying to use his personal connections and political influence to curry favor with the Court and stop the punitive campaign. Later in the 8th month, Tadatsune relayed that, if anything came of his machinations, he would be waiting for a reply at Mt. Ishimi in Kazusa.[90]

The army to punish Tadatsune marched as planned on the 5th day of the 8th month amidst onlookers anxious to catch a glimpse of the 200 or so soldiers Naokata led. On the 16th, Narimichi reported from Mino province that his mother was ill and that he wished to be released from his obligation. Sanesuke believed that the real reason for Narimichi's lack of enthusiasm was bad relations with the warrior commander Naokata. The Regent replied that Narimichi's mother was in good health and that the expedition should continue.

Because there is no source comparable to *The Tale of Masakado* for this rebellion, there is no way of knowing what the battles between Tadatsune and Naokata were really like, but there is reason to suspect that all did not go well for Naokata. In the 2nd month of 1029, the Court issued another search-and-destroy order to provincial headquarters throughout eastern Honshu. Later in the month, Naokata's father, Koretoki, who had helped convince the Court to appoint his son to lead the expedition against Tadatsune, left Kyoto for Kazusa to assume the governorship and lend a hand in the fighting. Yet in the 6th month, a report from the Kanto said that Tadatsune's behavior had become more violent; the Court searched Tadatsune's follower's house in Kyoto, began to discuss replacing Naokata, and issued another order to the provinces to destroy Tadatsune.

There seems to have been little progress against Tadatsune in 1029. In the 12th month, aristocrats discussed a report from Naokata and Koretoki, and as a result fired Nakahara Narimichi. The year 1030 saw no improvement, because, in the 3rd month of that year, Tadatsune attacked the new Governor of Awa and forced him to flee to the capital. Two days after the escaping Governor reached Heian, the Court appointed the warrior Taira no Masasuke to be the new Governor of Awa. As a condition of his appointment Masasuke demanded that every province contribute 20 ships and 500 *koku* of grain to crush Tadatsune.[91] According to Fujiwara no Sanesuke, "It is hard to ascertain whether or not a province has even 100 *koku;* the provinces with no grain would be difficult to tax."[92] Masasuke never arrived in the Kanto, as he fell to fighting in Ise with an archenemy within the Taira family.

On the 14th of the 5th month in 1030, Naokata made another request to tax the provinces. The Court refused because the information network of Sanesuke and others told them that Tadatsune had retreated to Mt. Ishimi with only a few soldiers. Six days later, the Court also learned that Tadatsune had become a Buddhist monk, a clear sign that he wished to fight no more. On the 23rd of the 6th month, the Court talked over another report from Naokata, Koretoki, and the Governor of Musashi. The report claimed that Naokata still did not know where Tadatsune was hiding, but Sanesuke rebuffed the assertion by pointing out that Tadatsune had been in contact with Naokata through a messenger. Even though Tadatsune had expressed a willingness to lay down arms, Naokata apparently preferred to keep on fighting until Tadatsune was dead. Sanesuke and others began to fear that Naokata was pillaging the Kanto to satisfy his desire for wealth and revenge. Early in the 7th month of 1030, the Court recalled Naokata.

In the 9th month, courtiers replaced Naokata with Minamoto no Yorinobu. By naming Yorinobu, they ensured that Tadatsune, who had surrendered to Yorinobu and become his vassal almost 20 years earlier when Yorinobu was Governor of Hitachi, would give in without a further fight. To make doubly certain, Yorinobu took one of Tadatsune's sons, a priest, with him. In the 4th month of 1031, a report reached the Court that Tadatsune, two of his sons, and three of his followers had surrendered. As the party returned to Heian, however, Tadatsune fell ill and died on the journey. On the 16th day of the 6th month of 1031, Yorinobu entered the capital with Tadatsune's head. Ten days later, the Court discussed the problem of Tadatsune's remaining sons, who were still at large; after numerous aristocrats aired opinions, they agreed to grant amnesty rather than risk greater destruction to the Kanto.

In many respects the revolt of Taira no Tadatsune is similar to Masakado's rebellion. Like previous violence in the Kanto, Tadatsune caused trouble by attacking and burning the Court's island of authority in the countryside, the provincial headquarters. Also like Masakado's uprising, the immediate cause for Tadatsune's insurrection was a quarrel over taxation, arising from economic decline and hardship. But when the Court sent Tadatsune's kinsman, Naokata, to smite him, the conflict took on the character of an intraspecific battle between two warriors seeking to establish their dominance within the Kanto Taira. Tadatsune tried to use his influence in the capital to halt the expedition sent to destroy him, and was somewhat successful; the Court vacillated in the face of rebellion. Finally, the Court utilized the old policy of setting one local strongman to catch another, as it had for Masakado. It is also likely that the troops sent to fight Tadatsune were provincial soldiers.[93] The system first promulgated in 901 for identifying and capturing criminals worked for the rebellion of Tadatsune as it had so many times previously.

There are two important effects of Tadatsune's revolt. First, Minamoto no Yorinobu, one-time Governor of Hitachi and victor over Tadatsune, gained prestige and political leverage which he used to build a base in the Kanto. At first Yorinobu pressed for appointment to the lucrative governorship of Tamba near the capital; in addition to a direct request, he made repeated presents to Sanesuke to further his chances. Later in 1031, however, Yorinobu changed his mind and asked for the governorship of Mino, allegedly because his mother's grave was there. As Yorinobu's messenger to Sanesuke put it, the real reason was that "[m]any men of the Bandō follow him, and, in making the journey [between the capital and the Kanto], Mino is somewhat more convenient."[94]

Yorinobu and the Minamoto, not Naokata and the Taira, built a base in the Kanto. Naokata was so impressed with Yorinobu's victory over Tadatsune that he took Yorinobu's son Yoriyoshi as his son-in-law and gave him Naokata's residence in Kamakura. Tadatsune's offspring also swore loyalty to Yorinobu after their defeat and followed Yorinobu's son and grandson into battle. The Court's use of Yorinobu to secure the submission of Tadatsune marks a shift in policy from the use of enemies to the use of a rebel's lord to obtain his surrender.[95]

The second and more significant effect of Tadatsune's revolt was the destruction it caused.[96] As in the rebellion of Masakado, the combatants relied on scorched-earth tactics, resulting in unprecedented pillage. The following passages reveal the extent of the damage:

1031 — 3rd month, 1st day:
. . . Sanesuke replied: "Because of the punishment of Tadatsune, the destruction in Shimōsa is especially severe. . . .
Awa, Kazusa, and Shimōsa have become devastated provinces."[97]

1031 — 6th month, 27th day:
. . . The Governor of Shimōsa, Tameyori, said: . . . "While we carried out the punishment of Tadatsune, people and things both were exhausted. It will be difficult to recover quickly. . . ."
. . . He spoke of the application of three men to be the Governor of Sagami. . . . In particular this province has performed military duties for a long time. Exhaustion is especially severe.[98]

1034 — 10th month, 24th day:
. . . The Governor of Kazusa, Tatsushige, came and said: "Since the smiting of Tadatsune, there has been no one who dares to resist taxation in the Bandō. But, after having carried out the punishment, the

destruction is great. Amidst the havoc, this province was the residence of Tadatsune. Because of this, . . . tax items were collected for three years by the officer Naokata and the soldiers of the province (*shokoku no heishi*). Not one speck of dust remains.

To wit, the former Governor [of Kazusa], Koretoki no Ason, brought on his person a copy of the tax-collection order and showed it to me. 'Total fields farmed in this province — altogether 18 *chō* plus [about 54 acres or about 22 hectares].' The signature of the previous Governor was clear. No one dares to doubt this figure. The basic fields [noted in maps] of this province are more than 22,980 *chō*, it is said. Even though there was great destruction during the revolt of Masakado, it was not yet as bad as this time.

But in the year when Tatsushige arrived at his post, there were more than 50 *chō*. In the next year and years thereafter, more has been cultivated. This year the survey of fields shows more than 1,200 *chō*. Many of the people who scattered to other provinces have returned. This is only because we have obeyed the letter of the law, and until now have not collected even one bundle of tax. Gradually we are recovering.[99]

These excerpts point out the severity of the destruction resulting from Tadatsune's rebellion. The devastation affected not just Kazusa, Shimōsa, and Awa provinces, but also reached the more distant Sagami and Hitachi provinces, where the Court granted 2-year tax relief to the peasantry.[100] In Kazusa, the home of Tadatsune, the disaster was so complete that, at one time during the revolt, farmers cultivated only 18 of nearly 23,000 *chō*, less than 0.1 percent of all arable land in the province (1 *chō* = 3 acres). The new Governor Tatsushige boasted that in 1034 peasants had returned and tilled 1,200 *chō*, still only 5 percent of arable land in the province.

Destruction of such magnitude set economic growth back several generations in the Kanto region. The years of Tadatsune's revolt were also a period of drought and disease, twin killers that were especially harmful to western Japan.[101] Smallpox, with a long history in Japan, was rampant, striking harsh blows in 993–995, 1020, and 1036. Measles entered Japan for the first time in 998, and returned in 1025. Enteric diseases also claimed their share of victims in 1016, 1025, and 1027. An unknown infection played havoc with the populace in 1030 and 1044, and drought was a constant threat to the harvest, being especially noted in 1035 and 1043–1047.

While all these epidemics had disastrous results for Japan, the outbreaks dating from 1025–1030, the era of Tadatsune's revolt, seem to have been especially harsh.[102] Records indicate that at least two killer diseases, measles and dysentery, afflicted Japan in 1025. Fujiwara no Sanesuke wrote in his diary for the 3rd month of 1025 that pestilence was rife in the northern Kanto on the eve of Tadatsune's upheaval; 7 district magistrates (half the total) had died of the disease.[103] Drought followed in the 7th month, along with Japan's second encounter with measles. Sanesuke described the roads of the capital as being filled with the sick, and *A Tale of Flowering Fortunes*, a history of the Fujiwara family, stated that the outbreak "was claiming victims of every class."[104] The plague lasted through summer and fall of 1025. It is likely that measles returned in 1026, since four orders dated the 13th day of the 5th month commanded nearly every province in the country to offer prayers to eliminate epidemics.[105] In 1027, an enteric disease was present, and in 1030, while Tadatsune rebelled in the Kanto, an unknown but severe epidemic killed many throughout Japan. The Court was particularly concerned about the adverse effects on agriculture.[106] Sanesuke was worried about an unlucky triple conjunction of heavenly bodies, and ordered his subordinate to search for precedents in the Tempyō era (729–749), another time of harsh epidemics. He wrote in 1029: "I believe in my heart that the decline of the realm is especially severe; we can only try to be frugal and await an answer from heaven!"[107]

The epidemics and droughts of the late tenth and first half of the eleventh centuries, in combination with Tadatsune's revolt, had two disastrous effects on Japan. First, both killed people in great numbers, especially adults. Reports of the smallpox outbreaks of 993–995, 998, and 1020 all show evidence of killing adults in the prime of their lives. For the epidemic of measles in 1025, a courtier wrote that "recently men and women, both clerics and lay people, throughout the empire have suffered from measles, regardless of age."[108] Second, to use William McNeill's terminology, both microparasites (plagues) and macroparasites (war) dealt severe blows to agriculture. The effects of Tadatsune's rebellion upon farming in the Kanto have already been catalogued; disease had equally disastrous results in western and central Japan:

> Mino province: . . . Manju 1/10/23 (1024): . . . The aforementioned estate has long been in the temple's domain. . . . [L]ast year when a great epidemic struck, the estate officials and residents all died. The lands of the estate greatly went out of cultivation. . . . [109]

> Ōmi province, some time between 1000 and 1034: . . . But epidemics are prevalent and the residents die.[110]

There can be little doubt that, as one scholar argues, the devastation of farmland in the period between 990 and 1040 was "terrible."[111]

The ravages of these two Horsemen of the Apocalypse, disease and war, necessitated a reform of local government and tax structure.[112] Two of the reforms had effects on the military system of the tenth and eleventh centuries. First, the Court inaugurated a new system of villages. The new district was smaller than that of the seventh and eighth centuries and new terms for local government, such as *ho* and *in* appeared; warriors helped to found many of the new settlements.

Second, in 1045 the government issued a permit recognizing all estates (*shōen*) started before the term of the previous governor. Estates were farms owned by wealthy Court aristocrats or religious institutions, and paid most of their revenue to the owner rather than the state. Before 1045, the Court greatly restricted the formation of new estates, and, since these enterprises were difficult to finance and operate, they constituted only a small percentage of farmland throughout Japan. Whereas previous laws had restricted the growth of estates, the 1045 order was a boon to those desiring to open new fields.[113] As one historian has noted, the 1045 law allowing hitherto prohibited agricultural enterprises was unique, and it was no accident that the state issued the authorization immediately after a period of disease and drought. Taken together, the reforms of local government and landholding supported the reopening of land, which altered the economy and portended changes throughout society, including the military.

CONCLUSION

Japan's military system of the middle Heian era, from the end of the rebellions of Masakado and Sumitomo in 942 until 1050, had two pillars: the forces of the aristocracy in the capital and the soldiers of the provincial headquarters in the countryside. In Heian, forces were composed of those belonging to distinct offices, such as the Imperial Guards or the Investigators' Office, and those who attended civil aristocrats like Michinaga or Sanesuke, including the great military aristocrats of whom the Taira and the Minamoto are the best known. Yet this catalogue of capital armies is merely for analytical purposes, since in reality public and private loyalties were mixed.

The Imperial Guards and the Investigators were small and routinely conducted searches and collected overdue taxes. These men came from minor families who had their bases in the capital region. Soldiers who accompanied the great aristocrats were probably more numerous, but many also served in the government, and the organization of these aristocratic guards followed the Taihō model. Most were mounted fighters.

The greatest source of capital forces was the military aristocrat, who belonged to an hereditary warrior house. The most famous houses were the Taira and the Minamoto, but several other lineages also practiced the "way of the horse and the bow." The military aristocrat usually swore loyalty to a powerful civil leader like Michinaga, and received rewards such as official position or rank for their services. Many military aristocrats became provincial governors, thereby acquiring wealth and valuable political experience.

The rural military was composed of 4 parts, commanded by the governor and coordinated by the provincial headquarters. (1) Every governor surrounded himself with personal retainers, usually ex-officeholders who kept the provincials in line. (2) The provincial headquarters itself was a military center, where artisans manufactured weapons for officials to carry. Many minor officials joined the governor's army, and some had once been district magistrates or Strong Fellows. (3) Every province contained soldiers of the province, local men who had long association with the governor's office, through guard duty, official hunts, or service in shrine ceremonies. The governor also utilized the posts of overseer, arrest officer, and search-and-destroy commanders to forge alliances with soldiers of the province. Provinces kept registers of all families with a military background, as soldiers of the province were members of military houses just like warriors of the capital. (4) The most important element in the rural military was the local strongman who remained independent of the governor and the provincial headquarters. These strongmen possessed great wealth, built ties to the central aristocracy, maintained rivalries, and intermarried amongst themselves.

An example of the military of the era 942–1050 in action is the insurrection of Taira no Tadatsune, in the Kanto 1028–1031. It began as a resistance to taxation. After pillaging the provincial headquarters at Awa and Kazusa, Tadatsune fought a long war of attrition against his lifelong enemy, Taira no Naokata, the warrior chosen to head the Court's expedition of chastisement. Eventually Minamoto no Yorinobu, who had convinced Tadatsune to become his vassal around 1016, replaced Naokata, and used his prior relationship with Tadatsune to compel submission. Yorinobu obtained a governorship for his efforts and gained a following in the Kanto region. The most important result of Tadatsune's revolt was the destruction it caused. Coming in a time of severe epidemic outbreaks and drought, the revolt took 4 tragic years of fruitless fighting. The disaster opened the way for a reform of local government and taxation, and a modification in the military system forged in 901.

Advocates of the Western-analogue theory believe that the era from 900 to 1050 was a period when Japan lacked effective political or military institutions, analogous to the time when barbarians destroyed the Western Roman Empire in European history. The samurai, reason these historians, must have had a short history, because they appeared only after these turbulent conditions forced them to take arms. The public institutions of the Taihō Codes could never have produced a private political arrangement such as feudalism.

But the middle Heian epoch had its own customary military system in the capital (aristocratic armies) and countryside (the provincial headquarters). These forces were not too different from their Chinese-style predecessors; the Taihō Codes mandated both followers for the great aristocrats and a role for the provincial headquarters in the eighth century. Such a similarity was no accident, because the military system of 900–1050, the "missing link" between the era of the Taihō Codes and the age of the samurai, grew out of Taihō institutions, just as assuredly as did the samurai himself.

chapter six
Warriors and Land, 1050–1150

A houseman [a warrior serving the military government in Kamakura,
1185–1333] is defined as a person who has been a land-clearance lord from
long ago. . . . A land-clearance lord is defined as one who holds
ancestral private lands.
— A legal guidebook of the early fourteenth century

Yet the official of Uzura [Minamoto no Kunifusa, a warrior] assembled force by
himself, and without fear of imperial restrictions, tore out boundary stakes . . . ,
violated cultivators, and probably planned to kill them. . . . During this period,
people's dwellings have disappeared and land has greatly gone to waste.
— from Mino province in 1117

Historians have long considered land to be a fundamental part of
the medieval warrior's heritage, along with lineage and the right to
practice the martial arts. An early-fourteenth-century legal handbook defined many military men as "land-clearance lords," who
possessed ancestral fields developed centuries earlier. Based upon
this definition, Western-analogue theorists have posited that the
period from 1050 to 1200 was Japan's "age of widespread land clearance," led by a new class of fighting men destined to seize political
power and establish feudalism.

But legal sources of the early fourteenth century do not reveal
when and how soldiers acquired their holdings. Warriors may have
assembled the capital and labor necessary to lead Japan's "age of
widespread land clearance" in the eleventh and twelfth centuries;
they also may have inherited fields opened by their forebears of the
tenth century or even earlier. Or they may have been like Kunifusa
in Mino and obtained their parcels by force and forgery.

Examination of the record for the era 1050 to 1200 suggests that the connection between fighters and the expansion of arable land was tenuous at best. Many, perhaps most, leaders of land clearance were not even warriors, and, when military men did take up farming, a large number chose to use their skills to terrorize cultivators and owners into handing over established crops and fields. Even in instances where warriors attempted to open new parcels themselves, yields may have been no higher than in 800; the few technological improvements in the late eleventh and the twelfth centuries were not sufficient to guarantee that most fields stayed productive for long.

Much evidence indicates that people who cleared fields in the late eleventh and twelfth centuries were really re-opening previously abandoned parcels. Before the so-called "age of widespread land clearance," that is, between 990 and 1050, the revolt of Tadatsune in the Kanto and cycles of unusually harsh epidemics and droughts in western and central Japan caused many cultivators to die or flee from their lands. As a result, between 1050 and 1200 not much new farmland was created out of virgin territory; but there was rejuvenation of fields abandoned by their former cultivators. The period from 1050 to 1200 is more appropriately called the "age of the widespread re-opening of abandoned lands."

During the middle and late eleventh century, just as farmers were beginning to take up their hoes and spades once again, warriors engaged in two wars in northeastern Honshu. In the Former Nine Years' War (1051–1062), the Court authorized Governor Minamoto no Yoriyoshi to punish the Abe family, tax-evaders of "barbarian" lineage, in accordance with the precedent of 901. Yoriyoshi's son Yoshiie also led troops in the Latter Three Years' War (1083–1087), and became a hero for his individualistic efforts in battle, indicating that the samurai style of ritualized, one-on-one combat had at last become prominent.

Reforms in provincial administration and land tenure modified the rural military system of the tenth and early eleventh centuries. By 1100, most governors, who had previously commanded provincial soldiers, were either unwilling or unable to lead local armies; in 1135, when pirates hampered shipping along the Inland Sea, the Court debated whether instead to have proprietors of estates raise soldiers or to employ Japan's leading military aristocrat to suppress the brigands. The government finally designated Taira no Tadamori to do the job, a choice that fueled the struggle among military nobles for the privilege of being "chief of all warriors."

THE LATE HEIAN ERA: AN OVERVIEW

Many scholars consider the period from 1050 to 1200 the starting point for the rise of the warrior (*bushi*). They believe this was the time when the wealth (tax and rent income from land) of fighting men increased, and a dramatic jump in productivity afforded the excess of goods necessary for the formation of a new class of feudal lords. *The Novice's Guide to Legal Judgments* (*Sata miren sho*), a judicial handbook of the early fourteenth century, contains two articles that portray most warriors of the Kamakura age as creators of farmland:

> Point: A houseman [a vassal of the Kamakura Shogunate] is defined as a person who has been a land-clearance lord [*kaihotsu ryōshu*] from long ago. . . .
> A land clearance lord is defined as one who holds ancestral private lands [*kompon shiryō*]. These lands are also called ancestral holdings [*honryō*].
>
> Point: An ancestral holding [*honryō*] means tenure of wet and/or dry fields as a land-clearance lord [*kaihotsu ryōshu*].[1]

Many have interpreted these two articles as evidence that the possession of land was an essential attribute of a warrior's line long before the fourteenth century, and that the way fighters acquired their holdings was through the opening of new parcels.

Based upon these two articles plus other evidence, many Japanese and Western proponents of the Western-analogue theory have asserted that the period from 1050 to 1200, which saw the establishment of a new system of land tenure (the *shōen-kokugaryō* system), was an era of widespread land clearance (*dai kaikon jidai*) led by a new type of military man.[2] Warriors became a wealthy, landowning class for the first time. The standard interpretation gives local warriors of the late eleventh and twelfth centuries the vague title of "country lords" (*zaichi ryōshu*), the newly ascendant leaders of feudalism. Conventionally, scholars believe these warriors to have possessed economic resources greater than "private proprietors" (*shiei den ryōshu*) like Taira no Masakado or Tadatsune, and far superior to local strongmen (district magistrates) of the eighth century. Many go on to assert that the new "country lords" organized their followers into loyal bands (*bushi dan*), which, unlike the peasant soldiers of Masakado, did not flee battle at the first sign of defeat.[3]

It is tempting to agree with the conventional view that the "rise of the warrior" began in the late eleventh century and coincided with an agricultural revolution. The middle and late eleventh century saw the first unmistakable signs of the individualistic fighting style of the Japanese soldier, although the samurai's weapons had appeared much earlier. The Taira and Minamoto each took turns in claiming a share of political power in the twelfth century, and surely there must have been an economic underpinning for their control.

Yet it is helpful to remember that Japan had supported martial specialists and systems of armament, conscription, and deployment since about A.D. 500. Military men had earned incomes long before 1050; district magistrates maintained households with holdings of land, grain, livestock, and other items in the 700s and 800s. Later, the Court had provided offices (such as provincial governorships) with tax-collecting privileges to worthy fighters to support their retinues. A major component of these earlier forces had been the mounted soldier, and armies and navies had defended Japan from invasion from the mainland.

Furthermore, the land-clearance articles from the early-fourteenth-century handbook may be subject to more than one interpretation. The legal source defines land-clearance lords as holding ancestral lands, which may have been brought into cultivation at any time. The title could imply a duty to open and maintain fields in production.

Finally, the Western-analogue theory implies a questionable view of premodern Japanese social structure, seeing horizontal class relations as all-important. Warriors are presumed to have been conscious of a common class economic interest which drove them to open lands and form the new mode of production for a feudal age. This preconception of medieval social structure probably does not even fit Western Europe very well, much less traditional Japan where vertical ties between people of different classes usually predominated.[4]

Historians make assumptions about the new-found wealth of twelfth-century warriors from both macroeconomic and microeconomic data. From the macroeconomic perspective, the evidence for such an interpretation rests on 3 points. (1) Many scholars can trace the lineages of most warrior houses of the medieval period (1185–1600) only back to the late eleventh century, which suggests a major break with earlier times. (2) The eleventh and twelfth centuries saw an unprecedented growth in the creation of new estates (*shōen*), the form of agricultural enterprise that sprang up after the devastation of the era 990–1050. (3) Records indicate that, after 1050, the Court recognized numerous new units of village administration which replaced the system first established by the Taihō Codes of 702.

The first argument relies heavily on martial genealogies, a weak reed at best.[5] As mentioned in the discussions of Masakado (Chapter 4) and Koremoto (Chapter 5), the problem with genealogies from after 1200 is that they treat the Heian family as a patrilineal unit when in fact it may not have been. One social scientist has proven that women were powerful and adoption of heirs was prevalent in Japanese society before 1200; another scholar has argued for a system of bilateral kinship.[6] The prevalence of bilateral kinship relations would mean that postdated, patrilineal genealogies do not reflect reality. For example, if a military family of a district magistrate in the Kanto adopted a Taira man into their family to continue the line, a patrilineal genealogy would show only the Taira man as head of the family; genealogists would have omitted the adopting family, native to the Kanto and with its own military credentials. In the words of one historian, genealogies do not provide conclusive evidence for the view that a new class of warrior families had their origins in the eleventh century.[7]

The second argument relies on the widespread creation of estates that commenced in the middle of the eleventh century and continued intermittently for 250 years.[8] An estate was formed when a local leader (such as a warrior or monk) obtained land, either through clearance, purchase, or some other means, and petitioned the Court to give the land immunity from taxation and official entry. A patron at Court ensured the status of the estate, and received a portion of the estate's produce for his or her protective services.[9] The warrior could use the remaining income from the land to pay his expenses, such as feeding and supplying troops and raising horses.

Most estates mentioned in the sources came into existence in the late eleventh and twelfth centuries. In the Kanto region, the home of the Japanese warrior, only 10 of 50 known estates predated 1050, and only 2 continued uninterrupted from 800 to 1200.[10] One scholar has noted that founders created numerous estates during the reign of the Retired Emperor Toba (1129–1156).[11] (Retired Emperors became the chief powerholders at Court in 1086). It has been assumed that warriors cleared new lands that they then commended to some powerful patron, such as the Fujiwara Regent's house or the Retired Emperor, who could protect the land from taxation by the provincial office.

But there are at least two problems with equating the formation of estates with a rise in warrior income through the expansion of arable land. First, it is not always clear that warriors were the agents of land clearance. Most Japanese historians jump to the conclusion that those persons clearing new lands were "country lords" (*zaichi ryōshu*, in opposition to the absentee lords in the capital in Heian, *zaikyō ryōshu*). The term *country lords* is supposed to mean warriors (*bushi*). Yet many different persons were responsible for creating new estates between 1050 and 1200, including Buddhist monks.[12] If one posits the predominance of vertical connections within institutions over horizontal class relations, a supposition supported by evidence from this and other eras of Japanese history, then it makes sense that temples and shrines would have chosen their own kind, rather than military men, to clear land and create estates. An agricultural historian has found that most local warriors did not even own farming tools.[13]

Second, the creation of new estates did not necessarily mean an increase in land under cultivation. Scholars once thought the area of Japan covered by estates was great, and that estates were composed entirely of arable land; recently these views have been reassessed. One historian has pointed out that temples and aristocrats held about 70 percent of the lands of tiny Noto province on the Sea of Japan in the early 1200s; Wakasa province also contained about the same proportion of land held in estates.[14] But Hitachi and Shinano provinces in eastern Honshu displayed an equal ratio of estates and land administered by the province (*kokuga ryō, kōryō*), and Sagami and Musashi may have possessed 4 times more *kokuga ryō* than estates.[15] John Hall has argued that Bizen, Iwami, and Awaji all had high percentages of provincially administered domain.[16] Thus estates may not have been so dominant as once assumed; a common estimate of the proportion of total land held in estates in Japan is 40 percent, which supports a picture of continued vitality for the provincial headquarters and the Court.

Founders created many estates at the expense of lands administered by provincial headquarters. Twelfth- and thirteenth-century records provide abundant evidence of disputes between estate lords and provincial officials over whether a parcel of land belonged to the *shōen* or *kokuga ryō* domain. One historian has argued that the process of estate formation occurred when "local strongmen (*chihō gōzoku*) conspired with Court aristocrats, separated a region supposed to belong to the provincial governor originally, and made it into land they [the local strongmen and Court aristocrats] controlled by themselves."[17] Others also emphasize that estate lands increased at the expense of provincially supervised fields.[18] There was little or no increase in the total land under cultivation, only a shift in management and profits from provincial parcels to estates, which were under the control of individual aristocrats or religious institutions.

Finally, even if estates were more widespread than provincially administered lands in the twelfth century, most specialists acknowledge that provincial lands were more important to warriors.[19] One has analyzed the transformation in the provincial headquarters that took place during the era 700 to 1200 and pointed out that several important martial families obtained their lands, status, and power from the provincial administration rather than from estates.[20] He lists such famous *bushi* families as the Chiba, Hatakeyama, Miura, Chichibu, Kawagoe, Oyama, Yuki, Kusano, and Ōuchi as holding important positions in the provincial headquarters. Of course, a warrior could hold lands in both sectors of the *shōen-kokugaryō* system. Yet the emphasis on the crucial role of the provincial headquarters confirms the interpretation presented in this book.

Another scholar presents the third argument implying new-found agricultural wealth for fighting men by documenting the formation of many new villages in the late eleventh century.[21] As noted briefly in Chapter 5, the Court created a novel system of village administration which subdivided or reduced in size the district of the Taihō Codes of 702, while additional names for rural settlements, such as *ho, beppu,* and *in,* appeared. Presumably, the creation of new villages indicates population growth in the countryside and a dramatic improvement in the rural economy over which the warrior presided. In addition, the government announced a new law on estate formation in 1045 which, unlike previous laws, did not attempt to stop the creation of new estates, but legalized and encouraged the development of uncultivated lands.

There is, however, a problem in this third argument as well. As indicated in Chapter 5, the creation of new settlements and estates followed a period of unprecedented destruction. In the Kanto, the revolt of Taira no Tadatsune caused sizable tracts of farmland to go out of cultivation; armies devastated almost all of Kazusa province. Moreover, the years 990–1045 saw repeated attacks of killer epidemics, including a deadly combination of smallpox and measles.[22] As demonstrated in Chapter 5, the epidemics were widespread and killed adults; as late as 1020 smallpox entered Japan from the continent and afflicted all those in the capital aged 28 and below, a sure sign that the disease was not yet endemic. Evidence shows that peasants in central and western Japan perished or fled from their lands. Finally, an unparalleled spate of drought from 1043–1047 motivated the Court to promulgate a law in 1045 promoting the opening of new fields as estates.

Epidemics and natural disasters did not end in the eleventh century. In 1108, Mt. Azama erupted, spewing volcanic ash widely over the Kanto; the province of Kōzuke suffered especially great damage. Archeologists who have discovered paddies buried underneath a thick layer of lava have dated the site at the early twelfth century.[23] A record from Mino province indicates that drought

211

and disease led to death and land abandonment among the cultivating class as late as 1133.[24] Drought reduced yields in 1063,
1065–1067, 1077, 1082, and 1107.

One Japanese historian has suggested a link between natural
and man-made disasters and the formation of new estates.[25] In the
tenth and first half of the eleventh centuries, drought, cold, epidemics, and wars drove peasants from lands previously administered by the provincial headquarters. Because these fields had
paid taxes to the Court, revenues to aristocrats decreased. Once
the cause for land abandonment, such as drought or warfare, had
abated, peasants and local strongmen were able gradually to bring
some fields back into production. But, instead of the province
administering the reopened fields, local inhabitants commended
their newly reopened parcels to aristocrats, supplementing the
courtier's decreased revenues. If this thesis is true, then the establishment of new estates did not mean an increase in cultivated taxable land, but quite the opposite.

One is therefore forced to ask whether the expansion of farmland which began around 1050 added new fields, or just replaced
parcels that had gone out of cultivation in the previous half century. This question is difficult to answer, primarily because the
early and mid-eleventh century is so poorly documented.[26] One is
tempted to rely on the opinion of Japanese experts, but they do
not speak with one voice. The scholar who discovered the reform
of village administration in the eleventh century believes that
lands under the plow before 1050 went totally out of cultivation,
and that peasants brought virgin lands into cultivation; he argues
that the cause of the shift in farming was the resistance of peasants
to government tax collectors.[27] A Kyoto University historian has
also implied that the expansion of arable land that took place after
1050 was accomplished in areas never cropped before, but he
omits any reference to land that was devastated.[28] A specialist in
military affairs from Tokyo University seems to believe the land
clearance that occurred after 1050 included both virgin territory
and parcels that had been abandoned.[29] Another scholar of medieval agriculture appears to agree with this position.[30]

A younger historian from Tokyo has studied one of the new
units of rural settlement, the *ho*.[31] Very little is known about these

villages, except that they were much smaller than the district of the eighth century and flourished mostly on provincially administered lands from 1100 to 1600. In total there were about 150 of these units; 109 new settlements originated in the 1100s, 13 in the 1000s, and 20 after 1200. But the overwhelming majority of these new units, 111 in all, were located in western Japan, with only 18 in eastern Honshu. Moreover, this specialist has identified only 3 cases in which a warrior acted as either the proprietor or local agent of land clearance for the new unit. Religious institutions and officers of the central government were more common.

Eighteen of the new village units are particularly well documented.[32] A large area of newly cleared land appeared in 4 cases; in one area the amount of new fields may have been 185 *chō*. (One *chō* = 3 acres or 1.2 hectares.) But in 5 settlements, cultivators reopened previously devastated fields, while in 3 others plans to clear land may well have never come to fruition. Thus one can not easily equate the establishment of this new unit of local control either with an increase in arable land or with military leadership in farming activity.

The real issue in the debate over the role of the warrior in land clearance between 1050–1200 is agricultural development. In *Population, Disease, and Land in Japan, 645–900,* I have written of the cyclical cultivation and devastation of land in Japan's early history.[33] The difficulty of keeping parcels constantly productive stemmed from both technological and demographic factors. A scholar from the Kyoto area, who first noticed this pattern, has analyzed records for 1050 to 1300, and concluded that the same cycle of clearance and abandonment held for this later period as well.[34] He argues that (1) the percentage of farmland was extremely low when compared with available tracts, or totals from other periods; (2) the turnover of land from clearance to abandonment was exceedingly rapid; and (3) few parcels were of a high grade. Yet this historian borrowed Marc Bloch's term *the age of widespread land clearance* to describe the late eleventh and twelfth centuries.

Not all Japanese historians are as ambivalent about the era 1050–1200. One specialist in medieval Japanese agriculture has criticized the work of scholars who emphasize the low level of agricultural productivity between 1100 and 1300, and has asserted that several important improvements occurred in Japanese farming in the twelfth century.[35] He has found evidence that fields produced at a steady pace near the capital, where rapid devastation previously had been the rule. It should be noted, however, that the evidence to prove stability in rice production derives from the study of only 18 *chō* (54 acres), and the dissemination of techniques to stabilize cultivation in other areas is doubtful.

Other advocates of the "era of widespread land clearance" point to technological improvements. The price of iron had dropped from about 7 to 2–4 sheaves of rice by 1100; it is likely that more middle-class peasants could afford iron-tipped hoes and shovels by 1200.[36] Transplanting rice seedlings from prepared beds also became a more common practice, as indicated by poetry from the Heian era.[37] One scholar has argued that local strongmen (warriors), who forced the peasants to labor for them, controlled the seed beds.[38] Double-cropping appeared for the first time in Ise in central Japan in the early twelfth century, and some agrarian historians cite even earlier examples.[39] Peasants dug irrigation ponds and ditches, and there is more evidence of reliance on manure, green manure, and ash for fertilizer.[40] A new strain of early-ripening, drought- and blight-resistant rice entered Japan from China, but perhaps too late for cropping in the twelfth century.[41] Despite the addition of a moldboard, the Japanese plow was still useless for deep plowing; hoes and spades remained the chief tools of Japanese farmers.[42] Dry fields became somewhat more valuable and prevalent, although farmers could not consistently crop them.[43] Land continued to be reclaimed from the sea, as cultivators had done centuries earlier.[44]

Yet, even those who point to these technological improvements and defend the period 1050–1200 as an era of dynamic agricultural activity often hedge. One advocate states that he has doubts about the strength of the agrarian economy over these 150 years, and that the twelfth century could not compare with either the eighth century or the early Tokugawa (1600–1720) as an epoch of land clearance.[45] He emphasizes fields going out of cultivation through epidemics, famine, and other causes.[46] Another historian of dry farming and the author of a recent article entitled "The Age of Widespread Land Clearance," states that *every* farmer who cleared new fields between 1050 and 1200 was cropping land that had been cultivated earlier and was merely being re-opened.[47]

An understanding of population trends from 1050 to 1200 can contribute to the debate. One demographer has calculated Japan's population in 1150 at less than 7 million, only slightly more than in the 700s.[48] His estimate derives from a source he claims lists the total arable land in 1150; given the shifting pattern of cultivation, one wonders if even his appraisal of 7 million might not be too high. This demographer suggests that the population of eastern Honshu grew relative to western Japan, an observation that could indicate a relative shift in the regional economic balance of power.

Adding up all the evidence on both sides of the issue from a macroeconomic point-of-view, I propose the following hypothesis. In the late tenth and early eleventh centuries, Japan encountered a severe subsistence crisis and farmers could no longer cultivate their parcels because of war, drought, and disease. Beginning in the late eleventh century, land clearance commenced anew, but did not significantly increase farmland above the amount that had existed in prior eras. Some advancements in agricultural technology may have occurred, and land use may have intensified somewhat. But the improvements were relatively small; nothing approaching Western Europe's age of widespread land clearance or "medieval agricultural revolution" occurred. To test this hypothesis, one is forced to fall back on individual case studies.

THE LATE HEIAN ERA: CASE STUDIES

KANTO. The best documentation for land clearance by warriors comes from estates in eastern Honshu. The most famous example is the Sōma Estate in Shimōsa province, which the Chiba family managed for a while.[49] When tillers first brought Sōma into cultivation is not clear, but it was most likely in the late tenth or early eleventh century. In 1130, Chiba Tsuneshige commended Sōma to Ise Shrine to ensure that control of the estate remained in his hands. In 1136, however, the Provincial Governor arrested Tsuneshige for failing to pay his taxes, and transferred Sōma to provincial control. By 1143, Minamoto no Yoshitomo, a military aristocrat and 5th-generation offspring of Yorinobu, pressured the Chiba into signing the property over to him. Two years later, in 1145, Yoshitomo also commended Sōma Estate to Ise, and Chiba Tsunetane (Tsuneshige's son) re-commended the land in 1146. Little more is known until 1161, when Tsunetane found himself competing with another warrior for Sōma. Eventually, Tsunetane lost out, and Sōma Estate became the property of his rival, an ally of the powerful Taira family who was in control of the government at that time.

Three points about Sōma and the Chiba are significant. (1) Some land was cleared. One historian has located Sōma Estate at the present-day Abiko City, east of Tokyo; it began as Fuse village (*gō*), a rural unit that did not exist in the 700s, but came into being sometime after 900.[50] Furthermore, he has estimated the area of Sōma Estate in 1146 at about 140 square km., but Sōma included not only many settlements, but also roads and uncultivated lands. Each time the Chiba commended the estate to Ise, the area of the estate was different.

(2) The challenges to Chiba proprietorship can hardly have encouraged much land clearance. In a matter of 40 years, the Governor, a relative, and two other warriors assailed Chiba control over Sōma, an area the Chiba had opened. The struggle over the land, much of it already under cultivation, makes one wonder how enthusiastic the Chiba would have been about opening still more new fields, and also indicates just how desirable and rare productive fields were.

(3) The historian who analyzed land use at Sōma has studied the other Chiba holdings of the Kamakura period (1185–1333), which numbered about 30 properties. The Chiba cleared only 2 areas before 1185, and they lost Sōma Estate, which they first opened in the early eleventh century, to a rival three times in the twelfth century (finally in the 1160s). The overwhelming majority of Chiba holdings were rewards for their participation in Yoritomo's revolt in the Great Civil War of 1180–1185, not new fields they had opened and commended as estates. Many other "land-clearance lords" were undoubtedly like the Chiba, opening 1 or 2 areas for cultivation and acquiring the rest of their holdings by conquest in war.

Furthermore, Shimōsa and its neighboring provinces, where

Sōma and other Chiba properties were located, still contained large stretches of wilderness in the 1100s. Through the late twelfth and the thirteenth centuries, Yoritomo's military government in Kamakura issued orders to "invite vagabonds to stay and clear new lands," and applied special tax incentives to the region.[51] One student of the medieval warrior has suggested that the origins of the preferential treatment for the eastern Kanto lay in the destruction caused by Tadatsune's revolt of 1028–1031.

Ōba Estate is a second well-known case study in the Kanto. Ōba was situated in Sagami province, named after an eighth-century village. The founder was Taira no Kagemasa, who fought with the Minamoto house of military aristocrats in the late eleventh century. When he first obtained the property, Kagemasa claimed that Ōba was all mountains and wilderness without wet or dry fields, but a historian of Ōba believes that Kagemasa must have been reopening old lands.[52]

According to a record from 1141, Kagemasa was unable to clear the land by himself, and so he garnered help from the provincial staff to "invite vagabonds and have them clear land."[53] He then commended the property to Ise Shrine. Ise replied by granting a tax rebate for three years and made Kagemasa the foreman (*gesu*) of Ōba Estate. According to one historian, Ōba covered about 63 square km., but this area was not all fields.[54] Moreover, the area commended probably included land administered by the province (*kokuga ryō*). Products collected from Ōba for Ise Shrine included rice, beans, fish, and hemp cloth. According to the scholar who estimated Ōba's area, the yield of Ōba's rice paddies was barely more than standards established for wet fields in the early 800s.

In 1144, the aristocrat Minamoto no Yoshitomo again appeared on the scene. Yoshitomo's home was nearby Kamakura; in the 9th month, Yoshitomo had his followers and the provincial staff invade Ōba, steal fish and beans, and round up the local peasants. In the 10th month, Yoshitomo's men forced their way into Ōba with "more than 1,000 horsemen," and showed falsified documents to sustain their claim to the estate. Yoshitomo's men also tore up the boundary stakes and stole 47,000 sheaves of rice.[55] Apparently warriors counted falsifying documents, changing boundary stakes, and assaulting the populace among the ways they "cleared land."

Nitta Estate in Kōzuke province provides another example of late Heian land clearance.[56] Like Shimōsa, Kōzuke had suffered terribly from Tadatsune's rebellion; the government granted tax relief to the province throughout the eleventh century. Minamoto no Yoshishige, another scion of the aristocratic line, was born at the beginning of the twelfth century, and must have been in charge of land clearing as a youth. Yoshishige and his father, Yoshikuni, obtained help from the Ashikaga (Hidesato-line), who possessed "several thousand *chō*" of land and political power in Ashikaga district in Shimotsuke.[57] Yoshikuni and Yoshishige began clearing land in Nitta district in Kōzuke province, just across the Watarase River from the Ashikaga.

By the middle of the twelfth century, Yoshishige had managed to become the district magistrate of Nitta, and also opened new lands there. However, there were already settlements in Nitta, and Yoshishige secured some lands by purchase. In 1157, Yoshishige commended his holdings to a Court aristocrat; from a later document, it is known that his land included much wilderness.[58] In 1168, Yoshishige transferred the wilderness to his wife and son, and by 1170 he had succeeded in taking over all of Nitta district. By 1170, Nitta seems to have comprised 56 villages (*gō*), with over 202 *chō* of rice paddies, almost 100 *chō* of dry fields, and 248 taxable households (*zaike*). How much of this land was opened as a result of Yoshishige's efforts is debatable, but he and his offspring may have been responsible for some expansion.

The Kumagai of Musashi province provide a fourth and final example of land clearance in the Kanto.[59] The Kumagai probably first became associated with Kumagai village (*gō*, low-lying land about 25 meters from the coast) sometime between 1126 and 1147. They had ties with the provincial administration through marriage, and also served as guards in Kyoto. The land in Kumagai was poor and swampy, and farmers could crop only about 30 percent; even that land was not always in good condition. However, under the leadership of the Kumagai, the re-opening of formerly abandoned fields improved so that tillers could farm 64 percent of the parcels. Thus the Kumagai seem to have overseen an increase in the percentage of parcels yielding a good harvest.

CENTRAL JAPAN. The best case of warrior activity on the land in central Japan comes from Mino province.[60] The Court appointed Minamoto no Yorimitsu, progenitor of the Mino Genji, to be Governor of Mino twice early in the eleventh century. Yorimitsu's grandson, Minamoto no Kunifusa, held land in Mino since at least 1064; he battled his Minamoto kinsmen near his residence in 1079. In 1096, monks of the venerable temple Tōdaiji appointed Kunifusa to be the foreman (*gesu*) of their Akanabe Estate in Mino, probably because it abutted his own land in Uzura village (*gō*). It is usually assumed that Kunifusa or one of his ancestors had cleared the parcels around Uzura.

From the beginning, there was trouble between Kunifusa and Tōdaiji. In 1096, Tōdaiji complained that Kunifusa had raised troops, attacked cultivators who fled to the surrounding hills, and harvested 21 *chō* of land for his own use. When the peasants reappeared at the behest of Tōdaiji officials, Kunifusa attacked again.

In 1117, Tōdaiji protested that, while "Kunifusa was an official at [Akanabe] Estate, he willfully dug up and took land which measured 2 *chō* east and west and over 10 *chō* north and south."[61] Tōdaiji dismissed Kunifusa from the foreman's post, but he was not finished:

> Yet the official (*gōshi*) of Uzura assembled force by himself, and without fear of imperial restrictions, tore out the boundary stakes once again, violated the cultivators, and probably planned to kill them. There was no one to farm out of trepidation from these actions. During the time when the fields went out of cultivation, within the land which he had recently dug up and taken, he forced the local peasants (*zaike*) to move, and had them cultivate wet and dry fields and mulberry trees, which he had also taken from within the estate. Also, the residents of Uzura robbed the horses, cattle, and implements from within the estate; they killed cultivators and burned farmhouses. . . .
>
> During this period, people's dwellings have disappeared and the land has greatly gone to waste. . . . The destruction of this estate derives solely from the disorder of the people of Uzura.[62]

To add insult to injury, Kunifusa's son then tried to commend his father's illegal holding to a capital aristocrat to secure the claim. In 1142, Kunifusa's family still held part of Tōdaiji's Akanabe Estate. Thus, while Kunifusa may have cleared Uzura, he supplemented his domain by falsifying boundaries and impressing cultivators.

THE CAPITAL AND ENVIRONS. The oft-cited activities of Hata Tametatsu in Harima province provide the classic example of land clearance in the late Heian era.[63] Although no documentation survives
to certify his first efforts, it seems probable that Hata, forerunner
of a warrior family of the Kamakura period (1185–1333), opened
the land for Hisatomi village (*ho*) sometime in first half of eleventh
century. Not long after he brought the land into cultivation, the
ditches became damaged, and Tametatsu was unable to return the
fields to use, even though he could command authority from a post
in the provincial headquarters. Enrolling about 5,000 laborers
with the aid of the district magistrate, Tametatsu opened several
tens of *chō* in 1075. Advocates of the "age of widespread land clearance" usually describe Tametatsu's efforts as emblematic of expansion of arable land in that era. But what scholars often fail to note
is that, 3 years later in 1079, another ditch became damaged and
30 *chō* of land—about as much as Tametatsu had opened—went
out of cultivation. In Hata's words, repair of the ditch was "not
within human powers."[64]

Not all land clearance ended in disaster. A record from 1184 tells
of Minamoto Suetada, who cleared a parcel of land called Mizu-
hai in Kawachi district in Kawachi province.[65] Unlike many other
instances, his record specifically states that Suetada "accomplished
the great labor of clearance" and passed his land to his son Yasu-
tada, who became a houseman for the first warrior government in
Kamakura in 1185. It is unclear, however, whether Suetada was
clearing wilderness or merely re-opening devastated parcels.

One is impressed by the frequency with which warriors in western Japan attempted to confiscate lands illegally, just as in the
Kanto. For example, most of the lands in Tomoda village (*mura*) in
Iga province had belonged to Tōdaiji since the eighth century.[66]
In 1097, however, Taira no Masamori, the warrior Governor of
remote Oki province, commended about 20 *chō* of land in Tomoda
and nearby settlements to the politically powerful Retired Emperor, precipitating a conflict with the temple. Despite protests
from the temple, Masamori claimed a legal right to the land; in
1109 Masamori, who had subsequently been appointed to the lucrative governorship of Wakasa province through the influence of
the Retired Emperor, commended another 53 *chō* of Tōdaiji's land

to his patron, and also impressed Tōdaiji's lumbermen to be cultivators. The cultivators cooperated with Masamori in exchange for lighter tax burdens and a chance to serve as his footsoldiers. A later document shows that Masamori had indeed commended a small amount of privately cleared land, but most of the fields belonged to Tōdaiji. The conflict continued for at least another 25 years, and, even though both Masamori and his son, Tadamori, gave repeated orders to their followers at Tomoda to submit to Tōdaiji's claims, these subordinates persisted in their violations. Thus the Taira commanded their men at Tomoda to obey Tōdaiji when they themselves were simultaneously snubbing the temple by commending land to a different patron at Court.

Other documents from Iga province show that warriors did not always win conflicts over land. Although Tōdaiji had held land in Iga since the eighth century, it was only in 1034 that monks formed Kuroda Estate, and a local pioneer in land clearance at Kuroda mostly re-opened lands that previous farmers had abandoned. Throughout the late eleventh century, Tōdaiji and the provincial headquarters fought over both land and cultivators, who moved back and forth from *shōen* to *kokugaryō;* in the 1050s, Tōdaiji and the provincial headquarters twice came to blows. In 1066, Tōdaiji granted the district magistrate the right to open lands in return for 3 years' tax relief. By the mid-twelfth century, the magistrate had tripled the land under the plow, but it is thought that he merely rebuilt earlier dikes and ditches that had fallen into disrepair. The magistrate's family took the warrior name Minamoto, and formed a band of soldiers, while inheriting the foreman's position (*gesu*) for Kuroda. In 1162, however, a monk journeyed to Kuroda with over 300 soldiers and evicted the warriors. One scholar has called the incident "the defeat of the medieval" (that is, warriors) in Japan.[67]

Yet another case from Kii province suggests that fighters from western Japan in the 1100s did not always belong to a new class of land-clearing "country lords."[68] The Sakanoue were a warrior family who traced their lineage all the way back to the pre-645 era, and had been district magistrates in the 700s. They cleared some land in Kii and eventually became foremen on estates of the monasteries on Mt. Kōya, but, like the Minamoto at Kuroda, the institution later confiscated the warrior family's holdings.

Finally, one example from 1164 indicates that falsified land clearance was common in western Japan.[69] In Ōmi province, a person fabricated a story that he had developed some land in order to take control away from a temple. Monks and warriors had good reason to forge records concerning newly opened fields, since owners of these properties could claim tax exemptions, exclusive ownership, and other advantages.

These cases do not exhaust the examples of land clearance by warriors in the late Heian era. Indeed, a compilation of documents extant from 1050 to 1185 contains about 150 explicit examples.[70] About three-quarters of the cases originated in western Japan, and, in about half, temples and shrines owned the fields. I could identify only about 30 explicit instances of land clearance performed by warriors. Of the 61 cases in which the deeds made any reference to acreage, the average size of a new parcel was over 8 *chō,* but the median was only 1.5 *chō.* It is interesting that the number of references to land going out of cultivation almost equaled terms signifying newly opened land (about 197 to 226, respectively).

Critics may dismiss these statistics. Yet this chapter has cited the clearest, most relevant, and best-known examples. These case studies suggest that, while military men did clear land, a sizable percentage must have been land that tillers had cultivated in earlier times and abandoned. Warriors also reveled in appropriating others' lands by falsifying documents, changing boundary stakes, and applying brute force. Even when farmers brought new lands under the plow, the average yield per unit does not seem to have been much greater than that of 300 years earlier. And warriors always faced temples and aristocrats who were able to wrest their hard-won gains from them. The case studies examined here confirm the earlier hypothesis that, while some improvements may have occurred in Japanese agriculture between 1050 and 1200, nothing approaching Western Europe's age of widespread land clearance took place in the late Heian period.

THE MILITARY IN THE FORMER NINE YEARS' WAR, 1051–1062

While Japan suffered through a subsistence crisis in the eleventh century, and cultivators took up their hoes and spades to bring some of the abandoned fields back into use, the Court in Heian faced the need to preserve law and order. During the late eleventh and early twelfth centuries, three major conflicts broke out: two wars in northeastern Honshu, and piracy in the Inland Sea. The Minamoto garnered fame and followers from battles against recalcitrant barbarians in the Tohoku, while a Taira leader cemented claims to be "the chief of all warriors" by suppressing seagoing brigands in 1135. These conflicts reveal the final elaboration of the samurai fighting style, the growing importance of estates in warrior life, and the continuing paramountcy of the provincial headquarters for raising an army.

THE FORMER NINE YEARS' WAR. The 12-year conflict known in Japanese history as the Former Nine Years' War occurred in northeastern Japan, primarily in the province of Mutsu[71] (see Map 8). It was the first major disturbance in the Tohoku since the rebellion of the late ninth century, and, like earlier conflicts, set those of supposedly "barbarian" (*emishi*) blood against the "civilizing" mission of the Court. The leader of the northeastern natives was Abe Yoritoki, whose family had ruled over the Six Districts of Mutsu for at least three generations, according to *A Tale of Mutsu* (*Mutsu waki*), the major source on the war.[72] The Six Districts included Fort Izawa and the basin of the Kitakami River, the region first pacified by Sakanoue no Tamuramaro in the early ninth century. *A Tale of Mutsu* describes Abe Yoritoki as a "native chieftain of the Eastern Barbarians" (*tōi no shuchō*), and there can be little doubt that Yoritoki held the hereditary post of district magistrate, collecting taxes and keeping the peace among his fellow pacified *emishi* on behalf of the Heian Court.

The war had 3 phases: 1051–1057, a stalemate which lasted until the death of Yoritoki; 1057–1061, a time of Abe victories and Court reverses; and 1061–1062, the final triumph of the Court under Minamoto no Yoriyoshi. In the first period, sources depict Yoritoki as arrogant and proud, a leader who "refused to pay taxes"

Map 8. THE FORMER NINE YEARS' WAR, 1051–1062

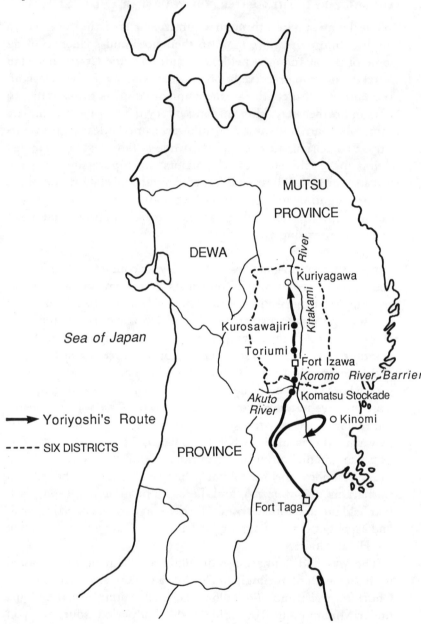

Sources: Shōji Hiroshi, *Henkyō no sōran,* p. 11; Kajiwara Masaaki, etc., *Mutsu waki.*

and "failed to provide men for corvée duty."[73] The Governor of Mutsu raised an army to punish Yoritoki, but Yoritoki's barbarian troops defeated him.

The Heian Court determined that Abe had to be destroyed, as Tadatsune and other tax evaders had been, and sent Minamoto no Yoriyoshi to be Governor of Mutsu and General of the Military Headquarters at Fort Taga. Yoriyoshi was the son of Yorinobu, who had been responsible for the suppression of Taira no Tadatsune in 1031. Yoriyoshi was renowned for his archery, and *A Tale of Mutsu* reports that he commanded many mercenaries from eastern Japan.[74] He had served both at Court and as the Governor of Sagami, and had married the daughter of Taira no Naokata, the first envoy charged with crushing Tadatsune's revolt.

Just as Yoriyoshi arrived in Mutsu about 1051, the Court issued a general amnesty that included the Abe; Yoritoki then laid down his weapons and politely served Yoriyoshi. Towards the end of Yoriyoshi's term, in about 1056, however, the camp of a provincial official located at the Akuto River, was attacked and many people and horses were slaughtered. The official blamed Yoritoki's son, Sadatō, because earlier the official's relatives had refused a marriage proposal from Sadatō — in the process slandering the Abe's barbarian background. Yoriyoshi quickly took advantage of the incident to punish the Abe. This incident, which would escalate into the Former Nine Years' War, was another intraspecific conflict. Like Masakado's rebellion, it began with a quarrel over marriage and lineage.

Each side raised troops, but, despite an initial victory, Yoriyoshi was unable to finish off Yoritoki. Yoriyoshi followed the traditional procedure required since 901 and sent a request to the Court to form an army. The Heian courtiers issued an order to the provinces of eastern Honshu to send soldiers.[75] Not long thereafter Yoritoki died of a wound inflicted in battle, but his family continued to resist. Yoriyoshi requested and received another order for "soldiers of the provinces" and provisions.[76]

Aid never arrived. In an ill-advised move late in 1057, Yoriyoshi marched to Kinomi and fought a pitched battle with Sadatō and the rest of the Abe, who soundly defeated the forces of the Governor of Mutsu, despite several individual acts of heroism. Sadatō collected taxes from the inhabitants to fund his campaign while Yoriyoshi complained that "I have seen nothing of the munitions and men supposedly requisitioned for me from other provinces. All the men in Mutsu have gone to Dewa to avoid conscription."[77]

The tide turned decisively in the final stage of the war in 1062. In the 7th month, Yoriyoshi convinced a powerful local strongman and pacified barbarian, Kiyowara Mitsuyori of Dewa, to join forces with him. Yoriyoshi's band, which had numbered only 1,800, increased to more than 10,000, according to *A Tale of Mutsu*. In 5 short months Yoriyoshi annihilated the Abe. On the 17th of the 7th month, Yoriyoshi utilized horsemen and foot soldiers to capture the Komatsu Stockade. After a respite, during which Yoriyoshi's men suffered from the effects of a poor harvest (about half deserted), Yoriyoshi repelled an attack by Sadatō on the 5th of the 9th month. Yoriyoshi, Mitsuyori, and their men pursued Sadatō through the Koromo River Barrier and, in a rare example of siege warfare in the Heian period, took the stockades at Toriumi and Kurosawajiri by the 11th. The Battle of Kuriyagawa took place from the 14th through the 17th of the 9th month; Sadatō and his closest allies died in battle. Munetō, another of Yoritoki's sons, surrendered soon after. On the 17th of the 12th month in 1062, Governor Yoriyoshi reported victory to the Court, and early in 1063 he presented the heads of Sadatō and others to the Investigators in Heian.[78] For his service, the Court promoted Yoriyoshi to the Senior 4th Rank, Lower Grade, and appointed him to the lucrative governorship of Iyo. His son Yoshiie, also a combatant in the war, assumed the Junior 5th Rank, Lower Grade, and the governorship of Mutsu.

CONSCRIPTION AND ORGANIZATION OF TROOPS. Some scholars view the Former Nine Years' War as a turning point, marking the decline of forces organized around the provincial headquarters and the first step in the rise of private, feudal warrior bands (*bushi dan*) as seen in the medieval period. According to this interpretation, the public military system of the Taihō Codes reigned supreme in the eighth and ninth centuries but had long since disappeared, and without an effective central government in the tenth and eleventh centuries local strongmen armed themselves for self-defense. By 1050, or about the time of the Former Nine Years' War, true samurai had appeared, leading private, feudal bands of vassals pledging undying loyalty to a lord.

This study presents a different argument. Rather than juxtapose the public system of the eighth century against the private feudalism of the eleventh century, I have stressed the strong similarities between military forces in the two eras. A political vacuum did not beget the samurai of the late Heian period; the Taihō Codes (and the related system of 901) did.

To be sure, *A Tale of Mutsu* tells of "[n]umbers of eastern warriors" (*kyūba no shi*) who "had long ago joined their fortunes" to Yoriyoshi's; the account lists 16 by name.[79] One Yoriyoshi loyalist from Sagami province, Saeki Tsunenori, even claimed to have served Yoriyoshi for 30 years.[80] Like Saeki, most of Yoriyoshi's followers probably signed on during Yoriyoshi's tenure as Governor of Sagami, when he could most easily reward his following with jobs.

But even those looking for the roots of Japanese feudalism have found little evidence for the formation of a vassal band during this war.[81] There was nothing new about a warrior-governor having followers. As argued in Chapters 4 and 5, a few warriors personally loyal to the provincial governor were an important component of Japan's military system since at least 900, and probably even before. One might expect such fighters to be especially numerous when the governor was of warrior lineage himself, as Yoriyoshi was. It is interesting to note that 3 of the men listed as Yoriyoshi loyalists possessed the title of *san'i*, which meant that they had Court rank but no government job; these men had undoubtedly served as low-level provincial officials. Soldiers with the same title also fought for the Abe.

In fact, as even one of the strongest advocates of the Western-analogue theory has admitted, "the principle of *ritsuryō* (eighth and ninth century) military organization was alive" in the Former Nine Years' War.[82] *A Tale of Mutsu* describes the organization of Yoriyoshi's troops on the eve of the final campaign in 1062 as having 7 lines; 6 were composed of Kiyowara Takenori's friends and relatives (Takenori was the local strongman who joined Yoriyoshi in the 7th month of 1062), and one included troops led by Yoriyoshi and a Mutsu provincial official. According to a northeastern wars specialist, the organization of Yoriyoshi's army was identical to his father's (Yorinobu's) in Hitachi, analyzed in Chapter 5.[83] Both military aristocrats led a personal retinue, provincial forces, and troops acquired through an important alliance with a local strongman.

As had been true of Japan's military since A.D. 500, the crucial variable in military success was the local strongman; in Yoriyoshi's case, the Kiyowara provided most of the forces. Before the Kiyowara joined the campaign, Yoriyoshi was on the run, but, after they threw in their lot, victory took only a few months.

The officials of the provincial headquarters tried to ensure the cooperation of locally powerful families in 1062 through the bestowal of titles and Court ranks. It is no accident that the leader of Yoriyoshi's first line, Kiyowara Takesada, held the post of overseer (*ōryō shi*), a military position in the provincial headquarters.[84] Takesada would be a good example of a "man of the province" who took an office in the provincial headquarters as his reward for fighting for the Court.

The numbers of Kiyowara fighters were so overwhelming, and Yoriyoshi had such trouble defeating the Abe with his own men, that one historian has written of the "fossilization" of the provincial military after 1050.[85] It is true that the Court could not easily fill Yoriyoshi's requests for troops from other provinces; Yoriyoshi complained in both 1057 and 1062 that other provincial headquarters were not answering his calls for soldiers and matériel.[86] What could have been the cause for the delays, if the provincial headquarters were still so important in raising an army?

The reasons Yoriyoshi had such trouble in putting together an army were bad weather and famine, undoubtedly part of the subsistence crisis then afflicting other areas of Japan as well. Most of Yoriyoshi's pleas for men and supplies were written in 1057, when, *A Tale of Mutsu* states, "a famine in the province cut off supplies of food and scattered the armies"; the same problem surfaced in 1062.[87] Like all armies, Japanese troops marched on their stomachs, and, when famine struck, provincial officials could not support fighters and the war stopped. The crisis in agriculture that made for abandoned lands and the *shōen-kokugaryō* system of land tenure nearly cost Yoriyoshi victory in Mutsu.

The Former Nine Years' War followed the procedure first established in 901 for conscripting military forces.[88] Once a serious crime was committed, local officials investigated and made a report to the Court. After conducting its own inquiry, the central government issued an arrest order (*tsuibu kampu*), thereby empowering the provincial headquarters, and eventually provincial police such as the arrest officer (*tsuibu shi*), to raise and reward provincial troops who punished the criminals. Several steps in this procedure are visible in the sources detailing the Former Nine Years' War, including the issuance of arrest orders to Yoriyoshi and the governors of the Kanto, and an account of the final campaign undoubtedly composed to justify claims for rewards.[89]

There were, however, two subtle modifications in the 901 system. First, the search-and-destroy officer (*tsuitō shi*) dispatched from the capital, Minamoto no Yoriyoshi, differed from such leaders of the tenth and early eleventh centuries, since he was not and never had been an Imperial Guard, as were most such officers before Tadatsune's revolt in 1028. Nor did other officials, organized into the 4-tiered hierarchy typical of Chinese-style posts, accompany Yoriyoshi.[90] Instead, the arrest officer was a famed warrior, given wide powers that might allow him to circumvent provincial governors and appeal directly to warriors based at the headquarters, thus increasing his personal following. Second, although the Court named Yoriyoshi to the governorship of Iyo as reward for his service, he refused to go to his post until 10 of his followers were also granted prizes.[91] His concern for his men paid off in a small but perhaps more loyal following that would stand the Minamoto in good stead in their uprising against the Court and the Taira in 1180.

MILITARY TECHNOLOGY AND TACTICS. *A Tale of Mutsu* provides the first real chance to analyze fighting style and weaponry since the rebellion of Masakado between 935 and 940. In Masakado's day, armies were composed of 3 parts: commanders on horseback; their close dependents, also mostly mounted archers; and a large majority of peasant foot soldiers. Archery was the favored style of combat, and sources reveal some evidence of coordinated, Chinese-style, mass tactics. Masakado's forces had characteristics of both the Taihō armies and the samurai of the twelfth century.

On the surface, battles in the Tohoku look similar to combat in Masakado's day. The Former Nine Years' War included both horsemen and foot soldiers, although mounted warriors received more attention from the author of *A Tale of Mutsu* than they did in *The Tale of Masakado*. While one can not be sure, it seems likely that each equestrian fighter commanded a few soldiers on foot, as had been the case in the eighth century and later. The bow and arrow was still the preferred weapon for the overwhelming majority of troops, but occasionally warriors resorted to swords, as Sadatō did when he met his end. Some soldiers also used spears, but there is no mention of shields.

Forces remained relatively small, usually from 1,000 to 3,000. The Kiyowara army was an exception, reported at "over 10,000," a figure suspiciously large and round.[92] There were often fewer than 20 casualties for each battle in the Former Nine Years' War, casting further doubt on the reports of large armies. Like troops in the revolt of Masakado, soldiers under Yoriyoshi showed a disconcerting predilection to flee battle as soon as the tide turned against them.[93]

But there are also subtle differences between the fighting style of men engaged in Masakado's revolt and the war in Mutsu, and some of the distinctions undoubtedly derive from the prevalence of siege warfare in the later conflict. The battle strategy of the Abe consisted primarily of retreating to the safety of fortifications that had been constructed in the eighth and ninth centuries; then placing archers on ramparts and firing rocks at their attackers, although probably not from catapults.[94] Sometimes the Abe even poured hot water on Yoriyoshi's men. When a fortress was about to fall, the Abe opened their gates and dispatched horsemen to deal with their assailants and make good their escape. Because of famine and the shortage of provisions, as well as the fact that most of his men rode horses, Yoriyoshi had little time for prolonged sieges. He tried using fire, tunneling, and assaulting bastions with picked horsemen and foot soldiers.

The presence of siege warfare does not, however, explain away another crucial difference between battles in Masakado's day and the mid-eleventh century: the increasing importance of individual mounted combat, as opposed to group formations, often employing foot soldiers. Like the rebellion of Masakado, the engagements of the Former Nine Years' War give some evidence of mass tactics. *A Tale of Mutsu* states that Yoriyoshi seized his opponent's flags as he engaged Sadatō after the retreat from the Komatsu Stockade in 1062; the Kiyowara may have used the flags to coordinate troop movements. Yoriyoshi also employed a Chinese maneuver known as the "two-headed snake" to chew into the enemy's line; when one "head" (group of men) fell under attack, the other lent support.[95]

But there can be little doubt that fighting by individual, mounted archers was more common and more deadly in the mid-eleventh century than it had been in Masakado's day. One hero was Yoriyoshi's son, Minamoto no Yoshiie. *A Tale of Mutsu* describes Yoshiie during an early battle:

> The great hero of the battle was Yoriyoshi's eldest son, Yoshiie. He shot arrows from horseback like a god; undeterred by gleaming blades, he lunged through the rebels' encirclements to emerge on their left and right. With his great arrowheads he transfixed one enemy chieftain after another, never shooting at random but always inflicting a mortal wound. He galloped like the wind and fought with a skill that was more than human. The barbarians fled rather than face him, calling him the first born son of Hachiman, the god of war.[96]

Although this account may be inflated, the portrayal of Yoshiie's skills, and the awe in which the Tōhoku chieftains held him, stands in marked contrast to the poor showing of Taihō forces against the native horsemen of northeastern Honshu in the late eighth century (see Chapter 3). After more than 250 years, mounted archers fighting for the Heian Court could at last hold their own against the barbarians of Mutsu and Dewa.

The author of *A Tale of Mutsu* repeatedly extols the acts of individual, horse-riding archers. In addition to the passage on Yoshiie, the storyteller lavishes great praise on 6 individuals who fought for Yoriyoshi in a losing battle late in 1057. One warrior "wheeled and entered the enemy cordon" by himself; his 3 retainers followed him to his death.[97] Another soldier was "a taciturn youth who excelled at mounted archery. Seven or 8 times during the battle he entered the enemy lines, killed a barbarian chieftain, and emerged again, imperturbable in the face of death."[98] Other examples of individual heroism, probably man-to-man combat on horseback, are present in the story.[99]

The numerous and conspicuous descriptions of single, mounted combat in *A Tale of Mutsu* suggest that, by 1050, the one-on-one fighting style characteristic of the samurai was nearing ascendancy, while mass tactics were much less important. Of course, one can question the perspective of the author of the tale; perhaps the exploits of the great military aristocrats like Yoshiie simply overawed the storyteller, and he ignored the common foot soldiers. Maybe the author of *The Tale of Masakado* was more sensitive to the plight of the commoner fighting for and against the rebellion. Yet evidence indicates that the compiler of *A Tale of Mutsu* relied upon the experiences of veterans of the war who actually saw the battles.[100] Thus the story of the Former Nine Years' War was not just one person's remote version of events.

In fact, the growing predominance of single, mounted combat had its roots in Japanese battle strategy from before 1050, as described in earlier chapters. In earliest times, horse-riding soldiers, who had learned their trade from the Koreans, probably fought as much as individuals as in groups; even after the adoption of Chinese-style battle formations in the late seventh century, it is questionable how regularly and seriously the Japanese actually practiced coordinated group maneuvers with horsemen and foot soldiers. "Struggling to be first," a method of individual combat, dated back at least to the Battle of the Paekch'ŏn River in 663, and reappeared regularly in the Japanese sources thereafter.[101] The trend away from mass tactics gathered momentum during the 40-year war against the "barbarians" of northeastern Honshu, spurred on, no doubt, by the spectacular failures of huge armies to subdue the barbarians. By the mid-tenth century, combatants were squaring off in man-to-man, mounted engagements, as shown by a story in *Tales of Times Now Past* entitled "The Battle between Minamoto Mitsuru and Taira Yoshifumi."[102] It seems probable that single, mounted combat always played a role in battles in Japan, but, as the lessons of the eighth century about the value of mass tactics faded from memory, individual fighting became more and more prominent.

Two considerations spurred the development of individualistic warfare after 900. First, Court aristocrats preferred mounted archery and showered rewards upon soldiers who could prove their bravery in this mode of confrontation. To receive a reward, however, the warrior needed trophies, which led to competition among combatants to perform individual acts of heroism. Second, as the Japanese economy sputtered and slowed in the ninth century, and as the Court became less concerned with day-to-day events in the countryside, the predatory seizure of territory and people became a less common cause of war, and intraspecific motives predominated. Warriors fought for their own survival and the future of their lines, as Masakado, Tadatsune, and the Abe did. In the search for hierarchy and dominance among military men, the fighter's identity and personal style of combat gradually became almost as important as the battle itself.

THE LATTER THREE YEARS' WAR: AN ILLEGAL CAMPAIGN

The Latter Three Years' War (1083–1087) was a private feud, an intraspecific conflict for dominance in the Tohoku from beginning to end[103] (see Map 9). The major combatants were the Kiyowara of Mutsu, the family who had come to Yoriyoshi's rescue in the war against the Abe, and Minamoto no Yoshiie, a hero of the Former Nine Years' War. The war revealed further aspects of samurai fighting style, the individual mounted form of combat seen 30 years earlier. Yet, because the Kiyowara had violated no Court laws, Yoshiie's display of his skills cost him wealth, hurt his reputation, and helped plunge the Minamoto into internal bickering and decline.

The origin of the Kiyowara is shrouded in mystery. One scholar believes they were descended from a military aristocrat who traveled to Dewa province to suppress the rebellion of 878.[104] After the siege of Kanezawa Stockade in 1087, the author of a source on the Latter Three Years' War calls the erstwhile chief of the Kiyowara family a "barbarian" (*ebisu*), a term that may indicate that the Kiyowara were natives of northeastern Honshu.[105] Prior to the annihilation of the Abe in 1062, the Kiyowara had their base in northern Dewa, but assumed the post of General of the Military Headquarters at Fort Taga after Yoriyoshi's victory in the Former

Map 9. THE LATTER THREE YEARS' WAR, 1083–1087

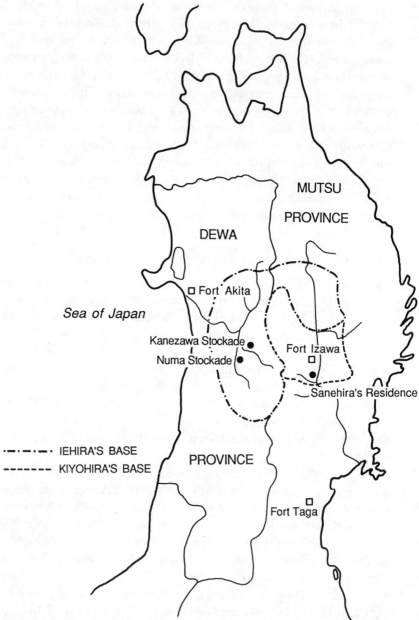

Source: Shōji Hiroshi, *Henkyō no sōran,* p. 88.

Nine Years' War. The Kiyowara also controlled the "Six Districts" of central Mutsu, where they prospered by "respecting provincial orders and fearing the authority of the court."[106]

THE WAR. The war between Yoshiie and the Kiyowara began as an argument within the Kiyowara family. The leader of the Kiyowara (Sanehira) was without child and adopted a boy, whom he married to a woman who was the granddaughter of a minor official from Hitachi and Yoriyoshi's daughter. At the banquet for the wedding, one of the Kiyowara vassals became insulted because his chief did not show sufficient appreciation of his gift of gold. He left. When Sanehira heard of the precipitous departure, he became angry and raised troops from the Six Districts of Mutsu for an expedition to Dewa.

The vassal realized that his troops were no match for the Kiyowara family and enlisted the aid of Fujiwara Kiyohira and Kiyowara Iehira, Sanehira's half-brother. Kiyohira and Iehira may also have been opposed to the marriage for reasons of inheritance. While the main body of Kiyowara forces was in Dewa, Kiyohira and Iehira attacked the Kiyowara base in Izawa, burning over 400 houses. When Sanehira heard of the attack, he returned to Mutsu, but his enemies were gone. He prepared for another campaign.

At that moment, in the fall of 1083, Minamoto no Yoshiie arrived to become the Governor of Mutsu. Sanehira postponed his battle plans to fete Yoshiie, and then set out for Dewa again. Kiyohira and Iehira proceeded to assault the main Kiyowara residence in Izawa again, and Sanehira's wife applied for help from two of Yoshiie's dependents from eastern Honshu who were in the vicinity on an investigation (*kemmon*). Yoshiie's followers sided with Sanehira and sent to the provincial headquarters for troops.

Yoshiie marched to the rescue and eventually prevailed over Iehira and Kiyohira. In the meantime, Sanehira died, and any reason for further fighting disappeared. Yoshiie accepted the peace offering of his assailants and divided the Six Districts of Mustu in 2 for Iehira and Kiyohira to share between them. Although the sources do not mention a conflict over the Kiyowara inheritance, it seems likely that Yoshiie was forced to decide such an issue, thus bringing down the wrath of the Kiyowara upon him.

Yet Iehira was not satisfied, and slandered Kiyohira to Yoshiie, who reacted by rewarding Kiyohira and forcing Iehira to live with his rival. Iehira then hatched a plot to assassinate his enemy, but the plot became public knowledge; Iehira still managed to burn Kiyohira's residence and murder his family. Kiyohira reported to Yoshiie, who marched against Iehira's Numa Stockade with "several thousand horsemen" in the fall of 1086.[107] A long siege followed in heavy winter snow, and Yoshiie's men suffered exposure and starvation. Eventually, Yoshiie was forced to withdraw his forces.

In the meantime, word of the conflict had reached the Court. Heian aristocrats debated about sending Yoshiie's brother (Yoshitsuna) to settle matters, but apparently did nothing. Later in the fall of 1086, as Yoshiie's position at Numa Stockade worsened, he applied to the Court for an arrest order, but the government refused.[108] A few days later the state summoned Yoshiie's brother to explain the war.

While Yoshiie was reassembling his army, Iehira's uncle, Takehira, marched to Numa Stockade and joined forces with his nephew.[109] Takehira advised his relative to withdraw to Kanezawa Stockade because it was more defensible. Meanwhile, Yoshimitsu, another of Yoshiie's brothers and a member of the Imperial Guards in the capital, left his position without authorization to assist Yoshiie, a deed for which the Court summarily dismissed him.[110] Yoshimitsu may have desired to fight side-by-side with his brother, but, as one historian implies, the real problem was that Yoshiie was in desperate need of men because the Court would not hand down an arrest order that would give him legitimate access to provincial forces.[111]

Even with his brother's aid, and despite spending the spring and summer doing nothing but calling up men, Yoshiie was unable to approach Kanezawa Stockade until after the harvest in the 9th month of 1087.[112] Again Yoshiie had to campaign during the harsh northeastern winter, reportedly with "several ten thousands of horse-riders."[113] Yet assaults against the fortification, which was armed with mighty warriors and crossbows, proved fruitless. The siege lasted well into the winter, as Yoshiie attempted to starve the Kiyowara into submission. Finally, on the 14th of the 11th month in 1087, Kanezawa Stockade fell; amidst the rape and pillage Yoshiie annihilated the Kiyowara confederates and their families. To prove their victory, Yoshiie and his troops took heads from the 48 main followers of the Kiyowara.

Yoshiie reported the demise of the Kiyowara on the 26th of the 12th month:

> "Takehira and Iehira's rebellion has been worse than that of [Abe] Sad-atō and Munetō. I have pacified them with my own personal power. I hope to receive quickly an arrest order and send the heads to the capital."
>
> But [the Court] heard that "the Kiyowara were Yoshiie's personal enemies. If we grant an order then we must give prizes." Thus they decided they ought not grant such an order.
>
> When he heard this, Yoshiie threw the heads on the road and returned to the capital empty-handed.[114]

The Court chose to regard Yoshiie's adventure in northeastern Japan as a private feud unworthy of reward and to punish Yoshiie for his actions. One year after Yoshiie reported his victory over the Kiyowara, the government discharged him from his post as Governor of Mutsu.[115]

FIGHTING STYLE. Sources for the Latter Three Years' War may not accurately reflect military technology of the late eleventh century. According to an entry in an aristocratic diary, no one wrote down the story of the Latter Three Years' War until 1171, almost a century after the events, when an artist painted a picture scroll on the order of the Retired Emperor, the most powerful politician at Court.[116] It would be unwise to accept this record of the Latter Three Years' War as a totally reliable portrayal of late-eleventh-century battle tactics.

But two points make stories of this conflict worthy of analysis. First, there was probably little difference between military technology in 1087 and 1171, since the samurai style of single, mounted combat had already evolved; storytellers would not have had much trouble understanding and preserving tales of Yoshiie and his men. Second, Japan has a strong tradition of oral literature, and veterans probably drifted to the capital to tell their stories, which literate persons would have then written down. Thus, although storytellers undoubtedly glorified individual acts of valor and enhanced descriptions of fighting styles, it seems likely that current records contain a kernel of truth about contemporary military technology, much like Homer's *Iliad*.[117]

Many tales give further evidence of the growing prominence of individual, mounted combat. Records tell of the heroism of Taira no Kagemasa, who later founded Ōba Estate in Sagami; he kept on fighting despite an arrow wound in the eye.[118] During the siege of Kanezawa Stockade, Yoshiie set up "cushions for cowards and the brave," with individual acts of courage or timidity determining where the warrior sat.[119] This custom was common in the Kamakura age (1185–1333), the heyday of single, mounted combat. As Yoshiie's stranglehold on Kanezawa tightened, the Kiyowara suggested a one-to-one mounted battle outside the stockade, won by Yoshiie's man.[120] The sources also mention giant arrows and gold-leaf armor, signs of the growing ritualization of intraspecific combat.[121] It is reasonable to conclude that all the characteristics of samurai fighting style were in place by the time of the Latter Three Years' War, except perhaps for the recitation of pedigrees by combatants.

One tale is especially interesting.[122] Just before Yoshimitsu arrived at camp in 1087, Yoshiie and his men were riding through a meadow. Yoshiie noticed a flock of birds which suddenly scattered in all directions. The commander immediately became suspicious, and directing his force to the place below the birds, spied 20 enemy horsemen, whom he and his men quickly dispatched. The reason this is worth citing is that an identical story occurs in *The Art of War*, written by the Chinese author Sun-tzu. While it is not clear that Yoshiie actually knew of the Chinese master of military tactics, the storyteller did. He chose the incident and described Yoshiie's action after the Chinese example, showing that, even in the twelfth century, the wisdom of the classics survived.

THE WAR, YOSHIIE, AND THE COURT. Historians of the Western-analogue theory have pointed out that, in the Latter Three Years' War, a soldier fought a major war without authorization from the Court, and that he was victorious without officially receiving access to the provincial headquarters. Moreover, Yoshiie seemed to gain stature among his fellow warriors; some even tried to commend land to him. Surely the Latter Three Years' War marked another stage in the growth of warrior power, and possibly even the inception of feudalism in Japan.

The late-eleventh-century conflict really shows, however, the weakness of Yoshiie, and the continued vitality of the Court and its military system. Yoshiie did not benefit from his 4 years of battling the Kiyowara; instead the government, still operating on the basis of the 901 system, decided that Yoshiie was carrying out personal vengeance and punished him by dismissing him from the governorship of Mutsu. Furthermore, as one scholar has pointed out, the Court did not promote Yoshiie in rank until he repaid tax revenues from Mutsu which he had interdicted and diverted to fight the Kiyowara.[123] The repayment must have been quite a burden since it took Yoshiie 10 years (until 1096) to obtain the proper receipts from Mutsu provincial headquarters, indicating that he had paid off the debt.

Why did the Court punish Yoshiie? Because Yoshiie's victims, the Kiyowara, had continued to pay their taxes and to respect the Court throughout the local dispute. To be sure, hostilities of the type waged between Sanehira and his vassal, or his relative Iehira and Kiyohira, were worthy of notice. But as long as the Kiyowara continued to pass along revenues and obey the Court, aristocrats considered private quarrels to be beyond official concern. The Heian Court took Masakado's revolt seriously only after he attacked the Hitachi provincial headquarters.

One can ask why Yoshiie risked the Court's wrath; the answer lies in his father's (Yoriyoshi's) relations with the Kiyowara. Recall that Yoriyoshi was losing the Former Nine Years' War until the Kiyowara joined him in 1062, and that most of the warriors that fought for Yoriyoshi were from the Kiyowara. According to one source, the Kiyowara claimed that Yoriyoshi had actually sworn loyalty to them by presenting his signed oath of allegiance (*myōbu*) to them.[124] After his victory at Kanezawa Stockade, Yoshiie vehemently challenged the Kiyowara to present their evidence for this claim, but they did not. It would not be surprising if Yoriyoshi had made promises to obtain Kiyowara support, and later, when

Yoshiie gave Fujiwara Kiyohira half the Kiyowara inheritance (the Six Districts of Mutsu), the Kiyowara perceived Yoshiie as violating his father's oaths. The war then became a struggle between Yoshiie and the Kiyowara to see who could enforce his will upon the other. Ironically, Yoshiie's victory, which should have guaranteed him dominance in the Tohoku, left the way open for another warrior family, the Fujiwara, to replace the Kiyowara as rulers of the Tohoku, and the Minamoto gained little advantage from their quarrel for dominance in the region.

Most historians agree that the Latter Three Years' War increased Yoshiie's reputation among warriors, especially in the Kanto. Records describe warriors such as Taira no Kagemasa as loyal followers of Yoshiie; his heirs continued to swear allegiance to the Minamoto in the twelfth century.[125] But the size of Yoshiie's following is open to dispute; many were undoubtedly mercenaries who left Yoshiie's service when the campaign ended.[126] The Kiyowara claimed to have had 48 major vassals (as evidence by the 48 heads taken by Yoshiie), and they resisted Yoshiie for quite a while.

Yoshiie's troubles did not end with his dismissal from the Mutsu governorship in 1088. In 1091, he fought with his younger brother Yoshitsuna. Later in 1091 and 1092, the government denied him the right to receive commendation of or to establish estates (*shōen*), but not, as Jeffrey Mass has stated, out of fear of Yoshiie's growing economic power.[127] Rather, the Court meant to punish Yoshiie for his quarrelsomeness and his failure to repay the revenues due the government from the Latter Three Years' War. One year after atoning for his sins, in 1097, the Court permitted Yoshiie the privilege of ascending into the Hall of Cool and Refreshing Breezes, the private residence of the Emperor; Yoshiie died in 1106, a favorite of the powerful Retired Emperor. Shortly after his death, one Heian aristocrat wrote:

> The late Yoshiie no Ason was for many years the chief of warriors [*bushi no chōja*]. It is said that he killed many who were without crime. In the end [would] the excess of his accumulated evil extend to his heirs?[128]

Rather than showing the ascendant private power of military lords, Yoshiie's experience in the Latter Three Years' War underlines the power of the Court and its adherence to the military system of 901. This war, which amounted to a personal battle for warrior dominance in northeastern Honshu, suggests the continued development of the samurai fighting style, but also indicates that even such bold practitioners as Yoshiie could not defy the Court with impunity.

RAISING AN ARMY IN THE LATE HEIAN PERIOD: TAIRA NO TADAMORI AND THE PIRATES OF THE INLAND SEA

Advocates of the Western-analogue theory have viewed both the Former Nine Years' War and the Latter Three Years' War as important events in Japan's shift to feudalism. Although I have argued that the provincial military system first established in 901 was still in operation throughout the eleventh century, it is true that historical sources for the two wars refer to the provincial headquarters less frequently, giving the impression of a new feudal military system in the countryside. Furthermore, the personal retainers of Yoriyoshi and Yoshiie figure prominently in literary accounts of the conflicts. It would be easy to conclude that private forces far outnumbered state troops, and that, by about 1050, Japan had emerged into European-style feudalism, leaving its earlier heritage behind.

An examination of other conflicts in the era from the conclusion of the Latter Three Years' War in 1087 to the outbreak of the Hōgen Disturbance in 1156 suggests that the provincial military system was not dead, but had only undergone further modification. The "rise of the warrior" continued to take place within the confines of the earlier institution. While one could cite several disturbances of the twelfth century to demonstrate the critical role played by provincial forces, none better illustrates this point than the suppression of pirates undertaken by Taira no Tadamori in 1135.[129]

Taira no Tadamori was a member of the famous warrior lineage that traced its origins back to Prince Takamochi of the late ninth century and boasted such eminent and lawless military men as Masakado and Tadatsune. As noted in Chapter 5, Taira no Korehira had established a base in Ise by the late tenth century. Tadamori was Korehira's great-great grandson and also controlled men and property in western Japan. By 1135, the Taira had obtained the favor of the Retired Emperor Toba, and competed with the Minamoto to serve the Court.[130]

Piracy on the Inland Sea was a crucial problem for the Heian Court because the brigands threatened the aristocracy's economic lifeline to western Honshu, Shikoku, Kyushu, and the Asian mainland. The Court's concern about piracy in western Japan is evident in its quick reaction to the revolt of Fujiwara Sumitomo in 939. In 1129, the Court dispatched Tadamori to suppress pirates in the Inland Sea after remarking that "governors feared the strength and bravery [of the pirates] and had no heart for capturing them."[131] In 1134, a prominent Court official recorded that one of Tadamori's men had received a prize for disarming pirates.[132] The year 1134 also saw widespread famine, flood, and epidemics, conditions that had fostered piracy earlier, in Sumitomo's time.[133]

The assault on aristocratic coffers continued. In 1135, the government issued an arrest order which asked provincial governors to "give instructions to the warriors (*mosa*) within their jurisdictions and . . . have them (the warriors) effect arrests."[134] The Court wished to use the provincial governors to raise forces, a standard procedure under the guidelines of 901.

But Minamoto no Morotoki, an official in the Imperial Consort's Quarters, scribbled in his diary that "[i]n my foolish opinion, this plan will not work." The reason he gave was that most of "the brave and powerful of the provinces [also] enjoyed piracy," and would intimidate the governors from capturing or killing the brigands. Instead, Morotoki hoped the governors would "tender a list (*kyōmyō*) of the warriors (*bushi*) of the province, and [the Court] would bestow a decree" upon each warrior. If the central government issued the order, then "wouldn't the aforementioned brigands come to respect us [the Court] of their own accord?"[135]

The author's comments suggest that the 901 system, which aimed at keeping peace in the countryside, was breaking down. Morotoki expressed reservations about how readily governors of the provinces along the Inland Sea could assemble warriors in their jurisdictions, especially since many of those soldiers were also pirates. Perhaps governors lacked the resources to reward warriors adequately, or perhaps they were profiting from the piracy themselves. Given the inability of the governors to rule effectively,

Morotoki suggested issuing arrest orders directly to warriors from the list of fighters in the provinces, which officials had been keeping since at least 901. Morotoki wanted to bypass the governors but still utilize the resources of the provincial headquarters.

On the 8th of the 4th month in 1135, Heian courtiers reconvened to discuss the matter. Fortunately, both Morotoki, who had disparaged the governors earlier, and the powerful Minister of the Right recorded the discussion, which took place before the most powerful member of the Court, the Retired Emperor himself. In his version of events, Morotoki emphasized the gravity of the threat: Pirates cut routes of trade and communication, and revenues could not reach the capital. This diarist included the remarks of another official who referred to relatives of the brigands residing in the capital and operating a network of spies plying the Inland Sea from Dazaifu to the capital, a situation reminiscent of Sumitomo's time.[136]

Morotoki also stressed that other officials perceived the provincial military as not working properly. The Court issued orders to governors who relayed them to warriors, but troops would not obey. According to Morotoki's version of the meeting, the Court decided to dispatch an arrest officer (*tsuibatsu shi*), presumably a famous warrior who could command the respect of other fighters, instead of relying on governors.

The Minister of the Right's description of the same meeting was somewhat different. It is quoted at some length both to show the disagreement and the collaborative nature of late Heian politics:

> The Regent [*denka*] proclaimed: "Recently pirates vie with each other to revolt. Boats coming and going to the capital are unable to pass. Because of this, the Court has issued a decree to the effect that the pirates ought to be pursued and struck down (*tsuitō*). Although an order has been sent to the provincial governors, until now it has not been implemented. What should we do? People should discuss among themselves and speak up."
>
> Akiyori stood and said: "[The Court] should decree to the effect that the residents of estates (*shōen*) here and there who act as pirates should be summoned by command of the guarantors (*honjo*) of their estates."
>
> People agreed with this.

I said: "What is wrong with issuing an order to the effect that Tadamori no Ason, the Governor of Bizen, or [Minamoto no] Tameyoshi, an Investigator (*kebiishi*), should pursue and destroy the pirates?"

The Regent remonstrated with the Retired Emperor through . . . the Head Chamberlain.

The Ex-Emperor expounded: ". . . Tadamori no Ason is the Governor of Bizen and ought to be right for the job. It ought to be proper to issue an order to Tadamori no Ason about quickly searching out and destroying the brigands."[137]

This version agrees in most respects with Morotoki's. The outline of the problem was the same, and the Regent shared the general frustration with the provincial governors of the Inland Sea. According to the Minister of the Right's notes on the meeting, eventually he himself made the suggestion to appoint an arrest officer, and the Retired Emperor Toba endorsed Tadamori.

The critical difference in the two versions of events concerns Akiyori's speech. The Minister of the Right recorded that, when the Regent called for people to express their opinions on the problem of piracy, Fujiwara no Akiyori, who held the post of Extraordinary Councillor, wanted to use a completely novel method to control the brigands: Command high-level estate (*shōen*) officials, the guarantors, to convince the pirates to come forward. Guarantors comprised the elite of twelfth-century Court society, including the Fujiwara Regent's house, the Imperial Family, and large temples and shrines.[138] Akiyori's plan to use these lords suggests that estates comprised a considerable proportion of land held in the new system of tenure implemented after 1045, and that many warriors were affiliated with the *shōen*.[139] Akiyori was also implying that the Court needed to modify the system of 901, in which governors led armies, because a new affiliation for warriors (*shōen*) had come into existence and governors were unable to exercise control there.

Thus Heian aristocrats considered 3 alternatives for raising troops to put down the pirates of the Inland Sea in 1135. (1) The Court tried to work through provincial governors, but they proved unreliable and ineffective. (2) The Court discussed military aristocrats who might be named to be arrest officers, and who could utilize their own personal forces along with the soldiers of the provinces. (3) One noble suggested enlisting the aid of the guarantors of estates, a method never attempted before.

In the end, the Heian aristocracy chose the second plan. However powerful estate guarantors might have been, the number of warriors associated with estates must have been too small and the method of rallying troops, through each guarantor, would have been too difficult. Even though new estates may have been widespread in western Japan, the Court must have felt that the proven method of dispatching an arrest officer of warrior lineage to command both his own following and the troops of the provincial headquarters was the best strategy. Unlike non-warrior governors appointed from the outside, military men named to be governors could take advantage of both the personal loyalties of local fighters as well as the official resources of the provincial headquarters. In the early twelfth century, the provincial headquarters (but not the governor) was as crucial as ever for raising and commanding military forces.

One might ask why governors were no longer reliable leaders of their provincial armies and navies. Ever since the end of the eighth century, many aristocratic governors refused to live in the provinces to which they were assigned. They stayed in the capital and traveled to the province a few times a year to hound residents into paying their taxes. By the late eleventh century, most governors employed an agent (*mokudai*) who stayed in the province to oversee the aristocratic governor's affairs. Soon it became apparent that the agent served the interests of the governor, which might be different from those of the other officials employed at the provincial headquarters.[140] Provincial officials must have looked upon the agent as an interloper; they did not cooperate with him in many areas, including military affairs. Without their help, the governor was no longer able to command the men and resources of the office to which the Court had appointed him. The Court came to recognize this problem, and decided to name military men as governors, as in 1051 when they appointed Yoriyoshi to circumvent the governors of the Tohoku.

Figure 8 represents the revised system of conscription and command in the twelfth century. At the local level, it was similar to the institution of 901, except that some warriors now dwelt in estates, beyond the immediate control of the government.

Figure 8. LOCAL MILITARY IN THE LATE HEIAN PERIOD

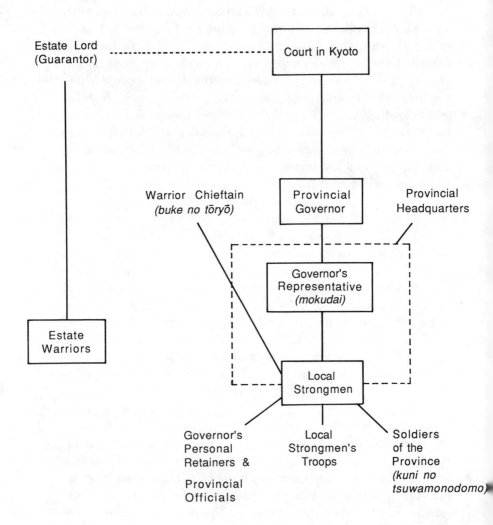

Sources: Ishii Susumu, *Kamakura bushi no jitsuzō,* p. 347; Shimomukai Tatsuhiko, "Ōchō kokka kokuga gunsei no kōzō to tenkai," *Shigaku kenkyū* 151:46 (May 1981).

The twelfth-century method for raising troops had one more important implication: Someone had to assume the position of "warrior chieftain" to command forces when the Court required. Presumably it would be someone from a military house, but it was unclear how such a leader would be chosen. Would the Court name him? Would other warriors recognize him? Would his exploits give him the title? Now the government officially recognized dominance and hierarchy within the warrior community; the existence of such a post, even if only by custom, had already led to conflict among military aristocrats. Official recognition of a warrior leader could open the door for internecine warfare on a national scale.

Tadamori's warrior blood was crucial to the decision to name him arrest officer. As the leader of the Taira, Tadamori boasted a personal following and could command the respect of other military men in the provinces along the Inland Sea. Moreover, as Morotoki put it in his diary, "Tadamori was rumored to have power in the Western Sea."[141] But before one makes too much of Tadamori's retainers, it is important to remember that he was also Governor of Bizen, with access to the warriors of that province. Therefore, Tadamori's appointment confirms that, by the twelfth century, troops were raised both through the personal connections of a leading military aristocrat and through the provincial headquarters.[142] At most, the 1135 plan for raising an army represented only a modification of what had gone before.

Dispatching Tadamori was the right move; news of his success against the pirates reached the capital by the 6th month.[143] On the 19th of the 8th month, Tadamori transferred about 70 captives to the Investigators, the legal representatives of the Court. Morotoki recorded that Tadamori and his men seized only about 30 pirates. He captured the other prisoners in an attempt to increase his reward.[144] On the 21st, Tadamori received a prize.

THE PROVINCIAL HEADQUARTERS IN OTHER CONFLICTS. Four more incidents reinforce the argument for the continued prominence of the provincial headquarters in the local military between 1087 and 1156. In 1091, Yoshiie and his brother Yoshitsuna became embroiled in a quarrel in the capital. The Court was concerned about reducing violence in its own city. On the 12th of the 6th month, the soon-to-be Regent wrote that the Retired Emperor had issued an order to the provinces "that the followers of the provincial governors desist [from entering the capital]."[145] In the late eleventh century, the Court still believed that provincial governors held the reins of Japan's military.

In 1107, the government dispatched Taira no Masamori, Tadamori's father, to deal with Minamoto no Yoshichika, Yoshiie's antisocial son. Yoshichika was Governor of Tsushima, where he had disobeyed orders from Dazaifu, and conspired with one of his own father's vassals to murder a state messenger. The Court banished him to Oki. Later Yoshichika violated the terms of his banishment and crossed over into Izumo, where he murdered the Governor's representative (*mokudai*) and stole provincial revenues. In the 12th month of 1107, the Court issued an arrest order which gave Masamori, Governor of neighboring Inaba, the right to "invite the fighters of the nearby provinces" (*kuniguni no heishi*) to punish Yoshichika.[146]

In 1139, the monks of Kōfukuji rioted in Nara and threatened to march on the capital. The upheaval arose when someone burned the residence of a temple official; arson and murder occurred at Kōfukuji throughout the 3rd month of 1139. To contain the disturbance, the Retired Emperor dispatched Tadamori, now Governor of nearby Mimasaka, and he and 6 other warriors destroyed the bridge at Uji that led to the capital from Nara. At the same time, he deployed "soldiers of the provinces" along the Yodo Crossing, another route to Heian.[147] The warriors stayed in place until the Court met Kōfukuji's demands later in the month.

In 1147, Taira no Kiyomori, the renowned son of Tadamori, quarreled with a lower official (*jῑnin*) of Gion Shrine (in the capital) while on a pilgrimage. Since Kiyomori's men wounded several persons and destroyed shrine property, the monks of Enryakuji became so enraged that they threatened to march on the capital. To defend against the monks, the Court dispatched "the soldiers of the provinces" to vital roads and bridges, although troops from the Retired Emperor's Northern Quarters probably played a more important role in this case.[148]

CONCLUSION

Many historians have viewed the period from 1045 to 1150 as a major turning point in the development of Japan's military. According to these accounts, estates in the countryside came to occupy a significant portion of the land under cultivation for the first time, and warriors (*bushi*), who led the "age of widespread land clearance" and founded most of these estates, gained the new wealth necessary to become rulers of all Japan. These military men used a new technology and fighting style that emphasized single, mounted encounters, and pledged personal loyalty to each other in martial bands. Many of these historians view the transition of the late eleventh and twelfth centuries as the victory of private ties over such public institutions as the system of the Taihō Codes. It was only natural, in these interpretations, that Japanese feudalism was seen to emerge from this period.[149]

This chapter has presented a different view of the same era. While agreeing that the development of the *shōen-kokugaryō* system of land tenure and the final elaboration of samurai fighting style were important, I have argued that underlying continuities were more impressive. The weapons and the preeminence of the mounted archer were not new to Japanese battle tactics in the twelfth century, but had been there all along. Fighters had organized themselves into military houses, with martial aristocrats leading armies and navies into combat. Other warriors had had sizable incomes, albeit from office and tax-collecting privileges.

The formation of the *shōen-kokugaryō* system did not represent a fundamental departure from the preceding system of land use and tenure. In *Population, Disease, and Land in Early Japan, 645–900*, I suggested that Japanese agriculture suffered from cycles of land clearance and abandonment, which derived from epidemics, famines, drought, and poor technology. The years 1045–1185 represent one of these cycles. Following a period of unprecedented devastation due to disease, war, and drought, warriors and many others began to clear lands. Much of the land they opened was actually a reopening of older parcels; it is possible that the total acreage under cultivation in 1180 exceeded earlier totals, but not by much. Warriors also enjoyed taking others' fields by forging deeds, altering boundaries, and using force. Yields and the population numbers they supported were probably not much greater than before, but cultivators may have farmed their parcels a little more intensively. The Japanese warrior (*bushi*), no less than his counterpart in the eighth century, was still a prisoner of economic and demographic trends beyond his control.

It is within the context of these trends that one must understand the reference to warriors as "lords of land clearance" (*kaihotsu ryō-shu*). Warriors did open parcels, but, since disasters had devastated so much land before the formation of the *shōen-kokugaryō* system in 1045, military men probably did not add much to total arable land. Thus fighters could have an important role in the revival of agriculture in the eleventh and twelfth centuries yet still fit into economic and demographic trends that had appeared much earlier.

While Japan was suffering and recovering from a subsistence crisis in the middle and late eleventh century, warriors fought two major wars with the residents of northeastern Honshu. In the Former Nine Years' War, Minamoto no Yoriyoshi subdued the Abe; the conflict had all the earmarks of another intraspecific battle between warrior families for dominance, although the Abe also brought down the wrath of the Court upon themselves by not paying their taxes. In the Latter Three Years' War, Minamoto no Yoshiie crushed the Kiyowara in a personal feud, and the Court refused to recognize or reward the chieftain for his efforts.

Both wars showed the final elaboration of the samurai fighting style of man-to-man, equestrian combat, but this change represented only a minor alteration in past patterns. The weapons preferred by mounted archers had evolved by the early ninth century, and the leading role of horsemen in the army was as true of Taihō forces or the troops of Masakado as it was of eleventh-century heroes like Yoriyoshi and Yoshiie.

Despite a continuing reliance on ties of loyalty among warriors, the critical role of the provincial headquarters continued. Yoriyoshi organized his men to rout the Abe in the Former Nine Years' War just like his predecessors: through the provincial headquarters and local strongmen. The government refused to reward and indeed punished Yoshiie, who tried to claim Court authorization and use provincial forces for a personal feud. When Taira no Tadamori suppressed the pirates of the Inland Sea in 1135, the Court considered utilizing estate guarantors to call upon their soldiers to lead the fight, but decided against such a method. Attempts to raise or command soldiers by means other than the provincial headquarters proved failures. The best way to crush an enemy of the state was to appoint a military aristocrat to a provincial governorship and allow him to employ both his own vassals and the considerable resources of the province.

By 1100, use of a prominent military aristocrat to lead Court forces had become the most common way for the Court to do battle. Appointment to such an expedition implied that the martial noble was "the chief of all warriors," at least for the time being. The rewards were great — prestige, influence among other fighters, Court rank and preferment, and governorships. Competition to be the sole military leader would make for constant warfare in the second half of the twelfth century.

chapter seven

The Quest for Independence and Political Skills, 1150–1185

*[Minamoto no] Yoritomo secretly . . . [said] . . . to the Retired Emperor: ". . .
[J]ust like old times, the Minamoto and Taira [should] stand side by side, and
. . . serve you. The Kanto would be under the control of the Minamoto, and the
Western Sea would follow the desires of the Taira. Both could be rulers. . . ."
. . . But before the late . . . [Taira no Kiyomori, head of the family] . . .
closed his eyes, with his dying words he said: "My sons and grandsons, even if
only one of you is left alive, you should die fighting against [lit. bleach your bones
in front of] Yoritomo."*
—from *The Jeweled Leaf,* the diary of Kujō no Kanezane, in 1181

By the twelfth century, the Japanese military needed a single
leader with full authority. Despite compromises such as the one
offered by Yoritomo to the Taira, martial aristocrats fiercely competed to determine who would hold the revered title "chief of all
warriors." Two factors encouraged such a contest, which was altogether new to late Heian Japan: the power struggles among military families, who sought to establish dominance within an accep-
table hierarchy of fighting men; and the system of command and
conscription, which required a single soldier to serve as an arrest
officer when trouble arose.

The keys to asserting leadership over other warriors were wealth
and power, both still dispensed mostly by the Court and the newly
ascendant Retired Emperor, who had assumed a prominent role
in politics ever since freeing the imperial institution from a Fujiwara stranglehold in 1086. A military aristocrat could gain riches
and clout at Court only through his use of political skills and his

acquired reserve of administrative and governmental acumen. A monopoly over brute force, organized into military houses and supported by a tenuous hold on small economic bases, had carried the warrior so far, but, by 1100, the game was mostly politics. Even improvements in the samurai's economic position had to come through war or political infighting, since basic demographic and agricultural advances would not come to Japan until after 1300.

At first the Kawachi line of Minamoto appeared to be the leading contender for supreme military command, as Yoshiie conquered the Kiyowara and garnered the favor of the first Retired Emperor. Yet, for most of the twelfth century, the Ise Taira held military power in the capital and countryside. Kiyomori, the most renowned head of the Taira, enhanced his ascendancy by displaying the greatest political ability of any warrior to date. He marshaled 300 horsemen on behalf of the Emperor Go-Shirakawa in the Hōgen Disturbance of 1156, and defeated the Fujiwara Regents and the main branch of the Minamoto. Kiyomori outmaneuvered his rival Minamoto no Yoshitomo politically, and then delivered the knockout blow to the hapless Minamoto in the Heiji War of 1159.

As the foremost military aristocrats of Japan, the Taira developed their own martial institutions from 1160. Holding nationwide military and police authority, they grew wealthy and politically adept; they built a national system of vassalage through grants of guard duty in the capital. They controlled many provincial headquarters and served the economic interests of their main followers, perhaps even by confirming them in their land holdings. By 1177, the Taira had become so powerful that they antagonized their powerful former ally, the recalcitrant Retired Emperor Go-Shirakawa, later confining him under house arrest and operating the military and the Court as they pleased.

In 1180, rebellions sprang up throughout Japan, fed by resentment of Taira dominance. But far from being a revolution into feudalism, the Great Civil War of 1180–1185 showed more continuity than change. The provincial headquarters was still crucial for raising and commanding armies for both sides, and samurai forces were the same size and used almost the same technology as those of the tenth century. Only a disastrous famine in western Japan allowed Minamoto no Yoritomo to reverse the pattern of outside control over the Kanto.

THE TAIRA'S ROAD TO POWER AND THE CAPITAL MILITARY

THE TAIRA OVERTAKE THE MINAMOTO. In 1100, the house of the Minamoto from Kawachi province, the line that had started its ascent with Yorinobu, hero of Tadatsune's rebellion, was the unquestioned leader of Japan's warriors. At that time, Yoshiie, "the son of Hachiman," was head of the family. He had attained fame, wealth, and the favor of the Retired Emperor, the most powerful figure at Court. But within ten years, the Minamoto had fallen upon hard times, and a new line, the Ise Taira, had started a march to power. How and why did this momentous turn of events take place?

Historians usually cite Taira no Masamori's commendation of land in and around Tomoda village to the estate of the Retired Emperor Shirakawa's late beloved daughter in 1097 as signaling the first step in the Taira's rise to fame (see Chapters 5 and 6 and Figures 9 and 10). The commendation of Tomoda lands, in tandem with ties to powerful civil aristocrats, began a relationship of mutual benefit to the Retired Emperor and the Ise Taira, a relatively obscure branch of the family.[1] As a result of the commendation, Masamori received appointment first to the governorship of wealthy Wakasa province and eventually to several other provinces.

There can be little doubt that there was an alliance of economic and political interests between the Retired Emperors and the Ise Taira, the former gaining land commendations from the Taira in return for governorships.[2] The Ise Taira also often served as the "teeth and claws" of the Retired Emperors, a position that allowed them to make contacts with other fighters throughout Japan. But, instead of adopting the position that the Retired Emperors unjustly favored an unknown branch of the inept Taira, it is more historically accurate to look at some objective factors that made the decision more reasonable and less capricious than one might think.

The most important factor was the lack of really capable military aristocrats from whom the Retired Emperor Shirakawa, who left the throne in 1086 at the age of 33 and held sway at Court until

Figure 9. THE IMPERIAL FAMILY IN LATE HEIAN JAPAN

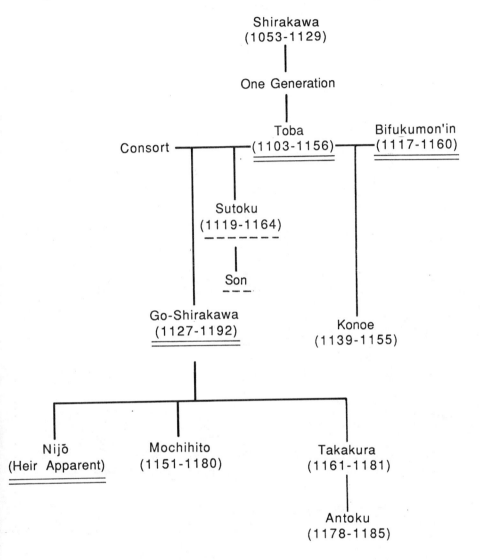

Regent's Faction in 1156 — — — — —
Imperial Faction in 1156 ═══════

Figure 10. THE ISE TAIRA AND THE MINAMOTO

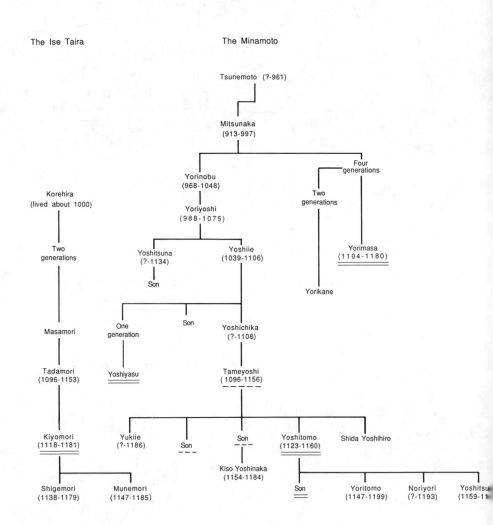

The Ise Taira

The Minamoto

Tsunemoto (?-961)

Mitsunaka
(913-997)

Yorinobu
(968-1048)

Four
generations

Korehira
(lived about 1000)

Two
generations

Yoriyoshi
(988-1075)

Two
generations
generations

Yoshiie
(1039-1106)

Yoshitsuna
(?-1134)

Yorimasa
(1104-1180)

Son

Yorikane

One
generation

Son

Yoshichika
(?-1108)

Masamori

Tadamori
(1096-1153)

Yoshiyasu

Tameyoshi
(1096-1156)

Kiyomori
(1118-1181)

Yukiie
(?-1186)

Son

Son

Yoshitomo
(1123-1160)

Shida Yoshihiro

Kiso Yoshinaka
(1154-1184)

Shigemori
(1138-1179)

Munemori
(1147-1185)

Son

Yoritomo
(1147-1199)

Noriyori
(?-1193)

Yoshitsu
(1159-11

Regents Faction in 1156 – – – – – –

Imperial Faction in 1156 =====

1129, could choose to serve as champions of the Court. When Shirakawa abdicated in 1086, the leader of the Kawachi Genji, the other major martial house, was Minamoto no Yoshiie (see Figure 10). As noted in Chapter 5, Yoshiie did not finish paying off his debts from the Latter Three Years' War until 1096; in 1098, he found favor with Shirakawa and obtained the privilege of rising upon the floor of the Hall of Cool and Refreshing Breezes, but by then he was almost 60 years old. Three years later, in 1101, Yoshiie's mad son, Yoshichika, was the object of an arrest order, and, in 1102, Yoshiie's vassal, undoubtedly dispatched to resolve the disorder before the Court intervened, conspired with Yoshichika to murder a government official (see Chapter 6). Yoshiie died in 1106.

Minamoto no Yoshitsuna, Yoshiie's brother and rival, was another capital aristocrat due consideration for duty under Shirakawa. Yoshitsuna had been guilty of raising troops against Yoshiie in 1091, but in 1094 he had received an arrest order to crush two villains with about 200 horsemen and 300 foot soldiers.[3] However, while Yoshiie cultivated Retired Emperor Shirakawa to obtain favor, Yoshitsuna chose the Fujiwara Regent, the traditional lord for the Kawachi Minamoto.[4] The Regent Moromichi protected Yoshitsuna from murder charges leveled by Enryakuji in 1095 when Yoshitsuna was Governor of Mino, but Yoshitsuna's champion died unexpectedly in 1099 at the age of 38, and the young son and heir to the regency lacked his father's political expertise and clout. It is likely that Yoshitsuna's tie with the Regent's house made him unacceptable to Shirakawa.

Thus, in 1101, when Minamoto no Yoshichika began his rampage, Yoshitsuna was not a serious candidate to lead a Court expedition. The same situation obtained in 1107 when government troops under Masamori beheaded Yoshichika. In 1109, the Minamoto descended into internecine struggle; Yoshiie's heir was murdered, and the Court accused and executed Yoshitsuna's child. Yoshitsuna was so enraged that he fled the capital and was obliged to surrender to the Court-appointed arrest officer, the 14-year-old son of Yoshichika, Minamoto no Tameyoshi. The Court banished Yoshitsuna and he never recovered politically.

By 1110, the Ise Taira had gained great favor through the subjugation of Yoshichika, while the Minamoto were in disarray. The young Tameyoshi, who had attained office in the Gate Guards through his actions against Yoshitsuna, led the Minamoto. Conventionally, historians have viewed the Retired Emperors as using the inexperienced Tameyoshi because they favored the demise of the Minamoto, but one scholar has challenged this interpretation,[5] and suggests that Shirakawa was really allowing Tameyoshi, the son of a convicted murderer and rebel, a chance to redeem himself and the Minamoto by handling his rival and relative Yoshitsuna in what could be considered a family affair. Tameyoshi must have been successful, since subsequently he became the adopted heir of Yoshiie and received an appointment to office for his efforts.

As head of the Minamoto, Tameyoshi tried diligently to reverse his family's decline. In his early life, Tameyoshi even followed his adopted father, Yoshiie, in preferring to serve the Retired Emperor over the Fujiwara Regents. Even though popular history has identified the Minamoto as usually working for the Fujiwara Regents, while the Taira monopolized the Retired Emperors, such thinking does not derive from the early twelfth century. Minamoto no Tameyoshi never acted on behalf of the Regents' house in his youth; he repeatedly followed the wishes of Shirakawa. He was even present to guard Shirakawa at Court meetings.

If Shirakawa held no animosity against Tameyoshi or the Kawachi Minamoto, then why did he prefer the Ise Taira over the Kawachi Minamoto? Part of the answer lies in circumstances beyond anyone's control. Tameyoshi began his career as Gate Guard and Investigator, just about the same time as his opposite number for the Ise Taira, Tadamori. But unlike Tadamori, Tameyoshi's adoptive father, Yoshiie, was dead and could provide no support: Tadamori's father, Taira no Masamori, lived on until 1121. Thus Tadamori assumed numerous governorships and ultimately became the Minister of Punishments, while Tameyoshi never rose above his initial offices.

A second reason Tameyoshi never succeeded as a military aristocrat was his own antisocial behavior. Between 1114 and 1154, Tameyoshi provoked 10 incidents, thrice hiding criminals, 6 times being responsible for quarrels, and once failing to prevent the disorder of his son in Kyushu. For one of these violations, in 1136, the

Court dismissed Tameyoshi from office. He remained without office for almost 10 years, from age 41 to 51.

Tameyoshi's bad reputation was so widespread that even the Retired Emperor, who wanted to employ him, knew of it. In 1135, when the government chose Tadamori to lead forces against the pirates of the Inland Sea, officials also considered Tameyoshi. But, in the words of the Retired Emperor, "If we dispatch Tameyoshi, the provinces along the way will naturally be devastated."[6] Tameyoshi was truly his father's (Yoshichika's) son.

The Retired Emperor turned increasingly to Masamori's Ise Taira to command Japan's military, not merely out of favoritism, but because the Taira were the most effective martial aristocrats available. The litany of Masamori's and Tadamori's triumphs in the provinces resounds through the first half of the twelfth century (see Chapter 6). In 1107–1108, Masamori killed Yoshichika and destroyed his force with soldiers of the province and about 200 horsemen and 40–50 foot soldiers.[7] In 1119, the Court dispatched Masamori to deal with pirates, and he selected 100 of the most famous warriors of the Inland Sea and Kyushu, returning in the 12th month with the heads of the culprits.[8] And in 1135, Tadamori routed the pirates again.

The Taira did not come to prominence without jealousy and complaints. Courtiers widely criticized Retired Emperor Shirakawa for giving a top prize (the governorship of Tajima) to such a lowly figure as Masamori, especially before the warrior had returned to the capital.[9] To counter this criticism, Masamori displayed his soldiers in full regalia before a properly awed capital throng. Still many doubted that a humble warrior like Masamori could behead Yoshichika. In 1117 and 1123, impostors posing as Yoshichika emerged in the Kanto, and in 1130 two more men masquerading as Yoshichika took up residence in the capital; the appearance of these impersonators implied that Masamori had not killed the rebel and that Shirakawa had shown undue favoritism in his relations with the Taira.[10] Yoshichika's wife discredited the frauds, or the Court had them murdered, and the Taira continued their rise. Despite these unusual events and the embarrassment they caused the government, the Retired Emperors continued to support the Taira because the alternatives lacked loyalty and reliability.

THE CAPITAL MILITARY. As the leading military aristocrats of their day, the Taira also naturally aided in protecting the capital. In the early and mid-twelfth century, defense of the capital was in the hands of three groups: military aristocrats like Masamori, the Investigators and the Imperial Guards, and warriors chosen by the Retired Emperor. Because the Taira held memberships in all three units by the early 1100s, and came to control military affairs in the Court and capital, a brief consideration of capital soldiery follows.

There were only slight modifications in the martial offices of Heian after 1050. The only entity from the Taihō capital forces to retain its military function after 1050 was the Gate Guards (Emon fu), although the unit guarding the Heir Apparent (Tachiwaki no toneri) regained a military function in the late eleventh century, as the Minamoto and the Taira entered its ranks. About three-quarters of the soldiers protecting the Heir Apparent were warriors from around the capital.[11]

The Investigators (Kebii shi) changed as well.[12] In the late Heian period, they became stronger as the Court appointed more men from the Taira and Minamoto, warriors who joined the organization in response to the Investigators' weak performance against monk armies who assaulted the capital to protest the Court's political and religious policies. The numbers and responsibilities of the Investigators also undoubtedly increased. The Retired Emperor often gave direct orders to them, but he could not issue commands to enter estates; in any case, the Investigators per se lost their military power during the Great Civil War of 1180-1185 and its aftermath.

A new institution, "the Warriors of the Northern Quarter" (Hokumen no bushi), counted many Ise Taira among its members. Established in 1087 by Shirakawa to guard the Retired Emperor, the Warriors of the Northern Quarter were either fighters with small bases in the capital region or Shirakawa's favorite governors.[13] They probably numbered only about 100 men or so, although in 1118, when the monks of Enryakuji attempted an advance on Heian, the Court responded by sending "about 1,000" fighters, including those who "served in the Northern Quarter and their followers."[14]

Many conflicts erupted in the streets of Heian during the twelfth century, but most did not differ fundamentally from those discussed in Chapter 5, whether wars between the followers of the civil aristocracy or robberies.[15] One form of violence was unique to the late eleventh and twelfth centuries — religious riots. Warding off bands of armed monks and their hired soldiers who assaulted Heian from time to time became a central concern for the Court and the Ise Taira as well. Monks took arms against the Court to protest temple appointments, gubernatorial land and tax policies, and conflicts with other religious institutions. The militarization of the great religious institutions was part of the general trend towards domestic violence in late Heian Japan, and was also a by-product of economic decline.

The state deployed the military against clerical protesters as early as 1039; by the close of the eleventh century, the frequency of attacks multiplied with religious militancy. In a 1081 attack by more than 1,000 monks of Mt. Hiei, 200 of whom wore armor and carried bows and arrows, the Court employed Investigators (Kebii shi), Gate Guards, and other warriors.[16] In other attacks in 1092, 1093, 1095, 1102, and 1104, it became the policy to use the Investigators and other minor military officials against the monks unless religious marchers were too numerous, in which case the Court would also call upon military aristocrats. Employing capital officials and military aristocrats to guard Heian had been common since at least the tenth century.

The Court first considered using the Ise Taira in 1107 against the monks of Enryakuji.[17] In 1108, the Court sent both the Taira and Minamoto as well as the Investigators to stop several thousand monks in their march on the capital. The most famous incident involving the Taira was the protest of 1113 (*Eikyū no gōso*),[18] which illuminates both the character of religious military forces and the workings of the capital military establishment as led by the Ise Taira in the twelfth century.

The combatants in the 1113 incident were the temples of Kōfukuji of Nara and Enryakuji located on Mt. Hiei just outside of the capital. Kōfukuji, which had connections to the Fujiwara Regents, petitioned on the 21st of the intercalary 3rd month in 1113 to have an appointment to its Heian branch temple of Kiyomizudera changed because monks at Kōfukuji's rival temple, Enryakuji, had trained the appointee. The petitition process was a violent one, in which monks, followers, and soldiers, altogether about 5,000 persons, marched on Heian bearing a sacred palanquin which contained an image of their god. Afraid of divine wrath, the Court withdrew its appointee and replaced him with a Kōfukuji-approved candidate.

On the 29th, Enryakuji's monks advanced on the capital and wrecked buildings at Kiyomizudera to protest Kōfukuji's actions. Shirakawa called upon Masamori and Tameyoshi to fend off the clerics with horsemen and foot soldiers:

> Warriors (*bushi*) formed a line and went on guard throughout the night. The voices of the monks calling out shook heaven. They came closer to the gate and the Governor of Dewa [Minamoto no] Mitsukuni and the Governor of Tango, Masamori, put on armor and moved forth.[19]

But the Court backed down and changed its decision again to favor Enryakuji.

This time the monks of Kōfukuji were enraged. They threatened to attack the capital and requested aid from other temples in Nara. The Court replied with orders to Kōfukuji and Enryakuji to cease all military preparations. Records state that the temples raised their troops from among "natives of Yamato province and those estate residents who could carry a bow and arrows."[20] Sources from a later conflict suggest that mercenary "soldiers of the provincial headquarters" composed as much as a third of the temple armies.[21]

On the 21st the Court issued orders to send warriors to Uji to defend against the monks of Kōfukuji, and to Sakamoto to ward off the clerics of Enryakuji. The scene at Uji, where newly appointed Investigators Masamori and Tadamori waited, became violent. The following excerpt begins with a description of the battle by a Kōfukuji monk, followed by the comments of the Minister of the Right, a leading Fujiwara aristocrat:

> While we [the monks of Kōfukuji] were waiting awhile, unexpectedly a deer appeared in front where we were carrying the treasures of the [Kasuga] Shrine. When the monks and their followers saw this they either became fearful or began praying. While we were expressing our

faith, a soldier from the midst of the government troops came forth and was about to shoot the deer. The monks and others saw this and became unruly. When the troops saw their clamor, they could do nothing but come forth and shoot arrows. The monks then retreated. At this time each monk stopped soldiers and the followers of Mt. Kombu (low-ranking clerics) and had them defend the monks by blocking errant arrows. Of their own accord we joined battle with the government troops for some time.

The clerics did not intend to stand face-to-face with government troops and do battle, I don't believe. This is truly beyond words and can not be fully described. The appearance of the deer was a strange coincidence. As I think about it, maybe it was something planned by the gods?[22]

The clerics viewed the deer as a sacred messenger from Kasuga Shrine, and reacted violently when the soldier threatened their animal. With this incident, the protest of 1113 came to a close; 30 monks, 3 Kasuga Shrine attendants, 90 religious troops, and only 2 government soldiers lost their lives. Monk armies were frightening because of their sacred authority, but proved no match for Masamori and his vassals on the battlefield. Apparently the deer incident brought the armies face to face and forced the monks to recognize the futility of further armed struggle at this time.

THE HŌGEN WAR OF 1156

The Hōgen Disturbance of 1156 was a result of Court infighting over the imperial throne that had been simmering for 50 years.[23] The issue divided the Imperial House, the Fujiwara Regents, and their confidantes, both civil and military, into competing factions, pitting members of families against each other (see Figures 9 through 11). The war led to a new constellation of forces at Court, with the Emperor Go-Shirakawa winning out over the Fujiwara, and Taira no Kiyomori securing warrior leadership instead of the feckless Minamoto no Tameyoshi.

The most serious schism was within the Fujiwara house, where Tadazane (1078-1162) favored his second son, Yorinaga (1120-1156), over his first heir, Tadamichi (1097-1164), to become head of the household, Regent, and Inspector of Orders before the com-

Figure 11. THE FUJIWARA REGENTS
IN LATE HEIAN JAPAN

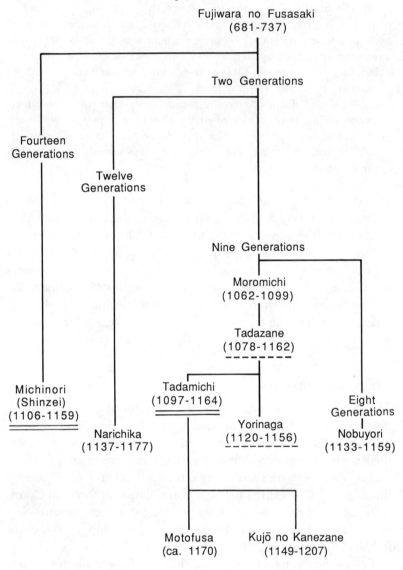

Regents Faction in 1156 ----

Imperial Faction in 1156 ====

mands were delivered to the Emperor for his approval. While Tadamichi was out of favor with his father, Tadazane, he was far from
powerless; Bifukumon'in (1117–1160), the consort of Retired
Emperor Toba, was Tadamichi's ally and had Toba's ear. Toba's confidantes, especially Shinzei (also known as Fujiwara no Michinori,
1106–1159), assisted Bifukumon'in in politicking for her candidate.

The specific problem over which these two factions fought was
the naming of an heir to the throne after the death of the sickly
Emperor Konoe in 1155. Toba's grandson and the son of the
Retired Emperor Sutoku (r. 1123–1141) was the logical candidate,
but Bifukumon'in pressed for her own favorite. Sutoku already
bore animosity towards Toba (his father) and Bifukumon'in
because they had forced him to abdicate in favor of the Emperor
Konoe. Eventually, Toba decided upon a third prince (Shinzei's
nominee) to become the Emperor Go-Shirakawa, and mollified
Bifukumon'in by establishing her man as Heir Apparent.

The Retired Emperor Sutoku had lost. So had Tadazane and
Yorinaga, because the new Emperor Go-Shirakawa assigned the
regency to Tadamichi, and Yorinaga lost the privilege of document
examination. Yorinaga, ever unpopular with the Court, retired to
his family's villa in Uji with his father Tadazane. Thus, by early
1156, the main line of the Fujiwara Regents, as represented by Tadazane and Yorinaga, opposed the chief authorities of the Imperial Household, Retired Emperor Toba, Bifukumon'in, and Go-
Shirakawa. Each had an ally in the other's household, Fujiwara no
Tadamichi for the imperial faction and the Retired Emperor
Sutoku for the Regents. As many historians have argued, the independence of the Fujiwara Regents from Toba and other Retired
Emperors was the crux of the matter.[24]

The losers in Court intrigue, the Fujiwara Regents and their
ally Sutoku, made plans to seize by force what they had not gained
by political maneuvering, and they decided to renew traditional
ties to the Kawachi Minamoto and ally themselves with another
"loser," Tameyoshi. Since his dismissal from office in 1135, Tameyoshi had been cultivating the Fujiwara Regents to help him
obtain office, the surest route to wealth and power. In 1142, the
Regent chose Tameyoshi to put down another riot at Kōfukuji. Kōfukuji was the Fujiwara's family temple, and a riot there was really

a private matter for the Fujiwara to handle; employment of Tameyoshi indicated his renewed favor with that family. After settling the riot and escorting the monkish culprits to Mutsu, Tameyoshi pleaded with Tadazane to help him retrieve his offices, but Tadazane refused. Tameyoshi continued to assist the Fujiwara until 1143 when he swore allegiance to Yorinaga.[25] In 1147, Tameyoshi achieved office again, probably with the aid of Tadazane and Yorinaga.

Meanwhile, Tameyoshi strove to improve his standing as head of the Kawachi Minamoto. He dispatched his eldest son, Minamoto no Yoshitomo, to the southern Kanto to enroll allies. This Yoshitomo did, raising warriors from Sagami, Shimōsa, and Kazusa to his cause, but Yoshitomo's success gave him other ideas. Instead of delivering his allies to his father, Yoshitomo kept them for himself. He left his son in charge in the Kanto, went to Heian, and proceeded to ingratiate himself with the very group his father's lords detested: the Retired Emperor Toba and company. In 1153 the Retired Emperor had Yoshitomo appointed Governor of Shimotsuke in the Kanto, and later added a post in the capital. A Japanese historian has uncovered other evidence of hostility between Tameyoshi and Yoshitomo; in one case the two Minamoto competed for men in Ōmi.[26]

Tameyoshi had to rethink his plans. He established a new heir and sent his second son to the northern Kanto to build another following in Kōzuke and Hitachi. Yoshitomo, the new governor of Shimotsuke, and Tameyoshi's second son arrived in the Kanto at almost the same time. It is interesting to note that the Fujiwara Regents claimed 5,000 *chō* of estate land in Kōzuke, where Tameyoshi's man was to do his work; Tameyoshi was undoubtedly looking for soldiers there.

But Toba blocked the plans of the Fujiwara-Tameyoshi faction. In the next year, 1154, another of Tameyoshi's sons caused trouble in Kyushu, and, when Tameyoshi was unable to control him, Toba dismissed Tameyoshi and his sons from office. Just a few months later Yoshitomo and his son did battle with Tameyoshi's second son and Kanto contact, first in Musashi and then in Shinano. When Yoshitomo pursued his brother into Shinano, Toba had Yoshitomo's action sanctioned with an imperial arrest order. One scholar has called these battles in the Kanto between Yoshitomo and Tameyoshi a "rehearsal for the Hōgen Disturbance."[27] A military center since the late sixth century, the Kanto once more was the scene of competition between rivals in search of soldiers.

On the 2nd day of the 7th month in 1156, the Retired Emperor Toba died after an illness of about two months. From the 1st of the 6th month, Yoshitomo and one of his kinsmen had guarded the palace, while other warriors had watched Toba's residence. Three days after Toba's death, the government ordered the Investigators to keep soldiers out of Heian; on the 6th, the police captured one of Yorinaga's troops who had slipped into the capital. On the 8th, the government mandated that the provincial headquarters prevent Tadazane and Yorinaga from raising troops from their numerous estates. Again this office stands out as the center of Court military activity in the countryside. Also on the 8th, the new Emperor Go-Shirakawa required Yoshitomo to search and seize Yorinaga's residence in Heian. On the 10th, each side organized its forces and made battle plans.

The battle took place in the streets of Heian on the 11th. The following passage lists troop strength for Go-Shirakawa's side, and shows how the Imperial Court received the news of victory:

At the crow of the cock, Kiyomori no Ason, Yoshitomo, and [Minamoto no] Yoshiyasu went to Shirakawa [to attack Yorinaga's and Sutoku's camp] with a total of over 600 mounted fighters. [Kiyomori brought over 300 horsemen from Nijō, Yoshitomo more than 200 from Ōi Gate, and Yoshiyasu more than 100 from Konoe.] . . .

. . . When it had been decided that a battle would take place, a messenger reported to Go-Shirakawa. At this time, the Lord Highness [Go-Shirakawa] sent up an entreaty for victory, and his servants prayed. Between 7 and 9 A.M., flames and smoke arose in the east. Go-Shirakawa's troops had already attacked and started a fire, it was said. Taking advantage of the rout, Kiyomori chased those who fled battle. The Ex-Emperor [Sutoku] and Yorinaga covered their tracks and fled. The Shirakawa residence was completely burned down.[28]

After the battle on the 11th, the Court meted out rewards and justice with equal swiftness. Kiyomori received promotion to the 4th Court Rank and appointment to the lucrative governorship of Harima, while Yoshitomo rose to the 5th Rank and a position in the imperial stables. The Court's preference for Kiyomori probably gave him an edge in acquiring loyal warriors and caused hard feelings on the part of a disgruntled Yoshitomo.

An arrow had struck Yorinaga during the fight, and he later died of his wounds; the government confiscated his lands and rescinded his posts. Tadazane fled to Nara and lost all power to his son Tadamichi, now Go-Shirakawa's choice for Regent, a transition signaling that the Fujiwara Regents had lost their independence. Soldiers captured the Retired Emperor Sutoku and the state banished him to Sanuki province, where he died in 1167. Police executed the inept Tameyoshi along with nearly 20 of his comrades. In the words of the monk-historian Jien, the Hōgen Disturbance introduced "the age of the warrior."[29]

THE MILITARY IN THE HŌGEN WAR: ORIGINS AND COMMAND. It is possible to analyze the forces fighting for each side in detail. According to one historian, the Sutoku-Fujiwara men came from 4 sources: (1) Sutoku's confidantes; (2) followers of the Fujiwara Regents; (3) Tameyoshi and his sons; and (4) the monks of Kōfukuji (who never arrived despite the machinations of Tadazane).[30] Thus the losing side probably had a small army from a narrow geographical base, which relied on the personal resources of its leaders; Tameyoshi's failure to raise men in the Kanto was critical in this regard. It is little wonder that one later chronicle states that Tameyoshi did not desire to fight at this time, but preferred to steal away with Sutoku to the Kanto where rebels were always on friendlier turf.[31]

In comparison with the Sutoku-Fujiwara forces, Go-Shirakawa had a truly national army. His generals included Yoshitomo, Kiyomori, and 5 other Taira and Minamoto chieftains. Yoshitomo's men alone hailed from 17 provinces in central and eastern Honshu, from Owari eastward (except Mutsu, Hida, and the provinces along the Sea of Japan).[32] When one recalls that Go-Shirakawa also had the Investigators and other officers at his command in the capital, and the provincial headquarters on his side in the countryside, one can see that his victory was ensured.

Taira no Kiyomori led the greatest number of horsemen (300 soldiers, mostly his kinsmen) into battle, and so students of Japanese history usually assume that he was the leader of Go-Shirakawa's forces. However, Yoshitomo, rather than Kiyomori, was the central figure of the battle and of *The Tale of Hōgen,* a literary account written 75 years after the event. Kiyomori was justifiably ambivalent about his participation in a battle against Sutoku. Of course, Kiyomori owed much to Toba, who had protected the Taira from criticism when two Yoshichika impostors had come to the capital in 1130, and had sheltered Kiyomori in 1147 when Kiyomori's men had shot the attendants of Gion Shrine (see Chapter 6). On the other hand, the lines of loyalty were complex: The wife of Tadamori, the great Taira chieftain, had served as wet nurse to Sutoku's son.[33] Had Tadamori been alive, Kiyomori and the Taira may have chosen to side with the doomed Sutoku-Fujiwara faction. The outcome of the Hōgen Insurrection would have been different, and the Taira's position atop Japan's military structure might have been placed in jeopardy.

FIGHTING STYLE AND TECHNOLOGY. Another important issue is the size of samurai forces employed in the Hōgen conflict. If armies used many large detachments of mounted warriors, that fact would support an interpretation stressing major change in Japan's military in the twelfth century. A small number of soldiers, however, would reinforce the historical continuity in military development stretching back to the era of the Strong Fellows in the late eighth century.

While scholars are not unanimous, most believe that even the national army fighting for the winning side in 1156 was modest in size.[34] According to the diary of the Minister of War, the three main generals, Yoshitomo, his kinsman Yoshiyasu, and Kiyomori, oversaw a force of 200, 100, and 300 mounted fighters, respectively. As part of the command structure of the day, every rider was accompanied by as many as 2 grooms/foot soldiers in the 1156 battle, a tradition dating back to the Strong Fellows of 792. If one assumes about 2 foot-soldier followers for each of these 600 horsemen, the total number of fighters for an army that decided the fate of the realm was about 2,000.[35]

To be sure, the literary account *The Tale of Hōgen* states that the victorious army had 4,500 men, but there are several reasons to doubt this figure. For example, *The Tale of Hōgen* notes Yoshitomo's following as 1,000 men, 400 supposedly important allies.[36] However, when it lists the names of Yoshitomo's chief vassals, the story mentions only about 80 and, of these 80, historians can verify only 1 man as fighting in the Hōgen War.

One scholar offers a compromise solution to the conflict between the diary and *The Tale of Hōgen*. He believes that the warriors whose names appear in the *The Tale* may have actually engaged in battle, but that the gross numbers are exaggerated, noting that the exploits of those named in *The Tale* are described in glowing detail. He also argues that civil aristocrats who wrote diaries (like the Minister of War) recorded only the most striking and famous warriors going to battle; they were less concerned with more humble fighters. Yet, even the historian who tries to reconcile the two sources appears to believe that the lower numbers of the diary are more accurate.[37]

One other piece of evidence appears to support the idea that samurai forces were still small. The Shirakawa Enclave where the battle took place measured only 0.15 square km. It seems doubtful that 4,500 mounted men and their estimated followers (9,000) could have fit in the small area and still left room for the other side.

While *The Tale of Hōgen* is not reliable regarding the size of armies, it does give a colorful description of samurai fighting style. All the elements long associated with twelfth-century engagements are present: single, mounted warriors bedecked in elegant and multicolored outfits, armed with oversized and personalized weapons, calling out their pedigrees to each other before seeking a kill. But it is important to remember that the full-blown, intraspecific combat of the Hōgen War owed its weapons and organization to another time. The primacy of the mounted warrior, the reliance on the provincial headquarters, even the emphasis of the individual over the group, all had their roots in the military establishments of earlier ages.

THE DISTURBANCE OF 1159

The poorly documented Heiji Incident was a battle among confidantes of the Emperor Go-Shirakawa, the victors of 1156.[38] Taira no Kiyomori outmaneuvered his rival, Minamoto no Yoshitomo, politically and defeated him in another battle in Heian. The conflict once again showed the political skills of Kiyomori, and cemented the Taira's place as the preeminent warrior family in Japan.

Go-Shirakawa retired from the throne in 1158. The wily Shinzei (Fujiwara no Michinori), once one of the Retired Emperor Toba's confidantes and now a client of Go-Shirakawa, became the central figure at Court after the 1156 Rebellion, taking the lead during Go-Shirakawa's reign as emperor and in his early retirement. Jealousy surrounded Shinzei's activities, and he was the special object of Fujiwara no Nobuyori's opprobrium, he having lost a coveted post because of Shinzei's influence.

Shinzei sought and gained a special tie with Taira no Kiyomori by marrying his son to Kiyomori's daughter. Minamoto no Yoshitomo had also tried to marry a son into Shinzei's house, but had been rebuffed for being too countrified. It is usually conceded that Yoshitomo harbored ill will towards Kiyomori as well. Yoshitomo was the real leader of Go-Shirakawa's forces in the Hōgen Rebellion, but the Emperor rewarded him only with promotion to the 5th Court Rank and appointment to the imperial stables, while Kiyomori assumed the 4th Rank and the rich governorship of Harima. Go-Shirakawa also promoted other members of Kiyomori's family, while Yoshitomo was forced to kill his own father, the incompetent head of the Minamoto, Tameyoshi.

In the 12th month of 1159, as Kiyomori and family went on a pilgrimage to their favorite shrine, Yoshitomo and Nobuyori seized the moment to capture Go-Shirakawa and the Emperor and hunt down Shinzei. They carried out an appointment ceremony in which they banished Shinzei's family, and the principals obtained high office. (Yoshitomo took the coveted governorship of Harima.) Kiyomori heard of the incident while in Kii province, and at first considered retreating to Kyushu where he could raise more troops.[39] But the Governor of Kii responded to a call to arms with 37 men —"a strong force for that day"— and Kiyomori returned to his residence at Rokuhara in Heian.[40] While Kiyomori was on his way back to the capital, Yoshitomo's forces under his son prepared to attack, but followed Nobuyori's ill-advised recommendation to delay.

For 10 days Yoshitomo and Kiyomori remained in a standoff in the capital. Kiyomori could do nothing without the sanction of the Imperial House, which was now in Yoshitomo's possession, and Yoshitomo awaited his soldiers from eastern Honshu. As Kiyomori bought time by sending a pleasant note to Nobuyori promising no tricks, other civil aristocrats became wary of Nobuyori and Yoshitomo. Two aristocrats who had originally sided with Nobuyori came to Kiyomori's aid by disguising the Emperor in women's clothes and conveying him to Kiyomori's mansion, while the Retired Emperor Go-Shirakawa fled to Ninnaji. Kiyomori then obtained an arrest order for Nobuyori and Yoshitomo and defeated them in battle at Rokujō Kawara in Heian. Nobuyori eventually fell from his horse and, with his nose bleeding, asked Go-Shirakawa for mercy. He was beheaded.

Yoshitomo fled for the Kanto, but before he reached the land of rebels, a retainer betrayed him while he took a bath at a supposedly safe haven. Kiyomori exterminated any of Yoshitomo's sons who were of age to threaten his house; only 13-year-old Minamoto no Yoritomo and the infant Yoshitsune survived. The Court exiled Yoritomo to Izu and put him in the custody of a trusty Taira ally, while Yoshitsune entered a temple.

THE MILITARY IN THE WAR. Unlike the Hōgen Rebellion, few sources survive to illuminate the military details of the Heiji Disturbance. *The Tale of Heiji,* a literary record written down by 1250 and the sole account of the war, once again describes single mounted combat in detail, complete with pedigrees and personalized weapons. The story also lists combat forces, stating that Kiyomori commanded 3,000 men while Yoshitomo commanded 2,000, but these figures are not reliable.[41] Perhaps by dividing these figures by 10, one might obtain the correct size for the armies.

Like *The Tale of Hōgen, The Tale of Heiji* is a glorified account of battle written down long after events had occurred. If one assumes that both storytellers were better at remembering the names of participants than their numbers, then there is another (admittedly fanciful) way to calculate the size of Yoshitomo's following. *The Tale of Heiji* lists the names of Yoshitomo's vassals, about 50 men from 7 provinces in eastern Honshu. Since *The Tale of Hōgen* named 80 of

Yoshitomo's dependents when he in fact had 200 horsemen (according to the more reliable diary of the Minister of War), by analogy one could conclude that Yoshitomo's forces comprised about 120 mounted fighters in the Heiji War. Of course, such calculation presumes that the same proportion would hold for 1159 as in 1156, a giant assumption.

Because *The Tale of Heiji* is the story of Yoshitomo's side, it is much more difficult to infer from it the size and structure of Kiyomori's army. The author mentions only 14 men by name as belonging to Kiyomori's army, most holding capital offices or governorships in western Japan. Fourteen men is unrealistic for Kiyomori's force; since he won the battle at Rokuhara, it is likely that his army was really somewhat larger than Yoshitomo's.

The crucial result of the failed Heiji coup was that it allowed Taira no Kiyomori to consolidate power. Kiyomori had shown remarkable political skill during the conflict. While he was away from the capital, he was tempted to flee to Kyushu to raise an army, but he wisely chose not to. Had he fled, he would have been branded an outlaw, a western Masakado, and the Court would have granted Yoshitomo and Nobuyori an arrest order and the right to use the soldiers of the provincial headquarters.[42]

After arriving in the capital, Kiyomori first waited patiently for rifts to appear among his foes; he even encouraged schisms by sending a friendly letter to Nobuyori. Once he had the Imperial House on his side, Kiyomori used it to secure victory. While it is impossible to be certain with such slim evidence, it seems likely that Kiyomori controlled both the capital and provincial military forces to defeat Yoshitomo. Yoshitomo may have been able to defeat Kiyomori in man-to-man combat as the stronger warrior, but Kiyomori had the political insights that fighting men had lacked for so long. Kiyomori deserved to be the chieftain of all warriors in 1160.

THE TAIRA AND THE LATE HEIAN MILITARY SYSTEM, 1160–1185

Historians have generally treated the Ise Taira of the late Heian era as failures, impostors who pretended to be Court aristocrats when they were in fact just mediocre warriors. For John Hall,

"Neither the posts, the sources of wealth, nor the lines of authority utilized by Kiyomori broke precedent. He essentially outdid the Fujiwara at an old game."[43] And for Jeffrey Mass, "That the Taira failed to establish themselves as military rulers can be demonstrated variously. The limited size of their core vassal band and the absence of any concerted effort to extend sway locally are two of the clearest indicators."[44] Anxious for preferment from the Retired Emperor, the Taira and their leader Kiyomori collected imperial offices, not lands. They ignored the interests of the warrior class to which they belonged and failed to attract a significant number of vassals. Only in 1179 did Kiyomori and his family seriously challenge the Court and Retired Emperor Go-Shirakawa, and by then it was too late to build their own warrior following or government. The Taira, who based their power on ancient foundations such as provincial governorships and capital offices, inevitably lost out to the medieval Minamoto, the champions of feudalism.

Even without examining the evidence, this characterization is questionable on 4 counts. (1) Members of both the Ise Taira and the Kawachi Minamoto were aristocrats; they were military nobles and had been since the rebellion of Masakado in the tenth century. (2) If Kiyomori sought imperial offices and provincial governorships, so had other warriors. Offices, especially provincial governorships, had been the surest route to wealth, arms, and men for centuries. (3) It is doubtful how strong and unifying class ties were in premodern Japan, and equally difficult to tell what a warrior's class interests really were. Most fighting men probably felt vertical and regional ties more strongly than class interests, and such ties fragmented the group into factions. (4) Labeling the Taira ancient and the Minamoto medieval is a misleading and highly abstract distinction derived from Western European history, and ultimately relies upon a false, modern dichotomy between concepts of public and private.

These and other problems have always troubled some Japanese historians.[45] In the last ten years, several scholars have reexamined the Ise Taira in the light of current knowledge of the Heian military.[46] Gomi Fumihiko of Tokyo University has focused on the Taira military base and divided the period from 1160–1185 into 3 phases: 1160 to 1176, when the Taira worked closely with the Retired Emperor Go-Shirakawa; 1176–1180, when the Taira began to develop an independent, national military system; and 1181–1185, when the Taira created a regional military in western Japan.

THE TAIRA MILITARY, 1160-1176. A crucial event in the first phase occurred in 1167, the year Kiyomori attained the highest office in the land, Grand Minister (*dajō daijin*), and three close relatives (including Shigemori, Kiyomori's heir) assumed prominent positions at Court (see Figure 10 for the Taira family). The Court also drafted a significant order that began by complaining of "robbers" in eastern Honshu and pirates in Kyushu who "stole taxes shipped by sea." Because it seemed "just as if imperial power did not exist," the government commanded "Lord Taira [Shigemori] to pursue and destroy bandits" throughout Japan.[47]

Three points about the 1167 order are noteworthy. (1) Its scope was nationwide. The law failed to mention only the provinces along the Sea of Japan explicitly in the edict and, according to the scholar who first pointed out the mandate, the intention of the authors was to grant national police and military authority. (2) The Court issued the order at a time when there were no revolts. The edict was not a temporary measure against a specified opponent but a general grant of military and police authority to be used as events warranted, at the behest of the Retired Emperor. (3) The state named Taira no Shigemori as commander. Shigemori was Kiyomori's son and heir; he was the perfect choice for a military specialist, since he was also a confidante of the Retired Emperor. Kiyomori used the opportunity afforded by his son's nomination to retire from his positions in government and take the tonsure at the family's mountain retreat in Fukuhara on the Inland Sea. From Fukuhara, Kiyomori could oversee his family's fortunes, while Shigemori directed military affairs for the Heian Court from the capital.[48]

Based upon the 1167 order, Shigemori conducted Court military operations at the bidding of Go-Shirakawa. For the most part these were aimed at monks who had the gall to march upon the capital. The best example comes from 1169, when the clerics of Enryakuji protested the actions of a provincial official of Owari, and demanded the banishment of a Go-Shirakawa confidante. Courtiers discussed the incident on the 23rd of the 12th month; the following except describes the atmosphere around the capital, the aristocratic decision-making process, and the size of Shigemori's army aimed at repelling the monks:

> Last night after the hour of the monkey [3 to 5 P.M.], the monks of Mt. Hiei came down to the capital. When it was heard that they had gathered at Kyōgokuji, the capital was in an uproar. The Investigators and warriors (*bushi*) came to the camp of the Retired Emperor as summoned. Their number was like clouds and mist. . . .
>
> The Retired Emperor pronounced: "In what manner ought we to deal with this situation? First the aristocrats ought to hold a discussion. Superintendent (*bettō*), inquire of the aristocrats how we should decide this matter."
>
> We (the aristocrats) had no choice but to hand down an order. If we did not act, then would the Retired Emperor dispatch warriors (*bushi*) into the Emperor's residence? But the Grand Minister, Minister of the Left, General of the Left, and Repairs Minister all said: "The Former Councillor Lord Shigemori and 3 others have brought 500 horsemen. (The aforementioned lord brought 200 riders, Consultant and Middle General [*saishō chūjō*] [Taira no] Munemori has 130, and Previous Head of Dazaifu [*daini*] Lord [Taira no] Yorimori has 150 horsemen.) While they are repelling the monks, it is clear that the situation could turn into a big incident. We should be very careful."[49]

The 1169 confrontation between Enryakuji and the Court is a good example of Shigemori's new authority. He and his lieutenants amassed 480 horsemen, nearly as many as the victorious side in the Hōgen Disturbance. With such military power, Go-Shirakawa was able to apply pressure to the Court to punish rowdy monks severely. But Shigemori never sent his troops to battle, and, even with Go-Shirakawa's strict stance, the Court caved into the demands of Enryakuji. Religious authority won out over military power.

During the early stage of Taira military preeminence from 1160 to 1176, Shigemori became a powerful man and the Taira a rich family. Shigemori was one of Go-Shirakawa's favorites, and his influence at Court was evident when his son provoked some servants of the Fujiwara Regent into wrecking the son's carriage.

Even though the Regent Motofusa tried several times to placate Shigemori, the Taira military specialist eventually sent his henchmen to Motofusa's residence to kidnap those in the Regent's household responsible for the insult. Shigemori's power derived not from his father, but from Go-Shirakawa.[50]

Taira economic strength had two foundations: trade with China and provincial offices. From 1170, Kiyomori and Go-Shirakawa engaged in trade with Sung merchants, who visited Fukuhara and exchanged gifts. Kiyomori saw to it that the Inland Sea provided the Chinese with friendly ports, as well as residences in Hakata Bay and harbors in Aki and Bingo provinces. One historian characterizes the Taira trade empire as an oceanic state in western Japan.[51]

During the same period, the Court granted the Taira 4 more proprietary provinces, more than doubling the number of Taira possessions from 3 to 7. (The government allotted proprietary provinces to aristocrats and temples, who thereby gained the right to collect taxes in the province.) The state also named 6 members of the Taira family to the upper aristocracy, holding the 3rd Court Rank or higher; many served as officials in Go-Shirakawa's estates.[52]

Taira ascendancy at Court and their trade empire in the Inland Sea are not new knowledge. But recently scholars have discovered that the Taira also used their new wealth and political influence to construct a nationwide system of vassalage, the first in Japan's history (see Map 10). Far from neglecting warriors, the Taira enrolled allies in unprecedented numbers; according to one authority, there is evidence for 612 followers of the Taira in the late Heian period.[53] This number is all the more impressive because few records remain to tell of those who served with the losing side in the Great Civil War of 1180–1185.

It is instructive to compare Taira vassals of the 1170s with those of Kiyomori and Yoshitomo in 1156, the year of the Hōgen War. While Kiyomori drew his men mostly from Ise, Iga, the capital region, and part of Kyushu in 1156, Yoshitomo's fighters hailed exclusively from eastern Honshu. By the 1170s, however, there were Taira followers throughout the nation. Thirty-one provinces included 1 to 5 individual soldiers; 12 provinces had 6 to 10; 8 provinces produced 11 to 20; and 6 provinces had more than 21. To han-

Map 10. TAIRA LANDS AND VASSALS

Taira Proprietary Provinces

• Taira Vassals

▪ Taira Estates

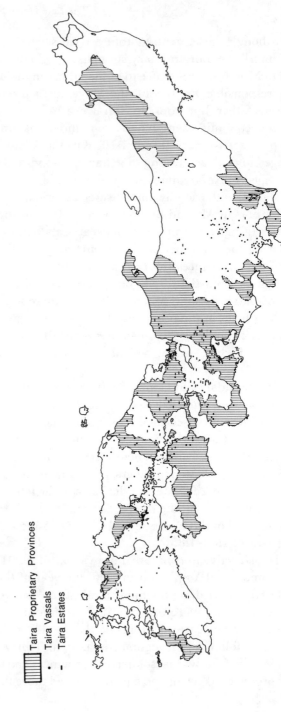

Source: Shūkan Asahi hyakka Nihon no rekishi 1, Chūsei 1, Genji to Heishi, p. 34–35.

dle these far-flung followers, one scholar has even suggested that the Taira had their own household office similar to the Office of Samurai in Japan's first warrior government in Kamakura after 1185.[54]

The greatest concentrations of vassals came from near the capital and in the Kanto. The capital region had a large number because it was a traditional Taira base, but the size of the Taira following in the Kanto is surprising. Taira influence in eastern Honshu was a result of both the multiplicity of warriors there and the seriousness of Taira effort.[55]

The methods by which the Taira built the first nationwide system of vassalage were many and varied. They offered a stay in the capital, usually protecting the Emperor's or an aristocrat's residence.[56] A tour of guard duty (ōban yaku) in the capital had always been most beneficial, especially to warriors from the distant Kanto. Rustic soldiers could seal marriage alliances with citified aristocrats, plead land and other cases, obtain official appointments, or secure an aristocratic patron. The status that service in the capital bestowed was considerable in eastern Honshu, and just breathing the air of Heian must have been exciting.

Country fighters had come to the capital for guard duty since the establishment of the Yamato state; the Taihō Codes of 702 had instituted Imperial Guards who traveled from their districts to take up arms on the Court's behalf. As these arrangements deteriorated in the ninth and tenth centuries, the Court was forced to fall back upon other means of raising troops for capital guard duty. The provincial headquarters, newly ascendant after the precedent of 901 and already providing guards for governors in the provinces and Heian, was a logical source (see Chapter 5). But just when the provincial headquarters began dispatching local warriors to protect government offices and aristocratic residences in the capital is a point of debate. One scholar believes the new system originated in the late eleventh century, while another has suggested that the Taira first developed the idea in the twelfth century.[57] When Yoritomo formed the first samurai government in 1185, he adopted the practice from his predecessors. As in the institution of the twelfth century, a soldier chosen by the provincial office for a tour of duty served in rotation in Heian. The

Kamakura system of capital guard duty was therefore not new but an outgrowth of an earlier invention, possibly a Taira institution.

One can cite several examples of guard duty in the capital from the twelfth century. In 1176, the police caught a few soldiers on guard duty at a noble residence stealing vegetables from the servants' garden. In the ensuing melee, these guards injured some servants and then fled. Later the aristocrat discovered that the warriors were from the band of Minamoto no Yorikane of Mino.[58] Another reference to guard duty appears in an 1177 entry in an aristocratic diary; yet another describes fighters from Mino, Echizen, and Ōmi coming to the capital for guard duty in that year.[59]

One specialist on the Taira has shown how that family used the enticement of guard duty in Heian to recruit allies. Takeda Ariyoshi was a well-known warrior from Kai province. Under the 1167 order, which granted Shigemori police and military powers in Kai and the rest of Japan, Shigemori commanded Ariyoshi to come to the capital to serve guard duty, and eventually Ariyoshi settled his family in Heian and became Shigemori's vassal.[60] Two Taira specialists have uncovered other examples of warriors' serving a tour of duty in the capital and becoming Taira men: Kawagoe Shigeyori of Musashi; Minamoto no Shigekiyo of Mino; Oyama Tomomasa and Utsunomiya Tomotsuna of Shimotsuke; Nitta Yoshishige of Kōzuke; and Chiba Taneyori of Shimōsa.[61]

Because the provincial headquarters made selections for guard duty in the capital, the Taira must have recognized the utility of that office.[62] One scholar indicates that the Taira controlled most or many important members of the headquarters in 21 provinces, including Hitachi, Kōzuke, Shimotsuke, Shinano, Shimōsa, Echigo, and Musashi in eastern Japan; Iwami, Aki, Nagato, Sanuki, and Iyo in western Japan; and Yamashiro, Yamato, Owari, Suruga, Mino, Noto, Inaba, Kii, and Awa in central Japan.

Specific cases show how the Taira manipulated the provincial headquarters. In Yamato, a warrior holding the Investigators' post assisted the Taira cause; in Shinano the use of Suwa Shrine enhanced Taira control. Taira power in Aki province is particularly well known, because the Taira used the governorship to enroll vassals and protect their lands from entry and taxation; but in Owari, too, "most of the officials of the headquarters followed the Taira."[63] As in the tenth century, command of the provincial headquarters was the sine qua non of rural military power.

Conventionally, historians have linked Taira control of the provincial headquarters to their holdings of proprietary provinces.[64] One specialist in particular has emphasized the importance of proprietary provinces, where an outsider came in to collect taxes, in raising troops for the Taira cause after their 1179 coup d'état against Go-Shirakawa. However, another scholar has found several Taira stronghold provinces that did not become proprietary provinces, such as Kai, Shimotsuke, Kōzuke, and others. Rather than serve the cause of Taira military strength, this source argues that an appointment to a proprietary province really hurt the Taira attempts to enroll vassals.[65] A third historian, who has listed over 500 Taira vassals by province, has found only a moderate correlation between the proprietary provinces the Taira held and their strength in vassals.[66] It therefore seems likely that collecting taxes as the chief of the proprietary province gave little advantage to the Taira, and that other methods such as a tour of duty in the capital or reliance on the 1167 order were more important.

In addition to guard duty and control of the provincial headquarters, the Taira also gathered men by serving their economic interests. In an era when supposedly loyal vassals regularly betrayed their lords, using economics to attract and retain fighters was particularly important. For instance, in Kōzuke province, Nitta Yoshishige was the foreman of Nitta Estate, where the guarantor (*honjo*) had married into Kiyomori's family. As Kiyomori rose in power at Court, Nitta Estate expanded to cover all Nitta district. Yoshishige was a Taira vassal who found it to his economic interest to ally with the Taira.[67]

Another example comes from Shimotsuke, where the Ashikaga won back an appointment to an estate with Taira help:

[Ashikaga] Toshitsuna . . . holds several thousand *chō* . . . During the recent Nin'an era (1151–1153), because of the harm done by some woman, he was dispossessed of his rights to Ashikaga Estate in Shimotsuke province. The guarantor of the estate, Taira no Shigemori, then granted the estate to the young lord Nitta Yoshishige. Whereupon Toshitsuna went to the capital to plead his case. Consequently, the estate was returned to him. Because of this debt to the Taira, he has been of late a supporter.[68]

Most historians say that the Taira never confirmed lands for warriors, but the tie between service and land is clear in this case. One specialist calls the relationship formed between the Ashikaga and the Taira "a medieval lord-vassal relationship."[69]

The Taira also enticed soldiers in western Japan. For example, in Kii province the Satō family originally served as officials in Tanaka Estate and as vassals of the Fujiwara Regents.[70] Beginning in 1156, the Satō illegally occupied parts of neighboring Arakawa Estate, which was in the portfolio of the Retired Emperor. Despite orders from the Fujiwara Regents to stop, the aggression became more open, and in 1161 Satō and forces of the Kii Governor attacked Arakawa again. In 1162, the Satō stormed the estate once more. Finally, in 1163, the Retired Emperor handed down an order demanding that the Satō cease their illegal activities, but the Satō ignored the order. The Taira supported the Satō at Court, according to an historian who first emphasized the role of the Taira, and this influence allowed the Satō to stay in Arakawa over the protests of the Go-Shirakawa and others.[71] The Satō became allies of the Taira and later received lands in Yamato province.

In Hizen province, the Taira held a mid-level post (*azukari dokoro*) in Kamisaki Estate. Kamisaki had been a center of the trade with Sung China since the time of Tadamori, 30 years before, and later records show that the Taira raised troops from Kamisaki by remitting estate taxes. The same scholar who studied the Satō believes that the remission of estate dues was also compensation for the residents' participation in overseas trade. The Taira considered access to sea routes and trade with the continent resources worth cultivating.

These four cases in the Kanto and western Honshu are the best-known instances of the Taira serving the economic interests of their allies, but not the only ones. There were many examples where vassals' residences and estates overlapped or were in close proximity. It seems natural to conclude that the Taira confirmed lands in exchange for martial service on a wide basis even before Yoritomo adopted the practice in 1180; the Taira had their feudal and medieval features, as well as relying on supposedly ancient means such as the provincial headquarters.

Other methods by which a warrior might become a Taira man include the use of marital ties and relatives, capital offices, and positions in the Retired Emperor's house administration. In addition, of course, the Taira had developed longstanding relations with traditional housemen residing in Ise and Iga from the late tenth century. However a warrior became a Taira follower, the network was nationwide and organized through the capital and provinces as the military of other eras had been.

In 1176 and 1177, the first stage of Taira military development came to an end, as increasingly the Taira and the Retired Emperor Go-Shirakawa came into conflict. In 1177, the monks of Enryakuji once again protested against the actions of a confidante of the Retired Emperor. This time, Kiyomori took the side of Enryakuji. On Kiyomori's command, the Taira twice refused Go-Shirakawa's orders to deploy, and the Court gave in to the demands of the temple. In the 6th month of 1177, Kiyomori captured and then banished many of Go-Shirakawa's favorites in the famous Shishigatani Conspiracy.[72]

A NATIONAL MILITARY, 1177–1180. Three major political events dominated the second stage in the development of Taira military power, when the warrior family attempted to build a national institution independent of the Court and Go-Shirakawa. (1) In 1177, Kiyomori learned of a plot by Go-Shirakawa confidantes Fujiwara no Narichika and others to destroy his family; in the 6th month of 1177, Kiyomori caught the conspirators and had them banished or killed. (2) In late 1179, Kiyomori marched "several thousand horseriders" into the capital and confined Go-Shirakawa to his residence at Toba.[73] Kiyomori had more confederates of the Retired Emperor discharged from their posts and took over their offices and economic resources. (3) In the spring of 1180, the Great Civil War between the Taira and the Minamoto began with revolts in the Kanto under Minamoto no Yoritomo and around the capital under Minamoto no Yorimasa and the clerics of Miidera. By the end of 1180, the Taira faced attacks throughout the country.

One scholar has listed 20 Taira military operations between the 5th month of 1177 and the end of 1180, and has noted two characteristics of Taira organization: the leading role of Kiyomori and the dual structure of martial organization (see Appendix Table 4). In both the Shishigatani Conspiracy of 1177 and the confinement of Go-Shirakawa in late 1179, Kiyomori was the central figure behind Taira moves, deploying troops on his orders alone. In the punishment of a Go-Shirakawa favorite in 1177, and in response to rebellions in the Kanto, Kyushu, and Mino in 1180, Kiyomori himself dispatched his loyal retainers. Kiyomori's authority on military matters at Court was so unassailable that he was able to circumvent some of the accepted customs concerning "search-and-destroy" missions.[74] One reason for the preeminence of Kiyomori was that Shigemori, the military specialist of the first stage, became ill and died in 1179, but a more important point was Kiyomori's growing power as Go-Shirakawa lost his political clout.

A second principle of Taira military organization was its dual structure. Forces consisted of the personal retainers of Kiyomori and government troops levied through the provincial headquarters. When Prince Mochihito, a disgruntled courtier passed over in the imperial succession and therefore hostile to the Taira, raised the standard of rebellion against the Court and the Taira in the spring of 1180, Kiyomori first dispatched his loyal allies in the Investigators' Office; these warriors went to battle not because they were Investigators but because they were Kiyomori's men. In case the Investigators failed to quell the rebellion, Kiyomori had mobilized other Taira kinsmen in the network. These warriors belonged to a state army conscripted through the provincial headquarters.[75] The opening combat against Yoritomo took on a similar cast; a Taira ally first fought Yoritomo at the Battle of Ishibashi in the 9th month of 1180, and a government force under the command of a Taira kinsman succeeded the small detachment of personal retainers about a month later. Taira expeditions against rebels in Kyushu, Mino, and Yamato consisted of the same two components. As one specialist has pointed out, Kiyomori raised most of the state forces through the provincial headquarters, where the Taira had worked so diligently to build a network of followers.[76]

The first signs of a new Taira military institution also appeared at this time. According to one historian, by 1179 Kiyomori began to use the title of land steward (*jitō*) to confirm warrior lands in return for military service in his beloved province of Aki.[77] If the Taira were indeed carrying out this practice, then it would be a significant historical fact. Rather than seeing the Taira as doomed to failure because of their fatal attachment to ancient means of raising an army, scholars could view the military family as feudal, using land as payment for service, like the Minamoto.

But Jeffrey Mass, who has also analyzed this case in detail, is hesitant to conclude that the Taira really did utilize the new office of land steward (*jitō*) in the way the Kamakura military government did after 1185.[78] He objects that no direct evidence establishes Kiyomori as the warrior lord who confirmed the position, and that the provincial office, usually not involved in Kamakura appointments, seems to have handled the Taira affair almost exclusively. He further argues that the warrior who received the land (Saeki Kagehiro) was already a powerful Taira follower and therefore not enticed into the Taira fold by the positions, and that the military government in the Kamakura period (1185–1333) did not call the Taira posts in Aki by the term *land steward (jitō)* when it later took over the area.

There are replies to these objections. While it is true that no unequivocal evidence testifies that Kiyomori confirmed Saeki in his lands, there is strong indirect substantiation for Kiyomori's role.[79] The provincial headquarters may have played a critical role in the process of confirmation for the Taira, but this point is consistent with the importance of the office in military affairs throughout the Heian period. Yoritomo also named strong allies to posts to maintain their loyalty, and, although later documents do not refer to the Aki land stewards as *jitō,* there are continuities between the Taira positions and Kamakura confirmations.[80]

Therefore many Japanese historians accept the idea that the Taira employed a forerunner to the Kamakura office of land steward to reward some of their followers.[81] Moreover, the Taira used this military office to reimburse their soldiers in areas other than Aki. One scholar cites examples from Hitachi, Suō, and northern Kyushu, while another has examined an instance from Satsuma.[82] Far from being limited to ancient or aristocratic methods of conscripting troops, the Taira were inventive in building their national army, thus paving the way for the medieval Minamoto in western Japan.

That the Taira operated an independent military from 1177 is controversial. Most historians have followed the conventional view, which argues that the Taira attempted to run state affairs and their own military machine for only a few months after the confinement of Go-Shirakawa late in 1179.[83] As a leading critic has noted, however, the 1179 event really has much less to do with the Taira rise than most believe. Go-Shirakawa had lost his authority as early as 1177, and his influence fluctuated thereafter until 1179. His confinement was important as a statement by Kiyomori of Taira independence from imperial influence, but it was not the sea change in power structure that many have supposed. In fact, even after the arrest of Go-Shirakawa in 1179, a Retired Emperor (Takakura) appeared in 1180, and the Taira reinstated Go-Shirakawa in 1181 with little detriment to their own power.

As they grasped the reins of power after 1177, the Taira promoted policies that alienated important segments of society. In 1178 and 1179, Kiyomori persuaded the Court to enact new laws against provincial disturbances by granting officials wide powers to deal with bandits and violent monks.[84] The authority given to the officials turned religious institutions and some warriors against the Taira. In addition, during this period the Taira took control of the lion's share of proprietary provinces, perhaps as many as 31. This also antagonized once-friendly warriors because the non-resident governors (Taira allies) and their representatives received tax revenues that could have gone to warrior-officials (*zaichō kanjin*) living in the province. Many provincial headquarters once receptive to Taira overtures now turned against the warrior family.[85] Rampant inflation from the importation of Sung cash in the capital and western Japan, another policy sponsored by Kiyomori and the Taira, focused more disapproval on the family. The Great Civil War of 1180–1185 was the result, and the second phase of Taira military development came to a close.[86]

A TAIRA REGIONAL MILITARY, 1181–1185. During the final act in the Taira tragedy that lasted from 1181 until their annihilation in 1185, the warrior family built a military base in central and western Japan. In the 10th month of 1180, the Taira expedition against Yoritomo in the Kanto met with defeat at the Battle of Fujikawa, and they fell back to the capital, never again to regain eastern Honshu. Perhaps at this point the Taira even considered a full-fledged retreat to their bases in northern Kyushu, as they had before they placed Go-Shirakawa under house arrest in 1179.[87]

Three months after the debacle at Fujikawa, in the 1st month of 1181, the Taira tried to create a regional military system for central and western Japan by establishing two new offices: commander-in-chief (*sōkan*) and estate foreman-in-chief (*sōgesu*).[88] Taira no Munemori, heir of the dying Kiyomori, became Commander-in-Chief and oversaw the capital region (Kinai) and the provinces of Iga, Ise, Ōmi, and Tamba, while the Estate Foreman-in-Chief, a vassal of Munemori, administered Tamba. According to the scholar who first analyzed these offices in detail, the commander-in-chief possessed the power to pursue and punish the rebels through the provincial headquarters; the estate foreman-in-chief had the authority to raise provisions from Tamba's estates.[89] The purpose of the new arrangements was to create a bloc of power in central Japan, an area where the Taira were already strong, to halt the rebels' advance and to rejuvenate Taira hopes.

When they set up the office of commander-in-chief, the Taira cited a law from 731 which sought to concentrate military power in the hands of the victors after a conspiracy in 729. Kujō no Kanezane, the twelfth-century aristocratic author of the diary *The Jeweled Leaf,* believed that a more appropriate precedent for the Taira action was the office established by Fujiwara no Nakamaro just before his fall from power in 764 (see Chapter 2). The Taira undoubtedly eschewed reference to Nakamaro's plan because they wanted to avoid a reminder of a failed precursor. It is interesting that the Taira referred back to the eighth-century state in their time of troubles; their plan suggests the staying power of the Taihō military system. The Taira may have been trying to establish their independence from the Court, but they could do so only within its military framework.

Because the Taira lost the Great Civil War of 1180–1185, historians have widely viewed the new offices as failures: Only two and one-half years after the appointments the Taira were forced to flee the capital. But as one specialist on the Taira points out, one's evaluation of the commander-in-chief and the estate foreman-in-chief really depends upon one's perspective.[90] After all, immediately after the establishment of the regional military, the Taira won one of their few victories at Sunomata in Owari in the 2nd month of 1181. For more than two years thereafter the Taira held their own; without the new offices rebels might have overthrown them even sooner.

One scholar has provided three examples of the effectiveness of the Commander-in-Chief in action,[91] pointing out that the Taira hoped the establishment of the office in such areas as Iga and Ise would reinforce their control in provinces where they were already strong. One instance shows a vassal of Munemori complying with an order to send boats from Ise for the impending Battle of Sunomata in 1181.[92] In another case, the Commander-in-Chief called upon Taira vassals from Izumi and Kawachi to resolve a land dispute in Kii.

In a third example from 1182–1183, vassals of the Taira levied troops from Yamashiro and Yamato for an expedition to Echigo against another rebel. In a reply to the conscription order, the leader of the lumbermen of Wazuka in Yamato complained that "strongmen were coming down to the lumber camp" and demanding that men join the Taira.[93] According to the lumbermen, force was useless against their number because "lumbermen do not make soldiers who carry bows, arrows, and swords"; yet the Taira tried to draft 27 of 36 lumbermen, an action "words could not describe."[94]

In raising men and supplies in the third stage, the Taira reversed their earlier hostility to Go-Shirakawa and made wide use of his power.[95] One might look upon Taira reliance upon the Retired Emperor as a weakness, a sign they could not overcome their dependence on the Court. Yet when the Minamoto, victors over the Taira in the Kanto, entered the capital in 1184, they followed Taira precedent in their relations with Go-Shirakawa and in their establishment of military institutions for western Japan. The commander-in-chief became a model for the constable (*shugo*) of the Kamakura era, and the estate foreman-in-chief was a forebear

of the province-wide land steward (*ikkoku jitō*) later created by Yoritomo.[96] Furthermore, there is evidence that the Taira also developed another new office, the messenger who promotes agriculture
(*kannō shi*), and placed him in the Aki provincial headquarters to
divide up land and dole out seed to peasants; the messenger was
a direct antecedent of the Kamakura-period constable in Aki.[97]

THE GREAT CIVIL WAR OF 1180–1185

The Great Civil War of 1180–1185 was the Japanese version of the
Peloponnesian Wars of ancient Greece (431–404 B.C.) — an asymmetrical battle between two different military traditions, one the
seagoing culture of western Japan and the other the horse-riding
civilization of eastern Honshu, especially the Kanto. Each side
tried to adapt to the other's mode of fighting, but in the end the
Kanto under Minamoto leadership was more successful. The war
toppled the Taira from power and resulted in the formation of a
martial government in Kamakura which gave formal recognition
to Minamoto no Yoritomo as "the chief of all warriors." At the
same time, the conflict was a battle for independence; after many
centuries of failed revolts, the Kanto attained formal political
autonomy, albeit still fragile and open to challenge.

Scholars usually divide the war into three phases: the year 1180,
which saw initial rebel (Minamoto) victories in the Kanto and the
Court's (Taira) failure to reconquer the same region; the time
from 1181 until the 7th month of 1183, when the Taira and Minamoto settled down to a stalemate; and mid-1183 until the 3rd
month of 1185, a period during which Minamoto no Yoritomo vanquished his rival and kinsman Kiso Yoshinaka and then annihilated the Taira at the Battle of Dannoura. Copious materials
document the war, including aristocratic diaries, Court chronicles, administrative records, and accounts written from the view-
point of the winners (Minamoto) and losers (Taira). The description that follows is a brief summary of the conflict, citing the major
battles and other points raised in later analysis[98] (see Map 11).
Appendix Table 5 lists the major battles and presents a summary
of the estimated size of armies fighting in the Great Civil War.

Prince Mochihito raised the standard of revolt against Taira

Map 11. BATTLES OF THE GREAT CIVIL WAR OF 1180–1185

1. Uji (Taira)
2. Ishibashi (Taira)
3. Fujikawa (Minamoto)
4. Ōmi (revolts against the Taira)
5. Sunomata (Taira)
6. Yokotagawara (Yoshinaka)
7. Kurikara (Yoshinaka)
8. Kyoto
9. Mizushima (Taira)
10. Bizen (Taira)
11. Hōjūji (Yoshinaka)

12. Mikusa (Minamoto)
13. Ichinotani (Minamoto)
14. Yashima (Minamoto)
15. Dannoura (Minamoto)
16. Kamakura

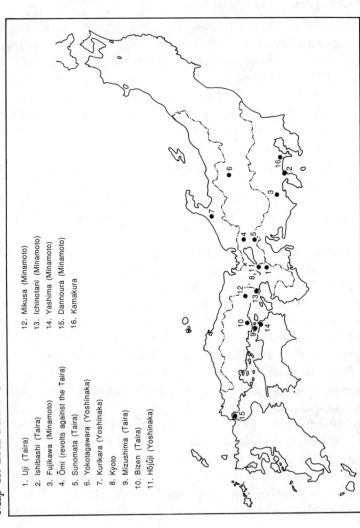

Source: Yasuda Motohisa, *Nihon no rekishi 1, Insei to Heishi,* map insert.

control of the Court in the 4th month of 1180. Mochihito, like the Emperor Temmu five centuries earlier, had lost his bid for the throne to a younger candidate, in Mochihito's case, the Emperor Antoku of Taira blood. *The Tale of the Heike*, a classic literary account of the war from the Taira perspective first put in writing about 1250, also accused the Retired Emperor Go-Shirakawa of complicity in the plot to overthrow the Taira, because of the harsh treatment meted out to the Retired Emperor and his favorites in the late 1170s.[99] In the end, the Taira monopoly of Court politics antagonized most of the imperial family, civil and military aristocrats, and important religious officials.

The first Minamoto warrior to respond to the call to arms was Minamoto no Yorimasa, once a reliable ally of the Taira. His forces, a mere 50 horsemen, met with defeat in the waters of the Uji River at the Battle of Uji in the 5th month of 1180; the Taira managed a frontal assault across a flooding river even though Yorimasa held the only bridge. Yorimasa and Prince Mochihito lost their lives. Yoritomo joined his kinsman in rebellion in the 9th month, and, after taking the Izu provincial headquarters, the Taira follower and Minamoto-hater Ōba Kagechika trapped Yoritomo's small force of 50 mounted soldiers in the mountains and defeated him at the Battle of Ishibashi before Yoritomo's main army could arrive. Yoritomo narrowly escaped death while he hid in the Hakone Mountains; unfortunately for the Taira, they were unable to kill Yoritomo then and there. Later, the Minamoto chieftain fled across the ocean to Awa, where he also captured the provincial headquarters.

Early in the 10th month, Yoritomo established himself at the traditional Minamoto base of Kamakura in Sagami province. For the next 6 weeks, he busily enrolled vassals and confirmed lands in preparations for the expected Taira expedition. Historians disagree on the speed and size of the response to Yoritomo's call to arms. One work written in the early 1960s emphasizes resistance to the Minamoto; a study from the 1970s stresses the great number of men siding with Yoritomo.[100] *The Mirror of the East*, a history of the war from the Minamoto point of view, boasts that 200,000 men flocked to Yoritomo's cause, but this figure is open to dispute.[101] Given the Taira control of the Kanto before 1180, and later signs of dissension within the Minamoto ranks, it seems likely that Yoritomo had far fewer men than *The Mirror of the East* reports.[102] While he amassed men and matériel, the Minamoto chieftain also directed his forces to capture the remaining provincial headquarters of the Kanto, just as Masakado had done in 939.

After bringing 11 provinces in eastern Honshu to heel, Yoritomo faced the Taira at the Battle of Fujikawa in the 10th month of 1180. Due to a major famine in western Japan, the Taira could not assemble either the men or supplies necessary for a campaign in the Kanto; in addition, rebels started a fearful rumor that Prince Mochihito was still alive and a member of their camp. Divided over a plan of attack, the Taira delayed too long after their victory at Ishibashi, and an important ally lost an early skirmish to superior forces just before the Taira main forces arrived at Fujikawa. Frightened that their route of retreat back to the capital would be blocked, and watching soldiers betray them constantly, the Taira expedition (which was reported in contemporary sources as comprising only 4,000 mounted fighters compared to Yoritomo's 200,000) fled without launching an attack. Sources note that, in the confusion, Taira vassals threw away their armor and leaped on the first horse they could find. Only 10 men returned to the capital with the Taira commander.

Other difficulties soon burdened the Taira. Minamoto kinsmen Takeda Nobuyoshi and Kiso Yoshinaka had revolted early in 1180 independently of Yoritomo in Kai and Shinano, respectively; Takeda had helped defeat the Taira at Fujikawa. Late in 1180 rebellions flared up in the capital region, Ōmi, and Mino, signaling a general conflagration against the Court. The expansion of the revolt into Mino and Ōmi as led by a faction of the Minamoto was particularly serious because it threatened the Taira's grain reserves in Ōmi. The Kikuchi led an insurrection in Kyushu, which also cut an economic lifeline. Worst of all, the temples of the capital region became hotbeds of anti-Taira sentiment, at least partly in reaction to the Taira's leading role in suppressing religious agitators in the twelfth century. In the 12th month of 1180, the Taira burned Miidera in Ōmi, the temple where Mochihito had hidden before Yorimasa's rebellion. Later that same month, the Taira burned the temples of Nara, including Kōfukuji and Tōdaiji, in an act which further alienated other courtiers from their cause. The Court and the capital, which had been moved to the Taira compound at Fukuhara in the 6th month, returned to Heian by the end of the year.

As the war entered 1181 and its second phase, the Taira stood alone to defend the capital. Kiyomori died of a long illness early in the year. Without their great leader, the Taira tried to use their monopoly of Court politics to plan countermeasures. It was then that the Taira had the Court create the offices of commander-in-chief and estate foreman-in-chief to turn the tide. The revolts in Kyushu, Mino, Owari, and Ōmi were serious, and the piratical monks of Kumano in Kii province also led an insurrection. Using the newly established offices, the Taira scraped together men and matériel from the capital and from noble houses, yet still barely had enough to get an expedition underway. Early in the 3rd month of 1181, the Taira won one of their few victories over the hapless Minamoto Yukiie at Sunomata on the border of Owari and Mino. The battle required the Taira to cross a river and land on the Minamoto-occupied opposite shore; in a 6-hour battle the Taira took almost 400 rebel heads; however, they did not have enough reserves to pursue their advantage.

The Taira next decided to move against the forces of Kiso Yoshinaka in the lands along the Sea of Japan. A Taira ally from Echigo raised an army and invaded Kiso's base in Shinano in the 6th month of 1181. After an initial victory, however, the vassal met with the combined forces of Kiso and the Takeda; despite being outnumbered more than 10 to 1, Kiso disguised his troops as Taira soldiers and crushed his enemy at the Battle of Yokotagawara. The northern front, too, settled into a stalemate.

Firmly in control of the Kanto in the summer of 1181, Yoritomo proposed a truce in the war. Yoritomo's suggestion and the Taira reply appears in the following excerpt:

[Minamoto no] Yoritomo secretly . . . said . . . to the Retired Emperor: ". . . Just like old times, the Minamoto and Taira [should] stand side by side, and . . . serve you. The Kanto would be under the control of the Minamoto, and the Western Sea would follow the desires of the Taira. Both could be rulers. . . ."

> . . . But before the late . . . [Taira no Kiyomori, head of the fam-
> ily] . . . closed his eyes, with his dying words he said: "My sons and
> grandsons, even if only one of you is left alive, you should die fighting
> against [lit. bleach your bones in front of] Yoritomo."[103]

This quotation not only indicates the depth of the enmity between
the Taira and Minamoto as they fought for military dominance in
Japan, but also points out that the division of the country into eastern and western regions was a widely recognized fact. Later, in the
10th month of 1181, the Taira at last pacified Kyushu. The victory
gained them little, for the year 1182 brought one of the worst
famines in Japanese history, and troops could not move.

Early in 1183, Yoritomo suffered a major defection, as Shida
Yoshihiro (Tameyoshi's son and Yoritomo's uncle) raised the standard against the master of the Kanto; but one of Yoritomo's allies
defeated Shida in battle.[104] Shida fled for protection to Kiso Yoshinaka, a rival leader who had earlier joined in the revolt against the
Taira. Relations between Kiso and Yoritomo declined to the point
of armed conflict, but Yoshinaka eventually repaired the rift by
sending a hostage to Kamakura.

The stalemate among forces of the Taira, Yoritomo, and Yoshinaka finally came to an end in the spring of 1183 as the Taira
mounted an expedition to recover the rich provinces along the Sea
of Japan from Yoshinaka. Although the Taira won some initial victories in Echizen, Yoshinaka lured them into the Kurikara Pass,
where he attacked at night and won a smashing victory. With the
Taira expeditionary force reduced from a reported 40,000 to 4 or
5 horsemen, the road lay open for Yoshinaka to take the capital.

The war entered its third and final stage. By the 7th month of
1183, rumors flew at Court that Yoshinaka was in nearby Ōmi.
The Taira tried to requisition enough troops to meet him, even
appealing to hostile Enryakuji for warriors; but the monks of Mt.
Hiei went over to Yoshinaka. With Yoshinaka's and Yukiie's armies
on Mt. Hiei and in Yamato, the Taira fled the capital to their base
in western Honshu on the 25th of the 7th month, taking along
with them the boy Emperor Antoku and the imperial regalia. Go-
Shirakawa, however, eluded them.

Throughout the campaign against the Taira, there had been

competition between Yoshinaka and Yoritomo for leadership of the revolt and dominance among all warriors; Yoshinaka was now seemingly in the catbird seat. He received appointments and Taira lands, and the Court ordered him to proceed against remnants of the Taira; but Yoshinaka was now on unfamiliar territory, facing an enemy that excelled at naval warfare. While rumors abounded that the Taira were gaining in strength, Yoshinaka dawdled. He finally marched to western Honshu in the 9th and 10th months of 1183, but, on the 17th, he lost to the Taira in Bizen. On the 3rd of the intercalary 10th month, the Taira wiped out the stain of previous defeats by mustering 1,000 boats against Yoshinaka's 500 at Mizushima in Bitchū. The Taira landed their mounts on the shore, took on Yoshinaka in single mounted combat, won again at Mizushima, and later overwhelmed Yukiie in Harima.

Relations between Yoshinaka and the other major players, including Go-Shirakawa and Yoritomo, worsened. Rumors surfaced in the capital that Yoshinaka would capture Go-Shirakawa and go back to the north, or that Yoritomo, now newly armed with court recognition of his rule in the Kanto, would advance on the capital.[105] Finally, in the 11th month of 1183, while Yoshinaka stalled in western Honshu despite orders from Retired Emperor Go-Shirakawa and the Court, Yoritomo sent a force to the capital under his brother Yoshitsune. Yukiie obeyed the Court and deployed his men against the Taira, but Yoshinaka instead turned against the Retired Emperor and surrounded and crushed Go-Shirakawa's numerically superior forces at the Battle of Hōjūji. Yoshinaka slaughtered the followers of the Retired Emperor and took military control of the capital.

Yoshinaka then compelled Go-Shirakawa to issue an order to destroy Yoritomo, and the uneasy alliance dissolved. He also received appointment as the Great General Who Quells the Barbarians, a position held by Sakanoue no Tamuramaro in 797 when the Court recognized him as the leading military man in Japan. Many people feared the Taira would re-enter the capital, or that Yoshinaka would ally himself with the Taira or with Fujiwara Hidehira, another independent warrior lord in Mutsu. Yoritomo's troops, under the command of Yoshitsune and another brother, Noriyori, advanced rapidly from the Kanto, first to Mino, then Ōmi. Meanwhile, the Taira occupied Kiyomori's old retreat at Fukuhara. Yoshinaka rushed his men to Ōmi, but was no match for Yoritomo's army. On the 20th of the 1st month in 1184, Yoritomo's armies entered the capital from Seta and Uji, and Yoshinaka was beheaded.

The Court wasted no time in turning against the Taira. One week after transferring Yoshinaka's head to the Court, Yoshitsune received an order to extirpate the Taira. First, Yoshitsune executed a surprise night attack and triumphed at Mikusa. The Taira then fortified a precipice called Ichinotani, but Yoshitsune outsmarted them by leading a small mounted force around behind the fortification and down a cliff. Yoshitsune routed the Taira in a series of battles, killing and capturing many warriors. However, Munemori, the Emperor Antoku, and a small force retreated with the imperial regalia into the Inland Sea.

Yoritomo now had the difficult task of arming and equipping his forces for sea battle in western Japan. It is not surprising that he spent the rest of 1184 outfitting an army and searching out the Taira. The Taira won a few victories during this period; the Court also charged Yoritomo with suppressing warrior transgressions against the government throughout the land, a job that exhausted his resources.

Finally, in the 2nd month of 1185, Yoshitsune attacked Taira headquarters, even though the other Minamoto general, Noriyori, was unable to move in concert. The Taira guarded their stronghold at Yashima on the island of Shikoku with about 1,000 horsemen. The Minamoto victory at Yashima on the 19th of the 2nd month was a masterstroke of naval and ground strategy; Yoshitsune discovered that the Taira had divided their men to cover several possible routes of attack and quickly overwhelmed a small group of defenders at the main Taira camp. A similar triumph at Shido (also in Sanuki) followed two days later, when Yoshitsune enticed the Taira into battle with a small force and then countered with his main army. Munemori and the main Taira contingent moved again, this time to Nagato province.

On the 24th of the 3rd month of 1185, Yoshitsune utilized supplies freshly arrived from eastern Japan to annihilate the Taira at the naval Battle of Dannoura, which ironically took place near the site of a provincial militia headquarters (*gundan*).[106] Although numerically inferior, the Taira fought valiantly until several allies betrayed their cause. The Emperor Antoku and several other Taira courtiers drowned rather than become prisoners of Go-Shirakawa and the Minamoto, while Go-Shirakawa and the Court rewarded Yoritomo with advancement to the 2nd Court Rank. The worst period of warfare in Japan's history had ended with a new head of all warriors ensconced atop an independent military government in the Kanto.

JAPAN'S MILITARY, 1180-1185

Conventionally, historians have interpreted the Great Civil War of 1180-1185 as a watershed, the event that marked off ancient Japan from the medieval period, much as the Meiji Restoration of 1868 is depicted as dividing traditional culture from modernity. The war was the crucible in which Yoritomo formed the Kamakura Shogunate and established Japanese feudalism; private customs and individuals prevailed over the public institutions of previous ages.

Though admittedly overstated, such a revolutionary view has merits. Scholars have seen in the conflict a general rebellion against all authority, an attempt by warriors and other groups to assert class interests over the narrow aristocratic elite which had controlled the Court and Japanese politics for centuries. It was partially in response to the explosion of warrior violence and rapacity that, during the course of the war, the rebel Yoritomo began a program of confirming his followers' landholdings, a policy that may not have been totally new, but was nonetheless notable for its systematic and national character. Out of necessity, Yoritomo had devised a new way to pay for the expensive military technology he had inherited from his ancestors, a method that took advantage of the land hunger of most warriors, and that many have likened to European feudalism. For the first time the Kanto could claim victory over and autonomy from western Japan, and with his mastery the Kamakura leader soon took over the military and police powers formerly held by the Court.

When considered from a military perspective, however, the remarkable point about the war is its continuity with the past. On all sides, commanders raised and equipped their men and fought battles much as they had since at least the time of Masakado, and quite possibly before. Technologically, weapons remained basically the same and the supremacy of the mounted fighter was unquestioned, while socially many fighting men were still members of a lineage privileged to follow the way of the horse and bow for centuries. The Japanese economy in 1180 was unable to support a military larger than that of 800 (probably smaller), and the provincial headquarters was still the fastest and most effective route for putting together a sizable force.

TECHNOLOGY AND FIGHTING STYLE. The Great Civil War was fought with ritualized, single-mounted combat, as had been true of the Former Nine Years' War, the Latter Three Years' War, the Hōgen Disturbance, and the Heiji Coup. The conflict displayed all the characteristics of a serious intraspecific battle, in which each side struggled to preserve itself and assert dominance over others. In this sense, the Taira-Minamoto rivalry is central to the conflict, and not, as Jeffrey Mass has asserted, an "impediment to understanding."[107]

Readers may make detailed observations of the rituals and tactics for themselves by perusing numerous translations of *The Mirror of the East* and that paean to the samurai, *The Tale of the Heike*. At their core, these descriptions of the Great Civil War are all about masculinity.[108] It is interesting to note that one phrase meaning "to do combat" in the Japanese of this era was *shiyū o kessuru,* which literally translates as "to determine who is male and who is female."

Of course, one might argue that the individual style of combat evident in the Great Civil War is feudal. To be sure, the knights of Western Europe did have rituals that were similar to the samurai's, even though the weapons were not the same. But one may also compare the ritualized, single fighting mode of the samurai to the tactics of Homer's ancient warriors in the Trojan War. The technology is widely different in all three cases, but the intraspecific content — the larger-than-life men who fought to assert their personal dominance in a hierarchy—is the same. Such conflict appears and reappears throughout history, not just in medieval France, and thus it is misleading to make exclusive comparisons of the samurai to Europe's feudal knight.

The Tale of the Heike is a treasure-trove of stories about warriors, and entire books are available on the topic of martial lore from the Great Civil War alone. One conversation seems to sum up the Great Civil War technologically, however; it dates from the Battle of Fujikawa in 1180, as the Taira expedition waited to fight the men of the Kanto:

> [Taira no] Koremori summoned Nagai no Saitō Bettō Sanemori, a man known to be acquainted with conditions in the east [i.e., eastern Honshu]. "Tell me, Sanemori, how many men in the Eight Provinces (the Kanto) can wield a strong bow as well as you do?" he asked.
>
> Sanemori uttered a derisive laugh. "Do you think I use long arrows? They barely measure 13 fists. Any number of warriors in the east can equal that: Nobody is called a long-arrow man there unless he draws a 15-fist shaft. A strong bow is held to be one that requires 6 stout men for the stringing. One of those powerful archers can easily penetrate 2 or 3 suits of armor when he shoots. . . .
>
> "I don't want to alarm you. As the old saying goes, battles are won by strategy, not by numbers. But I don't expect to return to the capital alive from the fight we face." All the Taira warriors trembled at his words.[109]

Sanemori's words do more than stress the skills of the Kanto warrior, one of the primary reasons for Yoritomo's victory; the remark about strategy suggests the nature of Japan's debt to Chinese martial thinking. The samurai had learned strategy from Sun-tzu and *The Art of War,* the Chinese classic of combat theory, and any number of battles described in tales and chronicles illustrate Japanese knowledge of terrain, command, and tactics as advocated by the Chinese master. In this respect, the samurai was a direct descendant of his Taihō ancestors.

By the late twelfth century, however, Japanese military thought had come a long way from the Taihō (and Chinese) emphasis on numbers and organization. It is unclear how committed the Japanese ever were to the Chinese belief in the superiority of well-drilled masses over a few experts, even in the eighth century; but, by the time of the Great Civil War, the Japanese warrior had abandoned all pretense of adherence to this principle. Thus Japan's adoption of Chinese military techniques had decidedly mixed results over the long term, as soldiers learned basic strategy but rejected coordinated tactics. No longer dependent upon numbers and organization, warriors fought the Great Civil War as a battle of individual expertise, a conflict the Kanto was bound to win.

THE SIZE OF ARMIES. Another subject of critical importance is the number of men who fought in the Great Civil War of 1180–1185. Sources frequently list numbers for expeditions and battles, but they contradict each other, and almost all figures are open to question (see Appendix Table 5). In particular, tabulations given in *The Tale of the Heike* and *The Mirror of the East*, usually in the several tens of thousands, are greatly exaggerated.[110] Japanese historians typically estimate that the authors could have overstated the competing forces by a factor of 10.

In contrast, aristocratic diaries give much smaller counts, a fact also true in the Hōgen War. Because civil aristocrats were literate and numerate while military men were probably not, the estimates of civil aristocrats are bound to be more accurate.[111] At the same time, as is also evident from analysis of the Hōgen numbers, civil aristocrats were probably more concerned with the chief warriors and less apt to count minor followers or foot soldiers.[112]

A few cases allow historians to compare the different sources (see Appendix Table 5). For example, at the Battle of Ishibashi in 1180 between Yoritomo and Ōba Kagechika, the diary *The Jeweled Leaf*, by Kujō no Kanezane, lists the Taira at 2,000 and Yoritomo at 500 horsemen; *The Mirror of the East*, the history of the Kamakura government, writes that Ōba had 3,000 and Yoritomo only 300, while *The Tale of the Heike* states that the Taira had only 1,000 men. These discrepancies may seem small, but note that *The Mirror of East* makes the odds worse for Yoritomo and *The Tale of the Heike* does the same for the Taira, probably to emphasize the valor of the side each author was supporting. Kanezane was likely the most accurate record-keeper.

In some cases there is wide disagreement between accounts. For the battle between the Taira and Minamoto no Yorimasa at Uji,

The Mirror of the East and *The Tale of the Heike* talk of Taira forces at 20,000 and 28,000, respectively, yet two aristocratic diaries list the Taira force at 200 and 300.[113] There is a chance that the aristocrats and the authors of the two literary works were describing two different armies; the Taira actually sent a few of their personal retainers against Yorimasa but also planned a large state expedition, which never arrived. But, even if it is true that the sources were referring to different forces, the warrior tales still wildly exaggerate the number of men in combat. Because the battle took place in an area close to Heian, it seems likely that the aristocratic count is more accurate. If one accepts those figures, the warrior histories are inaccurate by a whopping 100 times!

Figures are also available for other battles, but the numbers mostly show how inaccurate *The Tale of the Heike* and other martial chronicles are. Some battles involved larger forces, notably the Battle of Fujikawa, where even Kanezane agrees that the Minamoto had several tens of thousands of horsemen. Of course, since the battle took place in eastern Honshu where Kanezane could not witness it, one can not know how reliable his information was. A large host also participated in the Battle of Kurikara, with the Taira reportedly having 40,000 riders; and yet Yoshinaka defeated his enemy with a mere 5,000 men. It is also notable that the final battles in western Japan in 1184–1185 were often small; even the Battle of Ichinotani involved only a few thousand Minamoto horsemen.

Kanezane, author of *The Jeweled Leaf*, was acutely aware of the problem of counting warriors and knew how rumors tended to exaggerate the size of military forces. He made such an observation as he watched Taira soldiers departing for a last-ditch defense of the capital in 1183:

> [T]he search-and-punish mission [of the Taira] . . . left from Tawara and went by my house at the Eastern Small Road (at Tomi no kōji). Servants secretly observed, and the force was 1,080 horsemen. (They said they counted them for sure.) Recently, the estimates of the world have been as high as 7,000 or 8,000, even 10,000. But this force was only about 1,000. A rumor with no foundation![114]

A comparison of the sources and a knowledge of contemporary battle tactics suggests that most battles were fought between a few hundred horsemen; occasionally the count rose to a few thousand, but almost never above that.

Of course, every rider commanded 2 or 3 foot soldiers, a fact rarely alluded to in contemporary accounts. *The Tale of the Heike* occasionally mentions spears and shields, presumably wielded by foot soldiers, but little evidence shows that the Taihō tradition of trained infantry had survived. Any estimate of the battle strength of each side should take foot soldiers into account. But even with those fighters, it is highly doubtful that armies of the late twelfth century outnumbered those of 400 years earlier.

MILITARY INSTITUTIONS. As had been true for at least 300 years, military aristocrats and such offices as the Investigators composed armies in the capital, while in the countryside commanders organized their forces through the provincial headquarters or as personal followers. There is relatively little information about the capital military, since most battles took place in rural Japan. But, as long as the Taira held control of Heian, they continued to conscript troops through their position as military aristocrats and through the Investigators. For instance, when Yorimasa revolted in the spring of 1180, the Taira first sent Investigators (who also happened to be their vassals) to the Battle at Uji (see Appendix Table 4). All during the stalemate between 1181 and 1183, the Taira used their position as military aristocrats, as well as the post of commander-in-chief created in 1181, to try to conscript more soldiers. Even after the capital fell into Minamoto hands in 1184, a source speaks of "capital warriors (*kyōto no bushi*)."[115]

The picture of the military is clearest for the provinces. As in the previous age, generals raised, equipped, and deployed their troops either as personal retainers or through the provincial headquarters. I have already demonstrated the Taira use of this two-pronged system; the Minamoto also operated within the same arrangement. It is well known that Yoritomo had a close personal retinue, men such as Doi Sanehira and Chiba Tsunetane bound to him by ties of vassalage. But what most historians do not generally recognize is the extent to which Yoritomo relied upon the soldiers of the provincial headquarters.

Personal ties to troops (or the leaders of troops) were an important element of military success, as evident in the failure of non-warrior governors to command soldiers earlier in the twelfth century. But personal loyalty alone was not sufficient; commanders had to buttress their control by authority over the provincial headquarters. In an age when most warriors easily transferred personal loyalty (as witnessed by numerous betrayals), control of the provincial headquarters was crucial for mounting a campaign.

Records allude to the troops of the provincial headquarters with some frequency. For example, at the Battle of Fujikawa in 1180, one reason the Taira were unable to attack Yoritomo was that "the hearts of the soldiers [of the eastern Honshu] provinces were all with Yoritomo."[116] Later that same month, the same author confidently asserts that "the troops of the provinces" (*shokoku no gumpei*) will swell the ranks of Taira forces against the Mino rebels.[117] In the 4th month of 1181, the Taira ordered "the soldiers of Dazaifu's jurisdiction" to take up arms against the anti-government warriors of Kyushu.[118] In 1181, when Yoritomo sent his compromise suggestion to the Taira, the noted aristocrat Kujō no Kanezane lamented that "the warriors of the provinces" (*shokoku no bushi*) would not come to Munemori's aid.[119] After the Taira lost the capital, in the intercalary 10th month, the Court alerted "the soldiers of Yamato province" to be prepared for Taira strongmen in the region.[120] The "warriors of the province" (*kuni no musha*) appeared in a battle in Bizen later in 1183.[121] In 1184, as Yoritomo prepared to invade western Japan, he enrolled "troops of the provinces" through the provincial headquarters.[122] Other examples of the provincial headquarters serving as the chief center for raising and deploying troops are available.[123]

In fact, the Minamoto probably recognized the importance of the provincial headquarters even more than the Taira. Jeffrey Mass has pointed out several examples of Yoritomo's enrolling men through that office.[124] When Yoritomo began his revolt in 1180, his first military action was to take control of the Izu provincial headquarters by killing the Governor's deputy. When he fled to Awa, again his forces "hijacked" (to use a Japanese scholar's colorful phrase) the provincial office.[125] Yoritomo repeated the scene elsewhere in the Kanto when he seized control; as a military aristocrat out of power, he was committing a revolutionary deed through an age-old office, a pattern known only too well to scholars of Japanese history.

The provincial headquarters was located in a crucial strategic position in virtually every province upon the main routes to other provinces and the capital. The office held the keys to granaries in which warlords could find rice and other grains so essential to conducting military campaigns, and also contained seeds and equipment vital to peasant livelihoods. Every provincial center had small factories where artisans produced paper, cloth, weapons, and iron. And last, the provincial headquarters was the repository for land, loan, tax and other records and the home of the local officials who knew how to make use of them. Personal loyalty was easily transferred and warrior bands were amorphous entities, but the provincial headquarters was the fortress that held warriors together. In seizing and working through the provincial headquarters, Yoritomo acted in a revolutionary way, and at the same time showed his own dependence upon an institution laid out half a millennium earlier.[126]

REASONS FOR YORITOMO'S VICTORY. One typical explanation of Yoritomo's victory over the Taira and Yoshinaka is that the Minamoto represented a new feudal class, while the Taira and others were products of an outdated, ancient society. Such advocates of the Western-analogue theory see the establishment of a new order in Yoritomo's confirmation of landholdings, and view him as the champion of warrior (*bushi*) self-interest. According to this interpretation, the reason for Yoritomo's triumph lay in the new and advanced policies and institutions he put into practice.

As noted earlier in this work, the degree to which class interest motivated Yoritomo or any other warrior in the Great Civil War of 1180–1185 is debatable. Certainly a warrior's seizure of land had an anti-Court aspect, but it is important to remember that, when one warrior took over a parcel, another was usually ousted. And Japan in the twelfth century was not a land where communication among warriors, members of the same class but of different locales, was easy. Vertical and regional ties were probably more important to most fighting men than their presumed class attachments. In Marx's words, warriors were a class in themselves but not for themselves.

This work has emphasized continuities with the past and the relatively small institutional differences among warriors who battled in the Great Civil War. The Taira seem to have ensured land on a limited basis as the war progressed, retained a large group of vassals, and invented many of the feudal institutions, such as the land steward and constable, which were to become the hallmarks of the Kamakura regime. What is more, it is a widely accepted point that Yoshinaka also recognized the land of his followers, and yet he was unable to subdue either Yoritomo or the Taira. Yoritomo's confirmation of landholdings was an important step, crucial for rallying support in the Kanto in 1180, but one should see it for what it was: the only means available to Yoritomo to rally land- and reward-hungry fighters. He also relied on ancient means by raising his men via the provincial headquarters. There were few differences in the way various commanders drafted, equipped, and deployed their armies; other more important causes determined the outcome.

The major difference between the Taira and the Minamoto was geographical base. The Taira were located in western Japan, where temples, the Retired Emperor, and the rest of the aristocracy resided. The Taira succeeded in alienating all these potential allies both by their successes within Court society and by their high-handed tactics against the Retired Emperor, temples like Miidera, and the Fujiwara Regents' house. The Taira behaved as if one house or even one person (Kiyomori) could monopolize the Court. Kiyomori was a political genius, as was Yoritomo, but no one could dictate to a Court society that had dissolved into pluralistic factions over the past 200 years. Dissension cost the Taira cause mightily as they tried to conscript troops and acquire provisions, first in the Kanto, and later from aristocrats and temples.[127]

But, even had western Japan been united in its war against the Kanto, it still would have lost. The reason was a terrible famine that struck in 1180–1182, which is described a some length in the following twelfth-century literary account:

In [1181] . . . there were two years of famine, and a terrible time indeed it was. The spring and summer were scorching hot, and autumn and winter brought typhoons and floods, and as one bad season followed another the Five Cereals could not ripen. . . .

Some deserted their land and went to other provinces, and others left their houses and dwelt in the hills. . . .

. . . [W]hen we looked for some improvement during the next year it was even worse, for a pestilence followed, . . . [R]espectable citizens who ordinarily wore hats and shoes now went barefooted begging from house to house. And while you looked in wonder at such a sight they would suddenly fall down and die in the road. And by the walls and in the highways you could see everywhere the bodies of those who had died of starvation. And, as there was none to take them away, a terrible stench filled the streets, and people went by with their eyes averted. . . .

Another very sad thing was that those who had children who were very dear to them almost invariably died before them, because they denied themselves to give their sons and daughters what they needed. And so these children would always survive their parents. And there were babies who continued to feed at their mother's breast, not knowing she was already dead.

. . . And the number [of dead] that they counted within the city, in the space of four or five months, . . . was at least 42,300.[128]

The Great Famine of 1180–1182 was indeed a horror, one of the periodic subsistence crises that had plagued Japan, especially western Japan, ever since the eighth century, and perhaps as far back as the Neolithic age (10,000–300 B.C.). All fighting ceased for two years beginning in the middle of 1181, but this was not, as Jeffrey Mass has suggested, "phony war."[129] Neither side could muster the men or supplies necessary to do battle outside its own territory. The institutions developed by the Taira after 1180, such as the estate foreman-in-chief and the messenger who encourages agriculture in Aki, were responses to famine as well as to war.[130]

There can be little doubt that the famine and pestilence were most devastating in western Japan. For example, when the war moved to western Honshu after the defeat of Yoshinaka, Yoritomo's armies were under strict orders not to forage off the land, as had been customary in earlier campaigns. Yet, as *The Mirror of the East* indicates, Yoritomo was able to ship men, horses, and supplies to his generals Yoshitsune and Noriyori to fight the Taira.[131] Although the Kanto had not by any means developed all its agricultural potential, and although the area still suffered from its own agricultural and demographic maladies, the gradual recovery from the twin devastations of war and disease in the late eleventh and twelfth centuries in the Kanto, coupled with the harsh effects of the 1180–1182 famine in western Honshu, was enough to allow Yoritomo to provision his men adequately and secure victory. Demographic and economic realities were more critical than institutions; the Great Civil War of 1180–1185 proved that soldiers do indeed march on their stomachs.

Of course, one can not deny the considerable talents of Yoritomo and their role in his victory. He could deal with the Court more effectively than had other military aristocrats, with the possible exception of Kiyomori, and was the perfect leader for the Kanto Independence Movement. Unlike Masakado, he did not challenge the established order by naming himself emperor; he was content to stay in the Kanto away from wily politicians like Go-Shirakawa. When he began dealing with the Court and Go-Shirakawa, he worked through established channels and obtained proper imperial recognition for his regional rule. But, if Yoritomo had been dealing with a united and well-provisioned Court (as Masakado had), rather than the fragmented and devastated region that was late-twelfth-century western Japan, his independence movement may have died with him in the Hakone Mountains.

CONCLUSION

Historians have conventionally seen the late twelfth century as a time of great change. First the Ise Taira came to prominence as military aristocrats based on the favoritism of the Retired Emperors; their power derived from office and other ancient foundations. Even though they were warriors, they wanted to be like other civil aristocrats, and, when they came too close to succeeding, opposition arose. Eventually the Minamoto, true warrior (*bushi*) leaders, superseded the Taira, and they established a new military and social system based on the tie of land confirmation in return for service. Western-style feudalism had come to Japan.

In this chapter I have presented an interpretation that stresses continuities with the past and similarities among the rival camps. The Ise Taira became the preferred "teeth and claws" of the Court in the early twelfth century, not out of favoritism, but because they were actually better at the job. Faced with a generational change from their leader Yoshiie and internecine strife, the Minamoto lost their preeminent position as the "chief of all warriors" to Taira no Masamori and his descendants. Masamori proved his ability by subjugating the half-mad Minamoto no Yoshichika and suppressing pirates, while the Minamoto heir, Tameyoshi, destroyed everything in his path. By the middle of the twelfth century, the Taira were on a par with the Minamoto, and were consolidating a military base along the Inland Sea.

In the Hōgen Disturbance of 1156, Taira no Kiyomori and most of the Taira sided with Go-Shirakawa in vanquishing the Fujiwara Regents. Minamoto no Tameyoshi, always the political misfit, gathered his sons and fought for the Regents; only Yoshitomo served with the Taira and Go-Shirakawa. Go-Shirakawa's victory in 1156 meant that the Taira now had the upper hand, and, in the Rebellion of 1159 by Yoshitomo and some ambitious confidantes of the Retired Emperor, Kiyomori eliminated his last rival for military supremacy in Japan. Sources for both conflicts reveal that commanders raised and equipped their forces as they had earlier, through the provincial headquarters and personal ties. Armies in both revolts numbered only a few hundred horsemen and foot soldiers, and the style of combat was the single, mounted mode common since the 1050s.

With their enemies dead or under house arrest, the Taira began to construct the first nationwide system of vassalage. The basis for their authority was the imperial order of 1167; utilizing such enticements as office, aid in land disputes, and tours of guard duty in the capital, Shigemori built a Taira base in the Kanto as well as in the capital area and western Japan. As relations with Go-Shirakawa worsened in 1177, Kiyomori took complete control of the Court forces, still organized mainly through the provincial headquarters. In 1181, Munemori became the head of a regional military based in western Japan; his creation of the positions of commander-in-chief and estate foreman-in-chief helped breathe new life into the Taira cause. The arrangements found their roots in an eighth-century institution, and the Kamakura government was forced to copy them when Yoritomo invaded the capital region in 1184.

The Great Civil War of 1180–1185 was a nationwide revolt against Taira dominance of the Court. During the first year of battle, the Taira managed to quash rebels around the capital but lost the entire Kanto to Yoritomo; the Battle of Fujikawa resulted in Taira men fleeing back to the capital for their lives. From 1181 to 1183, the war settled down into a stalemate, as the Taira developed new institutions to deal with a terrible famine in western Japan. From mid-1183 until early in 1185, first Yoshinaka and then Yoritomo succeeded in taking over the capital from the Taira, who were annihilated at the Battle of Dannoura. Yoritomo was now the "chief of all warriors."

The Great Civil War saw few changes in Japan's military. Ritualized and individualized combat dominated the battlefield, as samurai simultaneously showed their debt to and their differences from the Chinese model. Figures on the forces that fought vary widely, but usually battles took place between a few hundred to a few thousand horsemen, assisted by foot soldiers. Military tales and warrior records typically exaggerate the size of forces by a factor of 10 or more; the head count of the combined armies certainly amounted to no more than it had several centuries before.

Military aristocrats raised capital troops primarily through personal ties, and the provincial headquarters provided most soldiers in the countryside. Yoritomo did confirm lands for his vassals on a widespread basis, but Yoshinaka and the Taira also may have embraced the same practice. In addition, the Minamoto relied heavily on the provincial headquarters to control first the Kanto and then other areas. Institutional differences among warriors were not as responsible for the Minamoto victory as the Great Famine of 1180–1182, the skills of the Kanto warrior, and Yoritomo's political acumen.

In the Introduction, I stated that, in defining the Japanese warrior (*bushi*), one should consider four factors: technology, social organization, economic base, and political expertise. The first two were in place early on, as the mounted archer was supreme in battle and organized into specialized military lineages. One could argue that the economic base also developed early on, as the Japanese economy was unable to produce significantly more horsemen in 1180 than it had in 800. Still, if the argument focuses narrowly on the Taira and Minamoto who fought in the Great Civil War, then they probably did not acquire their lands until the late eleventh and twelfth centuries, during the "great age of reopening of abandoned parcels."

Political expertise was another matter. Warriors had been naive in the days of Masakado, and it took the two great politicians, Taira no Kiyomori and Minamoto no Yoritomo, to lead fighting men to some degree of autonomy. Unfortunately for these two, they both were alive at the same time, and only one could become the head of all warriors. Despite the victory of 1185, however, political independence would prove most difficult to sustain.

chapter eight

Japanese Feudalism Reconsidered, 1185–1300

"This World of Transmigration is a place of impermanence, Lord Takeda.
What's going to happen, I wonder?"
Takeda replied, "Listen! Here's the truth of the matter. If Kamakura is victori-
ous, we'll adhere to Kamakura, and if Kyoto is victorious, we'll adhere to Kyoto.
Such is the way of those who wield the bow and arrow!"
— a warrior conversation in 1221

. . . within every 11 chō [1 chō = 3 acres] of wet and dry fields, 10 chō are
the allotment of the proprietor [Court aristocrat or religious institution] and the
provincial officers, and 1 chō is for the land steward [a Kamakura warrior].
— a law of the thirteenth century dividing land in estates

With the annihilation of the Taira in 1185, Yoritomo seemed unchallenged as the "chief of all warriors" throughout Japan. He
soon took the title of Great Barbarian-Subduing Generalissimo
(shogun), emblematic of his supremacy, and established a military
government in the Kanto, where he exercised police and military
powers for the Court and appointed favored soldiers to positions in
many estates and the army and navy.

Historians who endorse the Western-analogue theory are fond
of viewing the era after Yoritomo's victory in 1185 (known as the
Kamakura period, 1185–1333) as a watershed, even a revolution
into feudalism. In this view, manly warriors succeeded effete aristocrats as the rulers of Japan, and they did so by creating Western-
style feudalism in an East Asian country. For these scholars, the
establishment of feudalism meant that land was now the basis of
all wealth and served as the foundation for military service by the
loyal vassals of Kamakura; the thirteenth century was the heyday
of the warrior, who dominated politics, the economy, and society.

Recent scholars have modified this interpretation somewhat, but still see the Kamakura age as the beginning of medieval Japan.

The two excerpts from thirteenth-century sources quoted above raise doubts about just how applicable the term *feudalism* (by which I mean an exclusively martial ruling class bound by ties of dependence overseeing a stable agricultural society) really is to Kamakura Japan. How feudal could any society be when warriors acted more like mercenaries than vassals, repeatedly betraying their lords and switching their loyalties to the winning side? And how thoroughgoing could any revolution into feudalism be that left warriors, the supposed ruling class, with only one-eleventh of the farmland in much of Japan? No inquiry into the origins and rise of the warrior could be complete without considering how much change the founding of the Kamakura Shogunate actually wrought.

Here I shall briefly analyze 3 wars of the Kamakura era: the Northern Campaign of 1189, the Jōkyū Rebellion of 1221, and the Mongol Invasions of 1274 and 1281. In each, the provincial headquarters — a Chinese-style public institution that greatly predated Kamakura — was crucial in raising and deploying troops, just as it had been for commanders of the tenth century. The provincial headquarters reinforced ties of dependence, which were often too malleable to be useful. Furthermore, these wars reveal the continuing vitality of the Court in Kyoto and the limited power of the warrior government in Kamakura; it was not until the late thirteenth century and the military emergency induced by the Mongol menace that Kamakura obtained domination of the entire nation.

In addition to continuities in the ways soldiers fought, the Kamakura period reveals two other important time-honored trends. Tallies of warriors (*bushi*) in Japan in the 1200s indicate that the military class remained small, with perhaps 3,000 vassals of the shogunate and another few thousand non-vassals, figures about the same as tabulations for Strong Fellows and other mounted soldiers in 800. The unchanging size of the warrior class from 800 to 1200 is a measure of the stagnation in both the economy and population; the rise of the warrior and the formation of the Kamakura government were not revolutions of numbers, but a break-away movement of the Kanto warrior from Court domination.

A second evolutionary trend appears in military incomes. Analysis of legal sources, as well as three well-known cases from western Japan, demonstrates that warriors received only about a third of the harvest, and less than 10 percent of the land in that region of Japan throughout most of the Kamakura era. An example from Hitachi in eastern Japan, however, shows that fighters garnered the lion's share of land and revenues in the Kanto, where warriors predominated as they had ever since the late sixth century.

THE KAMAKURA MILITARY IN ACTION

By the late twelfth century, Yoritomo had created a military government in Kamakura that was separate from the court in Kyoto and complete with a bureaucracy and judiciary[1] (see Figure 12). The victor in the Great Civil War of 1180–1185 acquired the twin appointments of Arrest Officer-in-Chief of Japan (*Nihon koku sō tsuibu shi*) and the Land Steward-in-Chief of Japan (*Nihon koku sō jitō*), positions that gave him police and military powers throughout most of the country. As the culmination of his new-found authority, in 1192 the Court invested Yoritomo with the title of Great Barbarian-Subduing Generalissimo (*sei-i tai shōgun*) a term borrowed from the campaigns against the "barbarians" of northeastern Honshu. The nomination signaled the Court's recognition of his leadership of all warriors, and Japan's age of military rule seemed to be underway.

The Kamakura regime was a warrior government and possessed a body of laws which described the organization and duties of the military (see Figure 12). An individual vassal received the designation *houseman* (*goke'nin*) and owed loyalty to the shogun in return for service in battle; Kamakura organized its housemen by province and listed them in duty rosters. Yoritomo appointed many soldiers to lands to which his government had direct access and allotted them tax revenues for overseeing cultivation; he termed these followers *land stewards* (*jitō*). In addition, the constable (*shugo*), a prominent warrior of the province named by and directly responsible to Kamakura, led all retainers on guard duty and other police and military actions.[2] One historian also believes that warrior-officials took control of the flow of documents within many provincial headquarters.[3]

Figure 12. THE KAMAKURA MILITARY

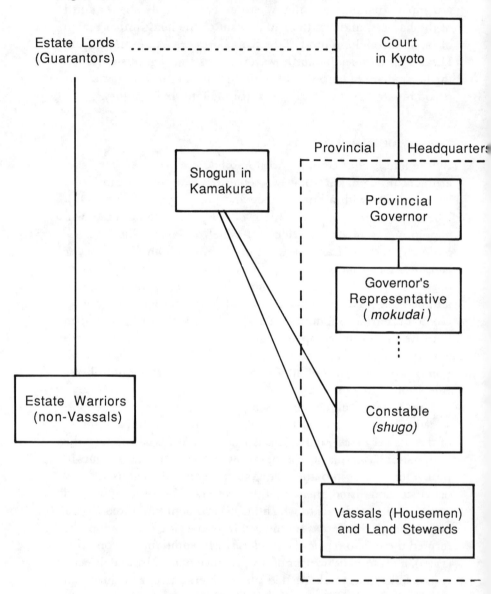

Sources: Ishii Susumu, *Kamakura bushi no jitsuzō,* p. 347; Ōyama Kyohei, *Nihon no rekishi* 9, *Kamakura bakufu,* p. 133; adaptations suggested by Hongō Kazuto of the Historiographical Institute of Tokyo University.

The shogunate was a new regime, but it is important to note how much Kamakura depended upon precedents.[4] The Court had defined military and police powers through the centuries-old practice of naming men to be arrest officers and overseers. The constable may have been a new position, but warriors had fulfilled similar functions (such as capital and provincial guard duty) in earlier eras. Most of Kamakura's power was articulated through the provincial headquarters, following a tradition going back to the Reform of 901.

Before drawing conclusions about Japanese feudalism and just how much change the founding of the shogunate really meant, one should supplement this short and abstract outline of the Kamakura military with instances of warriors in action.

THE NORTHERN CAMPAIGN OF 1189. The battles against the Fujiwara in Mutsu and Dewa provinces were really the concluding blows of the Great Civil War of 1180–1185.[5] After the defeat of the Taira, an open rift developed between Yoritomo and his younger brother, Yoshitsune. Yoritomo probably had good reasons to feel threatened: Yoshitsune was a brilliant field commander and enjoyed the support of many courtiers and of warriors who disliked Yoritomo. Beginning in 1185, Yoritomo carried out a national search for his brother, but failed to find him. In 1189, Yoshitsune fled to Mutsu, the independent kingdom of the Fujiwara (not related to the Fujiwara civil aristocrats at Court).[6] Worried about invoking the wrath of Japan's recently victorious military leader, the new Fujiwara leader, Yasuhira, forced Yoshitsune to commit suicide and sent his head to Kamakura on the 13th of the 6th month to placate Yoritomo. The Fujiwara had long been rivals of the Minamoto, who had previously subjugated the region in the eleventh century, first under Yoriyoshi and then under Yoshiie (see Chapter 6).

Yoritomo was not pleased with the news from the Tohoku because he now could prove that the Fujiwara had hidden Yoshitsune while he was conducting a nationwide search for his brother. Eleven days after he received Yasuhira's gift, Yoritomo decided to use the death of his brother, who had ironically been a threat while alive, as a pretext to go to war with the Fujiwara. Yoritomo accordingly followed proper legal channels and petitioned the Court for a pursue-and-punish order against the Fujiwara. Kyoto refused to issue the order, probably because the Retired Emperor Go-Shirakawa wanted to rein Yoritomo in and continue to use the Fujiwara as a counter to Kamakura. Yoritomo assembled his horsemen (1,000 according to the rosters of the 24th of the 6th month) and, following the advice of a sage elder, the commander of Kamakura decided to attack the Fujiwara even without an arrest order. On the 17th of the 7th month, he divided his command into 3 parts: Chiba Tsunetane and Hatta Tomoie oversaw forces approaching along the Pacific coast, including warriors of Hitachi and Shimōsa; Hiki Yoshikazu and Usami Sanemasa led an army marching along shores of the Sea of Japan (with soldiers of Kōzuke); and Yoritomo himself directed a middle unit (see Map 12). On the 18th, Hiki departed Kamakura; Yoritomo left the next day with a host recorded at 1,000. *The Mirror of the East* lists the names of 144 mounted archers in Yoritomo's expedition.[7]

On the 29th of the 7th month, Yoritomo crossed Shirakawa Barrier into the land of the Fujiwara. On the 7th of the 8th month, Yoritomo's middle command reached Mt. Atsukashi, where Yasuhira had constructed a fortification to hold 20,000 horsemen, according to *The Mirror of the East*. Aware that he might be forced to lay siege to mountain bastions, Yoritomo had ordered 80 laborers with spades and hoes to accompany his army. Now he had them fill a ditch 15 meters wide along the perimeter of the fortress and, for the next three days, the decisive battle of the Northern Campaign raged. At Iwana Slope near Mt. Atsukashi, Yoritomo's men took 18 heads despite many deadly shots from a crossbow, while 7 brave horsemen won the main battle at Mt. Atsukashi. In the foggy early morning of the 10th, one-on-one combat took place, and Yasuhira soon fled a losing battle. The Kamakura army captured 30 prisoners and killed Yasuhira's brother.

On the 12th of the 8th month in 1189, Yoritomo arrived at Fort Taga and met the army under Chiba and Hatta, and on the next day Yoritomo learned that his forces had won a decisive victory in Dewa as well. For the rest of the 8th month, Kamakura soldiers searched out Yasuhira. On the way north they encountered resistance from 40–50 horsemen and finally arrived at Hiraizumi,

Map 12. THE NORTHERN CAMPAIGN

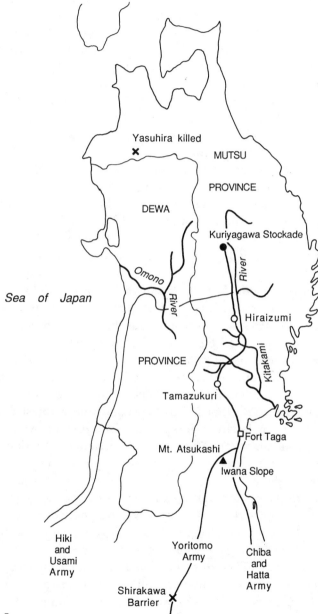

Source: Ōyama Kyohei, *Nihon no rekishi* 9, *Kamakura bakufu*, p. 142.

the Fujiwara capital, where his army took 30 prisoners. Late in the 8th month, Yoritomo's men caught Yasuhira, who begged for his life, but Yoritomo refused his entreaties. On the 3rd of the 9th month, Kamakura forces surrounded Yashuhira and one of his own retainers beheaded him. Kyoto's only choice was to express its agreement with Yoritomo's actions and, 6 days later, the Court handed down an order to punish the Fujiwara, just for appearance's sake. By that time, Yoritomo was busy hunting down the remnants of the Fujiwara forces, rewarding his major vassals, and resettling the people of Mutsu and Dewa.

Size of the Armies. The Northern Campaign poses many of the same questions examined during consideration of the Hōgen Disturbance and the Great Civil War of 1180-1185, seeming on the surface to be an engagement of massive armies, the apogee of Yoritomo's and Kamakura's military power. Yoritomo and his closest allies appear to have raised a gigantic host through ties of kinship and vassalage after ignoring the wishes of an impotent Court, and *The Mirror of the East* contains exciting stories of brave and loyal Kamakura warriors engaging the Fujiwara in single mounted combat.

The Mirror of the East lists the Kamakura army at an amazing 284,000 horsemen on the day after Yasuhira was beheaded (1189/9/4). If each equestrian fighter had 2 foot soldiers with him, then the army would have approached 1 million men. Most scholars contend that the number is greatly inflated, but Jeffrey Mass still believes that Yoritomo's host amounted to several tens of thousands of riders, and that it was "no doubt the greatest fighting force yet seen in Japan."[8] To support his argument, Mass notes that many names in *The Mirror of the East* belong to warriors from outside the Kanto, especially from central Japan and even as far away as Kyushu.[9]

Although the fighters gathered in the Northern Campaign may well have comprised a national force, and therefore the largest number of men that Yoritomo had ever commanded, a critical reading of *The Mirror of the East* raises great doubts about the overall size of the army. The roster of fighters leaving Kamakura with Yoritomo listed only 144 names, and, as in the Hōgen and Heiji Disturbances, generally military sources are much more accurate in naming than counting people. If one assumes that each of Yoritomo's followers had 2 foot soldiers, then the total force would have been 576, only about half of the 1,000 men reported under Yoritomo's command.

Furthermore, accounts of the Battle of Mt. Atsukashi relate that the numbers of dead and captured were small, which argues against the idea that observers counted forces in the hundreds of thousands. The battle itself turned on the actions of 7 riding warriors, and they used one-on-one combat. Like the mounted fighters throughout the period from 500 on, Kamakura armies relied on the technological advantage of their mounts, not on their sheer mass.

One can perform a calculation to arrive at an admittedly fanciful estimate of Yoritomo's army. If one assumes that the total of horsemen was 28,400 (by dividing the figure in *The Mirror in the East* by 10), and that every equestrian had 2 foot soldiers in train, then the sum would have been 85,200 men. This tabulation is nothing more than an educated guess, and is probably still too large, given the narrative of single combat and the small numbers of men in armies in the Hōgen Disturbance, the Great Civil War of 1180–1185, and the warrior class in general (see Chapter 7 and Chapter 8 below). Even if one accepts 85,200 as an accurate estimate, the 1189 campaign would still have been about the same size as some of the larger expeditions sent to northeastern Honshu in the eighth century. And it is well to remember that the numbers for the eighth-century wars may be found in fairly reliable Court histories, whereas the 1189 figure is mere speculation.

Organization and Technology. The organization of the armies showed no difference from the late Heian period: Once again the provincial headquarters was central. Chiba and Hatta conscripted their forces exactly as leaders had done in the twelfth century, using personal retainers of the generals (their families) and soldiers from Hitachi and Shimōsa provinces. The army under Hiki and Usami drafted men through the Kōzuke provincial office. Moreover, scholars have proven that the provincial headquarters was crucial in raising troops from outside the Kanto, as in the case of a roster from Mimasaka.[10]

In fact, the Kamakura Shogunate had already recognized in theory the importance of the provincial headquarters for their operations. Yoritomo had located his constables, the most power-ful warrior of each province, in that office to facilitate martial undertakings; his action was an effort to fill the vacuum created in the provincial headquarters when governors were no longer com-petent and obedient commanders. Nothing about the Kamakura forces in Mutsu suggests significant changes in the conscription and organization of the military since the late Heian period, but, by 1189, the powers to call up and reward had all fallen into the hands of a military aristocrat (Yoritomo), rather than the Kyoto Court.

Combat in the Northern Campaign appears to have been the tra-ditional samurai style of single mounted fighting, but there was an interesting twist. Although *The Mirror of the East* reports the eques-trian method of war-making in greatest detail, the crucial battle was against siege works, complete with crossbows and ditches. Engi-neers composed a critical element of Yoritomo's force, as they undoubtedly had in Tohoku wars since the eighth century.

Yoritomo and his Conquest. One final aspect of the Northern Cam-paign is crucial to an understanding of the Kamakura Shogunate. After the battles were over and Yoritomo had prevailed, he re-verted to a role as defender of the established order, confirming lands for temples and using the memories of elders to retrieve records destroyed in the burning of the Fujiwara capital at Hirai-zumi.[11] On the 1st of the 10th month, he gave explicit orders at the Taga provincial headquarters that provincial affairs were to oper-ate as they had under Yasuhira.[12] When Yoritomo established an organization for his new followers in northeastern Honshu, he util-ized the Investigators' Office (Kebiishi sho), a Heian bureau with-in the provincial headquarters.[13] The old system continued to serve the new.

THE JŌKYŪ WAR OF 1221. On the surface, the conflict between the Retired Emperor Go-Toba and the Shogunate arose primarily because Go-Toba turned a deaf ear to Kamakura's pleas for aid in selecting a candidate for the vacant post of shogun.[14] Yoritomo had died in 1199, and his two sons managed to hold onto the post of shogun for a combined total of 20 years. When the Minamoto line died out in 1219, officials of the warrior government hoped to adopt a member of the Imperial Family to fill the all-important position, but Go-Toba refused. Eventually Kamakura chose an infant shogun from among the aristocracy, despite the Retired Emperor's continuing resistance. In addition, *The Chronicle of Jōkyū* states that Go-Toba demanded the termination of two land stewards on estates belonging to his lover in Settsu province, a problem later forcefully resolved in favor of the land stewards.

Although, on the surface, the issues were succession to the shogun's mantle and a quarrel over land revenues, at the heart of the matter lay the Retired Emperor's questioning the military government's very right to exist. The "Great Barbarian-Subduing Generalissimo" was the highest official at Kamakura and the chief of all warriors; when Go-Toba denied the Shogunate the imperial heir he reasoned that such an appointment would upset the superior-inferior relationship between Kyoto and Kamakura.[15] Furthermore, the Settsu land stewards received their posts from the martial regime, and now Go-Toba wanted to reduce the Kanto's power in that regard as well. Without a shogun or the right to name military men to lands, Kamakura would cease to hold powers independent of the Court.

The war lasted only about a month in the summer of 1221, and had 3 phases: the hatching of Go-Toba's plot and his initial victories; the Kamakura response; and the Shogunate's victories in central Japan and the capital region. By the 14th of the 5th month, Go-Toba had assembled a force of 1,700 horsemen in Kyoto, using an archery tournament as the pretext for calling these men. While there are differences between the two major texts of *The Chronicle of Jōkyū*, it is clear that Go-Toba drafted these men from the provincial headquarters near the capital (*kuni guni no tsuwamono domo; kingoku no tsuwamono domo*).[16]

Perhaps realizing that these men would not be sufficient to overwhelm a united Kamakura, Go-Toba convinced Miura Taneyoshi, a powerful warrior and supporter of the Shogunate who was on guard duty in the capital, to join him and to try to convince his family to betray the Shogunate. If the Retired Emperor could entice the Miura into deserting the military government, then perhaps others would follow. Kamakura would fall of its own accord because of seeds of discord planted by Go-Toba. Although his plot was to fail, the idea must have been particularly threatening to the Shogunate, whose titular head was an infant.

Not long after gathering his force, Go-Toba handed down a pursue-and-punish order against Hōjō Yoshitoki, the true leader of the military government. Go-Toba issued the order to provincial headquarters throughout Japan and had it delivered specially by messenger to the Kanto. The Court conspirators arrested civil aristocrats in the capital with connections to Kamakura; of the two constables in residence in Kyoto, the Retired Emperor persuaded one to come over to his side, while Taneyoshi and "soldiers of the provinces" defeated the other in a mounted skirmish in the capital.[17]

The leaders at Kamakura had little faith that warriors of the Kanto would defy the imperial order to turn their backs upon the Shogunate, and they captured the messenger before he had a chance to reach the samurai of the region. Fortunately for Kamakura, the Miura rejected Taneyoshi's invitation to betray and attack the military regime. After a speech in which Hōjō Masako, Yoritomo's widow and stalwart of the Shogunate, rallied warriors to the Kamakura cause, the leadership decided not to await the next move by Go-Toba but to attack at once. According to *The Mirror of the East*, generals conscripted troops from the provincial headquarters of the Kanto. Hōjō Yasutoki, another leader of the Hōjō family and the martial government, departed Kamakura on the 22nd of the 5th month with only 18 horsemen at his side and without the hoped-for support of the men of Musashi. Three days later, however, sources state that the Shogunate had raised enough warriors to launch a 3-pronged attack on Kyoto and report that the 3 armies of southeastern, central, and northeastern Honshu as having 100,000, 50,000, and 40,000 riders, respectively (see Map 13).

The military regime released Go-Toba's messenger to return to the capital, and, when he told of Kamakura's plans, Go-Toba and his conspirators were badly shaken. The Retired Emperor dispatched mounted soldiers to meet each army but encountered nothing but disaster. On the 29th of the 5th month in 1221, at a battle in Echigo, Shogunate troops defeated 60 horsemen of Go-Toba. On the 5th and 6th of the 6th month, the armies of the Kanto dealt

Map 13. THE JŌKYŪ WAR, 1221

1. Settsu
2. Kyoto
3. Kamakura
4. Echigo Provincial Headsquarters, Route of Hōjō Tomotoki's Army
5. Ōido Crossing, Route of Takeda Nobumitsu's Army
6. Sunomata, Route of Hōjō Yasutoki's Army
7. Seta
8. Uji

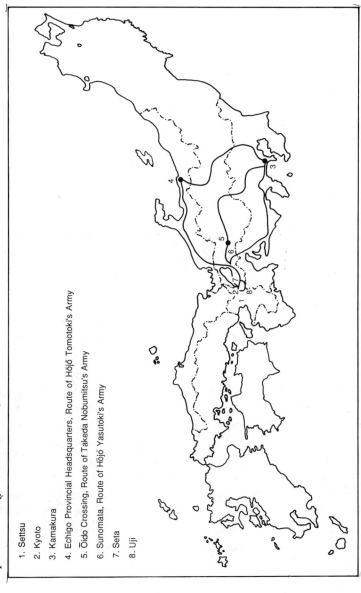

Source: Ōyama, *Kamakura bakufu*, p. 294.

staggering blows to Go-Toba's forces at Ōido Crossing, Sunomata, and several other sites in central Japan. These battles required crossing water on horseback, and occurred where the Minamoto and Taira had fought just 30 years earlier.

Before the critical Battle at Ōido Crossing, 2 warriors riding with the Kamakura forces had an interesting conversation about how serious their loyalties were:

> "This World of Transmigration is a place of impermanence, Lord Takeda. What's going to happen, I wonder?"
>
> Takeda replied, "Listen! Here's the truth of the matter. If Kamakura is victorious, we'll adhere to Kamakura, and if Kyoto is victorious, we'll adhere to Kyoto. Such is the way of those who wield the bow and arrow!"[18]

Despite the seemingly lopsided nature of the war, at least 2 important "vassals" of Kamakura were unsure of their fidelity.

In about a week, Kamakura armies arrived at Seta and Uji near the capital and annihilated the remaining Court troops, who tried to use the Uji River for defense; on the 15th of the 6th month, Hōjō Yasutoki entered the capital. Hōjō and his generals either executed or banished Go-Toba and his followers among the aristocracy for their roles in the affair.

Size and Organization of the Armies. The Mirror of the East cites the Kamakura army at 190,000, and the forces of Go-Toba reportedly numbered as many as 20,000. Although these figures may represent the correct proportion between Kamakura and Court men, again the actual numbers are greatly exaggerated.[19] Chronicles universally describe single mounted fighting, with occasional mention of foot soldiers who undoubtedly followed their equestrian lords into battle.[20] As in the late Heian period, such a method of combat characteristically used small forces.

A few specific examples point out how wildly *The Mirror of the East* overestimated battle forces. *The Tale of Jōkyū* states that Go-Toba collected 38 horsemen from 13 western provinces at the start of hostilities.[21] In a battle in Echigo, Kamakura men opposed 60 horsemen from Go-Toba's army, and later in Mino 30 archers behind shields made a stand for the Retired Emperor. In the battle against the Kamakura Constable defeated in Kyoto at the outset of the conflict, the Court presumably had 1,000 men, while the Constable led only 85.[22] At Jiki Crossing, another major battle, 100 Kanto troops fought against 19 men from western Japan; later near the capital, 300 riders from Go-Toba's side took on 3,000 from the Bandō. The numbers cited in these and other battles undermine the credibility of sources counting armies in the hundreds of thousands.

A final bit of evidence comes from *The Mirror of the East* itself, which lists casualties on both sides for the Battle of Uji. The account makes it clear that the battle was one of the more evenly matched encounters in the civil war, and records 98 Kamakura men as being either killed or wounded, while 255 died for Go-Toba. It is difficult to know what multiplier to use to reconstruct the original size of the forces, but, if one applies the same ratios of dead to combatants as at the Battle of Jiki Crossing, then the armies would have been 300 men for Kamakura and 500 men for Go-Toba.[23] If one uses a multiplier from another skirmish, such as the one between the Kodama League and Yamada later in the war, then the battle was between armies of 3,000 for Kamakura and 1,500 for Go-Toba. In either case, it is evident that scholars should radically reduce the standard counts of 190,000 horsemen for Kamakura and 20,000 for Go-Toba, probably by a factor of 10 or more.

The organization of soldiers, especially those of Go-Toba, is a controversial matter. On the Kamakura side, it seems clear that the Shogunate relied upon the provincial headquarters of the Kanto, since, on the 19th of the 5th month, not long after Go-Toba's initial overtures to Kamakura warriors, the Hōjō issued a notice to assemble forces through the provincial headquarters of Tōtōmi, Suruga, Izu, Kai, Sagami, Musashi, Awa, Kazusa, Shimōsa, Hitachi, Shinano, Kōzuke, Shimotsuke, Mutsu, and Dewa.[24] Jeffrey Mass believes, however, that the Shogunate may have bypassed the constables of these provinces and that the orders went directly to heads of various vassal families; the evidence for this claim is not clear.[25] Even if the military government used such a method, the results were admittedly poor; it seems likely that, as *The Mirror of the East* specifically states, the provincial headquarters played the most important role in transmitting orders and organizing armies for Kamakura.[26]

The origins and organization of Go-Toba's army are more uncertain, with interpretations varying according to the way one views the relative strengths of the Retired Emperor and Kamakura, and of western Japan and eastern Honshu. One historian originally proposed that Go-Toba's men came from his estates and listed 103 examples.[27] Although he correctly ascertained that most of the Retired Emperor's forces had their origins in western Japan, it is doubtful that estates were a major source of warriors because it was too difficult to raise troops through the various and sundry authorities in charge of *shōen*.[28]

Jeffrey Mass presents the most thorough analysis of Go-Toba's forces, arguing that the Retired Emperor's army was a weak and fragmented potpourri of odds and ends.[29] According to Mass, there were 6 sources for Court troops: disgruntled Kamakura vassals from central and western Japan who had not obtained nominations as land stewards; non-vassal estate officials from western Japan; warriors from the western and central provincial headquarters; disloyal Kamakura vassals; an elite Palace Guard favored by Go-Toba with honors and offices; and conscripts. It is interesting to note that Mass includes the provincial headquarters as one of the means by which Go-Toba raised his men, and the analysis presented in this book argues that it was an especially important means. This odd mixture of fighters for Go-Toba finds support in documents which tell of pressure tactics applied to warriors and even attempts to force men not of martial blood into service.[30]

Yet other historians portray the Court army as more powerful and united. One has examined the forces of Go-Toba, and discovered that 14 constables from the provinces of western Honshu sided with the Retired Emperor.[31] His study implies a relatively strong contingent for Go-Toba, and perhaps indicates that the Retired Emperor exercised some authority over western Japanese provincial headquarters. Another specialist from a different historiographical school has supplemented this work by establishing that many men were in the capital on guard duty.[32] Guard duty of the imperial residence was one of the services provided by warriors of western Japan to the Court and was regularly overseen by constables.[33] Taken together, these interpretations hint that the entire structure of the Kamakura military in western Japan, including the provincial headquarters, fell under the control of the Retired Emperor.

The most daring interpretation suggests that Go-Toba actually had the right to command provincial warriors of the entire central and western region.[34] Unlike views that stress the weakness of Go-Toba's soldiers, this argument holds that Retired Emperor's authority was unified, not fragmented.[35] If one follows this bold estimate of Court forces, then the Jōkyū War becomes not just a fight between Go-Toba and Kamakura, but a conflict between all western and all eastern Japan.

Whether one sees Go-Toba's power as fragmented or whole, there is little doubt that he made use of the provincial headquarters in western Japan to collect his men. *The Chronicle of Jōkyū* repeatedly asserts that Go-Toba relied upon the warriors of the provinces; in one case the list includes the 14 provinces of Yamato, Yamashiro, Ōmi, Tamba, Mino, Owari, Iga, Ise, Settsu, Kawachi, Izumi, Kii, Tango, and Tajima.[36] Another version of the same source adds Harima, Mikawa, and Iyo, while deleting Kawachi, Iga, Yamashiro, and Izumi.[37] The historic emphasis on the provincial headquarters in conscripting men remained, even though Japan had entered a feudal age when ties of vassalage supposedly were dominant.

Results of the Jōkyū War. In some respects, the conflict of 1221 was similar to the Great Civil War of 1180–1185. Eastern Japan was united while rifts appeared among the members of the Court, with some aristocrats supporting Go-Toba, some not. The Retired Emperor possessed more estates and thus perhaps more economic power than the Shogunate, but Kamakura was located in eastern Honshu where most of Japan's mightiest warriors lived. As long as the military government maintained control of the provincial headquarters in the Kanto, and the Court remained fragmented, the result of any clash was a foregone conclusion.

One may therefore ask why Kamakura did not obliterate the Kyoto Court once the Shogunate had won. There are at least 4 reasons for the continued vitality of the Court in the face of the military power of Kamakura. (1) Many of the members of the Court had not opposed the Shogunate, and it made no sense to punish all the aristocracy for the sins of a few. (2) The Court had a 600-year tradition of ruling Japan, and that precedent was difficult to ignore in a society that still lived by rules handed down from the past. (3) The Court carried out many important functions, especially political duties; the ceremonies acted out in the capital may seem useless to a twentieth-century observer but were essential for legitimacy. (4) The Court had too much economic and political power, particularly in western Japan, to be destroyed.

Thus the disparity in armies did not make for a Japan dominated by the Shogunate after 1221. Jeffrey Mass has stated that the Jō-kyū War saw the final downfall of the Court, and that "there was no doubt that Kamakura now stood supreme" in Japan.[38] But, as Kuroda Toshio has suggested, the Jōkyū War really represented the "stabilization" of the Kanto government within the aristocratic polity.[39] The war had virtually no effect on the civil aristocracy and religious institutions, while the power to decide on the imperial succession rested with the Court, not Kamakura.[40] The foundations of martial government continued to rest with the provincial headquarters. Of course, as a result of the conflict, Kamakura allies received appointments to posts as land stewards in western Honshu estates, but, as noted in a compendium of military law from 1232, the Shogunate was not to interfere in the administration of those lands and provinces.[41] For about a half-century after the war, the Shogunate respected Court prerogatives, and the dual polity continued. The warrior had at long last achieved an equal standing in Japan, but not yet a predominant place.

THE MONGOL INVASIONS OF 1274 and 1281. The Mongols, who had married their martial instincts and nomadic lifestyle to a new bureaucratic organization with merit promotion, presented the greatest threat the Japanese had ever faced, even more frightening than the Chinese and Korean armies that had opposed Temmu. Despite the eventual Japanese victory, the war resulted in changes in the polity and society that one historian marks as a major watershed in Japanese history.[42]

Mongol power on the continent had been on the rise since the late twelfth century, and, after conquering Korea in 1258, the Mongols dispatched several emissaries demanding that Japan enter into friendly diplomatic relations with them.[43] The Court in Kyoto vacillated while the Shogunate made preparations for war in accordance with its military authority; Kamakura issued orders to the constables of the provinces of Kyushu, western Honshu, and Shikoku to be on the alert. Another Mongol messenger arrived in Dazaifu in 1271, once again requesting peaceful relations, but the martial regime stood fast and made no reply. The Shogunate first encouraged Kanto warriors who had lands in Kyushu to go westward and put themselves under the command of the local constables, and then, in the 10th month of 1272, it required constables of the western provinces to submit land records to be used for conscription.

After the last Mongol emissary to Japan went home empty-handed in 1273, the Mongols prepared a force of about 90,000 men to invade Japan in the first month of 1274. The fleet set off from Korea on the 3rd of the 10th month and arrived at Tsushima on the 5th (see Map 14). When the Mongols landed, officials hurriedly rushed reports of the invasion to the land steward's office (*jitō sho*) within the provincial headquarters at Tsushima, and the Japanese reportedly met the Mongols with a mere 80 horsemen. After overwhelming all opposition, the Mongols pillaged the small island while news of the battle filtered back to Dazaifu.

When the Mongols attacked Iki, just off the coast of northern Kyushu on the 14th of the 10th month in 1274, the Japanese responded with 100 mounted soldiers, but again the steppe nomads prevailed with murder and mayhem. In the next few days, warriors of northern Kyushu, organized through Dazaifu, moved to defend the area. The Mongol fleet sailed to Hirado and Takashima, inflicted heavy casualties on the defenders, and then assailed Imazu where they came ashore. Other landing parties entered Sohara and Momochibaru; the main force attacked the area near Hakata and Hakozaki on the 20th. The following excerpt comes from a Japanese source, which describes the Mongol reaction to Japanese battle tactics:

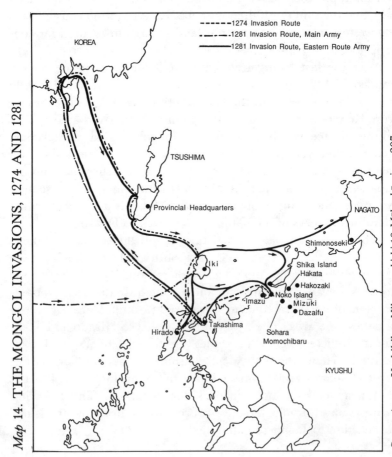

Map 14. THE MONGOL INVASIONS, 1274 AND 1281

- - - - - 1274 Invasion Route
- · - · - 1281 Invasion Route, Main Army
———— 1281 Invasion Route, Eastern Route Army

KOREA

TSUSHIMA

● Provincial Headquarters

NAGATO

Shimonoseki ●

Iki

Shika Island
Hakata
● Hakozaki
Noko Island
● Mizuki
● Dazaifu

Imazu

Takashima

Hirado ●

Sohara
Momochibaru

KYUSHU

Source: Ammo Yoshihiko, *Nihon no rekishi* 10 *Mōko shūrai,* p. 207.

The Mongols disembarked, mounted their horses, raised their banners, and began to attack. . . . [One Japanese] . . . shot a whistling arrow to open the exchange. All at once the Mongols down to the last man started laughing. The Mongols struck large drums and hit gongs so many times . . . that they frightened the Japanese horses and mounts could not be controlled. The Japanese side forgot about handling their horses and facing the enemy. . . .

Their [the Mongol] general climbed to a high spot and, when retreat was in order, beat the retreat drum. When they needed to race forward, he rang the attack gong. According to these signals, they did battle. . . .

Whereas we [Japanese] thought about reciting our pedigrees to each other and battling man-to-man in glory or defeat as was the custom of Japanese armies, in this battle the Mongols assembled at one point in a great force.[44]

The Mongol Invasions were more than just a turning point in Japanese political history; they were the convergence of two radically different military strategies. The Japanese, who had forgotten about the Taihō commitment to group combat, believed that their style of single mounted fighting was natural; the Mongols, who used mass tactics, were not impressed.

The Japanese at Sohara suffered heavy losses, but did manage to slow the Mongol advance. The main Mongol army at Hakata, however, proceeded rapidly and pushed the proud warriors back to the Mizuki, a fortification spanning the Hakata Plain originally built to defend Dazaifu in the seventh century. Then, as suddenly as they had come, the Mongols disappeared on the 20th of the 10th month in 1274.[45]

The Shogunate, in charge of military operations, assumed that the Mongols were not gone for long and was aware that a stiffer defense would be necessary. It ordered not only its own men, but also any fighting men who lived in estates normally beyond the control of Kamakura, to join in the preparations. For the first time a government was able to raise troops in sizable numbers from both provincial lands and shōen. In 1275, Kamakura summoned the soldiers of the provinces of Kyushu to guard duty along the northern coast. The Kanto government relieved Kyushu warriors from their normal guard duty in the capital and posted them to the northern coast. The Shogunate also thought that the Inland Sea was vulnerable and conscripted warriors from Aki and Suō to aid in the defense of Nagato, where there were too few soldiers. The military regime raised provisions from the wealthy and estate proprietors regardless of their legal standing, and warned warriors who had not had the stomach to contest the Mongols in 1274 that shirking would not be tolerated.

In 1275, the Mongols sent another emissary, but he was summarily beheaded. Kamakura then made a surprising about-face and copied its martial forerunners of seven centuries earlier by laying plans to invade Korea later the same year. It dispatched orders to constables in the provincial headquarters of Kyushu, as well as the rest of western Japan, to provide soldiers and helmsmen. Those warriors not involved in the invasion were to be responsible for constructing a wall across the coast of northern Kyushu; builders completed the wall in about a year, but the amphibious assault on Korea never occurred.[46]

In 1281, the Mongols raised two armies, one of 100,000 Chinese, and another of 40,000 Mongols, Koreans, and Chinese. The smaller force, called the Eastern Route Army, attacked Tsushima on the 21st of the 5th month, and next occupied Iki, at least two weeks ahead of the Mongol plan of attack. On the 5th and 6th of the 6th month, the foreigners struck at Nagato, but the wall there prevented any advance.

The main force made for Hakata, but there was a wall across Hakata, too, and the Eastern Route Army decided to wait at Shika and Noko Islands off the coast of northern Kyushu. Japanese warriors, including the famous Takezaki Suenaga, fought the Mongols fiercely from boats, and won individual victories, but the Mongol army managed to secure the two small islands. The Japanese still defended the wall built across Hakata Bay, and the Eastern Route Army decided to await the larger force of Chinese at Iki. While the Eastern Route Army bided its time for the massive second attack, an epidemic broke out and supplies dwindled.

At last the main army of over 4,000 ships and 100,000 Chinese troops arrived at Iki late in the 6th month of 1281 and made for Hirado in Hizen. The combined armies then began to advance towards the mainland, perhaps early in the 7th month, but, even while they were attacking, small forces of Japanese warriors in boats assaulted the Mongols. Then on the 1st of the intercalary 7th month, a great typhoon swept through northern Kyushu and wrecked the Mongol fleet; for several days, Japanese warriors like Takezaki Suenaga mopped up the remnants of the great Mongol force. The Mongols continued to plan invasions for several years, and the Japanese kept to their defense, but the Mongols never came again.

Conscription, Size of Forces, and Tactics. As in conflicts discussed previously, the provincial headquarters played a crucial role in drafting and organizing armies against the Mongols. When the first Mongol fleet sailed to Tsushima in 1274, officials immediately reported their arrival to the center for military preparedness, the land steward's office in the provincial headquarters. As the great Mongol army advanced on the mainland, Dazaifu saw to it that "the soldiers of the 9 provinces" (Kyushu) gathered.[47] After the initial attack in 1274, the Shogunate oversaw both the construction of the wall and guard duty through the provinces, listing warriors not simply as housemen (*goke'nin*), but as soldiers of a certain province.[48] The role of Dazaifu was similarly important in the second assault in 1281 when fighters of "the 9 provinces and 2 islands" opposed the Mongols.[49] Far from losing their importance, the provincial headquarters maintained the role of a military center throughout the thirteenth century, and constables in western Japan even used the Mongol invasions as an excuse to increase their power within this critical office.[50]

The number of warriors who resisted the Mongol advance is difficult to determine. One record mentions that there were 60,000 troops present for the second invasion, but it is not known how reliable this estimate is; the same source states that there were 46 vassals of the Kamakura Shogunate leading the fight.[51] One specialist on the Japanese warrior believes that most Japanese accounts greatly exaggerate the numbers of men engaging in combat for the Shogunate.[52] While one source uses the figure 100,000 for the first invasion, he notes that only 120 men actually received rewards; in the second invasion, the total was merely 400. Descriptions of the battles are of single mounted combat (at least on the Japanese side), and the numbers were small. In particular, Takezaki Suenaga, whose role in the invasions has been preserved in a picture scroll, rode into battle with as few as 5 mounted companions.[53]

Documents surviving from the attempts to conscript men from estates provide another means for estimating the size of the Japanese army.[54] In 1276, the warriors of Higo province in northern Kyushu listed the men and matériel that they could supply for an invasion of the continent. One warrior, Iseri Hideshige, noted his contribution as 4 warrior relatives (2 were over 60 years of age) and 3 followers from an area of 11.3 *chō*. In other words, he could provide 1 man per 1.6 *chō* of land. Because it is estimated that Japan had about 926,000 *chō* of land that could be farmed in the late twelfth century, one could calculate that all Japan could have produced 578,750 fighters at the rate cited by Iseri. Objections to this astronomical figure abound, since one cannot know how representative Iseri's case might have been or whether he and his relatives used other lands to support their levy. When one performs the same calculation using just the lands of Kyushu, then the figure is 63,600 men, a number close to one of the sources, but that result might be a coincidence.

The battles between the Mongols and the Japanese were a meeting of two different methods of combat, individual mounted warfare against group tactics. Unfortunately for historians but luckily for the Japanese, a typhoon intervened before the experiment in contrasting styles could be completed. However, even though the samurai fought bravely and prevented an immediate Mongol victory through their stout resistance, it seems likely that a well-coordinated Mongol attack would have succeeded had nature allowed it to proceed. The Mongols had numbers and technology on their side; there is little doubt that, with better sailing weather, the Japanese would have re-learned the lesson of the Battle of the Paekch'ŏn River and been forced to follow the example of Temmu all over again.[55] Individual bravery is important, but numbers, discipline, and technology win most of the time.

The Invasions and Japanese Politics. The impact of the Mongol Invasions on Japan has been discussed widely, but one point is worth emphasizing. The Mongol threat helped upset the balance between Court and Shogunate that had been in effect since the

Jōkyū War of 1221, and Kamakura began to encroach upon the lands and prerogatives of the Court in western Japan.[56] The growing power of the martial regime is especially evident in orders issued to raise soldiers and provisions from temple and aristocratic estates. The Court had been troubled about how to enlist warriors from estates since the twelfth century; the Mongols provided the means for Kamakura to do just that for the first time in Japanese history. From 1281 on, the warrior was on the verge of supremacy in Japan, after a long trek that had taken nearly eight centuries.

When one speaks of the Kamakura military, one normally calls to mind vassals who have pledged loyalty to the shogun in return for a grant of land: the operative paradigm is Western European feudalism. In this book, I have defined two of the major characteristics of feudalism as a predominance of ties of dependence within a warrior class holding land. As seen in the three cases of actual combat in the Kamakura age, this description is not totally inaccurate, but neither is it sufficient; the provincial headquarters, a public office inherited from the Heian period, was a crucial link between military men and their lords. In effect, the Shogunate merely took over the provincial headquarters and replaced the governor with a military specialist, the constable. In an age when personal loyalty was as changeable as the wind, and when land was still not continuously or highly productive, commanders needed another structure to ensure that soldiers turned out for battle. Like the fighting technology and style of Kamakura warriors, or the size of armies, the reliance on the provincial office was a heritage of earlier epochs, but it was not the only legacy.

COUNTING WARRIORS

The numbers of warriors in thirteenth-century Japan is a critical piece of information in any evaluation of the composition of the ruling class of the Kamakura period. Many *bushi* and great armies might suggest a country dominated by a military class, as my definition of feudalism requires, while few samurai and small forces could imply that the Shogunate was weak vis-à-vis the Court, and that the military was really only one part of the ruling class. The problem of counting troops has already been noted in descriptions of battles, and the tendency among all scholars is to cast suspicion upon the extraordinary numbers included in such sources as *The Mirror of the East*. In discussions of battles throughout this book, I have argued that the numerical strength of forces was perhaps only one-tenth the level indicated in war tales and other records.

How many warriors (*bushi*) were there? Is there any way to make a reliable estimate? I have conceived of 3 approaches: calculation from the total number of warrior bands (*bushi dan*) using a multiplier for the "average" group; comparison between the Court bureaucracy of the eighth century and that of the twelfth or thirteenth; and mere addition of the number of vassals of Kamakura to the figure of non-vassals listed in the sources. Each method has its weaknesses, and any tabulation will be imperfect.

Warrior bands, which were social units, usually included at least one family, often with distant kin and even unrelated persons.[57] A chieftain, who exercised some control over the members, headed every band. These martial groups were usually responsible for opening (or re-opening) a parcel of land, and they often took their surnames from the area they cleared.

Japanese scholarly journals overflow with analyses of warrior bands from all over Japan in the late Heian and Kamakura periods, going into great detail regarding the location of each military unit and its lands, relations among members, lineage of the main family, and other matters. For example, one study which examined these martial bands in the Kanto concluded that there were over 320 such groups in the region in the Kamakura era.[58] One might make a list of all the warrior bands in Japan as of 1200 and then use a multiplier to obtain the total number of fighters during the early Kamakura period.

One major problem that arises with this method is the great variety among martial groups.[59] In the Kanto, bands were normally large, perhaps including a whole district or more, while in western Japan the typical military unit was small. In particular, one type of warrior body was called a league (*tō*); a league had no chieftain, but individual member families fought as equals. Developing a multiplier that would fit the large fighting bands of eastern Honshu, the small ones in western Japan, and leagues in many areas would require many data for which there is no documentation.

A few examples help to show the amorphous quality of these martial groups. The Kōno were a well-known warrior band of Iyo province on Shikoku; in 1205, a document from the Shogunate listed the Kōno as having 32 members.[60] Yet, 16 years later in 1221, another record notes that the same unit possessed 129 members, an increase by a factor of 4.[61] If one accepts these numbers, it is clear that the Kōno underwent a fundamental change, explicable not only as an overall increase in the number of warriors but rather as the Kōno's absorption of some other bands.[62] Such martial groups were so amorphous that they are difficult to count, much less subject to a multiplier.

One of the most thoroughly studied fighting units is the Chiba of Shimōsa province in the Kanto, according to one scholar, a "great warrior band" of the Kanto, with a domineering chieftain, many lands, and dozens of warriors.[63] The Chiba were among the first to answer Yoritomo's call to arms, and Chiba Tsunetane was a close advisor to the first Shogun of Kamakura.

Recent historians, however, have modified this view of the Chiba. The biographer of Tsunetane has maintained that the Chiba probably controlled only one estate in Shimōsa before the Great Civil War of 1180–1185; the overwhelming majority of lands became Chiba territory only after the demise of rivals within the province.[64] Furthermore, the same historian found that the number of warriors Chiba Tsunetane rushed to Yoritomo's aid in 1180 really included only himself and his immediate family, 9 persons in all, rather than the 300 horsemen *The Mirror of the East* attributed to him.[65] One wonders if other supposedly great warrior bands were not also as small.

Every martial unit included not only mounted archers but their servants and vassals who also wielded weapons in battle. These supporting troops may not have been members of a distinct martial lineage, held any land, or fought as mounted archers. How far does one go in estimating fighting strength? Does one include only those who can be counted as warriors (*bushi*), or does one broaden the definition to encompass all men who played a role in the fighting? A meaningful multiplier is not easy to develop.

Because of problems such as these, and the growing realization that the provincial headquarters was more important in conscription and military organization, studies of warrior bands have declined markedly in recent years. Obstacles to calculating the total number of warriors from these amorphous and varied groups seem insurmountable. If one agrees that there were approximately 320 such units in the Kanto in 1200, and uses the Chiba as the standard for the multiplier (9 men per band), then one arrives at about 2,900 warriors in the Kanto. Many units were undoubtedly larger, and many smaller; this figure is open to question.

A second method of counting involves an extrapolation from the size of Court officialdom. When the Yamato King established a Chinese-style state in the late seventh and eighth centuries, he created a bureaucracy which contained innumerable offices, ranging from the highest minister in the capital to the lowest paper-pusher in an isolated district. Each office correlated to a rank, 9 in all, and every rank had 2 or 4 subdivisions (the entire 9-rank bureaucracy was divided into 30 gradations). Only a few men held aristocratic status at the 5th Court Rank and higher; probably only about 125 or so had that privilege at any one time in 750. But the entire bureaucracy was huge: The Codes contained over 6,000 offices, and the total number of officials was probably about 10,000.[66] One might conceive of the Court officialdom as a pyramid, with only a few fortunate aristocrats holding the top ranks, while the possessors of lower Court ranks were far more numerous.

As the Chinese-style state began to decline, the bureaucracy underwent a transformation. The government could no longer afford to pay lower-ranking officials; in any case those holding the last 3 ranks (Ranks 7, 8, and 9, or the last 12 gradations) were so far from becoming a part of the elite that their jobs and ranks eventually disappeared. Only officials at the 6th Court Rank, who still had a chance at reaching the 5th Rank and aristocratic status, and above, remained. At the same time, the numbers of people fortunate enough to enter the true aristocracy at the 5th Rank and above expanded. This "rank inflation" devalued the meaning of the 5th Rank of nobility (almost anybody could enter it), and "true aristocrats" sought distinction by occupying the 1st and 2nd Court Ranks, which had usually gone unfilled in the eighth century.

Thus, while the base of the bureaucracy had disappeared, the number of aristocrats in the tip of the triangle tripled or quadrupled to 500 persons or more. By the late twelfth century, the shrunken bureaucracy looked like a pyramid that was out of whack: The once-massive bottom had atrophied and the point had gotten fat.

Fighters belonged in the bureaucracy, too.[67] According to late Heian and Kamakura law, warriors normally possessed the 6th Court Rank, and had the title of *samurai*, "those who serve." These men were not alone in the 6th Rank; other individuals with special talents serving the elite, such as scribes and artisans, were also represented. As rank-holders, the samurai obtained certain privileges unknown to commoners (*bonge*), such as the freedom from interrogation when suspected of a crime, the prerogative to become a retainer of the Shogunate, and the right to use surnames and to wear certain clothes. From a legal point of view, only rank- and officeholders could be samurai; this excluded the followers of a warrior from being known as samurai if they held no rank and/or office. Above the samurai were the "gentlemen" (*taifu*) at the 4th and 5th Rank, and higher still were the high nobles (*kugyō*) in the first 3 ranks.

A comparison of the twelfth-century official pyramid with the original in the eighth century suggests a small military class. The bureaucracy in the 1200s amounted to far fewer persons than the 10,000 officials of the 700s, because the heavily populated bottom third of the pyramid had disintegrated by the time the Kamakura Shogunate had been formed in the late twelfth century. The expansion of the aristocracy in the 5th Court Rank and above could not even come close to making up for the absence of the lower bureaucrats; The total Court bureaucracy in 1200 may have been one-half (or 5,000 persons) what it had been at its acme in 750. Because warriors occupied only one rank in officialdom, and shared that rank with others, it seems likely that the number of fighting samurai was considerably below 5,000, perhaps only 2,000 to 3,000.

A third method for counting warriors (*bushi*), merely adding the number of Kamakura housemen (*goke'nin*) to those not pledging such loyalty (*higoke'nin*), is more precise and satisfactory. Chapter 6 mentioned that Kamakura law defined a vassal as a person who had cleared land recognized by the Shogunate. The same legal guidebook of the early fourteenth century (*Sata miren sho*) also described a non-houseman:

> A non-houseman (*higoke'nin*) is defined as one who, even though his status is that of a servant (samurai), does not hold a fief on land which inheres service (*tōyaku gonji*) [as a houseman].[68]

The distinction between vassals of the Shogunate and retainers with other loyalties developed gradually; it was not until the 1190s that each provincial headquarters composed rolls of housemen.[69]

Figures for vassals of the military government are not difficult to come by. For example, a passage in *The Mirror of the East*, which dates from 1185 when Yoritomo was pursuing his brother Yoshitsune, states that "the main housemen who gathered [at Kamakura] . . . numbered 2,096 men."[70] Although the Shogunate had succeeded in penetrating western Japan and enrolling followers there by this time, the figure 2,096 probably includes mostly residents of eastern Honshu, and perhaps under-represents western Japanese soldiers who were not yet affiliated with the Shogunate.

Fortunately, several rolls of housemen exist from western Japan in the 1190s and later; in addition, one can ascertain figures for housemen from some western provinces by other means, such as land records. To date scholars have estimated the number of housemen in the following provinces: Awaji (14), Izumi (30), Tajima (43), Harima (16), Wakasa (33), Sanuki (14), Hizen (140), Iyo (32), Satsuma (about 30), Ōsumi (35), Hyūga (11), and Buzen (34).[71] The average number of Kamakura retainers for each province is 36; if the unusually high count for Hizen is subtracted, then it is about 27. Because there were 37 provinces in western Japan (the area west of Owari, Hida, Mino, and Etchū, except Kyushu), then the number of housemen in that region emerges at about 1,100, assuming 30 retainers per province. The total figure for Shogunate vassals is about 3,200 men, a little less than 3,500 if one adds the 9 provinces of Kyushu.

The problem in tabulating warriors by this method comes not in counting housemen, but in counting the non-vassals. Estimates of those not pledging loyalty to Kamakura vary with assumptions about the relative power of the Court, the aristocracy, and religious institutions. The argument presented in this book has been that most warriors were associated with the provincial headquarters, and that Kamakura enrolled its vassals using this office. According to one specialist on warriors, aristocrats and temples forced their soldiers to avoid both the provincial headquarters, where the Kamakura constable was located, and status as a retainer of the Shogunate.[72] Non-vassals therefore probably resided mostly on religious and aristocratic estates, as far away from the power of the provincial headquarters as possible.

If one accepts the idea that most warriors maintained ties with the provincial headquarters, and that Kamakura controlled that office, then the number of soldiers not pledging loyalty to the martial regime must have been relatively small. The previous analysis of the Jōkyū War supports this conclusion, since Go-Toba raised his troops primarily by persuading constables and other Kamakura vassals to betray their lord; only a small portion of his force came from estates. Given these facts, it seems likely that non-vassals comprised a relatively small fraction of the total number of warriors by the Kamakura period, and an estimate of 2,000 non-vassals would appear to be more than reasonable.

Thus the total figure for warriors around 1200 would have been small, perhaps 5,000 or 6,000 men. If one assumes that every warrior had 2 followers to accompany him into battle, then the largest army that could have been raised in the Kamakura age was between 15,000 and 18,000 troops. This calculation is a far cry from the armies of 200,000 reported for the Battle of Fujikawa in 1180, 284,000 for the Northern Campaign in 1189, or 190,000 for the Jōkyū War. Even the armies of 40,000 to 55,000 conscripts who conquered northeastern Honshu in the eighth and early ninth centuries seem gigantic by comparison. Seen from this perspective, Japan's military experienced an overall decline in fighting strength, even as the age of the samurai was coming to fruition, probably because of population stagnation arising from disease, famine, and war. Once again one is reminded that Yoritomo's victory and the establishment of the Shogunate was no triumph of sheer numbers.

It is instructive to compare the changes in the sizes of Japanese armies over the period 800–1200 to the experience in Western Europe. Like Japan in 800, Roman armies were huge; estimates usually run into the hundreds of thousands.[73] By the year 900 and the beginning of high feudalism in the West, however, armies had shrunk dramatically, to perhaps 5,000 mounted men.[74] It is possible therefore to consider the shifts in Japanese military size as roughly parallel to those that occurred in Western Europe and to read into this parallel some support for the Western-analogue theory.

Yet a more critical examination of the evidence shows that such a parallel masks significant differences in the two cases. I have contended that even the great armies that conquered northeastern Japan in the late eighth century contained a large and effective contingent of mounted fighters, and that the samurai armies of horsemen of the twelfth century were the direct descendants of the eighth-century equestrian soldiers in technology, social organization, economic base, and other areas. In the West, however, Roman armies relied almost exclusively on the infantryman; such mounted men as there were did not possess the stirrup and served a minor role in battle.[75] The equestrian fighter became the heart of European armies only after the eighth century and the discovery of the stirrup. Thus in Western Europe the substantial reduction in the size of armies meant a true revolution in the way wars were fought, while in Japan a somewhat similar diminution in the number of troops can be read as a sign of slow evolutionary change.

The evolutionary nature of change in military matters in Japan becomes especially clear when the mounted fighters of the Kamakura age are compared to the Strong Fellows of 792 (see Chapter 3). Like the samurai of later times, the Strong Fellows were mounted soldiers, each accompanied by 2 foot soldiers. In addition, figures for the Strong Fellows, about 3,200 in 792 and 3,900 in the early tenth century, are strikingly similar to the sums derived for Kamakura housemen (about 3,200 warriors outside of the Tohoku and Kyushu). The numbers for individual provinces are also in many cases close for the Strong Fellows and housemen, respectively: Awaji (30, 14), Izumi (20, 30), Tajima (50, 43), Harima (100, 16), Wakasa (30, 33), Sanuki (50, 14), Iyo (50, 32). When the two lists are compared by region, the count for mounted warriors in western Japan seems to have decreased from the eighth to the twelfth centuries, while the figures for the Kanto increased somewhat. The shift in warriors from west to east was probably a result of nationwide demographic trends in the Heian period, which favored eastern over western Japan, as well as some further militarization of the Kanto.[76]

Of course, in addition to Kamakura housemen, there were also non-vassals, and, while they were probably few, their existence means that the total count of mounted warriors appears to be somewhat greater in 1200 than in 800. But, as one historian has pointed out, there were also other horse-riding fighters in the 800s besides the Strong Fellows, such as the barbarian *emishi* whom the Court had resettled in the Kanto and other provinces. According to this scholar's calculation, these Tohoku natives may have numbered about 10,000 riders in the provinces of the Kanto alone, a figure that more than makes up for the non-housemen of 1200.[77]

All these tabulations are controversial estimates derived from ancient, incomplete, and unreliable sources. Yet it seems unlikely that the population of mounted warriors increased dramatically from 792 to 1200. The ratio of followers for each horserider may have grown from 2 to 3 persons, although this calculation should also be subjected to further scrutiny.[78] In any case, the formation of a warrior government in the Kanto plain was not the result of a dramatic increase in warrior numbers, but was really part of the process of political and social fragmentation that had been going on for centuries.

A WARRIOR'S INCOME

The amount of revenue derived by a warrior from the land and other resources is as vital a question as the number of such fighters. The size of soldierly income, especially as compared to the lords of Kyoto, impinges upon estimates of the power of the military, symbolized by the Shogunate in Kamakura. If an individual warrior's income was large, then one might conclude that the "rise of the warrior" was accompanied by an economic revolution, and 1185 would become a watershed marking the establishment of Japanese feudalism (warriors ruling over a stable agricultural economy). On the other hand, if receipts to fighters were small even after 1185, then the power of the warrior and his government would still be limited. Without economic preeminence over land for military men, feudalism becomes an inappropriate concept to use for the Kamakura age, and the formation of the Kanto government takes on a different meaning.

The first source for an inquiry into the matter of warrior incomes is Shogunate law:[79]

> On incomes:
> Concerning the above, as in . . . [a] decree [of 1223], . . . within every 11 *chō* of wet and dry fields, 10 *chō* are the allotment of the proprietor (*ryōke*) and the provincial officers, and 1 *chō* is for the land steward (*jitō*). This proportion shall be distributed no matter whether the land parcel is big or small. In addition, a surtax (*kachō*) should be allocated at the rate of 5 measures (*shō*) per *tan* (.1 *chō*).[80]

By law, land stewards, who were Kamakura vassals, had 4 sources of income:

(1) the total revenues from one-eleventh of the land in any given estate;
(2) a surcharge of 5 measures per *tan* of land (1 *tan* = .3 acres; or .12 hectare; 1 measure = .24 liter).
(3) portions of mountain or wilderness products and later of mulberry groves and hemp fields; these products were shared equally with the proprietor or provincial officials.[81]
(4) one-third of the possessions of convicted criminals. Even though military men performed most of the police duties, two-thirds of the possessions went to the proprietor or to the provincial office.

Taken together, these laws of the early thirteenth century set a standard that made the rents of warriors seem greatly inferior to those of Court aristocrats, temples and shrines, and other big landowners in Kyoto.[82] The proprietor might reduce even this meager income if "customary levels" in the region were lower. These formulas were not empty rhetoric; the Shogunate acted vigorously to prevent fighting men from abusing their rights.[83]

The broader interpretation of these legal standards is an important question which varies widely according to one's perspective. On the one hand, the Shogunate decided upon these income levels right after its victory in the 1221 war against Kyoto; it seems unlikely that Kamakura would have accepted a low standard on the heels of its victory. At the same time, the martial regime named many of the new land stewards to estates in western Japan, where warriors were traditionally weak and the Court was powerful. A land steward in the Kanto may well have been better off.

The only way to be precise about martial incomes is to examine actual cases. Although few estates produced figures on the comparative allocation of revenues to proprietors and warriors, some data are available from which to form tentative conclusions. Before an analysis can be made, one must note that the tax structure of the thirteenth century included 3 types of levies: a rice assessment (*shotō*, or *nengu*), a commodities tax (*kuji*), and labor (*buyaku*). Because there is no record of the distribution of labor on estates, it will be excluded from this survey.

The most famous and clearest example comes from Ōta Estate in Bingo province in western Japan. Records of the late twelfth century list the amount of the land steward's income for the Kuwabara area in Ōta, as well as other production figures, while a later document relates the total lands and produce for the Kuwabara sector of the estate in about 1300.[84] Most of these records came into existence as a result of a conflict between Tachibana Kanetaka, the warrior at Ōta, and the religious institutions at Mt. Kōya, the proprietor of the estate.[85]

At Kuwabara in Ōta, the warrior received only 3 *chō* of land out of a total of nearly 264 *chō*, a mere 1 percent of the entire area. Tachibana may have had more land in other areas; in any case, he was also allotted the commodities tax from an additional 50 *chō* (*gesu myō*). The rate of rice taxation (*nengu*) for the Kuwabara area in Ōta was 3.37 *to* per *tan* (1 *to* = 10 *shō*), and, after calculation of the revenues from his own land and the 5-*shō*-per-*tan* surtax on all parcels, Tachibana obtained about 200 *koku* (about 400 bushels?) of rice, or about 22 percent of the amount taken by the proprietor. Because the proprietor allocated Tachibana the commodities tax from 50 *chō*, in addition to his own land (3 *chō*) and 10 *chō* of wilderness, he was relatively better off in respect to the commodities tax, collecting about 40 percent of the total receipts going to the proprietor.[86]

The picture portrayed by records from Ōta Estate is clear: The warrior Tachibana Kanetaka received considerably less than did the proprietor, Mt. Kōya (only about a third of Mt. Kōya's total receipts). Of course, Tachibana also had other revenues, such as a third of the proceeds from the mulberry patches (not one-half as in the law), and income from hemp fields and other areas. But in reality Tachibana's income may have been even lower, since one document states that he was to get only 3 measures (*shō*) for the surtax (*kachō*), not 5. When first appointed to Ōta, the proprietor allowed Tachibana only 1 *shō*, a figure that indicates how poorly off some warriors were in the late twelfth century.[87] Coupled with his mere 3 *chō* of land, the low rate of the surtax appears to have left Tachibana even worse off than the legal standard of 1223 would have made him.[88]

A second case, Nuta Estate in Aki province, is also from western Japan. In the middle of the thirteenth century, the land steward was Kobayakawa Shigehira and the proprietor was Saionji Kintsune, a Kyoto noble.[89] The estate was divided into two parts, and some comparative figures are available for the newer section in 1243, and the older area in 1252.[90] The land steward received all the revenues from 4.9 *chō* of land in the new section of Nuta, whereas the total for the new estate was 211.5 *chō;* thus the Kobayakawa land (*jitō kyū*) was only about 2.3 percent of the newer half of the estate. The amount of warrior land in the older half of the estate was slightly better, at 4.8 percent of 250.3 *chō*.

In addition, the two records list the amount of rice tax collected at Nuta. As in the case of Ōta Estate, the land steward collected the majority of rice through the surtax, which in this case was 5 *shō* per *tan*, the same as the 1223 standard. In the newer section of Nuta, the Kobayakawa got 37.5 percent of the revenues in rice, while the older parcels yielded 30 percent. Although there was some variation within the estate, the Kobayakawa acquired about a third of the total. (The commodities levy can not be calculated from the Nuta documents.) Therefore Nuta Estate seems to confirm a general pattern for warrior income in western Japan: a small amount of land and about one-third of the revenues.

A third example comes from Iriki Estate in southern Kyushu. A 1250 land survey notes the relative incomes of the land steward, the proprietor, and the provincial office.[91] Once again the small amount of land actually given over to the warrior is surprising: about 5 percent of the land (8 *chō*) produced taxes exclusively for the land steward. The three groups divided the rice tax more evenly, with the warrior receiving about 31 percent, the proprietor about 30 percent, and the provincial office 39 percent. Commodity tax revenues are unknown, although other documents show that the land steward obtained considerations such as silk cloth and thread. The figures from the Iriki case support the conclusions of little land and about one-third of the revenues for warriors, as seen at Ōta and Nuta.

Other examples from western Japan for which only partial data are available present the same picture. At Hitoyoshi Estate in Higo province in 1244, the land steward possessed 5.8 *chō* of land (*jitō kyū*), a mere 5.5 percent of the total productive paddies, as well as a rice surtax of 4 *shō* per *tan*.[92] However, the warrior also held 40 percent of the silk cloth and 70 percent of the hemp. At Sasakibe Estate in Tamba in 1238, when the land steward Ōyake Mitsunobu contested his small income with the proprietor Matsuo Shrine, the warrior had only 10 *chō* of the estate, which contained over 100 *chō*.[93] Over one-third of Ōyake's parcel was no longer being cultivated.

Ategawa Estate was located in Kii province; the warrior house was the Yuasa and the proprietor was Mt. Kōya, as at Ōta.[94] These lands were the scene of a famous protest by peasants against the land steward, who was accused of cutting the ears and noses off the wives and children of peasants who disobeyed his orders. The reason for the warrior's violence is not hard to fathom, for he had only 2 *chō* of land at Ategawa. A silk tax, paid in cash by the late thirteenth century, added significantly to the warrior's revenue, as he obtained about 43 percent of the receipts.

All the estates discussed so far were located in western Japan. Because this region was the home of numerous temples and the aristocracy, it is probable that warrior incomes were low in that region. What was the warrior's economic base in eastern Japan, the home of the Shogunate, where there were fewer temples and shrines? This question is a difficult one, because, in the absence of other proprietors such as temples and aristocrats, land disputes were relatively rare, and comparative records of estate officials' incomes were not formulated.

There is one case from which it is possible to infer relative warrior-proprietor shares of revenues in the Kanto. Shida Estate was a giant landholding of at least 600 *chō* in Hitachi province, originally opened by the Shida family.[95] The same warrior band had rebelled against Yoritomo in the Great Civil War of 1180–1185, and the Shogunate had doled out the lands to the Shida's conquerors, primarily Oyama Tomomasa. According to documents from 1223 and 1276, Shida Estate owed revenues in the form of silk cloth to the granddaughter of the Emperor Takakura (r. 1168–1180). The same record states that the 826-*chō* estate paid 300 units (*hiki*) to the noble in 1223 and 330 units in 1276.

Documents from Ategawa Estate allow an estimate of the ratio of land to silk cloth, the proportion being 1 *tan* of land for about .9 *jō* (approximately 2.7 meters) of silk cloth.[96] If the Ategawa ratio was standard for the country and is applied to Shida Estate, then the Kyoto proprietor in 1223 received only 24 percent of the silk revenue (if the area was 826 *chō*) or 32 percent of the silk revenue (if the area was 620 *chō*).[97] For 1276, the figures increase slightly to 27 percent (826 *chō*) and 35 percent (620 *chō*). Moreover, the silk took the place of the rice tax (*shotō*); no commodities or labor levies were due from Shida to the Kyoto proprietor at all. Therefore, it seems likely that, while warriors received a decidedly smaller percentage of land and assessments than proprietors in western Japan, the tables were turned in the warrior-dominated Kanto, where the warriors took the lion's share of revenues.[98]

The different proportions going to warriors and to Kyoto proprietors in the Kanto and in western Japan indicate the regional character of Yoritomo's victory and the Shogunate's tax base. By 1185, the Great Civil War had resulted in a redistribution of Kanto revenues away from the Court, to warriors generally, and the Shogunate specifically. In this respect, therefore, the triumph of 1185 looks like a revolution into feudalism, in which warriors at last seized control of taxation and their political destinies.

But this argument for dramatic change is difficult to prove, because scholars have no figures on comparative incomes for warriors and the Court from the Kanto before 1185. If warriors had most of the Kanto revenues before 1185, then the formation of the Kamakura government would have had little economic meaning; it becomes instead the culmination of a long-term political independence movement.

Furthermore, the economic weakness of soldiers in western Japan indicates that, despite the Shogunate's victory in 1221, big temples and powerful aristocrats still held sway in that area for most of the thirteenth century. Kamakura remained a regional power, dominant in eastern Honshu but relatively impotent not too far from its base. Such an analysis would suggest that, if the term *feudalism,* which implies that the military receives all farming revenues, is to be applied at all to thirteenth-century Japan, then it would best be used only for eastern Honshu, and perhaps just for the Kanto itself.

A LAND STEWARD'S SPHERE OF CONTROL. In addition to examining comparative Court-warrior incomes in various regions, it is instructive to focus on each land steward's individual unit and method of control. One historian from Tokyo University has created a schema made up of 3 concentric circles by which to better understand the nature of warrior (*bushi*) power over land and peasants[99] (see Figure 13; also note Chapter 5, Figure 7). The innermost circle included the warrior's house, usually a rectangular fort surrounded by a low wall called the *doi* or *hori no uchi*. The warrior's family and some of his closest vassals lived within the wall, and the warrior's power over those who dwelt there was great. In the second circle, the land steward possessed fields which he farmed using servile followers and from which he received all the revenues. Also known as the demesne (*tsukuda, mitezukuri*), these parcels were equivalent to the 1 out of 11 *chō* given over to the land steward in the 1223 laws. Such lands were often small in western Japan, and the relative size was an important measure of status among warriors. In the outer circle, there was the estate or village jurisdiction overseen by the warrior. The land steward collected his rice surtax and other levies from these lands, which included not just rice paddies, but also wilderness, rivers, and the seas. The warrior used his police and military powers to keep the peasants in line within this unit, but it is likely that his power was weaker than it was over the inner two areas.[100] The Tokyo scholar who developed this diagram believes the warrior's power was based on his strong control of those within his dwelling (the first circle), and he calls this authority "domiciliary control" (*ie no shihai*).

Figure 13. A LAND STEWARD'S SPHERE OF INFLUENCE

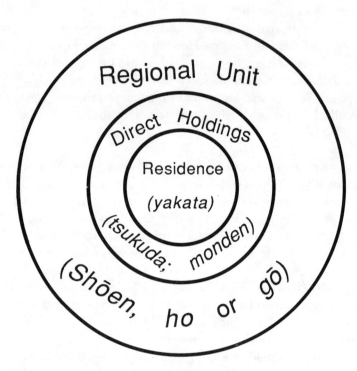

Source: Ishii Susumu, *Nihon no rekishi* 12, *Chūsei bushi dan,* p. 111.

The reader may recall that I created a similar outline to describe the life and power of the district magistrate of the eighth century, and one may ask how the base of each local official compared (see Chapter 2, Figure 4). To be sure, the nature of each administrator's power would have been different, with the magistrate's being more public and the land steward's more private. At least superficially, the Taihō Codes, not the Kamakura warrior's personal power over those within his residence, underlay the authority of the eighth-century official. But the contrast is not as strong as most authors have argued: The land steward also drew his authority from a public organization (the Shogunate and Court law), while the district magistrate had established his own residence (*ihe, yake*), and used special powers through his domicile.

The greatest difference between the local lords of 750 and 1250 lay not in the nature or even the strength of their control, but in the size of the unit over which they wielded power. In the 700s there were 550 district magistrates, while I have estimated that there were 5 or 6 times as many local officials (land stewards) in the Kamakura government. On average, the political unit the district magistrate oversaw could easily have been 10 times larger than the lands under the land steward's authority.

It is important to inquire as to why the change occurred. One immediate reaction would be to see the difference as population increase, but I find this answer too simple and not consonant with the facts. As I have argued elsewhere, the importation of severe plagues strongly hindered an increase of the Japanese population beginning in the eighth century.[101] As noted in Chapters 5 and 6, these foreign-borne epidemics continued unabated at least until the late eleventh century, when they depopulated the land that was eventually re-opened in the "age of widespread land clearance."

As population revived in the twelfth century, however, there are growing indications that formerly virulent parasites had begun to settle into endemicity; a "window of opportunity" for significant population and agricultural growth might have been possible by the mid-twelfth century.[102] But just as pestilence began to abate, climate worldwide became significantly colder and wetter; harsh famines resulted in Japan, especially in 1230–1231 (killing perhaps a third of the population) and in 1259–1260.[103] Although further study of Kamakura agriculture and population is necessary, the existence of such severe rural hardship suggests that peasants could not easily bring new lands into cultivation, particularly in eastern Honshu, the area of Japan where most virgin territory lay. Growth in Japanese population and agriculture was slowed once again to a standstill, until at least the end of the thirteenth century.

Instead of population growth, I believe that what happened between 750 and 1250 was just the opposite: Under difficult (perhaps stagnating) economic and demographic conditions, political and social disintegration set in. On the local level, the district became severely fragmented and more difficult to govern.[104] Although the land steward may have had more effective control over his unit, the *area* over which that control was held (the area from which he drew all tax revenues) was markedly smaller. This fragmentation was not a recent trend, but had begun even before the importation of Chinese institutions in 600.[105] It was a process that would not be reversed decisively until the sixteenth century.

CONCLUSION

Advocates of the Western-analogue theory have considered the Kamakura period a decisive turning point when samurai established European-style feudalism in Japan. In the Introduction, I defined a feudal society as one in which: (1) warriors comprised the ruling class; (2) ties of dependence bound soldiers to each other; and (3) military men took their revenues from land. This chapter has provided an analysis of three aspects of Kamakura society to test the viability of "a revolution into feudalism."

The first perspective was the way in which military commanders raised, equipped, organized, and deployed their forces. In the three major military operations of the Kamakura period — the Northern Campaign of 1189, the Jōkyū War of 1221, and the Mongol Invasions of 1274 and 1281 — it is evident that continuity, rather than change, was the rule. In all three, the provincial headquarters was just as important in conscripting and organizing warriors as in the Heian epoch. To be sure, a constable appointed by Kamakura was now in charge of housemen listed on rolls pledging loyalty to the Shogunate, but the essential element in military organization was still the provincial headquarters. Yoritomo had refined and revived the Heian system of 901. Armies probably remained small.

These three conflicts also trace the last stage in samurai political ascendancy. In the Northern Campaign of 1189, the Court and the Shogunate were on such bad terms that Kyoto refused to provide Yoritomo with a search-and-destroy order to smite the Fujiwara, as had been the rule for centuries. In 1221, the Retired Emperor attempted to destroy Kamakura first by political means, and then by military force; his defeat merely resulted in the Court's acceptance of the military government's legitimacy. Only in the late thirteenth century, after the emergency provoked by the Mongol Invasions did Kamakura begin to dominate the whole nation. The continuing vitality of the Court into the late thirteenth century shows that warriors made up only one part of the ruling class.

A second point of analysis was the number of warriors (*bushi*) throughout the country. Using three different methods, I have argued that the total for all warriors was perhaps 5,000–6,000, most of whom were allies of the Shogunate. This count probably did not significantly differ from the figure of Masakado's era, or even before. The number of Kamakura housemen just about equaled the sum of those named to provincial guard duty in 792 (the Strong Fellows), and the count of non-housemen was not so great as to offset mounted warriors used in the ninth century in other areas. The overall size of armies probably decreased from 750 to 1250. The small size of the warrior class reinforces the argument which holds that they made up only a part of the ruling class.

Finally, this chapter examined warrior incomes, which, even according to Kamakura law, were paltry in comparison to the revenues sent to the great aristocratic and clerical houses of Kyoto. The best-documented case studies originate from western Japan, where Kyoto was strong and warriors weak. In western and central Japan, warriors typically received a small amount of land from which to claim rents, usually less than the one-eleventh designated by Kamakura law. In addition, they obtained about one-third the amount of tax receipts going to the Kyoto proprietor. In the Kanto, the warrior fared much better, taking between two-thirds and three-quarters of the rice tax, and probably most of the land and the other taxes.

These three analyses suggest that the Kamakura era was not a revolution into feudalism, a sudden hurtling of Japanese society from the Chinese model into something resembling Western Europe. Rather, continuity was the rule; in most ways, life during the Kamakura era was no different than in the late Heian. Even the Kanto, where warriors were concentrated and received most of the wealth, and where scholars might be most tempted to use the term *feudalism,* confirmed the power of historical continuity: Most warriors had come from the wealthy families of the Kanto in 600, 800, and 1000. It is no exaggeration to say that the "rise of the warrior" was a regional political movement, an independence movement, and another aspect of the long-term process of political fragmentation.

The lack of a single strong, central authority affected soldiery in the Kamakura period. Intraspecific combat prevailed, as males fought almost exclusively in ritualistic one-on-one battles to secure their dominance in a hierarchy of masculinity. Intraspecific warfare was so commonplace in Japan that samurai resorted to it even when fighting the Mongols, a foreign invader; Japanese warriors could not understand how one could fight any other way. The customs and weapons of thirteenth-century intraspecific conflict were not very successful on the battlefield against the Mongols, but ironically soon became a part of the lore and legend of the samurai.

Conclusions

I will not from today
Turn back towards home —
I who have set out to serve
As the Emperor's stubborn shield.
— Imamatsuribe Yosofu,
a squad leader in the Border Guards in 755

From 500 to 1300 fighting men had acted as shields for the Court, defending it from enemies both at home and abroad. For approximately the first 400 years of this span, warriors had quietly, sometimes grudgingly acquiesced in their employment for the Court and the emperor. But as economic conditions changed after 900, service came at a higher and higher price, until finally samurai declared their political independence, which, despite Court machinations, they secured, in the thirteenth century. By 1300, Japan stood on the verge of a new era, when the samurai would come to dominate an improving economy and increasingly sophisticated society.

Historians have usually drawn upon Western European experience and put forth a Western-analogue theory to understand the way the soldier rose to political prominence in Japan. Reduced to its essentials, the Western-analogue theory is composed of 3 interrelated arguments: (1) that the Chinese-style government set up in the late seventh century was a civilian and public institution that paid scant attention to military development; (2) that the same administration disintegrated after 900, giving rise to a political vacuum in the countryside, where military specialists armed themselves out of self-defense and formed bands linked by ties of dependence and based in land; and (3) that in 1185 one warrior established a military regime which granted its retainers land in return for martial service, thereby creating a Japanese version of Western European feudalism.

Two characteristics of the Western-analogue theory are particularly important. First, advocates of this view depict the historical trends that led to Yoritomo's Shogunate as short-term. Most narratives of the "rise of the warrior" begin about 1050; at the earliest some experts push the story back to the age of Masakado in the 900s. Second, the Western-analogue theory sees a fundamental difference between the system imported from the Asian mainland in the late seventh century and Yoritomo's warrior government of the late twelfth century. Various scholars have portrayed the dichotomy in different terms, some preferring *public* and *private*, others employing familial models, still others using feudal terminology, but the intent is always the same.

In this study I have presented what might be called the "evolutionary model" to elucidate the development of Japan's military from 500 to 1300. I have divided these centuries into 8 distinct stages in which the Japanese warrior gradually came to dominate the country. During the first phase (A.D. 500 to 645), basic weapons and fundamental patterns of organization appeared. Even back in the New Stone Age (10,000–300 B.C.), the bow and arrow had been the deadliest armament a Japanese hunter could devise, and, by A.D. 500, men had learned to combine archery with horse-riding, a frightening new technology introduced from Korea. The demands of horse-raising and horse-riding meant that specialists, particularly from the Kanto, played a critical role in the military from the very start, but there was also room for ordinary foot soldiers wielding swords, spears, and shields. Both types of soldiers wore heavy iron armor modeled after continental designs, in an early example of the principle of counter-response and symmetry in weapons technology. The tactics used by the army are uncertain, but it seems unlikely that the Japanese employed techniques of mass, coordinated warfare to any significant degree.

Expeditions of the early seventh century which sailed to Korea from western Japan, where shipbuilding and the navy were based, give hints of Yamato military organization. Already the local strongman, a figure with political, military, economic, and religious authority over his region, was the crucial ingredient in any large military operation. The local strongman not only protected his bailiwick, but also sent his sons and brothers to serve as guards for the Yamato King in the Kinai. Military aristocrats, like the Mononobe and the Ōtomo, commanded the King's army; these houses are the first documented cases of exclusive martial families in Japan.

The second stage of military evolution (645 to 770) demonstrates the fundamental differences between the approach taken in this book and the Western-analogue theory. Rather than seeing this epoch as a military failure, I believe that the new Chinese-style government, really Japan's first martial regime, was ominously successful. Pressured by a violent coup, a disastrous foreign campaign, and a civil war, the Court became consumed by the need for arms and men to defend its shores from attack by China or Korea. The symbol for the military buildup was the Emperor Temmu, hero of the Civil War of 672, who set the tone for his new administration when he said that "in a government, military matters are the essential thing."

Temmu and his heirs followed the principle of counter-response and symmetry by adopting many Chinese ideas for their army and navy. Like the Chinese military, the Japanese drafted commoners and had them provide their own weapons, because such a system was inexpensive and a steady source of manpower. The Japanese Court put some weapons under state control, and sent experts on Sun-tzu's *The Art of War* to the provinces to instruct local commanders in strategy and mass tactics. The Battle of the Paekch'ŏn River in 663 had proven the superiority of Chinese-style warfare, in which numbers and organization were all-important; Japanese generals undoubtedly devoured Chinese books on this mode of fighting, although in practice drills often broke down into training in individual martial arts. The government also oversaw the construction of Korean-style siege works in northern Kyushu and western Japan to forestall any invasion from the continent.

This system, which absorbed so much from the Chinese model, departed from it in one critical way. Instead of severely restricting the role of local strongmen in the new army and navy, both law and practice handed command over to the local elite. The Chinese system was basically a defensive arrangement with only brief time for offensive campaigns, and it kept power out of the hands of local men, often barbarians. The Japanese Court was too weak to copy the Chinese model in that regard. In Japan, these local strongmen were among the few who had the time and wealth to master mounted archery and the martial arts, and the Codes gave a prominent place to local horse-riding military experts. They commanded local units of the provincial militia, they were Border Guards who went to northern Kyushu to defend the Court, and they were Palace and Gate Guards who journeyed to the capital to protect the emperor. The Codes put a special emphasis on training in the martial arts, by which was often meant fighting from horseback, as well as horse-raising, always in the hands of local strongmen.

Battles of the late seventh and eighth centuries show the prominence of local strongmen and the supremacy of equestrian fighters. In the Civil War of 672, Temmu rode to victory through his control of horse-riding local strongmen, while the Court crushed the rebellion of Fujiwara no Hirotsugu because it commanded superior numbers of district magistrates (local strongmen) with skills in mounted archery. *The Man'yōshū,* a poetry collection from the mid-eighth century, contains lyrics composed by local strongmen from the Kanto heading to Kyushu, frequently as horsemen. These same soldiers were also crucial to politics in the capital, where they took part in equestrian ceremonies when they were not menacing a political rival for their lord, as they did for Fujiwara no Nakamaro and others.

By the end of the second stage of Japan's military development in 770, many fundamental patterns had become established. The local elite led soldiers on horseback in the countryside and enrolled in political factions in the capital. The Kanto had already become Japan's largest military base, sending horse-riding local strongmen to defend northern Kyushu and the court.

During the third phase (770 to 900), the emphasis on martial specialists became even clearer. Between 774 and 812, the Court dispatched 5 expeditions against a people known in the records simply as the "barbarians"; these natives of northeastern Honshu fought in guerilla style as mounted warriors. When the huge Chinese-style armies of the government engaged those small forces

Conclusions

of *emishi* fighters, at first the result was disaster for the Court, as at the Battle of the Koromo River. Only with the determined and capable leadership of Sakanoue no Tamuramaro and the Emperor Kammu and after the near-exhaustion of the Kanto and western Japan did the Court prevail, extending its political control to the tip of northern Honshu and constructing fortifications throughout the Tohoku.

The government waged its long war within the framework of the Taihō Codes, calling up men to serve in large armies led once again by district magistrates (local strongmen) and veterans. Japan continued the custom of using military aristocrats to assume overall command, whether their names were Ōtomo, Saeki, or Sakanoue. But the wars also saw some subtle changes in the ways men fought and enlisted for combat. The success of barbarian tactics, which relied so heavily upon the heroics of a few mounted archers, undoubtedly encouraged their counterparts from outside the Tohoku to utilize symmetrical tactics. The technology of war altered subtly, as the curved sword and light armor of the barbarians replaced heavier continental prototypes. The provincial headquarters, especially in the Kanto region, increasingly became a center for conscripting and provisioning troops.

Forty years of fighting against the people of the Tohoku left the Court economically exhausted, and it quickly did away with the draft of commoners and related institutions such as the Border and Capital Guards. Serving in the army had always been a hardship for Japanese peasants, and, as labor became scarce and the quality of recruits declined, the Court had no choice but to do away with Chinese-style conscription. To replace the draft, the government turned to the very specialists who had always led the Taihō military—local strongmen. In 792, the Court designated the relatives of district magistrates as Strong Fellows, about 3,200 mounted fighters. The Kanto was home to a large proportion of these riders, and, until 1300, the early Japanese economy probably never supported more horsemen than it did at this time. The Strong Fellows were such a popular and effective force that the Court also established similar guards in the frontier provinces of Kyushu and northeastern Honshu. In addition to the Strong Fellows, the government deployed crossbow-bearing foot soldiers along the Sea of Japan to defend the country against invasion from Korea; but, although the crossbow was easy to use and effective against horsemen, the weapon proved too difficult to manufacture for general use.

In the fourth period (850 to 950), the Japanese military moved from foreign defense to domestic peacekeeping, as the system of the Taihō Codes now shifted focus from external to internal threats. This change arose partially from the decline of Japan's enemies on the continent, but mostly from the growing incidence of robbery, murder, and rebellion at home. Throughout the late eighth and ninth centuries, the Japanese economy and population slowly came to a standstill, leading to a zero-sum game which district magistrates and the average peasant lost and some Court aristocrats and "the rich" won. People turned to violence both to maintain their standard of living and express hostility against the government. In the Reform of 901, the Court responded to the mayhem by making the governors tax-farmers and reducing restrictions on their ability to raise and command troops.

Just when it seemed that the Reform of 901 had quieted the country, the Kanto exploded into rebellion between 935 and 940 with the revolt of Taira no Masakado. Unlike the wars in the Tohoku, Masakado's insurrection was an intraspecific conflict, in which the rebel and his rivals fought not to gain new territory, but for their own survival and continuation of their families. Soon after Masakado's revolt, Fujiwara Sumitomo led pirate raiders along the coast line of western Japan. Both insurrections ended in triumph for the Court; the Kanto continued its reputation for political independence and rebellion amidst the devastation of scorched-earth tactics.

Masakado's war underlines the slow, evolutionary way Japan's early military developed. His forces were composed of both horsemen and foot soldiers and used Chinese-style mass methods, although with a notable lack of success. Masakado himself was a mounted archer, and his army made war much like its Taihō predecessor, proving that the samurai had much more in common with his Chinese-style ancestor than is usually credited. Masakado's economic base included land, pastures, and ironworks, much the same sources of support an eighth-century district magistrate or a twelfth-century warrior would have depended on.

The rebellions of Masakado and Sumitomo also began new trends. The revolts legitimized and spread the Reform of 901 nationwide, as the provincial headquarters became the chief military center in the countryside and local men of influence sought appointments as overseers and arrest officers. Every warrior worthy of the name obtained rewards in office, rank, or other benefits, becoming in effect a mercenary for hire. The rebellions also propelled more groups of military aristocrats into prominence, the Taira, Minamoto, and Hidesato-line Fujiwara being the most important.

The fifth phase of warrior evolution (950 to 1050) marks another major difference between the interpretation presented in this book and the Western-analogue theory. Although it may appear at times as though there was no effective central government in the troubled middle Heian epoch, in reality a military system did exist for the capital and the provinces. In Heian, often the scene of violence, there were the Imperial Guards, the Investigators, and soldiers fighting for the great civil aristocrats (including martial nobles). Neither the Imperial Guards nor the Investigators controlled many police, although evidence indicates that a few warriors from small bases in the Kinai joined their ranks. The private armies of the civil aristocracy were mostly mounted archers, and they probably outnumbered the city's police; their leaders organized them into units of 10 after the Taihō model. Every civil aristocrat worthy of the name also received pledges of loyalty from a special category of soldier, the military aristocrat. These warriors were members of a lineage with the privilege of practicing the "way of the bow and horse," and the Court had granted them exalted rank for martial service. In the period from 950 to 1050, many families (not just the Taira and Minamoto) followed this occupation, and many of the best received appointments to governorships.

In the countryside, the provincial headquarters continued to serve as a center for conscription and deployment, with the governor taking command. His forces comprised: (1) his personal retainers; (2) officials of the province, such as Strong Fellows; (3) soldiers of the province allied to the governor through their participation in guard duty, hunts, Shinto ceremonies, and appointment to military posts such as arrest officer or overseer; and (4) independent local strongmen. The final category was composed of wealthy men who possessed personal access to capital aristocrats and had intermarried with families of district magistrates.

The revolt of Taira no Tadatsune between 1028 and 1031 severely tested the system of the middle Heian era. Although the insurrection appeared on the surface to be a tax rebellion, in fact it was another intraspecific conflict between two wings of the Kanto Taira vying for dominance in that region. After Tadatsune's defeat, his conqueror, Minamoto no Yorinobu, obtained a governorship and many loyal followers in the Kanto. But the real effect of Tadatsune's rebellion came in the destruction it caused to the Kanto, where it all but obliterated agriculture for decades. Coupled with a cycle of harsh epidemics and droughts in western Japan, the revolt left the country in ruins in the mid-eleventh century, and the Court enacted a new system of villages and estates to encourage agrarian recovery.

During the sixth stage of military evolution (1050 to 1150), advocates of the Western-analogue theory have asserted that a new class of feudal lords appeared, supported by an increase in rural wealth and a rise in productivity. They contend that warriors opened new parcels of land in what some Japanese scholars have termed the "age of widespread land clearance" comparable to Western Europe's agrarian take-off a century earlier. Some technological improvements, such as the invention of double-cropping and the diffusion of iron tools, support this view.

But military men had always possessed sources of wealth, such as land, cash, and office, and examination of macroeconomic trends and individual cases suggests that the late eleventh and the twelfth centuries saw no substantial progress in the agrarian economy. Local strongmen helped create many estates during this phase, but cleared little land from virgin territory, preferring to take over already productive provincially administered fields. In many cases it is not even clear that warriors were the leaders of land clearance, especially where temples and shrines were involved. A new system of village government came into existence, but it followed the era of unprecedented destruction from 990 to 1050, when Tadatsune's revolt, a cycle of harsh epidemics, droughts, and other natural disasters had depopulated the countryside. Instead of the "age of widespread land clearance," the era from 1050 to 1150 was really an age of widespread re-opening of formerly abandoned parcels.

Specific examples reinforce the impression of demographic and agricultural stagnation in the late Heian period. At Ōba Estate in the Kanto, the yield from rice paddies in 1150 was no better than it had been 350 years earlier. At Ōba, as well as lands in Mino and western Japan, warriors preferred to forge documents, move boundary stakes, and intimidate the cultivators and proprietors in order to acquire land, rather than open new parcels. Hata Tametatsu, a warrior of western Japan and supposed symbol of the productive energies of the new feudal class, cleared abandoned fields only to watch as the same land went out of cultivation a few years later for lack of reliable irrigation technology.

As Japanese peasants returned to their lands in the second half of the eleventh century, soldiers fought two wars in northeastern Honshu: the Former Nine Years' War (1051–1062) and the Latter Three Years' War (1083–1087). In the first, Minamoto no Yoriyoshi defeated the Abe in another intraspecific conflict, while, in the second, Yoriyoshi's son Yoshiie vanquished the Kiyowara, albeit without the recognition of the Court. Both wars showed continuities from the previous age — provincial headquarters central to the conscription and organization of forces, and small armies of mounted warriors supreme on the battlefield. By the late eleventh century, samurai had abandoned any pretense of mass tactics, a style to which Japanese fighting men had never been very committed, and had adopted individualized, ritualized mounted combat as the standard. Such a style was the result of the system of rewards, which required the recognition of individual fighters, and the intraspecific nature of wars, where men strove for dominance within a hierarchy. Yet overall strategic principles still owed much to Sun-tzu and Taihō precedents.

Subtle modifications within the Reform of 901 took place by the beginning of the twelfth century. When pirates threatened to cut off supply lines in the Inland Sea, the Court split on the issue of whether to have the governors, a renowned warrior, or soldiers on individual estates deal with the culprits. After some debate the Court sent the military aristocrat Taira no Tadamori to quell the pirates, suggesting that governors were too weak to lead their forces any longer and that estates were too small and varied to use. But even Tadamori still relied upon the provincial headquarters as a crucial military center, as did others throughout the twelfth century. The nomination of one man to lead Court expeditions helped spur competition among military aristocrats to see who would become the "chief of all warriors."

In the seventh stage of martial development (1150 to 1185), two warrior families vied for the privilege of leading the military establishment. The Minamoto, based in the Kanto, had produced such eminent fighters as Yorinobu and Yoshiie, but they fell upon hard times with Yoshiie's death in 1106. Meanwhile, the Ise Taira, a little-known family from western Japan, gained the favor of the Retired Emperors and proved effective in smiting the Court's enemies. By 1150, the Taira had ascended to prominence at Court and control of the capital military, while the Minamoto suffered under the incompetent leadership of Tameyoshi.

The Taira assumed control of the national military system through victories in the Hōgen Disturbance of 1156 and the Heiji War of 1159. In the former conflict, the Imperial House and the Taira took on the main Minamoto line headed by Tameyoshi and the Fujiwara Regents and defeated them in a battle in the capital. The imperial force was truly a national army, raised from the retainers of Taira no Kiyomori and Minamoto no Yoshitomo and the provincial headquarters, while the Regents and Tameyoshi depended upon their personal resources. Both armies were small: The imperial side comprised only 600 mounted soldiers, despite claims of greater forces in *The Tale of Hōgen*. The small size of armies shows the rise of the warrior was no revolution of numbers, and the fighting style was classic samurai man-to-man equestrian combat. In the Heiji War of 1159, Kiyomori destroyed his rival and former ally, Yoshitomo, and became the "chief of all warriors" through his remarkable political skills.

After their victories, the Taira placed their own indelible stamp upon Japan's military. Far from being failed courtiers as portrayed in the Western-analogue theory, the Taira took command of all warriors in the order of 1167 and began to build a nationwide warrior following based upon the use of capital guard duty and the provincial headquarters, especially in the Kanto. The Taira conducted a flourishing trade with Sung China and controlled 7 proprietary provinces, so they also tried to serve the economic interests of their men by confirming lands, giving tax exemptions, and in some cases possibly even appointing fighters to be land stewards. As Civil War approached after 1177, Kiyomori took over the military, issuing commands to his vassals and others through the provincial headquarters. By 1181, the Taira had alienated important segments of Court society and had lost the Kanto to the Minamoto, but showed their resourcefulness by establishing offices such as the commander-in-chief, the estate foreman-in-chief, and the messenger who promotes agriculture, forerunners of Kamakura institutions that lasted until the beginning of the fourteenth century in western Japan.

The Great Civil War of 1180–1185 was a clash of asymmetrical forces which was the downfall of the seagoing Taira and the triumph of land-based Minamoto no Yoritomo. It was also the quintessential intraspecific conflict among warriors for dominance throughout the land. The war was a rebellion against the authority of the Taira and the Court by warriors in eastern Honshu, and it brought about the political independence of the Kanto and the nationwide practice of using land to pay for military service.

But the conflict was not a revolution into feudalism, at least in the way soldiers fought and were conscripted for battle. Single equestrian combat still dominated, and armies were small. The provincial headquarters was still the key to raising troops, even for the revolutionary Yoritomo, who regularly "hijacked" the office, taking control and forcing the conscription of warriors in the province. Thus Yoritomo won out in the Great Civil War, not because of his feudal policies, many of which were not new or exclusively his, but because of his politically wise use of the establishment, the disunity at Court, and the disastrous Famine of 1180–1182.

No examination of Japan's early military evolution would be complete without a discussion of the era when feudalism had presumably come to fruition, the eighth phase (1185 to 1300). In ideal terms, Kamakura looks like a strong martial government, with a shogun taking over the Court's police and military powers, and constables and land stewards in the provinces carrying out the new authority. But the supposed establishment of feudalism really involved only minor changes to the military regime in action. In three wars—the Northern Campaign in 1189, the Jōkyū War of 1221, and the Mongol Invasions of 1274 and 1281—the Shogunate raised its relatively small forces through the provincial headquarters, just as commanders had done through most of the Heian period. In the Northern Campaign, Yoritomo reverted to being a defender of the entrenched order after his triumph over the Fujiwara. In the conflict of 1221, both sides used the provincial headquarters, and without that institution it is unlikely that either the Court or the Shogunate could have kept its mercenaries in line. During the Mongol Invasions, the same office once again came in for widespread use, as samurai attempted to do man-to-man battle with continental experts in mass tactics. As a result of the Jōkyū War, Kamakura at last achieved a measure of legitimacy in the eyes of the Court, but it took the military emergency created by the Mongols to enable the Shogunate to overcome the Court and extend its political authority into western Japan.

For a feudal society, where a martial ruling class bound by ties of dependence theoretically oversaw a land economy, Kamakura Japan was badly understaffed with warriors. Three different methods of counting fighters indicate there were about 5,000–6,000 warriors (*bushi*) and armies of 15,000 to 18,000 men in all of Japan. Such forces are far smaller than reported in contemporary sources and a fraction of the expeditions sent to the Tohoku to engage the barbarians in the eighth and ninth centuries. Even the number of horsemen shows almost no change from 800 to 1200, a sign of the demographic and economic stagnation Japan suffered in those four centuries.

The lords of feudalism also had distressingly small incomes in much of the country. Laws of the early thirteenth century gave warriors all revenues on a paltry one-eleventh of the land and a small surcharge on the rest. Cases from western Japan prove that warriors received full taxes on about 5 to 10 percent of the land and about a third to one-half the revenues of the big landowners of Kyoto. In eastern Japan the proportions were reversed, with Kyoto aristocrats and temples getting 30 percent of one tax, and perhaps nothing else. These comparative earnings point out the regional character of Kamakura power, and suggest that the term *feudalism,* if it is to be used at all, is probably applicable to the Kanto alone. The establishment of Kamakura was a political movement, an independence movement, and part of the long-term trend of fragmentation that saw power penetrate to the countryside in smaller and smaller units.

To sum up, the "evolutionary model" runs counter to the "Western-analogue theory" in several basic ways. The former interpretation emphasizes that most important conditions for the ascendancy of the warrior to a leading role in Japanese history came into existence early and did not change markedly, while the latter views the "rise of the warrior" as taking place almost entirely after 1050. The "evolutionary model" rejects juxtaposing the Chinese-style state and the Kamakura Shogunate as opposites; instead, it sees Japan's military development and the evolution of the samurai as a result of the martial emphasis of the Emperor Temmu and the Taihō system.

Another way to set forth the evolutionary model is to look at Japan's military development in terms of fundamental structures. When one does so, the year 800 emerges as a pivotal point. By the beginning of the ninth century, the basic technology of warfare was available and mounted warriors were supremely important on the battlefield; many soldiers organized themselves into houses with the exclusive right to practice the martial arts, either as aristocrats or local strongmen. At the same time, the early Japanese economy and population had produced all the support it could for a class of horse-riding local lords, and 400 years would bring little growth in agricultural production to increase the size of that class. The fundamental institutional patterns in which local strongmen controlled the provincial military as equestrian soldiers and also sent their relatives to the capital to guard the Court and make political alliances had become fixed. The only new institutional structure after 800 was the Shogunate itself, which inherited police and military powers previously held by the Court and was located in the Kanto, the home of most warriors for 500 years.

Of course, there were subtle changes after 800 within these fundamental patterns. During the wars in northeastern Japan between 770 and 900, Court forces moved from heavy iron armor like that used on the continent to the lighter variety characteristic of the barbarians, and from a straight to the curved sword, also well known among the residents of the Tohoku. The creation of a new generation of military houses (*tsuwamono no ie*) between about 850 and 1000 was another change, as the Taira, Minamoto, Hidesato line of the Fujiwara, and others received appointments to the aristocracy to reward their military efforts. A third subtle modification occurred between 1050 and 1200, when members of the Taira, Minamoto, and other military aristocrats and local strongmen acquired land during the age of widespread re-opening of abandoned fields, a movement that helped shift population and productive farmland slightly towards the Kanto. But these three changes were really minor alterations in the basic structures of warrior life, much like pouring new wine into old bottles.

One could then ask: If the underlying framework for the ascendancy of the samurai was in place by 800, why did warriors not form their own government then? Such counterfactual reasoning is always risky, but I believe that two changes occurring after the establishment of these fundamental patterns in 800 are crucial to understanding the "rise of the warrior" and also explain why advocates of the Western-analogue theory have for so long emphasized the period after 1050. The first factor is the change in the nature of violence in Japan after 800. Early Japanese society was usually violent, even in the supposedly quiescent eighth century (witness the wars in the Tohoku), but, when growth in the economy and population slowed to a standstill after 800, central control began to dissipate and society disintegrated, as people turned on each other as never before in Japan's recorded history. The increase in murder, rebellion, theft, and other crimes put the mounted soldier in a unique position to take advantage of his craft: He either initiated the disturbance or was needed to put it down.

But possessing the means of violence alone would not have

made for a Kamakura government, as can be seen by Masakado's and Tadatsune's fate. Warriors had to acquire political acumen, and the centuries following Masakado's demise were the time when military men gained that critical ability. The first martial leaders were politically naive; either the system used them, or they revolted against it and remained outside the power structure, like Masakado. He recognized the importance of the provincial head-quarters, which had gained in political and military function since the Reform of 901, but declared himself to be the "new emperor," antagonizing the Court. After Masakado's defeat, however, the government appointed many military men to provincial governor-ships and other positions which allowed them to gather valuable political experience and wealth. They gained control of soldiers, since troops continued to report to the provincial headquarters. Thus the Court's means of paying for its military—appointment to office—indirectly aided warriors in challenging Kyoto.

By the mid-twelfth century, several warriors could boast consid-erable expertise in political matters, but it was not until the appear-ance of Kiyomori (who dominated the Court) and Yoritomo (who used it) that warriors really had the political skills to vie with civil aristocrats and clerical authorities. Under the aegis of the Retired Emperors, Taira no Kiyomori conducted foreign relations from his capital at Fukuhara and developed his own institutions such as guard duty, nationwide vassalage, and perhaps even land steward-ship. In the end the Taira failed to become independent of the Court, but they heavily influenced the Kamakura Shogunate. Unlike Masakado, Minamoto no Yoritomo neither denied nor usurped earlier imperial institutions, but built his government on the foundations of the provincial headquarters. He placed consta-bles in the provincial offices to lead his men, and paid for expen-sive mounted archers by granting them land, not office. Yet even these two magnificent warrior-politicians could not guarantee the military control of all Japan; only the Mongols, another continen-tal threat like the one that confronted Temmu, could do that.

Another difference between the Western-analogue theory and the evolutionary model is the way each interpretation treats the relationship between the Chinese-style state and the Shogunate. The former explanation draws a dividing line between Taihō institutions and later feudalism. Because the Taihō system was public and civilian, so the theory goes, it must have been different from the Kamakura arrangement, which was private and military. But, as I have demonstrated, the division between public and private was meaningless in early Japan. Great aristocrats justified their private military forces through the public law codes of the eighth century, while the feudal army of the Kamakura period operated out of a civil government institution, the provincial headquarters. When one turns away from such anachronistic and artificial concepts, and instead looks at underlying institutional structures, technology, social ties, economics, and political skills, the evolutionary character of military development in early Japan becomes clear.

The continuation of many basic patterns over nearly a millennium implies that the Kamakura military owed a great debt to the Chinese-style state of the Taihō Codes, but one can arrive at such a conclusion only by correctly understanding the institutions of the eighth century. Applying the vague and rigid concepts of public and civilian of the Chinese-style state has led advocates of the Western-analogue theory to misinterpret Temmu's system as a short-lived aberration in Japanese history, lasting only a few decades. Such foreign institutions were doomed to failure because they were inapplicable to Japan and to human nature in general.[1]

Instead, the evolutionary model rests on the premise that Temmu and his heirs adapted many Chinese-style institutions to fit Japanese society, a task at which they were more successful than most Western historians have realized. But they accomplished their goals precisely because they recognized that certain fundamental patterns of Japanese society could not be altered for long, whether it meant allowing local strongmen to keep their horses and command the provincial militia, or permitting military aristocrats such as the Ōtomo to lead campaigns. The Chinese-style state lived on until 900 because it had been adapted to fit Japan reasonably well; those few institutions that were not well suited either never worked or died out relatively quickly. One could argue that in modifying the continental system the Court lost its Chinese spirit—a despotic, centralized state with vigorous imperial supervision—but that is a matter of definition.

Nor should one equate the persistence of the Chinese-style system over 200 years or the great longevity of individual institutions, especially the provincial headquarters, with an unchanging and all-powerful central government.[2] The Taihō Codes may have appeared to mandate a despotic, highly centralized government, with the power to set up a local government and military capable of lasting 500 years, but in fact Japan's level of economic development meant that eras of strong central rule would be brief and come in fits and starts.[3]

The early Japanese polity was no Roman or Han Empire. On the contrary, it was an alliance of Court aristocrats with 550 local strongmen (or district magistrates, in the Court terminology of the time), each supreme within his own region. As social and economic conditions changed in the countryside during the late eighth and the ninth centuries, the alliance between district magistrates and Court aristocrats was severed, and the Court had no alternative but to make the provincial headquarters preeminent in the Reform of 901, modifying the eighth-century institution by absorbing functions and officials from the district. Thus the Court's emphasis on the provincial headquarters as a center for drafting and organizing martial forces was really a product of the decline of the Chinese-style state of the Taihō Codes, not a sign of its potency.

The long life of the provincial headquarters as a martial center also shows the malleability of the Chinese-style institutions of the Taihō Codes.[4] The Court reinterpreted the Taihō Codes several times, the first occasion being after the Great Smallpox Epidemic of 735–737 when a short period of centralized, imperial rule came to an end. Leaders reconstituted the system once again in the late eighth century, and, when society and the economy declined even more in the 800s, the Court revised the institutions of the Taihō Codes a third time and created the Reform of 901. In the late twelfth century under a different set of circumstances, warriors also discovered that Chinese-style offices such as the provincial headquarters could be adapted to promote their own separatist goals. Social groups seeking to make changes in Japan have always tried to manipulate the old order to suit their needs.

A mistaken reading of the Chinese-style system, which stressed its civilian and public character, is only part of the problem with the Western-analogue theory; the other part is the use of the word *feudalism* to characterize twelfth- and thirteenth-century Japan. Of course, as many scholars have pointed out, there were some general parallels between Japan and Western Europe. Each region inherited its culture from cradles of civilization (Han-Tang China and the Greco-Roman world). Both areas were predisposed towards warrior rule in a semi-civilized epoch (the fourth through the sixth century), and in both cases a more centralized, imperial regime preceded the rise of the warrior. The Nara state and the Carolingian Empire each tried to copy true ancient empires and held a shadowy hegemony over their territories; both entities broke down after a short period of stronger central authority. In both societies this political fragmentation coincided with military rule, and the warrior values of a horse-riding elite became an important ethic for at least a portion of the ruling class.

But an answer to the age-old question of Western feudalism in Japan depends upon one's definition of the word. If one defines *feudalism* in a narrow sense, as an arrangement under which a grant of land is made in exchange for military service, then clearly Japan had fiefs and feudalism, certainly by the twelfth century.[5]

Yet, when this strict definition of the concept is employed, it is important to note that Japan continued to have non-feudal ways of paying for military service at the same time. In 1185 after the defeat of the Taira at the Battle of Dannoura, Yoritomo was required to issue a prohibition against his followers' going to the capital and accepting offices in the Imperial Guard.[6] Yoritomo took this offense so seriously that he stated he would punish offenders by confiscating their lands, a clear indication that these offices could eventually become bases from which to secure preferments like rank and wealth. Yoritomo had invented a new method of paying for Japan's military, and he preferred his men to owe their income and status to him alone, and not to him and the Court. But not all his soldiers saw it his way.

Even if one accepts the view that Japan had feudalism in a strict sense, I still believe that the differences are more striking than the similarities between late Heian and Kamakura Japan and medieval Western Europe. I started by defining *feudalism* as having 3 elements: a stable agrarian economy, a ruling class composed of warriors, and a predominance of ties of dependence binding members of the military class to each other.[7] I believe that twelfth- and thirteenth-century Japan lacked all three. First, along with a growing number of Japanese scholars, I doubt that Japan was a sustained, intensive agronomic order until at least the late thirteenth century, probably later.[8] Instead, erratic, non-intensive use of the land was the rule. I have detailed the agrarian problems faced by the Japanese peasant in the eighth and ninth centuries; livelihoods such as swidden farming, hunting, and fishing were common even in the late Heian and Kamakura periods.[9] William McNeill has argued that rice-growing was not preeminent in Japan until the seventeenth century.[10] The Japanese experience strongly contrasts with the history of the rich farming lands of Western Europe, which the moldboard plow and other factors turned into a home for an "agrocentric society" after 1050.[11]

Second, in a feudal society the ruling class must be military. To discuss this point, it is necessary to define the term *warrior* (*bushi*). Japanese scholars are divided on this issue, one camp seeing the *bushi* as a technical expert in warfare (*shokunō bushi*), the other as a rural landlord (*zaichi ryōshu*). Each definition has its merits: The former emphasizes the technology of war and corresponds better with the English word *warrior;* it also reveals the ancient roots of twelfth-century soldiers. The latter places emphasis of a fighting man's economic base, and leads to an analysis of the *bushi*'s ties to the peasantry.

Yet each definition has drawbacks. By defining a warrior (*bushi*) as an expert in the martial arts, one misses the important issue of how Japanese society paid for its horse-riding elite. The samurai-as-rural-landlord definition seems to solve this problem, but it has at least two shortcomings of its own. First, it presumes that all fighters had a base in land, an assumption that does not fit the evidence well, especially in western Japan. Second, it defines samurai as a class in Marxist terms, with their own consciousness struggling against the Court aristocracy. As I have remarked throughout this work, premodern Japanese social structure was probably vertical, not horizontal; the applicability of any concept of class is a much-debated topic even for modern Western nations.[12]

Recently two Japanese historians have proposed compromises to resolve the debate over the nature of the twelfth-century warrior. Ishii Susumu has combined the two definitions, stating that a warrior (*bushi*) was both a master of mounted archery and a rural landlord.[13] Amino Yoshihiko has also said that both concepts were correct, but his solution is to make a regional distinction: samurai in western Japan were experts in war, while samurai in eastern Honshu were really rural landlords.[14]

I endorse the efforts of both Ishii and Amino to reconcile the two groups of historians, but I prefer to define a warrior broadly, in such a way as to cover 4 aspects—technology, social organization, economic base, and politics, and to include fighting specialists from earlier eras. Therefore I would call a warrior anyone who specialized in the martial arts (usually mounted archery), was a member of a military house with its own economic base (often land), and/or served at one time or another as a local or national official. This definition is useful because it is specific yet comprehensive, embracing the district magistrate of the eighth century and the land steward of the thirteenth.

But even if one uses my broad definition, warriors still did not have a monopoly on political power in the late Heian and Kamakura ages. As late as the mid-thirteenth century, the civil aristocracy and religious leaders of Kyoto were significant parts of the political elite. By any definition, warriors probably numbered no more than 5,000–6,000 men throughout Japan, and their landholdings outside the Kanto were vastly inferior to those of major temples, shrines, and aristocrats. Thirteenth-century Japan had a dual polity based in Kyoto and Kamakura; the balance of eastern and western Japan continued after the Jōkyū War in 1221 until the Mongol Invasions in the late thirteenth century.

In a feudal society, ties of dependence must be prevalent and strong, especially among warriors. Yet, as indicated by the vacillation of soldiers between Kyoto and Kamakura during the Jōkyū War in 1221 (see Chapter 8), such ties were so insecure that leaders could not really count upon their men. A reward of land or office was absolutely necessary to retain the loyalty of most warriors. Jeffrey Mass has also indicated the weaknesses of late Heian and Kamakura vassalage and chieftainship.[15]

Throughout the later chapters of this book I have used the term *vassal* to refer to martial followers, but the single word masks a world of differences among fighting men. One historian has argued that there were two types of dependent ties in Heian and Kamakura Japan, relative to the vassal's degree of freedom.[16] In many cases, warriors were free to come or go as they pleased, with no real sign of dependence on their lord or lords. Of course, there were also those warriors who were absolutely subordinate, but they may well have been few in number.[17]

The use of offices within the established system of government to strengthen ties of loyalty raises a further objection to using the term *feudalism* to describe Japan. In European history, dependency was personal and non-statist, and the payoff for subordination was the fief. But in twelfth- and thirteenth-century Japan, loyalty was a public, not a personal matter; vassals of the Kamakura Shogunate in western Japan often never even saw their lord, much less swore fealty to him. The quid pro quo for many Japanese warriors was office — either in the provincial headquarters or in an estate as a land steward, from which warriors received a salary. By applying the term *feudalism* to both European and Japanese societies, one is missing the all-important distinction between two differing ties of dependence and means of rewarding subordination.

Another way to clarify the underlying differences between Japan and Western Europe is to compare the four factors of technology, social ties, economic base, and political skills in the two regions. In military technology, the two societies appear to be similar on the surface: Mounted fighters fought in small numbers in highly ritualized combat. But the similarity is only superficial, because, in their heyday (after 1050), European knights were shock troops riding large horses, wearing heavy armor and wielding lances, while Japanese equestrian fighters relied upon their swiftness and mobility on small horses and using the bow and arrow. In this respect, the Japanese samurai had more in common with other Asian modes of combat than with the European knight.

Moreover, the timing of the introduction of the stirrup and other horse gear, which made equestrian combat feasible, was different in each region. The stirrup did not enter Western Europe until the eighth century, long after fighters in that region had begun to use other weapons, whereas the Japanese had access to the same gear by 500, well before heavy influence from the Chinese. Therefore, eleventh-century Western European military technology displays a variety that seems to be absent in late Heian Japan; in medieval society in its prime, from 1150 to the early 1300s, Europeans used foot soldiers, crossbowmen, and light cavalry as well as knights. The mounted knight did not even become the predominant form of military power in Europe until well after Charlemagne, in the tenth century, while equestrian warriors decided battles in Japan as early as the seventh century. [18]

In the social realm, differences once again outweigh similarities. In Japan, lineages tracing kinship bilaterally and specializing in military matters became established early on, springing up almost as soon as horse-riding skills became widespread after A.D. 500. Intermarriage and adoption were commonly used to continue the line, and therefore there was only limited turnover in families specializing in military affairs over many centuries. The commitment to military nobility in the capital and local areas remained strong even as the names of the military aristocracy changed from the eighth to the twelfth century.

In Western Europe the break with Roman aristocracy was complete and abrupt; a new nobility based upon propinquity to the Carolingian royal house (and not military skills) came into existence in the 800s. [19] The Carolingian nobility lived on after the collapse of the Empire in the 900s, and, as military technology changed to favor the heavily armored mounted warrior, nobles began to use the military term *knight* (*miles*) to define themselves and legitimize their claims to power. Membership in the knighthood remained relatively open until the middle of the twelfth century, and the turnover in these families was much more rapid than in Japan. [20] By the late medieval period, fighters in Western Europe hailed from all social backgrounds. [21]

The contrast in economics is even more striking. In Western Europe, the rise of feudalism coincided with the opening of an entire continent. [22] Peasants developed the moldboard plow to cultivate the heavy, moist soils of England, Germany, and France; the high point of feudalism in the twelfth and thirteenth centuries saw the predominance of an agricultural economy that ended only in the Black Death of 1347–1351.

In Japan, the plow was unimportant. Iron agricultural implements and sophisticated irrigation technology were available in the 500s but took centuries to come into widespread use.[23] Yields did not increase much between 800 and 1200, and farmers opened new territory only with great difficulty. The "age of widespread land clearance" in Japan was mostly the recultivation of formerly abandoned lands. The lack of an agricultural revolution in Japan between 900 and 1200 meant that warriors had to take over lands from others, such as temples and civil aristocrats, if they were going to gain economic power. The slow pace of agricultural advance prevented the economic growth that could have supported Japanese feudalism.

Finally, politics was also fundamentally different. In Japan there was a non-military ruling class which had learned to manipulate political power, but, in Western Europe, the break with the Roman Empire was radical everywhere except Italy.[24] European fighters were not only blessed with an empty continent, but also a free hand politically; they responded by eventually absorbing other ruling elites and feudalizing monarchies. By contrast, in Japan local strongmen and military aristocrats had to serve a long apprenticeship before they could establish their own government in the Kanto, and even then they were on shaky ground. The imperial line remained important, and warriors legitimized their power through alliances with Kyoto and offices granted by the Court.

Western Europe and Japan were greatly different in the way they developed between 500 and 1300. Japan had both the technology of mounted warfare and specialized lineages early on, but warriors struggled to acquire economic and political power for centuries. In Europe, political and economic opportunities presented themselves at the outset, and then the technology of equestrian combat entered the picture. Almost as an afterthought European knights organized themselves into a noble class. The timing of all four factors was very close together in Europe, whereas in Japan the whole process took almost a millennium.

Whenever a comparison is drawn between Japan and Western

Europe, the contrasts seem to be more important than the parallels. But someone may object that all Western Europe was not feudal; less than 50 percent of the area of classical feudalism (between the Loire and the Rhine) was held in fief.[25] Could it be that comparing nations and continents blurs important distinctions, and that Japan, too, had its feudal region, that is, the Kanto? After all, the Kanto was the home to most warriors and the Shogunate, and military men collected almost all the region's revenues in the 1200s.

There seem to be two problems with likening the Kanto to Western Europe's feudal heartland. First, the powers Kamakura inherited had evolved over centuries at Court, long before the creation of the Shogunate. Second and more important, fighters, many of them mounted archers, had dominated the Kanto since the sixth century. When did the Kanto become feudal? If one chooses the most likely date, after the appearance of the Shogunate in 1185, then one gives the impression of a change much greater than actually happened. If one calls the Kanto feudal at an earlier date, then one is left to explain why warriors served and paid taxes to a distant Court.

No matter how one looks at the question of feudalism in Japan up until 1300, it is difficult to discover a satisfactory comparison. Therefore I believe it is insufficient and inaccurate to call Japan (or even the Kanto) feudal, at least before 1300. In the words of William McNeill, a well-known world historian, there are often parallels between civilizations that "may prove that there are norms in human history resulting from some kind of natural pattern of development."[26] The rise of the earliest river civilizations in the Middle East, India, and Central and South America may have such underlying similarities, but the civilizations of Japan and Western Europe between 500 and 1300 do not exemplify such a parallel.

Many Japanese historians recognize the great differences between Western Europe and Japan, and some have considered Japan's failure to establish European-style feudalism a tragedy. One specialist, for example, has spoken of "the defeat of the medieval" and "the reassertion of the ancient" in Heian Japan.[27] But one need come to this conclusion only if the course of Western European history is considered to be a paradigm. While I am wholeheartedly in favor of comparative history, devaluing Japanese history because it does not meet a Western European model serves no purpose.

If the term *feudalism* for late Heian and Kamakura Japan is inappropriate, then how should Japan be described? A Japanese critic of the Western-analogue theory has posited the evolution of a trifunctional aristocratic (*kemmon seika; kemmon taisei*) society over the period 1050–1300.[28] His use of the word *aristocratic* has appeal, because it implies a relatively small elite, dependent upon an economy that produced only a small surplus.

Employing the term *aristocratic state* also underlines the basic continuity of Japanese history between 500 and 1300. From 500 to 650, the elite looked to Korea as a model. From 650 to 900, adulation of China was the rule. From 900 to 1050, there was a synthesis of outside systems to fit changing Japanese experience. Beginning in 1050 to 1300, the elite evolved into three segments working together (a trifunctional unit): a civil aristocracy to make appointments and perform Court ceremonies, both of which legitimized the ruling class; Buddhist and Shinto leaders to carry out religious tasks; and a military aristocracy to handle police and military matters. Besides maintaining its own function, each segment of the elite had its own military forces, bureaucracy, and capital.

Of course, the aristocratic model has its drawbacks, especially since the creator defines the trifunctional elite after 1050 as the first stage of feudal Japan, again invoking a questionable Western model.[29] Furthermore, as one specialist has noted, the aristocratic interpretation may give the impression of political centralization, despite evidence of growing fragmentation, pluralism, and regionalism, between 750 and 1250.[30] Yoritomo's movement to establish the Kamakura government can be seen as the climax of all three trends.

One of the most important contributions of the aristocratic interpretation is to place the Kamakura period in its proper context. Japanese historians have long seen 1185 as the starting point for medieval Japan, the beginning of a whole new stage of history that lasted until Hideyoshi's dramatic reforms in the sixteenth century. But, although this traditional view has merit, the Kamakura epoch was more than just the start of something new: It was also a conclusion, really the last phase of the Chinese-style system (defined broadly) in Japan. The Kamakura era was the end of a great demographic and economic trend that had begun with the introduction of rice cultivation in the Yayoi epoch (300 B.C.–A.D. 300).[31] Institutionally as well, the Kamakura era had more in common with what had preceded it than with what came after. Yoritomo relied on the provincial headquarters and other aspects of Chinese-style government, changed though they were over 500 years.

In founding his Shogunate in the Kanto, Yoritomo drew from five centuries of military expertise and organization that started with the Emperor Temmu's dictum that in government military matters are essential. Faced with a national emergency, the Emperor Temmu had emphasized martial affairs and thus created the possibility for Yoritomo, centuries later, to become the "chief of all warriors" and head of a government exclusively for his own fighting men. By establishing his Shogunate, Yoritomo fulfilled the promise that began in the reign of the Heavenly Warrior Emperor.

Appendix Tables

Table 1. RESOURCES USED IN THE WARS IN THE
NORTHEAST: MEN

Date	Destination	Type	Number	Origins
709/3	Mutsu, Echigo	Soldiers		Tōtōmi, Suruga, Kai, Shinano, Kōzuke, Echizen, Etchū, Hitachi, Mutsu, Echigo
720/11	Mutsu, Dewa	Soldiers		Tōtōmi, Hitachi, Mino, Musashi, Echizen, Dewa
724/4		Army	30,000	9 provinces in eastern Honshu
737/4	Mutsu	Horsemen	1000	Hitachi, Kazusa, Shimōsa, Kōzuke, Shimotsuke, Musashi
		Guards (*chimpei*)	499	Mutsu
		Soldiers	5000	Friendly *emishi*
			249	Dewa
		Soldiers	500	Friendly *emishi*
			140	Kanto and Others
758/12	Ft. Monofu, Ft. Okachi	Horsemen		8 provinces in Kanto Friendly *emishi*
759/11	Mutsu	Soldiers	2000 or less per prov.	
767/10	Ft. Iji			Musashi, Sagami, Kōzuke, Shimotsuke
775/10	Dewa	Soldiers		Mutsu
776/2	Mountain and Sea Routes	Soldiers	20,000	Dewa
		Soldiers	4000	Hitachi, Shimōsa, Shimotsuke
/5		Horsemen		Mutsu
/11	Izawa	Army	3000	Mutsu
780/2	Mutsu	Soldiers	3000	

Table 1 (Continued)

Date	Destination	Type	Number	Origins
780/3	Ft. Kakubetsu	Friendly emishi		
/5	Military Post	Special soldiers		
/7		Draft soldiers		Kanto
783/6		Prepare soldiers	500–1000	8 provinces in Kanto
786/8		Inspect soldiers		Tōkaidō & Tōsandō
788/3		Horsemen & foot soldiers	52,800	Tōkaidō, Tōsandō, & Kanto
791/1		Soldiers		Tōkaidō & Tōsandō
794	Izawa	Soldiers	100,000	
801	Izawa, Hei	Soldiers	40,000	
811/3	Nisate, Hei	Friendly emishi	300	
/5		Soldiers	19,500	
/7		Friendly emishi	1000	
/10		Soldiers	1100	Mutsu

Table 2. RESOURCES USED IN THE WARS IN THE NORTHEAST: MATÉRIEL

Date	Destination	Item	Amount	Origin
709/7	Dewa Palisade	Weapons		Various provinces
	Dewa	Boats	100	Echizen, Echigo, Etchū, Sado
724/4	Mutsu	Cloth	17,200 units	9 provinces in eastern Honshu
		Weapons, tents, dishes		All provinces
759/9	Ft. Okachi, Monofu	Weapons		Sagami, Kazusa, Kōzuke, Shimōsa, Hitachi, Musashi, Shimotsuke
760/3	Ft. Akita	Rice		Echizen
775/5	Mutsu	Cloth for uniforms	10,000 units	Capital, Sagami, Kai
776/7	Mutsu	Boats	50	Awa, Kazusa, Shimōsa, Hitachi
777/5	Dewa	Armor	200 units	Sagami, Musashi, Shimōsa, Shimotsuke, Echigo
780/5	Dewa	Armor	600 units	Capital, various provinces
		Dried Rice	30,000 bushels	Kanto, Noto, Etchū, Echigo
/7		Uniforms	4000 units	Provinces of Tōkaidō and Tōsandō
	Mutsu	Armor	1000 units	Owari, Mikawa, and three other provinces
	Mutsu	Dried rice	16,000 bushels	Shimōsa, Hitachi
781/2	Mutsu	Grain	100,000 bushels	Sagami, Awa, Musashi, Kazusa, Shimōsa
/10	Mutsu	Grain		Owari, Kai, Echigo, Sagami, Hitachi

Table 2 (Continued)

Date	Destination	Item	Amount	Origin
783/4	Mutsu	Grain		8 provinces of Kanto
786/8		Weapons inspection		Tōkaidō & Tōsandō
788/3	Ft. Taga	Grain	35,000 bushels	Mutsu
	Mutsu	Dried rice, salt	23,000 bushels	Tōkaidō, Tōsandō, Hokurikudō
790/ Int.3		Leather armor	2000 units	Tōkaidō east of Suruga; Tōsandō east of Shinano
		Dried rice	140,000 bushels	Tōkaidō east of Sagami; Tōsandō east of Kōzuke
/10		Armor		Nationwide
791/1		Weapons inspection		Tōkaidō & Tōsandō
/3		Armor production		High officials
/6		Iron armor repair	3000 units	Various provinces
/10		Arrow production	34,500	Tōkaidō & Tōsandō
/11		Dried rice	120,000 bushels	Kanto
802/1	Ft. Okachi	Rice	Annually 10,600 b.	Echigo
		Salt	Annually 120 bushels	Sado
803/2	Ft. Shiwa	Rice	30 bushels	Echigo
		Salt	30 bushels	Echigo

Table 2 (Continued)

Date	Destination	Item	Amount	Origin
804/1	Nakayama Palisade	Dried grain & rice	14,315 bushels	
809/6	Mutsu			Convenient provinces
810/5	Mutsu	Rice		Kanto
813/9	Mutsu & Dewa			Shinano, Echigo

Source: Hirakawa Minami, "Tōhoku dai sensō jidai," in Takahashi Takashi, ed., Kodai no chihō shi 6 Ōu hen, pp. 176–179.

Table 3. NUMBERS OF STRONG FELLOWS (*KONDEI*) IN JAPAN, 792–905

Province	792 Order	Engi Ordinances (905)
Yamato	30	70
Kawachi	30	30
Izumi	20	20
Settsu	30	30
Yamashiro	30	40
The Kinai	140	190
Iga	30	30
Ise	100	100
Shima	—	30
Owari	50	50
Mikawa	30	50
Tōtōmi	60	60
Suruga	50	50
Izu	30	30
Kai	30	50
Sagami	100	100
Musashi	105	150
Awa	30	30
Kazusa	100	100
Shimōsa	150	150
Hitachi	200	200
Tōkaidō	1065	1180
Ōmi	200	200
Mino	100	100
Hida	—	30
Shinano	100	100
Kōzuke	100	100
Shimotsuke	100	100
Mutsu	—	324
Dewa	—	100
Tōsandō	600	1054
Wakasa	30	30
Echizen	100	100
Kaga	—	50
Noto	50	50
Etchū	50	50

Table 3 (Continued)

Province	792 Order	Engi Ordinances (905)
Echigo	100	100
Sado	—	30
Hokurikudō	330	410
Tamba	50	50
Tango	30	30
Tajima	50	50
Inaba	50	50
Hōki	50	50
Izumo	100	100
Iwami	30	30
Oki	30	30
San'indō	390	390
Harima	100	100
Mimasaka	50	50
Bizen	50	50
Bitchū	50	50
Bingo	50	50
Aki	30	40
Suō	30	50
Nagato	50	50
San'yōdō	410	440
Kii	30	60
Awaji	30	30
Awa	30	30
Sanuki	50	100
Iyo	50	50
Tosa	30	30
Nankaidō	220	300
GRAND TOTAL	3,165	3,864

Source: SZKT, Ruijū sandai kyaku, Enryaku 11/6/14 Order of the Council of State, pp. 558–559; SZKT, Engi hyōbu shō shiki, pp. 707–708.

Table 4. TAIRA MILITARY EXPEDITIONS, 1177–1180

No.	Date	Object	Commander and Organization
1.	1177/5/28	Enryakuji monks	Discussion between Kiyomori and Go-Shirakawa
2.	1177/6/1	Fujiwara no Narichika and other Go-Shirakawa confidantes	Kiyomori
3.	1177/6/9	Kaga governor	Vassals of Kiyomori in Owari
4.	1179/7/25	Enryakuji monks	Kiyomori's Pursue-and-Punish Force
5.	1179/10/3	Ōmi monks	State troops and private vassals
6.	1179/10/19	Enryakuji monks	State troops under Taira no Tomomori and Tsunemori
7.	1179/11/14	Go-Shirakawa and his favorites	Kiyomori and several thousand soldiers
8.	1180/5/21	Monks of Miidera and Mochihito	Munemori and others
9.	1180/5/26	Minamoto no Yorimasa; Mochihito; Miidera monks	Investigators; later Shigehira and Koremori
10.	Before 1180/8/2	Yoritomo	Kiyomori's personal retainer Ōba Kagechika
11.	Before 1180/9	Minamoto vassals in eastern Honshu	Nitta Yoshishige on Munemori's order
12.	1180/9/5	Yoritomo	Pursue-and-Punish troops led by Taira no Koremori and others; warriors of the Tōkadō and Tōsandō
13.	1180/9/19	Rebels of Kyushu	Kiyomori's personal vassals
14.	1180/11/7	Yoritomo and Minamoto no Nobuyoshi	Warriors of Mino, the Tōkadō, Tōsandō, and Hokunkudō led by Pursue-and-Punish Generalsi Yorimori and others

Table 4 (Continued)

No.	Date	Object	Commander and Organization
15.	1180/11/12	Mino Minamoto	Kiyomori vassals followed by a Pursue-and-Punish Force
16.	1180/12/1	Ōmi bandits	Troops of Iga and Ise
17.	1180/12/2	Eastern bandits of Mino and Ōmi	Pursue-and-Punish Force led by Sukemori and others
18.	1180/12/9–10	Monks of Miidera and Enryakuji	State force and others
19.	1180/12/22	Nara monks	Yamato and Kawachi residents
20.	1180/12/25	Nara monks	Pursue-and-Punish Force led by Shigehira

Source: Gomi Fumihiko, "Heishi gunsei no shodankai," *Shigaku zasshi* 88:1–36 (August 1979).

Table 5. FIGURES FOR ARMIES DURING THE GREAT CIVIL WAR OF 1180–1185

| | *Source* | | | | | |
Battle	GY	AK	HEI	SK	K	HRS
Uji	300v50	20,000	28,000	200v50		
Ishibashi	2000v500	3000v300	1000v300			
Fujikawa	5000v several 10,000	200,000*	70,000v 200,000	1000v several 10,000		
Ōmi	3000v 5000	1000s				
Sunomata	13,000v 3000 or 5000	690 dead*				3000; 690 dead*
Expedition against Yoshinaka	5-6000; 4-500 in capital		3000 in capital			
Yokotagawara			40,000v 3000			
Kurikara	40,000v 5000		100,000v 50,000			100,000
Taira loss of capital	1080; some say 7-8000					
Mizushima			1000v 7000			
Bizen			2000v 3000			
Yoritomo to capital		50,000*				
Hōjūji			20,000v 7000Y			
Defeat of Yoshinaka	5000;* 270*					
Yukiie v. Taira					300v 300	
Mikusa			3000v 10,000			

Table 5 (Continued)

Battle			Source			
	GY	AK	HEI	SK	K	HRS
Ichinotani	20,000v		7000v			
	2–3000		60,000			
Yashima	2–3000					
Shido	100	80*	80*			
Dannoura		500v	1000v			
		840 boats	3000			
			boats			

Key: Taira forces are given first. An asterisk indicates the Minamoto, and Y indicates Yoshinaka.

Sources: GY-*Gyokuyō;* AK-*Azuma kagami;* HEI-*The Tale of the Heike;* SK-*Sankai ki;* K-*Kikki;* HRS-*Hyakuren shō.*

Notes
Bibliography
Glossary
Index

Abbreviations Used in the Notes

DNK	*Dai Nihon komonjo*
DNKK	*Dai Nihon kokiroku*
DNS	*Dai Nihon shiryō*
HI	*Heian ibun*
KI	*Kamakura ibun*
NKBT	*Nihon koten bungaku taikei*
NST	*Nihon shisō taikei*
OCS	Order of the Council of State
SZKT	*Shintei zōho kokushi taikei*
ZST	*Zōho shiryō taisei*

Notes

INTRODUCTION

1. The word *samurai* is employed here in a general way to mean the horse-riding fighters of late Heian and medieval Japan. But in Japanese it also has a different meaning: "one who serves" or "one who attends" the high-born aristocracy. In early Japan after the adoption of Chinese-style Court ranks, the nobility occupied the first 5 rungs in the Court bureaucracy. Those holding the 6th Court Rank ministered to their betters in many forms, as soldiers, artisans, scribes, and messengers. Thus, technically not all warriors were samurai, nor were all samurai soldiers. See Tanaka Minoru, "Samurai bonge kō."

2. Ishii Susumu, "Chūsei shakai ron," p. 320. I borrowed the term *Western-analogue theory* from a discussion of the Meiji Restoration in Thomas Smith, "Japan's Aristocratic Revolution."

The Western-analogue theory is meant as a general characterization of most English works, and I do not have a particular author in mind. If pressed, I would cite E. O. Reischauer and A. Craig, *Japan: Tradition and Transformation*, pp. 1–49, or Peter Duus, *Feudalism in Japan*, as examples. Jeffrey Mass, *Warrior Government in Early Medieval Japan*, pp. 227–229, draws parallels between Yoritomo's feudalism (1180s) and the Carolingians (800s), implying that Japan was on the same track of historical development as Western Europe, but at a later time. Also see Mass, "The Early Bakufu and Feudalism."

The Western-analogue theory derives from two sources. One is the work of Asakawa Kan'ichi, a towering figure whose ideas permeate most Western writing on Japan. See, for example, "Some Aspects of Japanese Feudal Institutions." Second, prewar Japanese scholars such as Ōmori Kingorō, *Buke jidai no kenkyū*, and Hara Katsuo, *Nihon chūsei shi no kenkyū*, also developed this theory. For brief discussions of these works, see Sakamoto Shōzō, *Nihon no rekishi 6 Sekkan jidai*, pp. 342–346; and Yasuda Motohisa, "Bushi dan no keisei," pp. 124–125. Although most postwar Japanese historians have abandoned the Western-analogue theory, Western historians have generally not followed suit.

A few English-speaking authors have been uncomfortable with the Western-analogue theory, including John Hall, *Government and Local Power in Japan, 500 to 1700*, pp. 19–90, and "Feudalism in Japan—A Reassessment," pp. 39–41. But Hall uses the term *feudalism* to describe the Kamakura Shogunate and sets up the dichotomy between public and private. For another critique of the term *feudalism*, see Conrad Totman, "English-Language Studies of Medieval Japan: An Assessment."

Despite these doubts and criticisms of the last 25 years, the Western-analogue theory is still the most widely employed explanation in English of the rise of the warrior. Recently, see Martin Collcutt, "Daimyo and Daimyo Culture," pp. 1-7.

3. Yasuda Motohisa, *Nihon no rekishi 7 Insei to Heishi*, pp. 206-208.

4. On the age of widespread land clearance, see Tōda Yoshimi, *Nihon ryōshu sei seiritsu shi no kenkyū*, pp. 326ff., and Inagaki Yasuhiko, *Nihon chūsei shakai shi ron*, pp. 3-31. On the new class of proprietors, see Ishimoda Shō, *Kodai makki seiji shi josetsu*, pp. 26-40, 134-160, 182-196, and more recently Fukuda Toyohiko, *Chiba Tsunetane*, pp. 61-95.

5. On the terms *mononofu* and *tsuwamono*, see Sasayama Haruo, "Bunken ni mirareru senjutsu to buki."

6. Kuroda Toshio, *Nihon chūsei kokka to shūkyō*, pp. 16-23, and Takahashi Masaaki, "Kihei to suihei," pp. 68-69, are among those who describe the samurai as a specialist in mounted warfare.

7. Yasuda Motohisa, *Nihon shoki hōken sei no kiso kenkyū*, pp. 43-50, 173-229, 322-353; Nagahara Keiji, *Nihon hōken sei seiritsu katei no kenkyū*, pp. 489-502, and Ishimoda Shō, *Kodai makki*, pp. 134-160, and Ishimoda, *Chūseiteki sekai no keisei*, pp. 102-175, define the warrior (*bushi*) as a class of proprietors. (The evidence of these scholars from the Kanto region is drawn from the 14th-century handbook called the *Sata miren sho*.)

8. Ishii Susumu, *Nihon no rekishi 12 Chūsei bushi dan*, pp. 235-236, takes a middle position by defining the *bushi* as both a fighter and a landholder. Also note the discussion in Fukuda Toyohiko, "Ōchō gunji kikō to nairan," p. 117.

9. Elizabeth Brown, "The Tyranny of a Construct: Feudalism and the Historians of Feudal Europe," is highly critical of historians who use the term *feudalism* to describe Western Europe. Rushton Coulborn, ed., *Feudalism in History*, was an ambitious and largely unsuccessful attempt to define and apply the concept of feudalism in world history. For more on this problem, see note 2.

10. My definition of *feudalism* is essentially the same as Marc Bloch's in *Feudal Society*, II, 446.

11. Robert O'Connell, *Of Arms and Men*, p. 13.

12. Jacob Bronowski, *The Ascent of Man*, pp. 79-89.

13. William McNeill, *Plagues and Peoples*, pp. 47-48.

14. O'Connell, pp. 15-18.

15. Recent analyses of warfare and the military include O'Connell, *Arms;* William McNeill, *The Pursuit of Power*, and Martin Van Creveld, *Technology and War*.

16. O'Connell, pp. 7-9.

17. Ibid., p. 85.

CHAPTER ONE

1. Okamoto Isamu, "Genshi shakai no seisan to jujutsu," p. 82.

2. Gotō Shūichi, "Jōmon shiki bunka," p. 140.

3. Okamoto Isamu, p. 82, on arrowheads; Suenaga Masao, *Nihon buki gaisetsu,* p. 67.

4. Okamoto Isamu, p. 83.

5. Ibid., p. 84.

6. Takahashi Masaaki, "Kihei to suihei," p. 89.

7. Gotō, p. 140.

8. Okamoto Isamu, p. 85.

9. Sahara Makoto, "Nōgyō no kaishi to kaikyū shakai no keisei," p. 159.

10. Kawagoe Tetsushi, "Kinzoku ki no seisaku to gijutsu," in Sahara Makoto and Kanaseki Hiroshi, eds., *Kodai shi hakkutsu 4 Inasaku no hajimari,* p. 111.

11. O'Connell, pp. 46–49.

12. Sahara, p. 164.

13. Kondō Kyōichi, "Buki kara saiki e," in Higuchi Takayasu, ed., *Kodai shi hakkutsu 5 Tairiku bunka to seidoki,* pp. 69–77.

14. Kawagoe, "Kinzoku ki," p. 110–111.

15. Naoki Kōjirō, *Nihon no rekishi 1 Wakoku no tanjō,* p. 311.

16. Sahara, p. 158; Naoki, *Wakoku,* pp. 168–171; Inoue Mitsusada, *Nihon no rekishi 1 Shinwa kara rekishi e,* pp. 199–201.

17. On the destruction of Iron-Age villages, see *Inasaku no hajimari,* pp. 10–11; and Sahara, pp. 161–162. On the Civil War in Japan, see Inoue Mitsusada, *Shinwa kara,* pp. 199–201, 204–206; Wm. Theodore de Bary, et al., eds., *Sources of Japanese Tradition,* I, pp. 4–7.

18. *Inasaku no hajimari,* p. 17.

19. On Iron-Age boats, see Kishi Toshio, *Nihon kodai seiji shi kenkyū,* p. 123.

20. Inoue Mitsusada, *Shinwa kara,* p. 201.

21. Early Japanese-Korean relations are a controversial topic. Some historians, notably Egami Namio and Gari Ledyard, have argued that Japan was conquered by northeast Asian nomads in the 400s, but neither archeological nor written sources clearly support their position. See Gari Ledyard, "Galloping Along with the Horseriders: Looking for the Founders of Japan." For a critique of Ledyard's position, see Walter Edwards, "Event and Process in the Founding of Japan: The Horserider Theory in Archeological Perspective." Also note J. Edward Kidder, Jr., "The Archeology of the Early Horse-riders in Japan"; Kidder, "The Fujinoki Tomb and its Grave-Goods"; Kidder, "Saddle Bows and Rump Plumes — More on the Fujinoki Tomb." See also Roy Miller, "Linguistic Evidence and Japanese Prehistory," pp. 101–120. For standard Japanese views of Japanese-Korean relations, see Inoue Mitsusada, *Shinwa kara,* pp. 248–519; Inoue Mitsusada, *Nihon no rekishi 3 Asuka no chōtei,* pp. 36–137; and Hirano Kunio, "Yamato ōken to Chōsen," pp. 227–272. Hirano's article also contains numerous citations of Korean scholarship.

22. Inoue Mitsusada, *Shinwa kara,* p. 214; Naoki Kōjirō, *Nihon kodai heisei shi no kenkyū,* pp. 192–196; and Sasayama Haruo, *Kodai kokka to guntai,* pp. 14–19.

23. O'Connell, pp. 84–89.

24. On the introduction of the pike to Japanese warfare, see Satō Shin'ichi, *Nihon no rekishi* 9 *Namboku chō no dōran*, pp. 193–199.

25. William McNeill, *A History of the Human Community: I Prehistory to 1500*, p. 104.

26. Ibid., p. 72.

27. Lynn White, *Medieval Technology and Social Change*, pp. 57–69.

28. The following summary is taken from Hayashida Shigeyoshi, "Nihon zairai uma no genryū."

29. Ibid., pp. 236–240.

30. Korean horse riders seem to have armored their horses. See Kidder, "Saddle Bows," pp. 80–85; "Grave-Goods," pp. 69–70, 79–81. Kidder also notes some evidence for Japanese horse armor, but concludes that it was mostly ornamental.

31. Naoki, *Kodai heisei*, pp. 192–196; 201–207.

32. For example, see *Nihon koten bungaku taikei* (hereafter *NKBT*), *Nihon shoki*, I, Richū 5/9/18, p. 427; translation from W. G. Aston, *Nihongi, Chronicles of Japan from the Earliest Times to* A.D. *697*, I, 307.

33. Yamada Yoshimi, "Kofun shutsudo no bagu"; also note Naoki, *Kodai heisei*, pp. 201–207; and Inoue Mitsusada, *Shinwa kara*, pp. 288–289.

34. White, pp. 14–16.

35. Onoyama Setsu, "Bagu," in Onoyama Setsu, ed., *Kodai shi hakkutsu 6 Kofun to kokka no naritachi*, p. 83, for the bit; Yamada, "Bagu," p. 35, cites the saddle.

36. Mori Kōichi, "Kōkogaku to uma," p. 85.

37. Amino Yoshihiko, *Higashi to nishi no kataru Nihon no rekishi*, pp. 71–72.

38. Sasayama, *Guntai*, p. 20.

39. Suenaga, pp. 5–6.

40. Kobayashi Ken'ichi, "Yumiya to katchū no hensen," in Onoyama Setsu, ed., *Kodai shi hakkutsu 6 Kofun to kokka no naritachi*, pp. 98–102.

41. Sasayama, *Guntai*, p. 18.

42. *NKBT, Nihon shoki*, I, Yūryaku pre-accession annals, pp. 459–461; *Nihongi*, I, 336.

43. *NKBT, Nihon shoki*, II, Kimmei 14/8/7, pp. 105–106; *Nihongi*, II, 70.

44. Inoue Mitsusada, *Shinwa kara*, pp. 126–132.

45. The following discussion is based on Suenaga, pp. 8–11, 21–25, 44–48, 60–62, 66–68, 70–71, 79–91, 124–126; Ueda Hironori, "Nihon kodai no buki"; Kobayashi Ken'ichi, "Katchū," in Onoyama Setsu, ed., *Kodai shi hakkutsu 6 Kofun to kokka no naritachi*, pp. 78–79, 98–111; and Onoyama, "Bagu," pp. 80–83.

46. On the question of artisans, see the speculative essay by Onoyama Setsu, "Bagu no seisaku to kōjin no ugoki," in Onoyama, ed., *Kodai shi hakkutsu 6 Kofun to kokka no naritachi*, pp. 138–142.

47. Sasayama, *Guntai*, p. 19.

48. See, for example, *NKBT, Nihon shoki*, II, Kimmei 14/10/20, pp. 107–108; *Nihongi*, II, 70.

49. *NKBT, Nihon shoki*, II, Kimmei 14/10/20, pp. 107–108; *Nihongi*, II, 71.

50. Sasayama, *Guntai*, pp. 19–20.

51. *NKBT, Nihon shoki*, I, Yūryaku 18/8/10, pp. 495–497; *Nihongi*, I, 365–366.

My discussion of group tactics agrees with Sasayama Haruo, "Bunken ni mirareru senjutsu to buki," pp. 132-134.

52. For an example of a Korean fortress, see *NKBT, Nihon shoki,* II, Kimmei 5/11, pp. 89-91; *Nihongi,* II, 57. A discussion of Korean fortifications may be found in Kagamiyama Takeshi, *Kōkogaku Raiburari-4 Dazaifu iseki,* pp. 79-81.

53. Kishi, *Kodai seiji,* pp. 116-131.

54. Conrad Totman, *The Green Archipelago,* p. 10; Inoue Mitsusada, *Shinwa kara,* p. 398.

55. Takahashi Masaaki, "Kihei," pp. 85-86; Otomasu Shigetaka, "Chōkoku to saishiki hekiga," in Otomasu, ed., *Kodai shi hakkutsu 8 Sōshoku kofun to mon'yō,* p. 116. On ship construction in the period before 645, also see Shimizu Junzō, "Nihon kodai no fune," pp. 66-71. Most of the following discussion of early ship construction is based on Takahashi.

56. *Sōshoku kofun to mon'yō,* p. 14; Inoue Mitsusada, *Shinwa kara,* p. 398.

57. *NKBT, Nihon shoki,* II, Kimmei 15/1/9, pp. 109-110; *Nihongi,* II, 72.

58. *NKBT, Nihon shoki,* II, Suiko 10/2/1, pp. 178-179; *Nihongi,* II, 125-126.

59. On the number of states (*kuni*) in Japan in the early 7th century, see *Sui shu,* VI, 1826; and Niino Naoyoshi, *Kenkyū shi: kuni no miyatsuko,* pp. 91-93. For an example of the appointment of a local strongman, see *NKBT, Nihon shoki,* II, Ankan 1/Int. 12/4, pp. 54-55; *Nihongi,* II, 31.

Defining a term like *local strongman* is difficult. This phrase is inherently vague, as Aoki Kazuo, *Nihon no rekishi 5 Kodai gozoku,* pp. 16-23, admits. My usage follows Japanese scholars who employ terms such as *gōzoku* or *dogō.*

60. Naoki, *Kodai heisei,* pp. 180-181.

61. According to *Shintei zōho kokushi taikei* (hereafter *SZKT*), *Senjo-ryō no gige, Gunji no jō,* pp. 139-140, local strongmen (*kuni no miyatsuko*) of the pre-645 era were appointed to be district magistrates in the 8th century. In 792 (Enryaku 11/6/14), a government order found in *SZKT, Ruiju sandai kyaku,* pp. 558-559, required that members of the same families of district officials be named to military positions as "Strong Fellows" (Kondei). The Strong Fellows were all horsemen. See Chapters 2 and 3.

62. *NKBT, Nihon shoki,* II, Keitai 21/6/3, p. 34; *Nihongi,* II, 15.

63. Ibid., II, Keitai 21/6/3, pp. 34-35; *Nihongi,* II, 15.

64. Ibid., II, Keitai 22/11/11, pp. 36-37; *Nihongi,* II, 16-17.

65. Inoue Mitsusada, *Nihon kodai shi no shomondai,* pp. 101-184, first analyzed these royal military units. Slight revisions made on Inoue's initial work by other scholars are summarized nicely in Sasayama Haruo, "Nihon kodai no gunji soshiki," pp. 308-313.

66. Sasayama, *Guntai,* pp. 41-44, dates the origins of the quiver-bearers later, in the 500s.

67. *NKBT, Nihon shoki,* I, Keikō 40/10/7, pp. 306-307; *Nihongi,* I, 207.

68. Ibid., II, Kōgyoku 2/11/1, p. 250; *Nihongi,* II, 182.

69. *NKBT, Nihon shoki,* Kōgyoku 2/11/1, pp. 250-251; *Nihongi,* II, 182.

70. Naoki, *Kodai heisei,* pp. 113-118.

71. Inoue Mitsusada, *Shomondai,* pp. 171–182.

72. Amino, *Higashi to nishi,* p. 64. On the sword, see Anazawa Wakō and Manome Jun'ichi, "Two Inscribed Swords from Japanese Tumuli: Discoveries and Research on Finds from the Sakitama-Inariyama and Eta-Funayama Tumuli," pp. 375–396.

73. Ishii Ryōsuke, *Taika no kaishin to Kamakura bakufu no seiritsu,* pp. 52–66, 72–78; Amino, *Higashi to nishi,* pp. 59–69.

74. *NKBT, Nihon shoki,* II, Buretsu 11/8, pp. 10–11; *Nihongi,* I, 402.

75. Ibid., II, Suiko 34/5/20, pp. 212–213; *Nihongi,* II, 154.

76. Ibid., II, Kōgyoku 3/11, pp. 260–261; *Nihongi,* II, 189–190.

77. Naoki, *Kodai heisei,* pp. 117–118, discusses the supplies and cooks. Hirano Kunio, cited in Sasayama, "Gunji soshiki," p. 311, raises the possibility of salaries for royal retainers.

CHAPTER 2

1. The relationship between the Tang invasion and the Korean coups is posited by Inoue Mitsusada, "Taika no kaishin to higashi Ajia," pp. 134–136. Later, on pp. 136–139, Inoue discusses the factions at the Japanese Court and their views of the international situation; my argument on the palace revolution of 645 is derived from Inoue's work. For a simple version of his argument, see Inoue Mitsusada, *Nihon no rekishi 3 Asuka no chōtei,* pp. 275–291. On the politics of this period, also see William Wayne Farris, *Population, Disease, and Land in Early Japan, 645–900,* pp. 8–17.

2. *NKBT, Nihon shoki,* II, Taika 1/8/5, pp. 274–275; William Aston, tr., *Nihongi, Chronicles of Japan from the Earliest Times to A.D. 697,* II, 200–201. Slight alterations have been made in Aston's translation. *NKBT, Nihon shoki,* II, Taika 2/3/2, pp. 286–287; *Nihongi,* II, 212, shows that there were 8 governors.

3. *NKBT, Nihon shoki,* II, Taika 1/9/1, pp. 276–277; *Nihongi,* II, 203–204.

4. *NKBT, Hitachi fudoki,* p. 34.

5. There is some disagreement among Japanese historians about when the governors general were established, and how they were related to the governors (*kuni no mikotomochi*) of 645. Inoue Mitsusada, "Taika no kaishin," p. 140, and Ishii Ryōsuke, p. 74, believe that the governors general were identical to the *kuni no mikotomochi* dispatched in 645. Hayakawa Shōhachi, "Ritsuryō sei no keisei," p. 223, feels that the governors general were new officials named to their posts some time after the *kuni no mikotomochi.* Bruce Batten, "Foreign Threat and Domestic Reform," pp. 204–205, and Amino, *Higashi to nishi,* p. 61, have expressed approval of Hayakawa's position. *NKBT, Nihon shoki,* II, Taika 2/3/2, pp. 286–287; *Nihongi,* II, 212, indicates that at least 2 governors (*kuni no mikotomochi*) were dismissed in 646. Thus I follow the more recent work of Hayakawa.

6. Ishii Ryōsuke, pp. 53–54, 72–78; Amino, *Higashi to nishi,* pp. 60–66.

7. Inoue Mitsusada, "Taika no kaishin," pp. 150–152.

8. Yoneda Yūsuke, "Ritsuryōteki gundan no seiritsu sairon," pp. 164–170, dis-

cusses this new unit. My understanding of the evolution of the district follows Hara Hidesaburō, "Gunji to chihō gōzoku," pp. 203-213.

9. The authenticity of the 646 order is open to doubt. The first modern scholar to express doubt about the Taika Reform Edict was Tsuda Sōkichi, *Nihon jōdai shi no kenkyū*, pp. 221-224. Some recent historians who reject the edict outright include Hara Hidesaburō, "Taika no kaishin ron hihan josetsu," and Kadowaki Teiji, *"Taika no kaishin" ron*. I follow the argument of Inoue Mitsusada, "Taika no kaishin," pp. 142-152, who suggests that, while many phrases of the edict were doctored to match later records, some sections reflect neither the wording of the Taihō Codes of 702 nor the text of later Chinese pronouncements. Therefore the Taika Reform Edict probably existed in some form.

10. *NKBT, Nihon shoki*, II, Taika 2/1, pp. 280-283; *Nihongi*, II, 206, 209.

11. On the origin of the border guards, see Sasayama, "Nihon kodai no gunji soshiki," p. 326.

12. Inoue Mitsusada, "Taika no kaishin," p. 146; *NKBT, Nihon shoki*, II, 282-283.

13. Inoue Mitsusada, "Taika no kaishin," pp. 158-159.

14. Ibid., pp. 161-162. For more information on troop organization, see *Shintei zōho kokushi taikei* (hereafter *SZKT*), *Shoku Nihongi*, Keiun 4/5/26, p. 28; *NKBT, Nihon ryōiki*, pp. 90-91.

15. Inoue Mitsusada, "Taika no kaishin," p. 161.

16. *NKBT, Nihon shoki*, II, Tenji 2/8/17, p. 286; *Nihongi*, II, 279-280.

17. Inoue Mitsuada, "Taika no kaishin," p. 161. Also note the *Jiu Tang shu*, VIII, 2791-2792.

18. "Struggling to be first" to take the head of a rival was a common custom among the samurai of the 12th century. See Helen McCullough, *The Tale of the Heike*, pp. 286-288.

19. On the problem of command in Korea, see Muraoka Kaoru, "Ritsuryō kokka to gunji soshiki."

20. *NKBT, Nihon shoki*, II, Tenji 10/11/10, pp. 378-379; *Nihongi*, II, 297-298.

21. *NKBT, Nihon shoki*, II, Tenji 3/2/9, pp. 360-361. For a discussion of the reforms undertaken by the Emperor Tenji, see Inoue Mitsusada, "Taika no kaishin," pp. 163-165, and Hara Hidesaburō, "Taika no kaishin ron," pp. 31-43.

22. The fortifications in northern Kyushu are discussed in detail in Kagamiyama, pp. 27-114. Kagamiyama notes the likelihood of a moat on pp. 70-73.

23. Japanese historians debate whether or not Prince Ōtomo ever actually assumed the throne. I follow Inoue Mitsusada, *Asuka no chōtei*, p. 427, who argues that he did not.

24. Literature on the Civil War of 672 is plentiful. A good place to start is Hoshino Ryōsaku, *Kenkyū shi: Jinshin no ran*, pp. 244-305. My description is drawn mostly from Inoue Mitsusada, *Asuka no chōtei*, pp. 421-445. Also note Naoki Kōjirō, *Jinshin no ran*, pp. 90-201, and Kameda Takashi, *Jinshin no ran*, pp. 88-183.

25. Inoue Mitsusada, *Asuka no chōtei*, pp. 438-440.

26. Mizuno Yū, "Jinshin no ran," p. 199.

27. *NKBT, Nihon shoki,* II, Temmu 1/7/22, p. 400–401; *Nihongi,* II, 314.

28. Sasayama Haruo, "Bunken ni mirareru senjutsu to buki," p. 146.

29. For shields, see *NKBT, Nihon shoki,* II, Temmu 1/7/4, pp. 398–399; *Nihongi,* II, 313; on fortresses, see *NKBT, Nihon shoki,* II, Temmu 1/7/5, pp. 398–399; *Nihongi,* II, 313.

30. Sonoda Kōyū, "Waga jōdai no kiheitai," *Shisen* 23/24, 6–7 (March 1962).

31. *NKBT, Nihon shoki,* II, Temmu 1/6/26, pp. 390–391; *Nihongi,* II, 308.

32. Mizuno, "Jinshin no ran," pp. 202–203.

33. See *NKBT, Nihon shoki,* II, Temmu 1/6/29, pp. 396–397; *Nihongi,* II, 311; Temmu 1/7/9, p. 399; *Nihongi,* II, 314.

34. See Hoshino Ryōsaku, *Jinshin no ran,* pp. 255–258; Kameda, pp. 168–183; Inoue Mitsusada, *Asuka no chōtei,* pp. 432–435; Naoki, *Jinshin,* pp. 204–230.

35. On the military power of governors, see Hayakawa, "Ritsuryō sei," pp. 230–232; also Inoue Mitsusada, *Asuka no chōtei,* pp. 432–433.

36. *NKBT, Nihon shoki,* II, Temmu 13/Int.4/5, pp. 462–463; *Nihongi,* II, 363.

37. *NKBT, Nihon shoki,* II, Temmu 14/11/4, pp. 472–473; *Nihongi,* II, 372.

38. *NKBT, Nihon shoki,* II, Temmu 14/12/4, p. 473; also Kishi, *Nihon kodai seiji shi kenkyū,* p. 305.

39. Amino, *Higashi to nishi,* pp. 67–68.

40. *NKBT, Nihon shoki,* II, Jitō 7/12/21, p. 523; *Nihongi,* II, 414.

41. *SZKT, Shoku Nihongi,* Mommu 4/3/17, p. 6.

42. Hara, "Gunji," pp. 213–215; the classic article on this topic is Sakamoto Tarō, *Nihon kodai shi no kisoteki kenkyū,* II, 142–151.

43. *NKBT, Nihon shoki,* II, Jitō 3/Int.8/10, pp. 498–499; *Nihongi,* II, 394.

44. This opinion is expressed in Yoneda Yūsuke, "Ritsuryōteki gundan," pp. 154–157. Also note Sasayama Haruo, "Gunji soshiki," p. 316.

45. My description of the Chinese military comes from Mark Elvin, *The Pattern of the Chinese Past,* pp. 35–65; Arthur Wright, "The Sui Dynasty," in Denis Twitchett and John Fairbank, eds., *The Cambridge History of China 3 Sui and Tang China, 589–906,* I, pp. 97–103; Howard Wechsler, "The Founding of the T'ang Dynasty: Kao tsu," *Cambridge History,* pp. 175–176; T'ai-tsung (reign 626–649) the consolidator," *Cambridge History,* pp. 207–208; and Hamaguchi Shigekuni, *Shin kan zui tō shi no kenkyū,* I, 3–83.

46. Wright, "Sui History," p. 101.

47. Sasayama, "Gunji soshiki," p. 323.

48. Ishio Yoshihisa, *Nihon kodai hō no kenkyū,* p. 220.

49. Elvin, *Chinese Past,* p. 57.

50. Ibid.

51. *SZKT, Gumbō-ryō no gige, Heishi kanten no jō,* p. 183.

52. Urata Akiko, "Henko sei no igi"; Yoshida Takashi, "Ritsuryō sei to sonraku," p. 176.

53. Ishio Yoshihisa, *Nihon kodai hō,* pp. 222–223; Naoki Kōjirō, "Ikko ichi heishi no gensoku to tempeiritsu," pp. 35–37; Naoki Kōjirō, "Gundan no heisū to haibi no han'i ni tsuite," pp. 3–4.

54. *SZKT, Gumbō-ryō no gige, Bijūgu no jō,* p. 184.
55. *SZKT, Buyaku-ryō no gige, Toneri shishō no jō,* p. 122.
56. *SZKT, Gumbō-ryō no gige, Gundan no jō,* p. 185.
57. O'Connell, pp. 40, 99.
58. *SZKT, Gumbō-ryō no gige, Taigo no jō,* p. 183.
59. Hashimoto Yū, *Ritsuryō gundan sei no kenkyū,* pp. 153–168, lists the locations of the provincial militia.
60. The opinion of Kurita Hiroshi cited in Tsunoda Bun'ei, *Ritsuryō kokka no tenkai,* pp. 224–225; also note more recent criticisms by Tsunoda and others in Yamauchi Kunio, "Ritsuryō sei gundan ni kansuru kenkyū no dōkō," pp. 34–36.
61. Hashimoto Yū, *Gundan sei,* pp. 16–21; Noda Reishi, "Nihon ritsuryō gunsei no tokushitsu," pp. 36–42. Also note Noda's recent *Sakimori to eji* for a full exposition of his views.
62. On the examination of weapons, see *SZKT, Gumbō-ryō no gige, Kan'etsu jūgu no jō,* p. 183; on documents on campaigns see *SZKT, Gumbō-ryō no gige, Heishi ijō no jō,* p. 186.
63. *SZKT, Shikiin-ryō no shūge, Daikoku no jō,* pp. 164–165.
64. See Yoneda, "Ritsuryōteki gundan," p. 159; and *SZKT, Kōka-ryō no shūge, Kō gunji no jō,* pp. 641–643.
65. See Sekine Masataka.
66. Hashimoto Yū, *Gundan sei,* pp. 20–21.
67. Yoneda, pp. 158–164; Tōno Haruyuki, "*Shoku Nihongi* kanken nisoku," pp. 68–75.
68. *SZKT, Shikiin-ryō no gige, Gundan no jō,* p. 63.
69. *SZKT, Gumbō-ryō no gige, Gundan daiki no jō,* p. 185.
70. Hashimoto Yū, *Gundan sei,* pp. 16–26; Noda, "Ritsuryō gunsei," pp. 38–41.
71. Yoneda, p. 159.
72. Koguchi Yasuo, "Ritsuryō gundan sei no gunji kunren seido—zoku," pp. 24–25.
73. Ibid., pp. 26–28.
74. *SZKT, Ruijū sandai kyaku,* Tempyō Shōhō 5/10/21 Order of the Council of State, p. 553.
75. On notations in the registers, see Koguchi Yasuo, "Sekichō ni miru ritsuryō gundan heishi no bugei kunren." On drilling and the provincial manufacture of weapons, see Matsumoto Masaharu, "Saikaidō ni okeru shokoku kijō sei no seiritsu."
76. Hashimoto Yū, *Gundan sei,* pp. 120–133.
77. *SZKT, Shoku Nihongi,* Keiun 1/6/3, p. 20.
78. Hashimoto Yū, *Gundan sei,* p. 122.
79. For example, see *Shoku Nihongi,* Jingi 1/4/17, p. 101; Tempyō Hōji 5/11/17, p. 282.
80. *SZKT, Gumbō-ryō no gige, Heishi jōban no jō,* p. 185.
81. While all historians concede a major role to the men of the Eastern Prov-

inces among the Border Guards, some emphasize the primacy of eastern Honshu more than others. Kishi, *Nihon kodai seiji*, pp. 304–311, Naoki Kōjirō, "Sakimori to tōgoku" and Amino, *Higashi to nishi*, pp. 67–76, stress the importance of the fighters of the Eastern Provinces. Yamauchi Kunio, "Sakimori no shubi chi to shusshin chi," gives a larger place to men of western Honshu and northern Kyushu.

82. Kishi, *Nihon kodai seiji*, pp. 304–309.

83. *Mishima Jiicombo kofun gun*, p. 23.

84. *SZKT, Gumbō-ryō no gige, Heishi jōban no jō*, p. 185.

85. Hashimoto Yō, *Gundan sei*, pp. 51–59.

86. *SZKT, Gumbō-ryō no gige, Eji jōge no jō*, p. 185.

87. Hashimoto Yū, *Gundan sei*, pp. 99–118.

88. *SZKT, Gumbō-ryō no gige, Hyōe no jō*, p. 193.

89. *SZKT, Gumbō-ryō no gige, Nai roku i no jō*, pp. 195–196.

90. Inoue Mitsusada, *Nihon kodai shi*, p. 127.

91. For a good summary of work to date on the Laws of Army and the Defense (*Gumbō-ryō*), see the comments written by Sasayama Haruo in Inoue Mitsusada et al., eds., *Nihon shisō taikei 4 Ritsuryō*, pp. 619–629.

92. For a comparison of Japanese and Chinese laws on beacons, see Takigawa Masajirō, "Jōdai hōsui kō," pp. 57–72; "Tō hyōbu shiki to Nihon gumbō-ryō"; and Niida Noboru, "Tō gumbō-ryō to hōsui seido."

93. Several beacons are mentioned for Hizen province in northern Kyushu. See, for example, *NKBT, Hizen fudoki*, p. 393. Also note Okamoto Hironori, "*Hizen no kuni fudoki* ni okeru 'noroshi' no kenkyū."

94. On the Great General, see Noda Reishi, *Ritsuryō kokka no gunji sei*, pp. 106–175.

95. *SZKT, Ruijū sandai kyaku*, Enryaku 8/9/4 OCS, p. 540.

96. *SZKT, Shikiin-ryō no shūge, Sa meryō no jō*, p. 146.

97. *SKZT, Ruijū sandai kyaku*, Kōnin 6/3/20 OCS, p. 622.

98. *SZKT, Nihon sandai jitsuroku*, Jōgan 12/2/23, p. 269.

99. *SZKT, Kyūmoku-ryō no shūge, Kyū saima no jō*, third *koki*, p. 916.

100. Ibid., *Boku meuma no jō*, first *koki*, p. 919.

101. Fukuda Toyohiko, *Taira no Masakado no ran*, pp. 82–83.

102. *SZKT, Kyūmoku-ryō no shūge, Boku meuma no jō*, pp. 919–920.

103. For example, see *SZKT, Nihon sandai jitsuroku*, Jōgan 18/10/13, p. 383.

104. *Dai Nihon komonjo* (hereafter *DNK*), IV, 31.

105. Fukuda, *Taira no Masakado*, pp. 54–62.

106. On Haibara, see Isshi Shigeki, "Kamboku kō"; Isshi et al., "Nagano-ken Matsumoto-shi Kita Haibara suitei Shinano bokugen chōseki chōsa hōkoku." The following description is based upon these sources.

107. Nishioka Toranosuke, *Shōen shi no kenkyū*, I, 301–370.

108. Amino, *Higashi to nishi*, pp. 73–74.

109. *SZKT, Kōnin shuzei shiki, Ekiba chokuhō no jō*, p. 23.

110. *SZKT, Kyūmoku-ryō no shūge, Kyūba chō no jō*, pp. 917–918. Also cf. Fukuda, *Taira no Masakado*, p. 74.

111. *SZKT, Kyūmoku-ryō no shūge, Bokuba ōtai no jō,* p. 928.

112. Ishio, p. 220.

113. Some confusion exists over the course of events during Hirotsugu's revolt. I follow Sakaehara Towao, "Fujiwara no Hirotsugu no ran no tenkai katei," pp. 512–513, 525–528.

114. *SZKT, Shoku Nihongi,* Tempyō 12/8/29, p. 158.

115. Ibid., Tempyō 12/10/9, p. 160.

116. Ibid., Tempyō 12/9/24, p. 159.

117. Ibid., Tempyō 12/9/24, pp. 158–159.

118. Sonoda, p. 7. Also N.B. the presence of Hayato mounted archers on Hirotsugu's side. Nakamura Akizō, "Fujiwara Hirotsugu no ran," pp. 221–223.

119. Yokota Ken'ichi, "Tempyō jūninen Fujiwara no Hirotsugu no ran no ichi kōsatsu," pp. 295–297.

120. *SZKT, Shoku Nihongi,* Tempyō 12/10/9, p. 160.

121. This argument was first developed by Yokota, pp. 298–304.

122. Hall, *Government and Local Power,* p. 131.

123. *SZKT, Ruijū sandai kyaku,* Tempyō 11/5/25 OCS, included in Enryaku 21/12 OCS, p. 549. For a discussion of this new policy, see Kishi, *Nihon kodai seiji,* pp. 271–272.

124. Yamada Hideo, "Sei Hayato gun ni tsuite," pp. 293–318.

125. *NKBT, Man'yōshū,* X, #4321, pp. 408–409; The *Man'yōshū,* tr. Nippon gakujutsu shinko kai, p. 250.

126. *NKBT, Man'yōshū,* X, #4372, pp. 426–427; *Man'yōshū,* p. 254.

127. *NKBT, Man'yōshū,* X, #4374, pp. 428–429; *Man'yōshū,* p. 255.

128. This argument follows Kishi, *Nihon kodai seiji,* pp. 291–301.

129. The following composite of the district magistrate's power base is drawn from Hara Hidesaburō, "Gunji," pp. 217–223; Yoshida Takashi, "Ritsuryō sei," pp. 144–156; Aoki Kazuo, *Nihon no rekishi 3 Nara no miyako,* pp. 161–183; Hayakawa Shōhachi, *Nihon no rekishi 4 Ritsuryō kokka,* pp. 165–196; Aoki, *Nihon no rekishi 5 Kodai gōzoku,* pp. 98–171. For a list of the employees of a district, see SZKT, *Ruijū sandai kyaku,* Kōnin 13/Int. 9/20, OCS, pp. 279–280.

130. The following schema takes its inspiration from Ishii Susumu, *Nihon no rekishi 12 Chūsei bushi dan,* pp. 110–112. One must use caution in naming my diagram after Ishii's (*ie no shihai*), or drawing too many parallels, as Chapter 8 will show.

131. Hashimoto Yū, *Gundan sei,* pp. 69–92.

132. *DNK,* XVI, 393–399.

133. *SZKT, Shoku Nihongi,* Tempyō 12/10/23, p. 160. Many of the men under Nakamaro's command were Koreans. For a discussion of the role of the foreign troops, see Yokota, pp. 305–311, and Sasayama, *Guntai,* pp. 108–110. The Hata were probably sailors from Silla, while the Yamato no Aya hailed from various parts of Korea.

134. *SZKT, Shoku Nihongi,* Edict of the Emperor Shōmu cited in Edict of the Emperor Shōtoku, Jingo Keiun 3/10/1, p. 370.

135. Basic work on these troops has been done by Takigawa Masajirō, "Tachiwaki no toneri ni tsuite"; Inoue Kaoru, *Nihon kodai no seiji to shūkyō*, pp. 56–70; Naoki Kōjirō, "Kodai tennō no shiteki heiryoku ni tsuite," pp. 17–27; and Sasayama, *Guntai*, pp. 77–78, 95–98, 110–114.

136. *SZKT, Shoku Nihongi*, Tempyō Hōji 2/8/25, p. 255. On these troops, note Sasayama Haruo, "Chū efu no kenkyū"; and Sasayama, *Guntai*, pp. 98–102, 118–120.

137. *SZKT, Shoku Nihongi*, Tempyō Hōji 1/6/9, pp. 232–233.

138. Sasayama, *Guntai*, p. 117.

139. *SZKT, Shoku Nihongi*, Tempyō Hōji 8/9/18, p. 305. Also note Hashimoto Yū, *Gundan sei*, pp. 99–118.

140. The following discussion of Nakamaro's revolt has been taken from Hayakawa, *Ritsuryō kokka*, pp. 324–332; Kishi Toshio, *Fujiwara no Nakamaro*, pp. 382–410; and Tsunoda, pp. 244–274.

141. *SZKT, Shoku Nihongi*, Tempyō Hōji 8/9/18, p. 305.

142. Sonoda, p. 7.

143. See *NKBT, Man'yōshū*, I, #443–435, pp. 210–211 for *mononofu; Man'yōshū*, p. 185; *SZKT, Shoku Nihongi*, Yōrō 5/1/27, p. 84; Hōki 2/11/24, p. 396, for *bugei*.

144. Sonoda, pp. 9–10.

145. *SZKT, Shoku Nihongi*, Jingi 1/5/5, p. 101.

146. Ibid., Hōki 9/12/15, p. 445.

147. Sonoda, pp. 13–14.

148. *SZKT, Shoku Nihongi*, Yōrō 5/3/9, p. 85.

149. Yoshida Tokashi, "Ritsuryō sei," p. 176. Also note Urata, pp. 28–76, and the argument in Farris, *Population, Disease, and Land*, pp. 138–140.

CHAPTER 3

1. Thomas Cleary, tr., *The Art of War*, p. 98.

2. *NKBT, Nihon shoki*, Keikō 27/2/12, I, pp. 296–297; William Aston, tr., *Nihongi*, I, 200. Also note *Emishi shiryō*, p. 2.

3. Kudō Masaki, "Emishi Ainu setsu to hi Ainu setsu," pp. 54–94; Takahashi Tomio, *Emishi*, pp. 9–18.

4. Suzuki Naoshi, "Itai no jinruigakuteki kansatsu," pp. 23–44.

5. For a reference to the foreign tongue of these people, see *SZKT, Shoku Nihongi*, Yōrō 6/4/16, p. 92.

6. Itō Nobuo, "Inasaku no hokushin," pp. 24–27; Kudō, pp. 57–58.

7. On the penetration of Iron-Age culture into eastern Honshu, see Farris, *Population, Disease, and Land*, pp. 3–8.

8. Amino, *Higashi to nishi*, pp. 71–76.

9. *NKBT, Nihon shoki*, Keikō 40/7/16, I, pp. 300–303; *Nihongi*, I, 202–204. Also note *Emishi shiryō*, pp. 2–3.

10. Takahashi Tomio, *Emishi*, pp. 53–63.

11. For a list of appointments of *kuni no miyatsuko* to northeastern Japan, see *Emishi shiryō,* p. 1.

12. Inoue Mitsusada, "Taika no kaishin," pp. 157-158; Takahashi Tomio, *Emishi,* pp. 69-80.

13. *NKBT, Nihon shoki,* II, Saimei 4/4, pp. 330-331; *Nihongi,* II, 252.

14. *NKBT, Nihon shoki,* II, Saimei, 4/7/4, pp. 332-333; *Nihongi,* II, 254.

15. *NKBT, Nihon shoki,* II, Saimei 6/3, pp. 342-343; *Nihongi,* II, 263-264.

16. I follow here the periodization of Takahashi Tomio, *Emishi,* pp. 51-142. On Dewa province, note *SZKT, Shoku Nihongi,* Wadō 1/9/28, p. 37; Wadō 2/7/1, p. 39; Wadō 2/7/13, p. 39; Wadō 5/9/23, p. 49.

17. Ibid., Wadō 2/3/5, p. 38; Yōrō 4/9/28, p. 82.

18. Ibid., Jingi 1/3/25, p. 100; Jingi 1/11/29, p. 103.

19. Ibid., Tempyō 9/1/22, p. 142; Tempyō 9/4/14, pp. 143-145.

20. Ibid., Reiki 1/5/30, p. 60.

21. Ibid., Tempyō Hōji 4/3/10, p. 270.

22. Ibid., Tempyō Hōji 3/9/26, p. 265.

23. Ibid., Jingo Keiun 3/2/17, pp. 361-362; Jingo Keiun 3/6/11, p. 365.

24. Kuwahara Shirō, "Tōhoku no kodai jōsaku," pp. 97, 103. Also see J. Edward Kidder, *Early Buddhist Japan,* pp. 54-60. The most recent and best work on this topic has been done by Hirakawa Minami, "Kodai no jōsaku ni kansuru shiron," pp. 37-105. Archeologists update the work on forts in the northeast annually through meetings of the Forts and Palisades Research Group (Jōsaku kenkyū kai).

25. Komatsu Masao, "Shōnai Akio shi no 'Akita jō naigai kenshutsu no tateana jūkyo ato' o megutte," p. 24. See also the findings on Fort Shiwa in *Tōhoku jūkan jidōsha dō kankei maizō bunka zai chōsa hōkoku sho 13 Hotta hō hachi chō iseki,* pp. 23-243, 339-348, 416-432.

26. Hirakawa Minami, "Kodai ni okeru Tōhoku no jōsaku ni tsuite," believes that there is little archeological evidence to support calling the establishments of the Tōhoku "forts" or "palisades."

27. Note the rebuttal by Torao Toshiya, "Ritsuryō gyōsei no shosō," pp. 153-155.

28. Hirakawa, "Kodai ni okeru jōsaku," pp. 16-18.

29. Kadowaki Teiji, "Emishi no hanran."

30. Sasayama Haruo, "Heian shoki no seiji kaikaku," p. 240.

31. The following narrative is drawn from *Emishi shiryō,* pp. 34-68.

32. *SZKT, Shoku Nihongi,* Hōki 11/10/29, p. 464.

33. The Court chastised one leader, Ōtomo no Masutachi. See Ibid., Ten'ō 1/9/26, pp. 476-477.

34. *SZKT, Shoku Nihon kōki,* Jōwa 4/2/8, p. 64.

35. *SZKT, Shoku Nihongi,* Ten'ō 1/6/1, 472-473.

36. Murao Jirō, *Kammu tennō,* p. 142, argues that the real fighting force was only about 30,000, based on ibid., Enryaku 8/6/9, pp. 537-538. See text below.

37. *SZKT, Shoku Nihongi,* Enryaku 7/12/7, p. 432.

38. Ibid., Enryaku 8/6/3, pp. 536-537.

39. Ibid., Enryaku 9/10/21, p. 548.

40. Takahashi Takashi, *Sakanoue Tamuramaro,* pp. 1-30.

41. *SZKT, Nihon kōki,* Kōnin 2/5/23, p. 102.

42. *SZKT, Nihon kiryaku,* Enryaku 13/10/28, p. 268.

43. *SZKT, Nihon kōki,* Enryaku 15/11/21, p. 7.

44. *SZKT, Ruijū kokushi,* Enryaku 19/5/22, p. 335.

45. Takahashi Tomio, *Emishi,* pp. 136-137.

46. On this region, the heartland of *emishi* resistance, see Takahashi Tomio, *Izawa-jō,* pp. 13-41.

47. *SZKT, Nihon kōki,* Enryaku 24/12/7, pp. 48-49.

48. Ibid., Kōnin 2/4/19, p. 99.

49. On the permanent garrisons in northern Honshu, see Takahashi Tomio, *Emishi,* pp. 240-246; Takahashi Takashi, "Mutsu Dewa no gunsei."

50. Hall, *Government and Local Power,* pp. 132-133; Ōtsuka Tokurō, *Heian shoki seiji shi kenkyū,* pp. 388-394.

51. Hall, *Government and Local Power,* p. 90.

52. Cited in Hirakawa Minami, "Tōhoku dai sensō jidai," p. 174. The same wooden tablet is noted in Muraoka Kaoru, "Hasseiki matsu 'Seii' saku sai kentō," p. 126.

53. *Taga-jō urushigami monjo,* p. 35; *Kanoko C iseki urushigami monjo: hombun hen,* p. 126.

54. On the Codes' requirement for command structure, see *SZKT, Gumbō-ryō no gige, Shōsotsu shussei no jō,* pp. 188-189.

55. *SZKT, Shoku Nihongi,* Hōki 11/10/29, p. 464; Enryaku 2/1/8, p. 489; Enryaku 7/3/3, p. 528.

56. *SZKT, Shoku Nihongi,* Enryaku 2/6/6, p. 493; and Enryaku 7/3/3, p. 528. Other examples include *SZKT, Ruijū sandai kyaku,* Daidō 1/10/12 OCS, p. 309; *SZKT, Shoku Nihongi,* Hōki 11/3/16, p. 458; Enryaku 9/10/21, p. 548; and *SZKT, Nihon kōki,* Enryaku 24/2/5, pp. 38-39.

57. *SZKT, Shoku Nihongi,* Enryaku 7/3/3, p. 528.

58. For Sakanoue's genealogy, see Ishioka Hisao, "Sakanoue Tamuramaro to sono shūhen no kyūjutsu," p. 38.

59. In recent years, some Japanese historians have begun to deemphasize Sakanoue's leadership ability as a reason for the "barbarians"' defeat. Note Sekiguchi Akira, "Emishi no hanran to sono rekishiteki igi," pp. 42-43. Yet even Sekiguchi gives some credit to Sakanoue.

60. See Sekine Masataka, "Jōdai kijō ryō kō," pp. 9-11.

61. *SZKT, Ruijū sandai kyaku,* Ten'ō 1/4/10 OCS, p. 561.

62. Ibid., Enryaku 17/4/16 OCS, p. 518.

63. Takahashi Masaaki, pp. 90-91; Ishii Masakuni, *Warabite tō,* pp. 27-35, 132-144.

64. White, pp. 14-38.

65. Ōtsuka, pp. 390–391.

66. *SZKT, Shoku Nihongi,* Ten'ō 1/1/1, pp. 465–466.

67. Sasayama, "Heian shoki," p. 242.

68. Amino, *Higashi to nishi,* p. 61.

69. *SZKT, Shoku Nihongi,* Enryaku 9/11/27, p. 549.

70. *SZKT, Ruijū sandai kyaku,* Enryaku 11/6/7, Edict, pp. 547–548.

71. Ibid., Tenchō 3/11/3, OCS, p. 553.

72. Ibid., Tenchō 3/11/3 OCS, p. 554.

73. *SZKT, Ruijū sandai kyaku,* Tempyō Shōhō 5/10/21 OCS, p. 553.

74. Ibid., Kōnin 4/8/9 OCS, p. 551.

75. Ibid., Tenchō 3/11/3 OCS, p. 553.

76. *SZKT, Shoku Nihongi,* Yōro 3/10/14, p. 78. Cf. Kishi, *Nihon kodai seiji,* pp. 271–272.

77. *SZKT, Ruijū sandai kyaku,* Tempyō 11/5/25 Order of the Ministry of War cited in an Enryaku 21/12 OCS, p. 549.

78. *SZKT, Shoku Nihongi,* Hōki 11/3/16, 458. My interpretation of this law follows Nishioka Toranosuke, "Kihei sei no hattatsu to bushi," pp. 46–47.

79. *SZKT, Ruijū sandai kyaku* Enryaku 14/11/22 OCS, p. 548.

80. Scholars differ somewhat in their interpretations of these two edicts. Cf. Kishi, *Nihon kodai seiji,* pp. 307–308. Also note Yamauchi, "Sakimori no shubi chi to shusshin chi."

81. *SZKT, Ruijū sandai kyaku* Yōrō 6/2/22 Edict, p. 557. Also note the different version in *SZKT, Shoku Nihongi* Yōrō 6/2/23 Edict, p. 91.

82. Sasayama, *Guntai,* p. 156.

83. Literature on the decline of the Taihō military system in the capital is plentiful. For a brief summary, see Sasayama, *Guntai,* pp. 155–162; a more exhaustive treatment may be found in Sasayama, "Heian zenki no sa u konoe fu ni kansuru kōsatsu," III, 581–628; Sasayama, "Tōgu bō tachiwaki no toneri no kenkyū," III, 163–218; Ōboroya Hisashi, "Jūseiki ni okeru sa u emon fu kanjin no kenkyū"; *Nihon koda i gaku ronshū,* pp. 215–247.

84. *SZKT, Ruijū sandai kyaku,* Enrayku 11/6/14 OCS, pp. 558–559.

85. Nishioka Toranosuke, "Kondei ni tsuite," *Rekishi chiri* 37: 21–22 (January 1922). For an early use of the term *kondei,* see *NKBT, Nihon shoki,* II, Kōgyoku 3/11, pp. 260–261; *Nihongi,* II, 189. Inoue Mitsuo, *Heian jidai gunji seido no kenkyū,* pp. 30–32, is the most recent discussion of the relationship between the Japanese and the Tang systems.

Some Japanese historians still see the Strong Fellows as a dead letter from the start. See Nishioka, "Kihei sei no hattatsu," pp. 871–872; Inoue Mitsuo, *Heian jidai gunji seido,* pp. 47–53. I follow Sonoda, p. 16, and Hirano Tomohiko, "Kondei sei seiritsu no haikei to sono yakuwari," pp. 273–315, who see the *kondei* as a vital institution in the 9th century.

86. *SZKT, Ruijū sandai kyaku,* Tempyō 5/11/14 Edict cited in Daidō 5/5/11 OCS, p. 549; for abolition note *SZKT, Shoku Nihongi,* Tempyō 10/5/3, p. 152.

87. *SZKT, Shoku Nihongi,* Tempyō Hōji 6/2/2, p. 286.

88. Ibid., Hōki 11/3/16, p. 458.

89. Sonoda, pp. 14–16.

90. Ibid., p. 16.

91. *SZKT, Ruijū sandai kyaku,* Enryaku 21/12/? OCS, p. 548 (Nagato); Kōnin 10/11/5 OCS, p. 546 (Yamashiro).

92. Ibid., Jōgan 8/11/17, p. 560.

93. Ishii Susumu, "Chūsei seiritsu ki gunsei kenkyū no ichi shiten," pp. 10–11.

94. See *Dai Nihon shiryō* (hereafter *DNS*), 2nd series, V, 434; *Heian ibun* (hereafter *HI*), VI, 2268; VIII, 3138; X, 3837.

95. *SZKT, Ruijū sandai kyaku,* Tenchō 3/11/3, p. 554. Note the reduction of Kyushu conscripts in ibid. Kōnin 4/8/9, pp. 550–551.

96. Toda Yoshimi, "Kokuga gunsei no keisei katei," pp. 9, 40–45.

97. Ibid., p. 8.

98. *SZKT, Ruijū sandai kyaku* Kōnin 6/8/23, pp. 551–553.

99. Toda, "Kokuga gunsei," pp. 9–11.

100. *SZKT, Nihon sandai jitsuroku,* Jōgan 12/12/2, p. 280.

101. *SZKT, Shoku Nihon kōki,* Jōwa 4/2/8, p. 64.

102. *SZKT, Nihon shoki,* II, Suiko 26/8, 200–203; *Nihongi,* II, 146.

103. Ibid., II, Temmu 1/7/22, 400–401; *Nihongi,* II, 314.

104. *SZKT, Gumbō-ryō no gige, Gundan no jō,* p. 185.

105. A picture of a reloading crossbow appears in McNeill, *The Pursuit of Power,* p. 37. The recent traveling exhibit of clay Chin soldiers unearthed near Xian contains a simpler version, probably closer to 9th-century Japanese models.

106. Some archeologists have laid claim to the distinction of finding Japan's first crossbow. For example, see *Mishima Jiicombo kofun gun,* pp. 22–24; and *Iwate-ken Kitakami-shi Saraki chō Hatten iseki kinkyū chōsa hōkoku,* p. 14. In the Mishima case, only the arrowheads have been found; at Hattenhō, a wooden artifact that could be a crossbow was uncovered (but there was no trigger). Neither claim strikes me as convincing.

107. *SZKT, Engi hyōgo-ryō no shiki, Daijō e no jō,* p. 990.

108. *SZKT, Shoku Nihon kōki,* Jōwa 4/2/8, p. 64.

109. McNeill, *Pursuit,* pp. 37–38. McNeill's example is from China.

110. *SZKT, Shoku Nihon kōki,* Jōwa 2/9/13, p. 42.

111. Ibid., Jōwa 5/5/11, p. 76.

112. *SZKT, Ruijū sandai kyaku,* Jōgan 13/8/16 OCS, pp. 213–214.

113. Toda, "Kokuga gunsei," p. 17.

114. *SZKT, Nihon sandai jitsuroku,* Jōgan 8/7/15, p. 192.

115. *SZKT, Fusō ryakki,* Kampyō 6/9/5, p. 162.

116. *SZKT, Nihon sandai jitsuroku,* Gangyō 5/4/25, p. 497.

117. Hirano Tomohiko, "Kondei sei," pp. 273–315, summarizes the arguments that Japan still conscripted peasants for its military in the 9th century, the so-called *nimbei sei.* This view has gained proponents in recent years, including Toda, "Kokuga gunsei," pp. 16, 34; and Shimomukai Tatsuhiko, "Ōchō kokka kokuga gunsei no kōzō to tenkai," p. 62. While peasants undoubtedly played a role after

800, I find the argument for systematic, nationwide conscription lacking in evidence. Karl Friday, "Teeth and Claws: Provincial Warriors and the Heian Court," pp. 158-159, also expresses doubts.

118. Miyoshi Kiyoyuki, "Iken junikajō," in Takeuchi Rizō et al., eds. *Nihon shisō taikei* 8 *Kodai seiji shakai shisō*, p. 292.

CHAPTER 4

1. *SZKT, Nihon sandai jitsuroku*, Jōgan 8/7/9, p. 191.

2. *SZKT, Senjo-ryō no gige, Gunji no jō*, pp. 139-140.

3. *SZKT, Ruijū sandai kyaku*, Tempyō 10/4/19 OCS, cited in Tenchō 4/5/21 OCS, p. 307, which explicitly recognizes that heredity should not be a factor in appointment, and *SZKT, Shoku Nihongi*, Tempyō 14/5/27, p. 168, which does not mention heredity at all as a requirement for the district magistracy. Also note the reduction of district posts in Tempyō 11/5/23, p. 155. My understanding of these orders and other commands concerning the district magistrate follows Hara Hidesaburō, "Gunji to chihō gōzoku," pp. 215-216, and Imaizumi Takao, "Hasseiki gunryō no nin'yō to shutsuji," who sees the period from 735 to 742 as an era of reform away from hereditary families. For more on the relationship between the epidemic and the district office, also note *SZKT, Ruijū sandai kyaku*, Tempyō 11/7/15 OCS, pp. 304-305.

4. *SZKT, Shoku Nihongi*, Tempyō Shōhō 1/2/27, p. 197.

5. See Farris, *Population, Disease, and Land*, pp. 50-73, for this argument on the decline of the Chinese-style state. Farris, pp. 140-149, also summarizes and critiques other hypotheses.

6. *SZKT, Ruijū sandai kyaku*, Tempyō Hōji 7/9/1 Edict, p. 298.

7. See for example, ibid., Kōnin 3/8/16 OCS, p. 414-415.

8. Ibid., Hōki 10/10/16 OCS, p. 613.

9. The idea of "the rich" was developed by Toda, *Nihon ryōshu sei seiritsu shi no kenkyū*, pp. 14-45. The basis for the idea is primarily found in *SZKT, Ruijū sandai kyaku*.

10. For example, see *SZKT, Ruijū sandai kyaku*, Saikō 2/1/28 OCS, pp. 312-313. Also note the comments of Hayakawa, *Nihon no rekishi* 4 *Ritsuryō kokka*, p. 364.

11. *SZKT, Ruijū sandai kyaku* Enryaku 9/4/16 OCS, p. 625; Enryaku 14/Int. 7/15 Edict, p. 517; Jōgan 9/5/10 OCS, pp. 601-602.

12. Ibid., Kōnin 10/6/2 OCS, pp. 612-613; Gangyō 3/7/9 OCS, pp. 504-505; Jōgan 15/9/23 OCS, p. 418.

13. Ibid., Kōnin 13/3/26 OCS, pp. 526-527; Tenchō 7/4/29, pp. 527-528.

14. Ibid., Kampyō 6/2/23 OCS, p. 402.

15. *SZKT, Ruijū kokushi*, Enryaku 17/3/16, p. 124 (798 order); *SZKT, Nihon kōki*, Enryaku 18/5/27, p. 22. (799 order).

16. Examples of this problem are common in the late 9th century. See *SZKT, Ruijū sandai kyaku*, Jōgan 9/12/20 OCS, pp. 623-624; Kampyō 6/7/16 OCS, p. 624. These orders show the trouble that arose when capital aristocrats sent messengers

and housemen to ship aristocratic goods on the public transportation system. Also note the analysis of these orders by Toda Yoshimi, "Ritsuryō sei kara no kaihō," pp. 39-41. Other examples of aristocrats wreaking havoc in the countryside may be found in *SZKT, Ruijū sandai kyaku,* Kampyō 3/5/29 OCS, p. 616; Kampyō 3/6/17 OCS, pp. 616-617; Kampyō 6/11/30 OCS, p. 617; Engi 5/8/25 OCS, pp. 617-618; Engi 5/11/3 OCS, p. 618.

17. Work on the early estate is legion. Some of the best research is Iyanaga Teizō, *Nara jidai no kizoku to nōmin;* Kishi, *Nihon kodai seiji shi kenkyū,* pp. 317-375. In English, note Elizabeth Sato, "The Early Development of the *Shōen.*"

18. Farris, *Population, Disease, and Land,* pp. 67-68.

19. The first historians to discuss the metamorphosis of the provincial office were Takeuchi Rizō, *Ritsuryō sei to kizoku seiken,* II, 436-444, and Yoshimura Shigeki, *Kokushi seido hōkai ni kansuru kenkyū.*

20. There are many examples of ex-officials causing trouble in local politics during the second half of the 9th century. See *SZKT, Ruijū sandai kyaku,* Jōwa 9/8/15 OCS, cited in Jōwa 15/5/14 OCS, p. 248; and Kampyō 3/9/11 OCS, pp. 620-621. Also note *SZKT, Nihon sandai jitsuroku,* Jōgan 7/5/10, p. 155.

21. For details, see Takeuchi Rizō, "Shoki no bushi dan," pp. 194-197.

22. *SZKT, Nihon sandai jitsuroku,* Gangyō 8/6/23, p. 567; Ninna 2/5/12, pp. 609-610. Also note similar revolt in Tsushima in *SZKT, Nihon Montoku tennō jitsuroku,* Ten'an 1/6/25, p. 100.

23. *SZKT, Fusō ryakki,* Kampyō 1/4/27, p. 157. For a complete list of late-800 revolts, note Shimomukai Tatsuhiko, "Ōchō kokka kokuga gunsei no seiritsu," p. 13.

24. *SZKT, Ruijū sandai kyaku,* Shōtai 2/9/19 OCS, p. 565.

25. Miyake Chōbei, "Masakado no ran no shiteki zentei," pp. 69-72.

26. Ibid., p. 60.

27. For a discussion of a similar pasture in Shinano and its links with moving specialists like the "band of horse employers," see Kirihara Takeshi, "Shinano ni okeru shūba no tō no kōkogakuteki kōsatsu," pp. 271, 274-277.

28. Toda Yoshimi, "Chūsei seiritsu ki no kokka to nōmin," p. 30. Horiuchi Kazuaki, "Chūsei shoki buryoku no tokushitsu," objects to Toda's argument on 3 grounds. (1) He does not believe that 10th-century bands were permanent enough to oppress residents. (2) He shies away from the use of the term *tō* for these bands because he believes it is too easily confused with the same character used for some warrior bands of the 1100s. (3) He argues that the term *rui* is more appropriate, since it implies that the members did not constantly carry weapons, unlike members of 12th-century bands (*tō*).

29. These events are listed in Shimomukai, "Kokuga gunsei no seiritsu," p. 13.

30. Fukuda Toyohiko, *Taira Masakado no ran,* pp. 16-17.

31. *SZKT, Ruijū kokushi,* Kōnin 5/1/19; 5/2/10; 5/2/15; 5/5/18, p. 337.

32. *SZKT, Nihon sandai jitsuroku,* Jōgan 12/12/2, p. 280.

33. Sato Sōjun, *Heian zenki seiji shi josetsu,* pp. 233-234, emphasizes the famine,

while Niino Naoyoshi, "Gangyō no ran no shiteki igi," pp. 1-2, argues for the greed of the provincial governor.

34. Sato Sōjun, pp. 237-238.

35. Shimomukai, "Kokuga gunsei no seiritsu," p. 18. Note list pp. 20-21.

36. Takada Minoru, "Jūseiki no shakai henkaku," pp. 38-39. Also see Toda, "Ritsuryō sei kara," p. 43. Takahashi Masaaki, "Masakado no ran no hyōka o megutte," pp. 26-30, argues that Takamochi's forces were composed of "bad characters," such as those making up "the band of horse employers." Also note Morita Tei and Miyanaga Gen, "Heian zenki Tōgoku no gunji mondai ni tsuite," who point out that there is no proof for the inference that Takamochi went to the Kanto because he was a military aristocrat, and believe he left the capital because he had no political opportunities there.

37. Shimomukai, "Kokuga gunsei no seiritsu," pp. 17-22.

38. *SZKT, Hobō-ryō no gige, Shūkyū seijin no jō*, p. 303.

39. Ibid., *Yū tōzoku no jō*, pp. 303-304.

40. Ibid., *Tsuibu zainin no jō*, p. 304.

41. *SZKT, Gumbō-ryō no gige, Sahei no jō*, p. 186.

42. The following narrative is based upon *The Tale of Masakado* (*Shōmon ki*), the best edition of which is Kajiwara Masaaki, ed., *Shōmon ki*, 2 vols. Also of note is Hayashi Rokurō, ed., *Shōmon ki*, for its inclusion of numerous related materials. See also Takeuchi Rizō, ed., *Shōmon ki*, pp. 186-227. *DNS*, 1st series, VI and VII also includes a critical edition of *The Tale of Masakado* with all related materials. For a translation, see Judith Rabinovitch, *Shōmonki: The Story of Masakado's Rebellion*. An excellent guide to research on Masakado's revolt and related topics has been written by Ōshio Chihiro, Saeki Arikiyo, Sakaguchi Tsutomu, and Sekiguchi Akira, *Kenkyū shi: Masakado no ran*. For a fine treatment of the twin rebellions of Masakado and Sumitomo, see Fukuda, *Taira Masakado*.

43. Fukuda, *Taira Masakado*, p. 36.

44. Ibid., p. 37.

45. Ibid., pp. 120-122.

46. Ibid., p. 122.

47. Kajiwara, *Shōmon ki*, I, 27.

48. Ibid., I, 88.

49. Ibid., I, 140. Fukuda does not accept the idea that the statue was a psychological ploy because that would have violated "the way of the warrior." See *Taira Masakado*, p. 128.

50. Kajiwara, *Shōmon ki*, I, 155.

51. Ibid., I, 184.

52. Ibid., I, 215.

53. Ibid., I, 241.

54. The text of the *Shōmon ki* gives two different dates for Sadamori's return to the Kanto with the summons. I follow Uwayokote Masataka, who has argued that the real date must be the summer of 939, not 938 as the text says. See Uwayokote Masataka, *Nihon chūsei seiji shi kenkyū*, pp. 88-94. Also note Uwayokote's

recent explanation of the events of 939 in *"Shōmon ki shoshū no Masakado shojō o megutte,"* pp. 341–368 and Fukuda's explanation of events, *Taira Masakado,* pp. 132–134.

55. Kajiwara, *Shōmon ki,* I, 292.

56. *DNS,* 1st series, VII, 298, notes that Masakado's younger brother was the object of a Court search-and-destroy mission in Izu.

57. Kajiwara, *Shōmon ki,* II, 52.

58. Ibid., II, 149.

59. Ibid., II, 154.

60. Ibid., II, 130.

61. *DNS,* 1st series, VII, 556. Fukuda, *Taira Masakado,* pp. 154–156, is a leading advocate of Sumitomo's conspiring with Masakado to revolt at the same time.

62. *DNS,* 1st series, VII, 556.

63. Ibid., p. 556.

64. Ibid., pp. 443–444, 450, 462–463, 475–476, 485–487.

65. On the pirates of the Inland Sea, see Amino, *Higashi to nishi,* pp. 77–82.

66. *DNS,* 1st series, VI, 592, 629, 762.

67. Ibid., pp. 797–798, 816.

68. Ibid., 1st series, VII, 24.

69. Ibid., pp. 24–25.

70. Ibid., p. 553.

71. Ibid., p. 553.

72. Kajiwara, *Shōmon ki,* II, 196–201.

73. *DNS,* 1st series, VII, 583.

74. Ibid., pp. 592–593.

75. Fukuda, *Taira Masakado,* p. 163.

76. Kajiwara, *Shōmon ki,* II, 243.

77. Ibid., II, 270.

78. Ibid., II, 281.

79. *DNS,* 1st series, VII, 624.

80. This analysis of Masakado's forces is based on Fukuda, "Ōchō gunji kikō to nairan," pp. 85–88. There is a wide range of opinion among Japanese historians on this topic. At the other extreme from Fukuda is Uwayokote Masataka in Toda Yoshimi, ed., *Shimpojiumu Nihon rekishi 5 Chūsei shakai no keisei,* pp. 157–158, who believes distinctions between allies (*banrui*) and dependents (*jūrui*) are meaningless. Also note Yoshida Akira, "Masakado no ran ni kansuru ni san no mondai," pp. 13–18.

81. Fukuda, "Ōchō gunji kikō," p. 87.

82. Ibid., pp. 85–86.

83. Ibid., p. 86.

84. Kajiwara, *Shōmon ki,* I, 21.

85. Fukuda, *Taira no Masakado,* p. 91.

86. My definition of the term *banrui* follows Haruta Takayoshi, "Masakado no

ran ni okeru buryoku soshiki." Also note Yoshida Akira, "Heian chūki no buryoku ni tsuite," p. 8.

87. Yoshida Akira, "Heian chūki no buryoku," pp. 2–10.

88. Ishimoda, *Kodai makki seiji shi josetsu,* pp. 48–51.

89. For examples of lines and shields, see Kajiwara, *Shōmon ki,* I, 140, 241; II, 281.

90. Fukuda, *Taira Masakado,* pp. 94–98.

91. Yasuda Motohisa, "Bushi dan no keisei," p. 131.

92. Ishii Susumu, *Nihon no rekishi 12 Chūsei bushi dan,* pp. 113–115.

93. Fukuda, *Taira Masakado,* pp. 7–8.

94. Uwayokote, *Nihon seiji shi,* pp. 10–12.

95. Takeuchi, "Shoki no bushi dan," pp. 206–209.

96. The origin of this terminology is Ishimoda, *Kodai makki,* pp. 35–38, 40–53, 89–99, 101–105, 166–168.

97. Fukuda, "Ōchō gunji kikō," pp. 84–85.

98. Fukuda, *Taira Masakdo,* pp. 42–54; Fukuda Toyohiko, "Nihon kodai tetsu seisan no shoyōsō."

99. Fukuda, "Nihon kodai tetsu," pp. 45–46.

100. Shima Setsuko, "Masakado no ran no zaichi kōzō."

101. Takahashi Masaaki, "Masakado no ran no hyōka," p. 42.

102. Matsumoto Shimpachiro emphasizes Masakado as a revolutionary in "*Shōmon ki* no inshō," pp. 12–15.

103. Amino, *Higashi to nishi,* p. 92.

104. Uwayokote, *Nihon seiji shi,* p. 103.

105. Inoue Mitsuo, pp. 134–144.

106. Shimomukai Tatsuhiko, "Ōryō shi tsuibu shi no shoruikei," pp. 22–23.

107. Shimomukai, "Kokuga gunsei no seiritsu," pp. 5–6.

108. Shimomukai Tatsuhiko, "Keigo shi Fujiwara no Sumitomo," p. 16.

109. Ibid., pp. 13–15.

CHAPTER 5

1. This is a translation of a phrase used by Sakamoto Shōzo, the foremost advocate of the dynastic state (*ōchō kokka*). See *Nihon no rekishi 6 Sekkan jidai,* p. 16; for Sakamoto's general theories, see his *Nihon ōchō kokka taisei ron.* The precise Japanese phraseology Sakamoto uses is *kokka shihai naki ni hitoshiku muchitsujo jōtai.*

2. The idea that local strongmen were without weapons until after the 900s and armed for self-defense may be found in Hall, *Government and Local Power,* p. 130.

3. *DNS,* 2nd Series, XX, 56.

4. Sasayama, "Heian zenki no sa u konoe fu ni kansuru kōsatsu," II, 596–600; 605–610.

5. Sasayama, "Tōgū bō tachiwaki no toneri no kenkyū," pp. 176–180; 185–188.

6. *DNS,* 1st Series, IX, 232.

7. Ibid., pp. 301–302.

8. Ibid., 1st Series, XV, 386.

9. There is a great debate over exactly when the Kebii Shi was founded. The dates 815 to 834 come from Tanimori Akio, *Kebii shi o chūshin to shitaru Heian jidai no keisatsu jōtai,* pp. 14–18. Ogawa Seitarō, "Kebii shi no kenkyū," 17:46–52, argued that the Investigators only really became established in 894. More recently, the debate has continued between Watanabe Naohiko, *Nihon kodai kan'i seido no kisoteki kenkyū,* pp. 297–310, who argues for 815 or 816, and Ōae Akira, *Ritsuryō seika no shihō to keisatsu,* pp. 43–54, who proposes the date of 820. Inoue Mitsuo, pp. 105–114, suggests that the Investigators only really began their duties on a full-time basis in the 890s, a view that is close to that of Ogawa.

10. For an analysis of the Gate Guards of the 900s, many of whom served concurrently as Investigators, see Ōboroya Hisashi, "Jūseiki ni okeru sa u emon fu kanjin no kenkyū."

11. On the duties of the Investigators outside the capital, see Uwayokote Masataka, "Heian chūki no keisatsu seido," pp. 513–519.

12. *HI,* III, 886.

13. Morita Tei, "Kebii shi no kenkyū," pp. 12–23.

14. Uwayokote, "Heian chūki no keisatsu," pp. 525–529. Also Uwayokote Masataka, "Heian chūki no nairan to bushi dan," in Toda, ed., *Shimpojiumu Nihon rekishi 5 Chūsei shakai no keisei,* pp. 145–147; 165–166, where the author reasserts his belief in the non-warrior origins of the Investigators.

15. See Uwayokote, "Heian chūki no nairan," p. 146.

16. A comparison with the police forces of modern cities also provides a rationale for the small size of the Investigators. Knoxville, Tennessee, a city of 250,000 in 1990, had a police force of only 306 men and women. Surely Heian, a smaller city in the year 1000, would not have had more.

17. Ōboroya, "Jūseiki sa u emon fu," *Heian hakubutsu kan kenkyū kiyō* 5:127.

18. Horiuchi Kazuaki, "Heian chūki kebii shi no buryoku ni tsuite," pp. 342–347.

19. Ibid., pp. 342–354; Fukuda, "Ōchō gunji kikō to nairan," p. 99.

20. *SZKT, Chōya gunsai,* pp. 263–264. For an explication of this record, see Morita Tei, *Heian jidai seiji shi kenkyū,* pp. 359–361.

21. My argument follows Fukuda, "Ōchō gunji kikō," pp. 99–100.

22. *DNS,* 2nd series, II, 944–945. Also note *HI,* II, 507–508. For a similar analysis of this record, see Kawane Yoshihiro, *Chūsei hōken sei seiritsu shi ron,* pp. 29–42.

23. *DNS,* 1st Series, XII, 479.

24. Ibid., 2nd Series, I, 312.

25. Ibid., 2nd Series, II, 442–443, 448.

26. Ibid., 2nd Series, V, 327.

27. Ibid., p. 434.

28. Ibid., 2nd Series, VII, 722.

29. For examples, see ibid., 1st Series, X, 130; XXI, 17–18; 2nd Series, IV, 479.

30. Toda, "Kokuga gunsei no keisei katei," p. 23.

31. For an example, see Fukuda, "Ōchō gunji kikō," p. 99.

32. Ibid., p. 101.

33. *Dai Nihon kokiroku* (hereafter *DNKK*) *Shōyū ki*, 8, Chōgen 1/7/24, p. 71.

34. For example, see *NKBT*, IV, 75, 249; *Konjaku monogatari shū*, III, 463; IV, 75; IV, 249; V, 149.

35. *HI*, III, 775-778. This document lists Yorinobu's great-grandfather and imperial progenitor as the Emperor Yōzei, a fact that does not agree with conventional genealogies of the Kawachi (Seiwa) Minamoto.

36. Fukuda, "Ōchō gunji kikō, p. 98.

37. *DNS*, 2nd Series, X, 125-126.

38. *DNKK*, *Shōyū ki*, 9, Chōgen 4/7/6, p. 3.

39. Fukuda, "Ōchō gunji kikō," pp. 101-102.

40. *DNS*, 2nd Series, XVII, 100.

41. On Mitsunaka's Settsu base, see *NKBT*, *Konjaku monogatari shū*, IV, 65-70. For an excellent critique of this story and its overestimate of Mitsunaka's followers, see Yasuda Motohisa, *Nihon shoki hōken sei no kiso kenkyū*, pp. 53-72. On the role of Fujiwara Chiharu in the incident of 969, see Noguchi Minoru, *Bandō bushi dan no seiritsu to hatten*, pp. 26-30.

42. My description is drawn from Takahashi Masaaki, "Ise Heishi no seiritsu to tenkai." Also see Takahashi's recent book on the Taira, *Kiyomori izen*, pp. 11-21.

43. Fukuda, "Ōchō gunji kikō," pp. 104-105.

44. For more on the conflict between the two branches of the Taira, see Takahashi Masaaki, "Ise Heishi," pp. 20-22; *Kiyomori*, pp. 35-45.

45. *NKBT*, *Konjaku monogatari shū*, IV, 385. My translation depends to some degree on the work of William Wilson, "The Way of the Bow and Arrow—The Japanese Warrior in *Konjaku Monogatari*," p. 213.

46. Ishii Susumu, "Chūsei seiritsu ki gunsei kenkyū no ichi shiten," pp. 1-4. Also see the reports by Toda Yoshimi, Ishii Susumu, and Uwayokote Masataka, "Nihon chūsei shoki kenryoku kōzō no shomondai."

47. The classic study of the transformation of the provincial office is Yoshimura, *Kokushi seido hōkai ni kansuru kenkyū*.

48. *HI*, II, 474, 478, 479, 483, 484. The text included in *Heian ibun* is somewhat at variance with other texts, and in making my translations I also referred to Ienaga Saburō et al., eds., *Nihon shisō taikei 8 Kodai seiji shakai shisō*, especially p. 265.

49. Sakamoto Shōzō, *Sekkan jidai*, p. 299.

50. Toda, "Kokuga gunsei," pp. 29-30.

51. *SZKT*, *Chōya gunsai*, p. 523.

52. *Kanoko C iseki urushigami monjo: hombun hen*, pp. 126-128, 161, 164.

53. *SZKT*, *Ruijū sandai kyaku*, Kōnin 13/Int. 9/20 OCS, p. 279.

54. *HI*, IX, 3540.

55. *SZKT*, *Engi hyōbu shō shiki*, *Kuniguni taijō no jō*, p. 705.

56. Fukuda, "Ōchō gunji kikō," p. 108.

57. *NKBT*, *Konjaku monogatari shū*, III, 171.

58. Ibid., V, 181.

59. Takeuchi, *Ritsuryō sei to kizoku seiken*, II, 437-475.

60. Ishii Susumu, "Chūsei gunsei kenkyū," pp. 8-12.

61. Fukuda, "Ōchō gunji kikō," p. 106. Little work has been done on the Provincial and District Investigators. Cf. Watanabe, pp. 327-364, who argues for a strong military connection for the Investigators. Also note Ōae, pp. 268-286; Kuroda Kōichirō, "Jingū kebii shi no kenkyū," pp. 4-9.

62. For the sources on the Strong Fellows' Department, note Ishii Susumu, "Chūsei gunsei kenkyū," pp. 8-11. Also note the mention of *kondei* in Fujiwara Sanesuke's diary, the *Shōyū ki*, for Kankō 2/5/13 (1005), *DNS*, 2nd series, V, 434; *HI*, VI, 2268; VIII, 3138; X, 3837.

63. *NKBT, Konjaku monogatari shū*, IV, 374. Also see Wilson, p. 202.

64. Ishii Susumu, "Chūsei gunsei kenkyū," pp. 12-19.

65. *Zōho shiryō taisei* (Hereafter *ZST*) 7 *Shun ki*, Chōryaku 3/10/7, p. 43.

66. Ishii Susumu, "Chūsei gunsei kenkyū," pp. 13-14.

67. The text of this document is drawn from Ishii, "Chūsei gunsei kenkyū," p. 16. For the full unpunctuated text, see Toda, "Kokuga gunsei," p. 41.

68. Toda, "Kokuga gunsei," pp. 40-45.

69. Ishii Susumu, "Chūsei gunsei kenkyū," pp. 17-19.

70. Shimomukai, "Ōryō shi tsuibu shi no shoruikei," pp. 22-31. This idea was first suggested by Toda, "Kokuga gunsei," pp. 36-39. Also note Friday.

Shimomukai has complied a handy table of all appointments to positions as overseers, search-and-destroy officers, and arrest officers for the Heian and Kamakura periods. See "Shoruikei," p. 30, and "Ōchō kokka gunsei no seiritsu," pp. 23-27.

71. This point is made by Shimomukai, "Shoruikei," pp. 29-31; also by Ōae, pp. 313-319.

72. *SZKT, Chōya gunsai,* pp. 512-513.

73. Ishii Susumu, "Chūsei gunsei kenkyū," pp. 19-20.

74. Inoue Mitsuo, pp. 160-161, 194-195.

75. *SZKT, Azuma kagami,* Shōgen 3/12/15, p. 649.

76. Shimomukai, "Ōchō kokka kokuga gunsei no kōzō to tenkai," pp. 56-57.

77. For the translations of these records, I have followed the text provided in Ishii Susumu, "Chūsei gunsei kenkyū," p. 2.

78. Fukuda, "Ōchō gunji kikō," p. 118.

79. Ishii Susumu, *Nihon no rekishi 12 Chūsei bushi dan*, pp. 110-112.

80. The information for this reconstruction of events is provided in *DNS*, 2nd Series, XIV, 231-238.

81. Fukuda, "Ōchō gunji kikō," p. 118.

82. *DNS*, 2nd Series, XIV, 282.

83. *HI*, III, 777.

84. Ishimoda, *Kodai makki seiji shi josetsu*, p. 184.

85. This date appears in the *Shōki mokuroku*, a list of topics discussed in the parts of Sanesuke's diary no longer extant. See *DNKK, Shōyū ki*, 10, Chōgen 1/6/5,

p. 412. In recent years historians have discovered many new primary documents on Tadatsune's revolt. A neat summary is contained in *Ichikawa shi shi*, V, 186-203. Also note Noguchi Minrou, *Bandō bushi dan no seiritsu no hatten*, pp. 47-71.

86. It may be recalled that Taira no Koremoto and Tadatsune were long-time enemies. The hostility between Tadatsune and Koremoto dated back at least to their father's generation when the two families had fought over Koremoto's father's (Shigemori) pledge to copy and transport a sutra from the Kanto to Enryakuji in the capital. For this conflict, see Noguchi, pp. 64-66; Fukuda, *Chiba Tsunetane*, pp. 14-15; Ishii Susumu, "Chūsei gunsei kenkyū," p. 21.

The Sadamori wing of the Taira, to which both Naokata and his father, Koretoki, belonged, was close to Shigemori and Koremoto; according to Fukuda, *Chiba*, pp. 18-19, Sadamori had adopted several of his younger brother Shigemori's children. It was no accident that Koremoto had the same first character (Kore) in his given name as all of Sadamori's sons. Therefore it seems likely that Naokata was continuing a grudge of the Sadamori-Shigemori (Koremoto) wing of the Taira against Tadatsune and his immediate relatives.

87. *DNKK, Shōyū ki*, 8, Chōgen 1/7/15, p. 66.

88. Ibid., 8, Chōgen 1/7/15, p. 66.

89. Ibid., 8, Chōgen 1/7/23, p. 73.

90. Noguchi, pp. 53-55.

91. The *koku* is a measure of volume probably equal to approximately 2 bushels.

92. *DNKK, Shōyū ki*, 8, Chōgen 3/5/14, p. 175.

93. Fukuda, "Ōchō gunji kikō," p. 110.

94. *DNKK, Shōyū ki*, 9, Chōgen 4/9/18, p. 47.

95. Fukuda, "Ōchō gunji kikō," p. 113.

96. Ishimoda was the first to make this point. See *Kodai makki*, pp. 192-194.

97. *DNKK, Shōyū ki*, 8, Chōgen 4/3/1, p. 236.

98. *ZST* 6 *Sakei ki*, Chōgen 4/6/27, pp. 283-284.

99. Ibid., Chōgen 7/10/24, pp. 376-377.

100. *HI*, IV, 1311.

101. On disease in this period, see William Wayne Farris, "Disease in Japan, 500-1600."

102. For a brief description of epidemics from 990-1025, see Tsuchida Naoshige, *Nihon no rekishi* 5 *Ōchō no kizoku*, pp. 392-399.

103. *DNKK, Shōyū ki*, 7, Manju 2/3/2, pp. 93; Manju 2/3/24, p. 101.

104. Helen and William McCullough, tr., *A Tale of Flowering Fortunes*, II, 665.

105. *SZKT, Ruijū fusen shō*, pp. 65-67.

106. Ibid., pp. 87-89.

107. *DNKK, Shōyū ki*, 8, Chōgen 2/Int. 2/6, p. 129.

108. *ZST* 6 *Sakei ki*, Manju 2/7/22, p. 150.

109. *HI*, III, 1100.

110. Ibid., II, 701. The record deals with rice loans, and thus the adverse effects on agriculture may be inferred.

111. Sakamoto Shōzō, *Sekkan jidai*, p. 323.

112. For a discussion of these reforms, see Sakamoto Shōzō, *Nihon ōchō kokka taisei ron*, pp. 195–323.

113. Sakamoto Shōzō, *Sekkan jidai*, pp. 327–333.

CHAPTER 6

1. Satō Shin'ichi, Ikeuchi Yoshisuke, and Momose Kesao, eds. *Chūsei hōsei shiryō shū: Muromachi bakufu hō*, II, 36–62.

2. Toda Yoshimi originated the concept of the age of widespread land clearance, which he borrowed from Marc Bloch's *French Rural History*. See Toda, *Nihon ryōshu sei seiritsu shi no kenkyū*, pp. 326ff. Also note recent advocates Kimura Shigemitsu, "Dai kaikon jidai no kaihatsu," pp. 150–204, and Kuroda Hideo, *Nihon chūsei kaihatsu shi no kenkyū*.

3. Many Japanese historians see Tadatsune as the last of the "lords of privately operated land" (*shiei den ryōshu*). After Tadatsune, "country lords" (*zaichi ryōshu*) came into existence. The distinction between the two categories is subjective and vague. On the origin of these two terms, see Ishimoda, *Kodai makki seiji shi josetsu*, pp. 35–38, 48–53, 101–107, 167–173. Other historians have elaborated these terms. See Fukuda, "Ōchō gunji kikō to nairan," p. 113. Also see Fukuda's *Chiba Tsunetane*, pp. 32–94; and Ishimoda, *Chūseiteki sekai no keisei*, pp. 21–80, 161–259. For further discussion, see Chapters 4 and 5.

4. See Malcolm Hamilton and Maria Hirszowicz, *Class and Inequality in Pre-Industrial, Capitalist, and Communist Societies*, pp. 99–100, for criticism of the class definition of feudal lords. Also note R. S. Neale, *Class in English History, 1680–1850*, pp. 84–91, where a Marxist historian of Europe rejects the notion of Tokugawa Japan as a class society.

5. See Fukuda Toyohiko's report in Nagahara Keiji, ed. *Shimpojiumu Nihon rekishi 7 Chūsei kokka ron*, pp. 20–22.

6. Note Farris, *Population, Disease, and Land*, pp. 181, 196.

7. Fukuda report in Nagahara, *Chūsei kokka*, p. 21.

8. The best brief discussions of estate formation in this period are Ishii Susumu, "Insei jidai," pp. 196–200, 207–215; Sakamoto Shōzō, *Nihon ōchō kokka taisei ron*, pp. 206–207, 332; and Nagahara Keiji, "Land Ownership under the *Shōen-kokugaryō* System."

9. One place to begin the study of estate structure is Elizabeth Sato, pp. 91–108.

10. Fukuda report, in Nagahara, *Chūsei kokka*, p. 24.

11. Ishii Susumu, "Insei jidai," pp. 207–213.

12. Sakamoto Shōzō, *Nihon rekishi 6 Sekkan jidai*, pp. 345–346. Also see *HI*, VII, 2629.

13. Kuroda Hideo, pp. 49–52.

14. Ishii Susumu, "Insei jidai," pp. 208.

15. Nagahara, "Land Ownership," p. 274 (Hitachi and Shinano); Ishii Susumu, *Kamakura bushi no jitsuzō*, p. 120.

16. Hall, *Government and Local Power*, p. 160. Hall also lists *kokuga ryō* at 10%, less than 1%, and 5% for Satsuma, Hyūga, and Ōsumi, respectively.

17. Ishii Susumu, *Kamakura bushi*, p. 104.

18. Inagaki Yasuhiko, "Chūsei nōgyō keiei to shūshu keitai," p. 171.

19. The origin of this thesis is Shimizu Mitsuo, *Jōdai no tochi kankei*, pp. 132-157.

20. Takeuchi, *Ritsuryō sei to kizoku seiken*, II, 461-475.

21. Sakamoto Shōzō, *Ōchō kokka*, pp. 241-323; for a simplified exposition of Sakamoto's views, see his *Sekkan jidai*, pp. 321-339.

22. For a discussion of disease in this era, see Farris, "Disease in Japan."

23. Machida Hiroshi and Arai Fusao, "Kazan hai ni yoru iseki no nendai suitei," pp. 79-80.

24. See *HI*, V, 1985.

25. Minegishi Sumio, "Tōgoku bushi no kiban," pp. 35-40.

26. The lack of documentation gives implicit support to the idea that epidemics were of critical importance in the eleventh century; those striken by diseases rarely leave records.

27. Sakamoto Shōzō, *Sekkan jidai*, pp. 321-325.

28. Ōyama Kyōhei, "Kokugaryō ni okeru ryōshu sei no keisei," pp. 56-57.

29. Ishii Susumu, *Kamakura bushi*, p. 98.

30. Inagaki, "Chūsei nōgyō," p. 172.

31. Yoshie Akio, "Ho no keisei to sono tokushitsu."

32. Ibid.

33. Farris, *Population, Disease, and Land*, pp. 50-149.

34. Toda Yoshimi, "Chūsei no hōken ryōshu sei," pp. 231-232.

35. Inagaki, "Chūsei nōgyō," pp. 175-182, is aiming his criticism at Nagahara Keiji. Nagahara's argument is found in *Nihon no chūsei shakai*, pp. 157-164. For a summary of the Inagaki-Nagahara debate, see Kimura Shigemitsu, "Chūsei zenki no nōgyō seisanryoku to hatasaku," pp. 54-63.

36. Fukuda, "Nihon kodai tetsu seisan no shoyōsō," p. 45. Also note Farris, *Population, Disease, and Land*, pp. 103-104.

37. Furushima Toshio, *Furushima Toshio chosaku shū 6 Nihon nōgyō gijutsu shi no kenkyū*, pp. 162-164.

38. Miura Keiichi, "Chūsei ni okeru nōgyō gijutsu no kaiyūteki seikaku."

39. On double-cropping, see Kuroda Hideo, *Kaihatsu shi*, pp. 261-269; Kimura, "Dai kaikon jidai," pp. 169-177.

40. Kimura, "Dai kaikon jidai," pp. 183-193.

41. Kuroda Hideo, *Kaihatsu shi*, pp. 70-73.

42. Ibid., pp. 240-251.

43. Ibid., pp. 97-141.

44. Ibid., pp. 52-64. Kuroda claims that all 10 of his examples come from the 1100s, but in fact only 4 do.

45. Ibid., pp. 12-13.

46. Ibid., pp. 15–16.

47. Kimura, "Dai kaikon jidai," pp. 157–158.

48. Kitō Hiroshi, *Nihon nisen nen no jinkō shi*, pp. 12–13, 46–47.

49. Several scholars have treated the Sōma Estate expertly, including Mass, *Warrior Government*, pp. 48–54; Yasuda, *Nihon hōken*, pp. 185–199; Fukuda, *Chiba*, pp. 95–114; Noguchi, pp. 137–143.

50. Fukuda, *Chiba*, pp. 96–97.

51. *SZKT, Azuma kagami*, Bunji 5/2/30, pp. 319–320.

52. Again studies are legion. Cf. Mass, *Warrior Government*, pp. 45–46; Yasuda, *Nihon hōken*, pp. 185–199; and Ishii Susumu, *Kamakura bushi*, pp. 95–142. The expert cited in this paragraph is Ishii.

53. *HI*, V, 2054.

54. Ishii Susumu, *Kamakura bushi*, p. 109.

55. *HI*, V, 2148–2149.

56. For the exposition of this estate, I follow Minegishi, pp. 33–68.

57. *SZKT, Azuma kagami*, Yōwa 1/9/7, p. 77.

58. *HI*, VII, 2719.

59. Suzuki Tetsuo, "Musashi no kuni, Kumagai gō ni okeru ryōshu to nōmin."

60. I depend upon Miyazaki Yasumitsu, "Kodai makki ni okeru Mino Genji no dōkō," and Motoki Yasuo, "Settsu Genji ichimon."

61. *HI*, V, 1677.

62. Ibid., pp. 1677–1678.

63. Among the authorities on Hata are Toda, "Hōken ryōshu sei," p. 23; Nagahara, *Nihon hōken sei seiritsu katei no kenkyū*, p. 90; Nagahara, *Nihon chūsei shakai kōzō no kenkyū*, p. 515; Nagahara, *Nihon no chūsei shakai*, pp. 63–74; and Gomi Fumihiko, "Shugo jitō sei no tenkai to bushi dan," p. 81.

64. *HI*, III, 1177.

65. Cf. Toda, "Hōken ryōshu sei," p. 240; and Gomi Fumihiko, "Shugo jitō sei," p. 81.

66. On Tomoda Estate, see Tanaka Fumihide, "Heishi seiken no keisei katei," pp. 27–40. Also note Uwayokote, *Nihon chūsei seiji shi kenkyū*, pp. 334–337.

67. On Kuroda Estate, I follow Koyama Yasunori, "Shōen sei keisei ki no ryōshu to nōmin," pp. 107–138. Also note Ishimoda, *Chūseiteki sekai*, pp. 81–259, who is quoted here.

68. Uwayokote, *Nihon chūsei seiji shi kenkyū*, pp. 10–38.

69. See *HI*, VII, 2629–2630.

70. To complete this study, I examined all terms which mean land clearance and are found in the index to *Heian ibun* for the period 1050–1185. The drawbacks to this approach are manifold. (1) Land may be opened without documentation. (2) A new parcel may be cleared without stating so explicitly. (3) The index is flawed and undoubtedly omits some cases. (4) Often important information such as the size of the parcel, the agent of land clearance (as opposed to the owner), the date, or the place is vague or unknown. (5) Some examples of late Heian land

clearance are not available in *Heian ibun,* but appear in Kamakura sources such as the *Azuma kagami* or *Kamakura ibun.*

71. Primary sources dealing with the Former Nine Years' War are collected in Kajiwara Masaaki, ed., *Mutsu waki.* Also of note is *Nihon shisō taikei: Kodai seiji shakai shisō,* pp. 229-251. Helen McCullough, "A Tale of Mutsu," provides a translation of the major source. Shōji Hiroshi, *Nihon shi 5 Henkyō no sōran,* has written a thorough analysis of the war. I follow Shōji for the romanization of personal and place names.

72. For theories on the Abe's lineage, see Shōji, pp. 28-29.

73. Helen McCullough, p. 187.

74. Ibid., p. 188.

75. *SZKT, Fusō ryakki,* Tengi 5/8/10, p. 294.

76. Ibid., p. 294.

77. Helen McCullough, p. 193.

78. For the ceremony transferring heads from Yoriyoshi's men to the Investigators' Office (Kebii shi) of Heian, see *ZST* 8 *Suisa ki,* Kōhei 6/2/16, p. 2.

79. Helen McCullough, p. 187. The 16 are noted in Yasuda, *Nihon hōken,* p. 153.

80. Helen McCullough, p. 192.

81. See Jeffrey Mass, *Warrior Government,* pp. 35-37. It should be noted, however, that Mass presents feudal vassalage and government methods of raising troops as polar opposites. Mass is following the work of Yasuda in *Nihon hōken,* pp. 150-163. Also see Noguchi, pp. 164, 230-255.

82. Yasuda, *Nihon hōken,* p. 113.

83. Shōji, pp. 82-85.

84. Helen McCullough, p. 194.

85. Shōji, pp. 76-78.

86. *SZKT, Fusō ryakki,* Tengi 5/12 and 5/12/25, p. 295; Kōhei 5/12/28, p. 298.

87. Helen McCullough, p. 190.

88. Shimomukai, "Ōchō kokka kokuga gunsei no kōzō to tenkai," pp. 45-60.

89. The arrest orders are mentioned several times, including *SZKT, Teiō hennen ki,* Tengi 4/8/3, 5/8/10, p. 285. The battle account is preserved in *SZKT, Fusō ryakki,* Kōhei 5/12/28, pp. 298-299.

90. Shimomukai, "Ōryō shi tsuibu shi no shoruikei," pp. 29-30.

91. Fukuda, "Ōchō gunji kikō," p. 115.

92. Helen McCullough, p. 194. *SZKT, Fusō ryakki,* Kōhei 5/12/28, p. 298, reports the same figure.

93. See Fukuda, "Ōchō gunji kikō," p. 115, for reference to soldiers' fleeing battle.

94. Abe's men and women seem to have thrown stones and not used catapults. Cf. Helen McCullough, p. 200.

95. Flags and the maneuver appear in ibid., p. 197.

96. Helen McCullough, p. 191.

97. Ibid., p. 192.

98. Ibid.

99. Ibid., pp. 192-193, 195-197, 202.

100. Ibid., p. 181.

101. For example, warriors competed to see who could be first to scale the enemy's ramparts, a competition also evident in *Tales of Times Now Past* (*Konjaku monogatari*). Helen McCullough, p. 195.

102. *Nihon koten bungaku taikei, Konjaku monogatari shū,* IV, 368-370.

103. Sources on the Latter Three Years' War are scarce, fragmentary, and, with a few brief exceptions, date from a century after the conflict. For the following summary of the war, I have relied upon Shōji, pp. 100-132 and Miya Tsugio, *Kassen emaki,* pp. 35-36. For controversial personal and place names, I follow Shōji. A handy comparison of primary texts for the war is included in Furuya Minoru, "Go sannen kassen ekotoba kotobagaki shakubun to Ōshū go sannen ki taishō ichiran," pp. 155-169. In addition, a portion of the conflict is recorded in *ZST, Yasutomi ki,* II, Bun'an 1/Int. 6/25, pp. 68-69. Also note *DNS,* 3rd Series, Vol. I.

104. Takeuchi Rizō, *Nihon no rekishi 6 Bushi no tōjō,* pp. 65-66. Shōji, pp. 90-91, doubts Takeuchi's speculation.

105. Furuya, "Go sannen kassen ekotoba," p. 167.

106. Ibid., p. 157.

107. *ZST, Yasutomi ki,* II, Bun'an 1/Int. 6/25, p. 69. The date 1086 is derived from a terse entry in *DNKK, Go Nijō Moromichi ki,* I, Ōtoku 3/9/28, p. 141.

108. *DNKK, Moromichi ki,* I, Ōtoku 3/10/7, p. 142.

109. I follow Furuya, "Go sannen kassen ekotoba," p. 159, rather than the *ZST, Yasutomi ki,* which has Yoshiie's brother Yoshimitsu join the Governor before Takehira arrives.

110. *SZKT, Honchō seiki,* Kanji 1/9/23, p. 284. Also cf. *DNS,* 3rd Series, I, 214.

111. Shōji, pp. 108-112, 114-118.

112. Furuya, "Go sannen kassen ekotoba," pp. 160-161. Again the chronology is uncertain.

113. Ibid., p. 160.

114. Ibid., p. 169.

115. *DNKK, Moromichi ki,* I, Kanji 2/1/25, p. 181.

116. Miya Tsugio, "*Go sannen kassen ekotoba* ni tsuite," in Komatsu Shigeru, *Kassen ekotoba,* pp. 117-120.

117. It is important to note that Japanese historians have included sources on the Latter Three Years' War in *DNS,* III, 1.

118. Furuya, "Go sannen kassen ekotoba," pp. 159-160.

119. Ibid., pp. 161-162.

120. Ibid., pp. 162-163.

121. Ibid., p. 160 for the armor; p. 164 for the arrow.

122. Ibid., p. 161.

123. Fukuda, "Ōchō gunji kikō," p. 116.

124. Furuya, "Go sannen kassen ekotoba," p. 163.

125. Fukuda, "Ōchō gunji kikō," pp. 115-116. Also see Yasuda Motohisa, *Minamoto no Yoshiie*, pp. 100-117.

126. See Mass, *Warrior Government*, pp. 36-37, who emphasizes the ephemeral quality of Yoshiie's ties to other fighters.

127. On these points, see Yasuda, *Nihon hōken*, pp. 86-91; Mass, *Warrior Government*, pp. 36-37. My interpretation differs from the view presented by these two scholars, who believe that the ban on estates commended to Yoshiie shows the Court feared his great power.

128. *DNS*, 3rd Series, VIII, 738.

129. My analysis owes much to Shimomukai, "Kokuga gunsei no kōzō," pp. 45-47.

130. For a detailed discussion of the Taira in the 12th century, see Chapter 7.

131. *SZKT, Chōya gunsai*, Daiji 4/3, p. 288.

132. *ZST, Chūyū ki*, VII, Chōshō 3/Int. 12/12, p. 119.

133. See ibid., VII, Chōshō 3/*kotoshi no jō*, p. 122.

134. *ZST, Chōshū ki*, II, Hoen 1/3/14, p. 254.

135. Ibid.

136. Ibid., pp. 260-261.

137. *ZST, Chūyū ki*, VII, Hoen 1/4/8, p. 141.

138. On the *shiki* system, see Nagahara, "Land Ownership," pp. 269-296.

139. Shimomukai, "Shoruikei," pp. 26-27.

140. Shimomukai, "Kokuga gunsei no kōzō," pp. 64-66, notes the decline in the power of the governors due to the rise of estates; also see Gomi Fumihiko, "Heishi gunsei no shodankai," p. 24, who argues that agents sent in from the outside to collect taxes had trouble commanding the rest of the provincial staff. Also note Takeuchi, *Kizoku seiken*, p. 456.

141. *ZST, Chōshū ki*, II, Hoen 1/4/8, p. 261.

142. Takahashi Masaaki, *Kiyomori izen*, pp. 196-199.

143. *ZST, Chūyū ki*, VII, Hoen 1/6/8, p. 153.

144. *ZST, Chōshū ki*, II, Hoen 1/8/19, p. 301.

145. *DNS*, 3rd Series, II, 201-202.

146. Ibid., 3rd Series, IX, 715. Note that Takahashi thinks that Masamori's personal retainers, numbering between 200 and 250, were more important than the forces from the provincial headquarters in this case. Cf. Takahashi Masaaki, *Kiyomori izen*, p. 89. Yet Takahashi is the historian who emphasizes the role of the provincial headquarters in these incidents of the 12th century.

147. *Nanto taishu jurakki*, in *Zoku gunsho ruijū*, XXIX-B, p. 326.

148. *SZKT, Honchō seiki*, Kyūan 3/7/15, p. 558. Note that Takahashi Masaaki, *Kiyomori*, pp. 251-256, gives greater weight to the warriors of the northern quarter of the capital in this incident.

149. Yasuda, *Nihon no rekishi 7 Insei to Heishi*, pp. 206-208.

CHAPTER 7

1. On the role of one of these aristocrats, Fujiwara no Tamefusa, see Takahashi Masaaki, *Kiyomori izen,* pp. 71-72.

2. See Mass, *Warrior Government,* p. 16. Also see Mass, "The Emergence of the Kamakura bakufu," pp. 127-134.

3. Cf. *DNS,* 3rd Series, III, 260-262.

4. My argument follows Yasuda, *Nihon shoki hōken sei no kiso kenkyū,* pp. 86-94.

5. Uwayokote, "Insei ki no Genji," 163-168.

6. *ZST, Chūyū ki,* VII, Hoen 1/4/8, p. 141.

7. *DNS,* 3rd Series, X, 16-17. See note 145, Chapter 6. Tanaka Fumihide, "Heishi seiken no keisei katei," p. 33, notes that some of Masamori's men may have come from Tomoda.

8. *ZST, Chōshū ki,* II, Gen'ei 2/12/27, p. 188.

9. On criticism of Shirakawa for granting a prize to Masamori, cf. *DNS,* 3rd Series, X, 55. Also see note 32 below.

10. See Cameron Hurst, *Insei: Abdicated Sovereigns in the Politics of Late Heian Japan, 1086-1185,* p. 308. One false Yoshichika of 1130 was subsequently killed by 20 horsemen and 40-50 foot soldiers led by an embarrassed member of the Investigators, Minamoto Mitsunobu. See also *ZST, Chōshū ki,* II, Daiji 5/8/3, p. 22; 8/9, p. 23; 9/9, p. 30; 8/13, pp. 48-49; *ZST Chūyū ki,* VI, Daiji 5/8/5, pp. 217-218; 8/9, p. 219; 10/14, pp. 238-239; 11/13, p. 249; 11/15, p. 250. On the Yoshichika of 1117, see *DNS,* 3rd Series, XVIII, 264-265; XIX, 186-188. Also see Takahashi Masaaki, *Kiyomori,* pp. 180-189 for the Yoshichika of 1123. Takahashi also provides an excellent analysis of the 1130 events and Tadamori's handling of a difficult situation.

11. On these troops, see Sasayama Haruo, "Tōgū bō tachiwaki no toneri no kenkyū," pp. 192-217. Also note Sasayama Haruo, "Heian zenki no sa u konoe fu ni kansuru kōsatsu," p. 610.

12. On the Investigators, see Tanimori Akio, *Kebii shi o chūshin to shitaru Heian jidai no keisatsu jōtai,* pp. 189-278; and Ōae Akira, *Ritsuryō seika no shihō to keisatsu,* pp. 72-154, 184-193, 207-215.

13. On the Warriors of the Northern Quarter, see Yoshimura Shigeki, "In hokumen kō"; Ishii Susumu, "Insei jidai," pp. 202-204; Hurst, *Insei,* pp. 281-282; Hashimoto Yoshihiko, *Heian kizoku shakai no kenkyū,* pp. 106-109; Takahashi, *Kiyomori,* pp. 137-145.

14. *DNS,* 3rd Series, XX, 15-16.

15. Other incidents from 1115 to 1156 not included in Chapter 5 and worthy of a brief note are the Investigators against the monks of Miidera in 1116; Masamori against some robbers in 1119; Tameyoshi and Tadamori against the clerics of Enryakuji in 1123; Tameyoshi against murderers in 1128; the Kebii shi (including Tameyoshi) dispatched to Nara against monks also in 1128; the Investigators against Enryakuji at Sakamoto in 1133; Tadamori as an Investigator against the Nara monks in 1138; the Kebii shi against monks in 1150; the Investigators

against murderers in the capital in 1152; the same (including Tameyoshi) against Ninnaji monks in the capital; and in 1153 the Investigators catching criminals.

16. "Tamefusa kyō ki," Shōryaku 3/6/2, unpublished text cited in *Dai Nihon shiryō kōhon*. See *Shiryō sōran*, II, 278.

17. *DNS*, 3rd Series, IX, 459.

18. I follow Takeuchi, *Nihon no rekishi* 6 *Bushi no tōjō*, pp. 294-302 on this incident.

19. *DNS*, 3rd Series, XIV, 147.

20. Ibid., p. 164.

21. On the 1215 battle, see Tanaka Minoru, "Insei to Jishō Juei no ran," p. 210.

22. *DNS*, 3rd Series, XIV, 182-183.

23. The Hōgen Disturbance has been described ably by Hurst, pp. 171-177. Also see William Wilson, tr., *Hogen monogatari, Tale of the Disorder in Hōgen,* a partial and reductionist translation of *The Tale of Hōgen.*

24. Uwayokote Masataka, "Insei ki no Genji," pp. 181-182. The following description derives mostly from this work.

25. *ZST, Dai ki,* I, Kōji 2/6/30, pp. 91-92.

26. Uwayokote, "Insei ki no Genji," pp. 171-181. For Yoshitomo's followers in the Bandō, see Yasuda, *Shoki hōken,* pp. 131-136; Ishii Susumu, *Kamakura bushi no jitsuzō,* pp. 145-147.

27. Uwayokote, "Insei ki no Genji," p. 172.

28. *ZST, Heihan ki,* II, Hōgen 1/7/11, pp. 117-118.

29. *SZKT, Gukan shō,* p. 121. See the translation by Delmer Brown and Ishida Ichirō, *The Future and the Past; A Translation and Study of the Gukan shō, an interpretive history of Japan written in 1219,* p. 89.

30. Uwayokote, "Insei ki no Genji," pp. 173-175.

31. The plot to move Sutoku to the Kanto is recounted in *SZKT, Gukan shō,* p. 131. Brown and Ishida, *The Future and the Past,* p. 101. Also note similar plots in 810 and 842. See Sasayama, "Bunken ni mirareru senjutsu to buki," p. 147.

32. Uwayokote, "Insei ki no Genji," p. 175.

33. Cf. Takahashi Masaaki, *Kiyomori,* pp. 276-280. The same relationship is noted in *NKBT, Hōgen monogatari,* p. 80. Wilson, *Hōgen monogatari,* pp. 23-24.

34. Conversation with Ishii Susumu, Professor at Tokyo University, summer 1986. Also note Yasuda, *Nihon no rekishi 7 Insei to Heishi,* p. 245, where he uses the 600 figure. See note 3 above.

35. Ishii Susumu, *Nihon no rekishi 7 Kamakura bakufu,* p. 133, estimates 2 foot-soldier followers per horseman for the Kamakura age. Although it is not clear, it seems that Ishii's source is the picture from the Ippen Scroll cited on the same page.

36. *NKBT, Hōgen monogatari,* p. 95.

37. Uwayokote, "Insei ki no Genji," pp. 175-176.

38. The Disturbance of 1159 is described succinctly in Hurst, pp. 189-190. Also see *SZKT, Gukan shō,* pp. 136-145, and Brown and Ishida, pp. 107-117. Also see Edwin Reischauer, tr., "The Tale of Heiji."

39. *SZKT, Gukan shō,* p. 138; Brown and Ishida, p. 110.

40. Ibid.

41. *NKBT, Heiji monogatari,* pp. 217, 223; Reischauer, pp 435, 438.

42. *NKBT, Heiji monogatari,* pp. 207–208; Reischauer, p. 420.

43. Hall, *Government and Local Power,* p. 144.

44. Mass, "The Emergence of the Kamakura Bakufu," p. 129. See also Mass, *Warrior Government,* pp. 18–30. Mass's work is based on Ishimoda, *Kodai makki seiji shi josetsu,* pp. 384–402, 470–487. Also see Tanaka Minoru, "Insei," pp. 206–211. It should be noted that Mass has modified his argument slightly in a recent essay, "The Kamakura bakufu," pp. 49–52.

45. A pioneer in the study of the Taira is Tanaka Fumihide. Articles include "Heishi seiken"; "Heishi seiken no kokuga shihai"; "Heishi seiken no zaichi shihai kōzō." Also note the work of Takada Minoru, "Heishi seiken ron josetsu"; Uwayokote, *Nihon chūsei seiji shi kenkyū,* pp. 241–292; and Ishii Susumu, "Heishi Kamakura ryō seiken ka no Aki kokuga."

46. For example, Noguchi, pp. 181–255; Gomi Fumihiko, "Heishi gunsei no shodankai"; "Insei shihai ken no ichi kōsatsu"; Nishimura Takashi, "Heishi 'ke'nin' hyō," pp. 113–186.

47. *ZST, Heihan ki,* III, Nin'an 2/5/10, p. 259.

48. Gomi Fumihiko, "Heishi gunsei," pp. 11–15.

49. *ZST, Heihan ki,* V, Kaō 1/12/23, pp. 145–146.

50. Gomi Fumihiko, "Heishi gunsei," pp. 13–14.

51. Amino, *Higashi to nishi,* pp. 116–121.

52. Gomi Fumihiko, "Heishi gunsei," pp. 15–16.

53. Nishimura, pp. 116–182.

54. Ibid., p. 183. Also see Gomi Fumihiko, "Heishi gunsei," pp. 4–6, and Noguchi, pp. 185–215.

55. Nishimura, p. 184.

56. Gomi Fumihiko, "Insei shihai," pp. 6–9, first proposed this idea.

57. Ishii Susumu, "Insei jidai," p. 205; Gomi Fumihiko, "Heishi gunsei," p. 6.

58. *Gyoku yō,* I, Angen 2/6/29, p. 589.

59. *ZST, Kikki,* I, Jishō 1/4/30, p. 93; *Gyoku yō,* II, Jishō 1/5/29, p. 51.

60. Gomi Fumihiko, "Heishi gunsei," pp. 6–9.

61. On Kawagoe, Oyama, Nitta, and Utsunomiya, see Noguchi, pp. 192, 210, 214; on Minamoto and Chiba, see Nishimura, pp. 140, 143.

62. The first to make this point was Takada, "Heishi seiken," p. 98.

63. *SZKT, Azuma kagami,* Yōwa 1/3/19, p. 71.

64. The classic expression of this view is Kikuchi Takeo, "Heishi zuryō hyō." Recently Kikuchi's work has been updated and corrected by Ishimaru Hiroshi, "Insei ki chigyō koku sei ni tsuite no ichi kōsatsu," pp. 89–116. Also see Mass, *Warrior Government,* pp. 25–26.

65. Gomi Fumihiko, "Heishi gunsei," p. 6.

66. Nishimura, pp. 183–184.

67. Noguchi, pp. 210–211.

68. *SZKT,* *Azuma kagami,* Yōwa 1/9/7, p. 77. Note the translation in Minoru Shinoda, *The Founding of the Kamakura Shogunate, 1180–1185,* pp. 223–224.
69. Noguchi, p. 211.
70. Tanaka Fumihide, "Heishi zaichi shihai," pp. 188–195.
71. Ibid., pp. 192–194.
72. Gomi Fumihiko, "Heishi gunsei," pp. 16–17.
73. *Gyoku yō,* II, Jishō 3/11/14, p. 308.
74. Ibid., II, Jishō 3/7/27, p. 291.
75. On this point, see ibid., II, Jishō 4/5/26, pp. 408–409; *ZST,* *Sankai ki,* III, Jishō 4/5/26, p. 96.
76. Gomi Fumihiko, "Heishi gunsei," pp. 19–21.
77. Uwayokote, *Nihon chūsei seiji,* pp. 257–292.
78. Mass, *Warrior Government,* pp. 107–111.
79. Tanaka Fumihide, "Heishi kokuga shihai," p. 35.
80. Uwayokote, *Nihon chūsei seiji,* p. 281.
81. Ishii Susumu, "Heishi Kamakura ryō seiken," p. 11; Takada Fumihide "Heishi seiken," pp. 100–101, agrees that the Saeki (the Taira vassal) used the title of land steward but does not believe that Kiyomori necessarily made the confirmation; see Notes 78 and 79 above.
82. Uwayokote, *Nihon chusei seiji,* pp. 279–285; Ishii Susumu, "Heishi Kamakura ryō seiken," p. 11: Ishimoda Shō, "Kamakura bakufu ikkoku jitō shiki no seiritsu," *Chūsei no hō to kokka,* p. 70.
83. Ishimoda, *Kodai makki,* pp. 470–487.
84. *SZKT,* *Zoku sajō shō,* Jishō 2/7/18, pp. 69–71.
85. The trouble the Taira had in using the provincial headquarters between 1181 and 1185 suggests this point. Cf. *Gyoku yō,* II, Jishō 5/2/7, p. 474, where the Investigators and aristocratic followers (not warriors of the province) were enrolled to fight in Mino; *HI,* VIII, 3031, where orders to Kii warriors were not routed through the provincial office; and *HI,* VIII, 3014–3015, where orders were given directly to Ise Shrine. Of course the Taira may have lost their grip on the provincial headquarters through military defeat and political ineptitude.
86. Gomi Fumihiko, "Heishi gunsei," pp. 22–25.
87. For the Taira desire to flee to northern Kyushu, see *Gyoku yō,* II, Jishō 3/11/15, p. 309; *SZKT,* *Hyakuren shō,* Jishō 3/11/15, p. 99.
88. The order of appointment for the commander-in-chief is cited by Ishimoda Shō, "Heishi seiken no sōkan shiki setchi," p. 52. Also see the analysis by Mass, *Warrior Government,* pp. 28–29.
89. Ishimoda, "Heishi seiken no sōkan setchi," pp. 57–59; Ishimoda, "Ikkoku jitō," pp. 36–57. Note that Gomi Fumihiko, "Heishi gunsei," disagrees with Ishimoda on the establishment of the estate foreman-in-chief, p. 28.
90. Gomi Fumihiko, "Heishi gunsei," p. 28.
91. Ibid., pp. 29–30.
92. For the order to collect boats for the Battle of Sunomata, see *HI,* VIII, 3014–3016.

93. Ibid., VIII, 3084.

94. Ibid., VIII, 3084.

95. Gomi Fumihiko, "Heishi gunsei," pp. 31–32.

96. Ishimoda, "Sōkan setchi," p. 62; "Ikkoku jitō," p. 36.

97. Ishii Susumu, "Heishi Kamakura ryō seiken," pp. 8–11.

98. See the excellent summary of the war provided by Shinoda, pp. 48–100. Mass gives a strong account from the Shogunate's point-of-view, *Warrior Government*, pp. 59–92. Also see Helen McCullough, *The Tale of the Heike*. In Japanese, see Ishii Susumu, *Nihon no rekishi 7 Kamakura bakufu;* Takeuchi, *Nihon no rekishi 6 Bushi no tōjō;* and Ōyama Kyōhei, *Nihon no rekishi 9 Kamakura bakufu.*

99. *The Tale of the Heike*, pp. 183–184; Uwayokote, "Insei no Genji," pp. 182–185.

100. Note the difference of opinion between Shinoda, pp. 48–69, and Mass, *Warrior Government*, p. 61, who emphasizes the speed of warrior response to Yoritomo.

101. *SZKT, Azuma kagami*, Jishō 4/10/18, p. 51.

102. Given Taira control of the Kanto as indicated by Noguchi, pp. 181–228, it seems incredible that any warriors chose to join Yoritomo.

103. *Gyoku yō*, II, Jishō 5/8/1, p. 519.

104. *SZKT, Azuma kagami*, Yōwa 1/Int. 2/20, p. 67; Int. 2/23, pp. 67–68; Int. 2/25, pp. 68–69; and Int. 2/28, p. 69, places Shida's revolt in 1181, but I follow Ishii Susumu, *Kamakura bakufu*, pp. 90–92, who locates the rebellion in the 2nd month of 1183.

105. For a recent examination of the order that formally granted Yoritomo his power in the Kanto, see Amino, *Higashi to nishi*, pp. 131–134.

106. *Gyoku yō*, III, bunji 1/4/4, p. 72.

107. Mass, "Kamakura bakufu," p. 52.

108. There is only one example of a woman warrior in *The Tale of the Heike*. See *Heike*, p. 292.

109. Ibid., pp. 188–190.

110. For examples, see Shinoda, p. 63; Mass, *Warrior Government*, p. 61.

111. Literacy among warriors and civil aristocrats is a topic that requires further study. Scholars assume that civil aristocrats were both literate and numerate, because they kept diaries and attended the government university where mathematics and the classics were taught. Warriors have left no such records, and did not attend schools. Also note *SZKT, Azuma kagami*, Jōkyū 3/6/15, pp. 775–776, where none of Kamakura's 5,000 troops (including the commanders) could read a Court proclamation. Yet one would think that those warriors employed at the provincial headquarters would need to read and write to do their jobs. Counting skills would also have been useful in preparing men and supplies for battle.

112. Despite the prominence of mounted warriors, foot soldiers also occasionally figure in battle from 1180–1185. See, for example, *NKBT, Heike monogatari*, II, 207 (Helen McCullough, p. 309); and *NKBT, Heike monogatari*, II, 66 (Helen McCullough, p. 227).

113. *ZST, Sankai ki*, III, Jishō 4/5/22, p. 96; *Gyoku yō*, II, Jishō 4/5/26, p. 409.

114. *Gyoku yō,* II, Juei 2/7/21, p. 608.
115. Ibid., III, Genryaku 1/6/16, p. 23.
116. *ZST, Sankai ki,* III, Jishō 4/11/6, p. 132.
117. Ibid., III, Jishō 4/11/30, p. 136.
118. *ZST, Kikki,* I, Yōwa 1/4/14, p. 192.
119. *Gyoku yō,* II, Yōwa 1/8/1, p. 519.
120. Ibid., II, Juei 2/Int. 10/30, p. 648.
121. *ZST, Kikki,* II, Juei 2/11/28, p. 77.
122. *SZKT, Azuma kagami,* Genryaku 1/3/1, p. 105. Shinoda, pp. 254-255. Also note Bunji 1/3/29, p. 144; Shinoda, pp. 301-302.
123. Shimomukai, "Ōryō shi tsuibu shi no shoruikei," p. 30.
124. Mass, *Warrior Government,* pp. 65-66, 78-89. For two other examples of Minamoto use of the provincial headquarters, see *SZKT, Azuma kagami,* Jishō 4/9/29, p. 47 (Shinoda, p. 180); and Genryaku 1/2/15, p. 101 (Shinoda, p. 252).
125. Ishii Susumu, *Nihon no rekishi 12 Chūsei bushi dan,* p. 232.
126. Ishii Susumu, *Chūsei kokka shi no kenkyū,* pp. 291-292. The first scholars to note the Minamoto reliance on the provincial headquarters were Satō Shin'ichi, "Shoki hōken shakai no keisei," and Ishimoda Shō, "Kamakura seiken no seiritsu katei ni tsuite."
127. On this problem, see Ishimoda, "Ikkoku jitō," pp. 36-45.
128. *NKBT, Hōjō ki,* pp. 29-32; A. L. Sadler, tr., *The Ten Foot Square Hut and Tales of the Heike,* pp. 6-9.
129. Mass, "Kamakura bakufu," p. 58, note 19.
130. Ishii Susumu, "Heishi Kamakura ryō seiken," pp. 9-11.
131. *SZKT, Azuma kagami,* Bunji 1/3/12, p. 142; Shinoda, p. 298; and *SZKT, Azuma kagami,* Bunji 1/1/6, p. 131, and Bunji 1/2/22, p. 139.

CHAPTER 8

1. For a basic introduction to Kamakura government, see John Hall, *Japan: From Prehistory to Modern Times,* pp. 85-90; Ishii Susumu, *Nihon no rekishi 7 Kamakura bakufu,* pp. 108-111, 197-213.
2. On constables and land stewards, see Mass, *Warrior Government,* pp. 93-229.
3. I follow Ishii Susumu, *Chūsei kokka shi no kenkyū,* pp. 179-194. Note the basic agreement of Ōyama, *Nihon no rekishi 9 Kamakura bakufu,* pp. 186-189.
4. In this respect, I follow Shinoda's interpretation, pp. 139-141.
5. The only treatment of the campaign in English is Mass, *Warrior Government,* pp. 144-151.
6. Of the many works on the Fujiwara, see Takahashi Tomio, *Ōshū Fujiwara shi yondai,* and Amino, *Higashi to nishi,* p. 108. Takahashi has called Fujiwara Hidehira the "King of the North," but, in the late 12th century, Hidehira usually went by the title "Master of the Six Districts" in Mutsu, or other Court-appointed offices.
7. *SZKT, Azuma kagami,* Bunji 5/7/19, pp. 337-339.
8. Mass, *Warrior Government,* p. 146.

9. Ibid., pp. 147-149.

10. Ibid., p. 147.

11. *SZKT, Azuma kagami*, Bunji 5/9/14, p. 352.

12. Ibid., Bunji 5/10/1, p. 359.

13. Ibid., Bunji 5/9/22, p. 357; Bunji 5/9/24, p. 358.

14. Good work on the Jōkyū War is plentiful. For instance, see Jeffrey Mass, *The Development of Kamakura Rule, 1180-1250;* William McCullough, "Shōkyū ki: An Account of the Shōkyū War"; William McCullough, "The *Azuma kagami* Account of the Shōkyū War." My summary owes much to these sources.

15. Ōyama, *Kamakura bakufu*, pp. 285-286.

16. See *DNS,* 4th Series, XV, 921, 923.

17. Ibid., p. 961; William McCullough, "Shōkyū ki," p. 193.

18. William McCullough, "Shōkyū ki," pp. 194-195.

19. Mass, "The Kamakura bakufu," p. 73.

20. See, for example, *SZKT, Azuma kagami*, Jōkyū 3/6/15, p. 776. William McCullough, "*Azuma kagami* Account," p. 131.

21. *DNS,* 4th Series, XV, 958; William McCullough, "Shōkyū ki," pp. 189-190.

22. *DNS,* 4th Series, XV, 961-962; William McCullough, "Shōkyū ki," pp. 193-194.

23. About half the Court's force of 20 died at Jiki, while 35% of Kamakura's 100 men perished.

24. *SZKT, Azuma kagami,* Jōkyū 3/5/19, p. 767.

25. Mass, *Lordship and Inheritance in Early Medieval Japan,* pp. 55-56.

26. Here note Ōyama, *Kamakura bakufu*, pp. 294-295, for an interpretation that emphasizes the functions of the provincial headquarters.

27. Tanaka Minoru, "Jōkyū kyōgata bushi no ichi kōsatsu"; "Jōkyū no ran go no shin jitō bunin chi shui."

28. See Mass, *Development of Kamakura Rule,* pp. 16-17.

29. Ibid., pp. 16-31.

30. On these pressure tactics, see *KI,* VI, 264; the tale of the non-warrior is told in *KI,* VII, 43.

31. Ishii Susumu, "Heishi Kamakura ryō seiken ka no Aki no kokuga," pp. 6-7.

32. Uwayokote, *Nihon chūsei seiji shi kenkyū*, pp. 347-357; "Kamakura bakufu to kuge seiken," pp. 54-57.

33. On guard duty, see Gomi Yoshio, "Kamakura goke'nin no ban'yaku gonji ni tsuite." Also note Seno Seiichirō, "Kyoto ōban'yaku gonji ni kansuru ichi kō-satsu."

34. Gomi Fumihiko, "Insei shihai ken no ichi kōsatsu," pp. 4-5.

35. Note the criticism by Mass, *Development of Kamakura Rule,* p. 17.

36. *DNS,* 4th Series, XV, 923.

37. Ibid., p. 958; William McCullough, "Shōkyū ki," pp. 189-190.

38. Mass, *Development of Kamakura Rule*, p. 43. It should be noted that Mass has softened this extreme view in "Kamakura bakufu," pp. 46-47, 73, 78.

39. Kuroda Toshio, *Shōen sei shakai*, p. 178.

40. Uwayokote, "Kamakura to kuge," p. 57; *Nihon chūsei*, pp. 362-381; Amino, *Higashi to nishi*, pp. 200-212.

41. Amino, *Higashi to nishi*, pp. 202-203.

42. Amino's stimulating analysis is found in *Nihon no rekishi* 10 *Mōko shūrai*, especially pp. 441-445.

43. The following summary of events is based on Yamada An'ei, *Fukuteki hen;* Ikeuchi Hiroshi, *Genkō no shin kenkyū*, I, 130-150, 219-354; and Nitta Hideharu, "Kamakura kōki no seiji katei." Also see Kawazoe Shōji, *Chūsei shi sensho* 1 *Mōko shūrai kenkyū shi ron*, for a discussion of the development of studies on the Mongol assaults. Recently, Ishii Susumu, "The Decline of the Kamakura bakufu," has written an excellent summary in English.

44. *Hachiman gudō kun*, cited in *Gunsho ruijū*, I, 466-467. On military technology, also see Suzuki Keizō, "Mōko shurai ekotoba ni arawaretaru busō ni tsuite."

45. Most historians write that the retreat resulted from a typhoon; but that thesis is now suspect because of the late date. See Amino, *Mōko shurai*, pp. 161-164. Also note Ishii Susumu, "Decline of Kamakura," pp. 138-140.

46. On the wall and other monuments of the battles, see Miike Ken'ichi, "Genkō kankei no shiseki."

47. Yamada An'ei, II, 28.

48. For instance, see ibid., I, 21.

49. Ibid., IV, 14, 18.

50. Nitta, p. 18.

51. Yamada An'ei, IV, 29-30.

52. Cf. Ishii Susumu, "Decline of Kamakura," pp. 139, 141, 146.

53. "Takezaki Suenaga no ekotoba," cited in Ishii Susumu et al., eds., *Nihon shisō taikei* (hereafter *NST*) 21 (A) *Chūsei seiji shakai shisō*, p. 416.

54. *KI*, XVI, 244. Note the analysis of Aida Nirō, *Mōko shūrai no kenkyū*, pp. 137-138.

55. Amino, *Mōko shūrai*, pp. 219-220.

56. Amino, *Higashi to nishi*, pp. 212-215.

57. For my definition of warrior group, I am indebted to Mass, *Warrior Government*, pp. 38-39.

58. Katō Tsutomu, "Chūsei tōgoku bushi dan no ichiran."

59. For a recent taxonomy of warrior bands, see Gomi Fumihiko, "Shugo jitō sei no tenkai to bushi dan," pp. 106-114.

60. *KI*, III, 248-249.

61. The list is included in *DNS*, 4th Series, XVI, 388-391. Also see *KI*, V, 20.

62. Yamanouchi Jō, "Iyo no kuni ni okeru bushi dan no seiritsu to tenkai."

63. Yasuda, "Bushi dan no keisei," pp. 154-159.

64. Fukuda, *Chiba Tsunetane*, pp. 132-133.

65. Noguchi, p. 144; Fukuda Toyohiko, "Gempei tōjō roku, sono Chiba shi kankei no setsuwa o chūshin toshite," p. 81.

66. Farris, *Population, Disease, and Land,* p. 15.

67. The following points are made by Tanaka Minoru, "Samurai bonge kō."

68. Satō Shin'ichi, Ikeuchi Yoshisuke, and Momose Kesao, eds., *Chūsei hōsei shiryō shū: Muromachi bakufu hō,* II, 361.

69. On the development of the system of housemen, see Mass, *Warrior Government,* pp. 143–167; Yasuda Motohisa, *Nihon shoki hōken sei no kiso kenkyū,* pp. 322–353; Ishii Susumu, *Chūsei kokka shi no kenkyū,* pp. 174–178.

70. Ishii Susumu, "Kamakura bakufu ron," pp. 116–117; *SZKT, Azuma kagami,* Bunji 1/10/24, p. 178. Note that Hall, *Government and Local Power,* p. 182, appears to accept this figure (2,000) as being the total number of all Kamakura housemen throughout Japan. While I would place the number somewhat higher, Hall's analysis is not fundamentally at odds with the one presented here.

71. These figures are derived as follows. Wakasa, Awaji, Izumi, Tajima, and Harima are listed in Ishii, "Kamakura bakufu ron," p. 119. Also see Tanaka Minoru, "Kamakura bakufu goke'nin seido no ichi kōsatsu," for more on Wakasa. For Sanuki, see Tanaka Minoru, "Sanuki no kuni no jitō goke'nin ni tsuite." For Hizen, see Seno Seiichirō, *Chinzei goke'nin no kenkyū,* pp. 157–214. On Iyo, see Tanaka Minoru, "Kamakura jidai ni okeru Iyo no kuni no jitō goke'nin ni tsuite." Calculations for Satsuma can be found in Gomi Yoshio, "Satsuma no goke'nin ni tsuite." On Ōsumi, see Gomi Yoshio, "Ōsumi no goke'nin ni tsuite." On Hyūga, see Gomi Yoshio, "Hyūga no goke'nin ni tsuite." On Buzen, see Era Hiromu, "Kamakura jidai no Buzen no kuni goke'nin ni tsuite."

72. Tanaka Minoru, "Iyo no kuni no jitō goke'nin," p. 288.

73. O'Connell, p. 75.

74. Philippe Contamine, *War in the Middle Ages,* p. 25.

75. O'Connell, pp. 70–76, 87–89.

76. Kitō, pp. 12–13.

77. Fukuda, *Taira no Masakado no ran,* pp. 16–17.

78. *SZKT, Ruijū sandai kyaku,* Tempyō 5/11/14 Edict cited in Daidō 5/5/11, OCS, p. 560, states that each Strong Fellow was allocated 2 followers in the 8th century. Ishii Susumu, *Kamakura bakufu,* p. 133, states that every mounted warrior in the Kamakura era had 2 or 3 foot soldiers.

79. For another analysis of warrior rights in estates, which includes some comparison of warrior and proprietor incomes, see Mass, *Warrior Government,* pp. 171–202. Note especially pp. 172–173, where Mass lists 9 categories of land-steward income.

80. *Tsuika hō* cited in *NST, Chūsei shisō,* pp. 95–96.

81. Ibid., p. 98.

82. It is important to note, as Jeffrey Mass has, that these new standards did not apply to all appointments of land stewards after 1221. See Mass, *Development of Kamakura Rule,* pp. 48–55.

83. See ibid., which includes articles against a warrior's taking living expenses

from peasants while residing at the estate, against confiscating the contents of boats washed ashore on estate lands, against using both the income standards customary to an estate before 1223 and those established in 1223 at the same time, and against squeezing travelers for fees.

84. *KI,* I, 365-367; II, 314-315; XXVII, 162-163. Also note the analysis of Abe Takeshi, *Nihon shōen shi,* pp. 206-211, 226-228; and Kawane, pp. 121-152.

85. *KI,* I, 379-380.

86. My calculations were done as follows. For the rice tax, Kanetaka received the 5-*shō* surtax for 263.7 *chō* in Kuwabara, plus 5 *go* per 263.7 *chō,* plus 3.37 *to* and 5 *shō* for his own 3 *chō,* plus 3.37 *to* and 5 *shō* for 10 *chō* of unopened land, for a grand total of 193.5 *koku* of rice. The total earned by the proprietor (Mt. Kōya) was 889.6469 *koku;* thus Kanetaka received about 22% of the proprietor's receipts.

On the commodities tax, Kanetaka was allotted the earnings from his own 3 *chō* plus the 50 *chō* of *gesu myō,* plus 10 *chō* of wilderness. If one uses a standard for all Mt. Kōya estates from the early Muromachi era of 300 coins (*mon*) per *tan* of land, then Kanetaka's total receipts would have been 189 strings of cash (*kammon*), as compared with the proprietor's 462 strings, or about 40%.

It should be noted that my calculations for the rice tax at Ōta differ slightly from those made by Hall, *Government and Local Power,* pp. 174-176. He argues that the rice tax amounted to about 2.9 *to,* or about 24% of the yield and that lesser officials (warriors) received about .85 *to,* or 7% of the produce. By Hall's calculation, lower-level staff at Ōta received about 29% of the proprietor's receipts, as compared to my figure of 22%. The 7% differential between Hall's figures and mine is due to the fact my figures are from the late 12th century while his are from the mid-13th. The thrust of Hall's argument is similar to mine.

Hall relies on Egashira Tsuneharu, "Bingo no kuni Ōta no shō no kenkyū," p. 10, who miscalculates the rate of rice taxation for Kuwabara.

87. *KI,* II, 3.

88. Kanetaka's 3 *chō* were only 1% of the land at Kuwabara, instead of the 9% mandated by the 1223 laws. He drew the commodities tax from 23 *chō* of land in the 2 villages of Fukutomi and Uga Shigemitsu, which is about 9%. But, since Kanetaka received only the commodities tax from that 23 *chō,* he was still below the standard.

89. On Nuta Estate, see Ishii Susumu, *Chūsei bushi dan,* pp. 245-291.

90. *KI,* VIII, 410-418; X, 338-340.

91. *KI,* X, 214-218. See Nishioka, *Shōen shi no kenkyū,* III, 739-780, for an analysis of this record. For a translation of the document, see Asakawa Kan'ichi, tr. and ed., *The Documents of Iriki,* pp. 136-143.

92. For this record, see *KI,* IX, 87-91, and the analysis of Gomi Fumihiko, "Jitō shihai to kenchū."

93. *KI,* VII, 410-415.

94. On Ategawa, see *KI,* XV, 133-134; XVI, 46; XVI, 137-139; XI, 237-238. Also the analysis by Nakamura Ken, "Jitō hihō to katakana gonjō jō."

95. There is confusion about Shida's actual area. A tax record (*KI,* V, 197)

lists it as 826 *chō*, while the land record of Hitachi province gives Shida's area as 620 *chō* (*KI*, XVIII, 283).

96. The calculation works as follows. A document from 1137 (*HI*, V, 2015) lists the land for taxation at Ategawa at 43.7 *chō*, and the amount of 6-*jō* silk received as tax at 65.5 *hiki*. Division of the total number of *tan* (one-tenth of a *chō*, thus 437) into the total number of *jō* (1 *hiki* = 6 *jō*) yields .9 *jō* (2.7 meters) of silk per *tan*.

97. The calculation is as follows. The granddaughter of Emperor Takakura got 300 *hiki* in 1223, which is multiplied by 6 to obtain 1,800 *jō*. If the area of Shida was 826 *chō* and 1 *tan* produces .9 *jō* as at Ategawa, then the total produced was 7434 *jō*, of which 1,800 is about 24%. If the area was 620 *chō*, then the answer would be 1,800 *jō* divided by 5,580 *jō*, or 32%. In 1276, the granddaughter received 330 *hiki*, or 1,980 *jō*, divided by 7,434 and 5,580 to obtain 27% and 35%, respectively.

In both cases, there are two important underlying assumptions. The first is that 1 *hiki* of 6-*jō* silk (produced at Ategawa) and 8-*jō* silk (produced at Shida) were the same. While 6-*jō* silk had been the standard since the 8th century, the origin of 8-*jō* silk is unclear. Obviously, if the 8-*jō* silk was 2 *jō* larger than the 6-*jō* silk, then the answers would be altered. (For 1223, the calculation would be 2,400/7,434 = 32% or 2,400/5,580 = 43%, depending upon the area. For 1276, the new calculation would be 2,640/7,434 = 36%, or 2,640/5,580 = 47%. The Kyoto aristocrat receives less than the warrior in all cases and the outcome is not significantly different.)

A second assumption is that production of silk in the area around the capital at Ategawa was the same as that in the Kanto (Shida), an unverifiable premise.

98. Amino, *Higashi to nishi*, p. 207.

99. Ishii Susumu, *Chūsei bushi dan*, pp. 110-112; Ishii Susumu, "Chūsei shakai ron," pp. 348-350.

100. For this criticism of Ishii's diagram, see Ōyama Kyōhei, *Nihon chūsei nōson shi no kenkyū*, pp. 462-472.

101. See Farris, *Population, Disease, and Land*, pp. 50-73.

102. For this point, see Farris, "Disease in Japan, 500-1600."

103. Cf. Kitō, p. 53. His index of cold weather is highest for the period 1150-1350. Also note Yamamoto Takeo, *Kikō no kataru Nihon no rekishi*. His ideas are summarized in Yamamoto Takeo, "Rekishi no nagare ni sou Nihon to sono shūhen no kikō hensen." This phenomenon is already documented for Europe. See David Herlihy, "Ecological Conditions and Demographic Change," p. 35.

104. Cf. Ishii Susumu's characterization of the medieval era as having a "fragmented aspect" (*bunretsuteki sokumen*), "Chūsei shakai ron," pp. 341-347.

105. Farris, *Population, Disease, and Land*, p. 13.

CONCLUSIONS

1. On theories of the Chinese-style state, see Farris, *Population, Disease, and Land*, pp. 141-149.

2. Ishii Susumu, "Chūsei shakai ron," pp. 340–341. Also note Ishii's discussion of the power of the Chinese-style state of the Taihō Codes in *Chūsei kokka shi no kenkyū*, pp. 6–21.

3. Farris, *Population, Disease, and Land*, pp. 142–144.

4. Shimizu Mitsuo, cited in Ishii, *Chūsei kokka*, p. 12.

5. The leading advocate of such a definition is Brown, "The Tyranny of a Construct: Feudalism and Historians of Feudal Europe."

6. Ishii Susumu, *Nihon no rekishi 7 Kamakura bakufu*, pp. 159–160. The order is contained in *SZKT Azuma kagami*, Bunji 1/4/15, p. 146–149. Note Shinoda, p. 121.

7. The definition of *feudalism* employed here is essentially Bloch's, II, 446.

8. Amino, *Nihon no rekishi 10 Mōko shūrai*, pp. 441–445.

9. This thesis is explored in Farris, *Population, Disease, and Land*, esp. pp. 18–140.

10. McNeill, *Plagues and Peoples*, p. 124.

11. Robert Gottfried, *The Black Death*, pp. 16–32, 103.

12. The issue of class formation is much debated, even for early modern and modern English history. See, for example, E. P. Thompson, "Eighteenth-century English society: class struggle without class?"; Harold Perkin, *The Origins of Modern English Society;* or Ira Katznelson and Aristide Zolberg, *Working-class Formation.* Each of these historians differs in his theory of class and how applicable it is to modern England, much less premodern Japan.

Anthropology addresses classes and class formation. See especially Gerald Berreman, "Social Inequality: A Cross-cultural Analysis." Berreman has developed a schema describing stratification in different societies all over the world; he distinguishes between "category" and "group," the former having no consciousness of their common interests while the latter does. I would define Japanese warriors as a category according to Berreman's schema, but find it difficult to be more specific.

On the differences between class, status, and estate, see Reinhard Bendix and Seymour Lipset, eds., *Class, Status, and Power*, pp. 5–28; Kurt Mayer, ed. *Class and Society*, pp. 1–28; and Melvin Tumin, *Social Stratification.*

13. Ishii Susumu, *Nihon no rekishi 13 Chūsei bushidan*, p. 236.

14. Amino, *Higashi to nishi no*, pp. 152–172.

15. On the weakness of vassalage in the Kamakura period, see Mass, "The Early Bakufu and Feudalism."

16. Satō Shin'ichi, "Jidai to jimbutsu," pp. 7–9.

17. Fukuda, "Ōchō gunji kikō to nairan," p. 104.

18. Contamine, p. 31.

19. Georges Duby, *The Chivalrous Society*, pp. 59–80, 94–111, 134–148, 158–170, 178–185.

20. Contamine, p. 31.

21. Ibid., pp. 239–242.

22. Georges Duby, *The Early Growth of the European Economy*, pp. 157–270.

23. Farris, *Population, Disease, and Land*, pp. 94–117.

24. Contamine, pp. 15–17.

25. See Duby, *Chivalrous Society,* pp. 103, 106, 161.
26. McNeill, *History of the Human Community,* p. 332.
27. Ishimoda, *Chūseiteki sekai no keisei,* pp. 233–317.
28. Kuroda Toshio, *Nihon chūsei no kokka to shūkyō,* pp. 3–45.
29. Ibid., p. 32.
30. Ishii Susumu,"Chūsei shakai ron," pp. 332–341.
31. Kitō, pp. 11–17.

Bibliography

The place of publication is not given for works published in Tokyo.

Primary Sources

Azuma kagami (Mirror of the East). In *Shintei zōho kokushi taikei* (A library of Japanese history, revised ed.). Vols. XXXII–XXXIII. Yoshikawa kōbunkan, 1964.

Chōshū ki (Diary of Minamoto no Morotoki). In *Zōho shiryō taisei* (Historical materials, revised ed.). Vols. XVI–XVII. Kyoto: Rinsen shoten, 1965.
Chōya gunsai (Collected documents from Court and country). In *Shintei zōho kokushi taikei*. Vol. XXIX. Yoshikawa kōbunkan, 1938.
Chūyū ki (Diary of Fujiwara no Munetada). In *Zōho shiryō taisei*. Vols. IX–XV. Kyoto: Rinsen shoten, 1965.

Dai ki (Diary of Fujiwara no Yorinaga). In *Zōho shiryō taisei*. Vols. XXIII–XXV. Kyoto: Rinsen shoten, 1965.
Dai Nihon komonjo (Documents of Japan). Vols. I–XXV. Tōkyō daigaku shuppan kai, 1901.
Dai Nihon shiryō (Historical materials of Japan), Series 1, 2, 3, 4, 5. Shiryō hensan kakari, 1925–1986.

Emishi shiryō (Sources on the "barbarians" of the northeast). In *Tōhoku shi shiryō shū* (Collection of historical materials on the northeast). Vol. I. Yoshikawa kōbunkan, 1957.
Engi shiki (The Ordinances of Engi). In *Shintei zōho kokushi taikei*. Vol. XXVI. Yoshikawa kōbunkan, 1973.

Fudoki (Gazetteers). In *Nihon koten bungaku taikei* (A library of classical Japanese literature). Ed. Akimoto Kichirō. Vol. II. Iwanami shoten, 1958.
Fusō ryakki (Abbreviated annals of Japan). In *Shintei zōho kokushi taikei*. Vol. XII. Yoshikawa kōbunkan, 1965.

Go Nijō Moromichi ki (Diary of Fujiwara no Moromichi). In *Dai Nihon kokiroku* (Records of Japan). 3 vols. Iwanami shoten, 1956–1958.
Go sannen kassen ekotoba kotobagaki shakubun to Ōshū go sannen ki taishō ichiran (Comparative texts of the Annal of the Latter Three Years' War in Mutsu and the

picture scroll of battles in the Latter Three Years' War). Ed. Furuya Minoru.
In Komatsu Shigeru, ed., *Nihon emaki taisei* 15 *Go sannen kassen ekotoba* (A library
of Japanese picture scrolls: Picture scroll of battles in the Latter Three Years'
War). Chūō kōron sha, 1977.
Gukan shō (Humble interpretations). In *Shintei zōho kokushi taikei*. Vol. XIX.
Yoshikawa kōbunkan, 1964.
Gyoku yō (A jeweled leaf: Diary of Fujiwara no Kanezane). 3 vols. Geirin sha,
1975.

Hachiman gudō kun (Teaching my foolish children of Hachiman). In *Gunsho ruijū*
(Assorted writings). Vol. I. Keizai zasshi sha, 1898.
Heian ibun (Documents from the Heian period). Ed. Takeuchi Rizō. 13 vols.
Tōkyō dō, 1965.
Heihan ki (Diary of Taira no Nobunori). In *Zōho shiryō taisei*. Vols. XVIII–XXII.
Kyoto: Rinsen shoten, 1965.
Heiji monogatari (A tale of Heiji). In *Nihon koten bungaku taikei*. Ed. Nagazumi
Yasuaki and Shimada Isao. Vol. XXXI. Iwanami shoten, 1961.
Heike monogatari (A tale of the Taira). In *Nihon koten bungaku taikei*. Eds. Takaki
Ichinosuke, et al. Vols. XXXII–XXXIII. Iwanami shoten, 1959.
Hōgen monogatari (A tale of Hōgen). In *Nihon koten bungaku taikei*. Eds. Nagazumi
Yasuaki and Shimada Isao. Vol. XXXI. Iwanami shoten, 1961.
Hōjō ki (A tale of a ten-foot-square hut). In *Nihon koten bungaku taikei*. Ed. Nishio
Makoto. Vol. XXX. Iwanami shoten, 1957.
Honchō seiki (Chronicle of this Court). In *Shintei zōho kokushi taikei*. Vol. IX.
Yoshikawa kōbunkan, 1964.
Hyakuren shō (Manuscript of one hundred smeltings). In *Shintei zōho kokushi taikei*.
Vol. XI. Yoshikawa kōbunkan, 1929.

Ichikawa shi shi: shiryō hen (A history of Ichikawa city: Historical materials). Ed.
Takeuchi Rizō. Vol. V. Ichikawa city: Ichikawa shi shi hensan iinkai, 1973.
Iwate-ken Kitakami-shi Saraki chō Hatten iseki kinkyū chōsa hōkoku (Report on the
emergency investigation of Saraki Block Hatten. Site in Kitakami city). Sendai:
Tōhoku gakuin daigaku Tōhoku bunka kenkyūjo, 1972.

Jiu Tang shu (Old history of the Tang dynasty). Vol. VIII. Peking: Zhonghua,
shuju, 1975.

Kamakura ibun (Documents from the Kamakura age). Ed. Takeuchi Rizō. Vols.
I–XXVII. Tōkyōdō, 1971–1984.
Kanoko C iseki urushigami monjo: Hombun hen (Lacquer documents from Kanoko C
Site: Text). Mito: Ibaraki-ken kyōiku zaidan, 1983.
Kikki (Diary of Yoshida Tsunefusa). In *Zōho shiryō taisei*. Vols. XXIX–XXX.
Kyoto: Rinsen shoten, 1965.
Kōnin shiki (The ordinances of Kōnin). In *Shintei zōho kokushi taikei*. Vol. XXVI.
Yoshikawa kōbunkan, 1937.

Konjaku monogatari shū (Tales of times now past). In *Nihon koten bungaku taikei*. Ed. Yamada Takao, et al. Vols. XXII–XXVII. Iwanami shoten, 1961.

Man'yōshūt (Collection of myriad leaves). In *Nihon koten bungaku taikei*. Eds. Gomi Tomohide, et al. Vols. VII–X. Iwanami shoten, 1959.

Mishima jiicombo kofun gun (The tumuli at Mishima). Yamaguchi: Yamaguchi-ken kyōiku iinkai, 1983.

Miyoshi Kiyoyuki. *Iken jūnikajō* (Twelve-article opinion). In *Nihon shisō taikei: Kodai seiji shakai shisō* (A library of Japanese thought: Ancient politics and society). Ed. Takeuchi Rizō. Vol. VIII. Iwanami shoten, 1979.

Mutsu waki (A tale of Mutsu). Ed. Kajiwara Masaaki. Gendai shichō sha, 1982.

——. In *Nihon shisō taikei: Kodai seiji shakai shisō*. Ed. Ōzone Shōsuke. Iwanami shoten, 1979.

Nanto taishu jurakki (Annal of Nara monks' advance on the capital). In *Zoku gunsho ruijū* (Assorted writings, continued). Vol. XXIX-B. Zoku gunsho ruijū kansei kai, 1925.

Nihon kiryaku (Abbreviated Japanese annals). In *Shintei zōho kokushi taikei*. Vols. X–XI. Yoshikawa kōbunkan, 1929.

Nihon kōki (Latter chronicles of Japan). In *Shintei zōho kokushi taikei*. Vol. III. Yoshikawa kōbunkan, 1934.

Nihon Montoku tennō jitsuroku (The Veritable Records of the Emperor Montoku). In *Shintei zōho kokushi taikei*. Vol. III. Yoshikawa kōbunkan, 1934.

Nihon ryōiki (Miraculous stories of Japan). In *Nihon koten bungaku taikei*. Eds. Endō Yoshimoto and Kasuga Kazuo. Vol. LXX. Iwanami shoten, 1967.

Nihon sandai jitsuroku (The Veritable Records of three reigns). In *Shintei zōho kokushi taikei*. Vol. IV. Yoshikawa kōbunkan, 1934.

Nihon shoki (Chronicles of Japan). In *Nihon koten bungaku taikei*. Eds. Sakamoto Tarō, et al. Vols. LXVII–LXVIII. Iwanami shoten, 1965.

Owari no kuni gunji hyakusei ra ge (Report of the people and district magistrate of Owari). In *Nihon shisō taikei: Kodai seiji shakai shisō*. Ed. Takeuchi Rizō. Vol. VIII. Iwanami shoten, 1979.

Ritsuryō (Penal and administrative statutes). In *Nihon shisō taikei*. Eds. Inoue Mitsusada, et al. Vol. III. Iwanami shoten, 1976.

Ruijū fusen shō (Assorted orders). In *Shintei zōho kokushi taikei*. Vol. XXVII. Yoshikawa kōbunkan, 1933.

Ruijū kokushi (Assorted national histories). In *Shintei zōho kokushi taikei*. Vols. V–VI. Yoshikawa kōbunkan, 1933–34.

Ruijū sandai kyaku (Assorted regulations from three reigns). In *Shintei zōho kokushi taikei*. Vol. XXV. Yoshikawa kōbunkan, 1936.

Ryō no gige (Interpretations of the Administrative Codes). In *Shintei zōho kokushi taikei*. Vol. XXII. Yoshikawa kōbunkan, 1966.

Bibliography

Ryō no shūge (Collected commentaries on the Administrative Codes). In *Shintei zōho kokushi taikei*. Vols. XXIII–XXIV. Yoshikawa kōbunkan, 1966.

Sakei ki (Diary of Minamoto no Tsuneyori). In *Zōho shiryō taisei*. Vol. VI. Kyoto: Rinsen shoten, 1965.

Sankai ki (Diary of Nakayama Tadachika). In *Zōho shiryō taisei*. Vols. XXVI–XXVIII. Kyoto: Rinsen shoten, 1965.

Sata miren sho (A legal handbook). In *Chūsei hōsei shiryō shū: Muromachi bakufu hō* (A collection of medieval legal materials: Muromachi law). Eds. Satō Shin'ichi, Ikeuchi Yoshisuke, and Momose Kesao. Vol. II. Iwanami shoten, 1969.

Shiryō sōran (An overview of historical materials). Vols. I–V. Tōkyō daigaku shuppan kai, 1925.

Shoku Nihongi (Chronicles of Japan, continued). In *Shintei zōho kokushi taikei*. Vol. II. Yoshikawa kōbunkan, 1935.

Shoku Nihon kōki (Latter chronicles of Japan, continued). In *Shintei zōho kokushi taikei*. Vol. III. Yoshikawa kōbunkan, 1934.

Shōmon ki (The tale of Masakado). Ed. Kajiwara Masaaki. 2 vols. Heibon sha, 1975.

———. In *Nihon shisō taikei: Kodai seiji shakai shisō*. Ed. Takeuchi Rizō. Vol. VIII. Iwanami shoten, 1979.

———. Ed. Hayashi Rokurō. Gendai shichō sha, 1975.

Shōyū ki (Diary of Fujiwara no Sanesuke). In *Dai Nihon kokiroku*. 10 vols. Iwanami shoten, 1959–1982.

Shun ki (Diary of Fujiwara no Sukefusa). In *Zōho shiryō taisei*. Vol. VII. Kyoto: Rinsen shoten, 1965.

Sui shu (A history of the Sui dynasty). Vol. VI. Peking: Zhonghua shuju, 1973.

Suisa ki (Diary of Minamoto no Toshifusa). In *Zōho shiryō taisei*. Vol. VIII. Kyoto: Rinsen shoten, 1965.

Taga-jō urushigami monjo (Lacquer documents from Fort Taga). Sendai: Miyagi-ken bunkazai hogo kyōkai, 1979.

"Takezaki Suenaga no ekotoba" (The picture scroll of Takezaki Suenaga). In *Nihon shisō taikei: Chūsei seiji shakai shisō* (Medieval politics and society). Ed. Ishii Susumu. Vol. XXI. Iwanami shoten, 1972.

"Tamefusa kyōki" (Diary of Fujiwara no Tamefusa). Unpublished manuscript cited in *Dai Nihon shiryō kōhon* (Draft of historical materials of Japan). 10 vols.

Teiō hennen ki (Annals of the Emperor). In *Shintei zōho kokushi taikei*. Vol. XII. Yoshikawa kōbunkan, 1965.

Tōhoku jūkan jidōsha dō kankei maizō bunka zai chōsa hōkoku sho 13 Hotta hō hachi chō iseki (Report on the investigation of buried cultural properties related to the northeastern north-south highway: The site at Hotta hō Hachi chō). Morioka: Iwate-ken kyōiku iinkai, 1982.

Tsuika hō (Appended laws). In *Nihon shisō taikei: Chūsei seiji shakai shisō*. Ed. Kasamatsu Yūji. Vol. XXI. Iwanami shoten, 1972.

Yasutomi ki (Diary of Nakahara Yasutomi). In *Zōho shiryō taisei*. Vols. XXXVII–XXXIX. Kyoto: Rinsen shoten, 1965.

Zoku sajō shō (Medieval records). In *Shintei zōho kokushi taikei*. Vol. XXVII. Yoshikawa kōbunkan, 1965.

Secondary Sources

Abe Takeshi. *Nihon shōen shi* (A history of Japanese estates). Shinsei sha, 1970.

Aida Nirō. *Mōko shūrai no kenkyū* (The Mongol Invasions). Revised ed. Yoshikawa kōbunkan, 1982.

Amino Yoshihiko. *Higashi to nishi no kataru Nihon no rekishi* (Japanese history east and west). Soshiete bunko, 1982.

———. *Nihon no rekishi 10 Mōko shūrai* (Japanese history: The Mongol Invasions). Shōgakkan, 1974.

——— and Ishii Susumu, eds. *Shūkan Asahi hyakka Nihon no rekishi 1 Chūsei 1 Genji to Heishi* (Asahi weekly encyclopedia: The Minamoto and Taira). Asahi shimbun sha, 1986.

Anazawa, Wakō, and Manome Jun'ichi, "Two Inscribed Swords from Japanese Tumuli: Discoveries and Research on Finds from the Sakitama-Inariyama and Eta-Funayama Tumuli." In Richard Pearson, ed., *Windows on the Japanese Past: Studies in Archeology and Prehistory*. Ann Arbor: University of Michigan Press, 1986.

Aoki Kazuo. *Nihon no rekishi 5 Kodai gōzoku* (Ancient local strongmen). Shōgakkan, 1974.

———. *Nihon no rekishi 3 Nara no miyako* (Nara). Chūō kōron sha, 1965.

The Art of War. Tr. Thomas Cleary. Boston: Shambahla, 1988.

Asakawa, Kan'ichi. "Some Aspects of Japanese Feudal Institutions," *Transactions of the Asiatic Society of Japan* Series I 46: 77–102 (1918).

Batten, Bruce. "Foreign Threat and Domestic Reform," *Monumenta Nipponica* 41: 199–219 (1986).

Bendix, Reinhard and Seymour Lipset, eds. *Class, Status, and Power*. 2nd ed. New York: The Free Press, 1966.

Berreman, Gerald. "Social Inequality: A Cross-Cultural Analysis." In Berreman, ed., *Social Inequality*. New York: Academic Press, 1981.

Bloch, Marc. *Feudal Society*. 2 vols. Chicago: University of Chicago Press, 1961.

———. *French Rural History: An Essay on its Basic Characteristics*. Tr. Janet Sondheimer. Berkeley: University of California Press, 1965.

Bronowski, Jacob. *The Ascent of Man*. Boston: Little, Brown, 1973.

Brown, Elizabeth. "The Tyranny of a Concept: Feudalism and Historians of Feudal Europe," *American Historical Review* 79: 1063–1088 (April 1974).

Collcutt, Martin. "Daimyō and Daimyō Culture." In *Japan, The Shaping of Daimyō Culture, 1185–1868*. Washington: National Gallery of Art, 1988.

Bibliography

Contamine, Philippe. *War in the Middle Ages*. Oxford: Oxford University Press, 1984.

Coulborn, Rushton, ed. *Feudalism in History*. Princeton: Princeton University Press, 1966.

DeBary, Wm. Theodore, Ryusaku Tsunoda, and Donald Keene, eds. *Sources of Japanese Tradition*. New York: Columbic University Press, 1958.

The Documents of Iriki. Tr. and Ed. Asakawa Kan'ichi. Nihon gakujutsu shinkō kai, 1955.

Duby, Georges. *The Chivalrous Society*. Berkeley: University of California Press, 1977.

——. *The Early Growth of the European Economy*. Ithaca: Cornell University Press, 1974.

Duus, Peter. *Feudalism in Japan*. New York: Alfred Knopf, 1969.

Edwards, Walter. "Event and Process in the Founding of Japan: The Horserider Theory in Archeological Perspective," *The Journal of Japanese Studies* 9: 265–295 (Winter 1983).

Egashira Tsuneharu. "Bingo no kuni Ōta no shō no kenkyū" (Ōta estate), *Keizai shi kenkyū* (Economic history) 39: 1–27 (January 1933).

Elvin, Mark. *The Pattern of the Chinese Past*. Stanford: Stanford University Press, 1973.

Era Hiromu. "Kamakura jidai no Buzen no kuni goke'nin ni tsuite" (Buzen housemen), *Kyūshū shigaku* (Kyushu history) 20: 11–16 (August 1962).

Farris, William Wayne. "Disease in Japan, 500–1600." In Kenneth Kiple, ed., *The Cambridge History and Geography of Human Disease*. Cambridge: Cambridge University, in press.

——. *Population, Disease, and Land in Early Japan, 645–900*. Cambridge: Council on East Asian Studies, Harvard University, 1985.

Friday, Karl. "Teeth and Claws: Provincial Warriors and the Heian Court," *Monumenta Nipponica* 43: 153–185 (Summer 1988).

Fukuda Toyohiko. *Chiba Tsunetane*. Yoshikawa kōbunkan, 1973.

——. "Gempei tōjō roku, sono Chiba shi kankei no setsuwa o chūshin toshite" (A record of the battles between the Minamoto and Taira: Tales of the Chiba), *Tōkyō kōgyō daigaku jimbun ronsō* (Articles in the humanities from Tokyo Industrial University) 1: 65–91 (December 1975).

——. "Nihon kodai tetsu seisan no shoyōsō." (Iron production in ancient Japan), *Nihon shi kenkyū* (Japanese history) 280: 29–51 (December 1985).

——. "Ōchō gunji kikō to nairan" (Aristocratic military structure and rebellion), *Iwanami kōza Nihon rekishi* 4 *Kodai* 4 (Iwanami lectures in Japanese history, ancient). Iwanami shoten, 1975.

——. *Taira no Masakado no ran* (The rebellion of Taira no Masakado). Iwanami shoten, 1981.

Furushima Toshio. *Furushima Toshio chosaku shū* 6 *Nihon nōgyō gijutsu shi no kenkyū*

(Collected works of Furushima Toshio: A history of Japanese agrarian technology). Tōkyō daigaku shuppan kai, 1975.

The Future and the Past: A Translation and Study of the Gukan shō, an interpretive history of Japan written in 1219. Tr. Delmer Brown and Ishida Ichiro. Berkeley: Univerity of California Press, 1979.

Gomi Fumihiko. "Heishi gunsei no shodankai" (Stages in the Taira military system), *Shigaku zasshi* (Historical journal) 88: 1–36 (August 1979).

———. "Insei shihai ken no ichi kōsatsu" (Control under the Retired Emperor), *Nihon shi kenkyū* 158: 1–22 (October 1975).

———. "Jitō shihai to kenchū" (Land steward control and land surveys), *Nihon rekishi* (Japanese history) 390: 23–41 (November 1980).

———. "Shugo jitō sei no tenkai to bushi dan" (Warrior bands and the development of the constable and land steward), *Iwanami kōza Nihon rekishi* 5 *Chūsei* 1 (Medieval). Iwanami shoten, 1975.

Gomi Yoshio. "Hyūga no goke'nin ni tsuite" (Hyūga housemen), *Kagoshima daigaku bungakka ronshū* (Collected articles from the Literature Department of Kagoshima University) 7: 47–74 (December 1971).

———. "Kamakura goke'nin no ban'yaku gonji ni tsuite" (Guard duty for Kamakura housemen), *Shigaku zasshi* 63: 28–45 (September 1954); 63: 22–33 (October 1954).

———. "Ōsumi no goke'nin ni tsuite" (Ōsumi housemen), *Nihon rekishi* 130: 34–47 (April 1959); 131: 21–32 (May 1959).

———. "Satsuma no goke'nin ni tsuite" (Satsuma housemen), *Ka dai shigaku* (History at Kagoshima University) 6: 1–39 (September 1958); 7: 59–66 (August 1959).

Gotō Shūichi, "Jōmon shiki bunka" (Jōmon culture), *Zusetsu Nihon bunka shi taikei* 1 *Jōmon Yayoi kofun jidai* (Pictorial library of Japanese cultural history: Jōmon, Yayoi, and Tomb Periods). Shōgakkan, 1965.

Gottfried, Robert. *The Black Death*. New York: Free Press, 1983.

Hall, John. "Feudalism in Japan—A Reassessment." In John Hall and Marius Jansen, eds., *Studies in the Institutional History of Early Modern Japan*. Princeton: Princeton University Press, 1968.

———. *Government and Local Power in Japan, 500 to 1700*. Princeton: Princeton University Press, 1966.

———. *Japan: From Prehistory to Modern Times*. New York: Delacorte, 1970.

Hamaguchi Shigekuni. *Shin kan zui tō shi no kenkyū* (A history of the Chin, Han, Sui, and Tang Periods). Vol. I. Tōkyō daigaku shuppan kai, 1966.

Hamilton, Malcolm and Maria Hirszowicz. *Class and Inequality in Pre-Industrial, Capitalist and Communist Societies*. New York: St. Martin's Press, 1987.

Hara Hidesaburō. "Gunji to chihō gōzoku" (Local magnates and the district magistrate), *Iwanami kōza Nihon rekishi* 3 *Kodai* 3. Iwanami shoten, 1975.

———. "Taika no kaishin ron hihan josetsu" (A critical introduction to the debate over the Taika Reforms), *Nihon shi kenkyū* 86: 25–45 (September 1966); 88: 23–48 (January 1967).

Hara Katsuo. *Nihon chūsei shi no kenkyū* (A history of Japan's Middle Ages). 2nd ed. Heibon sha, 1969.

Haruta Takayoshi. "Masakado no ran ni okeru buryoku soshiki" (Military organization in Masakado's revolt), *Shigen* (Historical fountain) 2: 44–51 (May 1967).

Hashimoto Yoshihiko. *Heian kizoku shakai no kenkyū* (Aristocratic society in the Heian period). Yoshikawa kōbunkan, 1976.

Hashimoto Yū. *Ritsuryō gundan sei no kenkyū* (The provincial military system). Osaka: Hashimoto Yū shi ikōshū kai, 1982.

Hayakawa Shōhachi. *Nihon no rekishi 4 Ritsuryō kokka* (The Chinese-style state). Shōgakkan, 1974.

——, "Ritsuryō sei no keisei" (Formation of the Chinese-style state), *Iwanami kōza Nihon rekishi 2 Kodai 2*. Iwanami shoten, 1975.

Hayashida Shigeyoshi. "Nihon zairai uma no genryū" (Origins of the Japanese horse). In Mori Kōichi, ed., *Nihon kodai bunka no tankyū 9 Uma* (The search for ancient Japanese culture: The horse). Shakai shisō sha, 1974.

Herlihy, David. "Ecological Conditions and Demographic Change." In Richard DeMolen, ed., *One Thousand Years: Western Europe in the Middle Ages*. Boston: Houghton Mifflin, 1973.

Higuchi Takayasu, ed. *Kodai shi hakkutsu 5 Tairiku bunka to seidoki* (Excavations in ancient history: Continental culture and bronze articles). Kōdan sha, 1974.

Hirakawa Minami. "Kodai ni okeru Tōhoku no jōsaku ni tsuite" (Ancient fortresses of the northeast), *Nihon shi kenkyū* 236: 2–20 (April 1982).

——. "Kodai no jōsaku ni kansuru shiron" (Ancient fortresses), *Genshi kodai shakai kenkyū* (Primitive and ancient society). Vol. IV, Azekura shobō, 1975.

——. "Tōhoku dai sensō jidai" (The Great Northeastern War). In Takahashi Takashi, ed., *Kodai chihō shi 6 Ōu hen* (Local ancient history: The northeast). Asakura shoten, 1978.

Hirano Kunio. "Yamato ōken to Chōsen" (Yamato power and Korea), *Iwanami kōza Nihon rekishi 1 Genshi oyobi kodai* (Primitive and ancient history). Iwanami shoten, 1975.

Hirano Tomohiko. "Kondei sei seiritsu no haikei to sono yakuwari" (Background and function of the Strong Fellows). In *Nihon kodai shi ronkō* (Essays on ancient Japanese history). Yoshikawa kōbunkan, 1980.

Hōgen monogatari, Tale of the Disorder in Hōgen. Tr. William Wilson. Sophia University Press, 1971.

Horiuchi Kazuaki. "Chūsei shoki buryoku no tokushitsu" (Characteristics of military power in the early medieval period), *Ritsumeikan bungaku* (Literature at Ritsumeikan University) 306: 66–88 (December 1970); 307: 57–74 (January 1971).

——. "Heian chūki kebii shi no buryoku ni tsuite" (Military power of the Investigators in the middle Heian period). In *Ronkyū Nihon kodai shi* (Essays in ancient Japanese history). Gakusei sha, 1979.

Hoshino Ryōsaku. *Kenkyū shi: Jinshin no ran* (Research history: The Civil War of 672). Yoshikawa kōbunkan, 1973.

Hurst, Cameron. *Insei: Abdicated Sovereigns in the Politics of Late Heian Japan, 1086–1185.* New York: Columbia University Press, 1976.

Ienaga Saburō, et al., eds. *Zusetsu Nihon bunka shi taikei 2 Asuka jidai* (A pictorial library of Japanese cultural history: Asuka period). Shōgakkan, 1965.

——, et al., eds. *Zusetsu Nihon bunka shi taikei 4 Heian jidai* (The Heian period). Vol. I. Shōgakkan, 1966.

Ikeuchi Hiroshi. *Genkō no shin kenkyū* (The Mongol Invasions). 2 Vols. Tōyō bunko, 1931.

Imaizumi Takao. "Hasseiki gunryō no nin'yō to shutsuji" (Appointment and descent of district magistrates in the eighth century), *Shigaku zasshi* 81: 1–43 (December 1972).

Inagaki Yasuhiko. "Chūsei nōgyō keiei to shūshu keitai" (Medieval agriculture and forms of exploitation), *Iwanami kōza Nihon rekishi 6 Chūsei 2*. Iwanami shoten, 1975.

——. *Nihon chūsei shakai shi ron* (Medieval Japanese social history). Tōkyō daigaku shuppan kai, 1981.

Inoue Kaoru. *Nihon kodai no seiji to shūkyō* (Ancient Japanese politics and religion). Yoshikawa kōbunkan, 1961.

Inoue Mitsuo. *Heian jidai gunji seido no kenkyū* (Military institutions of the Heian period). Yoshikawa kōbunkan, 1980.

Inoue Mitsusada. *Nihon kodai shi no shomondai* (Problems in ancient Japanese history). Shisaku sha, 1949.

——. *Nihon no rekishi 3 Asuka no chōtei* (The Asuka Court). Shōgakkan, 1974.

——. *Nihon no rekishi 1 Shinwa kara rekishi e* (From myth to history). Chūō kōron, 1965.

——. "Taika no kaishin to higashi Ajia" (The Taika Reforms and East Asia), *Iwanami kōza Nihon rekishi 2 Kodai 2*. Iwanami shoten, 1975.

Ishii Masakuni. *Warabite tō* (Warabite swords). Yūsan kaku, 1966.

Ishii Ryōsuke. *Taika no kaishin to Kamakura bakufu no seiritsu* (Taika Reforms and the establishment of the Kamakura Shogunate). Sōbun sha, 1972.

Ishii Susumu. *Chūsei kokka shi no kenkyū* (A history of the medieval state). Iwanami shoten, 1970.

——. "Chūsei seiritsu ki gunsei kenkyū no ichi shiten" (Military system in the formative medieval period), *Shigaku zasshi* 78: 1–32 (December 1969).

——. "Chūsei shakai ron" (Medieval society), *Iwanami kōza Nihon rekishi 8 Chūsei 4*. Iwanami shoten, 1975.

——. "The Decline of the Kamakura bakufu." In Kozo Yamamura, ed., *The Cambridge History of Japan, Volume III, Medieval Japan*. Cambridge: Cambridge University Press, 1990.

——. "Heishi Kamakura ryō seiken ka no Aki kokuga" (The Aki provincial headquarters under the Taira and Kamakura), *Rekishigaku kenkyū* 257: 1–12 (September 1961).

——. "Insei jidai" (Era of the Retired Sovereign). In *Kōza Nihon shi 2 Hōken* shakai no seiritsu (Lectures in Japanese history: The establishment of feudal society). Tōkyō daigaku shuppan kai, 1970.

———. "Kamakura bakufu ron" (The Kamakura Shogunate), *Iwanami kōza Nihon rekishi* 5 *Chūsei* 1. Iwanami shoten, 1962.

———. *Kamakura bushi no jitsuzō* (Kamakura warriors). Heibon sha, 1987.

———. *Nihon no rekishi* 12 *Chūsei bushi dan* (Medieval warrior bands). Shōgakkan, 1974.

———. *Nihon no rekishi* 7 *Kamakura bakufu* (Kamakura Shogunate). Chūō kōron sha, 1965.

Ishimaru Hiroshi. "Insei ki chigyō koku sei ni tsuite no ichi kōsatsu" (On proprietary provinces under the Ex-Emperor), *Hokkaidō daigaku bungaku bu kiyō* (Articles from the Department of Letters of Hokkaido University) 28: 59–119 (March 1971).

Ishimoda Shō. *Chūseiteki sekai no keisei* (The formation of the medieval world). Iwanami shoten, 1985.

———. "Heishi seiken no sōkan shiki setchi" (Establishment of the commander-in-chief under the Taira). In Kurokawa Takaaki and Kitazume Masao, eds., *Ronshū Nihon rekishi* 4 *Kamakura seiken* (Essays in Japanese history: Kamakura power). Yūsei dō, 1976.

———. "Kamakura bakufu ikkoku jitō shiki no seiritsu" (Establishment of the province-wide land stewards under the Kamakura Shogunate). In Ishimoda Shō and Satō Shin'ichi, eds., *Chūsei no hō to kokka* (Medieval law and the state). Tōkyō daigaku shuppan kai, 1960.

———. "Kamakura seiken no seiritsu katei ni tsuite" (Formation of Kamakura power), *Rekishigaku kenkyū* 200: 2–16 (October 1956).

———. *Kodai makki seiji shi josetsu* (Political history at the end of the ancient era). Mirai sha, 1964.

Ishio Yoshihisa. *Nihon kodai hō no kenkyū* (Ancient Japanese law). Hōritsu bunka sha, 1959.

Ishioka Hisao. "Sakanoue no Tamuramaro to sono shūhen no kyūjutsu" (Sakanoue no Tamuramaro and his archery skills), *Kokugakuin daigaku kiyō* (Articles from Kokugakuin University) 5: 21–39 (May 1964).

Isshi Shigeki, "Kamboku kō" (State pastures), *Shinano* 2: 39–62 (April 1950); 2: 43–76 (May 1950).

———, et al., "Nagano-ken Matsumoto-shi Kita Haibara suitei Shinano bokugen chōseki chōsa hōkoku" (Report on the investigation of the pasture office for Shinano province at Kita Haibara, Matsumoto city, Nagano prefecture), *Shinano* 16: 1–31 (December 1964).

Itō Nobuo. "Inasaku no hokushin" (Northern advance of rice cultivation). In Itō Nobuo and Takahashi Tomio, eds., *Kodai no Nihon* 8 *Tōhoku* (Ancient Japan: The northeast). Kadokawa shoten, 1970.

Iyanaga Teizō. *Nara jidai no kizoku to nōmin* (Peasant and aristocrat in the Nara period). Jibundō, 1956.

Kadowaki Teiji. "Emishi no hanran" (Rebellion of the "barbarians"), *Ritsumei-kan bungaku* 96: 41–57 (May 1953).

———. "*Taika no kaishin*" *ron* (The debate over the Taika Reforms). Tokuma shoten, 1967.

Kagamiyama Takeshi. *Kōkogaku Raiburari-4 Dazaifu iseki* (Archeology library: The site at Dazaifu). Nyū saiensu sha, 1979.

Kameda Takashi. *Jinshin no ran*. (The Civil War of 672) Revised ed. Jibun dō, 1966.

Kanaseki Hiroshi and Sahara Makoto, eds. *Kodai shi hakkutsu 4 Inasaku no hajimari* (The beginning of rice cultivation). Kōdan sha, 1975.

Katō Tsutomu. "Chūsei tōgoku bushi dan no ichiran" (Warrior bands in medieval eastern Japan), *Musashino* 52: 39–61 (April 1973).

Katznelson, Ira and Aristide Zolberg. *Working-Class Formation*. Princeton: Princeton University Press, 1986.

Kawane Yoshihiro. *Chūsei hōken sei seiritsu shi ron* (Establishment of the medieval feudal system). Tōkyō daigaku shuppan kai, 1971.

Kawazoe Shōji. *Chūsei shi sensho 1 Mōko shūrai kenkyū shi ron* (Research history of the Mongol Invasions). Yūsan kaku, 1977.

Kidder, J. Edward. "The Archaeology of the Early Horse-riders in Japan," *Transactions of the Asiatic Society of Japan*. 3rd Series. 20: 89–123 (1985).

———. *Early Buddhist Japan*. New York: Praeger, 1972.

———. "The Fujinoki Tomb and Its Grave-Goods," *Monumenta Nipponica* 42: 57–87 (Spring 1987).

———. "Saddle Bows and Rump Plumes," *Monumenta Nipponica* 45: 75–85 (Spring 1990).

Kikuchi Takeo. "Heishi zuryō hyō" (Taira absentee governors). In *Sekai rekishi jiten* (Dictionary of world history). Vol. XXII. Heibon sha, 1956.

Kimura Shigemitsu. "Chūsei zenki no nōgyō seisanryoku to hatasaku" (Productivity of early medieval agriculture and dry fields), *Nihon shi kenkyū* 280: 52–82 (December 1985).

———. "Dai kaikon jidai no kaihatsu" (Age of land clearance). In Miura Keiichi, ed., *Gijutsu no shakai shi 1 Kodai chūsei no gijutsu to shakai* (A social history of technology: Ancient and medieval technology and society). Yūhikaku, 1982.

Kirihara Takeshi. "Shinano ni okeru shūba no tō no kōkogakuteki kōsatsu" (Archeology of the band of horse movers in Shinano). In *Chūbu kōchi no kōkogaku* (Archeology of the central uplands). Nagano: Nagano-ken kōko gakkai, 1978.

Kishi Toshio. *Fujiwara no Nakamaro*. Yoshikawa kōbunkan, 1969.

———. *Nihon kodai seiji shi kenkyū* (Ancient Japanese political history). Hanawa shobō, 1966.

Kitō Hiroshi. *Nihon nisen nen no jinkō shi* (Two thousand years of Japanese population history). Kyoto: PHP kenkyūjo, 1983.

Koguchi Yasuo. "Ritsuryō gundan sei no gunji kunren seido—zoku" (Military drills in the provincial militia—part 2), *Shoku Nihongi kenkyū* (Research on *The Chronicles of Japan, Continued*) 222: 1–34 (August 1982).

———. "Sekichō ni miru ritsuryō gundan heishi no bugei kunren" (Military drills of soldiers in the provincial militia as seen in household and tax registers), *Shoku Nihongi kenkyū* 225: 25–40 (February 1983).

Bibliography

Komatsu Masao. "Shōnai Akio shi no 'Akita-jō naigai kenshutsu no tateana jūkyo ato' o megutte" (On Shonai Akio's article entitled "Residences discovered within and outside of Fort Akita"), *Akita kōkogaku* (Akita archeology) 38: 18–26 (March 1984).

Koyama Yasunori. "Shōen sei keisei ki no ryōshu to nōmin" (Lord and peasant during the formation of estates). In Inagaki Yasuhiko, ed., *Shōen no sekai* (The world of estates). Tōkyō daigaku shuppan kai, 1973.

Kudō Masaki. "Emishi Ainu setsu to hi Ainu setsu" (Were the "barbarians" Ainu or not?). In *Kyūjō no kenkyū* (Palaces and forts). Vol. II. Seibun dō, 1983.

Kuroda Hideo. *Nihon chūsei kaihatsu shi no kenkyū* (A history of land clearance in medieval Japan). Azekura shobō, 1984.

Kuroda Kōichirō. "Jingū kebii shi no kenkyū" (Investigators at Ise Shrine), *Nihon shi kenkyū* 107: 1–20 (September 1969).

Kuroda Toshio. *Nihon chūsei no kokka to shūkyō* (The medieval Japanese state and religion). Iwanami shoten, 1975.

——. *Shōen sei shakai* (Society under the estate system). Nihon hyōron sha, 1967.

Kuwahara Shirō. "Tōhoku no kodai jōsaku" (Ancient fortresses in the northeast). In *Nihon jōkaku taikei bekkan* 1 *Jōkaku kenkyū nyūmon* (A library on Japanese fortresses: An introduction to research). Shin jimbutsu ōrai sha, 1981.

Ledyard, Gari, "Galloping Along with the Horseriders: Looking for the Founders of Japan," *The Journal of Japanese Studies* 1: 217–254 (Spring 1975).

McCullough, Helen. "A Tale of Mutsu," *Harvard Journal of Asiatic Studies* 25: 178–211 (1964–65).

—— and William McCullough. *A Tale of Flowering Fortunes*. 2 vols. Stanford: Stanford University Press, 1980.

McCullough, William. "The *Azuma kagami* Account of the Shōkyū War," *Monumenta Nipponica* 23: 102–155 (1968).

——. "Shōkyū ki: An Account of the Shōkyū War," *Monumenta Nipponica* 19: 163–215; 19: 420–455 (1964).

Machida Hiroshi and Arai Fusao. "Kazan hai ni yoru iseki no nendai suitei" (Estimating age of sites through volcanic ash). In *Kodai Nihon no tetsu to shakai* (Iron and society in ancient Japan). Heibon sha, 1982.

McNeill, William. *A History of the Human Community*, I, *Prehistory to 1500*. 2nd ed. Englewood Cliffs: Prentice-Hall, 1987.

——. *Plagues and Peoples*. Garden City: Doubleday, 1976.

——. *The Pursuit of Power*. Chicago: The University Press, 1982.

The Manyōshū. Tr. Nippon gakujutsu shinkōkai. New York: Columbia University Press, 1965.

Mass, Jeffrey. *The Development of Kamakura Rule, 1180–1250*. Stanford: Stanford University Press, 1979.

——. "The Early Bakufu and Feudalism." In Jeffrey Mass, ed., *Court and Bakufu in Japan*. New Haven: Yale University Press, 1982.

———. "The Emergence of the Kamakura bakufu." In Jeffrey Mass and John Hall, eds., *Medieval Japan: Essays in Institutional History*. New Haven: Yale University Press, 1974.

———. "The Kamakura bakufu." In Kozo Yamamura, ed., *The Cambridge History of Japan, Volume III, Medieval Japan*. Cambridge: Cambridge University Press, 1990.

———. *Lordship and Inheritance in Early Medieval Japan*. Stanford: Stanford University Press, 1989.

———. *Warrior Government in Early Medieval Japan*. New Haven: Yale University Press, 1974.

Matsumoto Masaharu. "Saikaidō ni okeru shokoku kijō sei no seiritsu" (Weapons in Kyushu), *Shoku Nihongi kenkyū* 227: 1–19 (June 1983).

Matsumoto Shimpachirō. "*Shōmon ki* no inshō" (Impressions of the *Tale of Masakado*), *Bungaku* 19: 6–21 (October 1951).

Mayer, Kurt. *Class and Society*. Revised ed. New York: Random House, 1955.

Miike Ken'ichi. "Genkō kankei no shiseki" (Sites of the Mongol Invasions), *Gunji shigaku* (Military history) 11: 58–63 (January 1975).

Miller, Roy. "Linguistic Evidence and Japanese Prehistory." In Richard Pearson, ed., *Windows on the Japanese Past*. Ann Arbor: University of Michigan Press, 1986.

Minegishi Sumio. "Tōgoku bushi no kiban" (The base of eastern warriors). In Inagaki Yasuhiko, ed., *Shōen no sekai*. Tōkyō daigaku shupan kai, 1973.

Miura Keiichi "Chūsei ni okeru nōgyō gijutsu no kaikyūteki seikaku" (Class character of medieval agrarian technology), *Nihon shi kenkyū* 82: 1–14 (January 1966).

Miya Tsugio. *Kassen emaki* (Picture scrolls of battles). Kadokawa shoten, 1977.

Miyake Chōbei. "Masakado no ran no shiteki zentei" (Historical premise for the Masakado revolt), *Ritsumeikan bungaku* 112: 57–73 (September 1954).

Miyazaki Yasumitsu. "Kodai makki ni okeru Mino Genji no dōkō" (The Minamoto of Mino in the late ancient period), *Shoryō bu kiyō* (Articles by the division of tombs) 30: 22–36 (February 1978).

Mizuno Yū. "Jinshin no ran, " in Ōbayashi Taryō, ed., *Nihon kodai bunka no tankyū: Tatakai* (War). Shakai shisō sha, 1984.

Mori Kōichi. "Kōkogaku to uma" (Archeology and the horse). In Mori Kōichi, ed., *Nihon kodai bunka no tankyū 9 Uma*. Shakai shisō sha, 1974.

Morita Tei. *Heian jidai seiji shi kenkyū* (Politics in the Heian era). Yoshikawa kōbunkan, 1978.

———. "Kebii shi no kenkyū" (Investigators), *Shigaku zasshi* 78: 1–44 (September 1969).

——— and Miyanaga Gen. "Heian zenki tōgoku no gunji mondai ni tsuite" (Military problems in the east in the early Heian period), *Kanezawa daigaku kyōiku gakubu kiyō* (Essays of the Education Department of Kanezawa University) 24: 230–242 (December 1975).

Motoki Yasuo. "Settsu Genji ichimon" (The Settsu Minamoto), *Shirin* (Historical forest) 67: 1–31 (November 1984).

Bibliography

Murao Jirō. *Kammu tennō* (The Kammu Emperor). Yoshikawa kōbunkan, 1963.
Muraoka Kaoru. "Hasseiki matsu 'Seii' saku kentō" (Policy to "subjugate the barbarians" at the end of the eighth century). In Takeuchi Rizō, ed., *Kodai tennō sei to shakai kōzō* (Social structure and the ancient imperial system). Azekura shobō, 1980.
———. "Ritsuryō kokka to gunji soshiki" (The Chinese-style state and military organization), *Rekishigaku kenkyū bessatsu tokushū* (Special ed.): 60–69 (November 1975).

Nagahara Keiji. "Land Ownership under the *Shōen-kokugaryō* system," *The Journal of Japanese Studies* 1: 269–296 (Spring 1975).
———. *Nihon chūsei shakai kōzō no kenkyū* (Social structure in medieval Japan). Iwanami shoten, 1973.
———. *Nihon hōken sei seiritsu katei no kenkyū* (The establishment of Japan's feudal system). Iwanami shoten, 1961.
———. *Nihon no chūsei shakai* (Medieval Japanese society). Iwanami shoten, 1968.
———, ed. *Shimpojiumu Nihon rekishi 7 Chūsei kokka ron* (Symposium in Japanese history: Medieval state). Gakusei sha, 1974.
Nakamura Akizō. "Fujiwara no Hirotsugu no ran" (The Revolt of Fujiwara no Hirotsugu). In Ōbayashi Taryō, ed. *Nihon kodai bunka no tankyū: Tatakai.* Shakai shisō sha, 1984.
Nakamura Ken. "Jitō hihō to katakana gonjō jō" (Land steward violations and peasant protest). In Inagaki Yasuhiko, ed., *Shōen no sekai.* Tōkyō daigaku shuppan kai, 1973.
Naoki Kōjirō. "Gundan no heisū to haibi no han'i ni tsuite" (Number of soldiers in the provincial militia and the limits of their deployment), *Shoku Nihongi kenkyū* 7: 1–5 (August 1960).
———. "Ikko ichi heishi no gensoku to tempeiritsu" (Draft rates and the rule of one soldier per household), *Nihon rekishi* 175: 34–37 (December 1962).
———. *Jinshin no ran* (The Civil War of 672). Hanawa shobō, 1961.
———. "Kodai tennō no shiteki heiryoku ni tsuite" (Private military power of ancient emperors), *Shirin* 45: 1–32 (March 1962).
———. *Nihon kodai heisei shi no kenkyū* (A history of Japan's ancient military system). Yoshikawa kōbunkan, 1968.
———. *Nihon no rekishi 1 Wakoku no tanjō* (The birth of Japan). Shōgakkan, 1974.
———. "Sakimori to tōgoku" (Border Guards and the Eastern Provinces), *Shoku Nihongi kenkyū* 4: 28–35 (February 1957).
Neale, R. S. *Class in English History 1680–1850.* Oxford: Basil Blackwell, 1981.
Nihongi, Chronicles of Japan from the Earliest Times to A. D. 697. Tr. William Aston. 2 vols. London: Kegan, Trench, Trubner, 1896.
Niida Noboru. "Tō Gumbō-ryō to hōsui seido" (Tang articles on military and defense and beacons), *Hōsei shi kenkyū* (Legal history) 4: 197–212 (1953).
Niino Naoyoshi. "Gangyō no ran no shiteki igi" (Historical significance of the Rebellion of 878), *Rekishi* (History) 41: 1–12 (June 1971).

——. *Kenkyū shi: Kuni no miyatsuko* (Local strongmen). Yoshikawa kōbunkan, 1974.

Nishimura Takashi. "Heishi ke'nin hyō" (Taira vassals). In *Nihon shi ronsō* (Essays in Japanese history). Kyoto: Hakubun dō, 1983.

Nishioka Toranosuke. "Kihei sei no hattatsu to bushi" (The warrior and the development of cavalry), *Shigaku zasshi* 37: 46–65 (September 1925).

——. "Kondei ni tsuite" (Strong Fellows), *Rekishi chiri* (Historical geography) 37: 21–29 (January 1922); 37: 23–30 (March 1922); 37: 8–11 (April 1922).

——. *Shōen shi no kenkyū* (History of estates). 3 vols. Iwanami shoten, 1953.

Nitta Hideharu. "Kamakura kōki no seiji katei" (Politics in the late Kamakura era), *Iwanami kōza Nihon rekishi* 6 *Chūsei* 2. Iwanami shoten, 1975.

Noda Reishi, "Nihon ritsuryō gunsei no tokushitsu" (Characteristics of the Chinese-style military system), *Nihon shi kenkyū* 76: 31–54 (January 1965).

——. *Ritsuryō kokka no gunji sei* (The military system of the Chinese-style state). Yoshikawa Kōbunkan, 1984.

——. *Sakimori to eji* (Border and Palace Guards). Kyōiku sha, 1980.

Noguchi Minoru. *Bandō bushi dan no seiritsu to hatten* (Establishment and development of eastern warrior bands). Kōsei shorin, 1982.

Ōae Akira. *Ritsuryō seika no shihō to keisatsu* (Police and judge under the Chinese-style system). Daigaku kyōiku sha, 1979.

Ōboroya Hisashi. "Jūseiki ni okeru sa u emon fu kanjin no kenkyū" (Officials in the Left and Right Gate Guards in the tenth century), *Heian hakubutsu kan kenkyū kiyō* (Research of the Heian Museum) 4: 123–169 (December 1971); 5: 81–137 (March 1974).

——. "Jūseiki ni okeru sa u emon fu kanjin no kenkyū." In *Nihon kodai gaku ronshū* (Articles on Japanese antiquity). Kyoto: Kodai gaku kyōkai, 1979.

O'Connell, Robert. *Of Arms and Men*. Oxford: Oxford University Press, 1989.

Ogawa Seitarō. "Kebii shi no kenkyū" (Investigators), *Waseda hōgaku* (Legal studies at Waseda University) 17: 1–87 (1938); 18: 88–199 (1939).

Okamoto Hironori. "*Hizen no kuni fudoki* ni okeru 'noroshi' no kenkyū" (Beacons in *The Hizen Gazetteer*), *Kodai bunka* (Ancient culture) 30: 25–35 (May 1978).

Okamoto Isamu. "Genshi shakai no seisan to jujutsu" (Production and superstition in primitive society), *Iwanami kōza Nihon rekishi* 1 *Genshi oyobi kodai* 1. Iwanami shoten, 1975.

Ōmori Kingorō. *Buke jidai no kenkyū* (Age of the warrior). Fusambō, 1923.

Onoyama Setsu, ed. *Kodai shi hakkutsu* 6 *Kofun to kokka no naritachi* (Tumuli and the establishment of the state). Kōdan sha, 1975.

Ōshio Chihiro, Saeki Arikiyo, Sakaguchi Tsutomu, and Sekiguchi Akira. *Kenkyū shi: Masakado no ran* (Masakado's rebellion). Yoshikawa kōbunkan, 1976.

Otomasu Shigetaka, ed. *Kodai shi hakkutsu* 8 *Sōshoku kofun to mon'yō* (Decorated tombs and patterns). Kōdansha, 1974.

Ōtsuka Tokurō. *Heian shoki seiji shi kenkyū* (Early Heian political history). Yoshikawa kōbunkan, 1969.

Bibliography

Ōyama Kyōhei. "Kokugaryō ni okeru ryōshu sei no keisei" (Formation of domains on provincially administered lands), *Shirin* 43: 46–69 (January 1960).
————. *Nihon chūsei nōson shi no kenkyū* (A history of medieval Japanese villages). Iwanami shoten, 1978.
————. *Nihon no rekishi* 9 *Kamakura bakufu*. Shōgakkan, 1974.

Perkin, Harold. *The Origins of Modern English Society 1780–1880*. London: Routledge and Kegan Paul, 1969.

Reischauer, Edwin O. "The Tale of Heiji." In Edwin O. Reischauer and Joseph Yamagiwa, eds., *Translations from Early Japanese Literature*. Cambridge: Harvard University Press, 1951.
———— and Albert Craig. *Japan: Tradition and Transformation*. Boston: Houghton Mifflin, 1978.

Sahara Makoto. "Nōgyō no kaishi to kaikyū shakai no keisei" (The origins of agriculture and the formation of class society), *Iwanami kōza Nihon rekishi* 1 *Genshi oyobi kodai* 1. Iwanami shoten, 1975.
Sakaehara Towao. "Fujiwara no Hirotsugu no ran no tenkai katei" (The revolt of Fujiwara no Hirotsugu), *Dazaifu kobunka ronsō* (Essays on the ancient culture of Dazaifu). Vol. I. Yoshikawa kōbunkan, 1983.
Sakamoto Shōzō. *Nihon no rekishi* 6 *Sekkan jidai* (Age of regents). Shōgakkan, 1974.
————. *Nihon ōchō kokka taisei ron* (The Japanese aristocratic state structure). Tōkyō kaigaku shuppan kai, 1972.
Sakamoto Tarō. *Nihon kodai shi no kisoteki kenkyū* (Ancient Japanese history). Vol. II. Tōkyō daigaku shuppan kai, 1964.
Sasayama Haruo. "Bunken ni mirareru senjutsu to buki" (Tactics and weapons as seen in written sources). In Ōbayashi Taryō, ed., *Nihon kodai bunka no tankyū: Tatakai*. Shakai shisō sha, 1984.
————. "Chū efu no kenkyū" (The Middle Palace Guards), *Kodaigaku* (Ancient studies) 6: 274–302 (October 1957).
————. "Heian shoki no seiji kaikaku" (Political reforms in the early Heian period), *Iwanami kōza Nihon rekishi* 3 *Kodai* 3. Iwanami shoten, 1975.
————. "Heian zenki no sa u konoe fu ni kansuru kōsatsu" (Early Heian imperial attendants). In *Nihon kodai shi ronshū* (Essays in ancient Japanese history). Vol. III. Yoshikawa kōbunkan, 1962.
————. *Kodai kokka to guntai* (The ancient state and the miltary). Chūkō shinsho, 1975.
————. "Nihon kodai no gunji soshiki" (Military organization in ancient Japan). In Ishimoda Shō, et al. eds., *Kodai shi kōza* (Lectures in ancient history). Vol. V. Gakusei sha, 1962.
————. "Tōgū bō tachiwaki no toneri no kenkyū" (Retainers of the Heir Apparent). In *Zoku Nihon kodai shi ronshū* (Essays in ancient Japanese history, continued). Vol. III. Yoshikawa kōbunkan, 1972.

Sato, Elizabeth. "The Early Development of the *Shōen.*" In John Hall and Jeffrey Mass, eds., *Medieval Japan: Essays in Institutional History.* New Haven: Yale University Press, 1974.

Satō Shin'ichi. "Jidai to jimbutsu" (History and personality). In Satō Shin'ichi, ed., *Nihon jimbutsu shi taikei* (A library of Japanese biography). Vol. II. Asakura shoten, 1959.

———. *Nihon no rekishi* 9 *Namboku chō no dōran* (Wars of the Northern and Southern Dynasties). Chūō kōron sha, 1965.

———. "Shoki hōken shakai no keisei" (Formation of early feudal society). In Toyoda Takeshi, ed., *Shin Nihon shi taikei* 3 *Chūsei shakai* (A new library of Japanese history: Medieval society). Asakura shoten, 1954.

Satō Sōjun. *Heian zenki seiji shi josetsu* (Politics in the early Heian period). Tōkyō daigaku shuppan kai, 1977.

Sekiguchi Akira. "Emishi no hanran to sono rekishiteki igi" (Historical import of the "barbarians" rebellion), *Rekishigaku kenkyū* 390: 35–45 (November 1972).

Sekine Masataka. "Jōdai kijō ryō kō" (Materials used in ancient weapons), *Yamato bunka kenkyū* (Yamato culture) 12: 1–15 (September 1967).

Seno Seiichirō. *Chinzei goke'nin no kenkyū* (Kyushu housemen). Yoshikawa kōbunkan, 1975.

———. "Kyōto ōban'yaku gonji ni kansuru ichi kōsatsu" (Kyoto guard duty), *Tōkyō daigaku shiryō hensan jo hō* (Report of the Historiographical Institute at Tokyo University) 9: 18–25 (1974).

Shima Setsuko. "Masakado no ran no zaichi kōzō" (Local structure of Masakado's revolt), *Nara shien* (A historical garden at Nara) 13: 1–11 (February 1965).

Shimizu Junzō, "Nihon kodai no fune" (Ancient Japanese boats). In Ōbayashi Taryō, ed., *Nihon kodai bunka no tankyū* 6 *Fune* (Boats). Shakai shisō sha, 1975.

Shimizu Mitsuo. *Jōdai no tochi kankei* (Ancient land relations). Itō shoten, 1943).

Shimomukai Tatsuhiko. "Keigo shi Fujiwara Sumitomo" (Watchguard Fujiwara Sumitomo), *Geibi chihō shi kenkyū* (Western Honshu local history) 133: 7–16 (October 1981).

———. "Ōchō kokka kokuga gunsei no kōzō to tenkai" (Structure and development of the provincial military of the aristocratic state), *Shigaku kenkyū* 151: 44–67 (May 1981).

———. "Ōchō kokka kokuga gunsei no seiritsu" (The establishment of the military system in the provincial headquarters in the aristocratic state), *Shigaku kenkyū* 144: 1–27 (July 1979).

———. "Ōryō shi tsuibu shi no shoruikei" (Types of overseers and arrest officers), *Hisutoria* 94: 17–33 (March 1982).

Shinoda Minoru. *The Founding of the Kamakura Shogunate, 1180–1185.* New York: Columbia University Press, 1960.

Shōji Hiroshi. *Nihon shi* 5 *Henkyō no sōran* (Frontier wars). Kyōiku sha, 1977.

Shōmonki: The Story of Masakado's Rebellion. Tr. Judith Rabinovitch. Sophia University Press, 1985.

Bibliography

Smith, Thomas. "Japan's Aristocratic Revolution," *Yale Review* 50: 370–383 (1961).

Sonoda Kōyū. "Waga jōdai no kiheitai" (Ancient horsemen), *Shisen* (Historical fountain) 23/24: 5–22 (March 1962).

Suenaga Masao. *Nihon buki gaisetsu* (Japanese weapons). Shakai shisō sha, 1971.

Suzuki Keizō. "Mōko shūrai ekotoba ni arawaretaru busō ni tsuite" (Military technology as seen in the picture scroll of the Mongol Invasions), *Kokugakuin zasshi* 45: 46–58 (December 1940); 46: 35–53 (January 1941).

Suzuki Naoshi, "Itai no jinruigakuteki kansetsu" (Anthropological autopsies on the cadavers). In *Chūsonji to Fujiwara yondai* (Chūsonji and the four generations of Fujiwara). Asahi shimbun sha, 1950.

Suzuki Tetsuo. "Musashi no kuni Kumagai gō ni okeru ryōshu to nōmin" (Peasant and lord in Musashi province, Kumagai village), *Chihō shi kenkyū* 163: 43–54 (February 1980).

Takada Minoru. "Heishi seiken ron josetsu" (Debate over Taira power), *Nihon shi kenkyū* 90: 89–103 (August 1967).

———. "Jūseiki no shakai henkaku" (Social change in the tenth century), *Kōza Nihon shi* 2 *Hōken shakai no seiritsu*. Tōkyō daigaku shuppan kai, 1970.

Takahashi Masaaki. "Ise Heishi no seiritsu to tenkai" (Establishment and development of the Ise Taira), *Nihon shi kenkyū* 157: 1–23 (September 1975); 158: 23–47 (October 1975).

———. "Kihei to suihei" (Horsemen and navy). In Toda Yoshimi, ed., *Nihon shi* 2 *Chūsei* 1. Yūhikaku, 1978.

———. *Kiyomori izen* (Before Kiyomori). Heibon sha, 1984.

———. "Masakado no ran no hyōka o megutte" (Evaluating Masakado's revolt), *Bunka shigaku* (Cultural history) 26: 25–44 (March 1971).

Takahashi Takashi. "Mutsu Dewa no gunsei" (Military system in Mutsu and Dewa), *Shigen* 15: 22–30 (November 1972).

———. *Sakanoue no Tamuramaro*. Yoshikawa kōbunkan, 1959.

Takahashi Tomio. *Izawa-jō* (Fort Izawa). Gakusei sha, 1971.

———. *Emishi* (The "barbarians"). Yoshikawa kōbunkan, 1963.

———. *Ōshū Fujiwara shi yondai* (Four generations of the Fujiwara of Mutsu). Yoshikawa kōbunkan, 1958.

Takeuchi Rizō. *Nihon no rekishi* 6 *Bushi no tōjō* (Rise of the warrior). Chūō kōron sha, 1965.

———. *Ritsuryō sei to kizoku seiken* (The Chinese-style system and aristocratic power). Vol. II. Ochanomizu shobō, 1958.

———. "Shoki no bushidan" (Early warrior bands). In Kawasaki Tsuneyuki, ed., *Nihon jimbutsu shi taikei*. Vol. I. Asakura shoten, 1961.

Takigawa Masajirō, "Jōdai hōsui kō" (Ancient beacons), *Shigaku zasshi* 61: 57–75 (October 1952).

———. "Tachiwaki no toneri ni tsuite" (Guards of the Heir Apparent), *Shoku Nihongi kenkyū* 3: 1–5 (April 1956).

———. "Tō hyōbu shiki to Nihon Gumbō-ryō" (Tang Ordinances of the War Ministry and Japan's Articles on the Military Defense), *Hōsei shi kenkyū* 2: 73–80 (1952).

The Tale of the Heike. Tr. Helen McCullough. Stanford: Stanford University Press, 1988.

Tanaka Fumihide. "Heishi seiken no keisei katei" (Formation of Taira power), *Nihon shi kenkyū* 95: 27–52 (January 1968).

———. "Heishi seiken no kokuga shihai" (Control of the provincial headquarters under the Taira). In *Joshi dai bungaku* (Literature at a women's college) 26: 21–43 (February 1975).

———. "Heishi seiken no zaichi shihai kōzō" (Local power structure of the Taira). In *Nihon shi ronshū* (Collected essays on Japanese history). Seibun dō, 1975.

Tanaka Minoru. "Insei to Jishō Juei no ran" (Politics of the Retired Sovereign and the Great Civil War of 1180–1185), *Iwanami kōza Nihon rekishi* 4 *Kodai* 4. Iwanami shoten, 1975.

———. "Jōkyū kyōgata bushi no ichi kōsatsu" (Warriors who fought for Go-Toba in the Jōkyū War), *Shigaku zasshi* 65: 21–48 (April 1956).

———. "Jōkyū no ran go no shin jitō bunin chi shūi" (New land stewards appointed after the Jōkyū War). In Kurokawa Takaaki and Kitazume Masao, eds., *Ronshū Nihon rekishi* 4 *Kamakura bakufu*. Yūsei dō, 1976.

———. "Kamakura bakufu goke'nin seido no ichi kōsatsu" (Kamakura housemen). In Ishimoda Shō and Satō Shin'ichi, eds., *Chūsei no hō to kokka*. Tōkyō daigaku shuppan kai, 1960.

———. "Kamakura jidai ni okeru Iyo no kuni no jitō goke'nin ni tsuite" (Land stewards and housemen in Iyo province in the Kamakura period). In *Shōen sei to buke shakai* (The estate system and warrior society). Yoshikawa kōbunkan, 1969.

———, "Samurai bonge kō" (Samurai and commoners), *Shirin* 59: 1–31 (July 1976).

———. "Sanuki no kuni no jitō goke'nin ni tsuite" (Land stewards and housemen in Sanuki province). In *Nihon shakai keizai shi kenkyū, kodai chūsei hen* (Social and economic history of Japan, ancient and medieval). Yoshikawa kōbunkan, 1967.

Tanimori Akio. *Kebii shi o chūshin to shitaru Heian jidai no keisatsu jōtai* (Police in the Heian period, focusing on the Investigators). Meishō sha, 1922.

The Ten Foot Square Hut and Tales of the Heike. Tr. A. L. Sadler. Rutland: Charles E. Tuttle., 1972.

Thompson, E.P. "Eighteenth-century English society: class struggle without class?" *Social History* 3: 133–165 (May 1978).

Toda Yoshimi. "Chūsei no hōken ryōshu sei" (Feudal lords in the medieval era), *Iwanami kōza Nihon rekishi* 6 *Chūsei* 2. Iwanami shoten, 1962.

———. "Chūsei seiritsu ki no kokka to nōmin" (State and peasant during the formation of the medieval period), *Nihon shi kenkyū* 97: 18–32 (April 1968).

———. "Kokuga gunsei no keisei katei" (Formation of the military in the

Bibliography

provincial headquarters), *Chūsei no kenryoku to minshu* (Medieval power and the masses). Sōgen sha, 1970.

———. *Nihon ryōshu sei seiritsu shi no kenkyū* (A history of the establishment of Japanese proprietary lords). Iwanami shoten, 1967.

———. "Ritsuryō sei kara no kaihō" (Liberation from the Chinese-style system). In Toda Yoshimi and Inagaki Yasuhiko, eds., *Nihon minshu no rekishi 2 Tsuchi ikki to nairan* (A history of the Japanese people: Local riots and revolts). Sansei dō, 1975.

———, ed. *Shimpojiumu Nihon rekishi 5 Chūsei shakai no keisei* (Formation of medieval society). Gakusei sha, 1972.

———, Ishii Susumu, and Uwayokote Masataka, "Nihon chūsei kenryoku kōzō no shomondai" (Problems of the power structure in early medieval Japan), *Hōsei shi kenkyū* 20: 133–202 (March 1971).

Tōno Haruyuki, "*Shoku Nihongi* kankei nisoku" (Two rules found in the *Chronicles of Japan, Continued*), *Shoku Nihongi kenkyū* 200: 68–75 (December 1978).

Torao Toshiya. "Ritsuryō gyōsei no shosō" (Chinese-style administration). In Takahashi Takashi, ed., *Kodai no chihō shi 6 Ōu hen*. Asakura shoten, 1978.

Totman, Conrad. "English-Language Studies of Medieval Japan: An Assessment," *The Journal of Asian Studies* 38: 541–551 (March 1979).

———. *The Green Archipelago*. Berkeley: University of California Press, 1989.

Tsuchida, Naoshige. *Nihon no rekishi 5 Ōchō no kizoku* (Aristocrats). Chūō kōron sha, 1965.

Tsuda Sōkichi. *Nihon jōdai shi kenkyū* (Ancient Japanese history). Iwanami shoten, 1947.

Tsunoda Bun'ei. *Ritsuryō kokka no tenkai* (Development of the Chinese-style state). Hanawa shobō, 1965.

Tumin, Melvin. *Social Stratification*. Englewood Cliffs: Prentice-Hall, 1967.

Ueda Hironori, "Nihon kodai no buki" (Weapons of ancient Japan). In Ōbayashi Taryō, ed., *Nihon kodai bunka no tankyū: Tatakai*. Shakai shisō sha, 1984.

Urata Akiko. "Henko sei no igi" (Significance of the household system), *Shigaku zasshi* 81: 28–76 (February 1972).

Uwayokote Masataka. "Heian chūki no keisatsu seido" (Police in the middle Heian era). In *Ritsuryō kokka to kizoku shakai* (Chinese-style state and aristocratic society). Yoshikawa kōbunkan, 1969.

———. "Insei ki no Genji" (The Minamoto in the era of the Retired Sovereign). In *Goke'nin sei no kenkyū* (The system of housemen). Yoshikawa kōbunkan, 1981.

———. "Kamakura bakufu to kuge seiken" (Kamakura and aristocratic power), *Iwanami kōza Nihon rekishi 5 Chūsei 1*. Iwanami shoten, 1975.

———. *Nihon chūsei seiji shi kenkyū* (Politics in medieval Japan). Hanawa shobō, 1970.

———. "*Shōmon ki* shoshū no Masakado shojō o megutte" (On Masakado's letter in *The Tale of Masakado*). In *Nihon seiji shakai shi kenkyū* (Political and social history of Japan). Vol. II. Hanawa shobō, 1984.

Van Creveld, Martin. *Technology and War*. New York: The Free Press, 1989.

Watanabe Naohiko. *Nihon kodai kan'i seido no kisoteki kenkyū* (Ancient Japanese ranks). Yoshikawa kōbunkan, 1972.

Wechsler, Howard. "The Founding of the T'ang Dynasty: Kao tzu." In Denis Twitchett and John Fairbank, eds. *The Cambridge History of China*, III, *Sui and T'ang China*. Cambridge: Cambridge University Press, 1979.

White, Lynn. *Medieval Technology and Social Change*. Oxford: Oxford University Press, 1962.

Wilson, William. "The Way of the Bow and Arrow—The Japanese Warrior in *Konjaku monogatari*," *Monumenta Nipponica* 28: 177–233 (February 1973).

Wright, Arthur. "The Sui Dynasty." In Denis Twitchett and John Fairbank, eds. *The Cambridge History of China*, III, *Sui and T'ang China*. Cambridge: Cambridge University Press, 1979.

Yamada An'ei. *Fukuteki hen* (Subjugating the enemy). Yoshikawa kōbunkan, 1891.

Yamada Hideo. "Sei Hayato gun ni tsuite" (Troops sent to subjugate the Hayato). In *Ritsuryō kokka to kizoku shakai*. Yoshikawa kōbunkan, 1969.

Yamada Yoshimi. "Kofun shutsudo no bagu" (Horse gear uncovered in tumuli). In Mori Kōichi, ed., *Nihon kodai bunka no tankyū* 9 *Uma*. Shakai shisō sha, 1974.

Yamamoto, Takeo. *Kikō no kataru Nihon no rekishi* (Climate in Japanese history). Soshiete bunko, 1976.

———. "Rekishi no nagare ni sou Nihon to sono shūhen no kikō hensen" (Historical climatic changes in Japan and vicinity), *Chigaku zasshi* (Geological journal) 75: 119–141 (March 1967).

Yamanouchi Jō. "Iyo no kuni ni okeru bushi dan no seiritsu to tenkai" (Establishment and development of warrior banks in Iyo province), *Nihon rekishi* 379: 16–34 (December 1979).

Yamauchi Kunio. "Ritsuryō sei gundan ni kansuru kenkyū no dōkō" (Trends in research on the Chinese-style provincial militia), *Shigen* 7: 30–65 (January 1969).

———. "Sakimori no shubi chi to shusshin chi" (Origins of and lands defended by the Border Guards), *Sundai shigaku* (Sundai history) 25: 20–56 (September 1969).

Yang Hung. *Zong guo gu bing qi lun cong* (Ancient Chinese weapons). Peking: Wen wu chu ban she, 1980.

Yasuda Motohisa. "Bushi dan no keisei" (Formation of warrior bands), *Iwanami kōza Nihon rekishi* 4 *Kodai* 4. Iwanami shoten, 1962.

———. *Minamoto no Yoshiie*. Yoshikawa kōbunkan, 1966.

———. *Nihon no rekishi* 7 *Insei to Heishi* (The Retired Emperor and the Taira). Shōgakkan, 1974.

———. *Nihon shoki hōken sei no kiso kenkyū* (Early Japanese feudalism). Yamakawa shuppan sha, 1976.

Yokota Ken'ichi. "Tempyō jūninen Fujiwara no Hirotsugu no ran no ichi kōsatsu" (The revolt of Fujiwara no Hirotsugu in 740). In *Ritsuryō kokka no kiso kōzō* (Basic structure of the Chinese-style state). Yoshikawa kōbunkan, 1960.

Yoneda Yūsuke. "Ritsuryōteki gundan no seiritsu sairon" (Establishment of the Chinese-style provincial militia). In *Genshi kodai shakai kenkyū*. Vol. II. Azekura shobō, 1975.

Yoshida Akira. "Heian chūki no buryoku ni tsuite" (Military power in the middle Heian period), *Hisutoria* 42: 1–16 (March 1967).

———. "Masakado no ran ni kansuru ni san no mondai" (Two or three problems on Masakado's revolt), In *Shōmon ki: Kenkyū to shiryō* (The *Tale of Masakado*: Research and materials). Shin dokusho sha, 1963.

Yoshida Takashi. "Ritsuryō sei to sonraku" (The Chinese-style system and the village), *Iwanami kōza Nihon rekishi 3 Kodai* 3. Iwanami shoten, 1975.

Yoshie Akio. "Ho no keisei to sono tokushitsu" (Formation and characteristics of the new unit called *ho*), *Hokkaidō daigaku bungaku bu kiyō* 22: 176–249 (January 1974).

Yoshimura Shigeki. "In hokumen kō," (Northern quarters of the Retired Emperor), *Hōsei shi kenkyū* 2: 45–71 (March 1952).

———. *Kokushi seido hōkai ni kansuru kenkyū* (Decline of the provincial government). Tōkyō daigaku shuppan kai, 1957.

Glossary

azechi 按察使
azukaridokoro 預所
Azuma 東, 吾妻
Azuma kagami 吾妻鏡

banchō 番長
Bandō 坂東
banrui 伴類
beppu 別符
bettō 別当
bokuchō 牧長
bokujū 僕従
bonge 凡下
bugei 武芸
buke no tōryō 武家の棟梁
bunretsuteki sokumen 分裂的側面
bushi 武士
bushi dan 武士団
bushi no chōja 武士の長者
buyaku 夫役

chihō gōzoku 地方豪族
chimpei 鎮兵
chinju fu 鎮守府
chinju fu shōgun 鎮守府将軍
chinsho 鎮所
chō 町
chōdai 帳内
chōsen 庁宣
chū efu 中衛府
chūnagon 中納言

daikaikon jidai 大開墾時代
daijin 大臣
daini 大弐
dai shōgun 大将軍
dajō daijin 太政大臣
denka 殿下
dogō 土豪
doi 土居
dōrui 同類
doshi 弩師

ebisu 夷
efu 衛府
Eikyū no gōso 永久の強訴
eji 衛士
emishi 蝦夷, 毛人
e mon fu 衛門府
Engi 延喜
ezo 蝦夷

fudai zu 譜代図
fugō no tomogara 富豪の輩
fushō 府生
fushū 俘囚

gesu 下司
gesu myō 下司名
go 伍
gō (measure) 合
gō (village) 郷
goho 五保
goke'nin 御家人

465

gon no suke (province) 権介
gōshi 郷司
gōzoku 豪族
Gumbō-ryō 軍防令
gun 郡
gundan 軍団
gunji 郡司
gunji shizoku 軍事氏族
gunken 軍監
gunki 軍毅
gunsō 軍曹
Gyokuyō 玉葉

haniwa 埴輪
Heian ibun 平安遺文
Heiji 平治
Heike 平家
heishi 兵士
higoke'nin 非御家人
hiki 疋
Hitachi 常陸
ho 保
Hōgen 保元
hoko 矛, 鉾
hokumen no bushi 北面の武士
honjo 本所
honryō 本領
hori no uchi 堀ノ内
Hyakuren shō 百練抄
hyō 評
hyōe 兵衛
hyōe fu 兵衛府

ichi no miya 一の宮
ichō 移牒
ie no shihai 家の支配
ifu 夷俘
ihe 家, 宅

ikkoku jitō 一国地頭
in 院
innen 因縁

ji'nin 神人
jinka 神火
jitō 地頭
jitō kyū 地頭給
jitō sho 地頭所
jō (province) 掾
jō (Gate Guards) 尉
jō (measure) 丈
jōhei 精兵
Jōkyū 承久
Jōsaku kenkyū kai 城柵研究会
jotei 助丁
jōtei 上丁
jū 従
jūrui 従類

ka 火
kachō (tax) 加徴
kachō (officer) 火長
kageyu shi 勘解由使
kaihotsu ryōshu 開発領主
Kamakura ibun 鎌倉遺文
kami (province) 守
kami (Gate Guards) 督
kampaku 関白
kammon 貫文
kannō shi 勧農使
kantō tachi 鐶頭大刀(太刀)
katchū 甲冑
kebii shi 検非違使
kebii shi chō 検非違使庁
kebii shi sho 検非違使所
kebii sho 検非違所
keigo shi 警固使

keikō 挂甲
kemmon 検問
kemmon seika 権門勢家
kemmon taisei 権門体制
ke'nin 家人
kenjō 傔仗
kenshi 健士
Kikki 吉記
kin 斤
kingoku no tsuwamono domo 近国ノ兵共
ko 戸
kohori 郡, 評
kokka shihai ga naki ni hitoshiku muchitsujo jōtai 国家支配が無きにひとしく無秩序状態
kyūba no shi 弓馬の士
koku 石
kokuga ryō 国衙領
kokusai 国宰
kompon shiryō 根本私領
kondei 健児
kondei sho 健児所
kōryō 公領
kubu tsuchi tachi 頭槌大刀
kugyō 公卿
kuji 公事
kuni 国
kun'i 勲位
kuniguni no heishi 国々の兵士
kuniguni no tsuwamono domo 国々の兵共
kuni no mikotomochi 国司
kuni no miyatsuko 国造
kuni no musha 国武者
kuni no tsuwamono domo 国の兵共

kuni no uchi no shikaru beki tsuwamono domo 国の内の然るべき（可然）兵共
kyōmyō 交名
Kyōto no bushi 京都之武士

Man'yōshū 万葉集
Masakado 将門
megurashi bumi 廻文
meryō 馬寮
mitezukuri 御手作
Mizuki 水城
mokudai 目代
mon 文
monden 門田
mononofu 武士
mosa 猛者
mura 村
Mutsu 陸奥
Mutsu waki 陸奥話記
myōbu 名簿

nai daijin 内大臣
nengu 年貢
Nihon koku sōjitō 日本国総地頭
Nihon koku sōtsuibu shi 日本国総追捕使
nimbei sei 人兵制
nōdo shu 農奴主

ōasari 大索
ōban yaku 大番役
ōchō kokka 王朝国家
ōryō shi 押領使

ri 里
ritsuryō 律令

467

rui 類
ryo 旅
ryōke 領家

sa eji fu 左衛士府
sa hyōe fu 左兵衛府
saishō chūjō 宰相中将
sakan (province) 目
sakan (Investigators) 志
sa, u emon fu 左, 右衛門府
sa, u hyōe fu 左, 右兵衛府
sa, u konoe fu 左, 右近衛府
sakimori 防人
sakko 柵戸
samurai 侍
sangi 参議
san'i 散位
Sankai ki 山槐記
Sata miren sho 沙汰未練書
sato 里
sei i taishōgun 征夷大将軍
senshi (warrior) 選士
settō 節刀
shi 士
shibi chūdai 紫微中台
shibi naishō 紫微内相
shiei den ryōshu 私営田領主
shijin 資人
shiki 職
Shikibu shō 式部省
shinnō 新皇
shishō 史生
shiyū o kessuru 雌雄を決する
shō 升
shōen 荘園, 庄園
shōen-kokugaryō 庄園国衙領
shōgun 将軍
shojin ōryō shi 諸陣押領使

shoka no heishi 諸家の兵士
shokoku no gumpei 諸国の
  軍兵
shokoku no bushi 諸国の武士
shokoku no heishi 諸国の兵士
shokoku ōryō shi 諸国押領使
shokoku tsuibu shi 諸国追捕使
shokunō bushi 職能武士
Shōmon ki 将門記
shoshō 書生
shotō 所当
shūba no tō 僦馬の党
shuchō 主帳
shugo 守護
sōgesu 総下司
sōkan 惣管
sōryō 惣領
suimon shi 推問使
suke (Imperial Guards) 佐
sumō 相撲

tachi (sword) 太刀
tachi (office) 館
tachi no monodomo 館の者共
tachiwaki no toneri 授刀舎人,
  帯刀舎人
tai 隊
taifu 大夫
tairyō 大領
taishō 隊正
takiguchi 滝口
tan 段
tankō 短甲
tate 盾
to 斗
tō 党
tobuhi 烽, 烽燧
tōgoku 東国

tōi no shuchō 東夷酋長
tokai no tagui 屠膾の類
tomo no miyatsuko 伴造
toneri 舍人
tōyaku gonji 当役勤仕
tsuibatsu shi 追罰使
tsuibu 追捕
tsuibu kampu 追捕官符
tsuibu shi 追捕使
tsukuda 佃
tsuitō 追討
tsuitō shi 追討使
tsurugi 劍
tsuwamono 兵
tsuwamono no ie 兵の家

udoneri 内舍人
u eji fu 右衛士府
u hyōe fu 右兵衛府
uji 氏

umaya 厩(厩, 廄)
unjō butsu ōryō shi 運上物押
　領使

warabite tō 蕨手刀

yabusame 流鏑馬
yakata 館
yake 宅
yari 鑓, 槍
yoriki 与力
yugei 靫負

zaichi ryōshu 在地領主
zaichō kanjin 在庁官人
zaike 在家
zaikyō ryōshu 在京領主
zuishin 随身
zuryō 受領

Index

Abe, in *A Tale of Mutsu*, 223
Abe no Ōmi Hirafu, 85
Abe Sadatō, 225-226
Abe Yoritoki, 223-225
Agata Inukai Harueme, 154
Agata Inukai no Sukune Kiyondo, 154
"Age of widespread land clearance," 204-205, 206-207, 249-250; re-interpretation, 212, 213-215
Agriculture: Iron Age, 13-14; and disease, 11th century Kanto, 199-200; 11th, 12th century, 213-215; 362-363; double-cropping, 214; Kamakura period, 373
Agricultural development: Western Europe, 376-377; Japan, 377
Akanabe Estate, 219
Akiyori. *See* Fujiwara no Akiyori
Allies, 418; in Revolt of Taira no Masakado, 136, 137; 10th century, 150, 151-152; military duties, 151
Ancestral holding, 206
Antoku: ascension, 291; in Great Civil War of 1180-1185, 294, 296; death at Dannoura, 297
Arakawa Estate, 282
Archery contests: 8th century, 76; provincial, 185-186
Aristocratic forces: Yamato period, 29-30; in Revolt of Fujiwara no Nakamaro, 69, 70-77; 756 limits on, 71-72; "feudal" ties, 75-77; 721 limits on, 77; 8th century, 79; in Rebellion of Sumitomo, 159; composition, 169-172; 10th, 11th century, 169-172; military technology, 170-172; numbers, 170-171; and Investigators, 171, 172; and Imperial Guards, 172; organization, 172. *See also* Soldiers of noble houses
Aristocratic state, 379
Armies: raising, 61, 63, 64, 65, 100, 160-161, 225, 227, 268, 321, 326-327, 383-384,
418, 429-430; provisioning, 103-104, 195, 306-307, 331-332, 334-335
Armor: iron breastplate, 19, 21 (figure); chain mail, 19-22, 21 (figure); Yamato period, 19-22; iron, 101; leather, 101
Army size: in Yamato expeditions to Korea, 26; in Revolt of Fujiwara no Hirotsugu, 61, 63; in Wars in the Northeast, 94-95, 97-98; in Rebellion of Taira no Tadatsune, 180 (figure); in Hōgen Disturbance, 269-270; in Heiji Disturbance, 272-273; in Great Civil War of 1180-1185, 291-292, 294, 296, 300-302, 392-393; in Northern Campaign of 1189, 318-319; in Jōkyū War, 322, 324-325; in Mongol Invasions of 1274 & 1281, 329, 332, 333-334
Arrest officer: in western Japan, 158; provincial, 187; as "Warrior Chief," 252
The Art of War, 299; accounts of Latter Three Years' War, 238
Ashikaga Estate, 281-282
Ashikaga Toshitsuna, 281-282
Ategawa Estate, 347
Aterui. *See* Taibo no Kimi Aterui
Mt. Azama, 211
Azuma kagami. *See* *The Mirror of the East*
Azumabito. *See* Ōno no Ason Azumabito

Bandō, definition, 90. *See also* Kanto
Banrui. *See* Allies
Battle of Fujikawa, 301
Battle of Ishibashi, 300
Battle of Kurikara, 301
Battle of the Koromo River, 92
Battle of the Paekch'ŏn River, 39-40
Battle of Uji, 300-301
Beacons, 408; in Taihō Codes, 56; in Revolt of Fujiwara no Hirotsugu, 61
Bifukumon'in, 265
Border Guards: in Taika Reform Edict, 37; and the Kanto, 54-55; in Taihō Codes,

Index

Index

Harvard East Asian Monographs